MUSSOLINI'S ENEMIES

THE ITALIAN ANTI-FASCIST RESISTANCE

MUSSOLINI'S ENEMIES

The Italian Anti-Fascist Resistance

BY CHARLES F. DELZELL

PRINCETON, NEW JERSEY

PRINCETON UNIVERSITY PRESS

1961

10-16-61

To
Gena

PREFACE

A FEW HOURS after they had broadcast the news of Italy's armistice with the Allies, King Victor Emmanuel III and his chief minister, Marshal Pietro Badoglio, fled with undue celerity from German-threatened Rome in the early dawn of September 9, 1943. The fugitive royal government made its way to Brindisi on the heel of the Italian boot to join the Anglo-Americans, the bulk of whose forces were still desperately trying to secure their Salerno beachhead while others pushed up from Taranto. The inhabitants of northern and central Italy soon realized to their horror that instead of a quick exit from the war that they had all come to hate, they faced on their own a grim new ordeal of Nazi occupation of the peninsula as far south as Naples. To make matters worse, Adolf Hitler restored to nominal power in northern Italy the decrepit *Duce* whom they thought they had repudiated for good in the *coup d'état* of July 25, 1943.

For the next twenty months a small but determined minority of Italians in the upper half of the peninsula took up arms in a perilous underground struggle against Benito Mussolini's refurbished Fascist regime and his German masters. Many of them at the time (though fewer in later years) regarded their Armed Resistance as Italy's finest hour—as a veritable "Second Risorgimento." But this time it was a rebirth that was participated in by a considerably broader cross section of the populace than was the case in the nineteenth century. Co-ordinated by anti-Fascist Committees of National Liberation (CLN's) and manned by puissant partisan forces in both the mountains and the cities, Italy's Resistenza Armata proved itself to be one of the most effective clandestine movements in Nazi-dominated Europe. It succeeded in liberating most of the major cities of the Po valley hours, or even days, ahead of the juncture of the Allies, with whom the Italian patriots usually worked in liaison.

Doubtless one reason for the effectiveness of the Italian Resistenza Armata of September 8, 1943, to April 25, 1945, was that it represented the culminating phase of a longer Resistenza Antifascista that had been going on for more than two decades at home and abroad.[1] The present study seeks to elucidate the record of this comprehensive underground struggle against Mussolini's dictatorship. Though the history of Italian anti-Fascism cannot logically be divorced from that of Fascism itself, any book would be unwieldy indeed that tried to cover in equal detail both sides of the story. This book deals primarily with the record of the clandestine opposition to Mussolini, for that aspect of Italian history is, regrettably, the least well known.

The first year and a half of Mussolini's coalition government produced one important political crisis—the debacle of the new Catholic Popular Party at its Turin congress in April 1923. Mussolini's own position was not seriously threatened, however, until June 1924. In the wake of the brutal assassination by Fascists of Giacomo Matteotti, secretary of the "revisionist" Unitary Socialist Party, a large bloc of oppositionists in Parliament seceded to a symbolic Aventine with the hope of inducing the King to dismiss his compromised premier. The Aventine strategy failed. With no small degree of skill Mussolini rode out the violent storm. By January 3, 1925, he was ready to clamp down the totalitarian regime and harry his foes either into foreign or domestic exile, and some to their death.

It was the Matteotti murder that marked the beginning of a truly determined, albeit long abortive, anti-Fascist Resistance. From that point on, the story of the Opposition becomes increasingly detailed, dealing as it must with the vicissitudes of both the *émigrés* and the stay-at-home passive and militant groups—for there was no permanent dichotomy in their labors. Certainly anti-Fascism was never the monopoly of any single party or class; yet most of the militant leadership came from the ranks of the proscribed leftist parties, outlawed labor organizations, stifled journalists, and harassed academicians and professional men. In the shadows behind these "activists" stood another variety of anti-Fascism, the "quiet" type, that won the tacit support of numerous Catholics and conservative-minded Liberals.

[1] Almost all Italian historians now use the term "Resistenza" in this broader sense and "Resistenza Armata" to denote the climactic 1943–1945 phase of the struggle.

From 1943 until 1945 anti-Fascism and anti-Nazism were more keenly felt by the mass of Italians in the unredeemed North than was the case in the Allied-emancipated South. Republicanism and socialism were also mounting more rapidly in the North because of intense popular resentment at the way in which the royal government had botched the armistice and left Rome to its fate, and because of the social structure of the more industrialized Po valley. Whereas the Northerners had to clench their teeth in clandestinity until the final liberation enabled their sharp political *vento del nord* to cleanse the atmosphere, the Southerners could indulge fairly freely and overtly in politics. Thus in every liberated zone bitter rivalry came to the surface between the leftist parties in the new CLN's and those rightist groups who preferred the retention of the essentially Aventine-inspired bloc that had effected the *coup d'état* of July 25, 1943. The Anglo-Americans, who prior to the war had evinced little interest in or sympathy for the more radical Italian foes of Mussolini, discovered rapidly after September 1943 that they could not ignore the heterogeneous leftist groups in the CLN's, even though many British Conservatives (from Winston Churchill on down) and some Americans were inclined to treat these committees with scant respect.

Anti-Fascist Resistance directors succeeded in pushing the political pendulum farther to the left for a few short months after the liberation in April 1945—despite all foreign-imposed handicaps, vast differences in wartime experiences and outlook between South and North, and their own blunders committed in an emotion-charged atmosphere. One of their major victories was the dislodgment of the timorous monarch whose telephone call had brought Mussolini to power in October 1922. To be sure, that same King twenty-one years later managed to screw up courage to dismiss the *Duce* who had brought Italy to ruin; but by this time his crown had become so tarnished by daily contact with Fascist tyranny that a majority of the Italian electorate (particularly in the North) discarded the monarchy altogether in June 1946 when they had their first opportunity in more than a quarter of a century to vote in a free election. In this and in other aspects of the moral, political, and constitutional reconstruction of Italy the anti-Fascist veterans played an influential, though in some respects transitory role. If Italian democracy has managed to avoid a complete reversion to the not always commendable patterns of public life that prevailed before Mussolini's dictatorship, this can be credited in considerable measure to the impact of the more idealistic segment of the Resistenza.

My curiosity about the nature and extent of the anti-Fascist Resistance was pricked during service with the American army in Italy from 1943 until 1945. In 1946 I returned to Italy and other Mediterranean countries as overseas representative of the Hoover Institution and Library of Stanford University, in order to collect records dealing with the recent political and socio-economic history of that region. I should like to express heartfelt gratitude to Professor Harold H. Fisher, who was then chairman of the Hoover Institution and Library, and to former President Herbert Hoover, its founder, for making that mission possible. While in Italy on that occasion I met several of the Resistance leaders whose names appear in this study. With the help of them and others I was able to collect a substantial number of books, newspaper and periodical files, and other documentation. In Milan I was permitted to microfilm some of the Resistance documents in the archives of the Corps of Volunteers of Liberty.

Returning to Stanford University in 1947 to work toward a doctorate in modern European history, I wrote as my dissertation a preliminary study of the Italian Resistance. In this effort I received helpful guidance from Professors Ralph Haswell Lutz and Charles D. O'Malley of the Department of History. Thanks partly to a scholarship awarded by the Italian Istituto per le Relazioni con l'Estero, I was able to spend the academic year 1948–1949 studying at the Naples Istituto Italiano per gli Studi Storici, which was founded after the recent war by the late Senator Benedetto Croce as a center for graduate study in history. While I was there, the late Professor Federico Chabod, Director of the Institute and himself an underground leader in Val d'Aosta, gave me encouragement and criticism in my research, as did others of the teaching staff and student group. It is impossible for me to list all those in Italy who provided helpful orientation at different stages of my research, but I must thank especially three historians—Professor Giorgio Vaccarino; Avv. Alessandro Galante-Garrone, President of the Tribunal in Turin;

and Dr. Vittorio Gabrieli—for their repeated assistance. Of course, none of these people should be held responsible for any errors I may have made.

Postdoctoral investigation of the subject has been carried on at the Hoover Institution, the Library of Congress, the Allied Military Records Branch, the Istituto Nazionale per la Storia del Movimento di Liberazione in Italia (Milan), the Biblioteca G. G. Feltrinelli (Milan), and the Joint University Libraries in Nashville—to all of whom I am grateful for generous assistance. I am particularly indebted to Chancellor Harvie Branscomb, Vice Chancellor Rob Roy Purdy, Deans Leonard B. Beach and Ewing P. Shahan, and Dr. Harold W. Bradley of Vanderbilt University, and to its Institute for Research and Training in the Social Sciences, headed by Dr. George W. Stocking, for making available both time and research grants to complete this study. Finally, let me express special words of appreciation to my wife, without whose help and understanding this enterprise could not easily have been completed, and to my young children, who have patiently put up with their father's work hours.

The present account makes no claim to being either definitive or completely impartial—doubtful of attainment under the best of circumstances and certainly unlikely when one chooses so contemporary and controversial a subject as the Italian Resistance. Each year has brought forth new information (much of it highly tendentious) to be fitted into the already involved story. The tenth anniversary of the liberation, celebrated in 1955, was especially productive of new documentation. No doubt more will appear.[2] I have tried to consult primary sources—memoirs, diaries, overt and covert newspapers and pamphlets—whenever this was feasible. In a few instances I have had access to non-Italian official documentation that was not readily available to others. Yet when one studies so complex a subject as this, it is physically impossible for one investigator to examine all the primary source material scattered in many countries. Necessarily

[2] Professor Mario Bendiscioli has offered commendable advice regarding the kinds of source materials that still must be assembled before anything even approaching a "definitive" history of the Resistance can be written. See "La ricostruzione storica della Resistenza," *Il Movimento di Liberazione in Italia, Rassegna di Studi e Documenti* [hereafter cited as *MLI*], No. 52/53 (1958), pp. 72–92.

one must often rely on the monographic and secondary studies of others.

Much valuable spadework has been done by a host of Italians who were directly involved in the underground. Such non-Communists as Gaetano Salvemini, Luigi Salvatorelli, Giovanni Mira, Aldo Garosci, Armando Gavagnin, Silvio Trentin, Ernesto Rossi, Carlo Sforza, Luigi Sturzo, Giuseppe Rossini, Renato Carli-Ballola, Nino Valeri, Piero Pieri, Paolo Monelli, Franco Catalano, Giorgio Vaccarino, and others in the Istituto per la Storia del Movimento di Liberazione in Italia have unearthed much material and offered suggestive interpretations of various facets of the Resistance. Communist chroniclers like Roberto Battaglia, Luigi Longo, Palmiro Togliatti, Paolo Robotti, and Giovanni Germanetto have done likewise. So have such heretical ex-Communists as Angelo Tasca, Leo Valiani, Fulvio Bellini, Giorgio Galli, and Valdo Magnani. Foreign scholars, including Max Salvadori, H. Stuart Hughes, Charles R. S. Harris, Elizabeth Wiskemann, Daniel A. Binchy, Max Ascoli, Norman Kogan, Howard McGaw Smyth, and others, have made signal contributions. I am deeply indebted to all of these writers, not only for much factual data but often for shrewd interpretations. My own work of synthesis embraces a somewhat longer span than that of several of the writers mentioned, and my geographical and political focus often tends to be broader. I shall be content if this *cronistoria* becomes a point of departure for new investigations of this tangled subject.

Though I have tried to be fair to all the political currents, my own bias should be stated frankly. It is that of an American Democrat who feels sympathy for at least several of the goals sought by the non-Communist groups in the Italian Resistance and who firmly opposes totalitarianism of whatever hue. Whether I have avoided the pitfalls of local partisanship and nationalism, of temporal proximity and personal involvement, or of certain ideological straitjackets that have marred some of the pages of previous studies is not for me to say. I hope that my relative disinterestedness has kept me from stumbling into an excessive number.

CHARLES F. DELZELL

Nashville, Tennessee
September 1960

CONTENTS

xiii

ABBREVIATIONS

AAF	United States Army Air Force
ACC; AC	Allied Control Commission. After 1944 Allied Commission
AFHQ	Allied Force Headquarters. In Algiers; later in Caserta
AMG	Allied Military Government
ANPI	National Association of Italian Partisans
AVNOJ	Tito's Anti-Fascist Council for the National Liberation of Yugoslavia
B/G	Fulvio Bellini and Giorgio Galli, heretical Communist authors of *Storia del PCI* (Milan, 1953)
CCLN	Central CLN. In Rome
CG/CVL	General Headquarters, Corps of Volunteers of Liberty. In Milan
CGIL	Italian General Confederation of Labor. Created in 1943 by fusion of CGL and Catholic Italian Confederation of Laborers
CGL	General Confederation of Labor. Marxist-dominated
CIL	Italian Corps of Liberation. Fought alongside Allied armies in Italy after October 1943
CLN	Committee of National Liberation. Composed usually of five or six anti-Fascist political parties after September 8, 1943
CLNAI	CLN for Upper Italy. In Milan after January 1944
Confindustria	Confederation of Industrialists
Consulta	Consultative Assembly. Appointed advisory body, 1945–1946
Costituente	Constituent Assembly. Elected June 2, 1946
CPLN	Piedmont CLN. In Turin
CTLN	Tuscan CLN. In Florence
CVL	Corps of Volunteers of Liberty. The military organization of the consolidated patriot movement, 1944–1945
DC	Democrazia Cristiana ("Christian Democratic Party"), 1942 ff.
DL	Democrazia del Lavoro ("Labor Democratic Party"), 1943–1945
DZ	Drop Zone for parachuted supplies
EAM/ELAS	Greek Liberation Movement and its guerrilla arm
FUCI	Italian Catholic University Federation

GAP; Gappisti Groups of Popular Action. Communist urban terrorists

GIL Italian Youth of the Littoral. Fascist youth organization

GL; Giellisti Giustizia e Libertà ("Justice and Liberty"). Led by Carlo Rosselli, 1929–1937; later merged into Pd'A

GNR Republican National Guard. Fascist militia in RSI

GUF Fascist University Youth Groups

IRI Institute for Industrial Reconstruction. Originally a Fascist economic agency somewhat analogous to American Reconstruction Finance Corporation

LIDU Italian League of the Rights of Man. *Émigré* anticlerical welfare organization, with headquarters in Paris

MFE European Federalist Movement. Headed in Italy by Altiero Spinelli

MLI *Il Movimento di Liberazione in Italia: Rassegna di Studi e Documenti.* Historical review devoted to the study of the Resistance. Printed in Milan by the Istituto Nazionale per la Storia del Movimento di Liberazione in Italia

MTO Mediterranean Theater of Operations in World War II

MUP Movement of Proletarian Unity. Socialist faction led by Lelio Basso that fused with PSI in 1943 to form the PSIUP

MVSN Fascist Volunteer Militia for National Security

NOVJ *See* AVNOJ

NYT *New York Times*

OF Osvobodilna Fronta. Titoist Slovene Liberation Front

ONB Opera Nazionale Balilla. Fascist youth organization. Initials also used facetiously by journalists in 1945 to refer to ex-Premiers Orlando, Nitti, and Bonomi

ORI Organization of Italian Resistance. Headed by Raimondo Craveri and worked with OSS

OSS American Office of Strategic Services

OVRA Fascist secret police. Organization for Vigilance and Repression of Anti-Fascism

OWI American Office of War Information

PCI Italian Communist Party. 1921 ff.

Pd'A Party of Action. 1942 ff.

PFR Fascist Republican Party. In the North, 1943–1945

PLI Italian Liberal Party. 1943 ff.

PNF National Fascist Party. Until 1943

POOF Inter-Regional Committee of the National Front for the Slovene Littoral. Titoist. *See* OF

PPI; Popolari — Italian Popular Party. Catholic party of Luigi Sturzo, 1919–1926

PR — Proportional representation

PRI — Italian Republican Party. Mazzinian current of Randolfo Pacciardi

PSI — Italian Socialist Party. Largest Socialist current; fairly maximalist in its program. *See* PSLI; PSIUP

PSIUP — Italian Socialist Party of Proletarian Unity. Title of consolidated party, led by Nenni, 1943–1947

PSLI — Socialist Party of Italian Laborers. Revisionist; superseded PSU abroad, 1926; in 1930 merged with PSI

PSU — Unitary Socialist Party. Giacomo Matteotti's revisionist party; known abroad after 1926 as PSLI

PW — Prisoner of war

PWB — Psychological Warfare Bureau. Anglo-American

RSI — Italian Social Republic. Mussolini's neo-Fascist puppet regime in the North, 1943–1945

SAP; Sappisti — Squads of Patriotic Action. Covert Communist squads, 1944–1945

SF — Special Forces. Usual designation for British SOE in Italy

SIM — Italian Military Intelligence Service

S/M, *Sdf* — Luigi Salvatorelli and Giovanni Mira, *Storia del fascismo: l'Italia dal 1919 al 1945* (Rome, 1952)

SOE — British Special Operations Executive. Better known in Italy as SF. Analogous to American OSS

SS — Nazi Elite Guards

UPI — Italian Popular Union. Social-Communist "front" organization abroad, 1937–1939

X^{ma} MAS — Decima Flottiglia Motoscafi Anti-Sommergibile. Neo-Fascist Tenth Flotilla of Torpedo Boats, headed by Prince J. V. Borghese and used as a land force in the North against the partisans, 1943–1945

PART I
THE CLANDESTINE OPPOSITION
1924–1943

CHAPTER I · THE DEBACLE

Advent of Mussolini

ON OCTOBER 30, 1922, Benito Mussolini obtained the post of President of the Council of Ministers of Italy. He achieved his goal by cynical opportunism, compounded by bluff and intimidation, and in the face of myopic blunders by the factious Socialists and Catholics, who refused to form a majority bloc in Parliament. Yet in the last analysis it was the deliberate action of the timid King Victor Emmanuel III, fearful lest he lose his throne and dubious of Army support, which brought Mussolini legally to power via the so-called *"wagon-lit revolution"*—a fact which the anti-Fascists were not inclined to forget.

According to the orthodox Fascist interpretation, Mussolini's advent "saved" Italy from Bolshevism. This facile notion has been thoroughly disproved by many historians, who have shown that such danger had ended after the failure of the sit-down strikes in the metallurgical plants in the summer of 1920.[1] Never-

---

[1] The most detailed critical account of the Fascist rise to power is Angelo Tasca, *Nascita e avvento del fascismo* (rev. ed.; Florence, 1950), a book that appeared in earlier versions abroad, the English one being *The Rise of Italian Fascism* (London, 1938), under the ex-Communist author's pseudonym, "A. Rossi." Of basic importance is the broad study of the whole Fascist era by the liberal historians Luigi Salvatorelli and Giovanni Mira, *Storia del fascismo: l'Italia dal 1919 al 1945* (Rome, 1952) [hereafter cited as S/M, *Sdf*]. With minor changes this was republished as *Storia d'Italia nel periodo fascista* (Turin, 1957); whenever this edition is cited the title will be given in full. Salvatorelli has trod much of the same ground in his essay, "L'opposizione democratica durante il fascismo," in *Il Secondo Risorgimento: scritti di A. Garosci, L. Salvatorelli, C. Primieri, R. Cadorna, M. Bendiscioli, C. Mortati, P. Gentile, M. Ferrara, F. Montanari, nel decennale della resistenza e del ritorno alla democrazia, 1945–1955* (Rome, 1955), pp. 95–180. Other studies are Nino Valeri, *La lotta politica in Italia dall'unità al 1925* (Florence, 1945); his *Da Giolitti a Mussolini: momenti della crisi del liberalismo* (3rd ed.; Florence, 1957); Paolo Alatri, *Le origini del fascismo* (Rome, 1956), a collection of essays most of which appeared in *Belfagor*; and the first two of Giacomo Perticone's three-volume *La politica italiana nell'ultimo trentennio* (Rome, 1945–1947).

The Fascist interpretation is best presented in G. A. Chiurco, *Storia della rivoluzione fascista* (5 vols.; Florence, 1929).

Interpretive accounts in English include H. Stuart Hughes, *The United States and Italy* (Cambridge, 1953); Denis Mack Smith, *Italy: A Modern History* (Ann Arbor, 1959); Cecil Sprigge, *The Development of Modern Italy* (New Haven, 1944); Carl T. Schmidt, *The Corporate State in Action* (New York, 1939) and *The Plough and the Sword* (New York, 1938); Herman Finer, *Mussolini's Italy* (New York, 1935); William Ebenstein, *Fascist Italy* (New York, 1939); and Arnold J. Zurcher, "Government and Politics of Italy," in James Shotwell (ed.), *Governments of Continental Europe* (New York, 1940).

theless, the way for Fascism's triumph was opened by the unrest fomented in a tightly stratified society by Marxists and others during the war and postwar years. Landowners in the lower Po valley and elsewhere dreaded the program of agrarian reforms preached by the powerful new Catholic Partito Popolare Italiano (PPI); small businessmen feared the ascendancy of socialistic municipal governments; industrialists were terrified by the growing power of organized labor; capitalists distrusted those politicians who seemed unwilling to intervene decisively to safeguard their property; many white-collar workers and professional men felt vaguely insecure and feared they might become *déclassés* in the turbulent postwar era; and a host of nationalistic war veterans resented the failure of Italy's diplomats to gain all the territorial spoils they coveted.

⌊In a country where liberal democracy was barely a decade old and serious social, economic, religious, regional, and other cleavages had hampered the development of a stable political and economic order, it was easy for the dissatisfied groups to turn hopefully to a new and vigorous movement led by a flamboyant demagogue.⌋ For a time many neurasthenic nationalists had looked to Gabriele d'Annunzio, the poet-*condottiere*; but after his debacle in Fiume, they turned their eyes to Benito Mussolini. Mussolini had already toyed with republicanism, anarchosyndicalism, and socialism before creating in 1919 his violent, irrational, and amorphous Fascist movement propelled by nationalism, illiberalism, anti-Marxism, and syndicalism. During the three years since the movement's birth Mussolini had cynically and pragmatically discarded planks (including republicanism and anticlericalism) whenever he thought this would increase his popular appeal. Despite Fascism's elaborate philosophical "foundations" (formulated many years *after* its establishment) Fascism in Italy was simply "Mussolinism"—as the *Duce* frankly conceded in a moment of candor.[2] Yet Fascism was also more

[2] See his conversation with one of his dwindling band of disciples on Lake Garda in 1945, quoted in Roman Dombrowski, *Mussolini: Twilight and Fall*, tr. by H. C. Stevens (New York, 1956), p. 145.

Regarding Mussolini's personal history, see Paolo Alatri's bibliographical essay, "Benito Mussolini (note biografiche e bibliografiche)," in Ettore Rota (ed.), *Questioni di storia contemporanea* (4 vols.; Milan, 1953–1955), III, 759–796, and reprinted in Alatri, *Le origini del fascismo*, pp. 323–390. Fundamental studies are Gaudens Megaro, *Mussolini dal mito alla realtà* (Milan, 1947), a revision

REGIONAL AND RELIEF MAP OF ITALY (pre-1947)

than an Italian phenomenon: it became a fairly ubiquitous twentieth-century "armed reaction" to unsolved, frustrating problems sired by an industrialized, nationalistic, and class-conscious world confronted by overwhelming crises unleashed by World War I and the Great Depression—an "armed reaction" that soon escaped the controls that certain conservative forces had hoped to maintain over it.

During the first few months after his assumption of power Mussolini headed a cabinet of "national concentration," composed of Fascists, Nationalists, several Liberals and Populars, but of course no Socialists or Communists. He asked and secured from Parliament a vote of confidence and special powers for a period of one year in order to effect economies by decree. Most Italians seemed to welcome the strong executive leadership (many had been conditioned for it by the partial relegation of Parliament during the war); moreover, Mussolini's relatively moderate program reassured them, and they could perceive little evidence at this juncture that he contemplated outright dictatorship.

Catholic dissidence

None the less, some deputies began to resist the new premier. Though this was customary practice in liberal states the world over, it was anathema to Mussolini, who demanded complete docility. A serious crisis arose in the spring of 1923 when the puissant PPI, acting at the behest of its secretary and founder, the redoubtable Sicilian priest, Don Luigi Sturzo, passed a resolution at its fourth congress in Turin condemning Fascism. Promptly Mussolini demanded the resignation of those Populars who were in his cabinet, whereupon most of the 100-odd Catholic deputies made ready to join the opposition.

Yet Sturzo's victory turned out to be his last as PPI secretary. His party already was rife with factionalism. Its right wing, especially sensitive to the thinking of high churchmen around the

of his *Mussolini in the Making* (New York, 1938), dealing with the *Duce*'s early career; Paolo Monelli's breezy but informative *Mussolini piccolo borghese* (Milan, 1950), which has appeared in English as *Mussolini: The Intimate Life of a Demagogue* (New York, 1954); and Guido Dorso, *Mussolini alla conquista del potere* (Turin, 1949). From the Fascist viewpoint are Yvon DeBegnac, *Vita di Mussolini* (3 vols.; Milan, 1936–1940); and the multivolume study of Giorgio Pini and Duilio Susmel, *Mussolini: l'uomo e l'opera* (4 vols.; Florence, 1953–1955).

conservative new Pope Pius XI (1922–1939), was becoming Fascistophile. They were impressed favorably by Mussolini's recent orders for compulsory religious instruction in elementary schools, restoration of the crucifix in courtrooms and schools, and the appointment of chaplains in the armed forces, to say nothing of his fulminations against Freemasonry. Many concluded that Fascism was Italy's best bulwark against materialistic Marxism, and they saw in the new regime a chance of ending the embittered relationship that had smouldered for half a century between the Vatican and the unified kingdom. Thus, on July 10, 1923, less than two months after the congress, Sturzo was obliged to resign from the secretariat as a result of pressure from ecclesiastics who feared, in his words, "obscure Fascist threats of armed reprisals against the Church." [3]

After that sensational event leadership of the fast-crumbling PPI passed to Giulio Rodinò, president, and Giovanni Gronchi and Giuseppe Spataro, secretary and vice-secretary, respectively. Sturzo's able lieutenant, Alcide DeGasperi, remained a potent figure in the inner council, and on May 19, 1924, that austere Tirolean replaced the "triumvirate" as party secretary.

Soon after Sturzo's resignation, Blackshirt squads in the lower Po valley stepped up their cudgel-swinging forays against Catholics and Socialists. It was in the town of Argenta on August 23, 1923, that Fascist *squadristi*, carrying out orders from the party *quadrumvir* Italo Balbo, waylaid and beat to death Don Giovanni Minzoni, an energetic archpriest who had been organizing rural co-operatives. Thus, a year before the assassination of the right-wing Socialist Giacomo Matteotti, the Catholics could claim a martyr; but, overcautious in their relations with Mussolini, they made little effort to exploit their tragedy. [4]

---

[3] See L. Sturzo, *Popolarismo e fascismo* (Turin, 1925), p. 137 ff. (republished in 1956 in the second volume of his *Il Partito Popolare Italiano*); his *Italy and the Coming World* (New York, 1945), pp. 81 and 126; Giuseppe Petrocchi, *Don Luigi Sturzo* (Rome, 1945), pp. 90–91; Arturo Carlo Jemolo, *Chiesa e stato in Italia negli ultimi cento anni* (Turin, 1949), pp. 603–607; Daniel A. Binchy, *Church and State in Fascist Italy* (London, 1941), pp. 147–153; Edith Pratt Howard, *Il Partito Popolare Italiano* (Florence, 1957), pp. 405–433; and Michael Fogarty, *Christian Democracy in Western Europe, 1820–1953* (London, 1957), pp. 324–325. See also Richard A. Webster, *The Cross and the Fasces: Christian Democracy and Fascism in Italy* (Stanford, 1960).

[4] The trial of Don Minzoni's assassins was a farce, though some anti-Fascists got in a few barbed remarks. See *Il processo di Don Minzoni* (Rome, 1945).

Parliamentary elections of April 6, 1924

In the wake of the crisis produced by the PPI, Mussolini decided to alter the electoral system so that he could gain a strong working majority in Parliament. Thus far he had fewer than 50 deputies in his National-Fascist bloc (Partito Nazionale Fascista); the remaining 485 belonged either to his uncertain allies or to the opposition. To this end he sponsored, in July 1923, a new electoral law that took its name from Giacomo Acerbo, the premier's undersecretary who drafted it. This new form of political arithmetic provided for a hybrid system of partly proportional and partly unproportional representation to replace the democratic PR system inaugurated in 1919. It authorized "national party lists" and entitled whichever party polled a plurality (so long as it was at least 25 per cent of the total vote) to a bonus of no less than two thirds of the seats in the lower house, the remaining seats to be distributed proportionally among the other parties.

The editors of the Milan *Corriere della sera*, the Turin *La Stampa*, and a few other papers bitterly denounced the travesty, while in Parliament Giovanni Amendola, the rising chieftain of the Constitutional Democrats, attacked it. So did the Socialists and many of the Populars who had helped introduce the 1919 system of PR. On the other hand, most Liberals (including ex-Premiers Giovanni Giolitti, V. E. Orlando, and Antonio Salandra) welcomed the Acerbo bill, for they blamed PR for the striking gains achieved by the Socialists and Catholics in the postwar elections as well as for their own poor showing. These conservative-minded Liberals deluded themselves with the notion that they could "domesticate" the Fascists once they eliminated the bulk of Socialist and Popular deputies. When the votes were counted the Fascists and their friends had 235 "yeas"; the "nays" (mainly Socialists) numbered 139; the abstentionists (mostly Populars), 77.[5]

If the elements in the democratic opposition (and especially the two "mass" parties of Socialists and Populars) could have composed their differences long enough to weld an electoral bloc, conceivably they could have prevented the Fascists from winning

[5] Zurcher, "Government and Politics of Italy," in Shotwell (ed.), *Governments of Continental Europe*, p. 619; and Sturzo, *Italy and the Coming World*, p. 81.

8

clear-cut control of the new Twenty-seventh Legislature to be elected on April 6, 1924. This was not to be the case. Most Italian Socialists were not yet capable of shedding their outdated revolutionary slogans and collaborating in a "bourgeois" cabinet.[6] And

[6] The Italian Socialist Party (PSI) dated from the Genoa Congress of 1892, when the Marxists separated from the Anarchists and adopted a contradictory program that often led to confusing vacillation between the "revisionists" or "minimalists" (who stressed the priority of short-term, "minimum" goals of democratic reforms) and the left-wing "maximalists" (who insisted upon nothing less than the long-term "maximum" goal of truly revolutionary social change). Despite the increasing membership in the party, factionalism always threatened to sunder it. After Caporetto the revisionists Filippo Turati and Claudio Treves offered their support to the hard-pressed bourgeois government, though the orthodox "maximalists" stubbornly continued their wartime policy of "neither collaboration nor sabotage."

The postwar period brought a resurgence of Italian Marxism, thanks to the economic chaos and the attraction of Lenin's regime. One of the many maximalists to be attracted by the Russian experiment was Giacinto Menotti Serrati, who with some others made a pilgrimage to Moscow in 1920. Returning in early autumn, they brought back disconcerting information that if Italian Socialists wished to gain admittance into the Moscow-sponsored Communist ("Third") International, they must first rid their party of all revisionists and accept unequivocally Lenin's stern "21 Conditions" for membership. Coming in the wake of the ill-fated sit-down strike in the metallurgical plants, this precipitated the greatest crisis yet in the history of the turbulent PSI.

During the ensuing few weeks the PSI leaders first approved and then hastily rejected the "21 Conditions." The revisionists Turati, Treves, G. E. Modigliani, and Giacomo Matteotti, supported by such powerful General Confederation of Labor (CGL) spokesmen as Bruno Buozzi and Lodovico D'Aragona, firmly resisted all pressure to renounce their democratic and gradualist program. Though the revisionists had no dearth of brainy leadership, this was more than offset by the inconstancy of their mass following. In time they were to label themselves the Unitary Socialist Party (PSU).

The largest faction within the PSI was the center group, which sought to maintain the fiction of party unity by paying lip service to both social-democratic and maximalist slogans. The inconsistency of such a position appeared not to bother them. By 1922 Pietro Nenni was emerging as the dominant spokesman for this faction. Next year he became director of the PSI newspaper, *Avanti!*, after successfully resisting Serrati's efforts to fuse with the Communists. Perhaps the Socialists' most adroit maneuverer, Nenni was almost as versatile as Mussolini; indeed, he too had militated in the Republican Party, shared a prison cell with Mussolini in 1911, and served briefly in 1919 in a Bologna Fascist group.

The PSI's extreme leftist group consisted of men who favored acceptance of the "21 Conditions." Enough of this contingent favored creating a separate Italian Communist Party (PCI) on Leninist principles to lead a secession at the Leghorn Congress in January 1921. The first secretary of the new PCI was Amadeo Bordiga, Neapolitan editor of *Il Soviet*. Bordiga was opposed to collaboration with the Socialists; he also insisted that battles in Parliament were futile and therefore recommended Communist abstention from them. The "abstentionist" leader urged that labor syndicates should, instead, seize power by revolutionary action. Other early PCI chieftains included Professor Antonio Graziadei; Giuseppe Tuntar, editor of the Trieste *Lavoratore*; and the Romagnole Nicola Bombacci, who eventually was to become a Fascist (and the *Duce*'s partner in death on the shore of Lake Como).

9

most of the Popolari were equally unready to take the initiative in working shoulder to shoulder with atheists. Bitter years of dictatorship elapsed before both groups appreciated their folly.

But these extremists were displaced from PCI leadership during the next few years by a clique of Torinese intellectuals headed by Antonio Gramsci and Palmiro Togliatti. The former was born in 1891 in Sardinia of a poor farming family; he joined the island's Marxist movement when just a boy, and soon thereafter moved to Turin, where with the aid of scholarships he worked his way through the university and was graduated with distinction along with his Genoese classmate, Togliatti. Gramsci spent the war in Turin as a Socialist writer and activist. Lenin's "October Revolution" and his use of "soviets" deeply impressed Gramsci, who perceived an analogous type of organization in the Italian workers' "shop committees" or "factory councils" ("*consigli di fabbrica*"), which were then emerging by election of the workers in the vast Fiat plants. These *consigli di fabbrica*, in his opinion, should exist not just for the purpose of negotiating agreements on wages and working conditions but as a means for gaining control over factory management. He dreamed of linking *consigli* throughout the nation. They could replace the old political organs and serve as a means for Communist seizure of power and "dictatorship of the proletariat." With the help of Togliatti, Umberto Terracini, Angelo Tasca, and others, Gramsci had founded in Turin in May 1919 the influential weekly newspaper, *Ordine nuovo* ("New Order"). The Piedmontese *Ordinovisti* took an active part in the backstage maneuvers that surrounded the birth of the PCI in January 1921, and in the next year or so they won the favor of Gregory Zinoviev and Nicholas Bukharin, pivotal figures in the Comintern. The friendships Gramsci shrewdly cultivated during the year and a half he spent in Moscow after June 1922 served him well in his fight to oust Bordiga from PCI leadership.

While this intraparty contest shaped up, Mussolini's Fascists marched to power. The PCI, primarily interested in bringing about the revolutionary overthrow of the capitalistic regime, professed at this time to see very little difference between the Blackshirts and the rest of the *bourgeoisie*; consequently, Communists made no serious effort to defend the beleaguered Liberal government, despite certain propagandistic talk about a "united front" with Socialists.

Among the important works to consult regarding the early period of Italian Marxism are Richard Hostetter, *The Italian Socialist Movement,* of which the first of three volumes, *Origins, 1860–1882,* has appeared (Princeton, 1958); Aldo Romano's projected 9-volume *Storia del movimento socialista in Italia* (Rome, 1954 ff.); Leo Valiani, *Storia del movimento socialista* (Florence, 1951); Gastone Manacorda, *Il movimento operaio attraverso i suoi congressi: dalle origini alla formazione del Partito Socialista (1853–1892)* (Rome, 1955); Roberto Michels, *Storia critica del movimento socialista italiano* (Florence, 1926); Alfredo Angiolini and Eugenio Ciacchi, *Socialismo e socialisti in Italia: storia completa del movimento . . . dal 1850 al 1919* (Florence, 1920); Leo Valiani, "Storia del movimento socialista in Italia dalle origini al 1921: studi e ricerche nel decennio 1945–1955," in *Rivista storica italiana,* LXVIII (1956), pp. 447–510, 620–669; and Rosario Romeo's critique of Marxist writers in *Nord e Sud,* III, Nos. 21 and 22 (1956), pp. 5–37 and 16–44.

On the post–World War I period, see also Aldo Garosci's chapter in Mario Einaudi (ed.), *Communism in Western Europe* (Ithaca, 1951); Gaetano Arfè, *Storia dell'Avanti!* (1896–1926; 1926–1951) (2 vols.; Milan-Rome, 1956–1958); Pietro Nenni, *Storia di quattro anni (1919–1922)* and his *Sei anni di guerra civile* (Milan, 1945); Fulvio Bellini and Giorgio Galli, *Storia del Partito Comunista Italiano* (Milan, 1953) [hereafter cited as B/G, *Storia del PCI*]; the subsequent revised and more fully documented work by Giorgio Galli alone,

Meanwhile, the Fascists carefully prepared their national ticket, popularly nicknamed the *listone* ("big list"). They made it eye-catching by persuading Salandra and Orlando to affix their names to it, and Giolitti to appear on a "parallel list." To remind voters of their "patriotic duty," *squadristi* set about intimidating many speakers who criticized the regime. Thus they broke into the home of ex-Premier Francesco Saverio Nitti on November 29, 1923, and they beat up Amendola on December 26. Several times they arrested the latter and the Socialists Pietro Nenni and Luigi Mascagni. And in a speech on January 28, 1924, Mussolini fumed, "When it is a matter of the Fatherland, or of Fascism, we are ready to kill and to die!" [7]

The Fascists claimed 64.9 per cent of the ballots, their strength concentrated chiefly in central and southern Italy. Apart from the numerous electoral irregularities (which Matteotti was soon to expose), the victory derived from a widespread "wait-and-see" attitude of many who doubtless were impressed by the country's recent economic improvement and by Mussolini's bold bombardment of Corfu. In any event, Mussolini gained two thirds (374) of the new Chamber of Deputies; in addition, he could count on the support of 15 Liberals, 10 Social Democrats (formerly known as Radicals), and 4 Peasant deputies.

The "constitutional opposition" consisted of 39 Populars and 14 Constitutional Democrats. The "extreme Left" ("*Sinistra estrema*") numbered 24 Unitary (*i.e.*, moderate revisionist) Socialists; 22 Maximalist (*i.e.*, orthodox revolutionary) Socialists; 19 Communists (an increase over their previous 13); and 7 Republicans. Finally, there were 2 Sardinian Actionists; 4 deputies from the Germanic and Slavic border zones; and 1 dissident Fascist.[8] It is worth noting that in some northern compartments (Piedmont, Lombardy, Venetia, Liguria, and Venezia Giulia) the combined total of the largest opposition parties was greater than the number of votes polled by the Fascists. Through-

---

Storia del Partito Comunista Italiano (Milan, 1958); Palmiro Togliatti (ed.), *Trenta anni di vita e di lotte del PCI* (Quaderno No. 2, "Rinascita," Rome, 1952); and Paolo Robotti and Giovanni Germanetto, *Trent'anni di lotta dei comunisti italiani, 1921–1951* (Rome, 1952).

[7] Salvatorelli in A. Garosci, *et al, Il Secondo Risorgimento*, p. 116.

[8] Mario Vinciguerra, "I partiti politici," in Corrado Barbagallo (ed.), *Cento anni di vita italiana* (2 vols.; Milan, 1950), I, 226–227. The following statistics are cited in S/M, *Sdf*, pp. 223–224:

out the next two decades the foes of Fascism counted these regions among their bastions.

Murder of Matteotti

Most foreigners accepted the April 6, 1924, election results as a valid reflection of Italian opinion and a posterior legalization of the Fascist March on Rome. But many Italians did not. During the next few weeks numerous editors and deputies were calling the Fascist electoral triumph a swindle. Giacomo Matteotti, secretary of Filippo Turati's revisionist Unitary Socialist Party, raised the most persuasive criticisms. His challenges signalled the start of a determined but long-frustrated anti-Fascist Resistenza that was to continue underground and abroad for the next two decades.

The 39-year-old Unitary Socialist was the son of a prosperous family of Fratta Polesine in Rovigo province. After graduating brilliantly from the University of Bologna law school, Matteotti had started his political career by founding Socialist organizations along the lower Po, a section long noted for its bitter seasonal struggles between migrant farm hands and landowners. Such practical experience he supplemented by extensive travel abroad, where he became acquainted with many of the Socialist and Labor Party leaders of western Europe. From the day he was elected to Parliament in 1919 he impressed almost everyone in Palazzo Montecitorio with his conscientiousness. He made it a practice

Party	Percentage of popular vote	Seats	Popular vote
Fascists	64.9	374	$\dfrac{4,305,936}{347,552} = 4,653,488$
Liberals	3.3	15	233,521
Social Democrats (Radicals)	1.6	10	111,035
Populars	9.0	39	645,789
Unitary Socialists	5.9	24	422,957
Maximalist Socialists	5.0	22	360,694
Communists	3.7	19	268,191
Republicans	1.9	7	133,714
Constitutional Democrats	2.2	14	157,932
Piedmontese Peasants	1.0	4	73,569
Sardinian Actionists	0.3	2	24,059
Germans (Alto Adige) and Slavs	0.9	4	62,451
Dissident Fascists	0.3	1	18,062
Total	100.0	535	7,165,462

to collect detailed data on every subject that interested him and he quickly won a reputation for intellectual honesty. Matteotti fought Fascism with facts and conviction.[9]

On May 30, 1924, he rose in the Chamber to deliver a blistering two-hour denunciation of the newly elected Fascist majority. He enumerated specific instances where Blackshirt toughs had employed physical intimidation and surveilled the ballot boxes. On the basis of this evidence he concluded that Mussolini could not truthfully claim overwhelming popular support. When he demanded "that the Government render account for its conduct of the elections," [10] Rightist deputies railed at him: "Hireling! Traitor! Demagogue!" To some of his own colleagues Matteotti whispered wryly, "And now you can prepare my funeral oration." [11]

The speech elicited angry replies both in Parliament and in the Fascist press, with some suggesting that physical reprisals be taken against the defiant Socialist. A few days later, June 10, Fascist gangsters led by Amerigo Dumini, a *squadrista* who already had perpetrated a dozen political murders, kidnapped Matteotti near his residence along the Tiber River, stabbed him numerous times in the getaway car, and then half buried his body in a grove fourteen miles from the capital. Several weeks passed before the mutilated corpse was found, though from the moment of Matteotti's forcible capture it was obvious that he was the victim of foul play.[12]

The assassination climaxed the wave of Fascist hooliganism and sundered anew the hybrid government. For at least a week Mussolini suffered intense fear for his own political future; indeed, for six months the country was convulsed *diminuendo* by a crisis the like of which the *Duce* was not to see again until

[9] Alessandro Schiavi, *La vita e l'opera di Giacomo Matteotti* (Rome, 1957), pp. 17–121; Piero Gobetti, *Profilo di Giacomo Matteotti* (reprinted in Rome, 1944), p. 4; and A.N.P.P.I.A. (ed.), *Matteotti* (Rome, 1957). Gaetano Arfè is editing Matteotti's complete works.

[10] Quoted from the official transcript, reprinted in G. Matteotti, *Reliquie* (Milan, 1924), pp. 263–282; also in Frances Keene (ed.), *Neither Liberty Nor Bread: The Meaning and Tragedy of Fascism* (New York, 1940), pp. 45–57.

[11] Nenni, *Sei anni di guerra civile*, p. 174.

[12] Gaetano Salvemini, *Fascist Dictatorship in Italy* (New York, 1927), Ch. v; cf. Schiavi, *Vita e opera di Matteotti*, p. 157 ff., for the unfolding and discovery of the crime.

13

the fateful summer of 1943. For days much of the foreign press headlined the domestic repercussions.[13]

Stirred deeply, the Italian public took two views of the crime. Many believed that Mussolini personally had ordered the assassination, while others suspected that the murder was undertaken, rather, by individual Fascists acting either on their own volition or at the instigation of some lower PNF official. Yet almost everyone conceded that, regardless of whether Mussolini had deliberately ordered Matteotti's removal, he had repeatedly incited his followers to acts of violence and thus could not escape a certain moral responsibility.[14] In the capital, therefore, demands arose from many quarters for him to resign. Unfortunately for those oppositionists who dreamed of persuading the King to intervene and ask for the resignation of his chief minister, Victor Emmanuel III was away on a state visit to Spain, where (according to charitable critics) perhaps he did not fully appreciate the furor. That he would have repudiated his premier had he gauged the popular feeling at first hand seems most unlikely, judging by the Savoyard's record before and after.[15]

Shaken by the commotion, Mussolini informed the Chamber on June 12 that he personally had ordered the police to intensify the search for Matteotti; he insisted that only his worst enemies could have dreamed up such a deed.[16] Years later he confided to his physician that perhaps as few as fifty or even twenty determined men could have upset his regime during that critical period.[17]

Before long Dumini and four others in the execution squad were arrested. But who had issued the mandate? Suspicion fell

[13] Mussolini was much concerned with foreign reaction. His correspondence with his diplomats on this subject fills a large section of Volume III (23 febbraio 1924—14 maggio 1925) of I Documenti Diplomatici Italiani: Settima serie, 1922–1935 (Rome, 1959), pp. 154–393.

[14] In Popolo d'Italia at the end of May and early in June there had been references to Matteotti as "an agent provocateur in the Chamber," and the warning, "If Matteotti gets his head broken, he will only have himself and his obstinacy to thank." Quoted in Monelli, Mussolini, p. 112.

[15] See Mussolini's cable to Victor Emmanuel III, Aug. 17, 1924, and the reply of Aug. 18, in I Documenti Diplomatici Italiani: Settima serie, 1922–1935, Vol. III, 262–264. Cf. Emilio Lussu, Marcia su Roma e dintorni (Rome, 1945), p. 167; S/M, Sdf, p. 248; and P. Alatri, "Le origini del fascismo e la classe dirigente italiana," Belfagor, July 31, 1950.

[16] Benito Mussolini, Scritti e discorsi (1924) (Milan, 1934), IV, 182.

[17] Carlo Silvestri, Turati l'ha detto (Milan, 1946), pp. 111–112.

on several ranking Fascists, and in time some were arrested: Giovanni Marinelli, PNF administrative secretary; Cesare Rossi, head of the press office of the prime minister; Aldo Finzi, Undersecretary of Interior; and Filippo Naldi, a journalist who enjoyed close ties with party hierarchs. Meantime, Filippo Filippelli, a Fascist newspaper publisher whose auto had been used but who personally was uninvolved, wrote an exposé (not immediately publicized) accusing the *Duce* of ordering the crime.

Hoping to silence the uproar, Mussolini resigned his portfolio as Minister of Interior in mid-June, while Emilio DeBono (one of the four *quadrumvirs* of the March on Rome) stepped down from the headship of the investigative police. By June 24 the harried prime minister had recovered some of his nerve. Standing before the Senate in a ceremony commemorating the murdered PSU secretary, he spoke eloquently in favor of a "reign of law." This hypocrisy reassured conservative Solons who were ready to accord him the benefit of the doubt. Thus two days later (notwithstanding trenchant arguments by ex-Foreign Minister Carlo Sforza, ex-Labor Minister Mario Abbiate, and Luigi Albertini, director of *Corriere della sera*) the Senate expressed confidence in Mussolini by a vote of 225 to 21, with 6 abstentions.[18] Senator Sforza, it may be noted, had suggested to some of his colleagues a few days after the assassination that they ought to arrest Mussolini in his office then and there, but no one acted.[19]

Secession to the Aventine

The lower house was less favorably impressed with Mussolini's promises. On the basis of strategy devised on June 18, some 150 Socialists, Populars, Republicans, and Constitutional Democrats withdrew from the *aula* on June 27 rather than participate in a commemorative ceremony alongside the Fascists. Repairing to another auditorium in the same building which was open to the public, the anti-Fascist bloc listened to Filippo Turati,[20] the elder statesman of Matteotti's party, speak in memory of the

[18] Carlo Sforza, *Contemporary Italy: Its Intellectual and Moral Origins* (New York, 1944), pp. 317–318; Schiavi, *Vita e opera di Matteotti*, pp. 199–203.

[19] Lussu, *Marcia su Roma e dintorni*, p. 170; Antonio Carcaterra, *Storia dell'Aventino* (Rome, 1946), pp. 68–69.

[20] The most recent biography is Franco Catalano, *Filippo Turati* (Milan-Rome, 1957).

15

deceased. Alluding to the historic last stand of Gaius Gracchus and his plebs around the Temple of Diana on the Aventine hill, white-bearded Turati called for immediate abolition of the Fascist Militia and then proclaimed, "The only real representatives of the people are those who now stand on the Aventine of their own conscience, whence no wiles shall move them until the sun of freedom dawns once more, until the rule of law is given back, and until the representation of the people ceases to be the ghastly jest to which it has been reduced." [21]

The Aventinian bloc thus decided to remain outside the regular Chamber, thereby assuming a virtually revolutionary stance, though only a few seemed to realize fully the logical implications of their move. Later a handful of Communist deputies joined them temporarily in their conventicles. Remaining in the usual place to carry on the legislative functions were some 380 Fascists and right-wing Liberals; but soon they recessed until November 12, which rendered the Aventinian foil less conspicuous. Fearful of anything that might open the door to Communism, three Liberal ex-premiers—Giolitti, Salandra, and Orlando (Turati facetiously dubbed them the "three Magi")—refused to participate in the Aventine.[22] Yet toward the end of the year they and the Piedmontese Marcello Soleri belatedly voiced timid criticism of the government.

The most authoritative spokesman of the constitutional opposition was Giovanni Amendola, a square-jawed 42-year-old Neapolitan deputy who probably would have become premier had the ill-starred Aventine succeeded. In his youth Amendola had gained a scholarly reputation from his philosophical treatises;[23] and for a period before the war he had been a university professor in Pisa. Then he switched his activities to journalism, becoming Rome correspondent of *Corriere della sera* after 1914.

[21] Quoted in Wayland Hilton-Young, *The Italian Left: A Short History of Political Socialism in Italy* (London, 1949), p. 138. *Cf.* Filippo Turati and Anna Kuliscioff *Carteggio*, Vol. VI, *Il delitto Matteotti e l'Aventino (1923–1925)* (Turin, 1959), pp. 236–237; Milan *Corriere della sera*, June 28, 1924.

[22] To a friend Giolitti wrote that the Aventine consisted of "well-meaning people who hold family get-togethers in order to make speeches to each other, which very few read, and who waste their time. We are in the midst of two abnormalities—one violent, the other, let us say, ridiculous." Gabriele de Rosa (ed.), *Giolitti e il fascismo in alcune sue lettere inedite* (Rome, 1957), p. 25.

[23] These included *Filosofia e psicologia nello studio dell'io* (Geneva, 1909); *La volontà e il bene—etica e religione* (Rome, 1911); and *Etica e biografia* (Milan, 1915).

16

He served as an artillery officer during the war and was decorated for valor. Ever more interested in politics, he won election to the Chamber in 1919 and occasionally held cabinet posts.[24] Unlike many of his leftist contemporaries (and even his own son [25]), Amendola was not overly impressed by Russia's Bolshevist revolution, and he never repudiated the tenets of democratic liberalism. His great ambition was to weld a powerful, genuinely democratic Left that would include revisionist Marxists, liberal Catholics, and other moderates.[26]

During the summer and autumn of 1924, and with the help of Alberto Cianca and Mario Ferrara, he carried on an almost incessant campaign against Mussolini in the columns of *Il Mondo*, an influential journal founded in Rome in 1921. Day after day Amendola sought to persuade the King of the imperativeness of dissolving Parliament, of insisting upon the resignation of Mussolini, and of calling for new general elections—but always in vain.[27] In November, for example, some Aventinians showed Victor Emmanuel III startling testimony by the Fascist Cesare Rossi which revealed much "inside information" about the Matteotti case and other affairs; but the monarch refused to read more than a line or two. To ex-Premier Ivanoe Bonomi's remonstrance that he thereby was assuming grave responsibility for the nation's future, the Savoyard replied that he feared no such danger.[28] He preferred to hide behind the constitutional fiction that his only eyes and ears were Parliament, and not any disjointed segment of it. If there was no alternative majority in

[24] G. Amendola, *Una battaglia liberale: discorsi politici* (1919–1923) (Turin, 1924), pp. 232–233; *cf.* the Marxian-oriented biographical sketch by Giampiero Carocci, *Giovanni Amendola nella crisi dello stato italiano* (1911–1925) (Milan, 1956); and Franco Rizzo, *Giovanni Amendola e la crisi della democrazia* (Rome, 1956).

[25] His son Giorgio attorned to Communism while living in exile and by January 1932 was roundly denouncing democratic *émigrés* for allegedly restricting the anti-Fascist struggle to a fight for merely "formal," "bourgeois" freedoms. See reply of Carlo Rosselli in *Quaderni di "Giustizia e Libertà,"* No. 1 (Paris, Jan. 1932) to an earlier article of Amendola in the *émigré* PCI review, *Stato operaio*.

[26] See his letter to Turati in August 1923, published by Alessandro Schiavi (ed.), *Filippo Turati attraverso le lettere di corrispondenti* (1880–1925) (Bari, 1947), p. 241 ff.; *cf.* Giovanni Amendola, *La democrazia italiana contro il fascismo, 1922–1924* (Milan-Naples, 1960), *passim*.

[27] Mario Ferrara, "Amendola nei ricordi di un compagno di lotte: antifascismo perenne," Rome *Il Mondo*, Jan. 31, 1956.

[28] Ivanoe Bonomi, *Diario di un anno, 2 giugno 1943–10 giugno 1944* (Milan, 1947), pp. xxvi–xxvii.

Parliament he could do nothing.[29] He was impervious to all arguments that some of the seats held by the Fascists had been gained improperly and that the 1848 *Statuto Albertino* need not be construed so narrowly. As a matter of fact, nineteen years later he overcame these legal scruples when he replaced Mussolini with Marshal Pietro Badoglio. But during the Aventine crisis he believed that any intercession would simply "open the way" to the Bolshevists, or at the very least to his unbeloved cousin and dynastic rival, the Duke of Aosta.[30] If Victor Emmanuel had decided to demand the resignation of Mussolini in the summer of 1924, probably he could have relied upon the support of the Army in case of a clash with the Fascist Militia; but he preferred to wait until 1943, when his country was in ruins and it was too late even to save his throne.

In the wisdom of hindsight one can argue that the Aventine secession was *controproducente,* to use a favorite neologism of the *Duce.* The oppositionists could have done more in the way of formal investigations from the floor of the Chamber than from outside. Moreover, by voluntarily withdrawing, they made it unnecessary for Mussolini to do what Adolf Hitler later was obliged to do with his Reichstag foes, namely, expel them by force.

Amendola was relatively more successful, but still very slow,[31] in promoting the National Union of Liberal and Democratic Forces, which he inaugurated on November 8, 1924, with the help of Mario Vinciguerra (its secretary), the historian Guglielmo Ferrero, and dozens of prominent scholars, journalists, and politicians.[32] They drew up a manifesto espousing "popular sovereignty," "a new democracy of liberty and work," "freedom of the press, speech, education, religion, and economy"; and seven

[29] For a defense of the King, see Mario Viana, *La monarchia e il fascismo* (Rome, 1951).

[30] Maurice Vaussard, *Histoire de l'Italie contemporaine* (1870–1946) (Paris, 1950), p. 209. Again in June 1925 the King listened without a word of reply to an oral exposition of the problem presented to him by DeGasperi, Amendola, and DiCesarò. Salvatorelli in *Il Secondo Risorgimento,* p. 146.

[31] Turati snapped wryly that Amendola was "inflexible in his immobility." Giancarlo Vigorelli, *Gronchi: battaglie d'oggi e di ieri* (Florence, 1956), p. 286.

[32] Among the signers were Amendola, Vinciguerra, Sforza, Bonomi, Ferrero, Cianca, Meuccio Ruini, Guido DeRuggiero, Luigi Salvatorelli, Mario Abbiate, Corrado Alvaro, Corrado Barbagallo, Mario Borsa, Piero Calamandrei, Giorgio Levi della Vida, Giovanni Mira, Enrico Molè, Nello Rosselli, Francesco Ruffini, Cesare Spellanzon, Silvio Trentin, and Vito Volterra. S/M, *Sdf,* p. 253.

months later (June 14–16, 1925) they convened in three well-guarded rooms the first and only congress of their new Democratic Party.[33] Noble as their slogans were, such phrases were incapable of toppling a government which had battened on widespread disillusionment with democratic liberalism.

During the first weeks after the initiation of the Aventine some of the Populars (among them DeGasperi and Gronchi, a Tuscan labor leader and ex-minister in Mussolini's first cabinet) discussed with Turati the possibility of joining in an eventual coalition if Mussolini could be unhorsed.[34] But rule by such a "revolutionary" bloc was resisted on the one hand by such conservative older statesmen as Orlando and Salandra, whose advice the King was then seeking. They preferred to take their chances with Mussolini, who, they believed, could be tamed and normalized.[35] Vigorous hostility to the Socialist-Popular gambit came also from the Jesuits. The editor of *Civiltà cattolica* published an article on August 16, 1924, in which he objected that such a bloc would be neither "decent, opportune, [nor] lawful"—despite DeGasperi's observations that similar coalitions had emerged in Germany and Austria.[36] If the PPI still stood in need of a *coup de grâce*, this was administered by Pius XI himself on September 9 when he pointedly told an audience of Catholic University students that he could not countenance "co-operation with evil" for "whatever reason of public welfare." [37]

PCI tactics

In November 1924 the Italian Communist Party deserted the Aventine. That young party's history thus far had been replete with factionalism and police harassment.[38] Early in 1923, for example, the police had discovered in a Rome tailorshop the covert provisional headquarters of its executive committee—a

---

[33] Meuccio Ruini, *La democrazia e l'Unione Nazionale* (Milan, 1925), pp. 271–299.

[34] Vigorelli, *Gronchi*, pp. 280–282.

[35] Howard, *Il Partito Popolare Italiano*, pp. 448–457.

[36] Mario Einaudi and François Goguel, *Christian Democracy in Italy and France* (Notre Dame, 1952), pp. 18–20; Binchy, *Church and State in Fascist Italy*, pp. 156–158; G. Candeloro, "Movimento cattolico in Italia," *Rinascita*, x (Aug. 1953), p. 474 ff.; Webster, *The Cross and the Fasces*, pp. 96–97.

[37] *L'Osservatore romano*, Sept. 10, 1924, cited in Stefano Jacini, *Storia del Partito Popolare Italiano* (Milan, 1951), p. 234 ff., and in Binchy, pp. 157–158.

[38] See *supra*, n. 6.

discovery that led to the arrest of several key members, including Amadeo Bordiga and Ruggiero Grieco, as well as hundreds of "lesser fry"; but after a highly publicized trial most of them were acquitted before the end of the year.[39] Luckily for the PCI, Palmiro Togliatti evaded the dragnet and moved from Rome to Milan, while Antonio Gramsci prudently stayed in Moscow most of 1923. Reeling from Fascist blows, the PCI lost two thirds of its members that year; [40] yet in April 1924 it won nineteen seats in Parliament—rather impressive under the circumstances. Its strength centered in Italy's northwestern "industrial triangle" and in Emilia and Tuscany.

Intermittently in 1923 and 1924 Gramsci (but not Bordiga) talked of the advantages offered by a united front with the Socialists. They glossed over the fact that this would have to be organized on their own terms. "Unity" always was one of their favorite cries; they used it as the rubric for their newspaper, *L'Unità*, founded in February 1924, a sheet which managed to appear openly and later clandestinely throughout the dictatorship. In line with the "united front" shibboleth, Gramsci, upon his return from Russia, led his party into the Aventine bloc. He was anxious to keep the PCI identified with the masses and he thought that the secessionists were arousing popular support. Soon after joining the Aventine, however, Gramsci decried its "sterile," constitutional strategy which looked to the King for solution of the crisis. Gramsci preferred at the very least to change the Aventine into an effective legislature—a true "Anti-Parliament." Still more important, he argued, was action on the barricades by hastily formed committees of workers and peasants.[41]

Gramsci's arguments for a "descent into the piazzas" were voiced also by the pugnacious Sardinian Republican, Emilio Lussu, and by such war-veteran groups as the Associazione Nazionale dei Combattenti and the Associazione dei Mutilati e Invalidi, which toyed with such a move in conclaves in Assisi and Fiume in July, only to drop it.[42]

More resolute action came from a republican veterans group,

[39] B/G, *Storia del PCI*, pp. 89, 102–104; Garosci, "Italian Communist Party," in Einaudi (ed.), *Communism in Western Europe*, pp. 160–164; and Guido Leto, OVRA, *Fascismo-Antifascismo* (Rocca S. Casciano, 1951), p. 43.
[40] Galli, *Storia del Partito Comunista Italiano*, p. 82.
[41] *Ibid.*, p. 97 ff.
[42] Salvatorelli in *Il Secondo Risorgimento*, pp. 113–114.

Italia Libera, which was instigated after Matteotti's assassination by General "Peppino" Garibaldi,[43] and the war heroes Raffaele Rossetti and Gigino Battisti. Soon they boasted nuclei in a couple of dozen cities, where Italia Libera sought to promote street demonstrations and at night pasted posters on walls calling for dissolution of the Blackshirt Militia, honest elections, an unemasculated Parliament, and freedom of the press and assembly. But Italia Libera was unable to spark revolt.[44]

The great majority of Aventinians regarded the PCI formula of violence as a "kiss of death" to their plans for winning the King's benison.[45] By late autumn the Communists themselves stopped such talk, and in November they returned to their old parliamentary benches, to the bewilderment of their own rank-and-file. From the Chamber they denounced any and all, amid noisy heckling from the Fascists.

One can only speculate whether violence in the early summer (and possibly as late as the autumn) of 1924 could have overturned Mussolini. In retrospect Communist writers boast of their own audacity and seem to have persuaded themselves that such a program would have won.[46] They can find some support in the memoirs of Guido Leto, who headed Mussolini's secret police (OVRA). He has suggested that an insurrection might have achieved its goal, at least in July.[47] In later years Mussolini saw fit to endorse this interpretation (perhaps to flatter himself on his own victory).[48] And the reputable Socialist historian, Giacomo Perticone, inclined toward this view,[49] as did the radical

[43] He was one of the grandsons of the ubiquitous nineteenth-century liberator. A soldier in six wars, he had been Francisco Madero's chief of staff during the 1910–1911 Mexican revolution, and he was to lead 3,000 Venezuelan rebels against dictator Cipriano Castro in 1930.
[44] Ernesto Rossi, "L' 'Italia Libera,' " in his *Non Mollare!* (1925) (Florence, 1955), pp. 43–67; and reprinted also in his *No al Fascismo* (Turin, 1957), pp. 23–48; Armando Gavagnin, *Vent'anni di resistenza al fascismo* (Turin, 1958), pp. 182–188; and Aldo Garosci, *Storia dei fuorusciti* [hereafter cited as *Sdf*] (Bari, 1953), p. 21.
[45] Carcaterra, *Storia dell'Aventino*, pp. 68–69 ff.; Lussu, *Marcia su Roma e dintorni*, p. 170.
[46] See PCI, *Per la libertà e l'indipendenza d'Italia: relazione della Direzione del PCI al Vº Congresso* (Rome, 1945), pp. 1–4; Togliatti (ed.), *Trenta anni di vita e di lotte del PCI*; Robotti and Germanetto, *Trent'anni di lotte dei comunisti italiani, 1921–1951*, pp. 45–50.
[47] Leto, *OVRA, Fascismo-Antifascismo*, p. 17.
[48] Silvestri, *Turati l'ha detto*, pp. 53–54, 116–117.
[49] Perticone, *La politica italiana nell'ultimo trentennio*: Vol. II, *La crisi della democrazia e la dittatura fascista*, pp. 243–244, 218.

21

Gaetano Salvemini.[50] The conservative Popular, Stefano Jacini,[51] and some others not necessarily to the right of center contended, on the other hand, that Gramsci's party did not yet exercise enough influence among the workers to enable it to carry out such an ambitious scheme.[52]

If one concedes that the Aventinians were correct to shy away from bloody revolution, there is still room for criticism of some of their constitutional actions. For example, they tarried too long in forming their Democratic Union, and they could have published sooner and to better issue some of the evidence they possessed. Even though the Filippo Filippelli and Cesare Rossi testimonials may not have contained enough information to support impeachment charges against Mussolini, they could have offered adequate grounds for the oppositionists, if they had returned to the Chamber, to propose the appointment of a parliamentary committee of inquiry, which conceivably could have further aroused the public.[53] Instead, the Aventinians failed to keep alive the moral indignation that had been widespread early in the summer.[54] Apathy was endemic from the Quirinal and Vatican to the workers' quarters. A great many people seemed anxious to give Mussolini a chance to clean house in his own way. Meantime, some of the anti-Fascists' moral arguments were weakened by unfortunate (and unauthorized) acts of violence by some of their outraged supporters, the most notable being the murder of a Fascist deputy in a Rome tram by an unbalanced youth.

By this time Mussolini was regaining his composure, thanks to the encouragement of such henchmen as Roberto Farinacci, the bellicose PNF *ras* of Cremona, and thanks also to the absence of any effective action by the Aventine. In a speech to the Senate on December 5, 1924, Mussolini felt confident enough

[50] Gaetano Salvemini, *Italy between the First and Second World Wars, 1919–1939* (Cambridge, Mass., 1942; mimeographed copy in Widener Library), Ch. 25, pp. 22–23, cited by Howard, *Il Partito Popolare Italiano,* pp. 473–474.
[51] Jacini, *Storia del PPI,* p. 240 ff.; *cf.* Salvatorelli in *Il Secondo Risorgimento,* p. 136.
[52] Giuseppe Turcato, "Il Partito Comunista Italiano," in Giovanni Gambarin (ed.), *I partiti dell'Italia nuova* (Venice, 1945), p. 31; and B/G, *Storia del PCI,* pp. 143–148.
[53] Salvemini, *Fascist Dictatorship in Italy,* pp. 283–284.
[54] Corrado Barbagallo, *Lettere a John: che cosa fu il fascismo?* (Naples, 1946), pp. 111–114.

to promise, "If His Majesty the King should call me at the termination of this session and tell me that I must go, I would stand at attention, salute, and obey." [55] He well knew that his only danger lay in royal rejection, and during the next few weeks he did his best to frighten Victor Emmanuel out of any such move.

"Coup d'état" of January 3, 1925

When Amendola and Cianca published the Rossi memorandum in *Il Mondo* on December 28, they were sure it would create a sensation and force the premier into a public trial in which he would have to testify. It did the first but not the latter. Mussolini lunged forth with a violent counteroffensive on January 3, 1925. In an impassioned half-hour speech in Parliament he took full responsibility for the previous violence—castor oil, blackjacks, and all. Shouting that "force" was the "only solution," he promised that "within forty-eight hours" he would "clarify" the situation in all respects.[56] He did. Dictatorship was his solution, and it grew steadily tougher during the next two years.

After the premier's pronunciamento, three prominent Liberals (Salandra, Alessandro Casati, and Gino Sarrocchi) who had held cabinet posts resigned, but without making their reasons crystal clear to the public. In the Chamber Orlando and Giolitti uttered desultory criticism of a radical new electoral system proposed by the government, but it passed in February by 307 to 33. Certainly such paltry dissent did not suggest to the circumspect monarch the existence of any realistic parliamentary alternative to the existing government.[57]

Though the Aventinians reaffirmed on January 8 their determination to hold firm, their cause had failed. Any chance of action in the streets by such a group as the Associazione Nazionale dei Combattenti was skillfully blocked when the Fascists seized control of its directory.[58] In any case, most Italians seemed frankly unready to risk their skins in defense of the seemingly pedestrian and humdrum virtues of constitutional government

[55] Mussolini, *Scritti e discorsi* (1924), IV, 411.
[56] Mussolini, *Scritti e discorsi* (1925), V, 13–16.
[57] Marcello Soleri, *Memorie* (Turin, 1948), p. 184; Salvatorelli in *Il Secondo Risorgimento*, p. 141.
[58] *Ibid.*, pp. 144–145.

after the menacing speech of January 3 and in the face of the powerful Militia. Democratic liberalism seemed to have lost whatever appeal it once had held out to them (but it must not be forgotten that they had experienced the simulacrum of democratic processes only since 1912). The steady din of ridicule heaped upon "bourgeois freedom" not just by Fascists on the right but by Marxists on the left had helped to undermine constitutional government.

Almost by reflex action, the Aventinians prepared for a future election campaign. But their front was already disintegrating. The PCI had defected in November 1924, and on January 24, 1925, some Populars talked also of returning to the Chamber, for it was clear that the Vatican disliked their program and was quite willing to sacrifice both the PPI and the Catholic labor organization (Confederazione Italiana dei Lavoratori) to the rival Catholic Action "apostolate of the laity" movement, in the hope of appeasing Mussolini.[59]

April and May were the months of the "battle of the rival manifestoes" issued by Giovanni Gentile and Benedetto Croce.[60] June provided the occasion for the one and only congress of Amendola's infant Democratic Party and for the fifth and final conclave of the PPI,[61] while July 13 saw the last public act of the Aventine—release of a document intended to demonstrate the guilt of the Fascist General DeBono in several crimes.

A week later (July 20) thirty *squadristi* brutally beat Amendola at the spa of Montecatini. They dragged him from his car and pommelled him so viciously he never fully recovered. Soon he emigrated to Cannes, where he died on April 7, 1926, at the age of 44—his death resulting from a tumor which physicians believed was caused by the blows he had received.[62] The death of Amendola, less than two years after Matteotti's death, deprived the constitutional opposition of its principal chieftain.

The Aventine had suffered a mortal blow. Already on September 18, 1925, the Maximalist Socialists had deserted it, and the Republicans followed suit on October 2; but neither party re-

---

[59] Regarding Catholic Action, see *infra*, Ch. III.
[60] *Ibid.*
[61] *Ibid.*
[62] S/M, *Sdf*, p. 266.

entered the old Chamber. The Populars, who had seen their courageous editor Giuseppe Donati hounded into exile in June and DeGasperi resign from the party directorate in December, began to look for a suitable occasion to return to the Chamber without giving the appearance of surrendering. They thought they had found it on January 16, 1926, when a memorial ceremony was scheduled for the late Queen Mother; but, to their discomfiture, Mussolini barred them unless they agreed to "surrender unconditionally," and only three deigned to do that.[63]

Against that backdrop and after innumerable delays the trial of Matteotti's murderers got under way in the fall of 1925, first in Rome and then in the remote provincial town of Chieti, far from the spotlight. The state prosecutor was a brother-in-law of Farinacci. By a curious interpretation of the evidence, the court persuaded itself that the kidnappers had not really meant to assassinate Matteotti but only to abduct him, and that the orders issued by Giovanni Marinelli and Cesare Rossi to the gang were simply to this effect. Thus the charges were reduced to "unpremeditated manslaughter." [64]

[63] Howard, *Il Partito Popolare Italiano*, pp. 466–469, 473–485.
[64] The two men who presumably had sat in the front seat of the car (Giuseppe Viola and Augusto Malacria) were acquitted. Dumini, Albino Volpi, and Amleto Poveromo were sentenced to six years but were freed after two months in the wake of a convenient amnesty announced on July 31, 1925, with the Matteotti case in mind. Partly because of it, neither Marinelli nor Cesare Rossi was brought to trial. In disgrace with Mussolini because of the damaging evidence he gave the opposition, Rossi fled to France in February 1926. There he engaged in journalism and associated with anti-Fascist *émigrés*. But in August 1928 Fascist agents tricked him into motoring into the Italian enclave of Campione on the Swiss side of Lake Lugano; there they arrested him. Charged with conspiring to assassinate the *Duce*, he was condemned by the Fascist Special Tribunal on Sept. 27, 1929, to thirty years. Marinelli, on the other hand, stayed in the *Duce's* good graces until the fateful Grand Council session of July 24–25, 1943, at which time he voted against his master. As a result, Mussolini had him tried for treason and he was executed with Count Galeazzo Ciano in January 1944.

After the Allied liberation of Rome in June 1944 the new democratic government of Premier Bonomi annulled the old trial of the Matteotti murderers and ordered the Rome Court of Assize to prepare for a new trial of the surviving suspects. Five were available in 1947 for the *processo*: Dumini, Rossi, Poveromo, Francesco Giunta (PNF secretary-general in 1924), and F. Panzeri (accused of having helped shove Matteotti into the auto). Viola, Malacria, and Filippelli could not be found and were tried *in absentia*. The testimony tended to show that the deceased Marinelli was the chief instigator of the crime. On April 5, 1947, the court sentenced Dumini, Poveromo, and Viola to 30-year terms; the others were acquitted under the Amnesty Act of June 5, 1946. See *New York Times*, July 10, 28; Aug. 3, 4, 9; Sept. 28, 1944; and Jan. 22, 23, 25, 28; Mar. 1, 2; and Apr. 5, 1947. See also Salvemini, *Fascist Dictatorship in Italy*, pp.

Heroic phase of the anti-Fascist press

Standing out in bold relief against the prevailing moral apathy of the period when democratic liberalism was being crushed in Italy was the brave determination of a handful of Liberal, Socialist, and Catholic journalists to speak the truth as they saw it. Luckily for them, Mussolini was slower than either Hitler or Lenin in forcing the opposition newspapers into gramophonic renditions of "His Master's Voice," though off and on in 1924, and especially in 1925, he interfered illegally with the freedom of the press.[65]

Thus Amendola in the Rome *Il Mondo* and Albertini [66] in the Milan *Corriere della sera*, flanked by Salvatorelli in the Turin *La Stampa* and Donati in the Rome PPI organ *Il Popolo*, headlined almost daily attacks against the tarnished government. Circulation of *Corriere della sera* soared to an all-time high of 800,000 during the Matteotti crisis.[67] Scarcely less energetic were such party organs as the PSI *Avanti!*, PSU *La Giustizia*, PRI *La Voce Repubblicana*, and the satiric Rome sheet *Becco giallo*, promoted by Cianca and Alberto Giannini.

When the government began systematically to violate freedom of the press, Salvatorelli (acting in behalf of the three great metropolitan dailies, *Corriere della sera*, *La Stampa*, and the Rome *Giornale d'Italia*) presented the King with a petition in January 1925, signed by twenty-five dailies, protesting such infringements. The King passed it on, without comment, to Mussolini. There it rested.[68]

269–296; S/M, *Sdf*, pp. 491–493; Gavagnin, *Vent'anni di resistenza*, pp. 254–255; Garosci, *Sdf*, pp. 16–17; Cesare Rossi, *Trentatre vicende mussoliniane* (Milan, 1958); and Mauro del Giudice, "Cronistoria del processo Matteotti," in A.N.P.P.I.A. (ed.), *Matteotti*.

[65] Armando Gavagnin, "Il giornalismo dell'opposizione dal 1922 al 1926," *MLI*, No. 21 (Nov. 1952), pp. 27–38; and his *Vent'anni di resistenza*, pp. 176–188.

[66] Regarding him, see Alberto Albertini, *Vita di Luigi Albertini* (Rome, 1945); the collection of his editorials and speeches in L. Albertini, *In difesa della libertà: discorsi e scritti* (Milan, 1947); and Nino Valeri, "Liberali e Fascisti dopo la marcia su Roma," Rome *Il Mondo*, May 17, 31, 1955.

[67] Max Ascoli, "The Press and Universities in Italy," *The Annals of the American Academy of Political and Social Science*, cc (Nov. 1938), pp. 235–253. *Cf.* L. Salvatorelli, "L'ultima battaglia per la libertà di stampa," in *Lezioni sull'antifascismo* (Bari, 1960).

[68] *Non Mollare!* (1925), Table XXI.

THE DEBACLE

Piero Gobetti's "Rivoluzione liberale" (1922–1925)

No less courageous than the daily press were several influential weeklies. Of these probably the most provocative was the Turin *Rivoluzione liberale*, founded and edited by the precocious Piero Gobetti. He was not directly identified with the Aventine, and his ideology was not molded in the same democratic matrix as Amendola's. His paper did not boast the circulation of the great dailies; still it was one of the most effective of the day.

Gobetti was well versed in Benedetto Croce's liberalism but found himself leaning much farther to the left. Unlike the Neapolitan philosopher-historian, Gobetti was very critical of the way in which Italy had been unified; [69] and he was no less faultfinding of the way in which the Liberals had ruled the country since. During his student days at the University of Turin, Gobetti also became acquainted with Gramsci, eleven years his senior, and later he served for a while as literary critic of the Communist editor's *Ordine nuovo*. Though he did not go so far as Gramsci in sensing the political possibilities of the *consigli di fabbrica* ("shop committees"),[70] he did perceive in the northern factory workers the germ of a new "ruling class." And he expressed the conviction that the "new liberalism must coincide in Italy with the workers' revolution." [71] Yet rather than try to found another *partito di massa*, Gobetti preferred to spend his energy training a new intellectual elite to push a thoroughly renovated brand of liberalism.[72]

To help prepare this elite, in Turin on February 12, 1922, he founded *Rivoluzione liberale*. It appeared regularly until sup-

[69] Gobetti minimized the role of the Savoyard royalty and stressed, instead, Piedmontese society; he also emphasized the absence of mass participation in the Risorgimento and attributed this to the political and moral immaturity of the people—caused, he suggested, by the absence in Italy of both a Protestant Reformation and a modern socio-economic system. See his posthumously published articles, *Risorgimento senza eroi* (Turin, 1926).

[70] See *supra*, n. 6.

[71] Turin *Rivoluzione liberale*, II, No. 8 (Apr. 3, 1923).

[72] See Nino Valeri's seventh chapter on Gobetti in his *Da Giolitti a Mussolini*, p. 213 ff.; Mario Vinciguerra, *I partiti italiani* (Rome, 1955), pp. 141–144; Ada Marchesini Gobetti, "Piero Gobetti," in Antonio Basso (ed.), *Dizionario di cultura politica* (Milan, 1946), pp. 299–301; Edmondo Rho, "Testimonianza su Gobetti," *Il Ponte*, XII (1956), pp. 401–408; Aldo Garosci, "Gobetti l'animatore," Rome *Il Mondo*, Feb. 28, 1956; and Barbara Allason, *Memorie di un'antifascista, 1919–1940* (Florence, 1946), pp. 7–8.

27

pressed by the Fascists on October 27, 1925. Quite eclectic (especially at first), it carried articles by men of almost every political hue, while its editor wrote his appraisals of the foremost Italian politicos of the day. Within a few months *Rivoluzione liberale* was winning close attention as one of the most progressive organs in the nation.

Gobetti hoped that the threat of Fascism would bring about an understanding between Liberals and Marxists. He did not foresee any easy compromise, but he insisted that in certain historical situations they could collaborate fruitfully. He regarded the Matteotti crisis as such a period. Denying the practicality of efforts to seek royal intervention, he advocated armed resistance. All of this was not greatly different from what Gramsci was preaching in the fall of 1924 when he withdrew the PCI from the Aventine. Some writers have thus concluded that Gobetti was fast becoming a Communist. Doubtless he did accept much of Marx's analysis of history, though not all his economics, and he and his wife learned Russian in order to read Lenin in the original. Yet in the opinion of none other than Gramsci, Gobetti never would have taken the final step into the PCI.[73] Several others (including his wife) think the same.[74]

Whatever might have been his course, one can only speculate; as things turned out, it was very short. Mussolini detested the militant editor and as early as February 1923 had him jailed briefly. Three years later he personally penned an order to the Turin prefect: "Make life difficult again for this silly opponent of the government and of Fascism." [75] Local *squadristi* quickly carried out these instructions and beat up Gobetti on his own doorstep. Finally they forced him to flee to Paris in February 1926. As he left his homeland Gobetti promised: "We shall write in Italian and also in French. First we may write badly, but then better; . . . and we shall keep the torch lighted." [76] The 25-year-old hoped to organize a new publishing house in Paris. "I do not intend to publish libels or trivial polemics like

[73] *Ibid.*, p. 18.
[74] Rho, *Il Ponte*, xii (1956), pp. 401–408; Gaetano Baldacci in his preface to Gobetti, *Matteotti*, p. 12; and Vinciguerra, *I partiti italiani*, p. 144.
[75] Quoted in Allason, *Memorie di un'antifascista*, p. 18; the original document in his own handwriting has been preserved.
[76] *Ibid.*, p. 36.

the displaced Russian granddukes; I wish to promote a cultural program in the sense of European liberalism and of modern democracy." [77] Instead, in his weakened condition (he suffered from a heart ailment in addition to the mauling) he came down almost at once with pneumonia and died in a Paris clinic on February 16.[78]

Perhaps more than any single Italian writer of the early 1920's, Gobetti stimulated thought and action in the non-Communist Left. Certainly he helped prepare the ideological terrain for Carlo Rosselli's Giustizia e Libertà movement in 1929 and for its World War II offspring, the Partito d'Azione ("Action Party").[79]

"Il Caffè" of Ferruccio Parri and Riccardo Bauer (1924–1925)

Another remarkable anti-Fascist weekly of the Aventine epoch was Il Caffè ("Coffeehouse"), printed in Milan during 1924 and 1925.[80] It derived its title from the distinguished 1765 publication edited by Pietro Verri, one of the first to dream of a unified, free, and republican Italy.[81] The liberalism of Il Caffè was less adulterated by socialism than that expressed by Gobetti's journal,

[77] So he wrote to Giustino Fortunato, an expert on the problems of Italy's South. Quoted in Gavagnin, Vent'anni di resistenza, p. 222.

[78] His widow and infant son did "keep the torch lighted." She became a teacher in Piedmont gymnasia and, upon encouragement from Croce, translated some thirty volumes of English literature. The family home in Turin remained a conspiratorial center throughout the dictatorship. During the 1943–1945 Armed Resistance mother and son participated in the Giustizia e Libertà underground. After the Liberation she became a vice-mayor of Turin and member of the National Consultative Assembly. See Ada Marchesini Gobetti, Diario partigiano (Turin, 1956), pp. 9–11, and passim.

[79] Regarding his impact see also Carlo Levi, "Piero Gobetti e la 'Rivoluzione Liberale,' " Il Ponte, v (1949), pp. 1009–1021; Natalino Sapegno, "l'insegnamento di Piero Gobetti," Rinascita, III (July 1946); Leone Bortone, "Piero Gobetti e la 'Rivoluzione Liberale,' " Il Ponte, III (1947), pp. 621–628; comments of Nino Valeri (ed.), Antologia della "Rivoluzione Liberale" (Turin, 1948); Gaetano Salvemini, "Gobetti: Non tutto è andato perduto," Il Ponte, XII (1956), pp. 513–514; R. Colapietra, "Piero Gobetti polemista politico," Mulino, v (1956), pp. 776–800; and Ricordo di Piero Gobetti nel xxx° anniversario della morte, 1926–1956 ("Quaderni della Gioventù Liberale Italiana," No. 5, Rome, 1956).

[80] Riccardo Bauer, " 'Il Caffè' (1924–1925)," Il Ponte, v (1949), pp. 76–82. Cf. Bianca Ceva (ed.), Antologia del Caffè: giornale dell'antifascismo, 1924–25 (Milan, 1961).

[81] See Donald A. Limoli, "Pietro Verri, a Lombard Reformer under Enlightened Absolutism and the French Revolution," Journal of Central European Affairs, XVIII (1958), pp. 254–280.

and its editorial policies reflected deep concern for both traditional civil liberties and social justice. According to the Milanese prefect who quashed it, it was "more dangerous than *Avanti!*" [82]

The editors of *Il Caffè* were two democratic Liberals, Professor Ferruccio Parri and Riccardo Bauer, both of whom remained vigilant tutelary numens of the Resistenza during the next score of years. Indeed, Parri was to become vice-commander (the so-called "General Maurizio") of the military wing of the Armed Resistance in World War II and the first postwar premier of the fully liberated nation. Tall, slight, and rather pale, he was most easily identifiable by his heavy shock of hair. Born in 1890 in Pinerolo in an ambient of Mazzinianism, he had been since his university days a schoolteacher, war hero, and editorial writer for *Corriere della sera*, before undertaking the publication of *Il Caffè*. In view of his background it was not surprising that he brazenly addressed a much-discussed "open letter" in his paper to "Signor Re" ("Mister King") in 1924, calling upon him to exercise his prerogative to dismiss the compromised prime minister.

Parri's collaborator, Bauer, six years his junior, was a level-headed, methodical, middle-class Lombard who had entered public life without benefit of a classical-school education. He bore witness to his optimistic faith in the essential goodness of man by serving as secretary for many years of a Milanese adult educational and vocational training organization, Società Umanitaria, which engaged in various cultural activities and provided its members with mutual assistance. [83]

"Non Mollare!" of Gaetano Salvemini and Piero Calamandrei (1925)

In Florence, meantime, the anti-Fascist clandestine press made its debut. Early in 1925 a group of university students, inspired by two eminent professors—the historian Gaetano Salvemini, who after leaving the Socialist Party in 1911 had edited the radical review *L'Unità* until 1920,[84] and the jurisprudent Piero Cala-

[82] Allason, *Memorie di un'antifascista*, p. 23.

[83] See R. Bauer, "L'Umanitaria," in *Esperienze e studi socialisti: scritti in onore di Ugo G. Mondolfo*, a cura di "Critica Sociale" (Florence, 1957), pp. 237–243; Bruno Widmar, "Ferruccio Parri," *Belfagor*, XIII (1958), pp. 177–199.

[84] Regarding Salvemini's place in Italian history and historiography, see Gino

mandrei [85]—organized the Circolo di Cultura, which in January sponsored the underground anti-Fascist periodical *Non Mollare!* ("Don't Give In!"). Eight issues of some 300 copies each appeared. The first was dated January 3 (to coincide with Mussolini's pronunciamento); the last, October 3, 1925. They circulated chiefly among Tuscan student groups but also among academicians in Milan, Padua, Rome, and elsewhere.[86] The two most exciting items to be published were the text of the Filippelli memorandum exposing the Matteotti murderers and in April 1925 a bold incitement to boycott a parade scheduled for Victor Emmanuel III when he visited Florence that month. The editors made no effort to hide their lack of confidence in the Aventine strategy. Professor Salvemini had convinced himself that the opposition could not wait indefinitely for the Crown to take action. It had no choice but to answer Fascist violence with countermeasures.[87]

The principal leaders of the younger contingent in *Non Mollare!* were the brothers Carlo and Nello Rosselli, Florentine reformed Jews. The former was born in 1899, and after fighting in World War I had entered the University of Florence as a student of economics and politics. Soon after Matteotti's assassination he joined the revisionist PSU. He was destined to become one of the Resistance titans.[88] His brother Nello, a more orthodox democrat who stoutly backed Amendola's National Union, was a promising historian, soon to become immersed in the study

Luzzatto, "Il merito di Salvemini," Rome *Il Mondo*, June 28, 1955; "Prospettive storiografiche in Italia: Omaggio a Gaetano Salvemini," *Itinerari*, IV (Dec. 1956), pp. 411–672; and Enzo Tagliacozzo, *Gaetano Salvemini nel cinquantennio liberale* (Florence, 1958). Regarding his *L'Unità*, see the anthology, L' "Unità" di *Gaetano Salvemini*, ed. B. Finocchiaro (Venice, 1958), and the essay of Cesare Vasoli, "*L'Unità* di Salvemini," *Il Ponte*, XIV (1958), pp. 1382–1406.

[85] Regarding Calamandrei, see the tributes to him in *Il Ponte*, XII (Oct. 1956), pp. 1635–1639, upon his death, and the special issue of *Il Ponte*, XIV (Nov. 1959), dedicated to him. He founded this review when Florence was liberated in 1944.

[86] A complete edition of this earliest anti-Fascist underground paper (very rare in the original now) has been reprinted by photo offset: *Non Mollare!* (1925), ed. Gaetano Salvemini, Ernesto Rossi, and Piero Calamandrei (Florence, 1955). See also Calamandrei's recollections reprinted in *Uomini e città della Resistenza: discorsi, scritti e epigrafi* (Bari, 1955), pp. 53–77; and Antonino Rèpaci, "Note e discussioni: *Non Mollare!*" in *MLI*, No. 42 (1956), pp. 39–47.

[87] E. Rossi (ed.), *No al fascismo*, p. 12.

[88] The fundamental biographical study is by his collaborator, Aldo Garosci, *La vita di Carlo Rosselli* (2 vols.; Florence, 1946) [hereafter cited as Garosci, VCR].

of certain left-wing Risorgimento currents.[89] The Rossellis were assisted in the *Non Mollare!* gambit by an irrepressible underground fighter and quondam political prisoner, Ernesto Rossi, author of many incisive attacks upon Fascism and the economic interests that buttressed it.[90] A young instructor at the British Institute in Florence, Miss Marion Cave, was also in the group; eventually she became Carlo Rosselli's wife. Nello Traquandi and Dino Vannucci joined the circle by way of the Italia Libera activist organization of republican war veterans.[91]

By the summer of 1925 the police had tracked down the place where *Non Mollare!* was printed. Ernesto Rossi escaped temporarily to France, but Salvemini fell foul of the police, who brought him up for trial in July.[92] Because of a postponement of legal proceedings, he gained provisional freedom. On August 4, 1925, he escaped to France, guided over the frontier by a young Valdaostan student of history at the University of Turin, Federico Chabod.[93] Though he had no other source of income, Salvemini resigned his chair at the University of Florence. Somehow the police dragnet missed Carlo Rosselli, who found it possible to move to Genoa, where he had been offered a teaching post, and thence to Milan. The covert foes of Fascism were lucky that the police apparatus often functioned poorly during this early phase of the dictatorship.

"Quarto Stato" of Carlo Rosselli and Pietro Nenni (1926)

In Milan young Carlo Rosselli teamed up with the vibrant 35-year-old former director of *Avanti!*, Petro Nenni, who was then engaged in writing his socialistic *Storia di quattro anni, 1919–1922.*[94] From March 27 until October 30, 1926, they published a weekly review, *Quarto Stato ("Fourth Estate")*, which

[89] See his *Carlo Pisacane nel Risorgimento italiano* (Genoa, 1936), and *Mazzini e Bakounine: 12 anni di movimento operaio in Italia (1860–1872)* (Turin, 1927).

[90] In addition to his *No al fascismo*, he has written *Una spia del regime* (Milan, 1955), and *I padroni del vapore* (Bari, 1955).

[91] See *supra*, n. 44.

[92] Garosci, *VCR*, I, 11–60; E. Rossi, "Il 'Non mollare!' " *Il Ponte*, I (1945), pp. 529–535; Enzo Tagliacozzo, "Il panno rosso," Rome *Il Mondo*, Mar. 29, 1955; Calamandrei's chapter, "Il manganello, la cultura, e la giustizia," in *Non Mollare!* (1925), pp. 69–112; M. Ferrara, "L'antifascismo del 'Non mollare!' " *Società*, XI (1955), pp. 758–764; and Rèpaci, *MLI*, No. 42 (1956), pp. 39–47.

[93] S/M, *Sdf*, p. 463. Cf. "Federico Chabod," *Rivista storica italiana*, LXXII, No. 4 (1960).

[94] After serving nearly three years as director of *Avanti!*, Nenni had recently resigned, chiefly because the maximalist PSI had turned down his proposal to

advocated Socialist unity in Italy on the basis of more or less revisionist economic theories coupled with an insurrectionary political program. Shrewdly (and probably necessarily) confining themselves to abstract discussions, the editors kept their review from being confiscated more than four times.[95]

Contributors included Max Ascoli, then a young instructor in legal philosophy at the University of Rome; Tommaso Fiore, a Bari educator; Alberto Pincherle, an historian of comparative religions; and Andrea Caffi, a brilliant journalist born in Russia of Italian parents. Along with almost every other patently anti-Fascist publication, *Quarto Stato* was quashed after the attempted assassination of Mussolini in Bologna on October 31, 1926.[96]

Tightening the dictatorship

A few days after Mussolini threw down his gauntlet on January 3, 1925, the PNF secretary warned all enemies of the regime that they would be punished mercilessly if they engaged in any hostile activity. Soon the authorities announced a series of repressive measures—not all at once, but spaced at sufficient intervals to enable the public to adjust itself to the new order. Several attempts upon the *Duce's* life provided him with convenient excuses for the harsh decrees regarding public security.

Zaniboni affair and the attack on Freemasonry

For example, on November 4, 1925, police arrested Tito Zaniboni (an ex-PSU deputy from the Veneto who had conspired for a time with the Garibaldis)[97] and General Luigi Capello, charging them with plotting to kill Mussolini. In reality, a police agent and a former Fascist cabinet minister had tricked them into this snare. According to the scheme, Zaniboni, attired in the uniform of a major of the Alpini, was to hide behind a Persian blind

---

amalgamate with the reformist PSU current of Turati, Treves, and Modigliani. Six years elapsed before he resumed in exile the newspaper's direction. See *infra,* Ch. 11.

[95] Garosci, VCR, 1, 72, 80; Gaetano Salvemini, *Carlo and Nello Rosselli, a Memoir* (London, 1937), p. 16.

[96] In the case of *Cronaca sociale d'Italia* (a Florentine labor review founded by the leftist Popular, Giovanni Gronchi, in February 1926) the end came even sooner; the authorities crushed it in August 1926. See Vigorelli, *Gronchi,* pp. 491–492.

[97] See *supra,* n. 43, and *infra,* Ch. 11.

in a hotel opposite Mussolini's office in Palazzo Chigi and shoot him when he appeared on the balcony to celebrate the 1918 military victory of Vittorio Veneto. His "friends" then tipped off the police ahead of the scheduled *attentat*. The court sentenced Zaniboni and Capello to thirty years' imprisonment.[98]

The government skillfully exploited the "plot" in order to break up what was left of Matteotti's PSU and to crush its paper, *La Giustizia*. Albertini, editor of *Corriere della sera*, was also compelled to resign his post.

Furthermore, the Zaniboni affair made it easy for Mussolini to step up his offensive against the Freemasons, since Zaniboni and Capello had close ties with the Grand Master of the Grand Orient branch of the lodge. It was somewhat ironic that Mussolini should have turned against the Masons so bitterly, as at least one of their wings (the Protestant-oriented Scottish Rite of Piazza del Gesù) had given financial aid to the Fascists in their fight for power. A group of high Masons naïvely contributed 3,500,000 lire (worth about $130,000 then) toward the expenses of the March on Rome.[99] Furthermore, many of Mussolini's local *fasci* had their origins in Masonic lodges between 1919 and 1922; the hierarchs Farinacci, Balbo, Acerbo, and Cesare Rossi were once Masons; and the original Fascist program was somewhat analogous to that of Italian Freemasonry.[100] After he attained power, however, Mussolini no longer needed the Masons, and he feared the possibility that their lodges might be converted into conspiratorial centers against him. Their cosmopolitanism also disturbed the archnationalist *Duce*. Then too, he seemed to think (wrongly, for the most part) that an attack against them might win him goodwill not only from ultraclericals who for years had fought the brotherhood but also from Marxists and such Liberals as Croce, who ridiculed much of the organization's religiosity and resented its political influence.[101]

[98] He was transferred from Alessandria penitentiary in 1942 to *confino* on the deportation island of Ponza. After the Allies arrived in 1943 they named him governor of the island and later High Commissioner of the Purge. See Zaniboni's version of the 1925 plot in Gavagnin, *Vent'anni di resistenza*, pp. 205-211.

[99] Eugenio Chiesa, *La mano nel sacco* (Rome, 1925), p. 6; Leto, OVRA, p. 22.

[100] Salvemini, *Fascist Dictatorship in Italy*, pp. 129-130; Binchy, *Church and State in Fascist Italy*, p. 146. Fascism also won recruits from the ranks of Syndicalists and Marxists, it should be noted in fairness.

[101] G. A. Borgese, *Goliath: The March of Fascism* (New York, 1938), p. 277.

Although as early as 1923 Blackshirts were bastinadoing indi-vidual Masons, and the PNF forbade its members to join the confraternity, wholesale persecution did not start until October 3, 1925. It was focused in Florence and resulted in many injuries and at least four deaths—as well as the end of *Non Mollare!* The Zaniboni incident followed soon afterward; henceforth Mussolini was bent on making Freemasonry a prime scape-goat.[102]

He hounded into exile the Grand Master of the atheistic Grand Orient wing of Palazzo Giustiniani, Domizio Torrigiani, who for a month after the March on Rome had intoned that "Fascism has a Masonic soul." [103] When Torrigiani unwisely slipped back sometime later, the police arrested and banished him to *confino* ("administratively imposed deportation") on Ponza. The Masons thereupon dissolved their higher echelons, the Grand Orient acting faster than the Scottish Rite. Many of the ranking officers found asylum in France, where they sought to reorganize inde-pendently of the foreign lodges—an expensive task. Early in 1930 Eugenio Chiesa, one of the mandarins of the suppressed Italian Republican Party (PRI), became Grand Master of the *émigré* brethren; but he died soon afterward (June 22). Arturo Labriola, a prominent syndicalist who later made his peace with Fascism and returned home during the Ethiopian War, was the next Grand Master. The last *émigré* Grand Master was Dr. Alessandro Tedeschi, a Jewish physician from Leghorn. He fell into the clutches of the Nazis when they invaded France in 1940.[104]

In the face of Mussolini's ceaseless blasts against Freemasonry, hundreds of individual Masons resisted as best they could, while many of the more pugnacious ones worked closely with the underground Republican Party.[105]

[102] Salvemini, *Fascist Dictatorship in Italy*, pp. 129–130.

[103] In an interview published in Rome *Giornale d'Italia*, Nov. 30, 1922, and in his pamphlet, "Massoneria e Fascismo" (Rome, 1923), cited by Binchy, *Church and State in Fascist Italy*, p. 146.

[104] Francesco Saverio Nitti, *Rivelazioni: dramatis personae* (Naples, 1948), p. 422 ff.

[105] Information from Prof. Giorgio Spini of the University of Florence; *cf.* Garosci, *Sdf*, pp. 272–273; Armando Borghi, *Mezzo secolo di anarchia* (1898–1945) (Naples, 1954), pp. 320–322. An objective history of Italian Freemasonry is greatly needed.

Meanwhile, other repressive measures followed the Zaniboni imbroglio. Decrees of December 24, 1925, and of January 31, 1926, transformed the 1848 *Statuto* without actually abolishing it. Mussolini acquired a new title, "Head of the Government [*Capo del Governo*] and Prime Minister." Thus he no longer was merely "first among equals" in the Council of Ministers; henceforth he was responsible only to the King. Parliament, moreover, could not discuss legislation until he assented, and his decree-laws acquired unquestioned legal sanction. Elected agencies of government at the municipal and provincial levels were abolished.[106]

It was on the occasion of senatorial debate of the foregoing acts that Gaetano Mosca, the venerable Sicilian sociologist and political scientist whose works hitherto had seemed sympathetic to Fascist "elitism," rose from his seat to lament the downfall of parliamentary government. From then until his death in 1941 Senator Mosca was quietly anti-Fascist.[107]

From time to time Mussolini announced important economic changes. The most significant early ones involved dissolution of the urban and rural co-operatives of the Socialists and Catholics, suppression of industrial shop-steward committees, and outlawry of both strikes and lockouts. To supersede the disbanded free labor organizations, Edmondo Rossoni and a phalanx of Fascist planners devised, amidst much deliberate confusion of terminology, a system of Fascist-manipulated workers' *sindacati* ("unions"). These were to parallel employer associations and to negotiate collective wage contracts and other matters. The new dispensation called also for a third category of "intellectuals' syndicates." The PNF ostensibly regimented everyone, but its whip scarcely bruised the employers, thanks to the Palazzo Vidoni Pact of October 12, 1925.[108] Unlike the employer agen-

---

[106] Finer, *Mussolini's Italy*, Ch. IX; S/M *Sdf*, pp. 271–272; and Vaussard, *Histoire de l'Italie contemporaine*, pp. 213–214.

[107] H. Stuart Hughes, "Gaetano Mosca and the Political Lessons of History," in H. Stuart Hughes (ed.), *Teachers of History: Essays in Honor of Laurence Bradford Packard* (Ithaca, 1954), pp. 146–167.

[108] On that occasion the employers' *Confidustria* (Industrial Confederation) had agreed to recognize only the new Fascist-sponsored labor syndicates; as its reward, the *Confidustria* could retain many privileges of self-management.

Regarding the confusing economic program of Fascism, see especially Gaetano Salvemini, *Under the Axe of Fascism* (New York, 1936); Louis Rosenstock-

cies, the new labor syndicates enjoyed no modicum of autonomy; their leaders were even designated by the PNF.

In the face of this destruction of the free labor movement, Bruno Buozzi—a revisionist Socialist who previously had headed the Italian Federation of Metallurgical Workers (FIOM) and had become secretary-general of the General Confederation of Labor (CGL) in January 1926—decided to emigrate. A year later (January 4, 1927) the skeletal CGL dismantled itself. Some older labor leaders (Lodovico d'Aragona, who had been CGL secretary-general before Buozzi, and Rinaldo Rigola, an organizer of textile workers in the Biella sector of Piedmont) decided to collaborate with Mussolini and his much-trumpeted *Carta del Lavoro* ("Labor Charter") of 1927, endeavoring to justify their action on grounds of realism.[109]

New acts of violence

The regime unleashed a new wave of violence after April 7, 1926, when a demented Irishwoman, Miss Violet Gibson, fired a revolver at Mussolini.[110] Luckily for him, the bullet lacerated only his nose. In line with his admonition to "live dangerously," he soon afterward ordered his Blackshirts, "If I advance, follow me; if I retreat, slay me; if I am killed, avenge me!"[111] Because of her foreign citizenship and her mental condition, Miss Gibson was transferred from prison to a mental hospital.

Another attempted assassination occurred in Rome on September 11, 1926. This time Gino Luccetti, a young Anarchist of Carrara who had just returned from abroad, threw a bomb at the *Duce's* passing automobile. He was condemned to thirty years.[112] Among other things, this incident led to a shake-up of the police command: Arturo Bocchini, a Fascist prefect, became Capo della Polizia for the next fourteen years.

Franck, *L'Économie corporative fasciste en doctrine et en fait* (Paris, 1934); William G. Welk, *Fascist Economic Policy: An Analysis of Italy's Economic Experiment* (Cambridge, 1938); Schmidt, *The Plough and the Sword;* Schmidt, *The Corporate State;* Finer, *Mussolini's Italy,* Ch. xvii; and Giuseppe Bottai, *Vent'anni e un giorno* (Milan, 1949).

[109] S/M, *Sdf,* p. 299.
[110] For details see Leto, *OVRA,* pp. 25–28.
[111] Mussolini, *Scritti e discorsi (1925 al 1926),* v, 312.
[112] Luccetti was liberated by the Allies in 1943 but soon afterward lost his life in a German bombardment of Capri.

The most sensational *attentat* took place in Bologna on October 31, 1926. On this occasion Anteo Zamboni, a 15-year-old whose family were Anarchists, fired at the *Duce* as he passed by in an open car. Again the bullet missed its mark but injured some bystanders. The crowd seized the boy and proceeded to stab him to death without further ado. Who, if anyone, encouraged his action remains a mystery.[113]

"Exceptional decrees" of November 1926

The Zamboni incident provided Mussolini with a fine pretext completely to stifle the opposition. This he did by a series of "exceptional decrees," issued after November 5, 1926. Covering a wide range of activities, some of the decrees provided for suppression of all "antinationalist" parties and newspapers. Another batch cancelled passports and set severe penalties for clandestine expatriation.[114] Still others inaugurated the Special Tribunal for the Defense of the State and elaborated the system of "administrative" justice. The death penalty was prescribed for those guilty of seeking the assassination of either the King or Capo del Governo, a revision of penal practice that evoked several strong protests in the Senate.[115] Finally, on November 9, 1926, the servile Chamber of Deputies passed a quite unconstitutional measure, the effect of which was to deprive of their seats all Aventinian "deserters" (and also Communists who had returned to the Chamber previously). Some 124 deputies were affected by this measure, which definitely marked the end of any semblance of normal political life in Italy.[116]

The Tribunale Speciale per la Difesa dello Stato began operations February 1, 1927, its members appointed by Mussolini. Cases were referred to it only upon specific recommendation of

[113] Leto, OVRA, pp. 37–38; Monelli, *Mussolini*, pp. 114–115, 279; S/M, *Sdf*, pp. 279–280; Gavagnin, *Vent'anni di resistenza*, pp. 311–312; and G. Salvemini, *Mussolini diplomatico* (Bari, 1952), p. 21.

[114] See *infra*, Ch. II.

[115] The exiled Venetian professor of jurisprudence, Silvio Trentin, soon published a comprehensive analysis and indictment of these decrees. See his *Les transformations du droit public italien. De la Charte de Charles Albert à la création de l'état fasciste* (Paris, 1929). The innocent title permitted many copies of the book to reach Italian libraries.

[116] S/M, *Sdf*, pp. 284–287. The most recent study of Fascistization is Dante L. Germino, *The Italian Fascist Party in Power: A Study in Totalitarian Rule* (Minneapolis, 1959).

the Capo della Polizia.[117] A person denounced to it was immediately put under arrest; bail was not allowed, and no time limit was set upon "preventive custody." The accused was entitled to no legal assistance until after the preliminary examination, and even then the defense attorney labored under handicaps. The Special Tribunal's decisions, which carried the force of martial law, could not be appealed. Some 720 audiences were held between 1927 and 1943; approximately 5,319 individuals were brought to trial, and of these some 5,155 were sentenced. All told, their prison terms added up to 28,115 years. There were 29 death sentences and 7 for life imprisonment. In order of cases handled, these years were busiest: 1928, 1931, 1935, 1942, 1939, 1938, 1934, 1941, 1936, 1932, 1930, 1940, 1937, 1929, 1943, 1927, and 1933.[118]

The exceptional decrees augmented the already widespread authority of Italian police agencies to handle "administratively" many political cases. Lowest in the scale of penalties was the *diffida* ("reprimand"), whereby persons suspected of anti-Fascism would be warned against indulging in politics. Vigilant surveillance and search of the suspect's house took place. More severe was the *ammonizione* ("admonition"), which could remain in effect for two years. The accused was required to hold a steady job and report weekly to the police to have his papers stamped. He could not leave his permanent residence without police permission and his daily movements were narrowly limited —restrictions that not only were almost intolerable socially but often disastrous economically for the accused.[119]

The harshest administrative penalty was *confino di polizia*

---

[117] Quite a number of political cases came up before the regular courts. Unlike most governmental agencies, very few of these regular courts became thoroughly Fascisticized; as a result, the accused could at least hope for a fair hearing. If found guilty, he might either be sent to *confino* or to a penitentiary. Mario Berlinguer, *La crisi della giustizia nel regime fascista* (Rome, 1944); cf. S/M, *Sdf*, p. 473.

[118] Ernesto Rossi, "L'altra campana," Rome *Il Mondo*, June 5, 1956; E. Rossi, "Il tribunale speciale per la difesa dello stato: la madre del diritto," in *ibid.*, July 24, 31, 1956; Cesare Rossi, *Tribunale Speciale* (Milan, 1952); E. Kohn-Bramstedt, *Dictatorship and Political Police* (New York, 1945), pp. 54–63; and Ebenstein, *Fascist Italy*, pp. 77–87.

[119] On July 3, 1956, the new Constitutional Court of the Italian Republic at last abolished this system. It ruled that *ammonizione* was "a kind of juridical degradation . . . in strident contrast with the constitutional precept that denies the administrative authorities the power of issuing regulations restrictive of personal liberty." Rome *Il Messaggero*, July 4, 1956.

("deportation") for a period up to five years. It was ordered by provincial commissions presided over by the prefect. Other members included the public prosecutor, chief of police, commander of the provincial Carabinieri ("the Royal police force"), and a high official of the Fascist Militia. The convicted were usually deported to the tiny islands of Ustica and Lipari, or in a later period to Ponza and Ventotene off the Neapolitan shore, and to Sardinia. When these became crowded, they were shunted instead to remote southern villages.[120] Though subject to almost constant surveillance, they occasionally enjoyed hours of limited freedom within restricted areas and now and then might be permitted to receive brief visits from their families. No doubt the system was relatively more humane than the extermination and forced labor camps that disgraced Hitler's Germany and Stalin's Russia; yet scarcely a prisoner escaped some form of abuse. During the entire period of Mussolini's dictatorship some 10,000 individuals were deported to *confino*. Another 15,000 were ordered into the scarcely less objectionable *domicilio coatto* ("compulsory residence"), while some 160,000 were subjected to the special vigilance that accompanied the issuance of an *ammonizione* or a *diffida*.[121]

From 1926 until his death in 1940, Arturo Bocchini was Capo della Polizia. Carmine Senise headed the apparatus during its final three years. Bocchini has been called an unscrupulous Italian Fouché. Though he may not have been a dyed-in-the-wool Fascist (on occasion he resisted the *Duce*'s orders), he generally

---

[120] Such was the fate of Dr. Carlo Levi of Turin, the versatile artist, novelist, and physician who, because of his membership in Carlo Rosselli's Giustizia e Libertà underground movement, was deported to backward, malarial Lucania. His autobiographical *Christ Stopped at Eboli*, published soon after the Liberation, was a revelation to Italian Northerners who had little direct acquaintance with the mores of the neglected *Mezzogiorno*.

[121] Leto, OVRA, pp. 58–67; E. Rossi, "La legge del sospetto," *Il Ponte*, XII (1956), pp. 1708–1731; the entire issue of *Il Ponte*, v (March 1949), devoted to "Prisons"; Ebenstein, *Fascist Italy*, pp. 69–93; William Elwin, *Fascism at Work* (London, 1934), pp. 96–100. For personal testimony of prisoners see also Emilio Lussu, *La catena: dalle leggi eccezionali alle isole* (Paris, 1929); Manlio Magini, *Una vita per la libertà: confinato politico* (Rome, 1956); Michele Giua, *Ricordi di un ex-detenuto politico, 1935–1943* (Turin, 1943); Alberto Iacometti, *Ventotene* (Milan, 1946); Mario Montagnana, *Ricordi di un militante* (Milan, 1947) and *Ricordi di un operaio torinese* (2 vols.; Rome, 1949); Massimo Salvadori, *Resistenza ed azioni (ricordi di un liberale)* (Bari, 1951); and Altiero Spinelli, "Gli antifascisti in galera," in *Lezioni sull'antifascismo*.

served his master well and reported to him almost daily.[122] He was responsible for the creation of two new sections—one for domestic political matters, the other for control of the frontiers and activities of the *émigrés*.

The first of these sections was the OVRA, established late in 1927 as a "special inspectorate" with headquarters in Milan, but soon extended throughout the country. The precise meaning of the initials is still uncertain, according to the knowledgeable Guido Leto, who headed the dread agency from 1938 until 1943.[123] While OVRA's operations may not have been so widespread as was commonly supposed at the time, they certainly aroused terror. The 900 informers whom it employed during seventeen years were responsible for many tragedies among the anti-Fascists.[124]

[122] Carmine Senise, *Quando ero Capo della Polizia, 1940–1943* (Rome, 1946), pp. 18–19; S/M, *Sdf*, pp. 322–325, 485; Leto, OVRA, p. 70.
[123] Three interpretations have been suggested: Organizzazione di Vigilanza e Repressione dell'Antifascismo ("Organization for Vigilance and Repression of Anti-Fascism"); Organo di Vigilanza dei Reati Antistatali ("Organ of Vigilance for Anti-State Crimes"); and Opera Volontaria di Repressione Antifascista ("Voluntary Agency for Anti-Fascist Repression"). Leto, OVRA, p. 52.
[124] Guido Leto, "I libri segreti dell'OVRA, aperti dal suo Capo," *Europeo*, March and April 1956. *Cf.* E. Rossi, *La pupilla del Duce (l'OVRA)* (Parma, 1956); and G. Cosmo, "Consuntivo dell'attività dell'Ovra," *MLI*, No. 14 (Sept. 1951), pp. 43–53, and No. 16 (1952), pp. 33–55.

CHAPTER II · ANTI-FASCIST EMIGRATION

Until August 1934

AFTER THE overthrow of traditional parliamentary government in Italy, the foes of Fascism remained split on questions of strategy and objectives. At the risk of oversimplification, it may be said that one broad wing, consisting of Liberals and many ex-Popolari, favored continuing the essentially constitutional form of oppugnancy that had been the trademark of the abortive Aventine. Most of them hoped that by such means the old monarcho-parliamentary system could be revived with little change. Not all, but most of the leaders of this faction preferred to remain at home in the hope that the King would repudiate the dictator. Certain Catholics hoped too that the Vatican would eventually reconsider its tolerant acceptance of the cynical and totalitarian regime.

The other wing of anti-Fascism, which included the three Marxian *partiti di massa*, the small Republican Party, and the votaries of a new intelligentsia cluster calling itself Giustizia e Libertà, doubted seriously that Victor Emmanuel III ever would have either the desire or the courage to turn upon Mussolini. Most of them, as a matter of fact, regarded him as co-responsible for the dictatorship. And in any case, their long-term goals included a republic and creation of a political and social system that would represent an advance over what they regarded as the oligarchic rule that had prevailed in Italy since the Risorgimento. Their specific prescriptions varied greatly. The Communists and bifurcated Socialists wished to establish a Marxian utopia of one sort or another. Republicans dreamed of something akin to either Giuseppe Mazzini's unitary republic or Carlo Cattaneo's federalistic republic. Dreaming romantically of luring a mass following, Giustizia e Libertà and some of the other intellectual circles advocated a judicious blend of political and economic reform. A large proportion of this anti-Fascist wing felt impelled to emigrate. In France and the other democracies they reorganized and for the next fifteen years nursed their visions of torpedoing the Blackshirt dictatorship.

The work of the *émigrés* and of the domestic enemies of the regime logically divides itself into four periods. Lasting until

August 1934, the first of these saw the birth in France of the Anti-Fascist Concentration ("Concentrazione Antifascista") and Giustizia e Libertà, and was characterized by rigid isolation of the Italian Communist Party from the other underground currents until after Hitler's advent to power. The second epoch, highlighted by spreading dictatorships and by the Ethiopian and the Spanish Wars, was the era of the Popular Front. During that phase the PCI emerged as the strongest force in the emigration, while inside Italy the intelligentsia suffered ever greater repression. The third period extended from the sudden Nazi-Soviet Pact of August 23, 1939, until the *coup d'état* of July 25, 1943, and Italy's subsequent clumsy breach with Hitler's Germany. The Resistenza Armata, from September 8, 1943, until April 25, 1945, formed the climactic final act.

Certainly the escape of many oppositionists from Mussolini's Italy was one of the salient aspects of the dictatorship.[1] One cannot know how many of those who crossed the borders were driven chiefly by political considerations and how many merely by economic or personal reasons. Doubtless the great majority fell into the latter category, especially when unemployment was at its worst; but eventually some 10,000 were to make the move mainly because of political persecution.[2]

Foreign versus domestic opposition

The relative efficacy of the *émigrés'* political activity compared with that of the anti-Fascists who stayed home is controversial. Fascist officials abroad who knew something of the ambient often ridiculed the work of the *fuorusciti* (as the Fascists disparagingly dubbed the *émigrés*) and regarded them as quite cut off from reality. Indeed, the exiles did have to labor under great handicaps. Most of them were reduced to penury, earning money by journalistic endeavors, language instruction, and other part-time jobs; they lacked secure channels of communication with their personal and political friends at home; they often found them-

[1] On this topic see also the author's "The Italian Anti-Fascist Emigration, 1922–1943," *Journal of Central European Affairs*, xii (April 1952), pp. 20–55; also available in Italian translation as "Il fuoruscitismo italiano dal 1922 al 1943," *MLI*, No. 23 (March 1953), pp. 3–37.

[2] The following statistics may give an impression of the fluctuation in emigration of all types. See Istituto Centrale di Statistica, *Annuario Statistico Italiano, 1944–1948*, Serie V (Rome, 1949), i, 49:

selves in serious trouble with foreign governments because of their agitation against Mussolini; and their ranks were repeatedly infiltrated by *provocateurs*.[3] While several of the more articulate poured out reams of clever propaganda exposing Fascism's brutality, others retreated into a conspirator's dream-world. And, as is so often the case among political exiles, the isolation and rigorousness of their lives produced many unseemly recriminations.[4]

Though never going so far as to denigrate the *fuorusciti*, Benedetto Croce, who was surely one of the most influential of the domestic passive opponents of Fascism, rated the efficacy of the *émigrés* low in comparison with that of the autochthonous opposition.[5] This judgment was in line with his contention that Cavour's work had been of greater importance than that of Mazzini and other exiles.

Aldo Garosci, on the other hand, has vigorously hailed the struggle of the *fuorusciti*. Himself a militant in Giustizia e Libertà both at home and (after 1932) abroad, Garosci has insisted that it is futile to dichotomize anti-Fascism into domestic and foreign compartments. He has argued persuasively that the work of the anti-Fascists, wherever they made their base, was

Year	Emigration to France	Emigration to all Europe (including France)	Emigration to non-European countries
1921	44,782	84,328	116,963
1922	99,464	155,554	125,716
1923	167,982	205,273	184,684
1924	201,715	239,088	125,282
1925	145,529	177,558	101,873
1926	111,252	139,900	122,496
1927	52,784	86,247	132,687
1928	49,351	79,173	70,794
1929	51,001	88,054	61,777
1930	167,209	220,985	59,112
1931	74,115	125,079	40,781
1932	33,516	58,545	24,803
1933	35,745	60,736	22,328
1934	20,725	42,296	26,165
1935	11,666	30,579	26,829
1936	9,614	21,682	19,828
1937	14,717	29,670	30,275
1938	10,551	71,848	27,994
1939	2,015	56,625	16,198

[3] See Garosci, *Sdf*, pp. 294–295, for a list of some of the OVRA spies abroad.
[4] See Carmelo Puglionisi, *Sciacalli: storia dei fuorusciti* (Rome, 1948), for an extreme indictment by a Fascist who for a time had enjoyed intimate contacts with some of the *fuorusciti*.
[5] See his comments in his *Quaderni della Critica*, No. 5 (Aug. 1946), p. 113.

part of a single Resistance; moreover, the two groups were largely reunited by 1943 for the culminating phase. Many of the returning exiles gained influential posts in the new party directorates, ministries, and Constituent Assembly. Certainly this new elite owed most of its training to the experiences it had passed through abroad.[6]

More or less similar judgments are implicit in the writings of Massimo Salvadori, Vera Modigliani, Gaetano Salvemini, and Armando Zanetti, who were active in the Diaspora.[7] Luigi Salvatorelli and Giovanni Mira (both of whom stayed at home but were in Giustizia e Libertà for a time) have assumed a middle position. They regard the *fuorusciti's* labors as less productive than those of the Risorgimento exiles but concede that the latter's foe was not so formidable as that of the twentieth-century exiles.[8]

The *fuorusciti* can claim credit for steadfastly presenting what they believed to be the true facts at a time when many Western statesmen had persuaded themselves that Mussolini's Blackshirts were respectable upholders of law, order, and capitalism. The exiles' progress was slow indeed, but in time they convinced many foreigners of the substantial truth of their description of Fascist terror—especially after Foreign Minister Ciano's Cagoulard agents brutally assassinated Carlo and Nello Rosselli in Normandy in June 1937.

In the absence of Italian military disasters, the *fuorusciti* could no more topple Mussolini than could the domestic resistants. No one has credited them with authorship of the plot that unseated him on July 25, 1943. Yet the leaven of their criticisms and proposals had filtered slowly into the consciousness of many Italians abroad and at home and had helped encourage them to think for themselves. Thus, despite all the difficulties in communication, the former could claim at least a small portion of the credit for creating the climate of opinion that became influential during Italy's military debacles of 1942–1943.

[6] Garosci, *Sdf*, pp. 109, 258–265, 295–298; and his "I fuorusciti," in *Lezioni sull'antifascismo*.

[7] See, *e.g.*, Salvadori, *Resistenza ed azione*; Vera Modigliani, *Esilio* (Milan, 1946); Gaetano Salvemini, *Memorie di un fuoruscito*, ed. Gaetano Arfè (Milan, 1960); Armando Zanetti, "L'emigrazione politica italiana nel 1931," first printed in the Belgian *Le Flambeau* (Dec. 1931–Jan. 1932); reprinted in MLI, No. 54 (1959), pp. 4–63.

[8] S/M, *Sdf*, pp. 459–460; Salvatorelli in *Il Secondo Risorgimento*, pp. 154–155.

First wave of emigration

The refugees from Mussolini's Italy poured out in three fairly distinct waves, according to Garosci, the most diligent historian of the exodus.[9] The first covered the months from October 1922 until January 1925. During that phase most emigrants left for economic reasons, to seek jobs in the labor markets of Switzerland, Belgium, and (most of all) France.[10] Among them, however, were numerous Anarchists and Socialists who had taken a militant part in the labor strife in Emilia, Romagna, and Tuscany.[11]

Most of the Anarchists who left did so with the intention of continuing abroad their "international of deeds" against the State (and, of course, against Fascism, which so passionately glorified the State). They often encouraged violence against those who erected *fasci* abroad. It was a young libertarian, Enrico Bonomini, who shot Nicola Bonservizi, a "Fascist of the first hour," in a Paris restaurant in 1924. After a widely publicized trial he was sentenced in October to eight years. Probably he would have gone to the guillotine had not the news of Matteotti's murder angered so many Frenchmen.[12]

Though one must not exaggerate the political complexion of the early emigration, it is notable that in Paris alone by 1924 numerous Italian-language periodicals of a political type were published: *Voce socialista* (Socialist); *Rivendicazione* (Anarchist); *La Riscossa* and *Campane a stormo* (Communist).[13] Elsewhere there were other anti-Fascist papers, some of which had

[9] Garosci, *Sdf*, pp. 11–14 ff.

[10] As of 1924 Italians were concentrated in the following zones of France (calculating approximately 1,000,000 as the grand total): 100,000 in Paris and environs; 300,000 on the Mediterranean shore; 100,000 in mining basins of the Meurthe and Moselle; 300,000 in war-devastated northeastern zones; 50,000 in Lyon and environs; 50,000 in Savoy and Upper Savoy; and 100,000 elsewhere. G. Salvi, "L'esodo degli Italiani in Francia," in *Almanacco socialista 1925* (Milan, 1924), pp. 199–211.

[11] Regarding such strife, see Tasca, *Nascita e avvento del fascismo*, Chs. 7, 9.

[12] Borghi, *Mezzo secolo di anarchia* (1898–1945), pp. 312–315. Borghi, a Romagnole Anarchist intellectual, left Italy in 1923 for Berlin and thence to Paris. After 1926 he lived in the United States for many years, evading the immigration authorities. His memoirs are an important source of information. *Cf.* Garosci, *Sdf*, pp. 13, 269–270; S/M, *Sdf*, pp. 461–462.

[13] Salvi, "L'esodo degli Italiani in Francia," in *Almanacco socialista 1925*, pp. 199–211.

been founded by a previous generation of emigrants—for example, the Anarchist *Risveglio* of Geneva and *Adunata dei Refrattari e Martello* of New York, and the Socialist papers, *La Parola* and *Corriere del popolo*, published in New York and San Francisco respectively.[14]

As early as November 1923 former Premier Francesco S. Nitti, a southern Liberal and university professor of somewhat radical bent, and well known for his Germanophile castigations of the Versailles settlement, decided that he must leave his country. Fascist hoodlums had sacked his residence in Rome and he was unable to get police protection. He applied for a passport; six months elapsed before he received it and could move his family to Zurich (June 1924). Right after the assassination of Matteotti a delegate of the PNF in Switzerland wrote to Mussolini to ask if he should take action against Nitti. Mussolini advised him not to, noting that under the circumstances "maximum discipline" was "indispensable." [15] Six months later, however, Mussolini dispatched a police agent to Switzerland to keep tab on Nitti.[16] Late in 1925 Nitti transferred his domicile to Paris. It served for fifteen years as a frequent meeting place for the *fuorusciti*. After the Aventinian debacle Nitti wrote, on March 5, 1925, a bitter letter to Victor Emmanuel III, in which he criticized him for tolerating Mussolini; this he followed up with another on March 9, 1926. Nothing resulted.[17]

Although Elder Statesman Nitti was held in respect by most of his fellow expatriates, he remained aloof from their political organizations. He believed that the programs of most of the *émigrés* leaned too much toward planned economies; moreover, he thought that these men displayed unseemly bigotry in excluding royalists from their inner circles. For the most part, Nitti occupied himself writing his widely circulated books: *Bolchévisme, Fascisme, et Démocratie* (Paris, 1925); *La Democrazia* (Paris, 1933); *L'Inquiétude du monde* (Paris, 1934); and *La Désagrégation de l'Europe* (Paris, 1938). A few days after

---

[14] Aldo Garosci, "Italia: L'emigrazione politica durante il fascismo," *Enciclopedia Italiana, Seconda Appendice, 1938–1948,* I–Z (Rome, 1949), p. 115.

[15] Mussolini to Italian Minister in Bern, June 19, 1924, in *I Documenti Diplomatici Italiani, Settima Serie, 1922–1935,* III (Rome, 1959), p. 171.

[16] Mussolini to Italian Consul-General in Zurich, Jan. 16, 1925, in *ibid.,* p. 416.

[17] His letters to the King are printed in his *Rivelazioni,* pp. 581–601.

Mussolini was overthrown in July 1943 Nitti was arrested by the Nazis in Paris and interned for the rest of the war in German camps.[18]

Italy's most well-known priest-politician of the decade, the impenitent Don Luigi Sturzo, felt compelled to seek refuge in London on October 25, 1924, after it was clear that the Vatican no longer favored his anti-Fascist leadership of the PPI.[19] In Paris on March 25, 1925, the Sicilian sacerdote delivered his maiden speech abroad, "Freedom in Italy," whereupon Mussolini passed the word to his embassies in Paris and London to hamper Sturzo's activities.[20] Sturzo explained to his listeners that "for ethical reasons" the Popolari could not support Fascism. It was their duty to oppose the notion that the nation-state was the only God. To foreigners who suggested that perhaps Fascism would soon tame itself, he replied passionately that no dictatorship had ever done so voluntarily. Either popular agitation or war must bring about such a change. "For us," he went on, "the present battle for freedom is like a second Risorgimento"—an epithet he did much to popularize among the anti-Fascists. "It has its phases and its difficulties, and it will have its epilogue; we do not know when or how, but we have faith that it will come . . . and the epilogue will be the reconquest of freedom." [21]

Thus he remained confident that ultimately the good sense of the people would prevail. To hasten that day, he supplied programs for future reform of political institutions, of the social and economic system, and for integration of Italy into a free and federated Europe. His own preference for a republican form of government came into the open after he left London in the summer of 1940 to take up wartime residence in Brooklyn.[22] Throughout his exile Sturzo wrote dozens of articles, essays, and books.[23] He had lived well beyond the Biblically allotted three score and ten when he returned to his homeland in 1946 to as-

[18] An autobiographical discussion of his activities may be found in the preface to his *Meditazioni dell'esilio* (Naples, 1947), pp. 5-47, and in his *Rivelazioni*.
[19] See *supra*, Ch. 1, Catholic dissidence.
[20] *I Documenti Diplomatici Italiani, Settima Serie, 1922-1935*, III, 505-513.
[21] Quoted in Achille Marazza, "I Cattolici e la Resistenza," MLI, No. 43 (1956), pp. 3-15.
[22] Sturzo, *Italy and the Coming World*, pp. 101-113.
[23] Soon after Sturzo's departure Piero Gobetti's press in Turin published three of his works: *Popolarismo e fascismo* (1924); *Pensiero antifascista* (1925); and *La Libertà in Italia* (1925). Perhaps Sturzo's politically most important publications abroad were *Italy and Fascism* (New York, 1927); *Politics and Morality*

sume the role of patron saint in the new Christian Democratic Party (DC), founded by his friend, Alcide DeGasperi. Despite their respect for Sturzo, most Christian Democrats paid little attention to his latter-day jeremiads on the perils of bureaucratic elephantiasis.

Second phase

The second phase of the emigration embraced the months between Mussolini's provocative speech of January 3, 1925, and the proclamation of the "exceptional decrees" in November 1926. During this period when the *Duce* tightened the screws of totalitarianism, emigration continued in fairly normal fashion because existing passports were still valid. Some of the new batch of *émigrés* were politicos who feared that if they stayed home in silence the public might misconstrue their behavior as tacit acceptance of the hated regime. And many fled simply because they did not wish their families to be exposed to further danger. It was violence that drove the Aventine chieftain, Amendola, to Cannes in July 1925 and his death a year later, and the Torinese journalist Gobetti to Paris and death in February 1926.[24]

In June and August 1925, respectively, two other articulate paladins of the opposition reached France. The first was Giuseppe Donati, the aggressive editor of the PPI newspaper, *Il Popolo*, who during the Aventinian secession had persistently advocated the return of the delegates to the Chamber and a trial of the assassins before a high court of justice.[25] The second was Professor Gaetano Salvemini of the University of Florence, in trouble because of his sponsorship of the underground *Non Mollare!* The two had been acquainted for years, and they were to share the grim distinction of being among the first thirteen *fuorusciti* to be deprived, in March 1926, of their citizenship and their property at home.[26]

(London, 1938); *Church and State* (London, 1939); *Italy and the Coming World* (New York, 1945); *Nationalism and Internationalism* (New York, 1946). His wartime articles were republished as *La mia battaglia da New York* (Milan, 1949). All of his works are currently being printed in an *Opera omnia* of several series by Nicola Zanichelli Editore of Bologna.

[24] See *supra*, Ch. 1, *Coup d'état* of January 3, 1925.

[25] Luigi Sturzo, "Il Partito Popolare: Note e ricordi," *Quaderni italiani*, No. 2 (New York and Boston, August 1942), p. 30; and Armando Cavalli, *Giuseppe Donati* (Faenza, 1945).

[26] The others were less well known. See Garosci, *Sdf*, pp. 15–16. For sprightly recollections of his exile, see Salvemini, *Memorie di un fuoruscito* (Milan, 1960).

While Salvemini busily delivered lectures in France, England, and America and published books exposing Blackshirt tyranny,[27] Donati promoted in Paris an Italian-language weekly (later daily) newspaper, *Corriere degli Italiani*. It enjoyed a circulation of several thousand in 1926–1927. The Catholic editor was helped at first by an aged Socialist, Oddino Morgari, and by a Republican, Carlo a Prato. Unfortunately for them, their enterprise ran into trouble. The editors lacked adequate sources of reliable information, which enabled the Fascist press mercilessly to ridicule their faulty reporting. The paper also lacked financial support, and in time fell into the hands of new directors who not only were less capable than Donati but in some cases were secretly in the pay of the enemy. When the *Corriere* published in 1927 an ill-advised editorial recommending the assassination of Mussolini, the French government had no choice but to order its suspension.[28] From 1929 until October 1930 Donati turned to directing the Paris *Pungolo*.[29] Thereafter he traveled to London, Malta, and back to Paris, where he died in July 1931 at the age of 42.

Still another journalist, Alberto Tarchiani, editor-in-chief of *Corriere della sera* and collaborator of Albertini, moved to Paris in 1925 when it became apparent that the "fourth estate" was to be shackled. A moderate democrat of cosmopolitan stamp, Tarchiani worked closely with Salvemini and with Carlo Rosselli during the initial phase of Giustizia e Libertà. After the fall of Fascism he became Free Italy's first ambassador to the United States.

Silvio Trentin, professor of legal philosophy at the University of Padua, successfully made his way to France in February 1926, where with scarcely a pause for breath he began to publish scholarly indictments of the dictatorship.[30] He was flanked by still other warriors of the pen—Carlo Sforza, Francesco L. Ferrari, Alberto Cianca, and later Ignazio Silone—who dispensed a

---

[27] The first was *The Fascist Dictatorship in Italy* (New York, 1927).

[28] Garosci, *Sdf*, pp. 32, 274; Garosci, *VCR*, I, 177–178.

[29] When Mussolini negotiated the Lateran Accords in February 1929, Donati denied his legal right to do so, though he approved the content (arguing that they realized Cavour's dream of a "free church in a free state"—a contention that was promptly rejected by anticlerical *émigrés*). See Giuseppe Donati, *Scritti politici*, ed. G. Rossini (2 vols.; Rome, 1956), II, 355–356.

[30] Gavagnin, *Vent'anni di resistenza*, p. 218; cf. *supra*, Ch. I, n. 115.

torrent of articles and books, political analyses and novels, news-papers and periodicals.[31] Their preachments were more effective abroad of course than in Italy, but some were smuggled into the peninsula and gave real encouragement to the underground.

The year 1926 witnessed a sensational attempt to field an anti-Fascist army in France. The idea had been gestating for a couple of years in the minds of General Giuseppe ("Peppino") Gari-baldi and his brother Ricciotti, grandsons of the Risorgimento hero.[32] They dreamed of recruiting a modern red-shirted legion among the radical emigrant workers in France and winning sup-port from other groups in Italy. In its earliest version the plan apparently called for Peppino to be in charge south of and in-cluding Rome; a brother, Sante, to be responsible for central Italy; a Venetian PSU ex-deputy, Tito Zaniboni, to direct affairs in the North; and Ricciotti to be the pivotal figure in France. Many hitches developed, and Zaniboni became disillusioned sometime in 1925 and broke with the Garibaldis. Yet by promis-ing Italian emigrants in France (especially the anarchistic ones) that he would lead them in a liberating expedition to oust Musso-lini, Ricciotti was able to attract several hundred to his legions, which were massing on various athletic fields. At first the French government raised no objection to the recruitment;[33] then sud-denly in early November 1926 French police arrested Ricciotti in Nice. Soon amazing revelations made it clear that he had been subsidized to the large amount of 645,000 *lire di Pesaro* by a Fascist police agent in France, LaPolla.[34]

[31] The fullest compilation of publications by and about the exiles is a 38-page pamphlet by G. Silvano Spinetti, "Bibliografia degli esuli politici sotto il fascismo," pref. by Aldo Garosci (Rome: Ed. di "Solidarismo," 1959). In 1938 Professor Michele Cantarella of Smith College prepared a listing for *Books Abroad*, XII, No. 1 (1938), of books written by the Italian exiles. This was reprinted in the appendix of the very useful anthology of excerpts from such *émigré* writings by Frances Keene (ed.), *Neither Liberty Nor Bread*. Cantarella later expanded this through 1945 in *Belfagor*, No. 3 (1949), 338–350. A useful bibliography limited to works by Socialist exiles is in Alessandro Schiavi, *Esilio e morte di Filippo Turati, 1926–1932* (Rome, 1956), pp. 559–565.

[32] See *supra*, Ch. 1, PCI tactics, regarding the Italia Libera veterans organization.

[33] According to Garosci, rumor had it that Ricciotti had some support from the Radical spokesman of the French *Cartel des Gauches*, Edouard Herriot (who would connive at the sequestration of some military supplies from garrisons near the frontier) and of the Czech Foreign Minister Édouard Beneš (who, because of his resentment of Mussolini's amity with Hungary, might provide some funds).

[34] At the same time Ricciotti was plotting a filibustering expedition into Catalonia with Colonel Francisco Macià, who later became first President of the

The scandal of the Garibaldi Legions not only injured the relationship of the *fuorusciti* with the French authorities but also disillusioned (until the Spanish Civil War) most anti-Fascists about the chances of encouraging direct action. As a result, many emigrants turned their backs on Italian politics and devoted their energies to the arduous task of making a living. In Italy the publicity about the Garibaldini furnished Mussolini with another pretext to nail down new restrictions.

Third phase

When Mussolini crushed the remaining political parties after the Draconian decrees of November 1926, many of the most conspicuous Socialists, Republicans, and Communists decided that both for personal safety and effective continuation of the struggle they must lose no time in getting away. Imaginative plotters hastily elaborated schemes to assist one another in escaping. The Socialists' general policy was to spirit out the older, prestigious men who manifestly were in danger but to leave as many as possible of the younger men to organize resistance.

Professor Ferruccio Parri was in the fore in planning the escapes of such PSU men as the elderly Claudio Treves, Filippo Turati, and the much younger Giuseppe Saragat. In November 1926 he escorted to the Swiss border the Jewish leader Treves and Saragat (who was destined to become Treves' chief ideological protégé in the ranks of the revisionists).[35] On foot they made their way over a mountain pass to Lugano, always a focal point of anti-Fascism. Treves then proceeded to Paris, while Saragat moved on to Vienna for the early period of his exile. Parri, meanwhile, repaired to Milan.

The most thrilling escape was that of Turati, the sickly "grand

---

Catalan Generalitat under the Spanish Republic. At the crucial moment in 1926 Garibaldi betrayed that enterprise. In later years the Garibaldis returned to Italy. "Peppino" died there in May 1950 at the age of seventy.

For the complex ramifications see G. Salvemini, *Mussolini diplomatico*, pp. 175–191; Gavagnin, *Vent'anni di resistenza*, pp. 205–209, 254; Borghi, *Mezzo secolo di anarchia*, pp. 313, 318–320, 327–328; Garosci, *Sdf*, pp. 21–24, 271–273; Garosci, *VCR*, I, 179–180; Arnold J. Toynbee, *Survey of International Affairs, 1927* (London, 1929), pp. 136–152; and Consul-General Lebrecht of Nice to Mussolini, Dec. 5, 1924, in *I Documenti Diplomatici Italiani, Settima Serie, 1922–1935*, III, 362–363, and *passim*.

[35] Many of Saragat's incisive articles abroad have been reprinted in his *Antifascismo, democrazia, socialismo: pagine attuali dell'esilio* (Rome, 1951).

old man" of revisionist Socialism. Since the *attentat* against Mussolini in the fall of 1926, Blackshirt marchers had been heard chanting up and down the streets of Milan, *"Con la barba di Turati—noi faremo gli spazzolini—per lustrare gli stivali—di Benito Mussolini!"* ("With Turati's beard we shall make some brushes to shine the boots of Benito Mussolini!") And when Turati's elderly wife, the colorful Russian revolutionary Anna Kuliscioff, had died on December 29, 1925,[36] Fascist hoodlums disturbed her funeral cortege. It was only after much difficulty in November 1926 that friends persuaded the septuagenarian widower that he must flee at once. Late that month Carlo Rosselli, Parri, Sandro Pertini, and some others sneaked him from his Milan home first to the residence of Camillo Olivetti in Ivrea, then to the Turin home of the parents of Dr. Carlo Levi, and finally (in a car driven by Adriano Olivetti) to the Ligurian coast. After several days' delay the group embarked in a small motor launch (manned by Italo Oxilia and Lorenzo DaBove) and made their escape to Corsica. From there Turati, accompanied by Pertini and Oxilia, soon made his way to the Riviera and Paris.[37]

Perhaps foolishly, Rosselli and Parri went back to the Italian mainland after depositing Turati in Corsica. Police arrested them (and Riccardo Bauer) almost at once, not for having assisted Turati to escape but for allegedly helping two journalists, Carlo Silvestri and Giovanni Ansaldo, to get out of the country.[38] They were eventually cleared of that charge, while Silvestri and Ansaldo received only brief sentences. Ironically, both of the latter became enthusiastic backers of Mussolini's dictatorship, Ansaldo accepting a post in the agency that regulated the press, thereby making life miserable for many of his former associates.[39]

Soon Rosselli and Parri were apprehended again, this time because of their complicity in Turati's flight. They were dispatched

[36] Before she married Turati she had been enamored, in 1877, of the famed Anarchist, Andrea Costa.

[37] Enzo Tagliacozzo, "L'evasione di Filippo Turati," in E. Rossi, *No al fascismo*, pp. 49–69; F. Parri, "All'alba, la Corsica: era la libertà," *Umanità*, Oct. 10, 1948. See also the recent biography by Franco Catalano, *Filippo Turati* (Rome-Milan, 1957), p. 303 ff. During a furtive return trip to Italy in 1929 Pertini was nabbed and condemned to ten years' imprisonment. Leto, *OVRA*, p. 120.

[38] Garosci, VCR, I, 111–116.

[39] Ascoli, *Annals of the American Academy*, CC (Nov. 1938), pp. 235–253.

to the isle of Ustica for a few weeks before being transported to Savona, in September 1927, for the so-called "trial of the professors." Luckily for them, they appeared before a regular court which had not been Fascisticized. Exploiting their good fortune, they achieved a tour de force in their denunciation of the dictatorship. Turati later dubbed their verbal battle the *"cinque giornate giudiziarie,"* in allusion to Milan's "five days" of insurrection in 1848. After listening to Rosselli and Parri evoke the spirit of the Risorgimento and appeal to principles of eternal justice superior to written law, the court ruled that the accused should benefit from attenuating circumstances. Their action, it noted, had been inspired by humanitarianism, since the aged and infirm Turati, who had vainly sought a passport, faced a real threat if he stayed in Italy. Thus his escape was not a political crime but simply a contravention of passport regulations. Apprised of the verdict, a prominent Genoese Fascist lawyer commented acidly, "Ten of these trials and the regime will be finished."

Rosselli and Parri had won a moral victory. Nevertheless, they had to submit to the minimum penalty of ten months' imprisonment, which, in view of the months already spent in detention, ended in January 1928. Parri then returned to Milan and freedom, but Rosselli, as a result of new "administrative" decisions by the police, was condemned to five years' *confino* on the barren isle of Lipari.[40]

Other prominent Socialists also fled. Giuseppe E. Modigliani and his resourceful wife Vera made good their escapes over the mountains to Austria and Paris, as did the hotspur Pietro Nenni.[41] Additional *compagni* to reach France were the aged writer Oddino Morgari; Bruno Buozzi,[42] who had organized Torinese metallurgical workers into the FIOM; Pallante Rugginenti, a young revisionist leader of the CGL; Nullo Baldini, promoter of co-operatives in Ravenna; Giuseppe Sardelli, a CGL militant

[40] Garosci, VCR, I, 120–125; Garosci, *Sdf*, pp. 29, 274; Tagliacozzo in E. Rossi, *No al fascismo*, pp. 49–69; letter of Pasquale Sarno, president of the Savona court, in Rome *Il Mondo*, Jan. 17, 1956; Barbara Barclay-Carter, *Il Mese*, IV, No. 19 (July 1945); and Fernando Santi, *Il Ponte*, V (April 1949), p. 532.
[41] V. Modigliani, *Esilio*, pp. 31–74; Garosci, VCR, I, 181 ff.
[42] For an anthology of his writings abroad, 1928–1934, see Bruno Buozzi, *Scritti dell'esilio*, ed. Alessandro Schiavi (Rome, 1958).

and parliamentary deputy; and Ugo Coccia, also a deputy and secretary of the maximalist PSI.[43]

Republican Party (PRI) moguls to leave Italy included Cipriano Facchinetti, Randolfo Pacciardi, and Egidio Reale, all of whom fled first to the Swiss Ticino. Eugenio Chiesa and some of the others traveled via Annemasse to Paris, while Fernando Schiavetti, ex-director of *La Voce Repubblicana*, and Mario Bergamo chose Austria.[44]

Senator Carlo Sforza, who had been very conspicuous in the Aventine, left Italy in March 1927 after repeated harassment, which included the burning of his villa. After a tour of the Orient he established his home in Brussels and later in France. One of the most respected figures in the non-Communist emigration, Sforza wrote many books and contributed a spate of fortnightly articles to the Brussels *Soir* and the Toulouse *Dépêche de Toulouse*.[45]

Avv. Francesco L. Ferrari of Modena, a member in 1923 of the PPI National Council, was another notable young democratic writer in exile, and like his friend Giuseppe Donati was to die prematurely abroad. At the University of Louvain he sustained a thesis, *Le régime fasciste italien*, published in Paris in 1928. From 1931 to 1933 he edited in Brussels *Res Publica*, a widely circulated French-language review which often carried articles by Sturzo, Sforza, Salvemini, and such foreigners as H. Wickham Steed, Cecil Sprigge, and Barbara Barclay-Carter. Before his death Ferrari wrote a work on the relationship of Italian Catholic Action to Mussolini's regime.[46]

Alberto Cianca, a vibrant orator and ex-director of Amendola's *Mondo*, escaped via Corsica to Paris in January 1927. That summer he revived *Becco giallo*, the satirical sheet which he and

[43] S/M, *Sdf*, p. 468.

[44] *Ibid.*, p. 474; Garosci, *Sdf*, pp. 28–29.

[45] Among Sforza's books in these years were *Diplomatic Europe since the Treaty of Versailles* (New Haven, 1928); *Les bâtisseurs de l'Europe moderne* (Paris, 1931); *Dictateurs et dictatures de l'après guerre* (Paris, 1931); *Les frères ennemis* (Paris, 1933); *L'âme italienne* (Paris, 1934); and *The Real Italians* (New York, 1938).

[46] Sturzo, "Il Partito Popolare," *Quaderni Italiani*, No. 2 (Aug. 1942), pp. 30–31. Ferrari's study, *L'Azione Cattolica e il "Regime"* (Milan, 1957), appeared posthumously.

Alberto Giannini had published during the Aventine. The paper was designed especially for covert circulation. Later Giannini deserted the anti-Fascists and bitterly denounced them.[47]

Political regrouping abroad

By 1927 enough authoritative politicians were abroad, chiefly in France, to reorganize some of the parties. Actually, only the leftist ones did so. The Liberals made no attempt, while the Populars, cognizant of the Vatican veto, dared not.

Among the first to regroup were the maximalist Socialists (PSI), led by their secretary, Ugo Coccia, who revived a weekly edition of *Avanti!* in Paris on December 10, 1926 [48]; the colorful Russian-born cosmopolite, Angelica Balabanoff, who had once befriended Mussolini; and the crusading advocate of Socialist solidarity, Nenni. Meantime, such prophets of revisionism as Turati, Treves, Modigliani, Buozzi, and Saragat shed their old PSU label of Matteotti days and reconsecrated themselves the Socialist Party of Italian Laborers (PSLI). In Zurich they published *Avvenire del lavoratore* ("Worker's Future").

The PRI likewise reorganized in Annemasse, Paris, and Lugano. Their directors included Chiesa, Facchinetti, Reale, Pacciardi, Chiostergi, and Pistocchi.[49] The PCI established in 1927 a Foreign Center in Paris and an Internal Center in Milan.[50]

Concentrazione Antifascista

Of greater moment than the reconstruction of the leftist parties was their decision (exclusive of the PCI) to band together in a Concentrazione Antifascista. The Anti-Fascist Concentration's birth dated from a conference held in Nerac in Lot-et-Garonne in April 1927. Issuing the invitations were two Italian residents

[47] See Alberto Giannini, *Memorie di un fesso* (Milan, 1941).
[48] Arfè, *Storia dell'Avanti!, 1926–1940*, p. 20 ff.
[49] Mario Pistocchi (whose citizenship was cancelled by Mussolini between 1926 and 1932) wrote a book on European federation, *Le destin de l'Europe* (Paris, 1931), that won second prize in a world competition sponsored by the *Revue des vivants*. Claudio Treves editorialized in Paris *La Libertà* on October 29, 1931, "We hope that the DESTINY OF EUROPE will be as sensible and full of realistic idealism as that set forth in the book." C. Treves, *Il fascismo nella letteratura antifascista dell'esilio: Antologia*, ed. A. Schiavi (Rome, 1953), pp. 99–104. Perhaps Treves would have been less enthusiastic had he known what was later revealed—that Pistocchi turned spy for OVRA. See Garosci, *Sdf*, pp. 15, 294.
[50] See *infra*, Ch. III.

of that town, Alceste DeAmbris and Luigi Campolonghi, top officials of the Lega Italiana dei Diritti dell'Uomo (LIDU; "League of the Rights of Man"), a nonpartisan, anticlerical society, established in 1922 and modeled after its French counterpart which dated from the Dreyfus Affair. The French society made its chief appeal to independent voters (especially Radicals, Anarchists, and Socialists) and often assumed a significant political role; the Italian LIDU busied itself mainly with defending the legal rights of the emigrants and providing economic aid to worthy people. DeAmbris, who in earlier years had been a revolutionary syndicalist, presided over LIDU; Campolonghi, a journalist who had emigrated during the unrest of 1898, served as secretary. When DeAmbris died Campolonghi inherited the gavel, and Cianca replaced him as secretary.[51]

At the Nerac conference DeAmbris and Campolonghi suggested creating an organization open to anyone, but the delegates of the two Socialist parties, the PRI, and Buozzi's skeletal CGL rejected that idea in favor of a bloc of the above-named groups and LIDU. This plan, drafted by Modigliani, was agreed to. Some eight months passed before the PSI ratified its adherence, but Nenni served from the outset as secretary-general of the Anti-Fascist Concentration, whose headquarters were in Paris at Rue du Faubourg St. Denis 103. Most of the adherents dwelt either in the environs of Paris or in southern France. The Communists would have nothing to do with this "social-fascist," "Masonic-inspired" "second Aventine." Populars and Liberals also steered clear, though individuals like Nitti and Sforza were good friends.[52]

The Nestor of the Concentration was Turati, who maintained an office on Boulevard Ornano. He provided the fulcrum for almost all of its activities until his death in 1932, and it was to him that most of the non-Communist refugees turned for moral inspiration on each anniversary of Matteotti's murder. In August 1927 he dedicated a statue to Matteotti in Brussels, erected by the Socialist International in the Maison du Peuple. The old gentleman devoted most of his declining years to writing articles,

[51] Lega Italiana dei Diritti dell'Uomo, *Il Programma, i metodi e l'azione della LIDU* (Paris, 1929); Borghi, *Mezzo secolo di anarchia*, pp. 154–160, and *passim*; Garosci, *Sdf*, pp. 33–37.
[52] *Ibid.*, pp. 40–48.

57

organizing propaganda displays, soliciting funds, attending congresses, and testifying in behalf of those *fuorusciti* whose overzealousness got them into trouble.[53]

The initial pronunciamento of the Concentration mentioned nothing of social reform, constituent assemblies, or a republic. It limited itself to promising to organize the exiles and to seek in every way possible to keep in touch with the Italian people. It would stimulate resistance, encourage a clandestine press, and offer aid to victims of Fascism. This cautious mandate reflected the predominantly Aventinian attitude of the leaders, most of whom had not yet given up all hope that Victor Emmanuel III might be persuaded to dismiss his prime minister. The Concentration decided to modify its stand the next year, however, when the Fascist Grand Council supererogated the sovereign's nominal right to name a new premier and even claimed a voice in matters affecting the dynastic succession. The King's failure to protest publicly dismayed the Concentration, which in June that year burned its royalist bridges and called for a republic. It also adopted a hostile line toward the Vatican after the Lateran Accords of February 1929.[54]

The Concentration's weekly newspaper, *La Libertà*, first appeared on May 1, 1927, and continued until May 1934. It enjoyed wide circulation among the emigrants, but when miniscule editions were mailed to Italy, Mussolini's police soon recognized the telltale format of the envelopes and confiscated most of the issues.[55] Treves, writing under the pen name "Rabano Mauro," served as editor-in-chief until his death in 1933.[56] In collaboration with Turati, he gave the paper a predominantly revisionist slant and harped upon the theme that the *fuorusciti* represented the authentic stream of Italian history while Fascism was but an aberration. The editors carefully listed the regime's deeds of violence and printed the names and sentences of people convicted by the Special Tribunal. For several weeks in mid-1927 Salvemini wrote a series of articles for *Libertà*, stressing the need

[53] Schiavi, *Esilio e morte di Filippo Turati*, 1926–1932, p. 6, and *passim*.
[54] Garosci, *Sdf*, pp. 38–41; S/M, *Sdf*, pp. 474–479; *cf*. mimeographed pamphlet by Pietro Montasini, *L'Organisation des antifascistes italiens à l'étranger* (Paris: 103 Rue du Faubourg St. Denis, March 1929), pp. 1–10.
[55] Leto, OVRA, p. 42.
[56] Many of his articles are reprinted in the Schiavi anthology (*cf*. n. 49 *supra*).

for unceasing self-criticism by the exiles and emphasizing the impossibility of any shortcut to eventual popular insurrection. Always a lone wolf, Salvemini soon severed his ties with the Concentration, however. His ideas found a more congenial habitat in Carlo Rosselli's Giustizia e Libertà movement after 1929.[57]

Meanwhile, Turati, Treves, and others sponsored exhibits in Cologne and Vienna in 1928 of exemplars of the clandestine press, and they often attended meetings of the Second International. After 1929 the Concentration also brought out a fortnightly information bulletin in French, and for a time Modigliani edited a fortnightly review, *Rinascita socialista* ("Socialist Rebirth").[58]

Whatever subsidization the Concentration received came mainly from such foreign working groups as the New York Lady Garmentworkers' Union, the Italian Society of Winterthur in Switzerland, a number of French labor organizations, and the International Transport Federation. In addition, some income accrued from sale of *Libertà* and contributions. But never was there money to spare, for most of the exiles earned their living by manual labor, and the oncoming Depression aggravated their misery. Only a handful of expatriates (for example, Carlo Rosselli and Eugenio Chiesa) were able to remove their savings from Italy in any substantial amount.[59]

It is not easy to measure the efficacy of the Concentration. Both the Communists and to a lesser degree Giustizia e Libertà ridiculed it as an outmoded recrudescence of the Aventine. Bocchini, head of the Fascist police, did not think it was very dangerous at first; his spies infiltrated it and informed him of many of its squabbles.[60] Nevertheless, there is reason to believe that the Concentration served some good purposes. Its newspaper was widely read abroad and enjoyed a good reputation, even though its propaganda was not well known in Italy. It provided a sounding board for discussion of politico-economic problems.

[57] Gaetano Arfè, "Salvemini nella Concentrazione antifascista," *Il Ponte*, xiii (1957), pp. 1168–1171; and G. Salvemini, "Gli antifascisti all'estero," *ibid.*, pp. 1172–1188.

[58] Garosci, *Sdf*, pp. 38–43; Schiavi, *Esilio e morte di Filippo Turati*, pp. 168–180, and photograph facing p. 224.

[59] Garosci, "Italia: L'Emigrazione politica durante il fascismo," *Enciclopedia Italiana, Seconda Appendice, 1938–1948, I–Z*, p. 115.

[60] Leto, *OVRA*, p. 41; Ermanno Menapace, *Tra i fuorusciti* (Paris, [1933]).

Furthermore, the Concentration helped clear the air of some of the confusion, recriminations, and misguided violence that had plagued the early phases of the emigration. Responsible Concentration chieftains gave no encouragement to anarchistic terrorism or to promotion of foolhardy filibustering forays. Thus they helped to restore the prestige of the *fuorusciti* after the fiascos of the Garibaldi Legions and of Donati's *Corriere degli Italiani*.

Giustizia e Libertà ("Justice and Liberty")

When 1928 drew to a close there were just two major organizations (apart from the Anarchists, who never were tightly welded) functioning in the active wing of the Resistance—the Anti-Fascist Concentration and the PCI. Early in 1929 a third took shape, composed of men dissatisfied with the programs of the existing parties and anxious to create a "supraparty" current that would flow somewhere between the left bank of Socialism and right bank of Liberalism.

Its initiators were located both in Italy and in France. Most had been previously connected with *Non Mollare!* in Florence or with *Il Caffè* in Milan. In the forefront was a cluster of Lombard democratic and republican Liberals. The *spiritus rector* was Professor Ernesto Rossi, who had fled to France for four months after *Non Mollare!* collapsed and then had sneaked back to a teaching post in the Bergamo Royal Technical Institute. For four years he had been distributing bushels of underground propaganda, and with much *sang-froid* had crossed the frontier five times without a passport.[61] Other promoters were Professor Parri and Riccardo Bauer, back from *confino*, and the journalist Giovanni Mira. In frequent contact with Professor Salvemini and Alberto Tarchiani in Paris, they began to draw up plans for printing pamphlets abroad which they would smuggle into Italy. They also envisioned coalescing scattered anti-Fascist groups both at home and abroad. To further this end, Tarchiani and some of the others plotted to assist the wealthy young Florentine Jew, Carlo Rosselli, to escape from Lipari, where he had been confined since the 1928 Savona trial.

The 29-year-old Rosselli was still enrolled in the PSU while on

[61] Ernesto Rossi, "Fuga dal treno," in E. Rossi (ed.), *No al fascismo*, p. 181.

Lipari. There he won the friendship of several other prisoners: Emilio Lussu, the tough-fibred parliamentary deputy of the radical Sardinian Action Party; F. Fausto Nitti, nephew of the former premier and son of a Methodist pastor in Rome, as well as being a high Mason; and Gioacchino Dolci, a young Republican worker from Rome who, freed ahead of schedule, was to escape to Paris.

From France in November 1928 Tarchiani dispatched a motor launch piloted by Raffaele Rossetti, a "gold-medal" war hero. The prisoners, hoping to catch his boat, remained in the water twenty minutes, but bad weather and other complications prevented them from doing so. On the next try, the night of July 27, 1929, Captain Italo Oxilia, piloting a 40-foot motor launch, *Dream V*, which had been purchased on the Riviera from an Egyptian prince, succeeded in rescuing Rosselli, Lussu, and F. F. Nitti, despite some anxious moments when the motor had to be started within earshot of the guards. The fugitives made their way first to Tunisia, where Tarchiani awaited them, and thence to Paris. At once they wrote and published in many lands romantic accounts of their daring escape.[62] At the end of his version, Rosselli swore that "one single thought will guide us in this hospitable land: to use this personal freedom which we have regained with so much effort as an instrument for the restoration of the freedom of an entire people." [63]

Shortly after his arrival and reunion with wife and child,[64] Rosselli decided to sever his tie with the party of Matteotti, stay clear of the Anti-Fascist Concentration, and instead launch a "supraparty" movement called Giustizia e Libertà which, he hoped, would magnetize the non-Communist opposition.[65] Parri,

[62] See Francesco Fausto Nitti, *Escape* (New York, 1930); Emilio Lussu, "The Flight from Lipari," *Atlantic Monthly*, CL (July 1930); Emilio Lussu, *La catena* (Paris, 1929; Rome, 1945); Carlo Rosselli, *Scritti politici e autobiografici* (Naples, 1944); Alberto Tarchiani, "L'impresa di Lipari," in E. Rossi (ed.), *No al fascismo*, pp. 71–126.

[63] Quoted in Garosci, *Sdf*, p. 56.

[64] The Fascists at first took reprisal by arresting Carlo's wife (an English citizen) and baby, but soon allowed them to emigrate. His brother Nello was also detained for some weeks on Ponza and then released. Since he was not overtly active in politics Nello could remain in Italy and carry on with little interference his historical researches on Risorgimento radicals and diplomacy.

[65] "Coming from diverse political currents," explained the initial manifesto, entitled "Giustizia e Libertà" and bearing the date November 1929, "we are for the present filing away our party membership cards and creating a union for action. A revolutionary movement and not a party, 'Giustizia e Libertà' is its name and

it seems, persuaded Rosselli to place "Justice" ahead of "Liberty" in the binomial title. The adherents of the new movement commonly called themselves "Giellisti" (the word being a combination of the sounds for "G" and "L").[66]

The Galahad of the Giellisti was Rosselli until his assassination in June 1937. He dominated not only because of the suppleness of his mind and the attractiveness of his somewhat erratic personality but also because he provided from his own fortune most of the subsidization. His philosophy did not evolve consistently, but the growth of many tenets can be traced through his numerous writings: *Non Mollare!*; *Quarto Stato*;[67] and the provocative *Socialismo Liberale,* composed in 1929 while he was on Lipari but not published till the following year in Paris, where it aroused the ire of Treves and other "orthodox" Socialists. Yet pragmatic considerations played a great role in shaping Rosselli's creed, just as they did with Mussolini. Except for unyielding insistence upon republicanism and bold deeds which would captivate the people's imagination and promote real uprisings, his program (whose early versions were largely drafted by Salvemini[68]) remained conveniently flexible. Its touchstone lay within a doctrinal triangle whose points were Liberalism, Revisionist Marxism, and Anarchism, but the precise locus shifted with changing conditions. Though there was much opportunism in GL, one must not minimize the moral fortitude and idealism that never failed Rosselli throughout his meteoric career.[69]

Rosselli was dissatisfied with the Concentration's "Aventinian passivity" and the willingness of some of its members to collaborate if necessary with the Crown and perhaps even with

----

symbol. Republicans, Socialists, and Democrats—we are fighting for freedom, for the republic, for social justice. We are no longer three different expressions but an indivisible trinity," Rosselli proclaimed with almost theological fervor. Quoted in S/M, *Sdf,* p. 501.

[66] Ferruccio Parri, "Nascita di G.L.," *Il Ponte,* XIII (1957), pp. 859–861.

[67] See *supra,* Ch. I, "Quarto Stato."

[68] E. Rossi (ed.), *No al fascismo,* p. 13.

[69] Rosselli's life and writings have been carefully documented and analyzed in the sympathetic study by his disciple, Aldo Garosci, VCR, and somewhat more compactly in the relevant chapter in Garosci, *Sdf.* Another highly favorable judgment may be found in Salvemini, *Carlo and Nello Rosselli, a Memoir.* Somewhat more objective assessments may be found in S/M, *Sdf,* and in Mario Vinciguerra's essay in Corrado Barbagallo (ed.), *Cento anni di vita italiana: 1848–1948* (2 vols.; Milan, 1948–1950).

the Army and Church. For Rosselli the Republic was a *sine qua non:* the Savoyards no less than the Blackshirts must go. To some extent he inherited his republicanism from his Mazzinian parents, though young Rosselli himself never subscribed to the Genoese Prophet's party; but it was chiefly his boundless contempt for Victor Emmanuel III during the Aventine that led him to nail down his intransigent republicanism.

Rosselli denied the Concentration's assumption that Fascism was but a roadblock in Italy's advance toward social democracy. Fascism, he contended, was rather the "expression of century-long weaknesses in the Italian nation [and] of unsatisfied elements among the youth," sentiments to which the Communists and moderate currents in the Concentration had been appealing unsuccessfully.[70] In his analysis of post-Risorgimento history, Rosselli shared some of the conclusions of the Fascists, and his emphasis upon "revolutionary action," his preference for the term "movement" rather than "party," and his flamboyant exuberance appeared to Modigliani to be redolent of Mussolini's own activism. No doubt Rosselli hoped to create a revolutionary force which would rival the Fascists in its mass appeal, but his long-term objectives were far more idealistic than theirs—a democratic republic, a "liberal-socialist" economy, preservation of civil liberties, achievement of social justice, and establishment of international peace.

In some respects Rosselli's program resembled that which Piero Gobetti had preached in *Rivoluzione liberale* almost a decade earlier, and among the Torinese Giellisti the links between the two were intimate. Yet there was a signal difference. Unlike Gobetti, Rosselli rejected out of hand any possibility of working closely with Communists. His economic program favored socializing only public utilities and certain heavy industries, establishing co-operatives, promoting agrarian reform, and inaugurating progressive income taxes.[71] All of this was too much for Togliatti to stomach. Scornfully the Hercules of Italian Communism contrasted the "rich dilettante" Rosselli's "superficial,"

[70] Aldo Garosci, "Profilo dell'azione di Carlo Rosselli e di 'Giustizia e Libertà,' " in *Quaderni del Partito d'Azione*, No. 9 (Liberated Italy, 1944), pp. 8–9.

[71] Vinciguerra, "I partiti politici," in Barbagallo (ed.), *Cento anni di vita italiana*, I, 232; Salvadori, *Resistenza ed azione*, p. 59.

"out-dated," "fascist-like" criticism of Marxism with the "poor intellectual" Gobetti's "studious," "revolutionary" attitude.[72]

Others besides Rosselli imparted to GL its peculiar tint. The Sardinian firebrand Lussu, for example, contributed perfervid republicanism and determination to stir the people's imagination by colorful, heroic deeds; he also stressed the Proudhonian theme of regional self-government and European federation.[73] Much more orthodox in their democratic convictions were Tarchiani, F. F. Nitti, Vincenzo Nitti (the latter the son of ex-Premier F. S. Nitti), Riccardo Bauer, and Luigi Salvatorelli (the last two still residing in Italy). They and a host of others made their views known through articles and verbal arguments in the councils of the movement. Some of them later broke away when they decided that GL was becoming too socialistic.

During its early phase Giustizia e Libertà was, above all, a movement preaching Dantonian audacity in order to win world attention and to rouse the people from their torpor. Such a strategy recalled the activist experience of numerous Risorgimento heroes—Orsini, Pisacane, the Cairolis, Cafiero, and others—but it ran the risk of degenerating into an unrealistic cabal sponsoring futile anarchistic terrorism.[74] Rosselli, for example, had barely launched GL when he found it necessary to take a stand regarding the attempted assassination of Crown Prince Humbert on his visit to his fiancée, Belgian Princess Maria José, October 24, 1929.

That *attentat* was committed by a 21-year-old Torinese Socialist, Fernando DeRosa, who received encouragement from at least some Giellisti.[75] In his teens the idealistic lad had been attracted to Fascism but had later shifted to a romanticized form of republican socialism, partly because of his reading of Jack London. Courageously he had slipped across the border several times on secret missions and had convinced himself that only an act of

---

[72] "Ercoli" [Togliatti], "Sul movimento di Giustizia e Libertà," Paris Lo Stato operaio (Sept. 1931), p. 463.

[73] Lussu published many anti-Fascist tracts, the most widely read being La marcia su Roma e dintorni (English edition, Enter Mussolini), and La catena. He also prepared propaganda designed for the Italian Army, which he hoped would increase its antipathy for the rival Fascist Militia (MVSN).

[74] Garosci, Sdf, p. 58.

[75] Aldo Garosci, "L'attentato di Bruxelles," in E. Rossi (ed.), No al fascismo, pp. 127–158.

violence could end tyranny in Italy. DeRosa fully realized the personal danger he ran, for he told the jurors at his trial: "My instinct recoiled with horror from the bloody deed; but my reason imposed it upon me as a supreme act of justice. Thus, when I decided to come to Brussels, after reading in a newspaper the news of the arrival of the prince, I underwent a long struggle with myself . . . and had to conquer myself. . . . I did not think I should leave the Brussels square alive. I did not want to harm innocent people. . . . It is true, I wanted to kill. I wanted to kill the hereditary prince of a reigning house that has killed freedom in my country. I felt that when this young prince behaved like a Fascist . . . , put on the Fascist uniform, was openly identifying himself with the assassins of Giacomo Matteotti . . . I wanted to do justice. . . ."[76] He really hoped to lose his own life and become a martyr; thus at the trial he deliberately accused himself.[77]

Giustizia e Libertà bestowed its unreserved blessing on the would-be assassin and furnished numerous defense witnesses (Salvemini, Tarchiani, Signora Rosselli, and Raffaele Rossetti) who were eager to confirm the tyranny of Mussolini. The PCI, on the other hand, denounced the plot as an "anti-class," "counter-revolutionary" gesture because it was diverting the "working masses" from their proper strategy.[78] The Concentration also assumed a rather typically Marxian posture toward individual terrorism, but unlike the PCI it tried to explain the motives of DeRosa, and the elderly spokesman of the bloc, Turati, testified for the defense. So did F. S. Nitti [79] and the Catholic exile, Avv. Ferrari. DeRosa's Belgian defense attorney was Paul-Henri Spaak. The court found the defendant guilty and sentenced him to five years. After serving two, DeRosa was freed for good conduct and expelled from the country.[80]

[76] Quoted in S/M, *Sdf*, p. 502.
[77] Gavagnin, *Vent'anni di resistenza al fascismo*, p. 265.
[78] Paris *Lo Stato operaio*, IV (July 1930), p. 449.
[79] Signora Luigia Nitti has edited a volume containing the testimony: *Le procès DeRosa* (Paris, 1931).
[80] DeRosa then migrated to the newly established Spanish Republic. There he helped stir up the abortive insurrection in Asturias in 1934 and was consequently jailed until the advent of the Spanish Popular Front government in the spring of 1936 facilitated his release. During the first weeks of the Civil War DeRosa commanded the "Octubre" battalion. He died at the front on September 16, 1936. See Gavagnin, *Vent'anni di resistenza*, pp. 266–267; Garosci, *Sdf*, pp. 59–

A couple of months after the DeRosa incident Paris police raided the residences of several GL leaders and arrested Cianca, in whose home they found seven packages of dynamite caps. This highly involved affair gave rise to sensational rumors, including an especially wild one that GL had intended to assassinate Italian delegates to the League of Nations. The Paris arrests resulted from a tip by Ermanno Menapace, an unsavory *provocateur* who had long intrigued among the *fuorusciti* and particularly with Camillo Berneri, a front-rank Anarchist and quondam student of Salvemini. It was Menapace who had planted the incriminating evidence in Cianca's home. The imbroglio led to brief incarceration of Cianca, Berneri, and Menapace in 1930 and acquittal of the others. The French at first ordered Lussu, Rosselli, and Tarchiani to leave the country but later let them stay on condition they periodically renew their documents. Henceforth they had to work under the handicap of increased police surveillance. After serving his sentence in 1931 Berneri fled from one country to another till he met violent death in May 1937 in Barcelona during the Civil War.[81]

In July 1930 Giustizia e Libertà sponsored one of the most daring deeds of the entire emigration—an airplane flight over Milan in mid-day. Giovanni Bassanesi, a Valdoastan student at the Sorbonne and president of the Paris section of LIDU, conceived the idea and volunteered for the task. Of delicate physique and precise in speech and mannerisms, Bassanesi hardly seemed the type for such a hazardous mission; after all, he did not even possess a pilot's license. When he first discussed the project with the Communist exiles they gave him no encouragement, but when he broached it to Cianca he won the support of GL. In due course the singular young student learned to fly, while Rosselli and others prepared a small landing field in the Swiss Ticino. Bassanesi managed to pilot his tiny craft safely across the Alps to the field, where he picked up his cargo of leaflets and took off for near-by Milan. For fifteen minutes during the noon

60, 275–277; and *Per la libertà del popolo spagnolo: documenti [di Fausto Nitti, Tommaso Toselli, Pietro Nenni, e Massimo Mila] sul contributo della Gioventù Socialista Italiana e sul sacrificio di Fernando DeRosa e Renzo Giua nella lotta contro il fascismo spagnolo* (Turin, 1956), pp. 1–55.

[81] Gaetano Salvemini, Rome *Il Mondo*, May 3, 1952; *cf.* his *Mussolini diplomatico*, pp. 188–191; Menapace, *Tra i fuorusciti, passim*.

hour, boldly circling the Lombard metropolis, he pitched out manifestoes which urged the people to boycott tax collectors and arm themselves for insurrection. On the return flight his plane crashed in the Alps and Bassanesi was injured. The Swiss police promptly locked him up, along with Rosselli and Tarchiani. Major defense witnesses at their trial in Lugano included Sforza and Turati. The accused were absolved but ordered to leave the country.[82]

The Bassanesi aerial invasion of Italy turned out to be the first of a series of similar attempts. This sort of *beau geste*, in the best tradition of the romantic Risorgimento, exerted a peculiar fascination on many exiles, who optimistically expected far too much to come of it. The last such project to be sponsored by GL occurred soon after the Spanish Revolution of April 1931 ousted King Alfonso XIII. Rosselli, Tarchiani, and Bassanesi proceeded hastily to Madrid to discuss with Spain's new Republican officials the possibility of using Iberian air bases for propagandistic flights over Italy. Among the Spaniards with whom they conferred were Manuel Azaña, Indalecio Prieto, and Ramón Franco. The latter came up with an audacious scheme for bombarding Mussolini's Palazzo Venezia. Oddly enough, Bassanesi rejected this, and in the upshot nothing came of these talks. Later that summer, however, Bassanesi attempted a flight from Constance into Italy, but his craft failed to get off the ground and the erratic pilot once more was apprehended.[83]

The most publicized and tragic aerial foray was that undertaken in October 1931 by the poet Lauro DeBosis, who was identified not with GL but with the Alleanza Nazionale. Both his deed and that political group merit special attention.

Alleanza Nazionale and the DeBosis flight

The National Alliance was a covert Liberal current that came into existence in Italy during 1930 and 1931. It was organized by Mario Vinciguerra, who once had been editor of Amendola's *Il Mondo* and secretary of the Aventinian Democratic Union. Subsequently he had collaborated with Lelio Basso in publica-

---

[82] Egidio Reale, "Il volo su Milano," in E. Rossi (ed.), *No al fascismo*, pp. 159–175; Garosci, *Sdf*, pp. 60–62 and 276.
[83] Garosci, VCR, I, 235–241.

tion of the short-lived Genoese *Pietre*.[84] Upon its suppression, Vinciguerra was admonished by the police to watch his step. But he remained obdurate, firmly believing that the people must be offered a reasonable, Liberal alternative to Fascism—an alternative based on constitutional premises. If this were not available, and if the Communists succeeded in "monopolizing the prisons," then the Italian people would never dare to repudiate Mussolini, he feared. Vinciguerra sought to be realistic; he concluded that no matter how much many of the anti-Fascists might dislike Crown, Church, and Army, these institutions were realities and must be used in the struggle. Certainly he did not want the oppositionists to become so radical that they would scare leaders of those institutions.[85]

The validity of Vinciguerra's contentions seemed to be borne out in July 1943 when Mussolini was felled by a plot rooted largely in those institutions; but of course the international situation and the domestic condition of war-weary Italy in 1943 were much different from 1930. Vinciguerra probably was unduly optimistic in hoping for the support of the King, Church, and Army in 1930. Yet one must remember that he was influenced by the contemporary hostility between Catholic Action and the regime.[86] Vinciguerra had contact with the beleaguered Catholic lay organization through Padre Enrico Rosa, S.J., director of the Jesuit periodical, *Civiltà cattolica*. Fr. Rosa was privately critical of the Lateran pacts, which he felt were a danger to the Church. Through Catholic Action Fr. Rosa "discreetly divulged the Alliance's literature." [87] Catholic support for the National Alliance also existed in Verona and perhaps elsewhere. In addition to support from certain religious leaders, Vinciguerra received encouragement from Croce. For a time there was also a link with Giustizia e Libertà, primarily through Professor Guido DeRuggiero of Rome, although (according to Vinciguerra) that eminent historian of liberalism found it hard to be antimonarchic in one underground group and royalist in another.[88]

[84] See *infra*, Ch. III, Anti-Fascism in the legal press.
[85] S/M, *Sdf*, pp. 520–521.
[86] See *infra*, Ch. III.
[87] G. Salvemini in his introduction to Lauro DeBosis, *Storia della mia morte e ultimi scritti* (Turin, 1948), p. xix.
[88] S/M, *Sdf*, pp. 520–522; Mario Vinciguerra in Lauro DeBosis, *Storia della mia morte*, p. 121.

The National Alliance employed the "chain letter" technique in the diffusion of its circulars, which began to appear fortnightly after July 1, 1930. These would be sent through the mails, the recipient being instructed to make six copies and to forward them to six others, including two Fascists. Much effort was required; the process was mechanical, and the envelopes often were quickly spotted by the police. None of the manifestoes called for uprisings; they simply discussed the necessity of an alternative to Fascism and Communism, and emphasized the need for co-operation by Monarchy, Church, and Army.[89]

Vinciguerra attracted several collaborators, the most important of whom was Lauro DeBosis, a 29-year-old poet.[90] DeBosis's father was a literary craftsman, while his mother (Lilian Vernon) was an American, the daughter of the founder of the Methodist Episcopal Church in Italy. Young DeBosis had studied in the United States and had taught one summer at Harvard. As a youth he was a moderate in politics. At first he had detected nothing objectionable in Fascism, but by 1925 he had turned against it; soon he was denouncing Mussolini's rule as "organized terror" and "systematic violation of justice." DeBosis's brilliant lyrical drama, *Icaro*, based upon the Greek myth of the slave Icarus who lost his life trying to fly to a free new world, expressed his own love of freedom. Written in 1927, that drama brought DeBosis the Olympic Prize for Poetry at Amsterdam the next year.[91]

Early in October 1930 DeBosis departed for the United States on a professional mission. He had scarcely left when the Rome police caught Vinciguerra, Umberto Zanotti-Bianco, Duca Di-Cesarò, Renzo Rendi, and others who held key posts in the Alliance. The police made every effort to wring confessions from Vinciguerra; their brutality, in fact, permanently injured his right ear. They searched the home of DeBosis's mother and arrested her when some clandestine literature was found on the premises. The lady was freed, however, after the police tricked her into signing a statement pledging fealty to Fascism. Vinci-

[89] S/M, *Sdf*, pp. 520–521.
[90] Among the others were Giovanni Antonio, Duca Di Cesarò, a former head of "Social Democracy"; Gino Doria, a Neapolitan writer; Umberto Zanotti-Bianco, a prominent southern economist; Romolo Ferlosio, a banker; and Renzo Rendi.
[91] S/M, *Sdf*, pp. 519–520.

guerra and Rendi were condemned by the Special Tribunal in December 1930 to fifteen years' imprisonment, even though none of their pamphlets called for insurrection.[92]

Upon his return to Europe young DeBosis heard of the misfortunes that had befallen the Alliance. Momentarily he thought of giving himself up, but instead decided to make a gesture of defiance in the manner of the mythical Icarus (and, more recently, of Bassanesi). He would learn to fly in order to drop the Alliance's manifestoes over the capital. Should he sacrifice his life, so much the better. By early 1931 DeBosis was becoming frankly republican and anticlerical, but he still thought it best to utilize the Monarchy and Church if they could be persuaded to fight Fascism.[93] He obtained money from Ferrari, editor-in-chief of Brussels *Soir*, secured employment as a clerk in a Paris hotel, and in his free time learned to become a pilot. After the loss of one craft, and with only five hours of solo flight to his credit, DeBosis took off in *Pegasus* from Cannes on October 3, 1931, intending to fly over Rome with his cargo of leaflets. The night before, he penned a moving essay, "Histoire de ma mort," which he mailed to Ferrari for publication in the event of his death. "I am convinced that Fascism will not fall until some twenty youths first sacrifice their lives to awaken the spirit of Italians," he wrote. "I shall be worth more dead than alive." [94]

DeBosis's plane reached the capital about 8 p.m. on the 3rd. Hovering for almost half an hour above Piazza Venezia, the Corso, and other crowded quarters, he threw out leaflets, some of which bore an urgent appeal to the King to take the lead in dismissing Mussolini: "Italians who are suffering the shame of being written off by the world as a servile herd do not know if you are with them or with the garrison of oppressors. Your Majesty: Choose! There is no third road." [95] Others appealed to the citizenry not to let themselves be intimidated. A foreign journalist who watched the sensational flight reported that De-Bosis "flew very low over the streets, and in places it seemed as if

[92] *Ibid.*, pp. 526–528; cf. Piero Calamandrei's commemorative speech on De-Bosis in *Uomini e città della Resistenza*, pp. 37–52.

[93] M. Salvadori, "Il sacrificio di DeBosis," in E. Rossi (ed.), *No al fascismo*, pp. 215–229.

[94] It was published in Italy (with a preface by Salvemini) after the Liberation: *Storia della mia morte* (Turin, 1948).

[95] Quoted in full in Gavagnin, *Vent'anni di resistenza*, pp. 318–325.

snow had fallen, so thickly were the leaflets strewn. He dropped them into the laps of spectators at an open-air cinema, and among the tables of cafés in the squares. One spectator recounted that the plane seemed to be mounting the Spanish Steps." [96] On the return flight DeBosis, pursued by Italo Balbo's airmen, apparently ran out of fuel and crashed in the darkness off Corsica.

With DeBosis's tragic death the National Alliance's brief existence came to an end. But his gesture had been a "ray of light in a dark sky" to dispirited anti-Fascists in Rome.

Giustizia e Libertà within Italy

During its first three years Giustizia e Libertà managed to establish several covert centers in Italy. At the end of that period its underground network, used chiefly for propaganda distribution, rivaled that of the Communists both in scope and efficiency, though it was admittedly aimed more toward intellectuals than was the PCI apparatus. Reliable statistics are difficult to come by, but some useful testimony has been offered by Professor Massimo Salvadori, who in those years was a GL activist in Rome. At the nadir of the Depression in 1933 there were in that city about 800 Giellisti, while some 2,500 to 3,000 were to be found in the central and southern provinces. In the North, where GL had its principal *point d'appui*, the number was substantially greater. Quite a few passed from GL to Communism, according to Salvadori, who noted that Communists made up slightly more than half the prisoners on Ponza where he was exiled early in 1933—the majority of them tightly disciplined Stalinists who kept mostly to themselves. Anarchists, chiefly of the Kropotkin collectivist breed rather than the violent bomb throwers, were next in number, while the Giellisti ranked third.[97]

Milan was the focal point of GL during 1930 as the result of yeoman labor by Ernesto Rossi, Riccardo Bauer, and Ferruccio Parri; but they and others also erected outposts quickly in Turin, Genoa, Florence, Trent, Trieste, and Rome.[98] As of the summer of 1930 Rosselli's *Socialismo liberale* had not come out in print, so Rossi and Bauer still had carte blanche to preach

[96] Quoted in Sforza, *Contemporary Italy*, pp. 326–327.
[97] Salvadori, *Resistenza ed azione*, pp. 73–74, 79, and 127–128.
[98] Garosci, VCR, I, 204–208.

their own creeds. Promoting a substantial bloc of Liberals, Republicans, and Socialists in Lombardy, they dreamed of forcibly overthrowing Fascist tyranny at once and replacing it with a democratic, republican, and socially progressive regime. They enthusiastically prepared and circulated a pamphlet, *Consigli sulla tattica* ("Tactical Advice"), which they hoped might galvanize latent unrest caused by the Depression and stir up the populace. They stressed the imperativeness of "revolutionary agitation" as opposed to mere "passive resistance," and offered suggestions as to the kind of work that could be undertaken— dispatching clandestine publications to bureaucrats, students, and factory workers, and various heroic gestures like demonstrating against tax collectors.[99]

It will be recalled that the latter was one of the specific measures advocated in Bassanesi's leaflets dropped over Milan in July. Such agitation had occurred during the Risorgimento, and conceivably it might win favor again. Rossi, Bauer, and Parri therefore discussed with Dr. Umberto Ceva, a sympathetic chemist who had often provided them with invisible ink, the feasibility of devising incendiary bombs which they could plant in tax offices during the autumn and time to explode at night in the empty buildings.

But they were too optimistic. As was so often the case, one of the conspirators (in this instance, Avv. Carlo Del Re) was a police informer. As a result, twenty-four of the principal Giellisti in Milan were apprehended on October 30. Rossi managed to elude his captors, but only for a short time, while being escorted by train from Bergamo to Rome.[100] To escape further torture, Dr. Ceva committed suicide on Christmas night in Rome's Regina Coeli penitentiary.[101] The turncoat Del Re—a truly Dostoyevskian type—fled to Argentina where he nonchalantly tried to blackmail the Fascist police.[102] During the course of preliminary hearings in February and March 1931 Parri was absolved but sent back

[99] *Ibid.*, I, 206–208; Salvatorelli in *Il Secondo Risorgimento*, p. 166.
[100] E. Rossi (ed.), *No al fascismo*, pp. 177–192.
[101] See the study by the sister of the martyr: Bianca Ceva, *1930: Retroscena di un dramma* (Milan, 1955); F. Parri, "Umberto Ceva," *MLI*, No. 38/39 (1955), pp. 90–91; Manlio Magini, "Il processo degli intellettuali," in E. Rossi (ed.), *No al fascismo*, pp. 193–214; Garosci, *VCR*, I, 215–223; Leto, *OVRA*, pp. 78–79; and S/M, *Sdf*, p. 528.
[102] Regarding the amazing career of Del Re, see Ernesto Rossi, *Una spia del regime* (Milan, 1955), which is largely a collection of documents from police

to *confino*. Most of the others were hailed before the Special Tribunal in Rome. On May 30, 1931, it sentenced Rossi and Bauer to twenty years' imprisonment, where they remained until the fall of Mussolini in 1943. In prison they became even more ardent advocates of European federation and critics of the economic "masters of the Fascist ship of state." [103] Remnants of the Milanese group wrote an impudent postscript to their covert work when by a ruse, on May 9, 1931, they published in *Corriere della sera* and *Tribuna* the emblem of GL (a torch of freedom bearing those initials on either side of it and the slogans around the square design "Il Vero Ricostituente" and "Il Vero Rigeneratore").[104]

In June 1931 another group of Giellisti from central Italy and Sardinia were dragged before the Special Tribunal. It handed down ten-year sentences to Francesco Fancello of Rome and Cesare Pintus of Sardinia, and a seven-year one to Nello Traquandi of Florence.[105]

Turin became the pivot of GL underground operations after the smashing of the Milanese conventicle.[106] Many Torinese Giellisti were academicians who had been stirred by Gobetti's

---

files which Rossi managed to photograph when he became an undersecretary in Premier Ferruccio Parri's postwar government in 1945. The first document is a letter to Mussolini from his *Capo della Polizia*, dated September 27, 1930, telling that Del Re had become an *agent provocateur*. No mission was too hard for this lawyer who held four university degrees. His masters took care of his legal and financial problems. But when he had gotten Rossi and the others arrested, Del Re did not hesitate to blackmail his employers; he did the same when Ceva committed suicide, blandly making pathetic references to the needs of his poor "mamma." The last document in the book is from the World War II top German police official in Italy, Herbert Kappler. It closes, ". . . at the moment [Del Re] is working for the German Secret Police as an informer, so he is, after all, working for the common cause. . . ." Del Re returned to Rome to practice law in the postwar era, much to the fury of Rossi, Parri, and others who had suffered at his hands. *Cf.* review note of Antonino Rèpaci, "Una spia del regime," *MLI*, No. 40 (1956), pp. 53–55.

[103] *I padroni del vapore* ("Masters of the Ship") was the title of one of Rossi's most provocative books after the Liberation. A selection of the many interesting letters his mother wrote to him while he was in prison have recently been published: Elide Rossi, *Lettere ad Ernesto* (Florence, 1958).

Other conspirators to be convicted included Vincenzo Calace, Bernardino Roberto, and Giordano Viezzoli, who received six- to ten-year terms. Mario Damiani and Pietro Zari were absolved for insufficient proof.

[104] See photographs in Gavagnin, *Vent'anni di resistenza*, pp. 129, 306.

[105] Magini in E. Rossi (ed.), *No al fascismo*, pp. 195–198.

[106] For a brief discussion of anti-Fascism in Piedmont see Raimondo Luraghi, "Lotta antifascista in Piemonte dal 1926 al 1943," *MLI*, No. 28/29 (1954), pp. 3–40; D. Zucàro, "Il primo antifascismo clandestino a Torino e in Piemonte," *Rivista storica del socialismo*, No. 11 (1960).

Rivoluzione liberale, especially as interpreted by Dr. Carlo Levi.[107] Nominal head of the group was Avv. Piero Zanetti, but the real director was young Mario Andreis, a Catholic who had joined the Republican Party after reading *De Regimine Principum.* Others included the young historian Aldo Garosci; Professor Lionello Venturi, historian of art; his son Franco, specialist in the history of the Enlightenment; Avv. Riccardo Poli from Emilia; Barbara Allason, a noted writer and translator; and Luigi Scala, a young botanist who with 16-year-old Renzo Giua helped spread GL's gospel into the lyceums.[108] Dubious of terrorism, all of them sensed that anarchistic violence did not meet with popular favor. Instead, they advocated social and agrarian reforms, and closer ties with factory workers in order to vie with the Marxists. To the latter end, Andreis and Garosci mimeographed *Voci d'officina* ("Factory Voices").

Tragedy befell the Torinese conspirators in January 1932 when the police net hauled in most of them. Andreis and Scala were condemned to eight years' imprisonment. Garosci and the Venturis were luckier. They escaped to Paris, where they helped persuade Rosselli of the merit of their own kind of resistance.[109]

In Rome, meantime, Salvadori, aided by Cencio Baldazzi and others, continued his anti-Fascism. Holding dual citizenship in Britain and Italy, Salvadori admired Anglo-Saxon democratic liberalism and favored pursuing more traditional methods of party organization and agitation. Drawn to GL by its talk of agrarian reform, co-operatives, socialized public utilities, progressive income tax, and a federated Europe, he encouraged such things as publication of books dealing with Risorgimento democratic champions, translation of provocative foreign authors, conversion of teachers and intellectuals, and tightening of bonds with other underground leaders. By the summer of 1932 the police arrested Salvadori. He spent the next several months in *confino* before he could emigrate.[110]

In due course a new covert GL group emerged in Turin under the guidance of Professor Leone Ginzburg, a brilliant young Russian Jew who had become a naturalized Italian and was a

[107] Regarding Dr. Carlo Levi, see *supra,* Ch. I, n. 120.
[108] Garosci, VCR, I, 227–229.
[109] *Ibid.,* p. 259.
[110] Salvadori, *Resistenza ed azione,* pp. 53–104.

university instructor of Slavic literature. Other participants were the economist Vittorio Foà; the young chemist Renzo Giua; the music critic Massimo Mila; professor of history Luigi Salvatorelli; professor of literature Augusto Monti; and Mario Levi, son of the scientist Giuseppe. During the spring of 1934 several members of the Jewish families in this ambient were arrested—anti-Semitism thus becoming an apparent factor for the first time in modern Italian history. Dr. Carlo Levi, patron of the conspirators, was sent to *confino* in Lucania at this juncture. In 1937 he was able to emigrate to France, where he resumed his work with GL. He finally returned to Italy in the late summer of 1943.[111]

Largely because of the Milanese debacle of 1930, the arguments in favor of longer-term action by the Torinese and Roman Giellisti, and the cessation of the aerial forays, Rosselli and his friends decided that they should emphasize the socialistic side of their program. For this purpose collaboration with the Anti-Fascist Concentration might be desirable after all. Thus they encouraged distribution of Rosselli's newly published vade mecum, *Socialismo liberale*, which he had written during internment on Lipari. Of still greater moment, they signed a working agreement with Nenni's reconsolidated Socialist Party (PSI) in the summer of 1931.

Socialist unity

Only after much reflection had the Socialist exiles finally reunited during the summer of 1930. It will be recalled that whereas some leaders like Turati, Treves, Modigliani, and Saragat had identified themselves with the PSLI (which had superseded the PSU in 1927 and won recognition from the Second International), most of the rank-and-file had stayed loyal to the maximalist PSI, dominated by Nenni, Coccia, and Balabanoff. In view of the enforced isolation of the *fuorusciti* and the hostility of the PCI, Turati had argued from the first in favor of a reunion of the two Socialist parties. In time he had won over Coccia and Nenni, the latter having convinced himself that Mussolini's triumph in 1922 was the direct result of the Socialist

[111] Allason, *Memorie di un'antifascista*, pp. 133–137; Garosci, VCR, II, 35–39; S/M, *Sdf*, pp. 650–652; Sandro Contini-Bonacossi and Licia Ragghianti-Collobi, *Una lotta nel suo corso* (Venice, 1954), p. 340; and Massimo Mila, "La mia opposizione al fascismo: testimonianze," *Il Ponte*, XVI (1960), pp. 32–43.

split, and that consequently Socialists must close ranks if ever they were to defeat him.[112] While Nenni wished the merger to be along maximalist lines, Turati and Saragat preferred revision-ism as the new program.[113]

At last in Grenoble on April 16, 1930, a maximalist PSI con-gress discussed fusion with the PSLI. By a large majority it came out in favor of a "charter of unity." This program was ratified unanimously by a joint "congress of Socialist unity" held July 19-21 in Paris. The consolidated party voted to retain its PSI label. It was quickly admitted into the Second International. For a time, though, there was confusion about the newspaper organ. A small wing of maximalists led by Balabanoff insisted upon continuation of the old *Avanti!* The new party therefore had to content itself with *Nuovo Avanti!* edited by Nenni first in Zurich and later in Paris, and with the adjective "New" in as small-size type as possible. *Rinascita*, an organ of the old PSLI, fell by the wayside.[114]

Inevitably there was semantic confusion in the new charter, which declared that the PSI, "basing itself on Marxian doctrine" and experience of past struggles, sets as its goal "the liberation of humanity from the political and economic servitude of capital-ism." This was to be achieved through class struggle, "organizing workers on a syndical and political basis, and struggling for the conquest of public powers with the intention of transforming them from instruments of oppression into instruments for libera-tion of the exploited class." An important third paragraph pro-claimed: "The PSI fights for the organization of a democratic regime in which the free development of each is the condition for the free development of all. Democratic in its aim, it is also in its methods. The PSI considers insurrection as the exercise of the inalienable right of the proletariat to repel the violent on-

[112] This theme ran through his *Six ans de guerre civile en Italie* (Paris, 1930); *La lutte des classes en Italie* (Paris, 1930); and *Ten Years of Tyranny in Italy* (London, 1932).

[113] Turati did not preclude a future split on this vexing issue, but he seemed to think that the impact of Fascism had changed everything. *Cf.* Turati in *Critica sociale*, XL (1948), pp. 263 and 1191, reprinted in Paolo Emiliani, *Dieci anni perduti: cronache del Partito Socialista Italiano dal 1943 a oggi* (Pisa, 1953), pp. 7-9. *Cf.* Garosci, *Sdf*, p. 71; and S/M, *Sdf*, pp. 511-512.

[114] Angelica Balabanoff, *Ricordi di un socialista* (Rome, 1946), pp. 358-363; Puglionisi, *Sciacalli*, pp. 96-97; S/M, *Sdf*, p. 512; and the detailed history of the party's covert publications by Gaetano Arfè, *Storia dell' "Avanti!" 1926-1940*. *Cf.* comments of Vittorio de Caprariis, "Nenni e Saragat nella storia dell'*Avanti!*," *Nord e Sud*, VI, No. 53 (April 1959), pp. 53-56.

slaughts of the dominating classes against the autonomy of the working class and common freedoms." Class struggle and even insurrection, therefore, were to be wrapped in democratic clothing.

The fourth paragraph rejected the policy of aloofness which in pre-Fascist years had kept the Socialists from considering sharing political power with bourgeois parties. It gave its blessing to political blocs so long as the anticapitalistic nature of the PSI was maintained. The penultimate paragraph termed Fascism a "coalition of capital, monarchy, and papacy," and appealed "to the working masses and to all free spirits" to find the "will and force to overthrow the dictatorship and install the democratic republic of the workers." The final paragraph confirmed the general program of the Second International—"a policy of war against war, [support of] arbitration, disarmament, and of solidarity among peoples united in a common will for peace, for the redemption of labor and liberty." [115]

The consolidated PSI reaffirmed its adherence to the Concentration, of which Nenni was secretary. In a more precise "pact of unity and action" signed on September 7, 1930, the Concentration declared that it stood for "absolute democracy" in a republican system which would prepare the emancipation of workers from all exploitation. It called also for local and regional self-government, tax reform, separation of Church and State; and abolition of the Lateran pacts.[116]

PSI and GL

Nenni and Saragat were receptive to the idea of PSI collaboration with GL, a policy which the latter also was beginning to favor, as has been observed. The Socialists saw the possibility of benefiting from access to GL's widespread *Apparat* in Italy, since their own was virtually nonexistent after Mussolini's police captured Sandro Pertini. "From that time on," according to two knowledgeable ex-Communist chroniclers, "nothing remained in Italy of the old Socialism except pictures of Matteotti which many workers preserved under their mattresses." [117]

Yet difficulties stood in the way of co-operation with GL, as

[115] Quoted from the document, excerpts of which are printed in S/M, *Sdf*, pp. 512–514.
[116] *Ibid.*, p. 550.
[117] B/G, *Storia del PCI*, p. 290.

77

many Socialists (both revisionists and maximalists) objected to the heterodox ideas in Rosselli's brand of "petty bourgeois," "liberal socialism," and neither group was ready to sacrifice its own identity. Although fusion of the renovated PSI and GL thus was out of the question, it was possible for them to work out a system of joint operations in the summer of 1931. This understanding permitted GL to assume the task of distributing inside Italy all material published by the Socialists and General Confederation of Labor, but such propaganda henceforth had to bear the label "GL." The PSI agreed not to promote any separate organizations of its own in Italy, and GL promised to do likewise abroad, except for maintenance of a small conspiratorial body.[118]

The accord between GL and the PSI presupposed a similar one with the Anti-Fascist Concentration. The Giellisti could profit from affiliation with that bloc, which would provide them with the opportunity of contributing articles to its widely read newspaper, *Libertà*. Rosselli therefore decided to lead his band into the Concentration in November 1931, notwithstanding some criticism from Giellisti in Italy and his own previous derogatory remarks. The Concentration professed to welcome the Giellisti and agreed to the expansion of the PSI-GL accord. Thus the Giellisti's right to direct underground operations in Italy was confirmed in return for agreement that the Concentration would guide such work abroad. In the six-member executive committee would be three Giellisti (Rosselli, Tarchiani, and Lussu); one member of PSI (Giuseppe Faravelli, who was friendly to GL); one representative of the PRI; and one from the CGL (Buozzi). Cianca of GL became co-editor, with Treves, of *Libertà*. The arrangement clearly worked to the advantage of GL.[119]

The honeymoon was brief. Instead of confining its work in Italy to operations in behalf of the Concentration, GL continued to act as a rival party (albeit still calling itself a "movement"). Especially annoying to the PRI and PSI was the news in January 1932 that GL, in violation of its bargain, had begun publication in Paris and Brussels of a thick pamphlet series, *Quaderni di "Giustizia e Libertà,"* twelve issues of which appeared during the

---

[118] Garosci, VCR, I, 245; Garosci, Sdf, p. 74.
[119] *Ibid.*

next three years. Some of them slipped through the censors into Italy under false covers of literary classics and provided a new link between the domestic Giellisti and those abroad. Rosselli and Caffi formulated editorial policy.[120]

The first issue contained a new "revolutionary program" of a socialistic type which entirely ignored the older parties and the traditional premises on which the Aventine and Concentration had rested. It called for a forceful revolution and a new state which would rest on local revolutionary committees. A constituent assembly thereafter would work out the details of the new republic, whose freedoms would be defended by a popular militia (presumably less fearsome than Mussolini's MVSN). There would be agrarian reform based on the principle of "land to him who tills it," and with indemnified expropriations, partial collectivization, and partial private enterprise. The issue called for socialization of certain key industries, to be administered through autonomous agencies;[121] workers' control and "factory democracy";[122] profit-sharing and progressive income taxes; abolition of the duty on grain and on other articles of mass consumption; progressive and general reduction of tariffs; and a public works program which would lead to municipal ownership. Moreover, it called for peace, disarmament, free exchange, and European federation. Schools should be freely open to everyone at all levels, and there should be separation of Church and State, with annulment of the Lateran Accords. To cap it all (and in some-

[120] Photographs of the camouflaged reviews are contained in Gavagnin, *Vent'anni di resistenza*, facing pp. 241 and 306. The series has recently been republished in book form by photo offprint: *Quaderni di "Giustizia e Libertà"* (Turin, 1959), with a preface by Alberto Tarchiani.

In addition to Rosselli and Caffi, the following contributed articles often: Max Ascoli, Umberto Calosso, Nicola Chiaromonte, Guido DeRuggiero, Luigi Emery, Giuseppe Faravelli, Vittorio Foà, Aldo Garosci, Leone Ginzburg, Michele Giua, Renzo Giua, Carlo Levi, Emilio Lussu, Luzzatto, Augusto Monti, Max Salvadori, Luigi Salvatorelli, Angelo Tasca, Silvio Trentin, Franco and Lionello Venturi.

[121] For the program see Garosci, VCR, I, 243–253. On this point Rosselli replied to the Marxists' queries: "Partial socialization is a guarantee of freedom, whereas total socialization means dictatorship, bureaucracy, destruction of individuality." Garosci, *Sdf*, p. 74.

[122] Rosselli took to task Giorgio Amendola, Communist son of the late Aventinian chieftain. In *Stato operaio*, Amendola had accused GL of fighting merely for "formal freedom"; Rosselli replied that GL stood with the proletariat, but not like the PCI which was reducing the proletariat to servitude under "Jesuitical discipline." Quoted by E. Rossi (ed.), *No al fascismo*, pp. 15–16.

what contradictory fashion), it called for the widest measure of local autonomy.

One sympathetic critic has commented that much of Rosselli's revolutionary program was more suitable for "Socialists who wished to drink of liberalism [than] for Liberals who wished to imbibe socialism." [123] And, according to Salvatorelli, the program created "a virtual schism within anti-Fascist democracy, which would later make itself felt in the postwar era when it met up with the dichotomy between 'Western democracy' and 'progressive democracy.' " [124] Certainly the Rossellian pronunciamento left many questions unanswered, especially the realistic ones of how power was to be administered in the revolutionary state.

The articles immediately angered both the socialistic and liberal wings of GL and led to the withdrawal of Vincenzo Nitti. The PRI was furibund. Many of the older Mazzinians denigrated the Giellisti as parvenus to republicanism via socialism and feared that they were outmaneuvering the PRI. No doubt GL was often tactless. Because of GL's new program, the PRI voted 236 to 187 in March 1932 to secede from the Concentration. For a year and a half it remained apart.

Oddly enough, the Concentration, assembling in Paris on November 12–13, 1932, proclaimed its broad approval of the GL prospectus, though it made certain reservations about its excessively Jacobinic and "Laborite" features.[125]

Soon the PRI reconsidered its stand. After persuasive arguments by its new secretary at a congress in Paris on April 22–23, 1933, it voted to rejoin the Concentration in September. But a leftist splinter faction captained by Fernando Schiavetti and calling itself Azione Repubblicana Socialista (ARS) declined and soon fused with GL.[126] Thus the PRI was weaker than ever.

Meantime, relations between the PSI and GL deteriorated. The death of Turati on May 29, 1932, and of Treves on June 19, 1933, deprived the emigration of its two most eminent revisionists. The new PSI directorate, dominated by Nenni, was less inclined to continue collaboration on a long term with such

[123] Guido Calogero, *Difesa del Liberalsocialismo* (Rome, 1945), p. 125.
[124] Salvatorelli in *Il Secondo Risorgimento*, p. 171.
[125] *Ibid.*
[126] Garosci, VCR, I, 260–263.

"bourgeois," unpredictable groups as GL, LIDU, and PRI; instead, it was disposed to seek a *rapprochement* with fellow Marxists on the left.

Collapse of the Anti-Fascist Concentration

Adolf Hitler's advent to power in 1933 and the unchecked spread of fascistic tendencies elsewhere led to some of the disputes which bedeviled the Concentration. Rosselli sensed faster than the Socialists that Fascism henceforth could not be looked upon as simply an Italian phenomenon. Turning his back on the Socialists' pacifist arguments that only arbitration and disarmament were valid means of preserving peace, he prophesied gloomily in his article, "La guerra che torna" ("War which is returning"), in the ninth (November 1933) issue of the *Quaderni*, that the Fascist-Nazi states would inevitably go to war. Thus Rosselli was one of the very first Italian resistants to realize the nature of the new world problem. He proposed that the anti-Fascists speedily close ranks and prepare themselves to fight "autonomously" in this coming war. Solidarity among all the anti-Fascist currents of all countries was indispensable, he argued, "for Fascism is truly the Anti-Europe." [127] Only "immediate intervention by the democratic powers in favor of revolution in both Italy and Germany" could stave off such a war. Meanwhile, that same year Rosselli tendered his support to a neo-Socialist French group led by Marcel Déat and André Montagnon who sought to outbid the Fascists in appeals to the middle class and ended in a kind of "national socialism" of their own.[128] All of these "unorthodox" actions caused both wings of socialists to denounce Rosselli.

The Anti-Fascist Concentration's death throes began in February 1934, when the Socialists raised objections to an article by Lussu in the tenth issue of *Quaderni*. It had mercilessly denounced the PSI as "a handful of mercenary brigands" and had proclaimed that GL represented authentic socialism. The PSI's fury became unbounded when in March GL launched a biweekly *Giornale degli operai* ("Workers' Journal"), which clearly

[127] Quoted in Gavagnin, *Vent'anni di resistenza*, p. 345; cf. Garosci, VCR, II, 22–27.
[128] Garosci, *Sdf*, p. 76.

aimed at competing with their own propaganda. The PSI thereupon demanded that the Concentration either censor GL publications in advance or end the existing pact so that each party
would be free to act on its own abroad and in Italy.

Faced with these choices, and unable to persuade the rest of
the Concentration to form a new consolidated Republican Socialist Party, Rosselli and his friends preferred to sever their tie
with the Concentration. Consequently it dissolved itself on May
5, 1935, and publication of *Libertà* ceased. A few days later GL
began its own weekly newspaper in Paris, *Giustizia e Libertà*.
The Socialists transferred publication of *Nuovo Avanti!* from
Zurich to Paris.[129] And that same year in Zurich, Ignazio Silone
(who had renounced Communism in favor of revisionist Socialism in 1931) published *Der Fascismus: seine Entstehung und
seine Entwicklung*.[130]

Eve of the Popular Front

The dissolution of the seven-year-old Anti-Fascist Concentration found its immediate cause in the circumstances noted, but
other factors included the reluctance of all *émigré* groups to
subordinate their separate programs and agencies to any joint
control, and the impact of the Communists' rapidly emerging
Popular Front policy.

The latter took shape in the months after Hitler's climb to
power, when Communist leaders belatedly awakened to the fact
that their previous tactics of hostility toward not only bourgeois
but Socialist parties (whom they contemptuously had dubbed
"Social-Fascists," while the latter had denounced them as "Red
Fascists") had simply hastened Hitler's victory. In addition to
the Russian inspiration there was also something spontaneous
about the Popular Front idea, which seemed so logical at a time
when the Nazis and Fascists were winning international support.

The chronology of this policy switch is of interest. Two or
three weeks after Hitler became chancellor, leaders of the Social-

[129] S/M, *Sdf*, pp. 646–647; Garosci, *Sdf*, p. 78; Garosci, VCR, II, 42–47; and
"La fine della Concentrazione," *Quaderni di "Giustizia e Libertà,"* II Série, No. 11
(Paris, June 1934), pp. 89–93; Arfè, *Storia dell' "Avanti!" 1926–1940*, p. 98.
[130] Some four years earlier Silone had brought out the anti-Fascist novel,
Fontamara, and in 1937 he was to publish *Bread and Wine*.

ist Second International in Amsterdam suggested forming a "united front" with the Comintern. Early the next month the Moscow agency replied. It was willing to tolerate only pacts worked out by the parties on a strictly national basis. The Second International found this objectionable; they preferred a world-wide policy of collaboration. In line with this attitude, the Italian PSI and PRI rejected one PCI invitation, even though Nenni personally favored such a "unity of action" agreement.[131] Most Socialists were vexed by Communist praise of Hitler's renewal of the German-Soviet friendship treaty. Thus the majority were unwilling to join the Red-sponsored "Amsterdam-Pleyel movement" of June 1933, a proposed "supraparty" front to oppose both war and Fascism.[132]

Next, the Socialist International sponsored a similar-type congress in August 1933 in Antwerp and Brussels, accompanied by great demonstrations. Then on August 21 in Paris a Socialist International Conference took up the theme "Strategy and tactics of the international workers' movement in the face of Fascist reaction." But the "Fascist reaction" they were concerned with was German rather than Italian. Propaganda was cast in so rigid a dialectical form as to be quite unattractive to the non-Marxians.[133]

After fascistic tendencies became increasingly visible in France and Austria during February 1934 the Italian Communist and Socialist parties began to sound each other out on the possibility of forming a "united front." So did the French Communists and Socialists, who announced theirs in June 1934.[134] The talks among the Italian exiles were conducted by Togliatti, Nenni, and Saragat, representing the three divergent currents of Marxism. The latter two probably sensed that an alliance with the PCI could not easily be consummated so long as the PSI remained linked to the GL in the Concentration. So, for reasons of

[131] For some of Nenni's reminiscences about this development, see his articles in Rome *Avanti!* July 16–18, 1944.

[132] S/M, *Sdf*, p. 643.

[133] *Ibid.*, p. 644; *cf.* Franz Borkenau, *European Communism* (London, 1953), pp. 115–162; and Hugh Seton-Watson, *From Lenin to Malenkov: The History of World Communism* (New York, 1953), pp. 176–183.

[134] Regarding the French aspects, see John T. Marcus, *French Socialism in the Crisis Years, 1933–36: Fascism and the French Left* (New York, 1957).

its own, the PSI was quite ready to allow that old instrumentality to commit suicide in May 1934. Three months later (August 17, 1934) Togliatti, Nenni, and Saragat signed the first of many "unity of action" pacts between the PSI and PCI. The Communists had emerged from their isolation.[135]

[135] S/M, *Sdf*, p. 670; B/G, *Storia del PCI*, pp. 305–306; Garosci, VCR, II, 111; Garosci, *Sdf*, pp. 80–83, 100–103, and 278–279; and Emiliani, *Dieci anni perduti*, pp. 10–13.

CHAPTER III · "QUIETISTS" AND COMMUNISTS

Until August 1934

A T HOME most Liberals and Catholics shied away from the kind of political reorganization and activism that characterized the work of the Socialists, Republicans, and certain other exiled groups. They favored, instead, a kind of passive resistance. These "static" noncollaborators often found it possible to keep the flame of freedom kindled in the privacy of their homes and religious conventicles. Occasionally they dared to state their views cautiously and subtly in the press and classroom,[1] and even from the Senate rostrum (until that body faded into desuetude). In effect they followed the advice that the departing Professor Salvemini had left behind: "Resist in silence, wait, don't make useless gestures: concentrate on saving your soul."[2]

Latent liberalism

After the doors of Parliament slammed shut against the Aventine secessionists in 1926 scarcely a deputy in the rump Chamber dared to utter a word against the dictatorship for more than a year. At last in 1928 two Piedmontese Liberals, ex-Premier Giolitti and Marcello Soleri, did speak up when the government proposed still another electoral "reform," designed to reduce the Chamber to 400 deputies, to be elected through a single national ticket (drawn up in the final analysis by the Fascist Grand Council). Giolitti had long since ended his tacit support of Mussolini and had voted against the measures of Fascistization; still, he had never gone so far as to make any hostile speech in public.[3] Such

---

[1] Many Italians never lost their wry sense of humor and did their best to needle Mussolini's regime in its most vulnerable spot—its swollen pomposity. Such gadflies liked to circulate light-hearted jokes, such as the answer of a teacher to a pupil's query, "How do we pronounce it—*régime* or *regíme?*" Teacher: "Why, *regíme*, of course, my children, just like *beccíme, mangíme,* and *concíme* (bird food, animal fodder, and manure)." Gavagnin, *Vent'anni di resistenza,* p. 271.

[2] Alessandro Galante-Garrone, "Calamandrei e la Resistenza," *Il Ponte,* xiv (supplement to special Nov. 1958 issue dedicated to Piero Calamandrei), p. 60.

[3] His shift can be seen in recently published correspondence with Camillo Corradini, 1927–1928: Gabriele DeRosa (ed.), *Giolitti e il fascismo in alcune sue lettere inedite* (Rome, 1957).

onerous tasks he had left to Soleri.[4] Yet on this occasion Giolitti felt impelled to "save his soul." He explained that he did not disapprove of a "national list" but did strenuously object to the unconstitutional manner whereby candidates would be placed on it. The Cassandra-like remonstrances of this aged politico (he died four months later) elicited only insults from the Blackshirts. They approved the new law on March 16 by a vote of 216 to 15—"with perfect Fascist style, without discussion, with absolute discipline." [5]

Henceforth the appointive Senate (that "clubhouse with commodious armchairs and a fine library" [6]) was the only public asylum for the renitent legislators. On May 12, 1928, a few Solons (Ettore Ciccotti, Luigi Albertini, and Francesco Ruffini) took their work seriously enough to criticize the new parliamentary structure. Though the Fascist press gave them no publicity, the gist of their arguments made the rounds.[7] The final Senate vote approved Mussolini's reorganization plan 138 to 49. Among the many who approved the blueprint was Pietro Badoglio— destined, ironically, to become Mussolini's rival and successor in 1943. The minority opposition included (in addition to Ciccotti, Albertini, and Ruffini) such men as Mario Abbiate, Alberto Bergamini, Alessandro Casati, Benedetto Croce, Luigi della Torre, Luigi Einaudi, Gaetano Mosca, Emanuele Paternò, Vito Volterra, Tito Sinibaldi, and Leone Wollemborg.[8]

That autumn Parliament dutifully enacted a startling law specifying the functions of the Fascist Grand Council as "supreme organ of the regime." It gained the right to present to the King nominations for a successor to the prime minister. Even more sensational was a clause giving it the right to be consulted in any legislation affecting succession to the throne.[9] There was no immediate likelihood that this would be in doubt, even though Prince Humbert was slow in begetting male offspring; but, in the opinion of ardent royalists, this measure inoppor-

[4] For his long career, see Marcello Soleri, *Memorie* (Turin, 1949); *cf.* Vincenzo Galizzi, *Giolitti e Salandra* (Bari, 1949).
[5] According to the PNF *Foglio d'Ordine*, quoted in S/M, *Sdf*, p. 327.
[6] Borgese, *Goliath*, p. 276.
[7] S/M, *Sdf*, p. 329; Albertini, *In difesa della libertà*, p. xi; Allason, *Memorie di un'antifascista*, pp. 39–42; Alessandro Galante-Garrone, "Francesco Ruffini e il Concordato," Rome *Il Mondo*, Aug. 12, 19, 1958.
[8] See S/M, *Sdf*, p. 330, for full list.
[9] *Ibid.*, p. 332.

tunely handed the Grand Council a sword of Damocles to dangle over Victor Emmanuel's already Lilliputian torso. Certainly the King was most distressed. Though he refrained from public protest, he complained to Mussolini (so the latter has reported) that "this measure is another mortal blow against my sovereign prerogatives. . . . Due to the imminence of an international crisis, I do not want to add fuel to the fire, but at any other time, rather than suffer this affront, I should prefer to abdicate." [10]

Benedetto Croce's moral leadership

The dying gasps of liberalism in the Senate were uttered almost alone by Benedetto Croce. The Neapolitan senator had taken over undisputed direction of the Liberals upon Giolitti's death in 1928. Though his anti-Fascism had not risen to the surface until Mussolini's brutal speech of January 3, 1925, few would deny that Croce, more than any other single Italian, best personified the unflinching, nonviolent type of resistance to Fascism. Antonio Gramsci, the Communist leader who stood at the materialist antipodes of Croce's philosophy, could write generously from his prison cell that "while so many intellectuals lost their heads and knew not how to orient themselves amid the general chaos, denying their very past, vacillating lamentably, in doubt as to who might prove to be the strongest, Croce remained imperturbable in his serenity and in the affirmation of his faith that, 'metaphysically, evil cannot prevail' and that 'history is rationality.'" [11]

The circumstances for Croce's brave, almost solitary criticism of the regime in Palazzo Madama on May 24, 1929, was Mussolini's submission of the Lateran Accords to the Senate for ratification.[12] Despite the negative votes of Croce and five others,

[10] Quoted by Benito Mussolini, *Storia di un anno (il tempo del bastone e della carota)* (Milan, 1944), pp. 179–180.

Before the Senate stamped its approval of the law, Mussolini went out of his way to note amiably that for six years he had been loyal to the Monarchy and that the King had been equally loyal to Fascism. S/M, *Sdf*, p. 333.

In actuality, Mussolini seldom convened the Grand Council—not even when he led Italy into World War II. Only on the night of July 24–25, 1943, did it assume a decisive role. Yet the law of December 9, 1928, was another major step in the emasculation of the 1848 *Statuto*. Egidio Reale, "The Italian Constitution under Fascism," *Foreign Affairs*, xviii (Oct. 1939), p. 157.

[11] Antonio Gramsci, *Il materialismo storico e la filosofia di Benedetto Croce* (Turin, 1948), p. 179.

[12] See *infra*, Ch. iii, Fascism versus Catholicism.

the documents were ratified; and, to the surprise of many, they were preserved by Communist votes in the 1948 Constitution of the Italian Republic.[13] After his speech Croce absented himself from the moribund upper chamber in protest against the *Duce's* unconstitutional gelding of Parliament and out of disgust for the moral flabbiness of his fellow legislators.

Senator Croce's relative immunity during the dictatorship has aroused considerable comment, especially abroad. It may be noted first that the Neapolitan landowner had a substantial income which could not easily be cut off by the enemy; thus he was under no economic compulsion to flee Italy. But he was the near victim of violence in October 1926 when Fascist hoodlums, intending to damage his huge library, broke into Palazzo Filomarino, his sprawling, book-lined home in the crowded heart of Naples. The police made no effort to protect him; instead, it was the indignant protest of Signora Croce that shamed the toughs away. The incident (considerably exaggerated abroad) made it clear to Mussolini that he risked alienating world opinion if he permitted harm to come to the renowned scholar.

Actually Mussolini regarded the Neapolitan intellectual titan with some awe (as he did also, for a time, Croce's ex-colleague, the Sicilian Giovanni Gentile, who had voluntarily subscribed to Fascism and had thus timely endowed it with his neo-Hegelian and ethereal brand of "actual idealism"). The *Duce* boasted to a Fascist congress on June 22, 1925, that he had never read a page of Croce;[14] yet later he asserted (doubtless with equal hyperbole) that he had "read everything" Croce had written. If he really had, it was no mean task. It seems a fair assumption that Mussolini suspected that continued release of Croce's books and bimonthly literary review, *La Critica*, by the Bari publishing house of Giuseppe Laterza was less perilous than the adverse publicity that surely would have resulted from their ban. He may even have thought that only a paltry number of intellectuals would be stirred by Croce's scholarly output, which in no instance advocated violence. But he erred.

[13] For postwar developments see Leicester C. Webb, *Church and State in Italy, 1947–1957* (Victoria, Australia, and New York, 1958).
[14] Croce's retort was: "But of course what he says may be true, for his writings are written for him by others." Quoted by Cecil Sprigge, *Benedetto Croce, Man and Thinker* (Cambridge, Eng., 1952), p. 18.

Even though the "man in the coffeeshop" seldom read or fully understood the meditations of Don Benedetto, he sensed the fact that a renowned thinker was critical of the regime. And the educated, thoughtful minority who did read Croce with understanding were heartened by his skillful defense of freedom and justice as the permanent aims of mankind, his contention that despotism was transient, and his belief that history's judgment was inexorable. Whenever he jibed against the regimentation of culture by the Reds and the Brownshirts, his readers could easily detect that he referred also to the bombastic lictors nearer home. It is reported that whenever Croce left Naples to visit other cities, his disciples welcomed him as the early Christians did St. Paul.[15]

The texture of most of Croce's historical studies during the dictatorship was watermarked with anti-Fascism, quite visible against the light. For example, his *History of Italy from 1871 to 1915*, which Laterza published in 1927, was avowedly intended to rehabilitate the record of liberalism in an era so maligned by Fascists. He deliberately refrained from writing the history of the Fascist epoch, which to him was repugnant,[16] just as he usually preferred to bypass periods of war and violence. In 1932 Laterza brought out *Ethics and Politics*, which contained some of Croce's clearest thoughts on the problems of liberalism. The next year saw release of *History of Europe in the Nineteenth Century*, a predominantly intellectual history whose theme revolved around the conflict of the rival "religious faiths" of liberalism, legitimacy, democracy, and socialism. In it Croce identified irrationalism as the cause of the twentieth century's disintegration and moral chaos. *History as Thought and Action* (1938) marked the culmination of Croce's historico-philosophical speculation.[17]

[15] Guido Calogero, "Some Personal Recollections," in *Benedetto Croce, A Commemoration* by Gilbert Murray, Manlio Brosio, and Guido Calogero (London, 1953), p. 33.
[16] See his explanation to students at his Istituto Italiano per gli Studi Storici in Naples, published in his *Storiografia e idealità morale* (Bari, 1950).
[17] See Federico Chabod, "Croce," *Rivista storica italiana*, LXIV (1952), pp. 473–530, for a brilliant, balanced critique of Croce's historiography. For a résumé of the literature interpreting Croce since his death in 1952, see Giovanni Mastroianni, "La polemica sul Croce negli studi contemporanei," *Società*, IV (1958), pp. 711–737.

For a quarter century the doughty Neapolitan kept the dim flame of Italian liberalism aglow and served as a beacon to a host of anti-Fascists. He advised them to seek a deeper understanding of the nature of liberalism and to follow the example of Boethius, who in another Dark Age had taken refuge in a life of scholarly reflection. To an activist like Professor Salvemini, this seemed not enough; he later berated Croce for quietly "gazing at his navel," Buddha-fashion, instead of martyring himself on the cross. Such a criticism seems unfair, for Croce was not a politico; he preferred to fight Fascism on the intellectual ground he knew so well.[18]

Not all readers stayed on the rather narrow path Croce trod. The democratic Liberal, Mario Vinciguerra, saw fit to organize in 1930 an underground National Alliance, as has been seen.[19] And some of the younger men on the left suspected that Croce erred in thinking the solution of Italy's problems lay simply in restoration of old patterns of public life.[20] Thus many questioned the accuracy of his assertion in 1943 that Fascism was but a temporary "aberration" in Italy's liberal evolution.[21] The "liberal revolutionist" Gobetti and the "liberal socialists" Rosselli, Calogero, and Parri sympathized with much of the senator's ideology but felt that it must be updated in a socialistic direction to cope with the practical problems of an industrial age.

Fascism and academic freedom

One of the *beaux gestes* of anti-Fascism in which Croce took greatest relish was his "Reply" to Giovanni Gentile's April 21, 1925, "Manifesto of the Fascist Intellectuals." For a score of

[18] G. Salvemini, "Politica di Benedetto Croce," *Il Ponte*, x (Nov. 1954), cited in Valeri's chapter, "Il liberalismo di Croce e il fascismo," *Da Giolitti a Mussolini*, p. 198 ff. Yet Croce's anti-Fascism was not entirely static, for he covertly encouraged in 1927 the Torinese underground current, Young Italy, and in 1933 he slipped to Dr. Leone Ginzburg of Turin an article about Fascist Minister of Education Ercole for publication in the clandestine *Quaderni di "Giustizia e Libertà*," No. 9 (Nov. 1933). Domenico Zucàro, "L'antifascismo democratico torinese: Croce clandestino," Rome *Il Mondo*, May 27, 1958.
[19] See *supra*, Ch. II, Alleanza Nazionale and the DeBosis flight.
[20] Lucio Lombardo-Radice, *Fascismo e anti-comunismo: appunti e ricordi, 1935–1945* (Turin, 1946), p. 27.
[21] Croce used the terms "sudden illness," rude "parenthesis," and unexpected "invasion of the Hyksos" to describe the "malady" of Fascism in Italy. See his "Italia e la conferenza di San Francisco," Aug. 7, 1945, cited in N. Valeri, "Sulle origini del fascismo," in E. Rota (ed.), *Questioni di storia contemporanea*, III, 741.

years the two had been collaborators; they split soon after Gentile accepted Mussolini's bid to become Minister of Education (1922–1924) and received carte blanche to reform the entire school system. He and his practicing Catholic successor, Pietro Fedele, proposed many radical reforms, some of which (like "electives" and examinations over a wide range of studies instead of some specialty) may well have had merit. But they came too fast for the conservative faculties to swallow easily.[22] When Gentile issued his rhetorical "Manifesto" as part of his campaign to reconcile Fascism with the cultural world, it was too much for Croce. He penned a scathing "Reply" on May 1 that was signed by dozens of "anti-Fascist intellectuals" and published in some of the newspapers with Amendola's help. In it Croce described Fascism as "an incoherent and bizarre mixture of appeals to authority and demagogy, of professions of reverence for the laws, ultramodern concepts and moth-eaten bric-à-brac, absolutism and Bolshevism, unbelief and toadying to the Catholic Church, flight from culture and sterile reachings towards a culture without a basis, mystical languors and cynicism." [23]

Years later Croce reminisced smugly that "almost everyone" recalled his vigorous answer long after they had forgotten the contents of Gentile's declaration.[24] In the wake of the Lateran pacts Mussolini discarded (or, to use Gentile's own jargon, "transcended") his official philosopher, who nevertheless trailed along in the wake of the ever-changing movement until he was brought back into grace in mid-1943, a year before his assassination in a Florence street by young Communists.

Efforts to Fascisticize the school system continued none the less and met with some superficial success on elementary and intermediate levels, though more in the athletic and extracurricular activities than in substantive courses, except for the peculiarly vulnerable disciplines of history, economics, and political science.[25] In the universities freedom of expression generally survived several more years, despite occasional pressure against

[22] Ascoli, *Annals of the American Academy of Political and Social Science*, cc (Nov. 1938), pp. 235–253.
[23] Quoted by Sprigge, *Benedetto Croce*, p. 18.
[24] Croce, "Ricordi," Milan *Corriere della sera*, Apr. 2, 1949; *cf.* recent study of Emilio R. Papa, *Storia di due manifesti: il fascismo e la cultura italiana* (Milan, 1958).
[25] See L. Minio-Paluello, *Education in Fascist Italy* (London, 1946).

social science and law faculties. Not till August 1931 did the dictatorship try seriously to interfere with the universities.[26] Then it required every instructor to subscribe to an oath whereby he promised "to be loyal to the King, to his Royal Successors, *and to the Fascist regime* (italics mine), to observe loyally the *Statuto* and the other laws of the State, to exercise the office of teacher and fulfill all the academic duties with the purpose of forming citizens, industrious, honest, and devoted to the Fatherland *and the Fascist regime*. I swear that I do not belong to and will not belong to associations or parties whose activity is not conciliable with the duties of my office." [27]

Some 1,200 university teachers (the overwhelming majority) subscribed, much to the joy of Gentile, who exulted, "The undisciplined intellectual disappears from our midst." [28] Probably most did so in order to avoid the financial ruin they faced if they lost their posts. Some, of course, were indifferent, or perhaps felt the oath would not hamper presentation of subject matter outside the fields of social science and humanities. Certain ones adhered because the Vatican indicated its approval, explaining that "Fascist regime" was the equivalent of the expression "Government of the State." [29] Only about a dozen refused to join in this *trahison des clercs* (to use Julien Benda's phrase) and declared flatly that the oath was a violation of both academic and political freedom. The short list of eleven original nonjurors included some of Italy's most internationally recognized savants.[30] Similar oaths were required in October 1934 of mem-

[26] In 1927 Umberto Ricci, an economics professor at the University of Rome, was dismissed because he had criticized Mussolini's corporate economic policies. His case was exceptional. Ascoli, *loc. cit.*, pp. 235-253.

[27] Quoted in Finer, *Mussolini's Italy*, p. 482.

[28] Cited in Binchy, *Church and State in Fascist Italy*, p. 465.

[29] *L'Osservatore romano*, Dec. 4, 1931, cited by Binchy, p. 465.

[30] (1) Gaetano DeSanctis, an eminent Catholic and distinguished professor of ancient history at the University of Rome who was to become the reorganizer of Italy's university system after the Liberation; (2) Lionello Venturi, professor of art history at the University of Turin before he moved to Johns Hopkins University; (3) Senator Francesco Ruffini, professor of ecclesiastical law at the University of Turin; (4) his son, Edoardo Ruffini-Avondo, professor of legal history at the University of Perugia; (5) Ernesto Buonaiuti, an unfrocked "modernist" priest who was professor of the history of Christianity at the University of Rome and perhaps more consistent in his political convictions than in his religious beliefs; (6) Giorgio Levi della Vida, professor of comparative Semitic languages at the University of Rome and later at the University of Pennsylvania; (7) Vito Volterra, professor of mathematics at the University of Rome; (8) Piero Mar-

bers of the venerable and prestigious Accademia dei Lincei.[31]

From the beginning of the dictatorship the regime herded children into parascholastic youth groups,[32] and by the early thirties the PNF further expanded its activities to enroll as many university students as possible into Gruppi Universitari Fascisti (GUF), designed to co-ordinate sports, parades, political lectures and keep their members on the narrow path of Fascist orthodoxy.[33] Many of the older students resented such regimentation, and in the case of the Federazione Universitaria Cattolica Italiana (FUCI), led by Igino Righetti, there was undisguised hostility.[34] Some of the youths who joined GUF were only "half-Fascists"—i.e., they affected loyalty to the regime but took advantage of suitable opportunities to question its propaganda and the ability of its hierarchs. In due course some Communists and other unbending enemies of Mussolini infiltrated GUF and other youth agencies. But during the early dictatorship most dissidents were not yet actual members of specific underground parties.

Though the Fascists fired some of the best professors and forced others to teach under handicaps, they never could cancel out the ideals of academic freedom, strongly embedded in Italy's humanistic tradition. Independent thought and a measure of free discussion of controversial topics continued in the universi-

---

tinetti, professor of philosophy at the University of Milan; (9) Mario Carrara, professor of criminal anthropology at the University of Turin; (10) Giorgio Errera, professor of chemistry at the University of Pavia; and (11) Bortolo Negrisoli, professor of surgery at the University of Bologna. Since Professor Giuseppe A. Borgese, who taught esthetics at the University of Milan before moving to the University of Chicago, was abroad he was not immediately asked to take the oath; when he was, he refused, thus becoming the twelfth nonjuror. Two professors (the jurisprudent and ex-Premier V. E. Orlando and the economist Antonio DeViti de Marco) quietly resigned before the oath was requested of them. The others had to be relieved of their posts and pensioned. S/M, Sdf, pp. 409–410; Finer, Mussolini's Italy, p. 482; Borgese, Goliath, p. 304; Ebenstein, Fascist Italy, pp. 101–102; and Alatri's essay on Orlando in his Le origini del fascismo, pp. 421–422.

[31] The refractories were Croce, DeSanctis, Orlando, Volterra, DeViti de Marco, Giulio Alessio, Attilio Bresciani-Turroni, Francesco DeSarlo, Emanuele Paternò, and Umberto Ricci. S/M, Sdf, p. 410.

[32] Such as Opera Nazionale Balilla (ONB) and its subsection for girls, Piccole Italiane; the boys' Avanguardisti and the girls' Giovani Italiane. In 1937 these were rechristened Gioventù Italiana del Littorale (GIL) and incorporated into the PNF (as already had been the case with the young men's Giovani Fascisti and young women's Giovani Fasciste movements).

[33] Minio-Paluello, Education in Fascist Italy, pp. 135–151; Binchy, Church and State in Fascist Italy, Chs. 15, 16, 17; and Finer, Mussolini's Italy, Ch. 15.

[34] A. Baroni, Igino Righetti (Rome, 1948).

ties (as well as many lower schools) because the majority of the faculties remained basically uncorrupted despite their expedient oaths to the regime, and because many students outgrew their childhood indoctrination that *"Mussolini ha sempre raggione."* [35]

Anti-Fascism in the legal press

The dictatorship's ruthless *Gleichschaltung* of the press was much more successful than its attempts to regiment the universities. Nevertheless, Italian censorship was not nearly so iron-clad as that in Soviet Russia or in Nazi Germany. On several occasions criticism of Blackshirt tyranny appeared in cleverly phrased articles on the *terza pagine* ("literary page") of the newspapers, rather often in the periodicals and scholarly journals,[36] and, of course, in the Vatican *L'Osservatore romano* during the bitter fight between Catholic Action and the Fascists.

It was right after the 1926 exceptional decrees that one more-or-less openly hostile monthly review appeared legally in Genoa (and later as a fortnightly in Milan): *Pietre* ("Stones"), published by Lelio Basso, the young Socialist who had collaborated with Rosselli and Nenni in *Quarto Stato*. *Pietre's* slant was quite similar to that of Gobetti's defunct review; some of its contributors called themselves clandestine "friends of the *Rivoluzione Liberale*" and were also associated with the covert Giovane Italia current which had a precarious existence from early 1927 until April 1928.[37] Participants included Mario Paggi, Umberto Segre, Vittorio E. Alfieri, and a group of University of Pisa students and teachers. In April 1928 the censor smashed *Pietre*.

[35] Ascoli, *Annals of the American Academy*, cc (Nov. 1938), pp. 235-253; G. Salvemini, "Italian Intellectuals under Fascism," in Keene (ed.), *Neither Liberty Nor Bread*, pp. 121-131; Minio-Paluello, *Education in Fascist Italy*, pp. 219-225; Lombardo-Radice, *Fascismo e anticomunismo*, p. 12; Allied Commission, Committee on Education, *La Politica e la legislazione scolastica in Italia dal 1922 al 1943* (Rome, 1947), pp. 265-270.

[36] Ascoli, *loc. cit.* For a documented study of press censorship, see Francisco Flora, *Stampa dell'epoca fascista* (Rome, 1945); for censorship of the theater, see L. Zurlo, *Memorie inutili: la censura teatrale nel ventennio* (Rome, 1952).

[37] It owed its origin to a Socialist physician in Turin, Dr. Alberico Molinari. In romantic fashion it sought to maintain a "triad" security system among its secret members. Unable to resuscitate the old Socialist parties, it tried with equal unsuccess to organize anti-Fascist defense squads. All it really accomplished was the distribution of propaganda (mostly mimeographed copies of a weekly sheet, *Altoparlante*) in some of the northern cities. Later its personnel tended to gravitate into Giustizia e Libertà. See Gavagnin, *Vent'anni di resistenza*, pp. 257-302; and his *Una lettera al re* (Milan, 1960).

94

Basso and most of his helpers (along with several non-Communists) [38] were arrested in the wake of excitement caused by an unexplained attempt to assassinate the King when he visited Milan's Commercial Fair on April 12. So far as is known, none of these anti-Fascists had anything to do with that bomb plot, which missed its intended target and killed, instead, eighteen bystanders and wounded several dozen others on Piazzale Giulio Cesare.[39] After spending the next five years in *confino*, Basso swung over to Communism.[40]

In Genoa soon after the exceptional decrees, the ex-Socialist and CGL newspaper *Il Lavoro* was revived when it professed loyalty to Mussolini. At intervals, though, the editorials of Carlo Bordiga, and later of Giuseppe Canepa, revealed patent disagreement with certain Fascist syndical policies. *Il Lavoro* served also as an organ for a Milanese coterie of ex-CGL officials headed by Rinaldo Rigola who, although they had generally capitulated to Fascism, occasionally found heart to criticize mildly some of its syndicalism and corporatism. In 1927 they formed an Association for the Study of Labor Problems and published the small, well-edited *Problemi del lavoro*.[41]

Meanwhile, in Rome, Adolfo Tino and Armando Zanetti, aided financially by Albertini, tried in vain to breathe enduring life into *Rinascita liberale*. Two other mildly critical publications in Rome (*Studi politici* and *Conscientia*) fared no better.[42]

La Cultura, stamped by the Giulio Einaudi publishing house in Turin (always a focal center of resistance),[43] met with greater

---

[38] Among them were Dr. Alberico Molinari, Professor Gino Luzzatto, Max Ascoli, Mario Vinciguerra, Ugo LaMalfa, and Alberto Consiglio.

A young Socialist, Fernando DeRosa, who had issued a covert Torinese journal, *Umanità nova* (circulation, 500), and who soon plotted to assassinate Crown Prince Humbert, escaped to France and Switzerland, whence he sought to supply his friends back home with clandestine literature. By 1929 he was printing 500 copies of a small review, *La lotta politica*, in Lugano for Nello Rosselli, Carlo Levi, and Riccardo Bauer, but he got only one copy across the border. Garosci, VCR, 1, 186; *cf. supra*, Ch. ii, Giustizia e Libertà.

[39] Gavagnin, *Vent'anni di resistenza*, pp. 268–271; S/M, *Sdf*, p. 322.

[40] Gino Calzolari, *Outline of Italian Anti-Fascism* (London, 1943), p. 15.

[41] S/M, *Sdf*, pp. 296–299.

[42] Garosci, VCR, 1, 37, 41.

[43] In politics Giulio Einaudi stood much farther to the left than his father, who always remained a Liberal. Regarding the arrests of 1935, see *infra*, Ch. iv. Another collaborator of Giulio arrested then was Cesare Pavese, to become a noteworthy anti-Fascist novelist (*Prima che il gallo canti* [Turin, 1947]; *La bella estate* [1949]; and *La luna e i falò* [1950]).

success. This was a liberal literary and historical review akin to Croce's *La Critica*. Professor Cesare de Lollis edited it until his death in 1928; thereafter the Gobettian Arrigo Cajumi and Raffaele Mattioli directed it until it was banned in 1935 in the midst of a general Fascist clamp-down in Turin. The historians who wrote in *La Cultura* sought, among other things, to rehabilitate the liberal rationalism of the Age of the Enlightenment in the face of Fascist distortions: "We are rationalists, and we shall remain so, in times of spreading irrationalism," wrote Professor Salvatorelli in 1933.[44] The censor's axe also struck down *La Riforma sociale*, edited since 1908 by Professor Luigi Einaudi, the University of Turin's eminent economist and future President of the Italian Republic (1948–1955). In 1936, however, Einaudi launched the new and quite respectable *Rivista di storia economica*.[45]

Fascism versus Catholicism

When Fr. Sturzo fled in October 1924, he left his close friend Alcide DeGasperi as secretary and chief spokesman of the disintegrating Italian Popular Party (PPI). This tenacious mountaineer had been born forty-three years before in Borgo Val Sugana (then part of the Austrian Empire). After studying philosophy at the University of Vienna he propagandized the cause of *Italianità* in *Il Trentino* and *Voce cattolica*, joined the Austrian Christian Socialist Party, and won election to Parliament in 1911. There he intensified his irredentism and opposed Austrian war moves. After the armistice DeGasperi helped Sturzo launch the PPI and lead Italy's Catholic masses into political life. As soon as Italy formally annexed the South Tyrol, he was sent to the Chamber of Deputies by his Alpine friends. He distinguished himself quickly as an advocate of progressive reforms.[46] Though the frustrations of the Aventine revealed clearly

[44] Walter Maturi, "Gli studi di storia moderna e contemporanea," in Carlo Antoni and Raffaele Mattioli, *Cinquant'anni di vita intellettuale italiana, 1896–1946: scritti in onore di Benedetto Croce* (2 vols.; Naples, 1950), I, 249.

[45] Documentation Center, Presidency of the Council of Ministers of the Republic of Italy, *Italy Today* (Rome, 1955), p. 156; S/M, *Sdf*, pp. 293–296, 671; Maurizio Milan and Fausta Vighi (eds.), *La Resistenza al fascismo* (Milan, 1955), p. 59; and Pietro Paolo Trompeo, "Ricordi di Arrigo Cajumi, un uomo europeo," Rome *Il Mondo*, Oct. 18, 1955.

[46] Giulio Andreotti, *DeGasperi e il suo tempo* (Milan, 1956), pp. 1–109;

to DeGasperi the flaccidity of the King, he did not become outspokenly anti-royalist. Similarly, he bit his lips in silence when he learned of the Vatican veto of a coalition cabinet of Populars and right-wing Socialists.

DeGasperi dominated the fifth (and final) congress of the PPI in Rome in June 1925; and he was present six months later when the party directorate held its last session. Neither DeGasperi nor any of the others deemed it wise to make bitter denunciations of the government on the latter occasion. Yet the police took action against them. And, worst of all, Pius XI the same day delivered an address to a secret meeting of the Consistory in which he indicated his sympathy for the regime and his horror of liberalism and socialism "which lead to anarchy." The pontiff appended only a few mild warnings about the danger of ultranationalism.[47]

In November 1926 police in Vicenza apprehended DeGasperi and did their best to make him capitulate to Fascism. But unexpectedly, as a result of the intervention of a friendly official, DeGasperi gained his liberty. He hid in Rome for the next few months under the name "Carlo Rossi." Finally he decided to move to Trieste, where he hoped to enjoy greater freedom. As his train passed through Florence on March 11, 1927, he was again arrested. The court found him guilty of the unfair charge of seeking to emigrate furtively and sentenced him to four (later cut to three) years in Regina Coeli penitentiary (later he was transferred to a Rome clinic) and fined him 20,000 lire. Luckily he regained his freedom sixteen months later, after dogged intercession by the Holy See.[48]

From 1929 on, DeGasperi worked inconspicuously as a Vatican librarian and translator.[49] He continued his research and, using a pseudonym ("C. Iaspar"), slipped cautious political articles through the censors to *Studium* and *Rivista internazio-*

Giuseppe Petrocchi, *DeGasperi: La Democrazia Cristiana e la politica italiana* (Rome, 1946), pp. 13–40; Petrocchi, *Don Luigi Sturzo*, pp. 110–115; V. Crialesi and A. V. Rossi, *DeGasperi*; Dante Benedetti, *DeGasperi politico e statista* (Rome, 1949), pp. 1–88; and Igino Giordani, *Alcide DeGasperi* (Milan, 1955).

[47] S/M, *Sdf*, p. 341.

[48] Andreotti, *DeGasperi e il suo tempo*, pp. 115–122.

[49] He translated Ludwig Pastor, *History of the Popes*; René Fülop-Miller, *The Power and Secret of the Jesuits*; Valeriu Marcu, *Lenin*.

nale di scienze sociale.[50] His commentaries on the vexations of the old German Center Party were admittedly designed to "remind Italian Catholics of the example of the parliamentary struggles carried on . . . against the formidable dictatorship of Bismarck." In his studies on corporatism (1928), DeGasperi has explained that he "sought to demonstrate . . . that whatever good there was in the corporatist conception was to be traced more than half a century back [to Catholic writers], and that in any case the spirit of the Fascist system, enslaved by the dictatorship of a single party, was essentially something different—things which could only be insinuated with much caution, but which I hope may have helped put on guard some unduly ingenuous Catholics who might have been too ready to compromise with Fascism because of certain formal similarities." Only thus could he operate publicly; "to speak of the present was excluded and extremely dangerous; every time I tried to stick out my antennae, I had to pull them back quickly and continue to sputter and weep in my solitary cup of chocolate." [51] Despite his substantial seclusion DeGasperi shared from time to time his "cup of chocolate" with his own party colleagues and such amiable agnostics as Ivanoe Bonomi and Alessandro Casati.

So long as the tenacious Trentine lived, he overshadowed everyone else in Catholic political ranks (save the exiled Sturzo). But a rising luminary (and one of DeGasperi's cohorts) during the Aventine was the Tuscan Giovanni Gronchi, quondam secretary-general of the Catholic CIL ("white" confederation of workers) and a minister in Mussolini's first cabinet. When the PPI held its final congress in 1925, Gobetti wrote with prophetic insight: "If DeGasperi . . . is the man of today, everyone is saying that Gronchi will be the man of tomorrow." [52] So it was;

[50] Stefano Jacini wrote in the same way occasionally for *Hochland* review in Munich. Gavagnin, *Vent'anni di resistenza*, p. 286.

[51] Alcide DeGasperi, *I Cattolici dall'opposizione al governo* (Bari, 1955), pp. viii–ix. An earlier edition of some of his writings was *Studi ed appelli della lunga vigilia*, ed. Giorgio Tupini (Rome, 1946). In Tupini's estimation, DeGasperi's most memorable essay of the clandestine era was his critical review of Croce's *History of Europe in the Nineteenth Century*, which gave him the pretext to remind Catholics that their own greatest thinkers of that century had also fought for freedom. Tupini, *I Democratici Cristiani*, p. 42.

[52] Turin *Rivoluzione Liberale*, July 5, 1925, cited in Vigorelli, *Gronchi*, pp. 3–5; see pp. 4–32 for further judgments by Gobetti of Catholic leaders. Cf. Tupini, *I Democratici Cristiani*, pp. 32–37.

in 1955, two years after Premier DeGasperi's death, Gronchi, showing no disposition at all to play the role of *roi fainéant*, was to become President of the Italian Republic. But that lay in the future; from August 1926 (when Gronchi's Florentine *Cronaca sociale d'Italia* was quashed and his efforts to revive the Catholic labor unions frustrated) until 1942 he had to bide the dictatorship in silence.[53]

While DeGasperi and his disciples trod with dignity and honesty their *via dolorosa*, Mussolini went ahead with plans for winning over the Vatican.[54] By agreeing to restore the crucifix to schools and courtrooms and by scheduling masses for public functions (to say nothing of such gestures as combating Freemasonry), he paved the way for appointment, in February 1925, of a commission of expert laymen to review legislation affecting ecclesiastical affairs. Working without fanfare, this group presented a report at year's end.

Meanwhile, secret negotiations between the regime and the Vatican had been in progress outside Parliament since late in 1925 to solve the Roman Question as a prerequisite to settlement of other Church-State relations. Despite occasional moments of tension—such as the year-long dispute between the ONB paramilitary youth organization and the 100,000-strong Catholic Boy Scouts ("Esploratori Cattolici"), which was resolved by virtually disbanding the latter in 1928[55]—these negotiations went ahead fairly smoothly and were supervised by Cardinal Secretary of State Gasparri, Marchese Eugenio Pacelli, and Pius XI himself. Some of the final meetings took place at night in Mussolini's residence. At last (February 11, 1929) the momentous agreements, which included a political treaty settling the Roman Question, a religious concordat, and a financial convention, were signed by Gasparri and Mussolini in the Lateran Palace. Seminarists intoning the "Te Deum" competed with Militiamen on the square in front who shrieked, "Eia, alalà!"[56]

Mussolini's star soared throughout the Catholic world, while

[53] Vigorelli, *Gronchi*, pp. 294–320.
[54] *Cf. supra*, Ch. 1, Catholic dissidence. See Howard, *Partito Popolare Italiano*, pp. 466–496; Jemolo, *Chiesa e Stato in Italia, passim*; and Binchy, *Church and State in Fascist Italy*, pp. 121–138 ff.
[55] *Ibid.*, pp. 408–420.
[56] *Ibid.*, pp. 167–195; Jemolo, *Chiesa e Stato in Italia*, pp. 637–640; and Amedeo Giannini, *Il cammino della conciliazione* (Milan, 1946).

humble Italian peasants shed their wonted indifference for public affairs long enough to flock to church to pray for the pontiff who had "given back God to Italy and Italy to God." The reconciliation doubtless contributed to the *Duce*'s top-heavy victory in the plebiscite of March 24, 1929 (only 136,000 dared vote against him).[57]

On the other hand, news of the pacts dismayed those laic foes of the dictatorship who had clung to the hope that the Church might throw its moral weight to their side of the struggle with Fascism, or at least remain neutral.[58] To them it seemed as if Pius XI overstepped himself on February 13 when he referred glowingly to the *Duce* as "a man . . . whom Providence has caused us to meet." They were exasperated too by the pontiff's observation that Mussolini was a "man who does not have the preoccupations of the liberal school, of the men to whom all laws and regulations . . . were like fetishes—and the more ugly and deformed the fetishes, the more stubbornly to be worshipped." [59]

During the spring, objections to ratification mounted from lay groups, while at the same time both the dictatorship and the Vatican began to indulge in harsh polemics, much to the bewilderment of outsiders. A few anticlerical professors and students at the University of Turin, led by Umberto Cosmo and including Barbara Allason, Franco Antonicelli, Pietro and Paolo Treves, dispatched a message to Senator Croce, urging him to denounce the concordat when it came up for ratification. This he bravely did in a lengthy, involved argument on the senate floor May 24, amid the silence of scores of ostensible Liberals. Although he made it clear that he did not object to the principle of Church-State reconciliation, Croce expressed the fear that these accords would upset the equilibrium between Church and State which had been slowly and painfully established by experience during the previous half century. The press in Italy

[57] Binchy, *Church and State in Fascist Italy*, pp. 192–198.

[58] See "The Italian Liberals and the Lateran Treaties," in a clandestine pamphlet circulated in Italy and translated in *Italy Today, Documents Published by Friends of Italian Freedom* (London, 1929), reprinted in Keene (ed.), *Neither Liberty Nor Bread*, pp. 168–179; *cf.* Calzolari, *Outline of Italian Anti-Fascism*, p. 15; Ernesto Rossi (ed.), *La Conciliazione*, with introduction by Guido Calogero (Florence, 1959), a collection of documents and criticisms of the pacts.

[59] Quoted by S/M, *Sdf*, p. 371.

completely ignored his speech. When the ballots were counted, only Croce and five others (Albertini, Ruffini, Bergamini, Paternò, and Sinibaldi) dared to register their nays; 316 voted (many hypocritically) in favor of the Accords. Meanwhile, the Torinese instigators of the plea to Croce spent a month in jail for their temerity, and Cosmo found himself deported to Lipari.[60]

The fears of a good many Fascists and other nationalists that the King would become the "Pope's altar boy," and the converse fears of Catholics that the Pope might end up the "King's chaplain" (to use Mussolini's flippant phrases) led to sharp, even brutal clarification by the *Duce* of the meaning of the pacts. On May 13 in a long speech in the new, hand-picked Chamber of Deputies, he claimed state control over all education of youth. Finally, he boasted of the "ethical character" of the Italian State, which "is Catholic but also Fascist, indeed before all else exclusively and essentially Fascist." [61]

The Pope lost no time in flatly rejecting many of these claims. He declared himself "intransigent," though not "intractable" (Mussolini's word) about the Church's rights in the field of education, and he noted pointedly that "education for conquest" could only lead "to general conflagration." Harsh rebuttals and counterrebuttals were hurled by the spokesmen of the rival authoritarian institutions. Fr. Enrico Rosa, S.J., editor of *Civiltà cattolica*, defied the government's ban on replies to the *Duce*'s speeches and published a bristling article, "Between Ratifications and Rectifications"; whereupon the local prefect quickly confiscated the entire issue "because of the general anti-Italian and anti-Fascist content of the leading article." [62] On June 6, the eve of the date fixed for the exchange of ratifications, the Vatican published a long letter from the Pope to Cardinal Gasparri in which he refuted many of the interpretations that Mussolini had set forth. The Pope not only had the last word but the better of the argument, and Mussolini was clever enough to recognize this. Next day, swallowing his irritation, he drove to the Vatican to

---

[60] Allason, *Memorie di un'antifascista*, pp. 72–76. Regarding Croce's speech see *supra*, Ch. III, Benedetto Croce's moral leadership; Binchy, *Church and State in Fascist Italy*, pp. 211–213, 224; and Benedetto Croce, *Due anni di vita politica italiana* (1946–1947) (Bari, 1948), p. 91.

[61] Mussolini, *Scritti e discorsi* (1929–1931), VII, 34 ff.

[62] Fr. Enrico Rosa, "Tra ratifiche e rettifiche," *Civiltà cattolica*, III (1929), pp. 97 ff.; and Binchy, *Church and State in Fascist Italy*, pp. 83, 209–219, 428.

exchange ratifications in a ceremony that "was carried out with as much friendliness of both sides as if not a breath of contradiction had ever disturbed their harmony." [63]

Most Catholics seemed to console themselves with the hope that the *Duce*'s intentions were honorable and that on balance the Church had achieved most of its aims. As a result, civil authorities acceded to the desires of churchmen whenever these did not flout the interests of Fascism; by the same token, ecclesiastical authorities usually gave their *nihil obstat* to the works of Mussolini and prudently glossed over all but the most blatantly un-Christian aspects of Fascist doctrine and practice. Yet the judgment of the anticlericals Salvatorelli and Mira seems harsh: "The ensuing atmosphere of solidarity was the thing which was habitual; the conflicts were only episodic, even though in some instances grave, or acute (which is not the same thing)." [64] Binchy hit the mark more closely when he observed that the experiences with Nazi Germany and Fascist Italy in the 1930's eventually "led Pius XI, although by temperament inclined to sympathize with authoritarian government, to recognize in modern dictatorships the most formidable danger to Christianity in our time." [65] (And this was to be even truer of Pius XII.)

The basic divergence between totalitarian Fascism and authoritarian Roman Catholicism [66] was clearly revealed in an acrimonious dispute that simmered along from 1929 until it erupted violently in the spring of 1931 over the status of Azione Cattolica. This new *dissidio* was far more vehement than the one ended by the Lateran pacts. Early in the century Pius X had used a branch of Catholic Action to disseminate instructions to Italian Catholic voters, but with the emergence of Sturzo's PPI, Catholic Action's political role had become increasingly muffled, so that by the eve of the fight with Mussolini its work among the laity was chiefly social and educational.[67] In 1929 this "apostolate of

---

[63] *Ibid.*, pp. 219–220.

[64] S/M, *Sdf*, pp. 366–368; *cf.* L. Salvatorelli, *Pio XI e la sua eredità pontificale* (Turin, 1939). This judgment is essentially shared by the anticlerical Ernesto Rossi, *Il manganello e l'aspersorio* (Milan, 1958); Giulio Castelli, *La Chiesa e il fascismo* (Rome, 1951); and G. Salvemini and Giorgio LaPiana, *What to do with Italy?* (New York, 1943), pp. 80–99.

[65] Binchy, *Church and State in Fascist Italy*, p. 329.

[66] Regarding some of the doctrinal points of conflict, see *ibid.*, pp. 335–353.

[67] Regarding the background and role of Catholic Action, see *ibid.*, Ch. 18; Gabriele de Rosa, *L'Azione Cattolica: storia politica dal 1874 al 1919* (2 vols.; Bari, 1953–1954); and F. L. Ferrari, *L'Azione Cattolica e il "Regime."*

the laity" possessed in Italy some 250 diocesan committees, 4,000 men's sections, and 5,000 Catholic youth and university clubs. Determined to control all mass organizations, Mussolini was of course extremely jealous of Catholic Action, which in many rural areas was stronger than the PNF. He therefore sought a pretext to eliminate it, even though Article 43 of the Concordat grudgingly recognized its independence. Among other things, he suddenly accused it in the spring of 1931 of harboring leaders of the outlawed PPI and of carrying on social work in competition with Fascist syndical and welfare programs.

There was some truth to these charges, for Catholic Action, though in no sense an organ of the Populars, included within its ranks a great many veterans of the dispersed party, and its membership swelled considerably after 1929—a development which surely annoyed the *Duce*.[68] Not all these recruits were actuated by the sole desire to advance the "apostolate of the laity"; many were anxious "to join the only association where enthusiasm for a regime which they disliked was not compulsory." [69]

Ramifications of the dispute extended into the university and youth organizations. Thus FUCI, which during the Aventine had been accused of serving as a front for anti-Fascism, was again denounced in the spring of 1931. The newly created GUF led the onslaught. On May 30 the government suppressed the FUCI.[70]

Meanwhile, *L'Osservatore romano* skirmished with *Popolo d'Italia* and chronicled many incidents in which the dictatorship had interfered forcibly with Catholic associations, seizing their publications, illegally "inspecting" them, and encouraging violence against individual members. Pius XI's growing displeasure with Blackshirt totalitarianism became more evident in public statements, including the Encyclical Letter, "Quadragesimo anno," issued on May 25, 1931, the fortieth anniversary of "Rerum

[68] He warned: "Let nobody believe that the smallest parochial bulletin of the smallest parish is not known to Mussolini. We will not permit the revival of parties and organizations which we have destroyed for ever. Let everyone remember that the Fascist regime, when it begins a war, fights it to a finish and leaves but a desert behind." *Scritti e discorsi* (1929–1931), VII, pp. 34 ff.

[69] Binchy, *Church and State in Fascist Italy*, p. 509; cf. George Seldes, *The Vatican, Yesterday–Today–Tomorrow* (London, 1934), p. 396.

[70] A. Baroni, *Igino Righetti*; Petrocchi, *DeGasperi*, p. 44; and the Marxian account of Giovanni Berlinguer and Giancarlo d'Alessandro, "Sulle vicende interne delle organizazzioni giovanili cattoliche," *Rinascita*, XI (May 1954), pp. 342–344. Cf. Webster, *The Cross and the Fasces*, pp. 137–143.

novarum." In it he expressed grave fears about not only Marxism and unbridled *laissez faire* but also the "exclusively bureaucratic and political character" of the new Fascist syndical and corporative organizations which risk "serving particular political aims rather than contributing to the initiation of a better social order." [71]

It reached its climax on June 29, 1931, when he issued the Encyclical "Non abbiamo bisogno" ("We have no need"), written in vigorous Italian rather than in Latin, to emphasize its urgency. He took elaborate precautions to evade Fascist postal censorship; indeed, Mgr. Francis Spellman of New York flew several hundred copies direct from Vatican City to Paris. The text came out in newspapers abroad before Italians read it on July 5 in *L'Osservatore romano* (which, incidentally, went on sale in the kiosks five hours earlier than usual and thus escaped confiscation until the issue was almost exhausted). The effect was electrifying. The Pope had flatly rejected the charge that Catholic Action leaders were chiefly directors of the defunct PPI, and he complained that the Fascists' manner of dissolving Catholic organizations was such as "to give the impression that action was being taken against a vast and dangerous organization of criminals." Bitterly he condemned the Fascist charges as "inventions, falsehoods, and real calumnies diffused by the hostile press of the Party, which is the only press . . . free to say and to dare to say anything, and is often ordered or almost ordered what it must say." [72]

On July 9 the PNF declared that participation in Catholic Action was incompatible with party membership; whereupon thousands of "Azionisti" resigned from the religious society, thereby giving further substance to the witticism that membership in the PNF was only "Per Necessità Famigliale." On the other side of the ledger, a good many Catholic Actionists turned in their PNF cards. The two organizations warred for more than a month before they reached a shaky truce on September 2,

[71] *Four Great Encyclicals* (New York, 1931), Addenda, pp. 27–38.

[72] Quoted in Finer, *Mussolini's Italy*, p. 463, which, with Binchy's Ch. 18 and the sections of Jemolo and Salvatorelli/Mira, offers a penetrating analysis of the dispute. See also Giorgio Candeloro, *Il movimento cattolico in Italia* (Rome, 1953), p. 474 ff.; F. L. Ferrari, "The Christian Democratic Outlook," in Keene (ed.), *Neither Liberty Nor Bread*, pp. 180–190; and Gavagnin, *Vent'anni di resistenza*, pp. 289–295.

1931. This came in the wake of discreet negotiations by Fr. Pietro Tacchi-Venturi, S.J., and after Mussolini shoved aside two of his most vocal critics of Catholic Action (PNF secretary Giovanni Giuriati and Carlo Scorza). Doubtless the *Duce* was also disturbed by foreign criticism, and certainly he wished to avoid any *Kulturkampf*.

The chief terms of the compromise were that Catholic Action was to be diocesan (not national) in character and under direct control of the bishops (rather than under officers elected by the members), who would not select its officers from among those who had belonged to "parties averse to the regime"; that the professional sections were to have no syndicalist functions; and that youth organizations were to stay out of sports. On the surface it looked as if the dictatorship had gained the greater triumph, but the Church could rejoice that despite Catholic Action's decentralization, the organization survived and stayed independent of the secular power. Both parties greeted the settlement with unfeigned relief.[73]

To demonstrate the restoration of amicable relations, Mussolini paid his first official call on the Holy Father February 11, 1932 (anniversary of the Lateran pacts); they conversed for more than an hour. Next month he bestowed the coveted Collar of the Annunciation upon Eugenio Cardinal Pacelli (the future Pius XII).[74]

During the Spanish Civil War, Catholic Action often lauded Mussolini's intervention, and in general it avoided any friction with the regime. Nevertheless, Fascist purists remained dissatisfied so long as it stayed independent of PNF authority. There was to be a brief epilogue to the fight in 1938 when the regime introduced anti-Semitic measures and again in April and July 1939, just a few months after Pius XII's accession. To forestall what appeared to be a new onslaught, the pontiff brought the terms of the 1931 compromise to their logical conclusion by abolishing the last vestiges of curial supervision of Catholic Action in Italy and substituting, "as already obtains in other countries," a three-man commission composed of members of the diocesan hierarchy. At the diocesan level control was vested

[73] Binchy, *Church and State in Fascist Italy*, pp. 527–531.
[74] S/M, *Sdf*, pp. 406–407.

in a Catholic Action office under the personal oversight of the bishop, while at the parish level there was a corresponding office directly responsible to the priest. No lay control at all was permitted.[75]

Not much is known about Catholic Action's underground work during the dictatorship's final years, and one suspects there was not much. Yet, even if it did nothing, it "was anti-Fascist by reason of the simple fact of not being Fascist," as Professor Mario Einaudi has observed.[76] And there can be no doubt that it provided the cadres wherein a whole new generation of Italian politicians got their training. After the Liberation, Catholic Action was the only agency in Italy that compared in efficiency with Togliatti's PCI.[77]

Anarchists and ethnic minorities

The role of the Italian Anarchists in the anti-Fascist struggle has remained largely unexplored,[78] though recent memoirs of Armando Borghi have shed some light upon the early years.[79] Italy has a long tradition of anarchistic thought and action, inspired to some extent by Pierre Proudhon but more directly by the ubiquitous Michael Bakunin, who established his headquarters in the peninsula off and on during the 1860's and recruited such able lieutenants as Carlo Cafiero, Errico Malatesta, and Andrea Costa. Italy's Anarchists concentrated in Emilia-Romagna, the Marches, and Tuscany's marble quarries in the Carrara sector, but they also cropped up in distant Naples, Sicily, and elsewhere. Next to Malatesta, who died in Rome in July 1932, a prisoner in his own country,[80] the most famous Italian

---

[75] Binchy, pp. 531–537. An astute postwar analyst has observed that these changes "represented a move of desperation" for an organization that had been conceived as giving concrete expression to the "apostolate of the laity." Webb, *Church and State in Italy, 1947–1957*, p. 50.

[76] Einaudi and Goguel, *Christian Democracy in Italy and France*, p. 26.

[77] A Catholic right-wing critic of Christian Democracy declares that the brief success of the PPI from 1919 to 1922 tended to weaken Catholic Action, whereas the post-World War II period has seen the Christian Democratic Party and Catholic Action grow in strength and develop intricate techniques of co-operation. Giovanni Spadolini, *L'opposizione cattolica* (Florence, 1954), pp. 688–703.

[78] Leto, OVRA, p. 84; Garosci, Sdf, pp. 147–148.

[79] See his *Mezzo secolo di anarchia* (1898–1945). He published in Paris a scathing denunciation, *Mussolini en chemise* (1932), later translated in English as *Mussolini Red and Black* (London and New York, 1938). Borghi resided in the United States from 1926 until the end of the war.

[80] See biography by Armando Borghi, *Errico Malatesta* (Milan, 1947).

Anarchist of this century was young Professor Camillo Berneri of Reggio Emilia, a one-time student of Salvemini. Berneri was to be slain in Barcelona, presumably by Stalinists, during the Spanish Civil War.[81]

Occasionally the Anarchists' war against Mussolini impinged upon that of the PRI and Giustizia e Libertà, though generally they operated separately. The period of the Depression marked the acme of their direct action, which was characterized by several killings of consular officials abroad, some bomb hurlings in the streets, and foiled assassinations of Mussolini.[82] They seemed convinced that violent gestures against tyrants would somehow restore freedom in quick fashion—a notion the Marxists scoffed at.

Three highly publicized terrorist deeds took place in 1931 and 1932. The first involved Michele Schirru, a 32-year-old Sardinian libertarian who was a naturalized American. In the United States he had associated with the anarchistic circle in New York that published L'Adunata dei refrattari. With an American passport he returned to Italy via France in 1930. Apparently he had the vague intention of killing Mussolini, but after manufacturing some bombs he decided that his objective was unrealistic, gave it up, and turned his attention instead to women of the street. When authorities discovered that he had a venereal disease, they brought him to a police station for routine investigation on February 3, 1931. As soon as Schirru saw that they were going to search him, he pulled out a revolver and fired. Whether his intention was to commit suicide or to kill the officers is uncertain; in any case, he seriously wounded several of them as well as himself. He was tried by the Special Tribunal and immediately executed (May 28, 1931). His dying shout was "Viva l'anarchia!" According to Capo della Polizia Leto, numerous officials raised serious doubts as to the justification of capital punishment for

[81] Of some interest is his mother's emotional evocation: Aldagisia Fochi-Berneri, Con tè, figlio mio! (Parma, 1948).

[82] Garosci, Sdf, pp. 147–148; Leto, OVRA, pp. 84, 88; E. Rossi (ed.), No al fascismo, p. 14; Pane e Libertà, ed. Gruppo Anarchico Autonomo di Parigi (Paris, [1932]). There is much contradictory information about terrorist deeds. Though many consular officials were killed, it is uncertain how many of these murders were inspired by political organizations and how many may have been simply the work of individuals disgruntled over bureaucratic delays. About a dozen incidents seem to have been clearly inspired by Anarchists, or in some cases ultraleftist Socialists. See Salvemini, Mussolini diplomatico, p. 190; S/M, Sdf, pp. 478–479.

this young man who, it was claimed, had renounced his original intention.[83] Schirru's political "testament" was published in *L'Adunata dei refrattari* in June 1931 and reprinted in Paris.[84]

On June 4, 1932, the police seized another Anarchist, a 25-year-old Venetian bricklayer, Angelo Sbardellotto. When he was booked for suspicious behavior in Rome's Piazza Venezia, a search revealed him in possession of a bomb and an automatic pistol. Sbardellotto, it seems, was coerced into confessing that he recently had been in touch with Alberto Tarchiani and Carlo Rosselli of Giustizia e Libertà in Paris—an obvious fabrication, as they were not there during the weeks in question. But Sbardellotto did have associates in and out of Italy, and if he had received a little more help from them he might well have succeeded. All told, he had made three trips to Rome with assassination of the *Duce* in mind. Just before he entered Italy on the final mission he wrote: "I do not ask of men gratitude or honorary reward for the sacrifice which I am about to undergo. I ask only that those who will be able to understand the meaning of my act will follow the example." [85] Evidently they did not. Convicted by the Special Tribunal, he was executed on June 17, 1932. Witnesses reported that he met his death imperturbably and, like Schirru, yelled, "Viva l'anarchia!" [86]

On the same day Domenico Bovone, a 30-year-old Genoese industrial worker, fell before a firing squad. He had been arrested in Genoa the previous autumn after the accidental explosion of a bomb in his home had killed his mother and seriously injured himself and a sister. In earlier weeks a series of bomb explosions in Bologna, Turin, Genoa, and Milan had caused much excitement, some property damage, and the wounding of a *Carabiniere*.

Whether or not Bovone was involved in all of these affairs remains unknown. Mussolini, in any event, decided to smash opposition terrorism once for all; consequently he sought to implicate Bovone in all the episodes and link him to as many *fuorusciti* in the Concentration as possible. Most of the accusations in the highly bruited *processo* were patently absurd; several

[83] Leto, OVRA, pp. 83–88; Garosci, *Sdf*, p. 64.
[84] See *Almanacco Socialista per il 1932*, p. 48; and *Giustizia e Libertà Opuscolo No. 28* (Paris).
[85] Garosci, *Sdf*, p. 65.
[86] Leto, OVRA, p. 92; Gavagnin, *Vent'anni di resistenza*, pp. 316–317.

persons were condemned to long terms even though they had never known Bovone. Yet the Fascists achieved their purpose: creating the belief that all *émigrés* were criminal terrorists and traitors.[87]

Because of the general revulsion only a few deeds of direct action took place after 1932. The most publicized was the explosion of a time bomb in the pilgrims' baggage-deposit area of Piazza San Pietro in Rome on Sunday, June 25, of the Holy Year (1933). It wounded four people. The affair was designed to protest the Vatican's friendship toward the regime; actually it served to tighten that relationship and thus hindered the anti-Fascist cause. Three months later the police locked up Leonardo Bucciglioni as well as the brother (Renato) and nephew (Claudio) of the *émigré* journalist, Alberto Cianca, and charged them with responsibility for the deed. Again the government sought to convert the trial into one against the *fuorusciti*. The Special Tribunal sentenced the accused to terms ranging from seventeen to thirty years.[88]

A certain amount of active resistance to Mussolini was ethnic in origin. The peace settlement of World War I had brought substantial numbers of Germans, Slovenes, and Croats into Italy. The Fascists inaugurated a harsh, often brutal policy of "Italianizing" these peoples, modifying their surnames and interfering with linguistic patterns in schools and in cultural and religious bodies. The tough-fibred South Tyrolese hung on to a large measure of their *Deutschtum*. The hard-pressed Slavs were not so fortunate. They fought as best they could the policy of *Italianità* and provided Fascist police agencies with no little work. As early as November 1926 seven Communists in Fiume, four of whom bore Slavic names, were jailed. The Special Tribunal condemned between February 1927 and July 1932 some 106 Slavs to a total of 1,124 years of imprisonment.[89] In May 1931 Mussolini used the excuse of Slavic terrorism to justify continuation of the Special Tribunal. The most publicized case was that of Vladimiro Gortan, charged with inciting some Slavs to fire upon voters during Mussolini's plebiscite of March 24, 1929. The Special

[87] *Ibid.*, pp. 101–113; S/M, *Sdf*, p. 546; and Garosci, *Sdf*, p. 65.
[88] S/M, *Sdf*, pp. 649–650; Gavagnin, *Vent'anni di resistenza*, p. 317.
[89] Salvemini, *Mussolini diplomatico*, pp. 454–469.

Tribunal met in Pola for the case, found him (and four others) guilty, and ordered his execution on October 17. Marshal Josip Tito's Yugoslavia regards Gortan as one of its primitive martyrs. Relentlessly persecuted by the Fascists, opposition currents in Venezia Giulia veered leftward; even before Marshal Tito's Partisans moved into the frontier sector, Communists had become the strongest activist group.[90]

Communist conspiracies

Along with the Anarchists, the Italian Communist Party provided the Special Tribunal and prisons with the largest quotas of victims during the early phase of Mussolini's tyranny. Indeed, over the entire period of the dictatorship there can be little doubt that the PCI's work of propaganda, organization, and reorganization was on a broader scale than that of Giustizia e Libertà or any of the other active groups—a fact that has been freely conceded by most (though not all) non-Communists.[91] Unlike the Anarchists and GL, the PCI pursued long-term goals rather than hasty uprisings; it favored steady propaganda among the masses rather than sensationalism or acts of terrorism.

That the PCI had more cells, more messengers, and suffered more casualties was not too surprising in view of the advantages it enjoyed in the way of a foreign base to extend it financial support, to train its leaders, and to prepare much of the propaganda and false documentation. From the outset the PCI had established a covert apparatus alongside its overt one. Party chieftains studied carefully the conspiratorial techniques devised by their Muscovite mentors as well as those contrived by Risorgimento patriots. As early as the Aventine era the PCI followed the Bolshevik example and adopted a cellular-type organization, based on occupational as well as geographical divisions. In general, the rules for clandestine operations were about the same as those of the French Communist Party, so well described by

---

[90] S/M, Sdf, pp. 546–548; Gavagnin, Vent'anni di resistenza, p. 313; Comitato Cittadino dell'Unione Antifascista Italo-Slavo, Trieste nella lotta per la democrazia (Capo d'Istria, 1945), pp. 15–21, 31–32; and Elio Apih, Dal regime alla resistenza: Venezia Giulia, 1922–1943 (Udine, 1960), passim.

[91] E. Rossi in his preface to No al fascismo, pp. 14–16; Gavagnin, Vent'anni di resistenza, pp. 244–245, 256–257. For major bibliographical sources regarding the controversial history of the PCI, see supra, Ch. 1, n. 6; cf. critique of Garosci, "La prima storia del PCI," in his Pensiero politico e storiografia moderna (Pisa, 1954), pp. 261–273.

Angelo Tasca ("A. Rossi") who had firsthand acquaintance with both.[92] This elaborate system, in conjunction with the strict discipline, quickly demonstrated its virtue.[93]

Defeat of Bordiga at the Lyon Congress

No less urgent than the internal reorganization of the PCI was the campaign against the doctrinal "errors" of the party's first secretary, the Neapolitan engineer Amadeo Bordiga. This fight went on for the better part of two years after the Matteotti crisis. An extremist among extremists, Bordiga preferred a party structure resting on a purely geographical foundation, and he advocated PCI abstention from parliamentary struggles, as well as rigid isolation from "social-democratic" groups (except for labor organizations). He had insisted that the labor syndicates must seize power by violence.

During 1922 a faction led by Antonio Gramsci and Palmiro Togliatti had begun to think that under prevailing conditions abstentionism was a mistake. They were encouraged by Zinoviev and Bukharin, leaders of the Comintern in Moscow, where Gramsci prudently spent some eighteen months after June 1922, building his political fences.[94] Insisting upon more flexible tactics that might win them converts among the badly split Italian Socialists, the Gramsci-Togliatti faction made some headway, especially after the Fascists arrested Bordiga in January 1923.

With the PCI's ostensible leader in detention for the rest of that year, the Gramsci-Togliatti clique began to take over control of the party organization. By 1924 they had secured the appointment of an enlarged executive committee which prepared an indictment of the "Bordighist heresy." Drafted by the Venetian economist Mauro Scoccimarro, who was one of Gramsci's aides and an Italian representative to the Comintern, it denounced Bordiga as a "narrow sectarian." Yet inconsistently Gramsci's faction tacitly adopted Bordiga's isolationist position when they abandoned the "single front" policy and deserted their Aventine associates and re-entered Parliament in November 1924. Obvi-

[92] A. Rossi [pseud. for Angelo Tasca], *A Communist Party in Action: An Account of the Organization and Operations in France* (New Haven, 1949), pp. 166–179, and *passim*, tr. and ed. by Willmoore Kendall from *Physiologie du Parti Communiste Français* (Paris, 1948).
[93] Robotti and Germanetto, *Trent'anni di lotte dei comunisti italiani*, p. 48.
[94] B/G, *Storia del PCI*, pp. 71–74 ff.

ously the fight against Bordiga was egged on by Moscow. For several months charges and countercharges reverberated through party cells until finally Gramsci's group felt sure of enough support to summon a congress—the party's third—to meet in Lyon in January 1926 to discuss Bordiga's fate.[95] Most of the sixty-odd delegates had to cross the frontier in disguise.

To the surprise of hardly anyone, the Lyon Congress voted overwhelmingly to expel Bordiga from the central committee and thereby recognized Gramsci as the undisputed master. In desperation, Bordiga made a hasty pilgrimage to Moscow to appeal his case to the Comintern. He found no sympathy, though for the nonce he was permitted to keep his party card. Soon the Fascist police caught him and banished him into *confino* until March 1930. When he was freed the PCI (by then thoroughly Bolshevized) proceeded to expel him, charging him with "leftist," "Trotskyist" leanings and of behaving toward Fascism in an "unworthy" manner.[96] Disillusioned and disheartened, he withdrew from all political activity and dwelt quietly in Naples.

Another important decision of the PCI Third Congress was to promulgate the so-called "Lyon Theses." These ordered the party not to "abstain from supporting and joining in partial actions." They noted, too, that the fight in behalf of freedom "offers the best grounds for agitations and struggles having limited goals," and called for no discrimination in admitting workers into "agitation committees." [97] The "theses" went on to reaffirm such basic objectives as a republican assembly representing committees of workers and peasants, land for the peasants, and control of the state by the workers. The PCI slogan must be *unità*—and not just "formal" unity. It must be "substantial unity" of all the working class, peasants, and geographical sections. At the same time the party adroitly added to its propaganda talk of restoring and augmenting self-government in the South, the islands, and border zones. Finally, the party platform emphasized that the masses "must be led on the basis of their

[95] *Ibid.*, pp. 124–130, 171–190, and *passim*. All told, according to Togliatti's version, there were eight "errors" in *Bordighismo*. They are listed in the PCI handbook by Giulio Trevisani (ed.), *Piccola enciclopedia del Socialismo e del Comunismo* (2nd ed.; Rome, 1948), p. 35.

[96] S/M, *Sdf*, p. 510.

[97] Quoted by Garosci, "The Italian Communist Party," in Mario Einaudi (ed.), *Communism in Western Europe*, pp. 166–167.

experience"—policies must always be realistic and practical.[98]

When Mussolini proclaimed the exceptional decrees in November 1926 the PCI had to go under deep cover. But the police intervened before it could make the switch. They arrested Gramsci and several other deputies, despite their parliamentary immunities. In the next few months the dragnet hauled in dozens of party hierarchs as well as hundreds of the rank-and-file. Only a handful of leaders escaped—the most noted being Togliatti, then on a mission to Moscow.[99] Not till May 1928 did the accused come into court for a notorious *processone* ("supertrial").

Palmiro Togliatti's leadership

Upon Gramsci's arrest Palmiro Togliatti assumed *de facto* control of the PCI, and when Gramsci died in 1937 he became leader *de jure*. Togliatti was a native of Genoa, born on Palm Sunday in 1893. His father, a poor bookkeeper, had hoped that the son would study in a theological seminary; but the lad showed even less inclination for this than did Joseph Stalin. He spent his youth in Piedmont and in Sardinia. Winning a scholarship to the University of Turin, he studied jurisprudence, political economy, and Hegelianism. It is interesting to note that Togliatti placed second in the competition for scholarships, while Gramsci (probably more versatile) placed seventh.[100] After submitting a thesis on colonial tariff systems, Togliatti received his laureate with distinction. When not busy with studies he mingled with Torinese factory workers and joined in local Socialist Party activities. He had served in the Army a year when lung trouble made possible his discharge in 1917.

Two years later Togliatti and Gramsci launched *Ordine nuovo* upon its influential course. After the birth of the PCI at Leghorn in January 1921, Togliatti served as editor of its Rome newspaper, *Il Comunismo*, until the Fascists padlocked it late the next year. By 1923 he had gained a post in the party directorate, thanks to Comintern backing and to the temporary imprisonment of Bordiga. Next year he married Rita Montagnana, a

[98] Togliatti, *Gramsci*, pp. 52–54.
[99] Others included Ruggiero Grieco, Mario Montagnana, Giuseppe Dozza, Egidio Gennari, Felice Platone, and Ottavio Pastore.
[100] B/G, *Storia del PCI*, p. 22.

Torinese Communist dressmaker.[101] In 1925 he spent several months in jail until amnestied, whereafter he fled to France and Soviet Russia. Throughout this period "Ercole Ercoli" (as he was to be known in the underground) prepared the way for the anti-Bordiga decision handed down by the Lyon Congress.

He continued to represent the PCI in the Comintern so long as that agency existed, and eventually he joined its permanent secretariat. Shrewdly he kept in the good graces of whichever was the prevailing faction of the Communist Party of the Soviet Union.[102] Although generally amenable to Moscow's directives, Togliatti displayed a bit of restiveness in the late twenties. According to Ignazio Silone, who was a close party associate of those days, Togliatti had not fully reconciled himself to the arbitrary, dissimulating methods the Russian Communists employed to dominate the Third International. Thus at its Sixth Congress in Moscow in the summer of 1928, Togliatti "asked permission to repeat the words of the dying Goethe: 'Light, more light!' " In some respects that speech was Togliatti's intellectual swan song, Silone has declared. Within another year or two he capitulated.[103]

Clandestine apparatus

Better to co-ordinate their underground, PCI coryphaei established their Political Office in their so-called Foreign Center, which was situated first in Switzerland but after 1928 in Paris. During most of the early years that center was under the personal direction either of Togliatti or of such aides as Ruggiero Grieco ("Garlandi") and Angelo Tasca ("Serra"), until the latter's breach with the party.[104] It maintained communications with Moscow and other Communist parties and passed instructions to the Internal Center ("centro interno"), which was usually located in Milan. Though the PCI insisted that the anti-Fascist struggle should be conducted primarily in Italy, it also called

[101] Some years after World War II they were separated.

[102] B/G, Storia del PCI, pp. 203–220, and passim; cf. Mario Ciatti, Palmiro Togliatti (Rome, 1946), pp. 20–30; and the official biography prepared in honor of Togliatti's sixtieth birthday: Marcella and Maurizio Ferrara, Conversando con Togliatti (Rome, 1953).

[103] See Silone's autobiographical essay in Richard Grossman (ed.), The God that Failed (New York, 1949), p. 105; cf. B/G, Storia del PCI, pp. 224–228.

[104] See infra, Ch. III, Italian Communism in isolation.

for missionary work among emigrant groups in France and else-where. Those in France, it decreed, ought not to be recruited into a distinct PCI but rather enrolled as "Italian language groups" within the French Communist Party. Large-scale recruit-ment of emigrants did not take place prior to the Popular Front era.[105]

In Milan, meantime, the party's Central Committee quickly established an office in an apartment on Via Nino Bixio. At first it was managed by Pietro Tresso, responsible for party organiza-tion. Alfonso Leonetti was entrusted with clandestine publica-tions, while Paolo Ravazzoli served as liaison man with the new labor syndicates. Camillo Ravera was also a functionary.[106] In 1930 Tresso, Leonetti, and Ravazzoli were to be expelled for daring to doubt the imminence of a revolutionary situation in Italy.

In addition to the Foreign Center and the Milan office of the Central Committee, there was a third directing body, the Internal Center, whose specific task was technical co-ordination of covert operations. It issued orders to the eight inter-regional secretariats, which in turn passed them down to local cells. Initial leaders of this "shock-troop" Internal Center included the brilliant Abruz-zese writer, Ignazio Silone; [107] the Sicilian Girolamo LiCausi, in charge of operations in Piedmont and Liguria; and young Pietro Secchia ("Botte") from Biella, who represented the Com-munist Youth Federation.[108] To preserve their secrecy, couriers who traveled from abroad to the Milan headquarters changed their identity cards at least three times—upon entering the coun-try, again at their destination, and once more before leaving. An almost endless variety of forged passports, bogus documents, false-bottom luggage, and other paraphernalia dear to the con-spirator were used in this hazardous work. So impressed were Mussolini's police by some of the techniques that they en-deavored to imitate them.[109]

The PCI devoted most of its efforts in the mid-1920's to spread-

[105] Togliatti (ed.), *Trenta anni di vita e di lotte del PCI*, pp. 70–72; Garosci, *Sdf*, pp. 89–93.
[106] B/G, *Storia del PCI*, pp. 212–215.
[107] This was his eventual nom de plume. Silone was born into this world in 1900 as Secondino Tranquilli, and was known in the underground also as "Pasquini."
[108] B/G, *Storia del PCI*, pp. 215–217.
[109] Leto, *OVRA*, p. 44; B/G, *Storia del PCI*, pp. 217–218.

115

ing covert propaganda on as broad a scale as possible. *L'Unità*'s first clandestine issue appeared in Lilliputian format on January 1, 1927; the second on January 21; and the third on February 5. It came out in various editions (sometimes in as many as 5,000 copies) in Turin, Milan, and Rome, and was distributed at night by automobile over broad areas.[110] Other publications included *Avanguardia*, put out by the Youth Federation; *Battaglie sindacali* ("Syndical Battles"), circulated among the industrial workers; and a lithographed humorous sheet, *Galletto rosso* ("Red Cock").[111] In March 1927 the first issue of the authoritative theoretical journal, *Stato operaio* ("Worker's State"), was published; in 1929 it had a subscription list of slightly more than 1,000. This significant serial, which appeared regularly in France until August 1939 and thereafter in New York, is an invaluable source of information. Somewhat later the PCI also published a Paris newspaper, *Vita operaia* ("Worker's Life").[112]

On one occasion in this period the Reds sought to stir up labor trouble in Italy. They noted carefully that Fascism's "battle of the lira" had deflated the currency some 40 per cent in the year ending June 1927. It seemed to them that however satisfactory this deflation might be to certain creditor groups, it would rankle in the craw of the workers, for their wages declined faster and stayed down longer than did price levels. The Communists therefore decided to exploit this grievance. They called a strike among the rice workers near Vercelli and Novara in June 1927.[113] It was a complete failure. Incidentally, it seems to have been the only labor disturbance in Italy between the inauguration of the dictatorship and the advent of the Depression. Perhaps some of the explanation may be found in Mussolini's prohibition of strikes and in the workers' attitude of hopeful expectancy. After all, unemployment was still relatively low during this period (439,000 were listed officially in January 1928 and but 247,000

[110] Leto, OVRA, p. 45.
[111] S/M, Sdf, p. 483.
[112] *Relazione della Direzione del PCI al V° Congresso*, p. 7 ff.; Giorgi Dimitrov, "The Tenth Anniversary of *Stato operaio*," in *The United Front, the Struggle against Fascism and War* (New York, 1938), p. 221; and "Manfredo" [pseud. for Riccardo Boatti], "Il Partito Comunista dalle leggi eccezionali in poi: Breve sguardo retrospettivo," *Quaderni di "Giustizia e Libertà,"* No. 6 (Paris, March 1933), pp. 25–34; and Garosci, Sdf, p. 93.
[113] Raimondo Luraghi, "Momenti della lotta antifascista in Piemonte negli anni 1926–1943," MLI, No. 28/29 (Jan.–Mar. 1954), p. 13.

in June of that year).[114] Many may have felt that the country's economy was reasonably satisfactory, or at least no worse than before Fascism.

More important than stirring up labor disturbances was the PCI effort to resuscitate and capture the CGL, which had been one of the strongholds of the revisionist Socialists before the Fascists destroyed it in January 1927. To this end, a group headed by Ravazzoli called a meeting in Milan on February 20, 1927. It also was attended by a few maximalist Socialists, labor organizers, and nonparty people. The group called for determined reorganization of the workers and for reliance upon class struggle for eventual victory. Their slogan was "Leave the Fascist syndicates! Join the CGL!"

But the skeletal CGL which the Communists claimed to have rebuilt was denied recognition by the Amsterdam International Trades Union Federation, identified with the Second International. Instead, the revisionist Amsterdam body gave its blessing in September 1927 to a new CGL formed among the *fuorusciti* in France by Bruno Buozzi, the right-wing Socialist who had been secretary of the old CGL.[115] Not till after Mussolini's fall did the Communists win control of the great labor organizations.

Catastrophes of 1927 and 1928

Fascist police, meanwhile, threw out their second dragnet to pull in PCI commanders early in the summer of 1927. The penitentiary wardens who had welcomed Gramsci, Terracini, and others in November 1926 now opened their gates to take in dozens more. One of the key men to be caught was Giovanni Parodi, who had taken over direction of the party in Milan after Terracini's arrest. Another was Aldo Penazzato, inter-regional chief in Bologna. His apprehension led to the roundup of most of the PCI conspirators in Tuscany and Emilia—the gravest blow of the year.

Next to be discovered was the secret Internal Center in Milan. Because of a tip-off, the four members of the Central Committee (Tresso, Ravazzoli, Leonetti, and Ravera) escaped. Finally, in March 1928, the police caught up with LiCausi, one of the

---

[114] S/M, *Sdf*, pp. 418, 429, and *passim*.
[115] *Ibid.*, p. 486; cf. B/G, *Storia del PCI*, pp. 218–220.

national figures, who had fled to the coast near Pisa with incriminating evidence.[116] It was also during this phase that two imprisoned Reds died after torture—Gastone Sozzi (a native of Cesena and Imola) in a Perugia prison and Giuseppe Riva in Genoa. Their memory came to be hallowed in party hagiographies.[117]

Session after session of the Special Tribunal convened in 1927–1928 to condemn in a veritable litany the many dozens of PCI leaders, big and small.[118] The most trumpeted trials took place in May and June 1928 after long preparation. These monster *processoni* involved Gramsci and many of the top leaders. Because of Gramsci's parliamentary status the charges against him had to be somewhat vague; yet the public prosecutor insisted upon the need for not less than a twenty-year stint to "prevent this brain from functioning." [119] The court was obliging; on June 4 it found everyone guilty. Going beyond the call of duty, it handed to Gramsci a sentence 4 months and 5 days longer than that which the prosecutor had asked. Giovanni Roveda got some 20 years; Umberto Terracini of Genoa (co-founder of *Ordine nuovo*, close associate of Gramsci, and future president of the 1946 Constituent Assembly) was sentenced to 22 years, 9 months, 3 days. Mauro Scoccimarro of Udine, member of the secretariat and delegate to the Comintern, got 20 years, 9 months, 5 days; Girolamo LiCausi, a pivotal figure in the Internal Center, 21 years. The last three remained in detention until Badoglio released them in August 1943. All told, the sentences announced on June 4 amounted to 238 years.[120] On June 22 the court condemned six Roman Communists to 21 years each. And on October 17, amid some misgivings since there

[116] *Ibid.*, pp. 230–235.

[117] F. Chilanti, *Gastone Sozzi* (Rome, 1955).

[118] On July 23, 1927, it sentenced seventeen from the one small city of Imola; on October 17, nine more party directors; on January 31, 1928, in Florence, eleven more; on February 13, 1928, seven Venetians; on March 19, some twenty-eight Southerners; on April 6, Giovanni Parodi, Altiero Spinelli (a future paladin of the European Federalist Movement), and Vignocchi; later that month, sixteen Apulian Communists; on May 4, eleven from Messina; on May 8, fourteen from Taranto; and on June 8, twelve from Varese. And the list continued. S/M, *Sdf*, pp. 323–325.

[119] D. Zucaro, "A. Gramsci a S. Vittore per l'istruttoria del processone (con alcuni documenti inediti)," *MLI*, No. 16 (1952), pp. 3–16; B/G, *Storia del PCI*, pp. 235–240.

[120] Robotti and Germanetto, *Trent'anni di lotte dei comunisti italiani*, p. 266.

seemed to be no threat to state security, the court handed down its first death sentence to the Communist Michele della Maggiora, accused of murdering a Fascist who had bothered him and thereafter shooting a bystander.[121]

Gramsci in prison

Upon his apprehension November 8, 1926, the tubercular Gramsci had been sent to the isle of Ustica. In January 1927 he was brought to San Vittore prison in Milan, and after the *processone* he was transferred to the prison hospital of Tura di Bari. He rapidly lost strength and suffered grave hemorrhages and fainting spells in August 1931 and March 1933. When the Fascists suggested that he petition for clemency he proudly refused. Communists throughout the world, meantime, made a *cause célèbre* of his incarceration; they obtained support from such cultural leaders in the free world as Romain Rolland and the Archbishop of Canterbury. During the last months of his detention Mussolini had Gramsci transferred to a tubercular clinic near Formia, but it was too late for medical help. Realizing that Gramsci was near death, the *Duce*, for propagandistic purposes, reduced the sentence by several years, with the intention of letting him die a free man. Transferred to a Rome clinic, the 46-year-old Communist intellectual died there on April 27, 1937, three days after the expiration of his shortened sentence. His death was attributed to uremic poisoning. If not caused, it was at least aggravated by his prison treatment.[122]

While a prisoner Gramsci maintained some contacts with relatives and managed to obtain and read a great number of books. In addition to writing many letters to his Russian-born wife, he jotted down voluminous notes on a spate of philosophical, literary, and historical topics. Eventually these were transmitted by devious ways to the party faithful who preserved and published them after the war in an eight-volume collection, *Quaderni del Carcere*. To fool the censors Gramsci rendered "historical materialism" as *"filosofia della prassi"*; he referred to

[121] S/M, *Sdf*, pp. 324–326; Gavagnin, *Vent'anni di resistenza*, pp. 244–245, 312–313.
[122] Togliatti, *Gramsci*, p. 58; Lombardo-Radice and Carbone, *Vita di Antonio Gramsci*, pp. 231–233 ff.; and Domenico Zucaro, *Vita del carcere di Antonio Gramsci* (Milan-Rome, 1954).

Lenin as *"Ilic"* or *"Vilici,"* and to Stalin as *"Giuseppe Bessa-rione."* The notations took up such problems as the formation of an Italian intellectual class and the reasons for its different ways of thinking. He particularly subjected to searching analysis Croce's revisionist critique of Marxism.[123] In early years Gramsci had been deeply influenced by some of Croce's canons of criticism;[124] he always respected him, and he hoped that somehow the sage would go back to his turn-of-the-century object of intellectual curiosity.[125] Yet he also came to believe that the Neapolitan senator exerted an "unhealthy" domination over southern liberalism and prevented it from adopting "progressive," "class-conscious" positions. Among the other topics about which Gramsci ruminated were literary criticism, Machiavelli, the Reformation and Counter Reformation, the Risorgimento, Catholic Action, journalistic techniques, and Henry Ford's industrial "exploitation."[126]

In most of Gramsci's writings there was evidence of the traditionally powerful humanistic as well as positivistic tendencies in Italian scholarship. To be sure, Gramsci talked of dictatorship of the proletariat; yet he seemed to sense the need for at least some intellectual freedom. "Spiritually he dwelt in the pre-1914 world: he never understood totalitarianism in its twentieth-century incarnation," H. Stuart Hughes has averred; and another non-Marxist, Count Sforza, has raised seriously the question whether Gramsci, if he had lived beyond the Fascist era, might not eventually have gone through the kind of evolution that detached from rigid Marxism such men as Antonio Labriola, Croce, Silone, and Tasca.[127] Obviously this must remain a subject of speculation; certainly the Communist *pontifex maximus* could

[123] Of special interest are the critiques of Gramsci in Garosci's chapter, "Totalitarismo e storicismo nel pensiero di Gramsci," in his *Pensiero politico e storiografia moderna*, pp. 191–260; and in H. Stuart Hughes, *Consciousness and Society: The Reorientation of European Social Thought, 1890–1930* (New York, 1958), pp. 96–104.

[124] "In February 1917 . . . I was tendentially almost Crocean," wrote Gramsci in *Il materialismo storico e la filosofia di Benedetto Croce* (Turin, 1948), p. 199; cf. *ibid.*, pp. 84–86, 105, 200, 224–225, 243.

[125] See *supra*, Ch. III, Benedetto Croce's moral leadership.

[126] See preface to Antonio Gramsci, *Lettere dal carcere* (Turin, 1949), and the editors' note in Milan and Vighi (eds.), *La Resistenza al fascismo*, pp. 23–25.

[127] Hughes, *Consciousness and Society*, p. 102; Sforza, *Contemporary Italy*, p. 330.

120

hardly have been expected to desert his ideology during the years when he was one of Fascism's most celebrated victims.

Italian Communism in isolation (1928–1934)

The six years from the *processone* until the inauguration of the Popular Front would have been hard in any case for the depleted ranks of Italian Communists but were even harder because the Communists insisted upon remaining apart from the Socialists and other anti-Fascists. This noncollaborationism was prescribed in the summer of 1928 by the Comintern Sixth Congress, dominated by the victorious Stalin. Turning its back upon such "united front" experiments as had taken place in Italy from time to time between 1921 and 1924, it went even so far as to denounce revisionist Socialist parties as "Social-Fascists." The left wings of the Social Democratic parties were regarded as even more dangerous obstacles to revolution than their right flanks.[128] Thus any serious co-operation between Communists and Socialists was out of the question.

There is reason to suspect that Togliatti was not too well pleased. Certainly it did not correspond to Gramsci's policy (prior to November 1924) of seeking "united fronts" of democratic groups to fight Fascism. Gramsci had emphasized that Fascism was a political expression of the most backward *bourgeoisie* of the country (the great landowners) but he did not regard it as a typical manifestation of the *bourgeoisie* considered as a whole. Implicit in his definition, therefore, was the possibility that Communists might find support among the liberal *bourgeoisie*, who could play an active role in the struggle against Fascism. Gramsci had seemed to envisage a policy that was not to be adopted by his comrades until the Popular Front a decade later (and even more effectively in the last years of World War II, when the PCI advocated a national anti-Fascist, anti-German front).[129]

In 1928 Togliatti offered a definition of Fascism that was

[128] Franz Borkenau, *World Communism: History of the Communist International* (New York, 1939), Ch. 20; Isaac Deutscher, *Stalin: A Political Biography* (New York, 1949), pp. 402–406; Martin Ebon, *World Communism Today* (New York, 1948), pp. 20–22; and B/G, *Storia del PCI*, pp. 241–251.
[129] *Ibid.*, pp. 145–146.

121

basically similar to Gramsci's. Rejecting any notion that Fascism was an insane "parenthesis" in Italian history, he declared that it was an integral phase of capitalist development. Specifically it was "a reactionary movement of the large industrial and agrarian *bourgeoisie*. Above all one can state that Fascism is the most important system of integral reaction that has thus far existed in countries where capitalism has reached a certain grade of development." [130] Yet Togliatti and his colleagues meekly followed the Comintern line when Stalin declared that "Fascism is the militant organization of the *bourgeoisie* which bases itself on the active support of Social Democracy. Objectively, Social Democracy is the moderate wing of Fascism. . . . [Fascism and Social Democracy] are not antipodes but twins." [131]

Thus the Italian Communists held aloof from such agencies as the *émigré* Anti-Fascist Concentration, sponsored in France in April 1927 chiefly by Socialists, Republicans, and officials of the old CGL. [132] They ridiculed it as a "second Aventine" and said they "would not participate in the new political *combinazione* of Masonic inspiration, but fight it, mobilizing against it the independent and class forces of the proletariat." [133] And in similar vein, after its birth in 1929, [134] they scorned the fascistic Giustizia e Libertà of that "rich dilettante," Carlo Rosselli. That such tactics of isolation cost them recruits, they now concede. [135]

The rigorousness of the line was revealed unmistakably in 1928 when Stalin denounced personally the "rightist" Angelo Tasca (who recently had been awarded a position on the new executive committee of the Comintern). Tasca's chief sins in-

[130] Togliatti in *Stato operaio*, Aug. 10, 1928, cited by Pietro Secchia, "Palmiro Togliatti, capo del Partito Comunista e dei lavoratori italiani," *Rinascita*, x (March 1953), 146.
[131] Joseph V. Stalin, *Sochinenya* (Moscow, 1946–1948), vi, 282, quoted by Deutscher, *Stalin*, pp. 406–407.
[132] See *supra*, Ch. ii, Political regrouping abroad.
[133] Quoted in S/M, *Sdf*, p. 485.
[134] See *supra*, Ch. ii, Giustizia e Libertà. *Cf.* Ercoli, "Sul movimento di 'Giustizia e Libertà,'" *Stato operaio*, v (1931), pp. 463–473; E. R., "Il programma di 'Giustizia e Libertà,'" *ibid.*, vi (1932), pp. 87–96.
[135] "One cannot deny that the rigid orientation assumed toward the anti-Fascist struggle prevented for some time the party's gathering around itself strata of intermediate opinion, ideologically and politically opposed to Fascism; these fell into a generic anti-Fascism or into Catholic Action, or ended up easily absorbed by the infinite 'reserves' and 'safety-valve agencies' which the Fascist State had prepared, especially for the youth." Maurizio Ferrara, "La nostra lotta per l'unità," *Rinascita*, xi (January 1954), 4.

cluded criticism of Stalin's German policy and his collectivization of agriculture; advocacy of an accord with the Socialists;
and denial of the imminence of an economic crisis within the
capitalist system with attendant revolutionary possibilities (such
as Stalin was predicting at the Sixth Comintern Congress). In
March 1929 the PCI Central Committee called upon Tasca to
"explain." They rejected his arguments and expelled him from
the party.[136] Taking up residence in France, Tasca (henceforth
known as "A. Rossi") became chief editor (1929–1934) of Henri
Barbusse's Paris *Monde,* and from 1934 to 1940 was foreign-
policy editor of the SFIO daily *Populaire.* Meanwhile, in 1934
he attorned to the Italian Socialist "center" in France and directed *Politica socialista,* designed to circulate covertly in Italy.
In 1938 his most important book, *The Rise of Italian Fascism,*
came off the press.

Communist activities in Italy during 1929 were unimpressive.
In March when Mussolini permitted his people to vote in "pulp-
paper revels" for his hand-picked slate of 400 deputies, the Communists passed the word to their followers to vote "no," whereas
the *émigré* Anti-Fascist Concentration recommended abstention.
The government declared that 89.63 per cent of the electorate
voted and that 8,506,576 favored the parliamentary list, with
only 136,198 opposing it. All the figures were suspect, of course,
for the voting system was scandalously rigged.[137]

During the summer the PCI concentrated its propaganda on
the theme of international peace, so desperately needed by the
Soviet Union, then intent upon industrializing itself. It was not
till October that the Communists formulated any clear policy of
entrenching themselves with the protean Fascist "mass organizations"—despite their own warnings against getting separated
from the masses. Secret conferences of labor leaders in Lyon and
Marseille heard Togliatti's instructions for infiltrating and subverting Fascist syndicates.[138] By year's end the PCI hopefully
reported an increase in the incidence of unrest in the northern

---

[136] Angelo Tasca, "Per una storia politica del fuoruscitismo," *Itinerari* (Genoa),
II (1954), No. 9–10, pp. 230–250, and No. 11–12, pp. 355–367; Angelo Tasca,
In Francia nella bufera (Modena, 1958), pp. 7–9; S/M, *Sdf,* p. 509; B/G, *Storia
del PCI,* pp. 247–251; Garosci, *Sdf,* p. 97.
[137] S/M, *Sdf,* p. 375; Togliatti (ed.), *Trenta anni di vita e di lotte,* pp. 100–110.
[138] *Ibid.,* Ch. 3; S/M, *Sdf,* pp. 507–508.

factories. To what extent this was politically inspired can only be conjectured.[139]

If 1929 was a fairly quiet year, 1930 was not. In *Stato operaio* in January and February Togliatti and Luigi Longo of the Youth Federation announced a sensational *svolta* (*i.e.*, "sharp new twist in strategy"). They proposed to the external Political Office that the majority of available party members be sent back to Italy for undercover work. Chiefly responsible for this decision was the line adopted by the Comintern Sixth Congress—a pronunciamento which seemed to be borne out by the Wall Street "crash" of October 1929. (Even Mussolini seemed to subscribe to the Comintern forecast of an imminent economic crisis of capitalism, with consequent revolutionary possibilities, when he declared that the Depression was a crisis "of" the very capitalist system itself and not just a cyclical maladjustment "within" it.) If this judgment were true, then the days of capitalism were numbered, especially in a country whose economy was as precarious as Italy's, and it would be imperative for the Communists to throw in their reserves for the showdown.[140]

This *svolta* met with much hostility from three members of the internal Political Office—Tresso, Leonetti, and Ravazzoli. Knowing the domestic situation firsthand, they doubted the chances of an immediate revolution and advocated, instead, careful preparation and renewal of collaboration with Socialists. In the voting this "group of three" (as the cabal came to be dubbed in PCI chronicles) found themselves opposed by Togliatti, Longo, and Ravera.[141] Because of the tie vote, Togliatti called in Pietro Secchia, a representative of the Youth Federation but not formally in the Political Office, to cast the deciding ballot. Secchia obediently cast his in favor of the anthropophagous "theses of 'Ercoli,' "[142] and in June the party expelled "the

[139] Togliatti (ed.), *Trenta anni di vita e di lotte*, p. 113 ff.

[140] Fidia Sassano, "La 'svolta' del PCI nel 1930," *Il Ponte*, XII (1956), pp. 1694–1707; Garosci, *Sdf*, p. 95; and S/M, *Sdf*, p. 508.

[141] Silone, a member of the Political Office, was opposed to the *svolta* but did not vote, as he was in Switzerland in poor health. He paired himself with another absentee, Ruggiero Grieco, then in Moscow and favorable to the *svolta*.

[142] Later Secchia was to write, "The crisis of the directing center of the party was the gravest that the PCI has ever passed through and was overcome and liquidated rapidly thanks especially to the work of Palmiro Togliatti and to the aid of the Communist International." "P. Togliatti," *Rinascita*, X (March 1953), p. 146.

three." Later they joined the Trotskyists in France.[143] The crisis marked the last time in the clandestine era when there was open dissension within the PCI (though there were other expulsions). Henceforth Togliatti kept a firm grip and shaped the leadership in the way it was to stay for the rest of the struggle.[144]

To replace "the three," Togliatti named Luigi Frausin, a native of Muggia (near Trieste); Luigi Amadesi; and Giuseppe DiVittorio, an experienced labor organizer from Apulia. Orders went out for conspiratorial work in Italy to proceed at full speed. The number of couriers traveling across the frontier increased greatly, and party cells emerged in some places where hitherto they had not existed or had been inactive. Naples was probably the most important of these new groups. There a handful of young intellectuals of the lower middle class who were interested in the economic problems of the *Mezzogiorno* took the initiative. Manlio Rossi-Doria was leader of the cluster. He had passed through a spiritual crisis in 1928–1929 when he renounced a theological career in favor of Marxism. (In later years he was to become a professor of agricultural economics at the University of Naples and repudiate all narrow Marxian interpretations of history.) [145] Traveling to Paris ostensibly for academic reasons in January 1930, Rossi-Doria received party instructions and upon his return organized a group, all of whom were to be prominent in years ahead. They included Emilio Sereni, who previously had been active in the Rome Jewish community, and two Neapolitans —Giorgio Amendola, son of the Aventinian chieftain, and Eugenio Reale, a medical student. The police caught all but the latter by October.[146]

News of strikes in Italy during the first half of 1930 cheered Togliatti and his companions. It was reported that 10,000 textile workers had quit their jobs for more than a week in Varano Borghi; that some 3,000 had struck against new wage cuts in a

[143] Ravazzoli died in sickness and poverty in France in 1936; Tresso disappeared mysteriously during the French Résistance in 1941 after being liberated from Nazi detention by Communist Maquis; Leonetti renounced all overt political activity.

[144] B/G, Storia del PCI, pp. 252–272; S/M, Sdf, p. 508; Garosci, Sdf, p. 98; Robotti and Germanetto, Trent'anni di lotte dei comunisti italiani, pp. 76–84.

[145] Cf. his paper read at the American Historical Association in December 1957: "The Land Tenure System and Class in Southern Italy," *American Historical Review,* LXIV (1958), pp. 46–53.

[146] B/G, Storia del PCI, pp. 275–277, 287.

Bergamo cotton mill; that in the Apulian town of Martina Franca people had assaulted Fascist clubs in protest against new taxes on wine; and that on May Day numerous slogans of a Communist type had been scrawled on walls.[147] PCI leaders abroad greatly overestimated their political import.

By early summer additional party officials reached the major cities. Of these the most important were Camillo Ravera, a member of the Political Office, and Pietro Tosin and Luigi Guermandi, both of whom were entrusted with reconstructing a central liaison office in Milan. Unhappily for their cause, the first two were apprehended in July. But others kept at the unending task of spinning the gossamer web of conspiracy as best they could. Vincenzo Moscatelli of Novara (who became a famed Communist guerrilla commander in the Resistenza Armata) was temporarily more successful. Only 22 years of age in 1930, he already had spent five years' training in party schools abroad. Sent to Bologna, Moscatelli was able to reactivate a promising network. His task was facilitated by Mussolini's slashing of factory wages 8 to 10 per cent, farm wages 10 to 25 per cent that autumn, and civil servants 12 per cent in the late autumn.[148] An imprudent Communist demonstration in Modena, however, led to mass arrests in November. Altogether, 114 were seized in the Romagna—25 of them in Parma alone and 18 in Ferrara. In the wake of this major blow to the underground, Moscatelli was condemned to 16½ years but released in 1936.[149]

PCI Fourth Congress in Germany (April 1931)

Meanwhile, the PCI directorate decided to schedule the party's Fourth Congress (the last during the Fascist era) for the spring of 1931 in Germany. The party modestly claimed a membership of 7,000 at this stage. In order to choose delegates from the internal apparatus, Togliatti dispatched Secchia to Italy at the end of 1930. He managed to reorganize the Internal Center in Milan and establish contacts with many in the underground before the police caught up with him in Genoa in March. According to some accounts, the police forced him to tell much; yet he succeeded in hiding the true nature of his mission, so

[147] S/M, Sdf, pp. 508–509; cf. Robotti and Germanetto, Trent'anni di lotte dei comunisti italiani, pp. 89–93.
[148] Salvemini, Under the Axe of Fascism, pp. 238–264; S/M, Sdf, p. 423.
[149] B/G, Storia del PCI, pp. 277–280.

that all of the delegates got to the congress. A few months later Secchia was condemned to 17 years and 9 months, and was not freed till Marshal Badoglio came to power.[150]

On April 10, 1931, some sixty leaders of the PCI (about three fourths of them straight from Italy) assembled in a well-guarded building in a woods near Düsseldorf, conveniently put at their disposal by comrades of the German Communist Party, and then moved on to Cologne for their final conclave a few days later. For many of the delegates this was their first sight of such bigwigs as Togliatti, Longo, Grieco, Gennari, and Dozza. They knew that it was men such as these who would tell them what to do; no one dared to question their line. The first big news they heard was Togliatti's announcement of the arrest of Secchia, which naturally dampened their ardor. Even Togliatti, it would seem, had sensed by this time that chances of a quick revolution had been overestimated, for his speech implied that the situation was not what he had assumed it to be during the 1930 fight against the junto of "the three."[151] Nevertheless, he doggedly reaffirmed PCI goals: "insurrection of the Italian people, led by the working class, against Fascism; the destruction of Fascism and capitalism by revolutionary methods; a workers' and peasants' government, a soviet Italy, the dictatorship of the proletariat."[152] He handed them a new slogan to take home: *"Per il pane, per il lavoro, per la terra, per la pace, per la libertà!"* ("For bread, for work, for land, for peace, for freedom!") The congress dutifully ratified the sundry expulsions and gave unanimous approval to all questions. Togliatti took special pains to denounce the Socialists (particularly Nenni and Saragat) and the "petty bourgeois" Anti-Fascist Concentration. Just before the delegates packed their bags they heard the news of the fall of King Alfonso XIII of Spain; to many this seemed a good omen of things to come in Italy.[153] Not long after the congress came the purge (in July) of Silone. A year later (August 1932) the

---

[150] *Ibid.*, pp. 280–283; Pietro Secchia and Cino Moscatelli, *Il Monte Rosa è sceso a Milano* (Turin, 1958), p. 65.

[151] PCI historians later explained with masterful understatement, "There is no doubt that in the first months of 1930 the directing organs of the party evaluated the immediate prospects in a somewhat exaggerated fashion, insisting that an acute revolutionary situation was fast approaching and launching watchwords that were premature." Quoted in S/M, *Sdf*, p. 509.

[152] Quoted in B/G, *Storia del PCI*, p. 284.

[153] Robotti and Germanetto, *Trent'anni di lotte dei comunisti italiani*, pp. 94–98.

Political Office, meeting in "enlarged session," announced still other expulsions.[154]

Meanwhile, a new Central Committee came into being, with Togliatti, of course, remaining secretary.[155] To direct the Internal Center Togliatti named Battista Santhià, an experienced Torinese revolutionary who had worked in the Fiat plants. Helping him in his labors (which were most fruitful in Piedmont and Liguria) was Sante Vincenzi. They paid special attention to volatile rice workers in the paddies near Vercelli and Novara, where strikes broke out in June 1931.[156] In Naples too underground operations were resumed, mainly by Eugenio Reale, who had evaded the police. In Emilia a certain painter (Carlo Alpi) took up where Moscatelli had left off. But history soon repeated itself. LaSpezia police picked up the trail of Santhià and arrested him. Vincenzi and others of the Internal Center were also nabbed, as were many in the Neapolitan and Emilian outposts.[157]

Seemingly undismayed, Togliatti and his comrades abroad resumed their Sysiphean labor and in mid-1931 chose Frausin, a trusted Triestian, to direct the Internal Center. He restored operations on a limited scale and spotted followers in major northern cities. But the dreary tale was the same. By spring police had demolished the Venetian nucleus and then the whole Internal Center. Frausin regained his liberty only after Mussolini's fall, at which time he became a partisan commander in his native region until he was captured and shot by the SS.[158]

So long as unemployment persisted on a mass scale [159] the PCI could not afford to give up the fight, even though most party

[154] *Ibid.*, pp. 83–84; S/M, *Sdf*, p. 510.
[155] Others included Grieco, Egidio Gennari, Anselmo Marabini, Battista Santhià, Giuseppe DiVittorio, Luigi Frausin, Giuseppe Dozza, Luigi Longo, Domenico Ciufoli, and Luigi Amadesi. B/G, *Storia del PCI*, p. 285.
[156] Robotti and Germanetto, *Trent'anni di lotte dei comunisti italiani*, pp. 99–103.
[157] *Ibid.*, pp. 103–104; B/G, *Storia del PCI*, pp. 285–288.
[158] *Ibid.*, p. 289; Robotti and Germanetto, *Trent'anni di lotte*, pp. 109–110.
[159] Unemployment mounted rapidly until the economic tide turned at last in 1934 and 1935. Doubtless true figures were higher than these "official" ones:

January 1928	439,000	December 1932	1,129,000
June 1928	247,000	December 1933	1,132,000
November 1932	945,000	November 1934	969,944

Statistics cited by S/M, *Sdf*, pp. 261, 418–422, 429; *cf.* Salvemini, *Under the Axe of Fascism*, pp. 238–264.

leaders seemed to sense after Frausin's capture that early revolution was impossible. Thus they tried doggedly to steer into political paths the popular demonstrations that occasionally broke out in the most depressed areas.[160] And in 1932 they appointed Gian Carlo Pajetta to supersede Frausin at the Internal Center. He met with some luck in Emilia until he was arrested in Reggio in February 1933 and sentenced to 21 years by the Special Tribunal. Meanwhile, police in Genoa caught Arturo Colombi and in April 1934 crushed a nucleus headed by Leonida Roncagli.[161]

Capture of these groups "marked the definite liquidation of every organized Communist activity in the peninsula." [162] Prior to 1934 the PCI, though possessing an apparatus abroad, had devoted most of its energies to clandestine work in depression-ridden Italy; after that date the PCI could claim very few links with the Italian scene, and necessarily turned its proselyting efforts toward the *fuorusciti*. The minimal Communist activity that took place in Italy after 1934 was conducted chiefly through "Trojan horse" infiltration of Fascist youth, cultural, labor, military, and other "mass" organizations.[163] "Operation Seduction" replaced "Operation Sedition" in the PCI manual of strategy.

By 1934 the Communist policy of rigid isolation from the Socialists and of reckless sacrifice of party cadres was drawing to an end. This happened none too soon, for it had played a part in helping Hitler to power. When fascistic forces almost overturned the French Third Republic in February 1934 it was manifest that the Communist line needed to be modified. The *svolta*

---

[160] Cf. Robotti and Germanetto, *Trent'anni di lotte dei comunisti italiani*, pp. 126–131, for some instances between 1931 and 1934.

[161] In this roundup, Longo's wife, Teresa Noce, who had organized a rice workers' strike that spring, escaped.

[162] B/G, *Storia del PCI*, pp. 307–308.

[163] The Executive Committee of the Comintern, meeting in its Twelfth Plenum in September 1932, advised the PCI to "come out from underground by developing the mass struggle against the Fascist dictatorship on the basis of the defense of the everyday interests of the toilers, taking advantage of Fascist meetings, organizing impromptu meetings in the factories, penetrating the Fascist trade unions, cultural and co-operative organizations, preparing and carrying on strikes and demonstrations. . . . Mass illegal work must be increased to the maximum extent." In the face of such criticism, Togliatti conceded that his party "failed to change its slogans, its methods of work and forms of organization with the necessary rapidity. This tardiness was utilized by Fascism and cost the party heavy losses." Ebon, *World Communism Today*, p. 233; Dimitrov, *The United Front*, pp. 221–222; and Togliatti, *Gramsci*, p. 54.

was signalled in June 1934 by "unity of action" pacts between the French Communist and Socialist parties, and on August 17, 1934, by agreements between the equivalent Italian parties. These opened the way for the Popular Front and a quick surge in Communist strength.[164]

Fascism solidified

While Red conspirators in Italy succeeded one another in kaleidoscopic confusion, Mussolini boasted of a measure of economic recovery in the nation. This was accompanied by much pump-priming by the IRI (Institute for Industrial Reconstruction), a large-scale public works program, promotion of agricultural autarchy, loud propagandizing of a new "corporate economy" to supersede moribund liberal capitalism, and—certainly not least—by a greatly stepped-up military program in anticipation of the wars that were indispensable to Fascism.[165]

Though the prosperity was flimsy at best, the regime seemed, outwardly, more robust than ever. Mussolini's prestige on the international stage was augmented by the march to power of Hitler, who in those years showed considerable deference to the older *Duce*. Membership in the PNF climbed from 807,034 in October 1932 to 1,416,289 a year later, though it should be recalled that many bureaucrats were obliged to join. The plebiscite of early 1934 was shamelessly rigged; yet one can not entirely ignore the results, which surely revealed no ground swell of opposition to the regime (or, perhaps more accurately, to its *Duce*). Clearly, the Depression, withering though it was for the democracies of the world, was not enough to fell Mussolini and his bombastic dictatorship.

[164] Galli, *Storia del Partito Comunista Italiano*, pp. 160–182.
[165] On economic trends see Salvemini, *Under the Axe of Fascism*, pp. 112–142; Schmidt, *The Corporate State in Action*; E. Rossi, *I padroni del vapore*; and Felice Guarneri, *Battaglie economiche tra le due guerre* (2 vols.; Milan, 1953).

CHAPTER IV · POPULAR FRONT ERA

August 1934 – August 1939

PCI-PSI "unity of action" pact

THE August 17, 1934, "unity of action" pact between the PCI and PSI marked a radical change in strategy, though it did not force either signatory to renounce its basic principles. The preamble conceded that "on the broad level of principles and of judgments regarding the international situation, there remain between the two [parties] fundamental divergences as to doctrine, methods, and tactics which are a barrier to a general political front . . . and organic fusion." [1] Many revisionist Socialists (including Modigliani, Morgari, Saragat, and Tasca) had strong reservations about Stalinist policies but preferred not to trouble the waters at this turn.[2] The pact offered the Italian Communists ideal soil for the sowing of tares at the expense of the Socialists, just as similar pacts did among the French Marxian parties.[3]

The two Italian parties agreed to publish in Paris the weekly *Grido del popolo* ("People's Cry"), edited by Teresa Noce. Making clear their hostility to corporatism and any new wage cuts, they also denounced support of the Austrian clerico-fascistic regime that had emerged after suppression of the Viennese Socialists in February 1934. But their most vociferous propaganda was concentrated on the need for abolition of the Special Tribunal, for prison reform, and for amnesties for political prisoners, beginning with the tubercular PCI director Gramsci, who was languishing in his eighth year of detention. The campaign reached its climax with mass demonstrations in Paris.[4]

Nenni was anxious to achieve still tighter union of Italian Marxists and was even ready to accede to Communist demands that Socialists promise to rush to the Soviet Union's aid in case it was invaded, while merely preserving neutrality should war occur elsewhere. It seemed as if Nenni had come to accept fully the Muscovite proletarian dictatorship; the last time during this

[1] Quoted in Garosci, VCR, II, 111.
[2] Arfè, *Storia dell' "Avanti!" 1926–1940*, p. 109 ff.
[3] *Cf.* John T. Marcus, *French Socialism in the Crisis Years, 1933–1936* (New York, 1958), Ch. 2, and *passim*.
[4] Garosci, *Sdf*, pp. 83–86, 169; S/M, *Sdf*, pp. 644, 669.

period he was to voice criticism of the Kremlin was in May 1935 when he was disturbed by Stalin's approval of French rearmament.[5]

Seventh Congress of the Comintern (1935)

Delegates of the Communist parties of the world trekked to Moscow in the summer of 1935 for the Comintern Seventh Congress. As soon as they had applauded a motion by Togliatti to dispatch comradely greetings to Stalin, they sat down to hear the major address of the conclave, delivered by Georgi Dimitrov, the new secretary-general. Speaking on the subject of the "united front" and the "popular front," he gave his approval to the "unity of action" pacts that had been signed in France. He made it clear that the old slogans about Fascists' and Social Democrats' being "two peas in a pod" must be discarded; the latter must no longer be smeared as "Social-Fascists." The "united front" of Socialists and Communists, fine as far as it went, must be expanded into a still broader "popular front" including "the great mass of peasants, the mass of the small *bourgeoisie*, assigning to their most pressing objectives a special place in the program of the anti-Fascist front. . . . We must [create] elective organs outside the party in the anti-Fascist front which can reach in their sphere of influence greater masses than can the parties and workers' organizations that thus far have come into existence." The culmination should be "a government that will carry out an effective struggle, not with words but deeds, against Fascism . . . ; then the Communists, although remaining irreconcilable enemies of any kind of bourgeois government and supporters of Soviet power, will nevertheless in the face of the rising Fascist danger, give their support to such a government." To this, Togliatti contributed an additional thought: "From the theoretical point of view there is no doubt about the possibility of the Bolsheviks' collaborating with capitalist states, even on the level of military co-operation." After all, the USSR had entered the League of Nations and had just signed alliance treaties with France and Czechoslovakia.[6]

Discussion made it clear that Communist-Socialist unity

[5] Garosci, *Sdf*, pp. 109–120.
[6] Quotations from B/G, *Storia del PCI*, pp. 310–311; *cf*. Garosci, *Sdf*, p. 136.

should continue as long as the proletariat was in a defensive position; whenever conditions permitted a new Communist offensive, the immediate program of anti-Fascist resistance should give way to the maximum goal of overthrowing capitalism. At that juncture Socialists would have to go along with the Communists or risk being abandoned. The Comintern did not indicate precisely how long or to what degree there should be an alliance with bourgeois groups willing to fight for restoration of parliamentary government, but it implied that this should endure as long as they had common interests.[7]

Togliatti, who held a post in the Comintern secretariat, remained in Moscow, while most of the other Italian delegates headed back to France to intensify their propaganda among their co-nationals. Since the April 1934 arrests of Pajetta and others within Italy, the PCI possessed no effective internal organization, but it did not halt plans to infiltrate Fascist youth and labor agencies—a policy which Dimitrov had preached vigorously.[8]

In the case of the Italians the Popular Front never became so formalized as it did among the French and Spaniards, who actually established Popular Front governments early in 1936. With the Italians the experiment achieved its maximum strength during the Spanish Civil War, and it drifted on till August 23, 1939, when the unexpected news that Foreign Ministers von Ribbentrop and Molotov had signed the ten-year Nazi-Soviet Neutrality and Non-Aggression Pact brought it to a jarring halt. Throughout the Italian phase of the Popular Front the Communists based their action on the "position of strength" afforded to them by their "unity of action" pact with the PSI—an alliance which was renewed without much difficulty on July 26, 1937, and which lasted till the eve of World War II. The Social-Communists were indisputably the sturdiest clandestine force during those years.

Giustizia e Libertà in crisis

After the breakup of the Anti-Fascist Concentration in May 1934, Giustizia e Libertà was a free agent. Rosselli still hoped to

[7] B/G, *Storia del PCI*, pp. 312–315.
[8] See his speech printed in Dimitrov, *The United Front*, pp. 47–53.

keep his movement aimed toward Italy, with an uprising there his prime objective—something which the Marxian parties were veering away from at this stage.

At once he launched his new weekly paper, *Giustizia e Libertà: Movimento unitario d'azione per l'autonomia operaia, la repubblica socialista, un nuovo umanesimo* ("Justice and Liberty: Unitary Movement of Action for Workers' Self-Government, the Socialist Republic, a New Humanism"). Despite the descriptive subtitle, GL's program remained rather ambiguous. The slogan "new humanism" meant something akin to what André Malraux was preaching—an amalgam of "humanitarianism" and the "religion of man." Rosselli wrote most of the lead articles. Though he was perhaps more tactful than Lussu and Tarchiani, his partners in the directing triumvirate, his editorials often were filled with caustic polemics, and he sternly took to task aspects of the defunct Concentration about which hitherto he had kept silent.[9] Certainly he was dismayed by the PCI-PSI pact of August 1934, for he had dreamed of enticing the Socialists into his own fold.

On the other hand, Rosselli's bitterness toward the Communists tended to subside a bit as a result of the changing world situation in which the Nazis and Fascists were smashing ahead. In November 1934, for example, he devoted an entire issue of his paper to a fairly sympathetic discussion of the anniversary of the Bolshevik Revolution. Rosselli maintained this attitude toward the PCI through his few remaining years. The new line was essentially political and opportunistic.[10]

All in all, the frenzied years from 1934 to 1937 were disappointing for Rosselli. His movement had no real headquarters with a full-time staff; instead, a number of bright young men like the historians Franco Venturi and Aldo Garosci in Paris looked after correspondence, propaganda dissemination, and lecture schedules. They spent much effort trying to attract Sigle ("Sympathizers of GL"), especially among the laborers. But establishment and maintenance of close ties with emigrant workers in sprawling Paris was not easy and the Giellisti were less successful than the Marxists.

Rosselli also looked to starboard for proselytes. Encouraged

[9] Garosci, VCR, II, 48–56.
[10] *Ibid.*, pp. 89–93.

partly by Louis Rosenstock-Franck, a perceptive student of corporatism, he flirted with such dissident left-wing corporatists as Tullio Vecchietti and Achille Corona, to no avail.[11]

Early in 1935, after the plebiscite in which the Saarlanders voted overwhelmingly to reunite with Hitler's Germany, Rosselli's editorials sounded a new *Leitmotiv*—an almost Hamiltonian skepticism of the political good sense of the untutored masses: "The mass as such is brutal, ignorant, impotent, feminine, prey of him who makes the most noise, or him who has the most strength, and success. Break the masses and mass-life, demolish Fascist totalitarianism with living and thinking nuclei —that is the task of the opposition. . . . We are not democratic in the excessively mechanical sense that the word has assumed; we do not attribute too much importance to majorities and minorities, if the majority conducts itself like peasants. We are liberals, anarchists, and revolutionaries." [12] This editorial, written in the mood of Ortega y Gasset, drew much criticism and Rosselli soon had to retreat, especially in view of the new PCI policy of subverting Fascist mass organizations. He too decided to pursue this tactic in order to "enlarge the horizons" of the opposition.[13]

Another novel facet of Rosselli's complex personality in this period of flux was his growing sympathy for Proudhonian ideas. He began to insist that post-Fascist Italy should consist of federated associations, as free and variegated as possible. Though he admitted the need for some central government, it must remain subject to the orders of society: "Man is the end—not the State." [14]

Such contentions provoked a vigorous reaction in Turin from Renzo Giua, a young idealist of the Crocean sort. He declared that the revolution must not produce just a "street-sweeping, letter-carrying, nursemaid 'state society,' but a truly 'ethical'— that is, political state, which co-ordinates the most disparate activities, maximizing instead of constricting them." [15] Whereupon Rosselli answered with asperity that he did not agree with

---

[11] *Ibid.*, 48–62; Garosci, *Sdf*, p. 129; S/M, *Sdf*, pp. 647–649.
[12] Quoted in Garosci, *VCR*, II, 69–70.
[13] *Ibid.*, p. 78.
[14] *Ibid.*, p. 80.
[15] Quoted in *ibid.*

all of Croce's theories, for in them the vital distinctions between force and consent, authority and freedom, state and society, *bourgeoisie* and proletariat, disappear easily and lead to the "acceptance of everything that exists." [16] Though continuing to be critical of any puissant state organization, Rosselli decided to let this debate peter out lest in all the fury GL become impractically "utopian—all thought and criticism." [17]

Manifestly such danger existed. The series of opportunistic modifications of GL's program caused some defections. For instance, Tarchiani resigned in February 1935, partly because he objected to the new policy of infiltrating hated Fascist agencies and partly because of his fondness for such old statesmen as Sforza and ex-Premier Nitti who remained apart from GL. Tarchiani continued, however, to write unsigned articles on foreign policy for *Giustizia e Libertà*.[18] Next came the secession of Lussu, who thought Rosselli was leaning too far toward anarchism, "intellectualism," and "reformism." In a public letter he announced his withdrawal and insisted that only a "revolutionary" and "democratic" Socialist Party with a paramilitary arm (such as the Austrian Socialists' *Schutzbund*) could arouse the "sole" revolutionary force within Italy, the proletariat.[19]

The crisis on the left was followed in September by one on the right. Andrea Caffi, Mario Levi, Renzo Giua, and Nicola Chiaromonte—all of them strong believers in the state—deserted GL on grounds that it was becoming libertarian.[20] Eventually they aligned themselves with the Socialists. Remaining loyal to Rosselli in France were Garosci, Venturi, Umberto Calosso, and Cianca, who helped edit the newspaper. In America he could count on the moral support of Professor Salvemini, recently named to a chair at Harvard.[21]

Within Italy, meantime, GL suffered its worst blow. In May 1935 *provocateurs* helped police track down the Torinese group, at that time the biggest in the country.[22] Among the first to be

[16] *Ibid.*
[17] Rosselli, *Scritti politici e autobiografici*, p. 194.
[18] Garosci, VCR, II, 93–94; Garosci, *Sdf*, p. 122.
[19] *Ibid.*, pp. 121–122; Garosci, VCR, II, 94–96.
[20] *Ibid.*, p. 102.
[21] Garosci, *Sdf*, p. 124.
[22] An indication of the scope of Rosselli's underground is revealed by the report that some 200 were arrested in Turin alone between 1929 and the eve of

arrested was Vittorio Foà, a keen economist who had headed the circle since the temporary arrest of the young Russian-born Leone Ginzburg. The police also rounded up Augusto Monti, professor of literature in a Turin lyceum; Michele Giua, chemist and father of Renzo; Massimo Mila, music critic; and Alfredo Perelli, a civil servant; and his son Giannotto. The Special Tribunal condemned most of them in February 1936 to long prison terms totaling fifty-nine years. These arrests shattered GL's major internal apparatus.[23]

Impact of the Ethiopian War

The active wing of anti-Fascism in Italy was perhaps at its weakest when the Ethiopian crisis began to come to a head early in 1935.[24] Through their recklessness during the early 1930's the Communists had sacrificed their internal echelons; no true PCI organization in Italy existed for several years after the apprehension of Pajetta, Colombi, and others in April 1934. Extirpation of the Torinese GL center ended for all practical purposes Rosselli's machinations in Italy. In France the exiles (apart from the new Social-Communist bloc) were split as badly as ever, with GL effectively boxed in.

In view of all this, the first reactions of anti-Fascists to the Ethiopian crisis were muffled and incoherent. Many nationalistic Italians were inclined to think that their country was justified in seeking "revenge" for the humiliation at Adowa. It was chiefly a handful of farsighted democrats (flanked by Social-Communists, once they got a cue from Moscow) who finally perceived that a Mussolinian triumph could produce a chain reaction of aggressions that might precipitate World War II. Some months passed before such analysts reached rough agreement on how best to criticize Mussolini's latest gambit and support the principle of collective security.

World War II. During the 1935 police roundup in Turin, promoters of La Cultura (published by the Einaudis) were also arrested. Cf. supra, Ch. II, Giustizia e Libertà within Italy; Ch. III, Anti-Fascism in the legal press.

[23] Garosci, Sdf, p. 123; Garosci, VCR, II, 97–114; Allason, Memorie di un'antifascista, pp. 217–218; S/M, Sdf, pp. 743–744; M. Giua, Ricordi di un ex-detenuto politico.

[24] For a detailed account of the international aspects of the Ethiopian crisis in which he spares no one, see Gaetano Salvemini, Prelude to World War II (London, 1953).

When the war of nerves started in February 1935, Marxian propaganda was still cast in anti-imperialist clichés: "Not one man, not one cent for the African adventure of capitalism!" Such a slogan made little impression on most Italians, who seemed ready to go along with the *Duce*'s contentions that seizure of African soil was not a "capitalist adventure" but a means for Italy to exert her civilizing influence, improve her economic position, export her burgeoning population, and revive the glories of the Roman Empire. During the next month delegations of the PCI and PSI drew up plans for *émigré* demonstrations against the "Ethiopian adventure." The PCI followed this in April with a unilateral appeal "to the workers, to the peasants, to the soldiers, to the aviators, to the oppressed peoples of Venezia Giulia, Alto Adige, the Dodecanese, and the African colonies, to the artisans, to the clerks, to the technicians, to the intellectuals, to the youth, to the women, to everyone" against the incipient war. Contending that the people wished to see the "military defeat of the Fascist government," it urged strikes, prevention of troop departures, fraternization with Ethiopian soldiers, and abandonment of the field of battle. Communists argued further that even if Italy won, the economic advantages would redound to the industrialists and bankers but not to the workers.

By the end of May, however, the Social-Communists showed signs of changing their line. Instead of preaching insurrection, for which the country clearly was unready, they pumped the theme of collective security to maintain world peace. They issued a joint manifesto, calling for a congress of Italians to foregather in mid-August in Basel to uphold the League of Nations. But the *fuorusciti* could not assemble in that city because of objections from the Swiss government.[25] Then suddenly in mid-July the PSI General Council in Paris reverted to the old line that the proletariat should expect nothing beneficial for themselves out of any war and should remember their duty to uphold the cause of peace and sustain the Soviet Union "which pursues a policy of peace." If hostilities should come, the world-wide proletariat must remember that its weapon was not imperialist

[25] S/M, *Sdf*, pp. 691–692; Garosci, *Sdf*, p. 106.

warfare but class struggle, for by converting the imperialist war into a civil conflict, the bourgeois state could be smashed and the triumph of socialism insured. On August 17, in a statement celebrating the "unity of action" pact, the PCI echoed that familiar shibboleth. Needless to add, this kind of talk tended to dissuade foreign conservatives from pushing a tough collective-security program lest it open Italy's portals to the Reds.[26]

Though Rosselli had predicted since 1934 that the inner logic of Nazi-Fascism signified war, he had doubted for some weeks in 1935 that Mussolini would dare risk a real conflict in Ethiopia. When the dictator proved him wrong, however, Rosselli favored taking advantage of the crisis. Thus he wrote a series of editorials between April 9 and May 3 entitled "How to conduct the campaign against the African war." Seeking an "up-to-date argument," he stressed that even if the Italians won, they would gain no colony suitable for emigrants, nor a region worthy of exploitation; they would simply be bled white. He also insisted (with only partial accuracy) that the whole crisis was really a domestic matter, a "private enterprise of the dictatorship." Nowhere in his ruminations did he emphasize the importance of collective security in the face of the growing Nazi-Fascist threat. He thought trust in the League would be as unrewarding as that entertained by the Aventinians in Victor Emmanuel III. Furthermore, he regarded the League as hypocritical, in view of its nonintervention against Japan and Germany in previous crises. Finally, he was anxious not to alienate nationalistic elements in Italy. On the constructive side, he recommended economic and cultural agreements with other countries to augment the possibilities of Italian emigration. He also suggested joint meetings with the Social-Communists to discuss common policy. But the latter declined, as did the PRI and LIDU.[27]

In September, however, Rosselli did persuade many exile factions to gather in Paris for an International Conference for the Defense of the Ethiopian People. Some spokesmen of the PCI, PSI, PRI, LIDU, CGL, and the Anarchists attended; but aside from voting to send a delegation to Geneva and approving a

[26] *Ibid.*, pp. 113–114; S/M, *Sdf*, p. 692; Arfè, *Storia dell' "Avanti!" 1926–1940*, pp. 128–136.
[27] Garosci, VCR, II, 124, 143–150; Garosci, *Sdf*, p. 107; S/M, *Sdf*, p. 693.

manifesto drafted by Rosselli and Calosso to the effect that the Fascist campaign in Africa signified "mass deportation of youth and police imperialism," the conference accomplished little.[28]

By this time Moscow was clarifying its propaganda line for the Social-Communists. An intimation of the collective-security approach was to be detected in a manifesto published in *Avanti!* on August 3, preaching the indivisibility of peace and calling for application of sanctions by the League against Italy. The manifesto emphasized that if the League failed, this might well be its deathblow.[29]

Soon the Social-Communists sponsored in Brussels on October 12–13 the major anti-Fascist demonstration of the year—a Congress of Italians Abroad. It convened ten days after Mussolini's minions marched into Ethiopia and one day after the League Assembly, by fifty votes, backed the Council's decision that Mussolini had violated the Covenant and was therefore the aggressor. With the notable exception of GL, virtually every *émigré* group attended. Some of the delegates, like the 24-year-old Torinese Socialist economics professor, Antonio Pesenti, came directly from Italy.[30] Luigi Antonini, Secretary of Local No. 89 of the Lady Garmentworkers Union and spokesman for thousands of Italo-Americans, arrived from New York. The great majority of delegates voted to send a telegram to President Beneš of the League Assembly, recommending a program of effective sanctions against Mussolini, now publicly branded the aggressor. Signed by elderly G. E. Modigliani (PSI), Egidio Gennari (PCI), and LIDU President Campolonghi, this plea underlined the importance of differentiating between the Fascist regime and the "real" Italy. It went on to urge the Italian people to oust their *Duce* and make immediate peace with the Ethiopians. The only contrary votes were cast by a tiny clique of Republican extremists, the Azione Repubblicana Socialista led by Fernando Schiavetti, who dissented mainly for nationalistic motives. Later the ARS affiliated with GL.[31]

On November 18, 1935, the League imposed economic sanc-

[28] *Ibid.*, p. 694; Garosci, VCR, ii, 141–142.
[29] S/M, *Sdf*, p. 694.
[30] He was arrested upon his return and condemned to long imprisonment, during which time he became a Communist.
[31] Garosci, *Sdf*, pp. 107–108; S/M, *Sdf*, pp. 709–710.

tions in accordance with Article 16. But, as is well known, oil and other strategic items were not included in the boycott, nor was the Suez Canal closed to Mussolini's vessels. Though the volume of trade with Italy by League members declined substantially, this was not enough to frustrate Mussolini's war effort; instead, it provided him the opportunity to pose as the persecuted paladin of *la patria*—a role which he exploited to the full.[32]

Rosselli did not back the Brussels Congress resolution because he doubted if underground resistants in Italy favored it. He feared (correctly) that sanctions might simply encourage Italians to rally round the *Duce* in paroxysms of nationalism and Anglophobia. Moreover, he argued that the huge sums spent on propaganda in Brussels might better finance revolutionary agitation in Italy.[33]

In February and March 1936 Rosselli conferred with Luigi Longo, one of the keenest PCI activists, and proposed that the Communists and Giellisti equip a large number of *fuorusciti* with leaflets and radios and dispatch them to Italy to stir up dissension. Longo remained unpersuaded, and repeated to Rosselli classical Marxian arguments against acts of violence directed at individuals. Though conceding that conversion of an "imperialist war" into a civil struggle was sound dogma, he insisted that terrorism was bootless unless the masses were first carefully prepared.[34] His judgment had much to commend it. So did that of *Capo della Polizia* Senise, who reasoned that there was little danger that a twentieth-century armed dictatorship could be toppled until and unless it was first dismantled by foreign military disasters.[35]

Soon after the Brussels Congress the PCI secretly infiltrated some of its youth leaders into the Italian Armed Forces to foment pacifism and rivalry with the Fascist Militia. To Egypt they dispatched Velio Spano, who intrigued under the alias of "Paolo Tedeschi." [36] Rosselli in the interim became the target of terror-

---

[32] Regarding sanctions cf. Moritz J. Bonn, "How Sanctions Failed," *Foreign Affairs*, xv (Jan. 1937), pp. 359–361; and Salvemini, *Prelude to World War II*, pp. 325–364.

[33] Garosci, *Sdf*, pp. 132–133, 138–139.

[34] *Ibid.*, pp. 131–132.

[35] Carmine Senise, *Quando ero Capo della Polizia* (Rome, 1946), p. 140; cf. Salvemini, *Prelude to World War II*, pp. 198–199.

[36] PCI, *Velio Spano* (Rome, 1947).

ism himself, narrowly escaping assassination in March 1936 at the hands of a mysterious agent named Carlo Zanatta, who vanished in the Paris Métro. For one more year Rosselli's luck held out.[37]

While Mussolini's aviators rained bombs and gas on Haile Selassie's barefoot troops, the Social-Communists stirred up a cloud of agitation. In January 1936 a committee appointed by the Brussels Congress issued a manifesto calling for preservation of Ethiopia's territorial integrity and denying that Fascism could ever be relied upon to join in a system of collective security. By February students from several European countries were successfully goading the *Duce* into debating the sanctions policy with them in the columns of *Popolo d'Italia*.[38] Also, that month a World Conference of Youth for Peace met in Brussels to call for a broader, more efficacious system of sanctions. Some 350 delegates from 23 nations attended, claiming to represent 12,-000,000 youth. The rising Social-Communist clamor inevitably frightened some foreigners into thinking that only Mussolini preserved Italy from new perils of Bolshevism—a contention which Sturzo, Borgese, and other exiles did their best to refute.[39] The winter of crisis culminated in March with Hitler's re-occupation of the Rhineland—a move which prompted a joint declaration from all the Italian anti-Fascist groups denouncing "the internal logic of the two Fascist regimes" which leads inevitably to war.[40] Rosselli, it will be recalled, had grasped this truth faster than the Marxists.[41]

During the Ethiopian War Rosselli's newspaper coverage of the conflict was quite inadequate. Until late spring he relied upon the opinions of an ex-Army officer who had convinced himself that the Italian forces were losing the fight (perhaps without his guidance?). Belatedly learning the truth about the military situation, Rosselli fired his counselor.[42]

By then the victorious forces of Generals Pietro Badoglio and Rodolfo Graziani were well on their way toward capturing Addis

[37] Garosci, VCR, II, 132-133, 147-148.
[38] See citations in Salvemini, *Prelude to World War II*, pp. 424-425.
[39] See articles by Sturzo in *The New Statesman and Nation*, Feb. 7, 1936, and statements by Borgese and other exiles in the *New York Times*, Feb. 2, 1936.
[40] S/M, *Sdf*, pp. 732-733.
[41] See *supra*, Ch. II, Collapse of the Anti-Fascist Concentration.
[42] Garosci, VCR, II, 144-147.

Ababa and Harrar. When they fell early in May 1936, the war came to an end. On the 9th Mussolini proclaimed "Victor Emmanuel III, by the Grace of God and by the Will of the Nation, King of Italy" also to be "Emperor of Ethiopia." Both the underground foes of Fascism and the League's champions of collective security had suffered clamorous defeat. Sanctions were lifted on July 15.[43]

Temporary zenith of Mussolini's popularity

Mussolini's quick victory in Africa caused his popularity at home to reach its peak.[44] Conversely, his store of goodwill abroad (at least in the Western democracies, where for some thirteen years many had sung the regime's praises) all but vanished.

From the outset the Ethiopian War had kindled the imagination of many Italians. Colonial expansion and revenge for the debacle of 1896 stirred the blood of many, as did the idea of Italy's singlehandedly defying haughty Britain and France and most of the world during the sanctions farce. And for many businessmen the war brought at least fleeting prosperity.

It was not surprising, therefore, that several erstwhile oppugners of Fascism wavered. Ex-Premier Orlando, for example, deserted his post in the "quiet opposition" and offered "patriotic support" to the fatherland. So did the dramatist Sem Benelli, who had been identified with the passive opposition since the Matteotti assassination. Two *fuorusciti*, Professor Arturo Labriola and Mario Bergamo, decided to return home and back the regime. Tens of thousands of ordinary citizens obediently, if not enthusiastically, turned in their gold wedding rings to help finance the war. Many of them, like Croce and Albertini, were "quiet" anti-Fascists who felt they could not refuse this gesture of solidarity with the boys at the front.[45]

Partial success in Mussolini's battle against unemployment also contributed to the general upswing in the dictator's popularity. In September 1935 there were 609,094 unemployed, compared to 887,345 a year earlier; during the war the number declined further, as a result of mobilization. Seasonal export of la-

[43] Salvemini, *Prelude to World War II*, pp. 439–468; S/M, *Sdf*, pp. 701, 710–711, 720.
[44] Salvemini, *Prelude to World War II*, p. 474.
[45] *Ibid.*, pp. 472–478; S/M, *Sdf*, pp. 701 and 720.

borers to Germany after the forging of the Axis in the fall of 1936 also reduced the total. Soon Fascist officials were boasting that they no longer needed to publish statistics on the shrinking problem! But economic recovery was spotty, and the costly African war, followed immediately by intervention in Spain's holocaust, led to new difficulties. Autarchy, undertaken during the sanctions era, was carried to absurd extremes and caused sharp price jumps; propaganda for a higher birth rate produced deleterious economic effects. By 1939 unemployment had climbed again to 1,000,000.[46]

When Mussolini's star was at its zenith a few Italians thought that the *Duce* would reward his people by liberalizing the regime, in somewhat the way Emperor Napoleon III had relaxed his "plebiscitarian dictatorship" during the 1860's.[47] Learning of these rumors, Communists in Paris sought to encourage such a possibility. They dug up Fascism's radical program of 1919 and declared their readiness to subscribe to it! From August until October 1936 *Grido del popolo* and *Stato operaio* hewed to this line, implying that Mussolini had committed heresy when he veered away from his original program (which, despite its hypocrisy, had expressed "basically democratic goals").[48] According to Salvatorelli and Mira, Mussolini in 1936 did toy abstractly with the thought of liberalization. He made a few concessions to Rinaldo Rigola and other ex-CGL chieftains in Milan and Genoa who edited a pamphlet series, "Problemi del Lavoro." While he let these writers proceed, he soon bowed to pressure from Fascist extremists and banned left-wing corporatist periodicals like *Cantiere* (Rome), *Camminare* (Milan), and *14 Novembre* (Ferrara and Ravenna).[49]

When all was done, however, no genuine relaxation had occurred. In fact, the regime became more pervasive than ever by the late 1930's. The fanatic PNF secretaries Achille Starace and Roberto Farinacci introduced a host of rituals and theatricalities

[46] *Ibid.*, pp. 766–767.
[47] See Leto, OVRA, pp. 140–141; Mario Fusti Carofiglio, *Vita di Mussolini e storia del fascismo: Predappio, Piazza Venezia, Piazzale Loreto* (Turin, 1950), pp. 288–289; Garosci, *Sdf*, p. 135; and S/M, *Sdf*, p. 741.
[48] *Ibid.*, pp. 742–743; Arfè, *Storia dell' "Avanti!" 1926–1940*, pp. 144–145; Valdo Magnani and Aldo Cucchi, *Crisi di una generazione* (Florence, 1952), pp. 7–8.
[49] *14 Novembre* took its name from a socialistic speech of Mussolini of November 14, 1921.

labeled *costume fascista* and *mistica fascista,* and organized a new propaganda agency, the Minculpop ("Ministry of Popular Culture"). In 1937 the PNF expanded its youth organizations, took over from the Ministry of Education the GIL (which superseded the ONB, Giovani Fascisti, and Giovani Fasciste),[50] and in every way possible monopolized the physical and political education of the young. GUF co-ordinated the university students. The party also inaugurated a none-too-effective "block warden" system of political surveillance. Farinacci aped Hitler's anti-Semitic policies and introduced the goose step. The regime even sought to change habits of speech, forbidding use of the "effete" third person singular form of the personal pronoun for "you" (*Lei*) and requiring, instead, use of the second person plural (*Voi*). In 1939 the corporate state reached its maturity when the lower house of Parliament was finally transformed into the Chamber of Fasces and Corporations.

Meanwhile, new sets of intriguers successively pushed their way into the *Duce*'s inner circle: Arturo Bocchini, head of OVRA; G. Buffarini-Guidi, Undersecretary of Interior; and Count Galeazzo Ciano, Mussolini's son-in-law and Foreign Minister. This also was the time when Claretta Petacci became the dictator's mistress and her profiteering relatives began to shuffle about behind the scenes. Had it not been "tempered by anarchy," the Fascist system might well have become intolerable.[51]

Spanish Civil War

Two months after the end of the conflict in Ethiopia a fratricidal struggle began in Spain. Dragging on almost three years, it cost the lives of hundreds of thousands and produced many international repercussions. It greatly affected the Italian anti-Fascist exiles who played an important part in the contest, for it strengthened the Popular Front at the expense of Rosselli's GL and it trained many in the art of guerrilla warfare.

Raising their standard against the recently elected Popular Front government of the five-year-old Republic, General Francisco Franco and his military, fascistic, and clerical forces invaded the peninsula from Spanish Morocco. Soon they won control of

[50] See *supra,* Ch. III, n. 32.
[51] S/M, *Sdf,* pp. 741–862.

a broad swath of land and established a provisional government in Burgos. But Madrid remained under the control of the legitimate or Loyalist government which, with the help of various workers' committees, hastily organized defenses. At first, liberal Republicans dominated the Loyalist government; not a single Communist was in it.[52] But after September 1936 when left-wing Socialist Francisco Largo Caballero became premier, effective power tended to pass to his faction and the Communists.[53]

Meanwhile, in Barcelona the autonomous Catalan republican government ("Generalitat") organized its own defenses under the leadership mainly of Anarcho-Syndicalists, who hated the Communists as bitterly as they did Franco's Insurgents, the Roman Catholic Church, and capitalism.[54]

Rapidly becoming a three-cornered fray, the Civil War was soon complicated by foreign intervention. Almost from the beginning Franco's rebels were assured of material support from Mussolini and, on a smaller scale, from Hitler. By January 1937 some 44,000 Italian Fascist "volunteers," co-ordinated by General Mario Roatta, had been dispatched to aid Franco, their primary naval and air bases being established on Majorca.[55] Britain and France meantime inaugurated a Nonintervention Committee, in the hope of localizing the war. Both Italy and Germany hypocritically agreed to participate in its work.[56] "Nonintervention" obviously hurt the Loyalists more than it did the Insurgents, because the latter continued to receive aid on a large scale from Mussolini and Hitler, who welded their Axis in October 1936. Certainly by that month (indeed, probably since early September) Soviet Russia was also intervening, furnishing

[52] Regarding the political background of the war see Gerald Brenan, *The Spanish Labyrinth* (New York, 1943), and Salvador de Madariaga, *Spain: A Modern History* (New York, 1958).

[53] On political trends during the early phase of the war, see Franz Borkenau, *The Spanish Cockpit* (London, 1937); on the general problems of Communism during the conflict, see David T. Cattell, *Communism and the Spanish Civil War* (Berkeley, 1955); for a brilliant discussion of the European intellectuals' attitude toward the war, see Aldo Garosci, *Gli intellettuali e la guerra di Spagna* (Turin, 1959).

[54] For the Catalan story cf. George Orwell, *Homage to Catalonia* (London, 1938).

[55] S/M, *Sdf*, p. 792.

[56] Regarding international complications, see Cattell, *Communism and the Spanish Civil War* and his *Soviet Diplomacy and the Spanish Civil War* (Berkeley, 1957); and Patricia A. M. van der Esch, *Prelude to War: The International Repercussions of the Spanish Civil War* (1936–1939) (The Hague, 1951).

some material and technical aid to the Loyalists and sending in numerous Red political advisers and intelligence agents.[57]

Rosselli's intervention in Spain

Throughout modern history the political links between Italy and Spain have been close.[58] The *fuorusciti* naturally sensed very soon the ideological nature of the Civil War and hoped to prevent a victory of Franco's Insurgents. They did not agree, however, upon the scope of their intervention, nor upon the question of whether it should be directed toward support of the Madrid Popular Front or of the autonomous and rival Catalan Anarcho-Syndicalists.

Carlo Rosselli apparently was the first to take a decisive step. He was influenced in part by messages from his friend, Umberto Calosso, who happened to be in Barcelona when the war began.[59] Sensing the opportunity of using Spain as a base for a great armed struggle that would culminate in an invasion of Mussolini's Italy, he invited spokesmen of various exile groups to meet in Paris on July 23–24, 1936, to discuss possible military intervention. These talks revealed that aside from GL only a small cluster of Anarchists and Trotskyists were willing to accept Rosselli's leadership in such an enterprise. The Social-Communists let it be known through Luigi Longo on August 11 that, in the absence of instructions from Moscow, they were not prepared to do more than ship medicine and certain supplies to the Loyalists. But a few weeks later, after the rise to power of Premier Largo Caballero, who invited them to come, they shed all hesitancy and intervened boldly. Stressing "democratic" goals, the Communists postponed talk of social revolution, but did not forswear their bitter fight against Spanish Trotskyists.[60]

Partly because of his inability to forge a common policy with the Social-Communists and partly because of his initial sympathy for the Anarcho-Syndicalists, to say nothing of his determination not to delay, Rosselli in August threw his support to the numeri-

[57] Cattell, *Soviet Diplomacy and the Spanish Civil War*, pp. 32–37; Max Beloff, *The Foreign Policy of Soviet Russia, 1929–1941* (London, 1947–1949), II, 28–38.

[58] See Amedeo Giannini, "I rapporti italo-spagnoli (1860–1955)," *Rivista di studi politici internazionali*, XXIV (1957), pp. 8–63.

[59] Calosso, *The Twenty-Year Struggle in Italy against Fascism*, p. 39.

[60] Garosci, *VCR*, II, 163; Garosci, *Sdf*, pp. 145–146; B/G, *Storia del PCI*, p. 321; Magnani and Cucchi, *Crisi di una generazione*, pp. 18–19.

cally weaker Catalan cause. This meant that GL soon found itself isolated, not only from the major Spanish political forces opposed to Franco but also from the European ones. Later Rosselli tried to rectify his blunder and achieve an accord with the Communists, but he was assassinated before he could carry this out.[61]

Before proceeding to Catalonia, Rosselli and his close friends assisted the writer André Malraux in his effort to recruit an *équipe* of aviators to defend Madrid. At least a half dozen Italians qualified as pilots; one of them (Giordano Viezzoli) helped defend the Loyalist capital until he was shot down on September 30.[62] But this recruitment was incidental to Rosselli's major ambition—organization of an Italian Column that would fight in Catalonia under its own banner and represent the political interests of the "coming Italian revolution." [63]

Groundwork for this column was laid by the libertarian philosopher, Camillo Berneri, together with Mario Angeloni, a PRI lawyer and Freemason who had hastened to Barcelona after the start of hostilities. Berneri was welcomed by the Catalan Anarcho-Syndicalists and was assigned a post in their Confederación Nacional del Trabajo (CNT; "National Confederation of Labor"). The Catalans soon made it clear to the Italians that foreign volunteers must align themselves with the Catalan Anarcho-Syndicalist Militia, which in turn took orders from the CNT. Although unhappy, Rosselli ostensibly acquiesced. With Berneri's help he sought to phrase the pact of August 17 establishing the Italian Column so as to safeguard its political autonomy. Time was to tell how meaningful this was.[64]

Anarchists made up the largest contingent within the 130-man column; the Giellisti numbered only some twenty. Understandably, therefore, the Anarchists were not easily persuaded to take orders from the latter. Choice for commander lay between Angeloni and Rosselli. Finally a compromise was reached: Angeloni, an ex-cavalry captain, took charge of some forty machine

[61] Garosci, *Sdf*, pp. 149–150; S/M, *Sdf*, pp. 797–798.
[62] Pietro Nenni, *Spagna*, ed. Gioietta Dallò (Milan-Rome, 1958), pp. 146–147.
[63] Garosci, VCR, ii, 164–166. *Cf.* Nicola Chiaromonte, "La guerra in Spagna," in *Lezioni sull'antifascismo*.
[64] The agreement is printed in the New York *Quaderni Italiani*, No. 3 (April 1943), and in Garosci, *Sdf*, pp. 279–280; *cf.* Garosci, VCR, ii, 167–173; Garosci, "Antifascismo democratico in Spagna: la Colonna italiana," Rome *Il Mondo*, June 26, 1956; and S/M, *Sdf*, p. 797.

gunners, while Rosselli led about ninety riflemen. Among their prize possessions were four brand-new machine guns and twenty-four "magnificent" mules. Rosselli had with him his Ford car, which he had driven from Paris.[65]

The Italian Column received its baptism of fire on the Aragonese front at Monte Pelato near Huesca on August 28, 1936. Repulsing an attack by a much larger enemy force, the column maintained its positions, but one tenth of its components were killed, including Angeloni. Rosselli suffered a minor wound.[66] On the eve of the battle the veteran conspirator wrote in his diary the reason for his intervention: "In view of the fact that Fascism won by force and is ruling by force, in view of the fact that the most basic freedoms have been snuffed out, in view of the fact that in certain hours a deed is worth more than a thousand speeches, we Italian exiles, volunteers of freedom, shall begin with force to combat Fascism in Spain." [67]

Despite the casualties, Rosselli could take pride that his unit was the first organized volunteer Italian group actually to enter the fray. Paris Giellisti headlined the story and later boasted that they did not wait for instructions from Moscow.[68]

Social-Communist intervention in Spain

Even before Rosselli's Monte Pelato victory and the formation in Madrid on September 4 of Premier Largo Caballero's government, some Italian Socialists and Communists had crossed the Pyrenees to rally to the Loyalists. Pietro Nenni hastened to Madrid on August 5 and quickly established links with Socialist leaders and with the Italian refugee Fernando DeRosa, who had taken command of the "Octubre" battalion of Spanish Socialist youths.[69] Vittorio Vidali (a Triestian Communist who under the alias of "Enea Sormenti" had promoted an Anti-Fascist Al-

---

[65] Garosci, VCR, II, 174–176; Calosso, The Twenty-Year Struggle, p. 39; C. Rosselli, "Partenza per il fronte," in his Oggi in Spagna, domani in Italia (Paris, 1938), and reprinted in E. Rossi (ed.), No al fascismo, pp. 231–235.
[66] Umberto Calosso, "La battaglia di Monte Pelato," in ibid., pp. 237–253.
[67] Quoted by Garosci in "Antifascismo democratico in Spagna: Il Battaglione Garibaldi," Rome Il Mondo, July 3, 1956.
[68] See facsimile of the newspaper in S/M, Sdf, p. 792; cf. Garosci, VCR, II, 183–189, and his Sdf, p. 154.
[69] Nenni, Spagna, pp. 121–126 ff.

liance in New York in 1926 and who in Spain affected the pro-sopopeia of "Carlos Contreras") was dispatched by the Com-intern to Madrid shortly before the revolt with instructions to help form paramilitary organizations.[70] Nino Nanetti was an-other early comer; he was to die in Bilbao after becoming a com-mander in the international brigades. Francesco Scotti and Gia-como Pellegrini reached Barcelona in August, while Luigi Longo passed through that city en route to Madrid later in the month. Wide-scale Communist intervention and co-ordination of volun-teer operations did not start till September, when the Comintern issued precise instructions and Longo hurried to Madrid.

Early in September Italian Social-Communists in Paris called a meeting of exile groups to decide upon a commander for their volunteer forces. As Rosselli was in Catalonia, GL was repre-sented by Venturi and Cianca. They quickly indicated that they would not collaborate with the Popular Front unless it gave due respect to the priority of Rosselli's volunteers in the Aragonese and Catalan sectors. An Anarchist representative also took issue with the Social-Communists, insisting that they were riding roughshod over autonomous Catalan units. Under these circum-stances no agreement was reached.[71] The Giellisti found them-selves farther out on a limb when Rosselli lost the support of the Catalan Anarcho-Syndicalists, who insisted upon dominating his column. When Berneri, who was devoting all of his energy to the internal struggle for power in Barcelona, made it clear he could not help, a rift occurred between the erstwhile friends.

The Social-Communists went ahead with their task of finding a commandant. Since their watchword at this stage was not social revolution but defense of the bourgeois Spanish Republic, they preferred to choose a non-Marxist. Thus they nominated Ran-dolfo Pacciardi of the PRI, a party which was sympathetic to the Popular Front government in Madrid. Pacciardi, a native of the Maremma and a veteran not only of World War I but of numerous street fights with the Fascists, had spent seven years in Switzerland since his departure from Italy in 1926. When the Swiss requested him to move on, he established residence in Mulhouse. During part of his exile he published a weekly news-

[70] Borghi, *Mezzo secolo di anarchia*, p. 343; B/G, *Storia del PCI*, pp. 322–323.
[71] Garosci, VCR, II, 200–204.

paper, *La Giovine Italia*. As soon as he was invited to take over command of the Italian volunteers, Pacciardi hurried across the Pyrenees in mid-September to discuss with Loyalist leaders plans for fielding an Italian Legion. Traveling via Catalonia, he visited Rosselli but did not explain to him his mission.[72]

After lengthy negotiations the Italian Social-Communists and Republicans signed a pact on October 27 with the Spanish Loyalists organizing the autonomous Italian Legion.[73] What emerged, however, was not a legion but the Garibaldi Battalion, forming part of the international brigades. At first there were slightly more than 500 men in the Garibaldi Battalion, which consisted of four companies bearing the names of anti-Fascist martyrs: Mario Angeloni, Lauro DeBosis, Fernando DeRosa, and Gastone Sozzi. A Biellese Communist, Antonio Roasio, served as political commissar. After a few weeks of hurried training the Garibaldi Battalion went into the line on November 13, 1936, at Cerro de los Angeles near Madrid's University City. Epic resistance by all the Loyalist forces saved the capital on this occasion.[74]

Several authoritative Communists meanwhile established the pattern for the international brigades which were to play so memorable a role in the war during 1937. Longo ("Gallo") and Giuseppe DiVittorio of Italy, aided by André Marty of France, Franz Dahlem of Germany, and others, were the chief initiators. In due course, Moscow dispatched the capable General Gregory Stern ("Emil Kleber") to take over supreme command of the international brigades, and with him came the Hungarian Mata Zelka ("General Paul Lukacs"). Each brigade consisted of several battalions, usually organized at first according to nationality. Alongside each military commandant was a political commissar, whose tasks included indoctrination of the soldiers, surveillance of the military officers, publication of newspapers, and dissemination of propaganda to civilians. All the commissars were Communists, and in some cases they were members of the Soviet GPU as well. Foreign Reds were enrolled in the Spanish Com-

[72] *Ibid.*, p. 203.

[73] The text of the agreement is printed in Garosci, *Sdf*, pp. 280–281; cf. *ibid.*, p. 152, and also Garosci, "Antifascismo democratico in Spagna: Il Battaglione Garibaldi," Rome *Il Mondo*, July 3, 1956.

[74] Regarding military and political aspects of this period, see Robert Garland Colodny, *The Struggle for Madrid: The Central Epic of the Spanish Conflict (1936–37)* (New York, 1958).

151

munist Party to insure discipline. The brigades were recruited from workers, artisans, and farmers; probably no more than one fifth of them had ever seen military service before. Most were at least thirty years old. In general they were quick to learn the new skills and languages. Echelons were fluid; a corporal or sergeant might suddenly be promoted to officer status, or the reverse might occur; political commissars and commanders sometimes switched posts. According to Salvador de Madariaga, there were eventually some 22,000 in the international brigades.[75]

The First International Brigade consisted of three battalions. Of these, one was composed of Poles, Yugoslavs, and Bulgarians; a second was made up of Germans and Austrians; and a third, of Frenchmen and Italians. DiVittorio ("Nicoletti") served as political commissar of the latter, which fought in the defense of Madrid. A little later the Second International Brigade was formed under the supreme command of the Magyar "General Lukacs"; its commissar was "Gallo" (Longo), a 36-year-old native of the Monferrato sector of Piedmont. One of its three battalions was Pacciardi's "Garibaldi." In later months three more brigades emerged.[76] Longo served as inspector-general of them all.[77] Headquarters were maintained much of the time in Albacete, about 150 miles southeast of Madrid. Nenni handled liaison in Madrid until August 1937.[78] That same summer Togliatti ("Ercoli," alias "Alfredo") arrived in Spain as chief political representative of the Comintern, replacing Hungarian Erno Geroe ("Pedro").[79]

[75] Madariaga, *Spain*, pp. 506–507; cf. Julio Álvarez del Vayo, *Freedom's Battle* (New York, 1946), pp. 124–129; Randolfo Pacciardi, *Il Battaglione Garibaldi: Volontari Italiani nella Spagna repubblicana* (Rome, 1945), pp. 97–98; and Colodny, *Struggle for Madrid*, pp. 58–64, and *passim*.

[76] Eventually all five brigades were incorporated in the Republican armies as the XI, XII, XIII, XIV, and XV brigades.

[77] Longo set out in 1939 to write a day-by-day history of the international brigades. One copy of the manuscript (taken away from him after his arrest in France at the outbreak of World War II) somehow escaped destruction. In 1956 Longo published it, editing it to emphasize the Italian aspects of the struggle. Though filled with encomiastic rhetoric and strictly Stalinist in its interpretations, it provides a useful firsthand description of military events and of political problems in forging the brigades. Longo's account ends with the battle of Brunete in July 1937. *Le Brigate Internazionali in Spagna* (Rome, 1956).

[78] Nenni, *Spagna*, pp. 148–163.

[79] B/G, *Storia del PCI*, p. 337.

During the winter of 1936–1937 Pacciardi engaged in some radio polemics from Madrid with a Fascist descendant of Giuseppe Garibaldi in Rome who challenged his right to use the Great Liberator's name for his battalion. On February 11 the Garibaldi Battalion successfully repelled an attack on the Jarama by the Insurgents. On that occasion Pacciardi suffered a minor injury.

Guadalajara, some thirty miles northeast of Madrid, was the site of the most remarkable engagement of the entire war, so far as Italians were concerned. There in mid-March, while Pacciardi was on a brief furlough and political mission in France, the enemy, which consisted mainly of Mussolini's "volunteers," unexpectedly attacked the Garibaldi Battalion and other contingents. The resultant week-long battle was fought without quarter. In Pacciardi's absence, Ilio Barontini, a PCI commissar from Leghorn, assumed command, but Pacciardi returned in time to take part in the last phase of the successful counteroffensive which ended on March 19. Exploiting to the full the propaganda value of the Garibaldi victory at Guadalajara, the *émigrés* stressed how much superior the "authentic" volunteers were to Mussolini's counterfeit Corps of Italian Volunteers Troops. The psychological significance of the victory was exceptional indeed; nothing hitherto had given the *fuorusciti* greater satisfaction, and many of them regarded it as a prelude to the civil war they were sure would eventually break out in Italy. Guadalajara produced newspaper headlines throughout the world and aroused the bitterest fury in Mussolini, who could not entirely ignore the defeat in his own press though he did his best to minimize it.[80]

The rapidly growing power of the Social-Communist bloc in Spain reached its pinnacle early in May 1937 when a bloody *coup d'état* occurred in Barcelona as a result of Comintern directives. The Catalan Anarcho-Syndicalists and Trotskyists were overthrown by Social-Communist forces supporting the Madrid Popular Front, now to be headed by Premier Juan Negrín. Among the hundreds of victims of the fratricidal *coup* in Barce-

---

[80] *Ibid.*, pp. 327–331; S/M, *Sdf*, pp. 799–806; Garosci, "Antifascismo democratico in Spagna: Guadalajara," Rome *Il Mondo*, July 10, 1956; Longo, *Brigate Internazionali in Spagna*, pp. 291–318; and Colodny, *Struggle for Madrid*, pp. 128–143, 237–238.

lona [81] were two of Italy's most prominent Anarchists, Professor Camillo Berneri and Giovanni Barbieri.[82]

From this time on, the exiguous Anarchist factions in the emigration ceased to exert much influence, though a few like Armando Borghi in New York, writing under pseudonyms, contributed articles to the libertarian *Adunata dei refrattari*.[83] Probably most felt like crying down a plague on both contending forces in Spain. During World War II they favored a neutral position "against all the capitalists"—a negative attitude which quickly reduced the strength and appeal of a movement that a decade or two before had been very active in Italy. In the Armed Resistance of 1943–1945 Anarchists were scarcely to be seen.[84]

Italian Popular Union (UPI)

In France, meantime, the Italian Social-Communist *fronte unico* ("united front") bent every effort to gain undisputed control of all the *fuorusciti*. In Lyon on March 28–29, 1937, it convened a congress under the honorary presidency of ex-Premier Edouard Herriot, the mayor of the city. Some 500 delegates attended, representing 17,000 adherents of the *fronte unico* and including numerous members of the PRI, LIDU, and GL. This Lyon congress decided to transform the Social-Communist front into a broad Unione Popolare Italiana (UPI; "Italian Popular Union") that would seek mass membership.

From the beginning the Social-Communists controlled the newly spawned UPI. To the irritation of many Republican, GL, and LIDU members, they opened the doors even to Fascist workers so long as they were willing to support the goal of "bread, peace, freedom, and the noblest expression of *Italianità*." They stressed the theme of patriotic solidarity by displaying prominently the Italian tricolor and blaring forth the "Garibaldi

[81] B/G, *Storia del PCI*, pp. 333–337; Garosci, VCR, ii, 262–268; Nenni, *Spagna*, p. 63. Orwell, *Homage to Catalonia*, offers an account sympathetic to the Catalan non-Communists. The orthodox Communist interpretation may be found in Longo, *Brigate Internazionali in Spagna*, pp. 329–335. Cattell, *Communism and the Spanish Civil War*, pp. 141–152, gives a picture of the affair. Of personal interest are the memoirs of Giovanni Pesce, *Un Garibaldino in Spagna* (Rome, 1955).

[82] Cattell, *Communism and the Spanish Civil War*, pp. 133–134 ff. Regarding Berneri's thought, see his posthumous *Pensieri e battaglie* (Paris, 1938).

[83] Borghi, *Mezzo secolo di anarchia*, pp. 357–358.

[84] Garosci, *Sdf*, pp. 156–158, 190.

154

Hymn." Since UPI defended the interests of its members against the French authorities in much the same way as did LIDU, some jealousy arose.[85]

Romano Cocchi ("Adami"), who had started out as a left-wing Popular before his conversion to Communism, was elected secretary of UPI. After announcement of the Molotov-Ribbentrop pact in August 1939, Cocchi broke with the PCI. During the war he died in the concentration camp of Buchenwald.

By July 1937 UPI had sponsored a daily newspaper in Paris, *La Voce degli Italiani,* under the direction of DiVittorio, who had returned, ill, from Spain. Later it was edited by Ambrogio Donini, Amedeo Ugolini, and Mario Montagnana. Its Communist slant was clear, though it sometimes printed articles by non-Communists.[86]

UPI, the Italian manifestation of the Popular Front, attracted at least 45,000 members before it collapsed under the blow of the Nazi-Soviet pact.[87] Certainly it was the strongest bloc in the emigration between 1937 and 1939. Its chief bastion was in the mining and industrial zones of eastern France. In the more rugged southern regions GL and other independent democratic groups managed to hang on to most of their old followers. UPI did its best to win support in Tunisia, where its propaganda was divulgated by *Italiano di Tunisi* for a few weeks until visiting Italian Navy personnel ransacked the newspaper plant and shot the local UPI secretary in September 1937. After a hiatus the PCI dispatched to Tunis in 1939 two of its most energetic youth leaders, Giorgio Amendola and Velio Spano. They promoted a newspaper, *Il Giornale di Tunisi.*[88]

Rosselli and the Popular Front

Since the autumn of 1936 Rosselli's Italian Column in Catalonia had found itself caught between two hostile forces—pressure from the local Anarcho-Syndicalists and rivalry from the Popular Front's puissant international brigades. Rosselli sought

---

[85] *Ibid.,* pp. 168–170, 187–189.

[86] *Ibid.,* pp. 171–172; PCI, *Giuseppe DiVittorio* (Rome, 1947), pp. 1–14.

[87] B/G, *Storia del PCI,* p. 308. The figure 70,000 has been mentioned by the Giellista Paolo Vittorelli in his *Dal Fascismo alla rivoluzione: storia della caduta del fascismo* (Cairo, 1945), p. 331.

[88] B/G, *Storia del PCI,* p. 355; Garosci, *Sdf,* pp. 172, 191–192.

to extricate himself by reshaping his column into a "motorized revolutionary force" that would take the offensive against Italian Fascist soldiers first in Spain and later at home. To instil "revolutionary discipline" among his predominantly libertarian troops, he was willing to copy the Communist system of political commissars.[89]

Late in October Rosselli decided to go back to Paris to drum up support in the democracies for his project. There in a broadcast on November 13 he sounded the keynote of his program: "Just as in the darkest stages of the Risorgimento when practically nobody dared hope, there came from abroad the example and initiative, so today we are convinced that from this modest but virile force of Italian volunteers a powerful will to achieve redemption will find its source. . . . TODAY IN SPAIN, TOMORROW IN ITALY."[90] But Parisian politicos gave him scant encouragement, partly because of his identification with the Catalan Anarcho-Syndicalists, who enjoyed little or no foreign support. Disappointed, Rosselli repaired to Spain late that year.[91]

During his absence he had lost touch with his fighting men. The Anarchist contingent, suspicious of him almost from the start, made it clear they wanted no part of his "revolutionary discipline." Because of the dissension, the column that Rosselli commanded for the last time in December at Almudévar (to the north of Saragossa) was a much weaker outfit than it had been in August at Monte Pelato. The two-day engagement at Almudévar was unsuccessful, and in the face of rising hostility from the volunteers, he resigned his command on December 6. He was too ill, in any case, to continue in the field, for he suffered from a recurrence of painful phlebitis of the legs.

Though very sick, he made his way back to Paris and his newspaper, still hoping somehow to capitalize on the Spanish War and prepare a military operation that would dislodge Mussolini. More firmly convinced than he had ever been since his clarion call that Fascism signified war, he exclaimed: "The dictatorship itself is but a means to an end. Fascism has been all things: *laissez-faire* and socialist, individualist and collectivist, bourgeois

---

[89] Garosci, VCR, II, 211–212.
[90] Quoted in *ibid.*, pp. 217–218.
[91] *Ibid.*, pp. 212–221.

and proletarian. On one point alone it has not changed: its dedication to war." [92] Force must therefore be met by force.

After Rosselli's departure a few of his friends in Barcelona tried to reorganize a unit that would follow his desires. Chief among them was Libero Battistelli, an intellectual who had passed considerable time in Brazil and who soon was to die in combat. In February 1937 Battistelli was joined by Cianca, who came from Paris. The best they could do was to enroll their followers in an Anarchist division and get a Giellista-appointed commissar. In March Garosci arrived in Barcelona with somewhat new instructions as a result of Rosselli's talks in Paris with the Social-Communists. Supported by Battistelli, Garosci recommended on the eve of the battle of Guadalajara that the Italian fighters in Catalonia identify themselves with Pacciardi's Garibaldi Battalion. But the Anarchist Berneri created trouble at this point; he wanted no strengthening of the Marxian cause. Any integrated policy was brought virtually to an end when the battle of Carrascal on the Aragonese front on April 10 led to dispersion of their unit. Many thereafter joined the Garibaldi.[93]

Confident the Italian people could be incited to revolt in case of world conflict, Rosselli decided to stir them up by flying over Turin and dropping provocative manifestoes. In mid-May he took off from Lyon, but when his plane landed near Grenoble, French police halted him and interned his craft.[94]

By June he had reconciled himself to the fact that military action would have to be organized within the framework of a broad program that would draw the support of the European democracies and the Popular Front. The triumph of Social-Communist forces at Guadalajara had made a vivid impression upon him; he could not help but appreciate their strength, unity, and political acumen even though he remained suspicious of the Reds' operational methods. Belatedly he realized that he would have to seek some kind of collaboration with them if he were to get out of his trap, for the Catalan Anarcho-Syndicalists no longer were a viable force.[95]

[92] *Ibid.*, pp. 230–231; Garosci, *Sdf*, pp. 152–153.
[93] Garosci, VCR, II, 238–247. Of interest for this era is the diary of the Giellista, Francesco Fausto Nitti, *Il maggiore è un rosso* (Milan-Rome, 1953), pp. 45–66.
[94] Garosci, VCR, II, 259–262.
[95] *Ibid.*, pp. 241–245, 262–270.

To achieve this, he discussed with the PCI the possibility of bringing GL into the Marxian "unity of action" pact and of sponsoring a new joint newspaper. (This was the period when the PCI was seeking by means of UPI to broaden its base and had not yet initiated a UPI newspaper.) Rosselli insisted that in such a consolidated enterprise he hold a key post, and he would not agree that the paper must stand willy-nilly for "unconditional defense of the Soviet Union." The most he would agree to was to promise not to indulge in "systematic campaigns against the Soviet Union." Just before his assassination on June 9 Rosselli was writing a series of articles illustrating the project he had in mind. They were entitled "For the political unification of the Italian proletariat." [96]

What the PCI may have thought about Rosselli's plan is uncertain. There was no doubt, however, about the PSI's coolness. In the PSI Third Congress, held in Paris from June 26 to 28, two weeks after Rosselli's murder, Nenni conceded the possibility that UPI could be reorganized and modernized, but that was as far as he would go.[97] On July 11 the Communists launched their new daily UPI organ, *La Voce degli Italiani*, and later that month renewed their "unity of action" pact with the PSI. Nenni's majority faction agreed to Communist insistence that they would seek to unify all parties and anti-Fascist organizations within the framework of UPI and would look forward to fruitful collaboration in the post-Fascist era. Among the Socialists only revisionist Modigliani expressed consistent opposition to renewal of the pact with the PCI.[98]

Assassination of the Rosselli brothers

Mussolini's anger at the *fuorusciti*'s intervention in Spain mounted to new heights upon their victory at Guadalajara. Compounding his anger were the impudent broadcasts of the gadfly Rosselli, "Today in Spain, tomorrow in Italy!" Though he forbade Italians to tune in to this type of foreign broadcast or to relay their messages, he could not erect an electronic curtain.

[96] *Ibid.*, pp. 247-259; Garosci, *Sdf*, p. 171; S/M, *Sdf*, p. 812.

[97] A few days earlier (June 21) at Annemasse, near the Swiss frontier, a joint meeting of the Comintern Executive Committee and that of the Socialist Second International took place. Longo came from Spain to represent the PCI. Togliatti had just come to Paris from Moscow and was soon to go to Spain. Longo, *Brigate Internazionali in Spagna*, pp. 363-370.

[98] Garosci, *Sdf*, p. 175; S/M, *Sdf*, p. 812.

During the spring a few manifestations of sympathy for the Spanish cause were reported in Milan and some other cities, as well as of protest against rocketing prices. Early in April a group of professionalists, students, artists, and workers belonging to a Milanese Anti-Fascist United Front, headed by the Socialist theoretician Rodolfo Morandi and inspired by the *émigrés* Pallante Rugginenti and Luigi Faravelli, were apprehended. The Special Tribunal condemned them in October to long imprisonment.[99] The dying PCI secretary, Gramsci, was also a problem of real concern to Mussolini, especially in view of the giant demonstrations abroad on his behalf.[100]

Against this backdrop the Fascist plot to assassinate Rosselli took form. Early in June 1937 Carlo had gone to the Normandy mud-bath resort of Bagnoles de l'Orne to recover his health before returning to Spain. He was joined by his brother Nello, who had continued to reside in Florence after his release from *confino* in 1929 and had resumed his historical research on the Risorgimento. On June 9, while driving in Carlo's Ford along an isolated road near the resort, the brothers were ambushed and pulled from their car. They put up a furious struggle against their assailants before the latter's trench knives butchered them. Two days later their bodies were found. In Paris agonized cries greeted the news. Indeed, only the murder of Matteotti in 1924 aroused as much indignation among the opposition as did the assassination of the Rossellis. A crowd estimated to be 200,000 strong marched in the funeral procession to Père Lachaise cemetery in Paris. Carlo's English-born wife, Marion, his son John, and his mother survived him.

Mussolini's press could not ignore the crime and spread wild rumors to the effect that the assassins were Social-Communists

[99] Receiving ten-year sentences: Morandi, Vittorio Ravazzoli, Mario Venanzi, Alfredo Testa, Aligi Sassu; another four received sentences ranging from one to four years; Lucio M. Luzzatto was absolved. S/M, *Sdf*, p. 814.

While in prison from 1937 until 1943 Rodolfo Morandi shifted from liberal socialism to Marxian socialism. In the days just before the final Liberation of German-held northern Italy in April 1945, he was to become President of the Committee of National Liberation of Upper Italy (CLNAI). His many writings are presently being published by Giulio Einaudi Editore, Turin, under the broad title, *Opere di Rodolfo Morandi*. See also Stefano Merli, "La formazione culturale e politica di Rodolfo Morandi (1923–1933)," *Rivista storica del socialismo*, 1 (1958), pp. 169–209.

[100] See *supra*, Ch. III, Gramsci in prison. The biggest demonstration occurred in Paris on May 22.

159

or perhaps Anarcho-Syndicalists. Almost no one abroad believed such fables, and it is doubtful that many did in Italy. From the first most exiles were sure that the assassination had been ordered by high Fascists, and postwar investigations by Professor Salvemini and others have confirmed this, though some aspects remain obscure. The deed was executed by French Cagoulards, the fascistic arm of the reactionary *Comité sécret d'action révolutionnaire*, for the price of one hundred Italian carbines. The Cagoulards perpetrated the crime upon instructions from Major Navale and Lieutenant Colonel Santo Emanuele of the Italian SIM ("Military Intelligence Service"), who in turn had been given the signal by Count Ciano, the *Duce*'s foreign minister and son-in-law. According to Salvemini, Filippo Anfuso (Ciano's *chef de cabinet*) also had knowledge of the affair. And it is hard to imagine that Mussolini himself was left completely in the dark.[101]

During the eight years in which Carlo Rosselli had dominated Giustizia e Libertà he had attracted much attention to his idealistic cause by courageous journalism, support of daring enterprises in Italy, and speedy intervention in Spain. To be sure, many had shaken their heads in bewilderment at the *"enfant terrible* of the emigration," and doubtless he had his foibles. He had often gone to extremes in his determination to be different from the older parties, and some of these distinctions seemed more verbal than real. No doubt there was much in GL that was pragmatic and opportunistic. Yet it would be hard to deny that the GL *condottiere* did more than almost any single person in the emigration to reawaken a desire for freedom and to prepare a new directing class of intellectuals, independent of the old Liberal and Marxian groups.

When Rosselli died, his followers were united more by a state of mind than by a common program; by an antipathy for the men and methods of the Aventine and of pre-Fascist Liberalism; and by an intense desire to bring about Italy's emancipation by the autonomous action of Italians themselves. The manner in

[101] See especially G. Salvemini, "L'assassinio dei Rosselli," in E. Rossi (ed.), *No al fascismo*, pp. 255–304; Garosci, VCR, II, 277–284; Garosci, *Sdf*, p. 161; and S/M, *Sdf*, pp. 814–815. An Italian Court of Assize in Perugia on October 14, 1949, acquitted Anfuso and the Italian military officers on the curious grounds of "insufficient proof." A Paris Court of Assize on November 18, 1948, convicted several of the Cagoulards involved.

which the nation was to be freed between 1943 and 1945 was different from what Rosselli had imagined in 1936 and 1937. It was to come about largely by the intervention of great foreign states, including non-European ones. Nevertheless, they alone did not liberate Italy, for they were aided by a valiant Armed Resistance, one of whose wings (the Partito d'Azione and its Giustizia e Libertà guerrillas) traced its inspiration straight to Rosselli. That such resistance could thrive between 1943 and 1945 was in no small way due to the moral inspiration that Carlo Rosselli bequeathed to an influential segment of his countrymen.

End of the Spanish Civil War

A month after its March 1937 victory at Guadalajara, the Garibaldi Battalion reorganized itself as the Garibaldi Brigade. During the early summer it tried in vain to impede General Franco's capture of the Basque and Asturias regions. In August the organization was rent by a bitter squabble between its PRI commander, Pacciardi, and the Communists. Pacciardi, who had become alarmed by their tactics since the overthrow of the Catalan libertarians, concluded that the Stalinists were acting selfishly rather than in the best interests of anti-Fascism and decided to resign. Increased Spanish membership in and Red domination of the international brigades was another factor in causing his defection. Nenni sided with him in the crisis, and because he was especially anxious to return to Paris to help fill the void left by Rosselli's murder, he accompanied Pacciardi back to France. From this time on the number of *fuorusciti* fighting in the Iberian peninsula steadily dwindled.[102]

After Pacciardi's resignation command of the brigade passed successively to Communist Carlo Penchienati, who later was to break with the party; a Socialist named Arturo Zanoni; and such obscure combatants as "Raimondi" and finally "Martini." The reorganized unit fought well through the rest of 1937 and into 1938 in many parts of the peninsula, including Estremadura [103] and the Ebro valley. Late in 1937 some remnants of

---

[102] See Pacciardi, *Il Battaglione Garibaldi*, pp. 239–240 and *passim*; his article, "Quando si sta con i comunisti," in Rome *La Voce repubblicana*, Mar. 27, 1949; Nenni, *Spagna*, pp. 160–163; Salvadori, *Resistenza ed azione*, p. 156; and Longo, *Brigate Internazionali in Spagna*, pp. 261–265 ff.

[103] In that sector ex-Giellista Renzo Giua lost his life in February 1938. See

Giellisti in Spain organized a new unit called the Rosselli Battery, commanded by Dino Giacobbe, which tried to collaborate with the Garibaldini.[104]

Not all of the *fuorusciti* looked upon the Spanish Civil War as a conflict to be won decisively by one side or the other. In London Fr. Sturzo, the principal Catholic leader in exile and the promoter in 1936 of the People and Freedom group,[105] deplored the religious hatred engendered by the fighting and perceived the dread possibility that it might lead to World War II, with immeasurable destruction of life and property. Sturzo hoped that such a conflict could be forestalled if the British and French governments undertook a resolute effort to conciliate the opposing factions in Spain. To this end, Sturzo, assisted by the British journalist Wickham Steed, promoted (as a subgroup of People and Freedom) the British Committee for Civil and Religious Peace in Spain. This agency co-ordinated its work with similar Spanish and French groups, headed respectively by Salvador de Madariaga and Jacques Maritain, and drafted a project which Lord Cecil and the Archbishop of Canterbury presented to Prime Minister Neville Chamberlain in 1938 with the hope that he, in turn, would seek Mussolini's support for it. But the work of Sturzo and his friends came to naught. The Prime Minister declined to intercede, not wishing "to raise any controversial topic" at that stage.[106]

In the course of 1938, however, the Negrín government let it be known that it could get along without the international brigades. This was partly because the military manpower shortage had been surmounted and partly because some irritations had arisen between Spanish officials and foreign Reds. But the chief reason was that the Negrín government was ready to follow the

---

Massimo Mila, "Destino spagnola," Milan *Rassegna d'Italia*, Nos. 6–10 (June–Oct. 1947).

[104] Garosci, *Sdf*, p. 184.

[105] People and Freedom sought to educate youth to participate in public life with moral and Christian perspectives. It took a deep interest in the plight of the Ethiopians and Basques. In August 1940 it decided to form an International Christian Democratic Union and promoted wartime conferences in London of Christian Democratic groups from several European countries including Italy. See Sturzo, *Nationalism and Internationalism*, pp. 124–127.

[106] Sturzo, *Italy and the Coming World*, p. 38, n.; Sturzo, *Nationalism and Internationalism*, pp. 124–126; Barbara Barclay-Carter, *Italy Speaks* (London, 1947), pp. 42–43.

advice of the London Nonintervention Committee, which favored disbandment of the brigades in hope that Franco would likewise send home the much more numerous Italian Fascist "volunteers." Thus in September 1938 Premier Negrín announced the immediate and complete withdrawal of all non-Spanish combatants from the Loyalist ranks.[107] Many components of the international brigades were interned temporarily in Catalonia before being evacuated to camps in southern France and Algeria. Some took up arms again under the command of Riccardo Formica ("Aldo Morandi"), an Italian Socialist, early in 1939 when it became apparent that the Loyalists were going to have to capitulate.[108]

As has been noted, Togliatti ("Alfredo") was in Spain after the summer of 1937 as the Comintern's *longa manus*. Following the collapse of Loyalist resistance in Barcelona in January 1939, he flew back to Madrid. He arrived about the time (March 5) Loyalist Colonel Segismundo Casado carried out a *coup* against Premier Negrín as a necessary step to signing an armistice with Franco. Casado's men arrested Togliatti near Alicante and were on the point of executing him. But when the Spanish Communists learned of Casado's intention of signing an armistice, they rose against him, with the result that some 9,000 were killed in this final civil war within a civil war. In the confusion Togliatti escaped by plane to Algeria on March 25 and thence to France, where he was interned briefly. Luckily for him, French police did not know who he was.[109]

All told during the Spanish War, perhaps as many as 3,000 *fuorusciti* fought alongside the Loyalists; of these, some 600 were killed and perhaps 2,000 wounded.[110] Most of the volunteers seemed to have been motivated by idealism; quite a number regarded themselves as an autonomous contingent in the world-

---

[107] Beloff, *Foreign Policy of Soviet Russia, 1929–1941*, II, 28–38; and Van der Esch, *Prelude to War*, p. 117 ff.; Garosci, *Sdf*, p. 167.

[108] *New York Times* correspondent Herbert L. Matthews has described the withdrawal of the brigades in his *Education of a Correspondent* (New York, 1946), pp. 140–142, 181–192.

[109] B/G, *Storia del PCI*, pp. 341–342; Ciatti, *Togliatti*, p. 45; Robotti and Germanetto, *Trent'anni di lotte dei comunisti italiani*, p. 184; Colodny, *Struggle for Madrid*, p. 147; and Colonel Segismundo Casado, *The Last Days of Madrid: The End of the Second Spanish Republic* (London, 1939).

[110] Statistics cited in *Quaderni Italiani*, No. 3 (April 1943), 139; Luigi Longo, *Un popolo alla macchia* (Milan, 1947), p. 26; cf. Garosci, *Sdf*, pp. 154–155.

wide struggle against fascistic forces. As a result of the exhilarating experience the *fuorusciti* recaptured a feeling of self-confidence, and, despite constant rivalry, more unity was attained than they had enjoyed before. Moreover, the veterans had learned first-hand about guerrilla warfare and an appreciation of the usefulness of factory workers in such a struggle—lessons that were helpful during Italy's Armed Resistance.[111] It was scarcely a coincidence, for example, that Longo ("Gallo"), who had gained practical experience as inspector-general of the international brigades, should emerge as the PCI politico-military commandant of the Garibaldi partisans in Italy from 1943 until 1945.

Finally, in weighing the significance of the Spanish Civil War in terms of the Italian struggle, one must remember that the two and one half years of bitter fighting greatly sapped Mussolini's regime. His troops had bogged down in Spain; he had lost not only far more manpower and equipment than in his Ethiopian adventure but also prestige. Furthermore, while Mussolini held on to the Spanish bull by the tail, not knowing how to let go, he obviously could not oppose (even if he had wished to) Hitler's annexation of Austria and seizure of the Sudetenland in 1938. Thus Nazi Germany emerged predominant in the Axis. Mussolini's cynical conquest of Albania in April 1939 could not begin to redress the imbalance. Italy entered World War II greatly weakened by the preceding military campaigns—a fact which hastened the domestic crisis that unseated the *Duce* in 1943.[112]

Giustizia e Libertà in decline

On the wane since 1934, GL almost collapsed after Rosselli's assassination in June 1937. Gone were the intellectual stimulation and personal magnetism, to say nothing of the financial underpinning which that enterprising director had provided;

[111] Roberto Battaglia, *Storia della Resistenza italiana* (*8 settembre 1943– 25 aprile 1945*) (2nd rev. ed.; Turin, 1953) [hereafter cited as Battaglia, SRI], pp. 32–33. The author of this important synthesis of the Armed Resistance was a militant of the Action Party during the war, but by the time he wrote this study he had shifted to the PCI. With Giuseppe Garritano he has also prepared an abridged edition, *Breve storia della Resistenza italiana* (Turin, 1955). The English version, *The Story of the Italian Resistance*, tr. and ed. by P. D. Cummins (London, 1957), rests on this latter shortened edition.

[112] See especially the discussion of Mussolini's ambassador to Franco's Spain in 1937: Roberto Cantalupo, *Fu la Spagna* (Milan, 1948); cf. Garosci, *Sdf*, pp. 163–164; S/M, *Sdf*, p. 844.

gone too was most of the popular base that had kept GL in motion. During the next two years its leadership was often split, though most of the spokesmen clothed their propaganda in socialistic garb, and some were even willing to collaborate with Social-Communists, as was shown by their joint statements at the time of Hitler's *Anschluss* and the Munich showdown.[113]

The principal Giellista in this critical period was Emilio Lussu, the Sardinian revolutionary and author of a 1936 tract on insurrection.[114] For two years Lussu had remained aloof from GL and had spent some of that time in Switzerland. He had conceived the idea of striking an accord with the PSI in order to wean it from the PCI and to bolster GL; but when his overtures failed to dent the "unity of action" pact, he turned toward Schiavetti's ARS splinter group and to a few Trotskyists for flanking support.[115]

Closely associated with Lussu in the final phase of GL was Professor Silvio Trentin, the distinguished exiled jurisprudent from Venice, who after working as a manual laborer had opened a bookshop in Toulouse.[116] Somehow he found time to write and publish a plethora of trenchant studies that did much to acquaint the outside world with the nature of Mussolini's regime.[117] Despite his repugnance for Stalinism, Trentin was an advocate of effective political unity among the *émigrés*.

Standing somewhat to the right of Lussu and Trentin in their desire to keep untarnished the "liberal" and "revisionist" ingredients in Rosselli's Socialismo Liberale were Garosci, Venturi, Calosso, Cianca, the Pierleoni brothers, and Paolo Vittorelli. To preserve a modicum of unity, however, they agreed to a new subtitle: Giustizia e Libertà: Movimento di Unificazione Socialista. Thus socialization, even though restricted to the sector of heavy industry, was taken for granted, and GL would simply offer itself as the instrument for bringing about fusion of the Socialist par-

---

[113] Garosci, *Sdf*, pp. 180, 190–191.

[114] See Lussu, *Teoria dell'insurrezione: saggio critico* (republished in Rome, 1950).

[115] Garosci, VCR, II, 247; Garosci, *Sdf*, p. 181.

[116] See *supra*, Ch. II, Second phase.

[117] Among them *L'Aventure italienne: légendes et réalités* (Paris, 1928); *Les Transformations récentes du droit public italien* (Paris, 1929); *L'Antidémocratie* (Paris, 1930); *Aux sources du fascisme* (Paris, 1931); and *Le Fascisme à Genève* (Paris, 1932).

ties. Under the circumstances, GL was ceasing to be an autonomous "movement" and becoming, potentially at least, a political
party.[118]

The deepening pinkish hue of GL caused a few members to
secede completely. So long as Rosselli had been alive, Tarchiani,
who was strongly opposed to any wide-scale socialization, had
maintained connection with the movement, even after the crisis
of 1935; but soon after Rosselli's death he withdrew. In December 1937 he and Pacciardi (who had severed his tie with the
Communists that summer) got together. They founded the
newspaper, *La jeune Italie*, not as a party organ but as the basis
for yet another broad anti-Fascist current. They enjoyed the frequent editorial collaboration of Sforza. Much of the time Pacciardi's paper carried on a running debate with the Communists;
on occasion the editor even engaged in fisticuffs with them. Still
another anti-Fascist resistant to sever his tie with GL at this time
and return to more familiar paths of liberalism was Massimo
Salvadori.[119]

Domestic underground (1935–1939)

After Mussolini's "liquidation" of the Communist underground in April 1934 scarcely any covert PCI agency worthy of
the name existed for some time. A year later GL had suffered an
equally devastating blow. Repercussions of the Ethiopian War
along with the economic upswing of the mid-1930's further
handicapped the stay-at-home anti-Fascists.

Though information about the years from 1935 to 1939 is
meagre, it seems likely that the PCI, hard-pressed though it was,
still was the sturdiest single clandestine force. It based its strategy
on Dimitrov's counsel at the Comintern congress of 1935:

"Our Italian comrades . . . have already been fighting under
the conditions of a Fascist dictatorship for about thirteen years.
Nevertheless, they have not yet succeeded in developing a real
mass struggle against Fascism, and therefore they have unfortunately been little able [to offer examples of infiltration into
mass organizations]. . . . Heroism alone is not enough. . . . In
our struggle against Fascist dictatorship it is particularly danger-

[118] Garosci, *Sdf*, pp. 181–182.
[119] Salvadori, *Resistenza ed azione*, p. 173; S/M, *Sdf*, p. 816; Garosci, *Sdf*, p. 187.

ous to confuse the wish with the fact. We must base ourselves on the facts, on the actual concrete situation. . . .

"What is the Achilles' heel of the Fascist dictatorship? . . . Since it is a dictatorship of the big *bourgeoisie*, Fascism must inevitably come into conflict with its heterogeneous mass social basis. . . . We can lead the masses to a decisive struggle for the overthrow of the Fascist dictatorship only by getting workers who have been forced into the Fascist organizations, or have joined them through ignorance, to take part in the *most elementary movements* for the defense of their economic, political and cultural interests. It is for this reason that the Communists must work in these organizations. . . . Communists must win elected positions in the Fascist mass organizations . . . and must rid themselves once and for all of the prejudice that such activity is unseemly and unworthy of a revolutionary worker." [120]

Quite a few of the younger comrades in the PCI (like Valdo Magnani and Aldo Cucchi, who broke with Togliatti after World War II) thought this "a ridiculous way to fight Fascism"; they thought, rightly, that Fascism could be overthrown only in a general European crisis.[121] Nevertheless, most of the younger Communists dutifully infiltrated GIL, GUF, and the armed forces, while older men tried to penetrate the Opera Nazionale Dopolavoro ("National Agency for Leisure-time") and even the Istituto Nazionale di Cultura Fascista.[122] For example, in Bologna in 1940 a group of ostensibly Fascist student members of GIL met in the home of Carlo L. Ragghianti, a stanch democrat. To his surprise, they were camouflaged Communists. That nucleus alone included Giaime Pintor, Mario Alicata, Antonello Trombadori, Carlo Muscetta, and Antonio Rinaldi, almost all of whom achieved reputations as Communist writers.[123] Doubtless there were several such nuclei in the major cities.

A Communist historian has suggested that PCI agitation led to unrest among Genoese port workers in 1937 and among some southern peasants; [124] however, non-Communist Professor Piero

---

[120] Dimitrov, *The United Front*, pp. 47–53.
[121] Magnani and Cucchi, *Crisi di una generazione*, pp. 19–23.
[122] Regarding these agencies see Minio-Paluello, *Education in Fascist Italy*, pp. 132–158.
[123] Carlo L. Ragghianti, *Disegno della liberazione italiana* (Pisa, 1954), p. 299.
[124] Battaglia, *SRI*, pp. 33–34.

Pieri has answered that local conditions accounted for such sporadic disturbances.[125] The PCI official report for these years does not claim much.[126]

Older men in the covert democratic circles identified with GL and its counterparts in Italy were reluctant to infiltrate Fascist agencies. Many of them felt there was something unethical and repugnant about "boring from within." Yet economic necessity in the 1930's compelled a good many to take out PNF cards, and a few skillfully took advantage of their status to spread subtle criticism. The younger generation which had grown up and received its schooling under totalitarianism could scarcely avoid at least nominal participation in Fascist student groups.

Though Mussolini's victory in Ethiopia in 1935–1936 won for him the hopeful allegiance of most Italians, it was precisely then that a number of youths began to feel perplexed, to go through a "crisis of their consciences," and to embark upon what one writer has called the "long journey" [127] that led them to active anti-Fascism. This was no isolated phenomenon, according to Mario delle Piane, who passed through this experience while studying at the University of Siena in the late 1930's. A substantial number of personnel in the GUF utilized its newspaper facilities to express their true feelings, he has explained. Ostensibly they wrote as loyal Fascists, but in reality devotion to the regime was simply their point of departure. It permitted and even imposed upon them the duty of pointing out shortcomings and proposing corrections. Their "legal action" rested on a dual myth: that Fascism was a "continuous revolution," barely initiated, which must be brought to its full realization; and that Fascism's origins were "pure" and "anti-bourgeois"—in a word, "left-wing." Criticism ranged from censure limited to particular episodes, offered with sincere conviction and the intention of serving Fascism, to activity that was the conscious result of an anti-Fascist outlook that at last had been fully attained.[128]

Of the latter type were the editorials of Eugenio Curiel, a Jewish student at the University of Pavia who became a Com-

[125] See his review-article, "Considerazioni intorno ad una 'Storia della Resistenza italiana,'" MLI, No. 32 (Sept. 1954), p. 55.

[126] PCI, Relazione della Direzione del PCI al V° Congresso, pp. 8–9.

[127] This phrase was first used in this context in a book by Ruggero Zangrandi, Il lungo viaggio (Turin, 1948).

[128] Mario delle Piane, "Alla ricerca di un'Italia civile," Il Ponte, XII (1956), pp. 975–987.

munist and edited the local GUF paper, *Il Bò*, in 1937–1938.[129] *Bò*'s format gave the appearance of political orthodoxy—so much so that some young resistants would not write for it, fearing that such action would aid the regime since outsiders might gain the impression that Italy really enjoyed freedom of the press. They feared that newspapers engaging in such "constructive criticism" might serve simply as "safety valves" for tyranny.

Both Delle Piane and Curiel's posthumous editor, Enzo Modica, have argued that, on balance, it was good that "legal action" against Fascism was conducted within GUF during the late 1930's. They have pointed out that most of the educated youth who joined in covert work on the eve of the Armed Resistance had started to do so in student organizations; indeed, it was an almost inescapable stage in their "long journey." Of course, if they had halted at that point, it would have been regrettable. But almost none did; instead, they moved on to positions of clear-cut enmity, sometimes as Communists, sometimes as liberal democrats, sometimes as Christian Democrats, and always at great danger to themselves.

World War II brought an end to the "legal action" phase, partly because of mobilization and the suspension of university publications and partly because of the arrests of the more daring students and the inauguration in 1938 of anti-Semitic decrees which silenced Jewish student writers.[130]

Guido Calogero's Liberalsocialismo

The most significant non-Communist, democratic underground current to emerge in academic circles during the latter period of Mussolini's dictatorship was Liberalsocialismo, founded in 1936 at the Scuola Normale Superiore in Pisa by a versatile 32-year-old professor of philosophy, Guido Calogero.[131] He was aided by Anglophile Umberto Morra and Aldo Capitini, the lat-

---

[129] Under the editorship of Enzo Modica, the writings of Curiel from the mid-1930's until his death in 1945 during the Armed Resistance have been published: *Classi e generazioni nel secondo Risorgimento* (Rome, 1955).

[130] Delle Piane, *Il Ponte*, xii (1956), p. 979; and Modica's introduction to Curiel, *Classi e generazioni nel secondo Risorgimento*. Regarding defection from Fascism of such Catholic youth as Dino DelBo and Teresio Olivelli, see Webster, *The Cross and the Fasces*, pp. 116–118.

[131] The basic source of information regarding the movement is Guido Calogero, *Difesa del Liberalsocialismo* (Rome, 1945); *cf.* his "Ricordi del movimento Liberalsocialista," *Mercurio*, 1 (1944), No. 2.

ter a theistic but anti-Catholic advocate of Gandhian nonviolent resistance whose anti-Fascism was intensified by the 1929 Concordat.[132] While Calogero's group consisted mostly of instructors and students, it also attracted thinking people beyond the academic corridors. Broadly speaking, the Liberalsocialists found their inspiration in the same principles that had motivated GL, though there was only tenuous contact (through Vittorelli and others) with the Giellisti exiles.[133] In selecting a label for his movement, Professor Calogero simply inverted the title of the book that Carlo Rosselli had written in 1929 while a prisoner on Lipari. Like Rosselli, he stressed that liberalism and socialism were co-important and not adjectival to one another—hence the unhyphenated title. Calogero argued that the basic problem confronting the twentieth century was not the relationship between socialism and economic liberalism but that between socialism and political liberalism. The Liberalsocialists hoped to create a "third force" which would combine the most valid elements of revisionist socialism and political liberalism.

In proposing their initial platform in 1936 and 1937 the youthful Liberalsocialists aroused Croce's scorn. Disdainfully, the Neapolitan dean of Italian liberalism termed the ideas of Calogero's academicians a "hodgepodge" of philosophical positions. With all the logic he could muster he insisted that a neat distinction between socialism and liberalism must be maintained.[134] After a couple of years, however, Croce softened his strictures of the new movement and kept in friendly communication with many of its adherents.[135]

---

[132] See Aldo Capitini, "La mia opposizione al fascismo," *Il Ponte*, XVI (1960), pp. 32-37; his "Liberalsocialismo nel 1937," *Mercurio*, II (1945), No. 12; and his "Sull'antifascismo dal 1932 al 1943," *Il Ponte*, XI (1955), pp. 848-854. Capitini also wrote *Elementi di un'esperienza religiosa* (Bari, 1936); regarding this, see his "Premessa a un libro del '36," *Il Ponte*, I (1945), pp. 536-543, and "Un'esperienza religiosa dell'antifascismo," *MLI*, No. 33 (Nov. 1954), pp. 60-64, which described a religious anti-Fascist movement at the University of Pisa in 1932. See also Nello Finocchiaro, "La 'Normale' Pisana," Rome *Il Mondo*, July 22, 1958; and C. L. Ragghianti's letter in *ibid.*, Aug. 5, 1958.

[133] Calogero may have derived some of his economic ideas from certain "left-wing" corporatists (Professor Ugo Spirito, Luigi and Arnaldo Volpicelli, and Agostino Nasti) who favored abolition of private property and creation of a harmonious unity of labor, management, and capital in industry wherein workers would share in management and profits. Vittorelli, *Dal fascismo alla rivoluzione*, pp. 181, 328-329; Max Ascoli, *Fascism for Whom?* (New York, 1938), p. 91.

[134] Croce, "Sul carattere teoretico del marxismo," *La Critica*, XXXV (1937), pp. 158 ff.; "Comunismo e Libertà," *ibid.*, pp. 238 ff.

[135] Calogero, *Difesa del Liberalsocialismo*, pp. 194-195.

The Liberalsocialists did not try to promote violent revolution; instead, they sought to clarify the ideas of those who were dissatisfied with the regime. They contributed notably to political thought by popularizing the idea of a supreme court and a new constitution to safeguard civil liberties—both of which were to be signal accomplishments of the anti-Fascist Resistance. Furthermore, they helped promote a broader front of intellectuals willing to collaborate temporarily and cautiously with the PCI in the common fight against Fascism. Though a small number of them (Lucio Lombardo-Radice, Gastone Manacorda, and Antonello Trombadori) ended up in the PCI camp, most remained vigorously independent.[136]

Spreading out from Pisa after 1936, the Liberalsocialists organized nuclei throughout central and parts of northern and southern Italy. Florence and Rome were the strongholds, but Turin, Milan, Bologna, Genoa, Naples, and Bari also claimed adherents.[137]

Ferruccio Parri's radicalism

Inevitably, the Liberalsocialists paralleled and overlapped other liberal democratic and radical currents, and especially Ferruccio Parri's.[138] As the years slipped by, Calogero and Parri pulled closer together, with the help of a competent young Bolognese art historian, Carlo L. Ragghianti.[139] Between 1940 and 1942 the Liberalsocialists, Parri's radical democrats, and remnants of GL merged to form the influential Partito d'Azione (Pd'A; "Action Party").

After his arrest in October 1930 Parri had been sent once more to the *confino* isles, where he bided his time, devoting every free moment to study. Gaining conditional liberty in 1934, he re-

[136] Lombardo-Radice, *Fascismo e anticomunismo*, pp. 79–80; Ragghianti, *Disegno della liberazione italiana*, p. 297.
[137] In Tuscany were Professor Piero Calamandrei, expert in constitutional law; Tristano Codignola, Rosselli's partner in *Non Mollare!* and later proprietor of La Nuova Italia publishing house; Mario delle Piane and Enzo Enriques-Agnoletti, political journalists; Rannuccio Bianchi-Bandinelli, art historian; Giorgio Spini, political historian; and Professor Carlo Francovich, cultural leader. In Rome key members included Professor Guido DeRuggiero, eminent historian of liberalism; Avv. Federico Comandini; Avv. Sergio Fenoaltea; Vittorio Gabrieli; Luigi Milani; Enzo Tagliacozzo; and Bruno Zevi. The latter two fled to the United States after the anti-Semitic decrees of 1938.
[138] See *supra*, Ch. II, Third phase; Giustizia e Libertà.
[139] See his essay on the origins of the Partito d'Azione in the appendix to his *Diesegno della liberazione italiana*, pp. 273–353.

turned to Milan to accept a post in the Edison Company's research office. The prestigious moral leader of the non-Communist resistance immediately resumed his clandestine crusade.

Parri's closest collaborator in Milan was Avv. Ugo LaMalfa, a native of the South who in his student days in Rome had been a disciple of Amendola. Now an economist, LaMalfa worked in the research office of the Banca Commerciale and published some of his articles in Professor Einaudi's Torinese economic history review.[140]

While space limitations preclude any listing of all the covert groups in Parri's underground, a word must be said about the major geographical centers. Turin was always a focal point of anti-Fascism. Most of its radical democrats had attorned to GL; but by the late 1930's several members of the legal and academic professions were identified with Liberalsocialism.[141] Standing somewhat apart were the more orthodox Liberals like Avv. Manlio Brosio and two eminent scholars, Salvatorelli and Einaudi. The last-named, Italy's most distinguished liberal economist, naturally had to be circumspect in his contacts with the underground, but he was well aware of its existence and inspired many by his writings, particularly on the subject of European federation.

The non-Communist underground in Rome kept in communication with the Torinese, Milanese, and Neapolitan groups partly with the help of Raimondo Craveri, a native of Piedmont, employee of the research office of Banca Commerciale, and husband of Croce's eldest daughter, Elena. Roman members of the democratic underground included Professor DeRuggiero, Vinciguerra, and Morra (incisive historians all), and a group of aggressive lawyers (Sergio Fenoaltea, Giuseppe Bruno, Stefano Siglienti, Achille Battaglia, and Mario Berlinguer). The Republican Reale family of Rome emigrated to Lugano during the mid-1930's;

[140] Some other members of Parri's covert group in Lombardy included Mario Paggi, Adolfo Tino, Vittorio Albasini-Scrosati, Riccardo Lombardi (an ex-Communist), Giovanni Mira, Bianca Ceva (sister of the chemist suicide), Cesare Spellanzon (federalist historian of the Risorgimento), Francesco Flora, Mario Borsa, Umberto Segre (to be re-arrested in 1940), and (after 1939) Mario Vinciguerra. All of them were critical thinkers and professionalists; many were writers.

[141] Most conspicuous were the magistrate Domenico R. Peretti-Griva, Giorgio Agosti, Ada Prospero (widow of Piero Gobetti), Carlo and Alessandro Galante-Garrone, Dante Livio Bianco, Carlo Mussa, and (after their return from prison) Mila, Monti, and Andreis.

there Egidio Reale inaugurated an impressive publication program, "Nuove edizioni di Capolago," first of which to appear (1936) was *Liberazione* by the *émigré* historian, Guglielmo Ferrero.

After 1937–1938 Bologna produced a spirited anti-Fascist nucleus. Besides Professor Ragghianti there was the law school professor Edoardo Volterra, the art historian Cesare Gnudi, and Avv. Jacchia. In the Romagna Arnaldo Guerrini was a key organizer, while at the University of Padua Norberto Bobbio, Mario dal Pra, and Egidio Meneghetti were magnets. In Vicenza lived Neri Pozza, later to head a publishing firm. In the southern half of the peninsula Professor Adolfo Omodeo, the University of Naples' renowned historian of the Risorgimento, was the leading radical democrat; both he and the philosophy professor Alfredo Parente were intimate friends of Croce. In Bari the educators Tommaso and Enzo Fiore and the junior members (Franco and Giuseppe) of the Laterza publishing house stood out.

Indeed, the covert democratic groups, though much less effective than they had been during the Depression and though faced with growing Communist competition, were by no means extinct in the "lean years" of anti-Fascism.

Monarchy, Church, and Jews

Shortly before World War II, the undercurrent of latent discord between the *Duce* and the King manifested itself again. Premier Mussolini had never felt true affection for Victor Emmanuel, and he resented the difficulties caused by their dual executive system (the "dyarchy"). The King, for his part, was irritated by Mussolini's increasingly pro-German orientation after the Ethiopian War. He resented the "Prussian" impact upon Army policies and found the goose step especially repugnant.[142]

When Hitler annexed Austria in March 1938 Mussolini spoke to the Senate in order to allay widespread national bewilderment. In the course of his remarks he declared that any future war "will be directed, under the King's orders, by one man alone, by the one who is speaking to you"—words later to be thrown back in

---

[142] In January 1938 the dictator spread unkind stories that Italy's *mezza-cartuccia* ("half-cartridge") monarch disliked the step only because he could not perform it, and hated the cavalry because he had to "use a step-ladder to mount a horse." *Ibid.*, p. 823.

his face. About the same time the obliging Parliament created a new rank, "First Marshal of the Empire," which it bestowed simultaneously upon King and *Duce*. Since this treated them as equals, the old Savoyard was in a rage. According to Mussolini, he said: "This measure is another mortal blow against my sovereign prerogatives. . . . Due to the imminence of an international crisis, I do not want to add fuel to the fire, but at any other time, rather than suffer this affront, I should prefer to abdicate." [143]

Rumors had it that Mussolini would get rid of the Monarchy as soon as the Spanish War ended. Actually, he prudently decided to postpone this till the aged King should die. When Reichschancellor-President Hitler visited Rome in May 1938, protocol required him to spend much time with the sovereign. Ribbentrop told Mussolini of his master's displeasure, whereupon the *Duce* responded dryly: "Tell the *Fuehrer* to be patient. I have been patient for sixteen years!" Later the King let it be known that he disliked Mussolini's anti-Semitic measures and his plan to invade Albania.[144]

On the eve of the vicennial anniversary of the Fascist movement, Victor Emmanuel feared some new humiliation. To forestall it, he proposed that Mussolini assume the title "Chancellor"; but the *Duce* would have none of this—to the King's embarrassment. Their relationship did not improve when the sovereign told his minister that he heard the Germans were calling the latter the "*Gauleiter* of Italy." [145] Despite the *Duce*'s arrogance the King swallowed his pride and accepted with seemingly childish joy the new title of "King-Emperor" which the Blackshirt dictator thoughtfully bestowed upon him after the African victory. Nor did he reject the Albanian crown. And though he heartily disliked the Germans, Victor Emmanuel did not block Mussolini's war move against France. Not till after a series of military disasters did the supine Savoyard turn against his prime minister with any degree of decisiveness, and only then when he was sure of support from high Army officers.

[143] Quoted by Mussolini, *Storia di un anno*, pp. 179–180; *cf*. Nino Bolla (ed.), *Colloqui con Umberto II; colloqui con Vittorio Emanuele III* (Rome, 1949), p. 123.
[144] S/M, *Sdf*, pp. 829, 831, 839.
[145] *Ibid*., pp. 859–860; Monelli, *Mussolini*, p. 168.

174

Occasional rumors of intraparty strife involving such Fascists as Edmondo Rossoni, Giuseppe Bottai, Dino Grandi, and Luigi Federzoni made the rounds in the late 1930's. Though they were "left-wing corporatists," they were not yet openly *frondeurs*, and, like the King, they too waited until the military debacles of World War II compelled them to plot against the dictator.[146]

With the Vatican Mussolini had enjoyed superficially amicable relations since settlement of the Catholic Action dispute. Though at least a fraction of parish priests and laymen certainly felt no fondness for Fascism, they prudently kept their thoughts to themselves. When the Ethiopian War and sanctions agitated the nation, most clergymen let themselves be swept along with the patriotic tide. Mussolini was pleased to learn that Milan's Ildefonso Cardinal Schuster and several dozen other eminent prelates had ardently supported the military campaign. Though it seems that no members of the papal curia overstepped the bounds of neutrality during the war, a few days after the armistice Pius XI let his native Italian patriotism get the better of him when he addressed (May 12, 1936) promoters of a World Exhibition of the Catholic Press. His prepared text contained a most imprudent phrase which, taken out of context, caused intense embarrassment to anti-Fascist Catholics: "May this Exhibition be blessed by Almighty God, Who has suffered it to begin in such an unexpectedly propitious atmosphere, general and local, near and far, to the point of an almost exact coincidence with the triumphant joy of an entire great and good people over a peace which, it is hoped and intended, will be an effective contribution and prelude to that true peace in Europe and the world of which this Exhibition wishes to be a clear symbol." [147]

Italian clergymen raised no objection to Mussolini's dispatch of "volunteers" to Spain. One could hardly have expected them to do otherwise in view of the Church's manifest sympathy for

---

[146] Salvadori, *Resistenza ed azione*, p. 183.

[147] *Civiltà cattolica*, II (1936), 422, cited by Binchy, *Church and State in Fascist Italy*, p. 648. See this liberal Catholic's discussion of the Ethiopian War, pp. 637–651 ff. It is a kind of rebuttal to the extremely anticlerical interpretation of Salvemini, "The Vatican and the Ethiopian War," *Christendom* (Winter, 1937), reprinted in Keene (ed.), *Neither Liberty Nor Bread*, pp. 191–200. Cf. S/M, *Sdf*, p. 858; and Jemolo, *Chiesa e Stato in Italia negli ultimi cento anni*, pp. 668–686.

Generalissimo Franco's "crusade" against the "Godless Reds" who in many cases were persecuting the Church in Spain.[148]

Not till the *Duce* abjectly copied Hitler's anti-Semitism did significant new discord between Fascism and the Church occur. In his Encyclical, "Mit brennender Sorge," Pius XI had made no secret of his intense horror of Germany's pogroms, and on occasion he had expressed relief that no such persecution took place in Italy. One can imagine his dismay, then, when but a few months later (July 14, 1938) the *Duce* and Farinacci—backed by a group of anonymous university professors who helpfully discovered ten curious "scientific bases" for an "Aryan" racial policy in Italy [149]—launched their anti-Semitic measures and spread blatant biological propaganda on the subject in a new periodical, *Difesa della razza* ("Defense of the Race"). Immediately and unequivocally the Pope censured these heresies. He made it clear that anti-Semitism, by its denial of the Fatherhood of God and the brotherhood of man, struck at the very roots of Christianity. "If there is anything worse than the various theories of racialism and nationalism, it is the spirit that dictates them," he declared on July 21. Then he especially infuriated Mussolini by taunting him over adopting policies in deliberate imitation of Nazi Germany and in direct violation of the noblest traditions of the Roman Empire which he supposedly was anxious to restore. The *Duce* was even more beside himself when on September 3 the Pope bluntly explained to Belgian pilgrims, "Spiritually we are Jews." [150] Mussolini's police sought to confiscate several issues of *L'Osservatore romano* and *Civiltà cattolica* in the midst of these recriminations. At least one churchman, Fr. Gemelli, Rector of Milan's Catholic University, spoke out (January 10, 1939) in favor of the racist policies.[151]

Italy's anti-Semitic decrees made life steadily more difficult for the country's twenty-six autonomous and relatively small native Jewish communities, estimated to have numbered about 56,000 people in 1937,[152] as well as for those additional refugees who

[148] Binchy, *Church and State in Fascist Italy*, pp. 651–654.
[149] They are printed in the *New York Times* [hereafter cited as NYT], July 15, 1938.
[150] Quotations cited in Binchy, *Church and State in Fascist Italy*, pp. 615–617.
[151] Herbert L. Matthews, *The Fruits of Fascism* (New York, 1943), p. 241; Webster, *The Church and the Fasces*, pp. 159–161.
[152] Binchy, *Church and State in Fascist Italy*, p. 605, n. 2; *cf.* his Chapter 21.

had escaped recently from Central Europe. First Mussolini closed the schools to foreign-born Jews; then he forbade such refugees to establish residence in Italy; next he drove all Jews from teaching and other public posts; and finally (over the protests of the Pope who announced it violated the Lateran Accords) he forbade marriage between Jews and Gentiles.[153] Yet Jews in Italy, unlike those in Nazi-ruled Europe, made out fairly well until 1943, thanks to the goodwill of most Italians and the discreet succor of the Roman Catholic Church. But when the Nazis seized northern Italy in September 1943, the plight of the Jews became desperate. Some 9,000 lost their lives.[154]

The deleterious results of anti-Semitism were most visible in the universities. Practically every field of research lost able scholars. Hardest hit were the faculties of science, medicine, and law. Among those harried out of the land was the brilliant atomic physicist and Nobel Prize winner, Enrico Fermi, himself not a Jew but married to one. Professor Fermi identified himself with the West in the postwar ideological conflict with the Soviet bloc, whereas another Jewish *émigré* physicist, Bruno Pontecorvo, eventually threw in his lot with Stalin's Russia after spending some time working with the French physicist and Communist, Jean Frédéric Joliot-Curie.[155]

Manifestly, not all who fled were anti-Fascists. Signora Margherita Sarfatti, for example, had once written an effusive biography of Mussolini.[156] Yet few who departed carried any affection for Italy's totalitarian regime now linked to Hitler's. Most of them gravitated into opposition circles abroad and infused them with new vigor, more up-to-date information of how superficial Fascism's fascination was in the hearts and minds of most Ital-

[153] *Ibid.*, p. 628; S/M, *Sdf*, pp. 834–838.
[154] Massimo Salvadori, *Storia della Resistenza italiana* (Venice, 1955), pp. 34–35 [hereafter cited as Salvadori, *SRI*].
[155] Garosci, *Sdf*, pp. 192–193. Minio-Paluello, *Education in Fascist Italy*, pp. 200–201, mentions other Jews dismissed: in mathematics, Tullio Levi-Civita, Federigo Enriques, Giacomo Fubini, Beppo Levi, and Giulio Fano; in physics, Franco Rasetti and Bruno Rossi; in medicine, Giuseppe Levi, Mario Donati, Carlo Foà; in law and economics, Edoardo Volterra, Giorgio del Vecchio, Adolfo Ravà, Giorgio Mortara, Marco Fanno, and Gustavo del Vecchio; in arts and letters, Benvenuto Terracini, Giorgio Falco, Attilio Momigliano, Adolfo Levi, Rodolfo Mondolfo, Lodovico Limentani, Arnaldo Momigliano, Marco Attilio Levi, Alessandro della Seta; and in other sciences, Roberto Almagià and Giacomo Levi.
[156] *Dux: The Life of Benito Mussolini* (New York, 1927).

ians.[157] Some of the anticlerical *fuorusciti* could not avoid being favorably impressed by the Church's sympathy for the Jews; to some degree this helped attenuate their hostility to the Church. Quite a number of Jewish refugees joined Giustizia e Libertà. The Rome architect Bruno Zevi, for instance, collaborated with Giellisti in the *Quaderni Italiani* in New York and Boston during World War II, while Enzo Tagliacozzo and Lamberto Borghi made their way to Massachusetts,[158] where they worked closely with Professor Salvemini, who from his Harvard desk kept up a barrage against the dictatorship, one of the most telling being *Under the Axe of Fascism* (New York, 1936).

By the time Cardinal Pacelli ascended the throne as Pius XII in February 1939 at least some of the friction between Church and State had abated.[159] The new pontiff forestalled more by tightening the Church hierarchy's control of Catholic Action.[160] But the relative harmony was brief. During the first months of the war there was no doubt that the Vatican was as unhappy over Nazi-Fascist aggression and racism as it was over Soviet annexation of much of Catholic Poland and the Baltic states. In the period of the *Duce*'s nonbelligerency certain Catholic leaders like Giorgio LaPira condemned the war through the pages of the short-lived Florentine periodical *Principî*.[161]

As the bleak news from the battlefronts caused Mussolini's prestige to plummet, the popularity of the Holy Father among the Italian masses soared correspondingly, so that by the eve of the crisis of July 25, 1943, millions were looking to the Vatican for leadership (just as they were also looking to the Crown).

End of the Popular Front

Even after the Communist exiles organized the UPI in March 1937, their "unity of action" pact with the PSI remained their strongest card. But the wisdom of this agreement, which operated in strict accordance with current Soviet needs, was questioned at intervals by revisionists like Modigliani and Tasca. The behavior

---

[157] Salvadori, *Resistenza ed azione*, pp. 174–178.

[158] Garosci, *Sdf*, pp. 192–194.

[159] S/M, *Sdf*, p. 858; *cf.* Giorgio LaPiana, "The Political Heritage of Pius XII," *Foreign Affairs*, XVIII (April 1940), reprinted in Keene (ed.), *Neither Liberty Nor Bread*, pp. 201–208.

[160] See *supra*, Ch. III, Fascism versus Catholicism.

[161] Published from January 1939 till February 1940 by Libreria Editrice Fiorentina; reprinted as Giorgio LaPira, *Principî*, ed. Angelo Scivoletto (Florence, 1955).

of the Communists during some phases of the Spanish blood bath, combined with the great purges in the USSR, aroused no little anxiety among Italian Socialists. But usually in the showdowns (as at the PSI congress in June 1937) the "doubters" stopped short of voting against the alliance. It was formally renewed on July 26 of that year. Nenni thus was able to keep tight rein on the PSI until the startling announcement of the August 23 Molotov-Ribbentrop Treaty of Neutrality and Nonaggression between Soviet Russia and Nazi Germany.[162]

This produced shock of the first magnitude among Italian Socialists and Communists. Only ten days earlier Togliatti and Longo had convened a party conference in Paris, attended by some directors who had just arrived from northern Italy. They had drawn up plans to transfer, in case of war, as many comrades as possible into Italy to spread propaganda. Moscow's *svolta* of the 23rd, however, made it mandatory for Reds everywhere to reverse their slogans and quit berating Hitler and Mussolini, for nothing must be done that could stir the Axis to declare war upon the USSR. Nor must Communists give aid to the war effort of "imperialist" Britain and France. Instead, the proper course should be that which Lenin had pursued—defeatism and conversion of the "imperialist war" into a "civil war." Doubtless most Italian Communists were momentarily as dismayed as their French comrades,[163] but (except for a handful) they obediently closed ranks and toed the new line.[164]

Virtually all of the PSI members, however, were indignant over the cynical pact. At first, Nenni was just as angry with it as were the spokesmen of his party's revisionist wing—Saragat, Faravelli, and Tasca.[165] But during the next few days he decided not to sever his bond completely,[166] whereupon his reformist colleagues accused him of betraying both democracy and socialism

[162] Garosci, *Sdf*, pp. 173–180.

[163] Tasca, *A Communist Party in Action*, p. 2 ff.; Tasca, *Les Communistes français pendant la "drôle de guerre"* (Paris, 1951); and Tasca, *In Francia nella bufera*.

[164] Noteworthy defectors included Romano Cocchi, secretary-general of UPI, and Leo Valiani, a journalist exile from Trieste who was to become a leader in the new Partito d'Azione. B/G, *Storia del PCI*, pp. 346–347, 352; Garosci, *Sdf*, pp. 173–180.

[165] See Paris *Nuovo Avanti!* Aug. 24, 1939.

[166] His position had indeed changed substantially since 1923. In that year he had been rewarded with the directorship of *Avanti!* after repulsing Serrati's efforts to fuse the PSI and PCI; in 1926 he had resigned after failing to persuade the maximalists to consolidate with the revisionists.

and demanded his immediate resignation. Since they could not assemble a formal congress, they summoned an autumn conclave of those party members who lived near Paris. There Tasca denounced Nenni for blindly following Moscow's line. Nenni retorted that there was more socialism in Germany and Russia than in any of the Western states. Calling attention to the distinguished historical role of the USSR, he expressed conviction that sooner or later the Kremlin would re-enter the anti-Axis lists.[167] Nenni might well have been expelled had it not been for timely intercession by the venerable Modigliani, who feared that the French police would arrest Nenni if his pro-Soviet attitude attracted further publicity. He therefore urged Nenni to become inactive. This he prudently agreed to, resigning both the secretarial and editorial posts he had held since 1930.[168]

The bombshell of the Molotov-Ribbentrop Pact thus disintegrated the substantial anti-Fascist solidarity that had been forged during the Popular Front era. It was to be restored only with difficulty between June 1941 and the summer of 1943.[169]

---

[167] P. Nenni, "Alleanza Social-comunista," *Mercurio*, No. 3 (1944), 13–18; *cf.* his *Pagine di diario* (Milan, 1947), p. 109 (June 10, 1940); and his articles in Rome *Avanti!*, July 16–18, 1944; *cf.* Arfè, *Storia dell' "Avanti!" 1926–1940*.

[168] Puglionisi, *Sciacalli*, pp. 137–139; Garosci, *Sdf*, pp. 203–204.

[169] Arfè, *Storia dell' "Avanti!" 1926–1940*, pp. 153–157, 212–225.

CHAPTER V · BEGINNING OF THE END

August 1939 – July 1943

Italian unpreparedness and intervention

THE Molotov-Ribbentrop Pact of August 23, 1939, removed the last major obstacle from the path of Hitler's Juggernaut by assuring him a one-front war as soon as weak Poland was knocked out. Within forty-eight hours after *Stukas* and tanks roared across the Corridor, Britain and France rallied to Poland's aid.

Drained of its physical vigor by four years of bloodletting in Ethiopia, Spain, and Albania, Mussolini's Italy was wholly unprepared to enter the war. By August 1939 Count Ciano had lost ardor for the Pact of Steel which he himself had negotiated with Nazi Germany three months before.[1] Along with the relatively independent-minded hierarchs Italo Balbo, Giuseppe Bottai, and Dino Grandi, he sought to dissuade Mussolini from joining the fray, arguing that even an Axis triumph would mean ultimate defeat for Italy, since Hitler would not long tolerate even a semblance of equality on the part of his Mediterranean ally. High prelates, Marshal Pietro Badoglio, and Sumner Welles all entreated Mussolini to stay neutral;[2] so did exiled former Premier F. S. Nitti in a letter from Paris on September 15, 1939.[3]

Ciano's diary reveals that the self-effacing King did consider rejecting the *Duce's* war plans. On March 14, 1940, the wily Minister of the Royal House, Count (later Duke) Acquarone, approached Ciano on the golf course and reported that the monarch was of the opinion that "it may become necessary for him to intervene at any moment to give a different direction to things; he is prepared to do this and to do it with despatch." Acquarone explained that the King felt for Ciano "more than benevolence— a real affection and much trust." Although Acquarone wished to go deeper into the subject, Ciano preferred to keep the conversation "on general lines."[4] During the rest of the spring, however,

---

[1] Hugh Gibson (ed.), *The Ciano Diaries, 1939–1943* (Garden City, 1947), p. 125 ff. *Cf.* Arnold and Veronica M. Toynbee (eds.), *The Eve of War, 1939* ("Survey of International Affairs, 1939–1946") (New York, 1958).
[2] S/M, *Sdf*, p. 886.
[3] Printed in Garosci, *Sdf*, pp. 282–283.
[4] Gibson (ed.), *Ciano Diaries*, p. 221.

Ciano became more passive, and so did the King. Indeed, the old monarch scorned the letter of May 30 which Count Sforza addressed to him from abroad, imploring him to reject any war gambit by Mussolini.[5]

For a while counsels of neutrality seemed to persuade the vacillating dictator, but one could never be sure that his mind would stay made up. Fearing the world would call him a welsher, Mussolini had entreated Hitler to send him a public telegram (which he did on September 1, 1939) explaining that Germany did not then need Italy's military help.[6] But when Hitler achieved his easy victory in the Low Countries and France, Mussolini was determined not to delay intervention, lest he lose forever the chance for booty and prestige. Ever the opportunist, he cast the die for war without even bothering to consult the Grand Council, let alone the robot Parliament. But he did confer with the King, who alone under the Albertine Constitution possessed power to declare war. Though disturbed, Victor Emmanuel did not seriously object. He confined himself to resisting the dictator's desire to take over the supreme command personally and agreed to entrust him only with command of troops actually in the field.[7] Little wonder, therefore, that embittered anti-Fascists stepped up their denunciations of the timorous Savoyard whom they held co-accountable for the war.

Responsibility for Italian entry into the conflict certainly lay with more than one man alone, but just how widely the blame ought to be apportioned is hard to determine.[8] Some of the crowd that surged into Piazza Venezia on June 10, 1940, to hear the *Duce*'s decision was genuinely enthusiastic. Yet there is no

[5] Printed in Carlo Sforza, *L'Italia dal 1914 al 1944 quale io la vidi* (Rome, 1945), p. 164.

[6] Cited in *I Documenti Diplomatici Italiani*, Ottava Serie, 1935–1939, Vol. XIII (12 agosto–3 settembre 1939) (Rome, 1953), p. 330; cf. *ibid.*, Nona Serie, 1939–1943, Vol. I (4 settembre–24 ottobre 1939) (Rome, 1954), pp. 10–12; Gibson (ed.), *Ciano Diaries*, pp. 135–141; S/M, *Sdf*, p. 879.

[7] *Ibid.*, p. 889.

[8] Roberto Battaglia, Communist historian of the Armed Resistance, has sought to blame especially "finance capital." However, he is compelled to concede that there were differences in attitude between capitalist cliques, and he admits that they tended to become disillusioned with the war and opposed Mussolini after November 1942. "Un aspetto inedito della crisi del '43: L'attegiamento di alcuni gruppi del capitale finanziario," *MLI*, No. 34/35 (1955), pp. 29–36. Salvatorelli has raised many doubts about Battaglia's economic interpretation; *MLI*, No. 34/35 (1955), p. 143.

reason to doubt the testimony of discerning observers that this mood did not characterize the populace at large.[9] If thousands of actual and potential anti-Fascists obediently shouldered arms, it was due largely to their instilled belief that in time of war one must fight for his country, right or wrong.[10]

The date Mussolini chose to hurl Italy into battle coincided almost exactly with the sixteenth anniversary of the murder of Matteotti and the third one of the assassination of the Rossellis. Just as those bloody deeds had outraged anti-Fascists, so this "stab in the back" of France disgusted the free world and ushered in a graver crisis than any Mussolini had confronted. This time the sagging dictator could not surmount the gale.

Italy's role in the war was inglorious.[11] Co-ordination was deficient at all levels of command. Most of the officer caste, inadequately trained for modern warfare and permeated by political ambitions, could not hold the respect of the men. Nowhere was the failure of the corpulent, tired regime more glaring than in the very sector it had always sought to glorify—the armed forces. Italians found scant cause to rejoice over the bits of French soil Hitler tossed to them. Still more humiliating was the ill-fated invasion of Greece, which Mussolini (with encouragement from Ciano) ordered in October 1940, without prior warning to his Axis partner. When the troops bogged down on this new front, the *Duce* had to ask his Teutonic ally for help. Henceforth the Germans scarcely bothered to conceal their contempt

[9] Matthews, *Fruits of Fascism*, pp. 308–311.

[10] A. Marazza, "I Cattolici e la Resistenza," *MLI*, No. 43 (1956), pp. 3–15.

[11] On the politico-military crisis after 1940, see Franco Ravà and Giorgio Spini, "Fonti documentarie e memorialistiche per la storia della crisi dello stato italiano (1940–1945)," *Rivista storica italiana*, LXI (1949), pp. 404–431 and 574–602; Mario Toscano, "Fonti documentarie e memorialistiche per la storia diplomatica della seconda guerra mondiale," *ibid.*, LX (1948), pp. 83–126; his numerous monographs on the "pact of steel" and diplomacy of this era; *Saggio bibliografico sulla seconda guerra*, prepared by Ufficio Storico, Corpo di Stato Maggiore Esercito (Rome, 1955); Ettore Anchieri, "Les rapports italo-allemands," *Revue d'histoire de la deuxième guerre mondiale*, No. 26 (April 1957), pp. 1–23; Katherine Duff, "Italy from June 1940 to July 1943," in A. and V. Toynbee (eds.), *Hitler's Europe* (London, 1954), pp. 283–337; Elizabeth Wiskemann, *The Rome-Berlin Axis: A History of the Relations between Hitler and Mussolini* (New York, 1949).

Regarding unpreparedness, see General Giacomo Zanussi, *Guerra e catastrofe d'Italia, 1940–1945* (Rome, 1946); Carlo Favagrossa, *Perchè perdemmo la guerra: Mussolini e la produzione bellica* (Milan, 1946). *Cf.* Vittorio Gorresio's articles, "I Fascisti alla guerra," Rome *Il Mondo*, Jan. 28, Feb. 4, 11, 18, 1958.

See Emilio Faldella, *Revisione di giudizi: l'Italia e la seconda guerra mondiale* (2nd ed.; Bologna, 1960), for a useful recent appraisal of Italy's role in the war.

for Italy's fighting ability. Searching for a scapegoat in Greece, Mussolini fired his Chief of the General Staff, Marshal Badoglio, in November 1940 and thereby propelled him into the tortuous plots that two and one half years later led to the *Duce's* own fall.[12]

In Africa the British struck at Graziani's men until they were groggy, and then reinstated Haile Selassie on his Ethiopian throne in 1941. When the Nazis invaded Yugoslavia in April, Hitler sliced off a bit of Slovenia for Mussolini and allowed him and the Croatian Fascist chieftain, Ante Pavelič, to organize a quisling Kingdom of Croatia. After Hitler turned upon Russia in June, the *Duce* unwisely dispatched some 240,000 poorly equipped troops to that theater and thereby scattered further his thinly spread manpower. At least half the Italian forces on the eastern front never returned.

Morale at home plummeted to new lows under the impact of aerial bombardments by the "Anglo-assassins" and the overbearing attitude of the Germans. Yet most of the time civilians were too busy with the elementary tasks of keeping their families housed and fed to think much about the foreigners. Their use of electricity, gas, and gasoline had been curtailed severely early in the war; basic articles in their diet had been rationed. Despite price and wage controls, inflation soared and the black market flourished. Honest people resented favoritism in distribution of commodities and grumbled about the ever-more-apparent corruption at all levels of government. By 1942 rogues and profiteers surrounding Mussolini's mistress, Claretta Petacci, had become a national scandal.[13]

Skeptical of propaganda from Rome, large numbers of people risked arrest to tune in on the BBC's Italian-language newscasts and incitements to anti-Fascism. Defeatism welled up. Replacement of one inept party secretary after another evidenced the internal crisis. The squabbles among the hierarchs could not be

[12] The incompetent Marshal Ugo Cavallero became the surrogate Chief of Staff till February 1, 1943. For a discussion of permutations in the Italian High Command, see Howard McGaw Smyth, "The Command of the Italian Armed Forces in World War II," *Military Affairs*, xv (Spring 1951), pp. 38–52.

[13] Monelli, *Mussolini*, pp. 201–205; S/M, *Sdf*, pp. 907–910, 932–936; Vaussard, *Histoire de l'Italie contemporaine*, p. 224; Matthews, *Fruits of Fascism*, pp. 305–306, 324; and Richard G. Massock, *Italy from Within* (New York, 1943), pp. 326–329, 369–377.

hidden; when Mussolini fired Badoglio, "ushers at the doors of the Palazzo Venezia were given instructions to accompany the most important Italian big shots into different rooms, in order to prevent a general brawl." [14]

Four days after the Japanese struck Pearl Harbor, Mussolini proclaimed in a "brief and incisive speech" that Italy was also at war with the United States. The people in the piazza responded with minimal applause, for most of them knew something of the New World's might. In July 1942 the *Duce* sojourned three weeks in North Africa in anticipation of a triumphal march into Alexandria; not only was that denied him, but Field Marshal Erwin Rommel failed to receive him. When he sneaked home a flare-up of his duodenal ulcer and gastroenteritis caused him rapidly to lose forty pounds. In his heart he must have sensed that the war was lost and that his own career was ebbing. [15]

Turning point of the war

For Italy the turning point of the war was November 1942, when General Dwight Eisenhower's forces landed in Morocco and Algeria and began their push to meet General Bernard Montgomery's British Eighth Army, which already had broken through Axis defenses at El Alamein. The new Allied bases facilitated stepped-up bombardments of Italian cities and rail centers and complicated hopelessly the already chaotic problems of transportation, production, and housing.

"Henceforth the strategic initiative lay in the hands of the Allies," while at home "all the enemies of Fascism . . . raised their heads," the *Duce* admitted candidly in his memoirs. [16] The same fact was attested to by Ciano, Bottai, Caviglia, and virtually everyone else close to the seat of power. [17] Ciano's diary entry of October 31, 1942, revealed that he "offered many olive branches" to a Swiss banker, for "we have great need" of Switzerland. On November 17 he expressed his doubts about the Militia's fidelity: "I believe that police and *Carabinieri* represent all that is left to

[14] Gibson (ed.), *Ciano Diaries* (Nov. 26, 1940), p. 315.
[15] S/M, *Sdf*, pp. 922–928; Monelli, *Mussolini*, pp. 11–17, 191–194.
[16] Mussolini, *Storia di un anno*, pp. 8–9.
[17] Giuseppe Bottai, *Vent'anni e un giorno* (Milan, 1949), pp. 230–236; Maresciallo Enrico Caviglia, *Diario (aprile 1925–marzo 1945)* (Rome, 1952), pp. 382–399.

guarantee our institutions." The King told Ciano on the 19th that he was worried, especially about the scarcity of troops in Rome. Four days later Ciano wrote: "In the country, pessimism and concern are growing beyond all measure. One cannot speak with any person of any class or station in life without hearing the same thing." [18]

Mussolini sought to silence some of the mounting criticism by ordering sweeping changes in the Army High Command and in his Cabinet; and with respect to the former the King almost certainly had a hand. On February 1, 1943, Mussolini named General Vittorio Ambrosio to replace Marshal Cavallero as Chief of the General Staff. Rumor had it that the latter and Farinacci were conspiring to unseat the dictator; in any event, they were patently subservient to the Nazis. "What is important" about Ambrosio, wrote Ciano, "is that at the head of our armed forces there is an Italian, a patriot who sees with honest eyes the reality of things, and who intends to put the interest of the country above everything else." [19] When Ambrosio sought to bring home troops dispersed in France and the Balkans, the Nazis at once were suspicious.[20]

The February 5 "changing of the guard" in the Cabinet affected all but two ministries and greatly augmented the already widespread hostility within the PNF toward the *Duce*. Outgoing officials included Ciano, Justice Minister Grandi, and Education Minister Bottai. Many speculated that these men were really *frondeurs* who favored slow evolution toward constitutional government and peace with the Allies; certainly they and Ambrosio all became archplotters against the dictator. Appointed ambassador to the Holy See (usually an innocuous post, but in wartime quite the reverse), Ciano noted significantly on February 5 that his new assignment might "open up many possibilities." The King was "happy" and Acquarone was "personally enthusiastic about it," he vouchsafed.[21] Hitler, it is now known, drew the quick inference that Ciano would seek a separate peace; to stiffen his wobbly ally, he dispatched Ribbentrop to Rome.[22]

[18] Gibson (ed.), *Ciano Diaries*, pp. 536–565.
[19] *Ibid.*, p. 575 (Jan. 30, 1943).
[20] S/M, *Sdf*, pp. 930–931.
[21] Gibson (ed.), *Ciano Diaries*, p. 577 (Feb. 6, 1943).
[22] Alan Bullock, *Hitler: A Study in Tyranny* (London, 1952), p. 645; Ulrich von Hassell, *The von Hassel Diaries, 1938–1944* (London, 1948), p. 256.

The dismissed cabinet officers were replaced by little-known party hacks. Mussolini himself took charge of Foreign Affairs and he kept the portfolios of Interior, War, Navy, and Air. Thus on the eve of the final crisis he was personally responsible for military decisions not only as *Capo del Governo* but as chief of the service ministries. The quality of performance did not improve.

While everywhere the war continued relentlessly, in Italy a crescendo of strikes and conspiracies testified ominously to the people's exasperation. In the forlorn hope of infusing new spirit into the defeatist-ridden party and nation, Mussolini announced on April 17 another "change of the guard" and named Carlo Scorza, an advocate of "get tough" measures, the new PNF secretary.[23]

Fighting "fuorusciti" (1939–1943)

Meanwhile, in France, after declaring war on September 3, 1939, Premier Edouard Daladier's government lost little time in suppressing Communist defeatist propaganda. Quickly it banned not only the French-language papers *L'Humanité* and *Ce Soir*, but the PCI periodical *Stato operaio* and newspaper *La Voce degli Italiani*, as well as most other Italian-language anti-Fascist publications; for Daladier was anxious to give no offense to Mussolini, at that time a nonbelligerent. Indeed, the French premier bent over backward to avoid giving the war any ideological coloration. For the present his propaganda stressed simply that the war was "in defense of *la patrie*," not a crusade.[24]

Within a matter of days police rounded up domestic and foreign Communist bellwethers, including Togliatti, Longo, and Giovanni Parodi. Togliatti was kept under arrest until February 1940, but luckily for him the police did not know his true identity. They interned Longo and Parodi with other veterans of the international brigades in camps near Toulouse.[25]

Since it was manifestly impossible to operate overtly in France, the PCI decided to dissolve its Central Committee there and transfer the Secretariat to Moscow as quickly as possible, leaving behind only a small Foreign Office. All this was done in the in-

[23] L. Salvatorelli, "Situazione interna e internazionale dell'Italia nel primo semestre del 1943," *MLI*, No. 34/35 (1955), 7–15; S/M, *Sdf*, pp. 936–937.
[24] Garosci, *Sdf*, p. 198.
[25] Robotti and Germanetto, *Trent'anni di lotte dei comunisti italiani*, p. 190.

terval between Togliatti's release and his arrival in Moscow in April 1940.[26]

Other PCI stalwarts were instructed to proceed to Tunisia and to the United States to carry on propaganda. To this end, Ambrogio Donini and Giuseppe Berti hastened to New York, where they resumed publication of *Stato operaio* and a weekly paper, *L'Italia del popolo*. These organs advocated American neutrality until Hitler attacked Stalin's Russia, after which they insisted just as loudly that the United States enter the war at once. Velio Spano and Giorgio Amendola went to Tunis to edit the daily *Giornale di Tunisi*; they got back to Italy in 1943 with the Allies.[27]

The PCI Foreign Office was left under the initial supervision of Agostino Novella, Umberto Massola, and Antonio Roasio— and, in a later period, of Celeste Negarville. Paolo Silvati, Emilio Sereni, and Giuseppe Dozza also worked out of that office. They undertook a threefold program: intensification of efforts to find dependable people for covert operations in Italy; publication of the clandestine *Lettere di Spartaco* ("Letters from Spartacus") to explain the party line and problems arising from the war; and assignment of party leaders to strategic places so that at the proper moment they could enter Italy without delay. After Mussolini pushed his nation into war on June 10, 1940, a cluster of Reds returned to Italy temporarily to disseminate a manifesto calling for union of all the people against the *"Duce's* war." [28]

Those Socialists who had been proponents of "unity of action" with the PCI also faced real danger of arrest in France. When Nenni resigned as secretary and editor of *Avanti!* in the late summer of 1939, neither of his most vocal critics, Tasca or Saragat, took his place. The former had become a French citizen and his time was taken up by writing for *Le Populaire,* delivering propa-

[26] During Togliatti's absence from Moscow since early in the Spanish Civil War, the PCI had been represented in the Comintern by Edoardo d'Onofrio. A few others had also been in Moscow: Ruggiero Grieco; the aged Egidio Gennari; Ottavio Pastore; Giovanni Germanetto, then Togliatti's secretary; Rita Montagnana, still Togliatti's wife; Paolo Robotti; Luigi Amadesi; and Luigi Polano. *Ibid.*, pp. 190–191; B/G, *Storia del PCI*, pp. 356–358; Garosci, *Sdf*, pp. 198–199.

[27] B/G, *Storia del PCI*, pp. 355–356; Robotti and Germanetto, *Trent'anni di lotte dei comunisti italiani*, p. 190; and Angelo Tasca, "I Comunisti prima e dopo," Rome *Il Mondo*, April 1, 1950.

[28] PCI, *Relazione della Direzione del PCI* at V° *Congresso*, p. 13; B/G, *Storia del PCI*, p. 360.

ganda broadcasts in Italian over Radio Française, and by his activities in the SFIO ("French Socialist Party").[29] Saragat lived
in a small town near Toulon, too far from the capital to be in
easy touch with party members there. Thus the aged and none-
too-robust Oddino Morgari (he died during the war) was called
upon to take over the secretariat. Much of the party work was
conducted out of Toulouse (where the French Socialist Federation of the Southwest had its headquarters) until the transfer of
operations to Zurich after the fall of France.[30]

Proposed military intervention

Several Italian Republicans, Socialists, Giellisti, and affiliates
of the LIDU expressed the desire to engage actively in the war
against Germany. Soon after its outbreak representatives of these
currents decided to collaborate in uniting the emigrant masses
"in the struggle alongside the French people and for the victory
of democracy in Europe." [31] In Paris they formed an Italian National Committee and launched a recruitment program for a
volunteer Giuseppe Garibaldi Legion. Pacciardi, Tarchiani, and
Sforza headed this effort.

Daladier raised no objections except that the legion must omit
any propaganda about "fighting Fascism." [32] As a matter of fact,
the French also permitted two rival recruiting agencies to work.
Romano Cocchi, who had just defected from the PCI and resigned his UPI secretaryship, headed one of these; later he died
in a Nazi concentration camp. Assisting him was the ubiquitous
Sante Garibaldi, brother of Peppino and Ricciotti and "veteran"
of the feigned filibustering "legion" of 1926. The third recruiting
agency was headed by a certain Signor Marabini, whose views
were much farther to the right.[33]

Late in the spring of 1940 Sforza, who ineffectually appealed
to King Victor Emmanuel III on May 30 to reject any war
gambit by Mussolini, met with more success with the French
government. He persuaded it to accept Italian emigrant contingents in its armed forces. These would fight against the Ger-

[29] Tasca, *In Francia nella bufera*, p. 15 ff.
[30] Garosci, *Sdf*, pp. 116, 206, 283–284.
[31] *Ibid.*, p. 200.
[32] *Ibid.*, p. 198.
[33] *Ibid.*, pp. 200–201.

mans, provided they could serve under their own banner; they would not be required to fight against Mussolini's Italy should it enter the conflict.[34] But recruitments met with very little result, and the *Blitzkrieg* ended before anything important had been accomplished. Perhaps it was just as well, for it would have been hard for the *fuorusciti* to maintain autonomy with respect to France's war aims. Furthermore, the type of volunteer units that had fought well in a conflict such as the Spanish Civil War scarcely made much sense in the mechanized struggle of World War II.

After Italy jumped into the fray on June 10, 1940, French officials wisely decided not to intern the *fuorusciti* lest such a move drive them into the arms of the *Duce*. All that they required was a simple *acte de loyalisme*, a promise not to disturb the war in any way. For the most part, the emigrants sympathized with France in her hour of defeat, and at war's end reasonably amicable relations between the Italianate groups and the rest of the Gallic citizenry were restored.

The inglorious collapse [35] of the Third Republic in June 1940 terminated any co-ordinated activity by the exiles. The German police in the occupied northern zones and the Vichy authorities in the Midi began to extradite as many of the *fuorusciti* as possible. This policy struck the Communists with great severity; eventually Longo, DiVittorio, Parodi, Barontini, Alberto Jacometti, Vittorio Flecchia, and others found themselves shipped home, where Mussolini's minions dispatched them to either the *confino* isles or mainland prisons.[36]

Most of the extradited Reds wound up on Ventotene, off the Neapolitan shore. Longo, who was interned there with DiVittorio, Terracini, Scoccimarro, Secchia, LiCausi, Roveda, and one hundred ex-Garibaldini from Spain has dubbed it the "capital" of the PCI underground. Communists were probably the largest contingent of the 1,000 prisoners interned there by the eve of

[34] Sforza, *L'Italia dal 1914 al 1944 quale io la vidi*, p. 200; V. Modigliani, *Esilio*, p. 284.

[35] Nenni, who was in Paris on June 12, told Communist DiVittorio he was shocked that there was not even a hint this time of an 1871-type Commune. Perhaps he momentarily forgot that the Communists were still defeatists. Nenni, *Pagine di diario*, p. 116 (June 12, 1940).

[36] Regarding Moscow's efforts in 1941–1942 to gain Longo's liberation in France by granting him Soviet citizenship, see Tasca, *In Francia nella bufera*, pp. 138–139.

the *coup d'état*. Twice weekly a small boat brought provisions and newspapers from the mainland. Though conditions fluctuated, secret messages occasionally could be slipped in and were passed surreptitiously from one *compagno* to another during daily exercise periods. PCI prisoners did their best to proselyte inmates; in the case of some Albanian military cadets they were quite successful. They also carried out rigorous study programs. A typical day's activities might include a half hour of gymnastics followed by studies until noon. After dinner and an hour of rest, party members often turned their attention to languages, mathematics, and other practical subjects (including the chapters on guerrilla warfare in an edition of Clausewitz they managed to obtain); toward evening they would discuss politics, whenever this was feasible.[37]

At least a handful of the Communists quartered on Ventotene became disillusioned with Stalinism and shifted to Socialism during their internment. This was the case wth Altiero Spinelli, who had started out in his youth as a PCI conspirator (attracted by the "internationalism" of the ideology) in Piedmont but after ten years of detention and much soul-searching had broken with the dogmatic party in 1937.[38] Along with two other inmates— Ernesto Rossi (the well-known Giellista) and Eugenio Colorni (who had served in the PSI Internal Center before his arrest in 1937)—Spinelli reflected on the international crisis and reread some perceptive essays that Professor Luigi Einaudi, the economist, had written in 1918 on the subject of a United States of Europe.[39] Sensing that the way was rapidly being cleared for Europe to escape from its Procrustean bed of nationalism, Spinelli and his friends turned for guidance to American and Swiss constitutional history and read avidly the writings of various Anglo-American federal unionists. In July 1941 they infiltrated

[37] Longo, *Un popolo alla macchia*, pp. 37–39; Jacometti, *Ventotene*; PCI, *Agostino Novella* (Rome, 1947), p. 12; and Pietro Secchia, "La Resistenza: organizzazione o spontaneità?" *MLI*, No. 55 (1959), pp. 177–179.
[38] Altiero Spinelli, "Pourquoi je suis européen," *Preuves*, No. 81 (Nov. 1957), pp. 33–39.
[39] First published in Milan *Corriere della sera* on January 5 and December 28, 1918, under the pen name "Junius," they were republished in book form under the same nom de plume: *Lettere politiche* (Bari, 1920), and reprinted in Luigi Einaudi, *La guerra e l'unità europea* (Milan, 1948), pp. 11–33. In them Einaudi compared the League of Nations to the American Articles of Confederation and argued that Europe really needed a replica of the American Constitution.

to the mainland a *Manifesto for a Free and United Europe*.[40] Federal union must have top priority among postwar tasks, it declared. Only in this way could the problem of Germany be solved, could socialism succeed, and could Italy raise her living standards. The manifesto went on to proclaim that henceforth "the dividing line between progressive and reactionary parties" would not be determined by the degree of democracy or of socialism they advocated but by their attitude toward the goal of a federated Europe. During ensuing months the authors stimulated noticeable federalist talk among the program drafters of the re-emerging Italian parties.[41]

A few PCI militants managed to stay in hiding in France after August 1939, pursuing for another year or so the defeatist line. Of course, Hitler's invasion of the "Socialists' Fatherland" on June 22, 1941, changed everything. Henceforth the Communists wholeheartedly joined the "patriotic struggle" of "democratic" states who were defending themselves against "Nazi-Fascist aggression," and cleverly sought to revive the Popular Front technique.

Their efforts bore fruit first in Toulouse, focal point in unoccupied France for many Italian *fuorusciti* and Spanish Republican exiles. Many of these worked closely with a local bookseller, Professor Silvio Trentin, the GL juridical scholar from Venetia. During the early war years he organized an autonomous "revolutionary movement for liberation and reconstruction," inspired by Rosselli's credo and bearing the label "Libérer et Fédérer." Its first publication on Bastille Day 1942 attested to the vivid dream of not just winning the war but of "winning the peace" through a federated, free Europe, and a kind of Proudhonian system of federated occupational groups within each country. Certainly it was a notable programmatic advance.[42]

Among those who took temporary shelter with Trentin in June 1940 was ex-Premier F. S. Nitti, who fled from Paris. Later, when officials intimated that it was safe to return to the German-

[40] See A. S. [Altiero Spinelli] and E. R. [Ernesto Rossi], *Problemi della Federazione europea* (Rome, 1944), with an intro. by Eugenio Colorni, who had then become editor of the underground *Avanti!* in Rome.

[41] See Charles F. Delzell, "The European Federalist Movement in Italy: First Phase, 1918–1947," *Journal of Modern History*, xxxii (1960), pp. 241–250.

[42] Henri Michel, *Histoire de la Résistance* (Paris, 1950), p. 21; *cf.* Tasca, *In Francia nella bufera*, pp. 62–65.

192

held metropolis, Nitti did so, accompanied by his very sick wife and dying son. He was in Paris when Mussolini fell three years later, but he scarcely had time to rejoice before the Germans deported him to the same camp in which Léon Blum was held. Not till 1945 did the old statesman get back to Italy, where he assumed a royalist stance.

Meanwhile, in Toulouse in October 1941 Trentin and F. Fausto Nitti [43] signed on behalf of GL an important pact with delegates of the PCI and PSI whereby a Committee of Action for the Union of the Italian People was established, which called upon Italy to make an immediate separate peace, to depose Mussolini, and to restore civil liberties.[44] Sereni and Dozza signed for the PCI, while Nenni and Saragat represented the PSI, which was trying hard to close ranks and silence the proponents of old-fashioned pacifism and of Rossellian "autonomous action." [45] The agreement had little practical effect outside southern France; indeed, so difficult were communications (usually via Switzerland) that its contents could be transmitted to the clandestine Turin Socialist Federation only in the summer of 1942.[46] Yet it signalled a momentous step toward revival of the Popular Front—a development that seemed more logical to anti-Fascists who stayed in Europe than to those who escaped overseas.[47]

Not long after the tripartite pact of Toulouse, Vichyite police nabbed Sereni in Nice and handed him over to an Italian military tribunal, which sentenced him to twenty years' imprisonment in Fossano. Sereni did not regain his freedom until after Marshal Badoglio's interregnum. Communist Giuliano Pajetta had somewhat better luck—at least till 1942, when he too was

[43] His book, *Huit chevaux—soixante-dix hommes* (Paris, 1946), gives an impression of Italo-French collaboration in this period.

[44] It also encouraged Italians abroad to resist tenaciously all efforts either to conscript them into forced labor in Germany or to repatriate them. For excerpts and discussion of the pact, see Tasca, *In Francia nella bufera*, pp. 57–62.

[45] In the PSI so-called "Lyon Theses" of late 1941, Nenni and Saragat called for unconditional solidarity with the anti-Fascist powers. Old Modigliani, on the other hand, held to the traditional pacifist line (just as he had in the era of Zimmerwald and Kienthal). Andrea Caffi, an ex-Giellista, supported by Faravelli, advocated the third thesis (of Rossellian stamp), calling for only conditional adherence to the Anglo–American–Soviet bloc, so as to preserve full autonomy for the Socialists at war's end. See Andrea Caffi, *I Socialisti, la guerra, la pace* (Genoa, "Quaderni del 'Gobetti,'" 1, 1958), and the review of it by Gaetano Arfè in *Il Ponte*, xv (1959), pp. 859–860.

[46] Battaglia, *SRI*, p. 63.

[47] Longo, *Un popolo alla macchia*, p. 30; Garosci, *Sdf*, p. 206.

caught (in Cannes). During the preceding year he had busily carried out instructions to reorganize PCI emigrants throughout France and had worked tenaciously amid much peril and achieved some success in Toulon, Nice, and the Maritime Alps. His diary entry on the eve of his incarceration at Grasse revealed his optimism.[48]

On February 8, 1943, three months after the German irruption into Vichy France, the police also arrested Nenni, who had been hiding most of the time in the eastern Pyrenees, where he put out six issues of *Nuovo Avanti!*, wrote a long essay on the Spanish War, and advocated "liquidation" of Socialism that was not also Social-Communism.[49] After a long odyssey through German prisons, this stormy petrel was finally sent to the *confino* isle of Ponza—partly, it would seem, as the result of Mussolini's intercession with Hitler.[50] Nenni's daughter died in Auschwitz and his son-in-law, a Frenchman, was executed in 1942 for having helped publish the Communist *L'Humanité*.[51] Other Socialists to be arrested in France and taken to Camp Vernet were Alessandro Bocconi and Giuseppe Faravelli. The latter, who had engaged in radio propaganda, was deported to Italy and condemned to twenty-two years' imprisonment; he was not freed during the Badoglio interlude but managed at a later date to escape during a bombardment. Tresso, the Trotskyist who had been expelled from the PCI during the 1930 "purge of the three," was jailed by the Vichy regime; eventually he gained his liberty, only to be killed, it is reported, by pro-Stalinist *maquis*.[52]

Though very few first-rank exiles were left in France by 1943, mandataries of the PCI, PSI, and GL met in Lyon on March 3 to reaffirm the Toulouse Pact.[53] And a few *fuorusciti* chose to remain in France, among them Tasca, Alfonso Leonetti,[54] Mario Levi, and Andrea Caffi (who died during the war). Most of them

---

[48] Giuliano Pajetta, *Douce France: diario 1941–1942* (Rome, 1956).

[49] Pietro Nenni, *Taccuino 1942* (Milan-Rome, 1955), *passim*; "Il dramma del non-intervento," in Nenni, *Spagna*, pp. 7–118; Tasca, *In Francia nella bufera*, pp. 135–137.

[50] Mussolini claimed the credit in a conversation with Carlo Silvestri in 1945. Dombrowski, *Mussolini: Twilight and Fall*, pp. 155–156; *cf.* Nenni, *Pagine di diario*, Part III.

[51] Two Italian accomplices, Riccardo Boatti and Stiatti, also went to their death.

[52] B/G, *Storia del PCI*, pp. 271–272; Garosci, *Sdf*, p. 206; Tasca, *In Francia nella bufera*, p. 133.

[53] Battaglia, *SRI*, p. 75.

[54] Author of *L'Italie* (*dès origines à 1922*) (Paris, 1953).

militated in the French underground, though Tasca and some other Socialists at first published the daily *Effort* in a vain attempt to encourage Marshal Pétain's Vichy government to lean in a socialist direction. When Tasca perceived the unlikelihood of this, he burned his bridges and joined the Résistance in February 1941.[55]

New foreign centers

As the Germans slugged their way toward Paris in the late spring of 1940, many *émigré* leaders managed to flee abroad in order to continue their fight. Some of them were aided by the British, *e.g.*, Sforza and Tarchiani, who escaped aboard one of His Majesty's destroyers from Bayonne and who later moved on to America. Several politicians were evacuated through Marseille and Casablanca to the United States, thanks to the help of American labor and religious organizations, as well as to President Franklin Roosevelt's issuance of emergency visas. Others sought to escape by way of Switzerland, or Spain, or Portugal. Not all succeeded. The young GL historian Franco Venturi, for example, was arrested in Spain and deported to Italy. But many finally made their way to such havens as Egypt, Uruguay, and Mexico.[56]

The labors of the scattered exiles between 1940 and 1943 can perhaps most clearly be summarized country by country. On the Continent, Switzerland offered the most suitable refuge. It had long permitted an Italian Socialist Federation to function among Italian immigrants who did not wish to join the Swiss Socialist Party. The mountain republic also had shown hospitality to the historian Guglielmo Ferrero, who died in Geneva on August 3, 1942; the ex-Communist Ignazio Silone, who resided in Zurich; and to such Republicans as Egidio Reale and Fernando Schiavetti. After the fall of France, old G. E. ("Menè") and Vera Modigliani sneaked into Geneva with the aid of Joyce Lussu. But the number of refugees in Switzerland during the early phase of the war was but a handful compared to the thousands who were to pour in from the German-seized Po valley after the announcement of the Italian armistice on September 8, 1943.[57]

---

[55] Tasca, *In Francia nella bufera*, pp. 43, 71–130, and *passim*.
[56] Garosci, *Sdf*, p. 208 ff.
[57] See *infra*, Ch. VII.

Prior to 1943 most anti-Fascist activity in Switzerland revolved about Silone's Zurich PSI Foreign Center. The famed writer had at last been persuaded to join the party and become its secretary in 1940. He was anxious to renovate the party creed and rid it of the Social-Communist clichés associated with Nenni. Silone therefore came out strongly in favor of an "ethical conception" of socialism and the reorganization of Europe along federalist lines; indeed, the motto of his newspaper, *L'Avvenire dei lavoratori* ("Workers' Future"), was "Liberare e Federare"—the same shibboleth Professor Trentin had proclaimed in France. "The old and reactionary system of national sovereignties" would have to be destroyed, Silone insisted; Europe must be unified and North Africa liberated. Moreover, a "third front" was necessary, for Fascism could not be felled by military force alone, but in the final reckoning only by action on the internal "third front." Thus in December 1942 Silone's group sought to infiltrate covert pamphlets calling upon the Italian people to engage in "civil disobedience." This conspiratorial work was supervised by Riccardo Formica ("Aldo Morandi"), who had commanded the Garibaldi Brigade early in 1939 during its final stand in Spain. A printer in Zurich, a bookdealer in Chiasso, and a railway stationmaster in Tirano served as the go-betweens. But Swiss police seized the material and its bearers at the end of 1942. Formia escaped; Silone was not so lucky. The Swiss did not free him until they were sure the Axis was losing the war. Thus contact between the PSI Foreign Center and Italy was severed during the critical weeks prior to the *coup d'état*.[58]

In Egypt small groups of Giellisti and Communists spread propaganda. The former were ably represented by Umberto Calosso, Paolo Vittorelli, and an ex-PW, Stefano Terra. They started a daily paper as well as an ambitious pamphlet series, "Nuovi Quaderni di Giustizia e Libertà." They made little headway among conservative Italian merchants in Alexandria and Cairo but gained some recruits among the prisoners held by the British.[59] Heading the PCI nucleus in Cairo was Renato Mieli,

---

[58] See Ignazio Silone's essay, "Nel bagaglio degli esuli," in *Esperienze e studi socialisti: scritti in onore di Ugo Guido Mondolfo*, ed. "Critica Sociale" (Florence, 1957), pp. 301–315; Crossman (ed.), *The God that Failed*, p. 76; and Garosci, *Sdf*, pp. 213–214, 284–289.

[59] Vittorelli, *Dalla rivoluzione alla caduta del fascismo, passim.*

who later returned to Italy with the British occupation forces and secured a post in the Military Press Censorship Division.[60]

Before the war Britain had never been the focal point of much intensive activity by the exiles, though a few stalwarts (Sturzo,[61] Salvemini,[62] and Max Salvadori—brother of Signora Joyce Lussu) had spent some time there. Because he held dual Anglo-Italian citizenship, Salvadori was called from North America to the War Ministry in London for consultation in the autumn of 1939. He learned that British Intelligence hoped to persuade "Capital, Crown, and Church" in Italy to keep Mussolini neutral. He conceded that this might be useful for the moment but he urged British officialdom to take a longer view of the problem and to extend aid to the genuine anti-Fascists who certainly would play a big role in the eventual rebuilding of Italian democracy. So long as Fascist Italy was not at war, however, the British were disinclined to go along with his suggestion. When the *Duce* did declare war upon them in June 1940, they rounded up most Italian residents, some of whom they deported to Canada and others they released for propagandistic and intelligence work.[63] British Intelligence sent Salvadori back to North America to help co-ordinate anti-Fascist newspapers for Italian-speaking communities, to propagandize PW's, and to promote Italian volunteer contingents.[64] It employed Paolo Treves, son of Claudio, to deliver broadcasts to the Italian people.[65]

Inevitably, many *fuorusciti* passed through London during the early war years, for it was then the major center of Allied propaganda broadcasts and of policy-making with respect to Italy. Giellisti who visited London included the Lussus, Calosso, and

[60] Garosci, *Sdf*, pp. 210–211.
[61] The Catholic leader, his health precarious, switched his base to the New World in the summer of 1940. In Brooklyn he resided in the modest home of friends and continued his writings, which included in this period a series of essays, subsequently published as *La mia battaglia da New York*, and the widely read *Italy and the Coming World*.
[62] Since 1933 Professor Salvemini had been teaching history at Harvard University.
[63] Aided by Ivor Thomas, a sympathetic Laborite MP, some of the exiles organized the Friends of Free Italy Society; under the pseudonym "Pentad," five of them published *The Remaking of Italy* (Harmondsworth, 1941).
[64] Salvadori, *Resistenza ed azione*, pp. 180–190.
[65] See collection of broadcast scripts in Paolo Treves, *Sul fronte e dietro il fronte italiano* (Rome, 1945). In 1942 he wrote *Italy, Yesterday, Today, Tomorrow* (London).

Dino Gentili. Emilio Lussu, after helping many of his co-nationals escape from France through the Iberian peninsula, reached London in 1942. More radical than his brother-in-law Salvadori, Lussu sought to disabuse the War and Foreign Offices of any dreams of a *coup d'état* by the Royal House, Marshal Badoglio, or Fascist dissentients, and instead to persuade them of the feasibility of sparking a guerrilla uprising in Sardinia. But his scheme was rejected, partly because of his refusal to become a British agent and partly because of London's skepticism of its practicality. In March 1942 Lussu visited the United States briefly, but, disheartened by the negative results of his clandestine diplomacy, he decided to return to France. With his wife he set out for Italy via Switzerland, arriving soon after Badoglio's advent to power.[66]

Some months earlier, British intelligence officers at last saw fit to extend their gaze beyond the coteries of Italian monarchists, industrialists, clerics, and Fascist *frondeurs* upon whom hitherto they had pinned all their hopes. They developed a certain interest in the democratic underground and drew up plans to slip trusted agents into Italy at the proper moment. With such a purpose in mind, they persuaded Max Salvadori, who had returned in January 1943 from his mission in the Western Hemisphere, to accept a captaincy in the "cloak and dagger" Special Operations Executive (SOE)—or Special Forces (SF), as it was more commonly known in Italy. He was to spend 1943 and 1944 in North Africa and southern Italy, and then early in 1945 was to be parachuted behind the lines to serve as Allied Liaison Officer with the Milanese headquarters of the northern Armed Resistance.[67]

United States

For political reasons the United States was the preferred goal of perhaps most displaced anti-Fascists. But many also made their way to Latin America, where they joined up with refugees of an earlier period.[68] Uruguay, Argentina, Chile, Brazil, and

[66] Emilio Lussu, "Diplomazia clandestina: 14 giugno 1940–25 luglio 1943," *Il Ponte*, xi (1955), pp. 13–30, 168–181, and 340–357, and reissued in book format under the same title (Florence, 1956). *Cf.* Joyce Salvadori Lussu, *Fronti e frontiere* (Bergamo, 1945), for an exciting account of their wartime peregrinations; Salvadori, *Resistenza ed azione*, pp. 185–201.

[67] *Ibid.*, pp. 193–195, 200 ff.; *cf. infra*, Ch. vii ff.

[68] Among prewar *fuorusciti* in Latin America were Francesco Frola, Luigi

198

Mexico all claimed their quotas of exiles, whose political complexions ran the gamut from monarchism to anarchism. Many of them made their way to Montevideo in August 1942 to attend a great Pan-American Anti-Fascist Congress, instigated by Sforza.[69] In Mexico the PCI *émigrés* included the Triestian Vittorio Vidali, the ex-Socialist Francesco Flora, and Mario Montagnana, one-time editor of *Voce degli Italiani* in Paris and author of the widely translated *Ricordi di un operaio torinese*. They and such Giellisti as Leo Valiani (who had broken with the Communists in 1939) and the Pierleoni brothers were able to keep in touch with friends north of the Rio Grande.

Those who reached the United States in 1940 and 1941 naturally found many established Italian immigrant communities. But most of the newcomers were shocked to discover that, prior to Pearl Harbor, anti-Fascists were definitely an exiguous minority among Italo-Americans.[70] Part of the explanation for this political lag (so different from the situation among Italian emigrants in France during the Popular Front) may lie in the fact that the United States had severely restricted immigration by the time Mussolini came to power; thus it was not at all easy for political refugees to reach that country. The majority of Italo-Americans were descendants of an earlier outpouring which had left the mother country (primarily the politically retarded South) for economic reasons. They had settled along the Atlantic seaboard, as well as in various great Middle Western cities and in California. These newcomers had become patriotic Americans; yet at the same time most of them retained a sense of nostalgia for Italy, though with scant understanding of its political currents.

Some Italian writers have suggested that because of a fairly widespread initial feeling of inferiority with respect to certain other ethnic groups in the New World, many Italian immigrants seemed determined to keep alive their old cultural nationalism. In any event, the "little Italies" of the bigger cities proved susceptible to much of Mussolini's theatrical propaganda, as can be seen by an examination of the Italo-American newspaper press.

Fabbri, Mario Mariani, Francesco Ciccotti-Scozzese, and Libero Battistelli. These were joined later by Renato Treves, Rodolfo Mondolfo, Gioacchino Dolci, and others.

[69] See *infra*, Ch. v, Montevideo Pan-American Anti-Fascist Congress.

[70] Salvadori, *Resistenza ed azione*, pp. 162–165.

Some papers saw no inconsistency in simultaneously lauding the *Duce*'s totalitarianism and President Roosevelt's New Deal. Probably Mussolini's prestige among Italo-Americans reached its zenith during the Ethiopian War. According to the Anarchist Borghi, who had been in New York since 1926, tens of thousands of Italo-Americans wearing black shirts could be relied upon to turn out for mass meetings in those years, whereas never could the anti-Fascists attract more than two thousand.[71]

Of course there were many politically heterogeneous clusters (Socialists, Anarchists, garment-workers' unions, clubs, and journalists) adamantly opposed to Fascism and active especially in Boston, New York, Newark, Paterson, Buffalo, Chicago, San Francisco, and Tampa. And in the universities, publishing houses, and artistic circles *fuorusciti* and native Italo-Americans often spoke out vigorously against the dictatorship. Since the early 1930's these included Gaetano Salvemini and Giorgio LaPiana of Harvard,[72] Giuseppe A. Borgese of the University of Chicago, Max Ascoli of the New School of Social Research in New York, Lionello Venturi of Johns Hopkins University, Michele Cantarella of Smith College, and the *maestro* Arturo Toscanini [73] of New York. Others arrived after 1938 because of anti-Semitic persecution and wartime necessity—Leonardo Olschki, Enzo Tagliacozzo, Renato Poggioli, Giorgio DeSantillana, Giuliano Bonfante, Alessandro Pekelis, Duccio Tabet, Bruno Zevi, and others. It must be repeated, though, that prior to Pearl Harbor such people were much less influential with Italo-Americans than they were with academic and certain other groups in the New World.

[71] Borghi, *Mezzo secolo di anarchia* (1898–1945), pp. 339–341; Garosci, *Sdf*, p. 216.

[72] They co-authored *What to do with Italy?* (New York, 1943). Salvemini was sad not to be able to influence politically apathetic Italo-Americans for several years after his arrival at Harvard in 1933. Before World War II he had almost no influence in the U.S. State Department, but during the conflict he did. Professor Michele Cantarella is now compiling a list of Salvemini's writings between 1939 and 1945: *L'Italia vista dall'America*, which will comprise two or three volumes. See Norman Kogan, "Salvemini in America," Rome *Il Mondo*, Oct. 8, 1957, pp. 9–10. *Cf.* Salvemini's memoirs: *Memorie di un fuoruscito*, pp. 169–179.

[73] Toscanini had been reared in a Parmesan anticlerical, Garibaldian environment. In May 1931 he was beaten up by Costanzo Ciano in Bologna. Taking refuge in the United States, he did not return to Italy until after World War II. In World War II he leaned more toward Salvemini than he did toward Sforza. Borghi, "I miei ricordi su Toscanini: esilio americano," Rome *Il Mondo*, May 14, 1957.

In 1940 and 1941 the last wave of exiles reached the United States, most of them from France—democrats like Sforza, Tarchiani, Garosci, Cianca, Pacciardi, Nicola Chiaromonte, the Lussus (briefly), Sturzo; and Communists like Ambrogio Donini and Giuseppe Berti. Only in the case of the small PCI junto was there much disciplined activity. The others found it easiest to disseminate propaganda on a nonpartisan basis, mainly because of the vast differences between the American two-party system and the European multipartite traditions with which they were familiar. Of these nonpartisan organizations by far the most salient were Italia Libera and the enterprising Mazzini Society.[74]

When the latter was founded in New York in 1941 Professor Ascoli served as first president. Tarchiani held the secretaryship until his return to Italy in 1943. From the beginning he, Sforza, and Borgese were pivotal figures in the society. Salvemini collaborated for a time, then disagreed, and finally left the group. In March 1942 the Mazzini Society undertook publication of the weekly (later biweekly) *Nazioni Unite* ("United Nations"). In its circles, according to Garosci, at least three broad problems came up repeatedly for discussion: Which political forces should be merged in a tight alliance and which left on the periphery of anti-Fascism? How could the democrats abroad best support the domestic Resistance in Italy? How could the force of Italian anti-Fascism retain its autonomous role and avoid being swallowed up by the national interests of certain belligerent powers?

With respect to the first, directors of the Mazzini Society—all of whom had felt keenly the shock of the Russo-German *rapprochement* of August 23, 1939—did not desire to repeat the Popular Front experience. This time they wished to maintain a resolutely democratic stance in the customary Western sense of the term. In other words, they favored a united Italian "democratic front," though they were willing to collaborate with the PCI so long as it was not formally included. Thus, initially, the factions in the Mazzini Society were the same as those that had collaborated in France from August 23, 1939, until the 1940 Diaspora. This led to bitter polemics with PCI exiles in the Western Hemisphere—especially those in Mexico, where Frola and Montagnana had instigated a Communist-dominated Gari-

[74] Salvadori, *Resistenza ed azione*, pp. 191–192; Garosci, *Sdf*, pp. 217–219.

baldi Alliance ("Alleanza Garibaldi"). The attitude of the Mazzini Society did not correspond to the feeling that prevailed among Resistance groups in Europe after Soviet Russia's entry into the war in June 1941. There the Popular Front tradition, reborn in the protean Committees of National Liberation, was to dominate.[75]

On the second question, Sforza and Tarchiani emphasized repeatedly that the democracies must carefully differentiate the Fascist regime from the Italian people. They should be firm in their enmity to Mussolini and refrain from making deals with Monarchists who were compromised with the regime, but they should seek to understand sympathetically the plight of the masses.[76]

Montevideo Pan-American Congress (August 1942)

The problem of how to keep Italian anti-Fascism autonomous in the world struggle came up most clearly at an important congress of anti-Fascist organizations from all over the Western Hemisphere held in Montevideo, Uruguay, August 17, 1942. The Mazzini Society was represented, of course, and Sforza was the dominant figure in the conclave. In fact, the essential features of an eight-point program that he had drawn up in New York soon after the United States entered the war were adopted unanimously by the several thousand delegates.[77] The congress recommended that as soon as Italy was liberated it should elect a constituent assembly, which should draft a new constitution to supersede the 1848 one. Italy should also replace the tarnished Monarchy with a "democratic and social Republic"; Italians abroad should form an "Italian National Council," whose purpose would be to co-ordinate the struggle against Fascism and to represent the "Free Italians" before the United Nations; Sforza, as the "spiritual head of the Italian anti-Fascists," should direct this proposed council; and Randolfo Pacciardi, in view of his military experience in Spain, should try to organize combat units, with the hope that they would be permitted to fight alongside the Allies as distinct entities in the campaigns against Mus-

[75] Ibid., p. 220; Salvadori, Resistenza ed azione, pp. 191–192; and Alberto Tarchiani, Dieci anni tra Roma e Washington (Milan, 1955), p. 13.
[76] Garosci, Sdf, pp. 215–219.
[77] It is printed in Sforza, L'Italia dal 1914 al 1944 quale io la vidi, pp. 175–176.

solini's Italy. The eighth point affirmed that, after the overthrow of Fascism, the Italians would be ready to "co-operate with courage and serenity toward the solution of any international problem concerning them, on only one condition: that there will be no discussion of Italian problems as such, but of Italian sides of European problems"—a statement that clearly reflected Sforza's "European federalist" outlook.[78]

The Montevideo Congress provided considerable publicity for the anti-Fascists and extended their influence in Latin America; it helped accustom people to the importance of distinguishing between the regime and the mass of Italians; it popularized the idea of seeking a postwar political system for Italy that would rest on democratic terrain rather than on old conservative forces; and lastly it gave a boost to a handful of prisoners on Ventotene who were irrepressible advocates of European federation.[79] Yet for various reasons the results of the congress did not measure up to expectations. Its goals were not easily attainable. Part of the trouble came from the fact that not enough factions were represented. For example, the Communists were deliberately excluded; the Socialists had only second-string men present; and the Catholics had no real organization backing the movement. In the absence of a broader coalition, the Allies could hardly feel obligated to pay attention to the congress's resolution. Jealousy on the part of some Italian politicians who alleged that Sforza and Pacciardi aspired to become Italianate "DeGaulles" also nullified some of the work. Moreover, many feared that the Italian oppositionists would lose their freedom of movement if the proposed National Council ever got beyond the drawing boards and gained Allied recognition.[80] Sensing the growing dis-

[78] *Ibid.*, pp. 187–188; *cf.* Sforza, *Problemi italiani*, a cura del Movimento Liberale Italiano ("Punti di orientamento formulati al Congresso di Montevideo, nell'agosto del 1942") (Naples, 1943).

[79] When news of the congress reached Altiero Spinelli (*cf. supra*, Ch. v, Proposed military intervention) on the prison island he tried, in vain, to send Sforza a message, urging him to go farther and advocate a precise European federation in contrast to the vague organization contemplated in the Atlantic Charter. In retrospect, it is interesting to note that Spinelli foresaw correctly the positive attitude the United States eventually would take toward the problem of European integration. See Carlo Sforza, *O' federazione o nuove guerre* (Florence, 1948), pp. xii–xiii and 103–110; and Spinelli and Rossi, *Problemi della federazione europea.*

[80] This argument was set forth vigorously by Garosci, Tagliacozzo, Zevi, and Poggioli in their new GL-type periodical, *Quaderni Italiani,* published in Boston

sidence among Italians and the undisguised hostility of Prime Minister Churchill toward any hasty casting aside of the House of Savoy, Sforza soon shelved the Montevideo program. But in the United States, at least, he managed to keep himself in the news and to win the sympathy of numerous State Department officials.

Pacciardi was undeterred by Sforza's loss of interest in the Montevideo program. Doggedly he went forward with plans to organize a military legion, and he founded a newspaper, *La Legione dell'Italia del popolo*, to push the cause. To the amazement of those familiar with his breach with the Communists in Spain in 1937, he made overtures to the PCI again and found it willing to be courted—a flirtation which led to polemics with the Mazzini Society.[81] But Pacciardi's coquetry did not last long; [82] furthermore, his military scheme collapsed, due to lack of support from the royalist British, ineffective contact with public opinion in Italy, and apathy among Italians overseas.

Concurrently with Pacciardi's unsuccessful efforts to form a legion, certain Giellisti carried on intermittent negotiations with the British and United States governments. When Emilio Lussu visited London and Washington between 1941 and 1943 he sought support for an insurrection he hoped to foment in Sardinia. As a prerequisite for such an irruption he sought to get the British to guarantee in writing the integrity of Italian national territory (excluding Ethiopia, Albania, and the Dodecanese Islands) and to promise a nonpunitive peace treaty. This London was not ready to do.[83]

In the United States Dino Gentili, a Milanese businessman associated with GL, continued this line of somewhat naïve negotiations (with some further concessions regarding the Slovenian sectors of Venezia Giulia, recommended by Salvemini).[84] Gentili talked mostly with Assistant Secretary of State Berle and eventually persuaded him to make a speech in the presence

and New York during 1942–1943. See No. 3 (April 1943), and Garosci, *Sdf*, pp. 221–223.

[81] *Ibid.*, pp. 222–223.

[82] By 1944 Pacciardi once more was roundly denouncing the PCI.

[83] Lussu, *Diplomazia clandestina, passim.*

[84] The "Gentili mémoire" and some related correspondence of Count Sforza are quoted in Garosci, *Sdf*, pp. 289–293; *cf.* Carlo Sforza, *Cinque anni a Palazzo Chigi* (Rome, 1952), p. 403.

of Sforza, assuring American recognition of Italian national interests. On November 14, 1942, at a banquet tendered him in New York by the Mazzini Society and the Italian-American Labor Council, Berle reassured his audience that the United Nations had assumed a pledge toward Italy no less than toward the entire world in the eight points of the Atlantic Charter. No American sought to destroy or minimize the "nationhood of Italy," he declared. Berle's statement obviously was vague, and certainly it did not bind anyone; still, it gave a moral boost to some Italians, despite disagreement over its meaning. In any event, the exiles could reply to their critics within Italy that they were doing their best to look after their country's national interests in the midst of a global war.[85] And in later months it became quite clear that the Americans intended to let Italy have full freedom to decide the nature of her political institutions—a policy which Churchill had to accept.

At the Casablanca Conference in January 1943, following the Allied invasion of French North Africa, President Roosevelt, supported by Prime Minister Churchill, announced the "unconditional surrender" formula. One of his reasons was to reassure Premier Stalin, who had often criticized Anglo-American delay in launching a second front and had seemed to imply that the West was not really committed to speedy defeat of the Axis. The surrender slogan immediately aroused anxiety among many Italians abroad. Sturzo denounced it publicly.[86] So did Modigliani in articles in the Swiss Socialist paper, *La Sentinella*.[87] Sforza, for his part, began to point out the advantages federation with France might hold for Free Italy.[88] Of course, none of these men desired a compromise peace; what they feared was that the Allies might jeopardize Italy's legitimate national sovereignty and, by needlessly emphasizing "unconditional surrender," delay rather than speed the end of the war. Though valid, their objections

[85] Garosci, *Sdf*, pp. 224–229.
[86] See his *La mia battaglia da New York, passim*.
[87] S/M, *Sdf*, p. 939.
[88] In "Italy and her Neighbors after the War," *Foreign Affairs*, xxii (Oct. 1943), pp. 106–113, Sforza suggested that such a federation might even be expanded to include a "purified" Spain and Portugal, as well as Belgium, Greece, and Yugoslavia. His proposal met with silence from French leaders in Algiers and hostility from Sturzo, who called it "meaningless, unless to counterbalance British or German influence in Latin Europe." Sturzo, *Italy and the Coming World*, p. 218.

seem ironic, as "unconditional surrender" of the Fascist regime had been and was to remain a cardinal principle of the underground.[89]

As soon as the invasion of Italy seemed imminent, several *fuorusciti* asked Allied permission to return home at the earliest moment. The Giellisti's tactic was purely practical and in line with Rosselli's recommendation for "autonomy" in his 1933 article, "La guerra che torna." Neither seeking nor promising any political commitments, they simply argued that they and the Allies had parallel interests in ousting Mussolini and furnishing additional leadership to the internal opposition. Their proposal won the support of President Roosevelt in the spring of 1943. Still smarting from the barbs he had received for backing Admiral Darlan and General Giraud instead of General DeGaulle in North Africa, he was anxious to avoid a similar imbroglio in Italy. Overruling certain advisers, he argued that since the Italians sooner or later would be free to choose the form of government they wished, leading exiles should be allowed to return as soon as the invasion was secured. In view of Churchill's support of the Gaullist exiles, the Briton could hardly reject the logic of Roosevelt's argument. Thus, soon after the invasion at Salerno in September 1943, Allied intelligence agencies transported several of them to Italy. Tarchiani, Cianca, Gentili, Spano, and later Sforza and Togliatti entered alongside Allied forces in the South. Others, including Garosci, Valiani, and Renato Pierleoni, quickly made their way behind the enemy lines by small boat, by parachute drop, or afoot.[90]

Revival of opposition parties

The underlying cause of the almost bloodless overthrow of Mussolini's dictatorship on July 25, 1943, was the disastrous military, economic, and psychological condition of the country as a result of the war. In this *mise en scène* high-placed officials identified with the Crown, Army, and Fascist Grand Council

[89] Regarding the relationship of "unconditional surrender" to Italian anti-Fascism, see especially Leo Valiani, "Antifascismo e Resistenza," *MLI*, No. 54 (1959), pp. 39–43.
[90] Garosci, *Sdf*, pp. 226–227; Salvadori, *Resistenza ed azione*, pp. 226–227; Leo Valiani, *Tutte le strade conducono a Roma* (Florence, 1947), Ch. 1; and Leo Valiani, "La Resistenza e la questione istituzionale," *MLI*, No. 52/53 (1958), p. 31.

acted out their rival conspiracies. Though the anti-Fascist underground did not play a stellar role in the *coup d'état*, it did its bit
to create the necessary climate of opinion, and it proferred the
bewildered nation certain alternative courses of action.

In the confusion leaders of the old opposition parties re-
emerged. And they were flanked by younger men who had experienced only the Italy of Fascism. By the fateful summer of
1943 six (in some regions more) opposition currents could be
identified. Soon they were to pool their resources in a new version
of the Popular Front, or, more precisely, in an Anti-Fascist National Front, precursor of the Committees of National Liberation
(CLN's). From left to right these parties on the revolutionary
hustings were the Communists (PCI), Socialists of Proletarian
Unity (PSIUP), Actionists (Pd'A), Christian Democrats (DC),
Labor Democrats (DL), and Liberals (PLI).[91]

PCI and northern strikes (March 1943)

In July 1941, a month after Hitler invaded Russia, the PCI
proclaimed that its aims were to overthrow the Fascist regime;
form a popular government which would conclude at once an
armistice with the USSR and Britain; re-establish constitutional
freedoms; release political prisoners; arrest Fascist hierarchs; and
confiscate wartime profits of Fascists.[92] Adopting the slogan
"Peace, Independence, and Freedom!" the PCI invoked revolution in the name of "democracy" rather than of "dictatorship
of the proletariat." From 1942 on, Communist propaganda
shrewdly omitted any attacks against the Crown or demands
for separation of Church and State. Speaking as "Mario Correnti," Togliatti beamed a series of radio messages from Moscow
to the Italian people.[93]

About the same time the PCI Foreign Office in France dispatched Umberto Massola to northern Italy to start the laborious
secret reconstruction of factory cells. Because of his efficiency,
Grido di Spartaco ("Spartacus' Cry") rolled off the presses in
Milan on October 24, 1941, while the *Quaderno del Lavoratore* ("Worker's Notebook"), containing documents, appeals,

[91] Leo Valiani, "I partiti antifascisti nel 1943," MLI, No. 34/35 (1955), pp.
134–137.
[92] Longo, *Un popolo alla macchia*, p. 30.
[93] His broadcasts were published after his return to Italy in 1944. See Togliatti
("Mario Correnti"), *Discorsi agli Italiani* (Rome, 1945).

speeches by Stalin, and other party news, appeared regularly each month from July 1942 until July 1943. On May Day 1942 the expanding Communist underground stamped a manifesto, "Viva il 1° Maggio '42!" urging workers to slow down war production. During the last months of the year Communists in Turin tried to carry out the intent of the Toulouse Manifesto of October 1941 and construct a "popular front" with Catholic, Liberal, and Socialist currents. The resultant Turin Anti-Fascist National Front Committee (even though it barely extended beyond the echelons of the PCI) can claim credit for being the precursor of the Piedmontese CLN which emerged in the summer of 1943.[94]

Communists of course did their best to stimulate industrial unrest or, at the very least, to turn such discontent to their own ends. They were helped markedly by the war-weariness which spread rapidly as Allied bombardments became more severe and inflation spiraled unchecked. Toward the close of 1942 an average of two strikes per month occurred, and this rate shot up to five and one half per month during January and February 1943.[95]

By March 1943 when almost everyone in Italy had realized that the war was lost, the strike wave reached its crest. Massola and Giovanni Roveda, who had just escaped from Ventotene, ordered a young party worker, Leo Lanfranco, to exploit unrest in the vast Fiat-Mirafiori plant in Turin, where a strike had broken out on March 5, nominally to secure payment of "evacuation compensation" (equal to the pay for 192 hours of overtime) promised in February to bombed-out personnel. Lanfranco and his nucleus of 80 PCI members in the 21,000-employee plant did their best to give the work stoppage a political complexion. To what degree it actually was PCI-controlled is disputed.[96]

During the next few days workers in other factories struck and agitators distributed thousands of leaflets bearing slogans

[94] Mario Giovana, "Ricerche sulla storia del CLN Piemontese," *MLI*, No. 34/35 (1955), pp. 69–74; Achille Marazza, "I Cattolici e la Resistenza," *ibid.*, No. 43 (1956), p. 7; and PCI, *U. Massola* (Rome, 1947).

[95] PCI, *Relazione della Direzione del PCI al V° Congresso*, p. 19.

[96] See especially the non-Communist account of Giorgio Vaccarino, "Gli scioperi del marzo 1943: contributo per una storia del movimento operaio a Torino," *Aspetti della Resistenza in Piemonte* (Turin, 1950), pp. 3–40; the Communist versions in Massola, *Marzo 1943, ore 10* (Rome, 1950); Longo, *Un popolo alla macchia*, pp. 39–41; Battaglia, *SRI*, pp. 70–74; and the comment of Senise, *Quando ero Capo della Polizia*, p. 171.

"For bread, peace, and freedom! Long live the strike!" In Turin on the 8th (Communism's "International Woman's Day") thousands of women gathered in Piazza Castello to protest the war. In little more than a week "hiccup strikes" spread throughout the Po valley, with particularly effective ones launched on March 24 in Milan at the Pirelli, Falck, and Ercole Marelli works. The government had to dispatch ace conciliators to the region. By means of widespread arrests (164 in the first week), blandishments, and approval of substantial wage increases on April 2, they brought the disturbances to an end. Yet the implications could not be laughed off, as the dissident hierarch Bottai observed in his diary on March 13; [97] for now that workers had won an economic round against the dictatorship, they probably would turn next to political goals.

The PCI's most effective organizational work was in Piedmont and in Lombardy, though noteworthy progress was also registered during the spring in the Veneto, Emilia, and Tuscany. In the South, however, the party was still very weak; propaganda among the peasants had scarcely begun. The PCI directorate on the mainland was buttressed during the spring by the arrival of Celeste Negarville, Giorgio Amendola, Agostino Novella, and Paolo Silvati. Many of the younger people who gravitated toward the party in these months were more inspired by the epic of Stalingrad than by doctrinal considerations, declared an ex-editor of *Unità* who belonged to the generation which entered the PCI during the years of clandestinity.[98]

A distinguished Latinist at the University of Padua, Professor Concetto Marchesi, and Ludovico Geymonat were the PCI's most versatile intermediaries with other opposition parties. Visiting Rome in May, they made it clear to two Liberal senators, Casati and Bergamini, that the PCI would welcome the King's playing a prime role in the overthrow of the *Duce*. This they reiterated in conferences with non-Communists in Milan and with General Raffaele Cadorna in Ferrara the next month. Quite clearly the PCI, though continuing its efforts to stir the masses to revolutionary fervor, sensed that at this stage the unarmed

[97] Bottai, *Vent'anni e un giorno*, p. 255.
[98] Emanuele Rocco, "Comunisti davanti al PC," Rome *Il Mondo*, Dec. 11, 1956, pp. 1–2.

populace could scarcely succeed by itself. Professor Marchesi's approaches also made it evident that the PCI, despite its special links with the republican Socialists and Actionists, was anxious to create a broad "National Front" of anti-Fascists that would include royalists too and postpone the institutional question of the Savoyard Monarchy till after the war.[99]

Socialist Party of Proletarian Unity (PSIUP)

Just to the right of the PCI in the underground political arena stood the Socialists. Prior to the Molotov-Ribbentrop pact, it will be recalled, these two parties had been linked by a "unity of action" agreement. The dispersed Socialists in France reaffirmed this pact on a *de facto* basis after the USSR's entry into the war in June 1941 and the fusion of the Nenni and Saragat factions. When Moscow dissolved the Third International in April 1943 some Italian Socialists anticipated a true reconciliation between Socialism and Communism, and at least a few were ready to liquidate the old Second International in Amsterdam. The PCI, for its part, according to a prominent postwar defector, worked hard to capture the PSI, whose support it perceived would be most useful in winning the complete devotion of the workers and their intellectual sympathizers.[100]

Within Italy the Socialists were still badly split in the spring of 1943. In the preceding decade they had lost many members to the PCI (and on a lesser scale to GL), and their old clandestine apparatus had largely rusted away. Those who kept the faith looked for guidance to such men as the quondam revisionist deputy, Giuseppe Romita, who had finally emerged from *confino*; a wine merchant, Oreste Lizzadri; and a physician, Dr. Nicola Perrotti. But by the beginning of 1943 the old guard PSI was being challenged in the Po valley by a new Movimento di Unità Proletaria (MUP), captained by younger men—Lelio

[99] See Paolo Monelli, *Roma 1943* (5th rev. ed.; Verona, 1948), p. 105; Mario Alicata, "Partiti e movimento popolare intorno al 25 luglio," *Trenta anni di vita e di lotte del PCI* (Rome, 1951), pp. 163–167; Negarville, "L'Origine del Comitato di Liberazione Nazionale," *ibid.*, p. 161; Gianni Corbi, "I partiti alla vigilia dei 45 giorni di Badoglio: solo i comunisti si fidavano del re," Rome *L'Espresso*, Aug. 16, 1956, p. 3; Raffaele Cadorna, *La Riscossa* (Milan, 1948), pp. 18–19; and Longo, *Un popolo alla macchia*, p. 43.
[100] Paolo Emiliani [pseud. for Valdo Magnani], *Dieci anni perduti: cronache del Partito Socialista Italiano dal 1943 a oggi* (Pisa, 1953), pp. 25–32.

Basso (who covertly edited in 1943–1944 the weekly Milanese *Bandiera rossa,* quite extreme in its "classism"),[101] Carlo Andreoni, Corrado Bonfantini, and Luigi Fabbri. In Rome emerged still a third faction of young men—Unione Proletaria Italiana, speared by Giuliano Vassalli and two other lawyers.[102]

It took much skill to achieve eventual fusion of this exiguous and disparate array. "Why, we are only a few!" exclaimed Nenni when he reached Rome on August 6, 1943, from *confino* and scanned Romita's membership rolls. "There is no party, there are only Communists." "Yes," Romita answered, "the party does not exist as an organization, but it exists in the conscience of many citizens." [103] Under their impetus and that of Bruno Buozzi, ex-CGL director and long-time exile, the three splinter groups merged by August 12 under the new label, Partito Socialista Italiano di Unità Proletaria (PSIUP). The consolidated party named Nenni secretary-general and director of *Avanti!* and Carlo Andreoni and Sandro Pertini national vice-secretaries.[104]

The Socialists were of course anticlerical and antiroyalist; yet, for the same expedient reasons as the PCI, they preferred not to stress these points in 1942–1943.

Action Party (Pd'A)

Slightly to the right of the PSIUP and vying with the PCI for top honors in clandestine enterprise was the highly articulate but (as was later proved) minuscule Partito d'Azione (Pd'A). It had been in *de facto* existence since July 1942, though it did not adopt its title till January 1943 and did not hold its first congress (in Florence) until September 3 of that year. It attracted its adherents from those ultrarepublicans and semisocialists who in the early 1930's had flocked to Rosselli's Giustizia e Libertà or who later in the decade had rallied either to Parri's radical republicanism or to Calogero's Liberalsocialismo.[105]

[101] *Ibid.,* pp. 23, 52–57.
[102] See "Documenti per una storia del PSIUP," *Iniziativa Socialista,* II, No. 13, p. 344; G. Vassalli, "Iniziativa Socialista nella storia del PSIUP," *ibid.,* II, No. 1, p. 3, cited by Emiliani, *Dieci anni perduti,* pp. 22–23 ff.
[103] Giuseppe Romita, *Origini, crisi, e sviluppo del socialismo italiano* (Rome, 1951), p. 28.
[104] Rome *Avanti!,* Aug. 26, 1943; Garosci, *Sdf,* p. 233; Corbi, Rome *L'Espresso,* Aug. 16, 1956, p. 3.
[105] See Ragghianti's essay on the origin of the party in *Disegno della liberazione*

As has been noted, Professor Calogero's underground academic contingent held frequent discussions with such spokesmen of Parri's group as Ragghianti of Bologna. Eventually seeing the merit of pooling their strength, they set about drafting a statement that would clearly express their socio-economic, laic, and republican aims. First written by Calogero, the manifesto went through several revisions before it was finally approved at a secret conclave in Assisi in May 1940. The Assisi conventiclers made a cogent appeal to Liberals, Marxists, and Catholics:

"You [who are Liberals] have been . . . in the vanguard of the struggle for freedom. . . . But you have also been distressed by uncertainty over the limits to which discipline of freedom is permissible. Thus, torn between the desire for a strong state and the fear of betraying freedom for authority, between the nostalgia for *laissez-faire* and your initial sympathy for Fascism, you have abandoned freedom to the enemies of liberty, and you have permitted dictatorship to be born, to grow, and to defeat you. . . .

"To the Marxists [we say] our aspirations are your aspirations, our truth is your truth when it is freed from the myths of historical materialism. . . . Remember Marx the agitator, inflamed by the ethical ideal of justice, and forget Marx the theoretician who, predicating that ideal into his economic investigations, thought . . . he was able to prove it from these very investigations. And above all, do not forget that Marx wrote the *Manifesto* and *Kapital* in London under the protection of English liberties. Make sure that the spirit of tomorrow may not deprive a new Marx of the chance of emerging. . . .

"Lastly, to the Catholics, to the Christians, to all men of real religious belief [we say] that the ideal of Liberalsocialismo is nothing but the eternal ideal of the New Testament. It is nothing more than a form of practical Christianity, of service for God, anchored in reality. Whoever loves his neighbors as himself cannot but work for justice and for freedom."[106]

During the rest of 1940–1941 the "conspiracy of the intellectuals" proceeded, with the group spending its free time discussing concrete programs that could meet with general approval. In February 1942 disaster befell them: the police arrested Calogero,

---

italiana, pp. 273–353; *cf*. Giuliano Pischel, *Che cosa è il Partito d'Azione?* (Milan, 1945), p. 71 ff.

[106] Quoted in Calogero, *Difesa del Liberalsocialismo*, p. 230.

Capitini (who had declined to support the Assisi fusion and had drifted closer to the Social-Communists), Codignola, Ragghianti, Enriques-Agnoletti, Francovich, and some others.[107] They were not tried before a court but simply banished administratively to *confino* for several months. As a matter of fact, the police never produced concrete evidence of the membership of these men in the movement nor did they find a copy of the manifesto; they were still searching for it in June 1943 when they jailed Professor DeRuggiero in Rome and Tommaso Fiore in Bari.[108]

February 1942 also marked another milestone in Parri's prison peregrinations. Police arrested him in Milan on the not-unlikely assumption that he was the guiding spirit of the radicals. The white-haired fighter stood just as resolutely before this Special Tribunal as he had before the Savona court in February 1927: "Before giving my answers to the interrogation, I intend to reaffirm before you, Fascist judges, my faith in the liberal and democratic ideal state," he declared. Lacking clear-cut evidence, the Tribunal had to free Parri in November. In association with the younger Ugo LaMalfa (a Palermitan transplanted in Milan), the Lombard Adolfo Tino, Mario Paggi, and other lawyers and professionalists, he immediately resumed his underground toil with as serene an outlook as could be expected.[109]

Meanwhile, in July 1942 the conspirators at last agreed upon and published a seven-point program (most of it formulated in December 1941):

"1. Abdication of the Savoyard dynasty, co-responsible with Fascism for the country's ruin, and establishment of a Republic;

2. Regional autonomy and economic equalization of the regions;

3. Nationalization on a flexible basis of large industrial monopolies;

4. Radical agrarian reforms and land redistribution;

5. Restoration of labor union privileges to factory workers and permission for them to share in industrial management;

6. Full religious freedom, and separation of Church and State;

[107] In Rome in 1941 Luigi Milani and Vittorio Gabrieli were also arrested.
[108] Calogero, *Difesa del Liberalsocialismo*, p. 199 ff.
[109] Sandro Contini-Bonacossi and Licia Ragghianti-Collobbi (eds.), *Una lotta nel suo corso: lettere e documenti politici e militari della Resistenza e della Liberazione* (Venice, 1954), p. 347.

7. Promotion of a European federation of free democratic states within the framework of still broader world collaboration." [110]

All of these proposals reflected the party's variegated background: the republicanism of Mazzini's earlier Partito d'Azione; the democracy of Amendola; the agitation of Cattaneo, Lussu, Salvemini, Dorso, Rossi-Doria, and others for regional autonomy and land reform; the campaigns of Gobetti and Rosselli for more participation in civic life by organized labor, peasants, and the lower middle class; the Marxian propaganda for a collectivist economy; the "religion of freedom" and historicism of Croce; and the internationalist, federalistic spirit of Ernesto Rossi and Altiero Spinelli (both still on Ventotene).[111] Naturally, there was much disagreement upon where to place the major stress.

At a meeting in Milan in January 1943 Mario Vinciguerra suggested the title, Partito d'Azione, which won out over such proposed rubrics as Labor Party and Liberalsocialist Party. The first issue of L'Italia Libera was circulated clandestinely in Milan the same month. It called for "immediate peace, overthrow of the dictatorship, and installation of a government founded on civil and political liberties, and on the representative institutions of public opinion." [112] Bitterly attacking the House of Savoy, it declared that the royal family "shared every responsibility with the authoritarian regime" and insisted that the dynasty "must die with the Fascist regime." [113] The third issue irritated Croce, who hitherto had been benevolently disposed toward the movement. He challenged some of the philosophical premises of the new party which, he thought, tampered too freely with pure liberalism.[114]

The Partito d'Azione's chief financial backers were in the North. They included certain officials in the Milan Banca Com-

[110] Manlio Rossi-Doria, Il Partito d'Azione ([Bologna], 1944), pp. 6-8; cf. Ragghianti, Disegno della liberazione italiana, pp. 314-317.

[111] Recently Leo Valiani has called attention to another matrix of the political philosophy of the Action Party: the pages of a Vicenza fortnightly of the post-World War I period, Volontà. Leo Valiani, Dall'antifascismo alla Resistenza (Milan, 1959), pp. 24-38.

[112] Quoted in Monelli, Roma, 1943, p. 60.

[113] Ibid.; cf. Ragghianti, Disegno della liberazione italiana, pp. 318-319.

[114] Croce, Per la nuova vita dell'Italia, p. 93 ff.; cf. Ragghianti, Disegno della liberazione italiana, pp. 273-353.

merciale Italiana, Olivetti Typewriter Corporation of Ivrea, Fiat in Turin, and the Pirelli Rubber Company.[115] Despite this consideration, Pd'A chieftains decided to transfer their headquarters to Rome in the spring of 1943 in order to be ready for any crisis. Control of the party in the capital at that stage lay in the hands of Professors DeRuggiero and Salvatorelli and the lawyers Sergio Fenoaltea, Federico Comandini, and Oronzo Reale. In Florence Professor Calamandrei and Enriques-Agnoletti held the reins, assisted by the artist Ragghianti. In the *Mezzogiorno* the eminent University of Naples Risorgimentalist Adolfo Omodeo and philosophy professor Alfredo Parente (both intimate friends of Croce) were the leaders.[116] The brilliant if headstrong leadership of the Pd'A during the next three years proved to be all out of proportion to its numerical strength.

Christian Democratic Party (DC)

At the hub of the political ring was the Christian Democratic Party ("Democrazia Cristiana"), whose birth took place in March 1943. Potentially the largest *partito di massa* in Catholic Italy, Alcide DeGasperi's new party was the direct heir of Sturzo's ill-fated Partito Popolare Italiano (PPI) of 1919–1926. It was also the beneficiary of the conservative Catholic Action laity organization which (in spite of its promises to Mussolini) had covertly preserved political cadres. For that reason the Vatican-controlled Catholic Action held a rather heavy mortgage upon the new DC. Lastly, the Democristiani were strengthened by their fusion in mid-1942 (effected personally by DeGasperi) with the Lombard Comitato dell'Azione Guelfa ("Committee of Guelph Action"), founded in Milan in 1928 on democratic, Catholic principles by Piero Malvestiti, Enrico Falck, and E. Clerici. The Guelphs had functioned on a modest scale, maintaining occasional contact with the Giellisti until Malvestiti was arrested and condemned by the Special Tribunal in 1933. After his eventual release he had emigrated to Lugano, where he published articles of a distinctly republican hue.[117]

[115] Elizabeth Wiskemann, *Italy* (London, 1947), p. 104.
[116] "Partito d'Azione," *Enciclopedia Italiana*, 1938–1948, *Seconda Appendice*, A–H, 345.
[117] Piero Malvestiti, *La lotta politica in Italia dal 25 luglio 1943 alla nuova costituzione* (Milan, 1948), pp. i–xii, and *passim*; cf. his *Parte Guelfa in Europa* (Milan, 1945); and Webster, *The Cross and the Fasces*, pp. 148–152.

Throughout the war years DeGasperi, still employed inconspicuously in the Vatican libraries, conversed regularly with close friends and elaborated a political creed under the pen name "Demofilo." [118] He was anxious that Christian Democracy follow Sturzo's counsel and avoid any suspicion of becoming a confessional party, lest the old rift between Church and State be reopened. He was firmly convinced that Catholics must collaborate with secular democratic forces if popular government were to succeed in a country like Italy, and he was even willing to march abreast the Communists for the duration of the battle against Nazi-Fascism. Co-operation with democratic secular currents remained the ideal so long as DeGasperi directed the DC. Some writers have insisted, however, that his party was more closely anchored to the Vatican (because of the situation in 1943 and Catholic Action's role) than Sturzo's PPI had been.[119]

In addition to DeGasperi, direction of DC devolved upon Professor Guido Gonella, ex-editor of *Osservatore romano* and member of Parliament, and now to become editor of the clandestine *Il Popolo*; the Roman Giuseppe Spataro, ex-secretary of the PPI; and the Sicilian journalist and ex-secretary of Sturzo, Mario Scelba (destined to become a postwar premier). At the party's nerve center were also three top-flight Catholic labor leaders—the Pisan Giovanni Gronchi (later to become President of the Italian Republic), Achille Grandi, and Giulio Pastore. Influential too were Giorgio Tupini, who had instigated the covert youth journal, *La Punta*, and the elderly rightist, Stefano Jacini (veteran of the Aventine and author of a history of the PPI).[120] In Sardinia Antonio Segni (to become still another postwar premier) was DC chieftain. In Naples Giulio Rodinò [121] was conspicuous. In German-held northern Italy after September 8, 1943, Achille Marazza was the key figure.[122]

[118] DeGasperi, *Studi ed appelli della lunga vigilia*, ed. G. Tupini (Rome, 1946), and the more complete collection of his clandestine publications, *I Cattolici dall'opposizione al governo* (Bari, 1955), pp. 477–510.
[119] Einaudi and Goguel, *Christian Democracy in Italy and France*, pp. 25–26; cf. Webster, *The Cross and the Fasces*, pp. 133–136.
[120] Cf. Petrocchi, *DeGasperi*, p. 42 ff.; Giorgio Tupini, *I Democratici Cristiani: cronache di dieci anni* (Milan, 1954), pp. 32–76; Vito G. Galati, *Storia della Democrazia Cristiana* (Rome, 1955); and Francesco Magri, *La Democrazia Cristiana in Italia* (2 vols.; Milan, 1954–1955).
[121] Cf. Giulio Rodinò, *Un uomo e un'idea: documentazione della vita politica di Giulio Rodinò*, ed. Giacomo Deuringer and Others (Naples, 1956).
[122] Marazza, "I Cattolici e la Resistenza," *MLI*, No. 47 (1956), pp. 3–15.

After the fusion of the DeGasperi and Malvestiti groups in the summer of 1942 the Christian Democrats hammered out a ten-point program, "Idee Ricostruttive della Democrazia Cristiana," which (with exegesis by "Demofilo") Gonella published in *Il Popolo*.[123] Inspired mainly by the ethical pronouncements of Pius XII, this manifesto naturally espoused co-operation between Church and State on the basis of the Lateran Accords. Though it demanded restoration of political freedom and of Parliament, a corporatist strain of thought called for reorganizing the Senate into a High Council, to be elected partly on a professional basis.[124] The manifesto favored creation of a Supreme Constitutional Court and establishment of some regional autonomy (though less than the PPI platform of 1919 had demanded). In the economic sphere it called for unfettered labor organizations and freedom from fear and want. The party's left wing (which included Gronchi and often DeGasperi in months to come) [125] favored land reform and acquiesced in a market economy based primarily upon small businessmen and widespread ownership of property. However, it favored the principle of profit-sharing and socialization of large monopolies in the electric, steel, mining, chemical, heavy construction, sea and air (railroads already were) transport fields. The right wing, dominated by big industrialists and landowners, stoutly opposed anything going beyond what Mussolini's IRI had already nationalized. Most of the controversy over the Monarchy had not yet gotten underway, though there was evidence that the party's northern leaders favored a republic. In general, the DC aspired to function as a broad center movement, tolerating many economic and political currents so long as religion remained the bond.

Labor Democratic Party (DL)

Still in the formative stage early in 1943 was a fifth faction, first known as the United Freedom Front ("Fronte unico della Libertà") and later as the Labor Democratic Party (DL; "Democrazia del Lavoro"). Although it was the smallest of the par-

---

[123] Reprinted in Tupini, *I Democratici Cristiani*, pp. 330–338, 48–57.

[124] It may be noted that Sturzo, perhaps as a result of his long sojourn in Anglo-Saxon countries, came to reject most of the corporatist planks that had been in the original PPI platform. Vaussard, *Histoire de la Démocratie chrétienne*, I, 272–273.

[125] DeGasperi, *Studi ed appelli della lunga vigilia*, p. 179.

ties, DL became important because it often pounded out compromises among them. Labor Democracy was sponsored chiefly by such older men as ex-Premier Ivanoe Bonomi, Meuccio Ruini, and Pier Felice Stangoni. Regarding itself as the heir of Italy's historic Left ("Sinistra"), it found its recruits almost exclusively in Rome and the South.

A native of Mantua and one-time teacher, Bonomi had been in the revisionist wing of the Socialist Party until he was expelled in 1912 at the instigation of Mussolini, who charged him with excessive conservatism and nationalism. In line with his interventionist views, Bonomi had joined the armed forces and fought in some early battles of World War I on the Austrian front. Later he had entered various coalition ministries. His attitude toward the early Fascist movement was somewhat equivocal, according to a recent study.[126] As Minister of War in 1921 he had helped Premier Giolitti and Foreign Minister Sforza negotiate the Treaty of Rapallo with Yugoslavia, whereby Italy gained Zara and some other Dalmatian territory. On that occasion King Victor Emmanuel III had awarded him the coveted Collar of the Annunciation. Premier from June 1921 until February 1922, Bonomi formed a cabinet from a coalition of center and left-of-center parties. Suffering defeat in the 1924 parliamentary elections (the same which Matteotti denounced), he had spent the next eighteen years quietly in Rome, studying and writing the history of modern Italy and making no compromise with the totalitarian regime. The moment was now approaching when the 70-year-old genro could take revenge on Mussolini.[127]

Standing midway between the Pd'A and the Liberal Party, the Labor Democrats sought to attract Freemasons, anticlericals, and radical bourgeois groups. They differed from the Actionists

[126] Roberto Vivarelli, "Bonomi e il fascismo in alcuni documenti inediti," *Rivista storica italiana*, LXXII, No. 1 (March 1960), pp. 147–157.

[127] "Ivanoe Bonomi," in *Chi è? Dizionario biografico degli Italiani d'oggi*, 1948 (5th ed.; Rome, 1948). His *La politica italiana da Porta Pia a Vittorio Veneto, 1870–1918* was published in Turin after the Liberation.

Ruini and Stangoni also had distinguished backgrounds. The former, a native of Reggio Emilia, had held a seat in the Senate and cabinet posts under Premiers Orlando and Nitti. During the Aventine he was associated with Amendola's Democratic National Union. After the inauguration of the dictatorship he had retired, devoting his time to legal studies. In 1947 he was to head a committee that helped draft the new Republic's Constitution. Stangoni was a native of Sardinia who embarked on a journalistic career in the capital, working on the staff of *Avanti!* until the Fascists suppressed it and jailed him for a time. *Cf.* "Pier Felice Stangoni," in *Chi è?* 1948, p. 890.

chiefly in their refusal to campaign resolutely against the House of Savoy and in their reluctance to advocate socialization of as many sectors of the economy. Some Labor Democrats held a low opinion of Victor Emmanuel III, to be sure, but most of them wished to preserve the Monarchy. The day after Mussolini was dismissed, Ruini published the DL platform in the Rome *Il Mondo*: ". . . popular self-government and parliamentary supremacy; . . . progressive and extraordinary taxation; the principle of the 'nation in arms'; regional autonomies; free public schooling, even through the university; inviolability of freedom of the press and of organization. . . . [The party] favors all reforms that may raise the dignity of labor and labor's rights with respect to capital, [provided] that the State's economic framework be not suddenly endangered. Above all, we are Unionists—of the United Freedom Front." [128] It was this last point that was most important about the fleeting DL. Even though Bonomi was unable to recruit many followers outside Rome, he performed a signal service in 1943 by encouraging secret talks among the anti-Fascist currents. Acting as mediary, the respected ex-premier soon emerged as the spokesman of the six parties.

Liberal Party (PLI)

Definitely to the right of the other parties stood the Liberals —heirs of Cavour's Right—who were slowly reorganizing into small, heterogeneous Gruppi di Ricostruzione Liberale that sought to restore the pre-Fascist system of constitutional government with as few changes as possible. Differences among the Liberals arose chiefly out of regional and occupational considerations. In the North where lawyers, teachers, and other professionalists joined the party, its outlook tended to be progressive. University of Turin Professor Luigi Einaudi, Milanese literary critic Senator Alessandro Casati, and the somewhat-radical Count Niccolò Carandini of Rome exercised considerable influence. In the South, on the other hand, landowners predominated, and whatever their liberal beliefs were on the surface they had "tradition, not to say reaction in their bones" [129]—though some features of Croce's idealist philosophy (variously interpreted) diffused enlightenment in their midst. Not till after the

[128] Rome *Il Mondo*, July 26, 1943.
[129] Muriel Grindrod, *The Rebuilding of Italy: Politics and Economics, 1945–1955* (London, 1955), p. 18.

219

armistice of September 1943 did the PLI emerge as a full-fledged party.

The PLI devoted most of its attention to political rather than economic issues. Many members were unenthusiastic about the reigning sovereign, but most were inclined to support the Monarchy as an institution. Indeed, several Liberals took the lead in attempts to work out a regency compromise in 1943–1944. In economics the PLI tended to follow Croce's curious dictum that the party of freedom need not descend to mundane affairs and formulate a specific program.[130] Almost certainly this reluctance to advocate concrete socio-economic reforms kept the Liberals from attracting many workers or young people. In religious matters the PLI advocated uncompromising separation of Church and State.

Republican Party (PRI)

The aforementioned six parties were the mainstays of the dozens of Committees of National Liberation that sprouted throughout the country after the summer of 1943 (though DL was seldom to be found north of Rome). These components of the so-called *esarchia* ("hexarchy") came up against a seventh party in central Italy which commanded a certain following, though it seldom joined the CLN's except on a local basis. This was the venerable Mazzinian Italian Republican Party (PRI), led by Randolfo Pacciardi. Doctrinally it stood slightly to left of center, where its chief competitor was the new Partito d'Azione.

The nonco-operative attitude of the PRI stemmed partly from Pacciardi's disillusionment with the Communists during the Spanish Civil War. When the other parties were driven willy-nilly into a "truce" with the House of Savoy in 1944 for the duration of the war, the PRI became more convinced than ever of the validity of its own intransigence. In economic affairs the PRI was agreeable to some nationalization, and it was willing to shy away somewhat from Mazzini's gospel of extreme centralism and move, instead, toward Cattaneo's federalistic ideas.[131]

---

[130] Benedetto Croce, *Quando l'Italia era tagliata in due: estratto di un diario (luglio 1943–giugno 1944)* (Bari, 1948), p. 94; English translation by Sylvia Sprigge entitled *Croce, the King and the Allies: Extracts from a Diary by Benedetto Croce, July 1943–June 1944* (London and New York, 1950).

[131] Vinciguerra in Barbagallo (ed.), *Cento anni di vita italiana*, I, 235.

Beginning of "unity of action"

Ex-Premier Bonomi took the initiative early in 1943 in sounding out the views of Rome's clandestine politicos during the growing crisis of Mussolini's regime. Throughout his talks Bonomi tried to maintain a neutral position as to the Monarchy, but his personal friendship for Victor Emmanuel III was no secret. These privy conferences helped lay the foundation for multipartite "unity of action" and the CLN's. Bonomi's most congenial friends were the Liberals Casati, Bergamini, and Marchese della Torretta, who visited him almost every Sunday in his modest Rome apartment.[132]

Bonomi was of course aware of the discussions that Communist Professor Marchesi and Antonio Giolitti, nephew of the famed statesman, were undertaking with Liberals and others for the purpose of creating an anti-Fascist "united front." In their approaches the Communists made it clear that despite their ties with the archrepublican PSIUP and Pd'A, they were ready to help the King remove Mussolini. They also indicated that they would not shirk responsibility in a post-Fascist government and intimated that they would be content with a "ministry without portfolio." This was the PCI's first hint of a reversal of its old policy of refusing cabinet responsibility in a bourgeois government. The Popular Front experience, combined with the practical necessities and opportunities of World War II, explained the new attitude. The PCI's task of persuading bourgeois groups to collaborate in the patriotic cause was helped by Moscow's dissolution of the provocative Comintern in April 1943.[133]

Bonomi also conferred harmoniously with such Christian Democrats as DeGasperi and Spataro, in whose law offices many of their *rendezvous* took place. The Catholics assured him that they were not averse to working with others (even the Communists) in a broad front and that they were not prejudiced on the institutional question. With Romita and some other PSIUP men in Rome Bonomi also enjoyed rapport. His relationship with

[132] Less often he conferred with Orlando, Carandini, Einaudi, Soleri, Marshal Enrico Caviglia, Bortolo Belotti, Leone Cattani, Enzo Storoni, Dante Coda, and Giustino Arpesani. *Cf.* Bonomi, *Diario di un anno (2 giugno 1943–10 giugno 1944)*, p. x ff.

[133] Longo, *Un popolo alla macchia*, p. 43; Monelli, *Roma, 1943*, p. 105; and Corbi in Rome *L'Espresso*, Aug. 16, 1956, p. 3.

Pd'A militants was less cordial, however, for they would brook no compromise with the Monarchy, even if Victor Emmanuel should dismiss Mussolini. Despite such diffidence, the essentially royalist Bonomi kept in touch with the Roman Actionists Fenoaltea, Comandini, and others.[134]

Out of these protracted talks emerged an informal understanding on April 27, 1943, shared by all except the Pd'A and PRI. Later it was put in writing and signed by Bonomi, Casati, Ruini, DeGasperi, Romita, and "an obscure Communist who had authority." Pledging the covert parties to temporary unity of action, the new Anti-Fascist United Freedom Front agreed that during the period of national reconstruction it would set as its common goal a democratic system in which "all powers, even the highest, should derive from the popular will." [135]

Discussions revealed two strategies for overthrowing the dictatorship. One called for collaboration with the Royal House. Proponents of this (chiefly Liberals and "realistic, practical" Communists, to use Bonomi's adjectives) were confident that the King, sure of Army support, eventually would oust the *Duce*. The other (advocated by the Pd'A and in lesser degree the PSIUP) insisted upon toppling Mussolini and the Monarchy simultaneously.

Though he doubted the practicality of the latter program, Bonomi tried to pursue a policy that would placate both factions. He was not too confident that he could persuade Victor Emmanuel III to repudiate his premier but he believed there was at least a chance. For this reason he sought an audience with the King in order to reveal to him the views of the political opposition. His conversations were closely linked with the plots that high Army officers and dissentient Fascist hierarchs were hatching against the *Duce*.

[134] Bonomi, *Diario di un anno*, pp. xxii–xxiii.
[135] *Ibid.*, p. xxiv.

CHAPTER VI · BADOGLIO'S
"FORTY-FIVE DAYS"

July 25 – September 8, 1943

Parallel plots

B Y EARLY SUMMER 1943 three opposition groups were scheming against Mussolini. One of them was the militant wing of anti-Fascism whose twenty-odd years of corrosive agitation has been the main theme of this study; but this group was not primarily responsible for the *coup d'état* of July 25, 1943. The *Duce* fell chiefly because of his own disastrous foreign policy, for when it became clear that Italy had lost the war, he forfeited the support of the powerful forces (Crown, capital, clergy, Army, and bureaucracy) which in the past had generally welcomed and benefited from his dictatorship.[1] Some of them went so far as to conspire against him in order to get Italy out of the war.

The second group consisted of Army men like Chief of the General Staff of the Armed Forces General Vittorio Ambrosio and his aide, General Giuseppe Castellano, who worked in conjunction with the wily Genoese Duke Pietro of Acquarone, Minister of the Royal House, and a few other intimates of the King. Their candidate was Marshal Pietro Badoglio, hero of the Ethiopian War and scapegoat of the Greek campaign.

The third category of intriguers included ambitious young PNF *frondeurs*. On the one hand were to be found the *Duce's* sardonic son-in-law Count Galeazzo Ciano, ambassador to the Holy See since February 1943; Dino Grandi, suave ex-ambassador to the United Kingdom; and Giuseppe Bottai, ex-Minister of Education and Civil Commissioner in Greece, who for several years had sponsored "constructive criticism" of the regime in his magazine, *Primato*, and had thereby attracted quite a number of Fascist-trained youths already bored by the stuffiness of the dictatorship. A rival cabal in the *gerarchia* consisted of such Germanophile fanatics as Roberto Farinacci and Carlo Scorza, newly appointed PNF secretary.

[1] Salvadori, SRI, pp. 36–41, 49; *cf.* his *Brief History of the Patriot Movement in Italy, 1943–1945* (Chicago, 1954), pp. 9–17.
  Manifestly, one must not make a blanket indictment of these classes, for there were some anti-Fascists among all of them, just as there were Fascists among other social groups.

Their plots produced a revolution "from above" instead of one "from below" which might have modified the social base upon which the regime rested. Efforts to achieve this deeper revolution had to await the armistice and debacle of the royal-military dictatorship of King Victor Emmanuel III and Marshal Badoglio on September 8, 1943.

High lights of the conspiracies

The leader of the military junto, General Ambrosio, who had become Chief of the General Staff of the Armed Forces in February 1943, owed his appointment at least in part to Ciano.[2] Castellano, a quick-witted Sicilian, was the Army's youngest general and Ambrosio's closest confidant. At home with intrigue, Castellano often spurred his superior on. From about February 1943 the two men were hard at work on various plans to arrest Mussolini, the details of which need not be recounted here. Once or twice weekly Ambrosio reported to the King on the course of the war, but seldom did the latter reveal to him his inner thoughts. One man, though, could often interpret the Savoyard's taciturnity and give encouragement to those who sought his intervention in the mounting crisis. He was Duke Pietro of Acquarone, Minister of the Royal House. Often he assumed responsibility for actions which his master disliked taking and could, if necessary, repudiate.

Several months after the *coup* King Victor Emmanuel asserted in a letter to Acquarone that his decision to replace Mussolini was made six months before the event.[3] Be that as it may (and there is some question as to the full candor of the King's claim), the selection of a specific date for the *coup* was long in the making and seems not to have been fixed firmly until July 19, 1943. Victor Emmanuel managed to keep his feelings concealed from most of the people who sought audiences to plead with him to dismiss Mussolini. As news of military disaster upon disaster reached Rome, pressure to act increased from retired military men Admiral Thaon di Revel [4] and Marshal Caviglia; [5]

[2] Ambrosio replaced General Ugo Cavallero, regarded by many as very pro-German. See Smyth, "The Command of the Italian Armed Forces in World War II," *Military Affairs*, xv (Spring 1951), pp. 38–52.
[3] Monelli, *Roma, 1943*, p. 95.
[4] The admiral told Ciano on February 4, 1943, that he expected Italy "to be saved by the Monarchy." Gibson (ed.), *Ciano Diaries, 1939–1943*, p. 576.
[5] Caviglia, *Diario* (Jan. 15–24, 1943), pp. 391–393 ff.

from older statesmen Bonomi, Soleri, and Bergamini; and from some members of the royal family. But to one and all the misanthropic monarch usually listened in silence, refusing to commit himself. On rare occasions when he did respond it was to the effect that there were (allegedly) constitutional limitations on his freedom of action.

Bonomi's Anti-Fascist United Freedom Front

Characteristic of such incidents was Bonomi's experience, recorded in detail in his diary.[6] As spokesman of the Anti-Fascist United Freedom Front, formed on April 27, 1943, he talked first with Crown Prince Humbert's wife, Maria José, about the problem of getting rid of the dictator. The Belgian-born Princess of Piedmont was known to be favorable to a move against Mussolini; wits were calling her the "only man in the House of Savoy." [7] Rumor had it that she favored a government headed by Grandi, Ciano, and Bottai. The princess assured Bonomi that her father-in-law, confident of Army support, had decided to dispense with the *Duce*.[8] At her suggestion, Bonomi visited the Undersecretary of War but learned nothing from him. Soon, however, he discovered that the official whose word counted most with the King was Acquarone. Through a mutual friend he kept informed of the Duke's discussions with the monarch.

Bonomi was more anxious than ever to confer personally with Victor Emmanuel when he learned via the British Legation to the Vatican that Churchill preferred a monarchical solution to the crisis and reportedly would help Italy if she withdrew from the war.[9] About the same time he was disturbed to learn that Ciano and Grandi were secretly conferring with the British envoy. Bonomi wished to forestall any deal by either the British or the King with the intriguing hierarchs.

To this end, Bonomi wrote an article, "The Decisive Hour," published in *Ricostruzione* in May, just before the Axis sur-

[6] Bonomi, *Diario di un anno*, p. xxvii ff.

[7] Leopoldo Piccardi, "Colpo di stato e Movimento di Liberazione," *MLI*, No. 34/35 (1955), pp. 120–124.

[8] Leopoldo Piccardi, "A dieci anni dal 25 luglio," *Il Ponte*, ix (1953), pp. 909–922; Domenico Bartoli, *La fine della monarchia* (Verona, 1947), *passim*.

[9] The British envoy, Sir d'Arcy Osborne, had so informed Christian Democrat Guido Gonella. It was of course no mystery that high Vatican officials wished to replace Mussolini's dictatorship with a royal government and get Italy out of the war. Raffaele Guariglia, *Ricordi, 1922–1946* (Naples, 1949), p. 493, and *passim*.

render in Tunisia. In it he noted that the people were turning to the King and to the Army for guidance. Acknowledging that the opposition was split on the question of the Monarchy's future, he insisted that this "institutional question" must temporarily be postponed. If the King acted decisively in the crisis, everyone would rally around him, he predicted; if he did not, no one would forgive him. The only satisfactory solution was "destruction of Fascist domination and installation of a government which [would be] clearly anti-Fascist and [would detach Italy] from Hitler's Germany and Nazism." Men identified with Fascism were unqualified to negotiate peace with dignity, he continued. "They can request unconditional surrender but they cannot lead Italy once again into the body of free nations. . . . [Royal intervention] must not be delayed beyond the eve of the great Russian offensives . . . and the Anglo-American ones on the European continent. . . . An intervention which precedes these impending events can preserve Italy from invasion, can save the remainder of [her] bombarded cities, can spare hundreds of thousands of human lives, and can insure the possibility of a new future." [10] The article was received favorably by many republicans and royalists. It may have helped dissuade the King from casting in his lot with Ciano and Grandi.

On May 26 Bonomi at last was able to confer privately with Acquarone. To him he emphasized the need for royal intervention, arrest of Mussolini, and formation of a government headed at first by an Army general who could cope with the immediate military problems. Then, at the earliest possible time, authority should be transferred to the anti-Fascist parties arrayed in the United Freedom Front. They would denounce the German alliance and end the war. He recommended that secret talks start at once with the Anglo-Americans. Acquarone interrupted at this juncture to declare that the King would never listen to such a move against the German ally. Bonomi remained adamant, declaring that the proposed anti-Fascist government would have to terminate the Axis with or without royal approval. At the end of the colloquy Acquarone arranged for Bonomi to see the King personally within a week. [11]

This audience finally took place in the Quirinale the morning

[10] Bonomi, *Diario di un anno*, pp. xxxiv–xxxv.
[11] *Ibid.*, pp. xxviii–xxix.

of June 2. Annoyed by Bonomi's visit, the King deliberately monopolized the conversation.[12] Bonomi did find an opportunity, however, to remind him of his legal power to dismiss Mussolini at any time and to insist upon the necessity of arresting him.[13] He suggested three men—Marshal Badoglio; the latter's jealous rival, Marshal Caviglia; and General Ambrosio—as suitable to head the brief military government. The Axis could be severed easily, he went on, because the phraseology in the preamble to the Pact of Steel referred to "two regimes," "two revolutions." Overthrow of the Fascist "regime" could therefore be construed to invalidate the pact. Diffident and hesitant as was his wont, the King gave no indication that he either accepted or rejected Bonomi's advice.[14]

The United Freedom Front was dismayed by the seemingly negative outcome. However, spirits rose again when Acquarone persuaded Soleri, a Piedmontese Liberal, to speak to the King in behalf of Badoglio, also a native of Piedmont.

Badoglio was a logical choice to head a new government. He had a long record of military service, including participation in the ill-fated Abyssinian campaign of 1896 and the Caporetto debacle of 1917. He had flirted with Fascism and had betrayed Premier Facta in October 1922, but he was a good friend of the King. He had held several high posts: senator, ambassador to Brazil, Chief of the General Staff, and President of the Army Council. Though he had opposed the invasion of Ethiopia in 1935, he had loyally brought that conflict to successful issue, whereupon the *Duce* had rewarded him with the title Duke of Addis Ababa and honorary status in the PNF.

In World War II, on the other hand, Badoglio's military role as Chief of the General Staff had been less resplendent. He had permitted the armed forces to go into battle with the weapons and tactics of 1918. In the midst of the bogged-down invasion of Greece, Mussolini had sacked him (December 6, 1940). This, of course, did not improve Italian military fortunes, and it was the Germans who eventually rescued their hard-pressed ally. Unquestionably Badoglio bitterly resented Mussolini's brusque ac-

[12] Piccardi, "Colpo di stato e Movimento di Liberazione," *MLI*, No. 34/35 (1955), p. 122.
[13] Article 65 of the *Statuto* and Article 2 of a law of December 24, 1925, provided the King with all the legal power, Bonomi explained.
[14] Bonomi, *Diario di un anno*, pp. 1–7.

tion and shrewdly kept in touch with the Crown Princess, Acquarone, and Ambrosio.[15] In one of his talks with Acquarone before the *coup d'état* Badoglio broached the suggestion that Victor Emmanuel III abdicate in favor of the Crown Prince (as his ancestor Charles Albert had done after Novara) in order to strengthen the institution of the Monarchy. Acquarone squarely opposed this. Prince Humbert was too inexperienced, he argued. "If you take up this matter," he warned Badoglio, "you will fail, as the King is determined to remain at his post. The only result will be a coldness in your relations with His Majesty which will certainly not ease the task of your government." Badoglio dropped the subject.[16]

The King's audience with Soleri took place on June 8. He too emerged with a noncommittal reply.[17] After that, Bonomi tried a new tack; he went to Prince Humbert. When the latter indicated that he too favored Badoglio, Bonomi suggested that they go together to talk to the King. This proposal elicited no enthusiasm from Humbert, who believed in letting but one Savoyard rule at a time.[18]

Soon bleak communiqués revealed the fall of Pantelleria (June 12) and the smashing Allied invasion of Sicily (July 10). All that the *Duce* had to offer his people at this point was fatuous "sand-line" strategy.[19] Bonomi decided it was time to talk personally with the man most apt to assume power—Badoglio. On

[15] On January 15, 1943, Caviglia observed, "Badoglio also is preparing himself for the succession to Mussolini." *Diario*, p. 391.

[16] Pietro Badoglio, *Italy in the Second World War: Memories and Documents*, tr. by Muriel Currey (London, 1948), pp. 46–47. His memoirs often omit important points. Regarding this, see Salvemini, "Pietro Badoglio's Role in the Second World War," *Journal of Modern History*, xx (1949), pp. 326–332, and his more detailed probe, "Badoglio nella seconda guerra mondiale," serialized in *Il Ponte*, viii–ix (1952–1953). Cf. Amedeo Giannini, "Pietro Badoglio," *Rivista di studi politici internazionali*, xxiii (1956), pp. 639–644, for a short, critical biographical summary that emphasizes Badoglio's lack of political vision; Luigi Mondini, "Pietro Badoglio: il soldato e l'uomo politico," *Nuova antologia*, xci (1956), pp. 467–474; Amedeo Tosti, *Pietro Badoglio* (Milan, 1956); and Vanna Vailata, *Badoglio racconta* (Turin, 1955).

[17] Marcello Soleri, *Memorie* (Turin, 1949), p. 240.

[18] Bonomi, *Diario di un anno*, pp. 8–15.

[19] On June 24 he had told PNF leaders that "Italy will not fail to block the enemy on the foreshore, the sand-line (*"linea della bagnasciuga"*) where the water comes to an end and the land begins. . . . Should any of the enemy occupy a piece of our land, it will only be by remaining there for ever in a horizontal position and not a vertical one!" This speech was published on July 6.

the 14th Bonomi explained to him his scheme for deceiving Germany by continuing the war for a few days after the overthrow of Mussolini. Bonomi's plan in this respect differed from Acquarone's, which called for a much longer continuation of the German alliance. Badoglio seemed to approve Bonomi's proposal. The ex-premier then offered a revised plan for the future government: it should consist of both military officers and politicians and should dissolve Fascist agencies and the Axis compact. Bonomi suggested that Badoglio become President of the Council of Ministers, leaving the vice-presidency to himself. In that body the six political parties should be represented, Badoglio selecting the military personnel and Bonomi the civilian ministers. Badoglio seemed to favor this suggestion, and for the post of Foreign Minister advanced the name of the Neapolitan Raffaele Guariglia, then minister to Turkey. After some hesitancy Bonomi concurred. Badoglio also declared that Orlando and Croce should hold high posts.[20]

Next day Badoglio conferred with the King, in hopes of winning his adherence. Instead, Victor Emmanuel (perhaps at the behest of Orlando and Acquarone) threw cold water on the scheme. He asserted that *coups d'état* never succeed and objected to a political government made up of what he termed "revenants," for it would be disruptive and resemble too much the "empty life" of the pre-Fascist era. Badoglio apparently did not dispute him. Thus everything was left in the air.[21]

Foregathering in Milan at this same time was a "committee of the opposition," analogous to Bonomi's in Rome and in close touch with it. It consisted of representatives of the PCI, PSI, MUP, DC, and Ricostruzione Liberale. After long discussion, this northern underground directory voted in favor of insurrection if there was no speedy action by the King and Army plotters. News of this "ultimatum" reached Bonomi on July 20 and won the support of his group, which laid down a deadline of July 25 for action by the Crown. This decision, however, had little if any effect upon the actual course of events during the next few days.[22]

[20] Bonomi, *Diario di un anno*, pp. 15–21.
[21] *Ibid.*, p. 22; Monelli, *Roma, 1943*, pp. 110–111; Badoglio, *Italy in the Second World War*, p. 43.
[22] Battaglia, *SRI*, pp. 80–81.

The King decides

Available evidence suggests that it was on July 19 that Victor Emmanuel III at last made up his mind to remove his *Capo del Governo*. His decision was hastened by two important events that day: the abortive conference between Hitler and Mussolini at Feltre in the Veneto, and the massive Allied bombardment of Rome. The military conspirators had been accelerating their plans for a *coup* since the invasion of Sicily a week before.[23] Ambrosio was ready to give Mussolini one last chance at Feltre to break with Hitler and neutralize Italy, should the *Fuehrer* fail to assure him a vast amount of material aid. But at the conference the *Duce* dumbly listened to his German partner harangue him for three hours.[24] Mussolini's abjection had revealed itself in all its nakedness to the Army leaders present; on their way back to Rome they decided they must get the King's signal.[25]

At the very moment the two dictators were conferring, the Allies launched their first precision-bombing attack upon Rome "in one of the most significant operations of the war." Almost the entire strategic air force in the Mediterranean, including more than 500 bombers, dropped 1,000 tons of bombs upon the Lorenzo and Littorio freight yards.[26] Unmistakably, the Anglo-Americans had revealed their proximity and power; if the "revolution from above" were to occur at this juncture, the Allies would be near enough to save Italy (and the House of Savoy) from German retribution.

The King made up his mind under this pressure and communicated his decision to Acquarone, who passed it on to Castellano, Senise, Soleri, and (presumably) Badoglio.[27] At this stage the plan called for seizure of Mussolini on Monday, July 26, when he would make his regular periodic report to the King. The

[23] Giuseppe Castellano, *Come firmai l'armistizio di Cassibile* (Milan, 1945), pp. 45–51 ff.

[24] Vittorio Zincone (ed.), *Hitler e Mussolini: lettere e documenti* (Milan, 1946), pp. 165–190; Dino Alfieri, *Dictators Face to Face* (London, 1954), pp. 233–249; Enno von Rintelen, *Mussolini als Bundesgenosse: Erinnerungen des deutschen Militärattachés in Rom 1936–1943* (Tübingen and Stuttgart, 1951), pp. 197–215.

[25] Castellano, *Come firmai l'armistizio*, pp. 54–56 ff.

[26] U.S. Office of Air Force History, *The Army Air Forces in World War II* (Chicago, 1949), II, 463–465.

[27] Senise, *Quando ero Capo della Polizia*, pp. 193–200; Soleri, *Memorie*, pp. 233–240 ff.; Monelli, *Roma, 1943*, p. 113; Bonomi, *Diario di un anno*, pp. 24–27.

date had to be advanced to the evening of the 25th as a result of action taken by the Fascist Grand Council in its emergency session on the night of the 24–25th.

Meeting of the Fascist Grand Council

This supreme agency in Mussolini's regime had long been in desuetude. Since early in July, however, various Grand Councillors had broached to Mussolini the need for a formal meeting to discuss the precarious situation. He acceded and promised on the 16th to convene it within two weeks. During the next few days several of the hierarchs accelerated their intrigues, which paralleled those of the Army officers and the Crown. Grandi, it seems, got wind of the secret plans of Acquarone and Castellano and hoped to use the Grand Council's action as leverage upon the King to persuade him to name a neo-Fascist triumvirate consisting of himself, Ciano, and Luigi Federzoni.[28]

When the twenty-eight Councillors (some of them bearing hidden arms) assembled in Palazzo Venezia at 5 p.m. on July 24, Mussolini almost surely had some inkling of their schemes; yet he underestimated the seriousness, thinking that somehow he could ride out the storm.[29] The well-known high lights of the dramatic night session need not be recounted in detail here.[30] The discussions were tense but seldom violent. Some criticized the dictator for being too indecisive; others berated him for not ridding the government of incompetent bureaucrats; most of them made it clear that the King must take over active wartime leadership. The ailing *Duce* labored hard to defend himself, but to no avail. Final balloting gave 19 out of a possible 28 votes to the Grandi-Bottai-Ciano resolution calling for royal leadership

[28] Bottai, *Vent'anni e un giorno,* pp. 268–287; Wilhelm Hoettl, *The Secret Front: The Story of Nazi Political Espionage* (New York, 1954), pp. 272–274; Monelli, *Mussolini,* p. 209.

[29] Grandi has declared that he informed Mussolini on July 22 of the nature of his resolution. "Dino Grandi Explains," *Life,* XVIII (Feb. 26, 1945), p. 81; Dino Grandi, *Memoriale* (Bari, 1944); and *Dino Grandi racconta* (Venice, 1945).

[30] The firsthand accounts vary somewhat in interpretations. See Grandi's versions (n. 30); Mussolini, *Storia di un anno,* pp. 73–83; Bottai, *Vent'anni e un giorno,* pp. 295–318; Alfieri, *Dictators Face to Face,* pp. 278–294; *cf.* secondhand versions of Monelli, *Roma, 1943,* pp. 136–158; Edmondo Cione, *Storia della Repubblica Sociale Italiana* (Caserta, 1948), pp. 78–79; S/M, *Sdf,* pp. 944–947; and F. Debyser, "La chute du régime," *Revue d'histoire de la deuxième guerre mondiale,* No. 26 (1957), pp. 24–48.

231

and the rehabilitation of moribund state institutions.[31] Seven voted for a substitute resolution by PNF zealot Carlo Scorza.[32] Intensely pro-Nazi Roberto Farinacci cast a lone ballot for his own "order-of-the-day." It seems likely that Grandi and Ciano, had they become the new executives, would have speedily sought an armistice.

"Coup d'état"

When the session adjourned at 2:30 a.m. on Sunday, July 25, few of the Councillors dared return to their own homes. About 4 a.m. Grandi met Acquarone to report what had happened. He told him that a government of men unsullied by Fascism (for example, Marshal Caviglia) was imperative and that the overthrow of Mussolini must be synchronized with an armistice.[33] Acquarone saw the King at dawn and got his approval to dismiss Mussolini that same day instead of Monday and to appoint Marshal Badoglio instead of Grandi, any other hierarch, or Caviglia to head the new government.[34] At 7 a.m. Acquarone went to General Ambrosio to co-ordinate plans for Mussolini's arrest, and then both visited Badoglio to hand him the King's nomination decree. Thereafter Badoglio put on his uniform and waited impatiently for the final summons.

During the day Mussolini did some work at his office, visited bombed sections of the city, and conferred with Farinacci [35] and Scorza.[36] At noon he requested to be received in special audience

[31] It demanded "immediate reinstatement of all the organs of the State, assigning to the Crown, the Grand Council, the Government, Parliament, and the Corporations the tasks and responsibilities established by our Constitution and laws." The King must "assume the effective command of the Army, Navy, and Air Force. . . ." Voting for it were Grandi, Bottai, Ciano, Alfieri, DeBono, DeVecchi, DeMarsico, Acerbo, Pareschi, Cianetti, Federzoni, Balella, Gottardi, Bignardi, DeStefani, Rossoni, Marinelli, Bastianini, and Albini. Senate President Suardo abstained. Next day Cianetti notified Mussolini that he was reversing his vote.

[32] Scorza's resolution called for "political commissars" and other "reforms and innovations" of an extremely Fascist sort. It referred sympathetically to the Church and the "valorous German soldiers." Scorza, Biggini, Polverelli, Tringali-Casanova, Frattari, Buffarini-Guidi, and Galbiati voted for it.

[33] Grandi, Life, XVIII (Feb. 26, 1945), p. 89.

[34] Castellano, Come firmai l'armistizio, p. 57; Monelli, Roma, 1943, pp. 114, 158–159.

[35] Later that day Farinacci took refuge in the German Embassy and was soon flown to Hitler. Louis P. Lochner (ed.), The Goebbels Diaries, 1942–1943 (Garden City, 1948), p. 413.

[36] Apparently Mussolini issued orders to apprehend Grandi and Ciano, but the police ignored them.

by the King at 5 p.m. in Villa Savoia. At the appointed hour he arrived bearing legal documents designed to prove that the Grand Council's vote was merely advisory. Victor Emmanuel III, however, had decided to exploit the Council's action and regard it as a perfectly constitutional vote of nonconfidence.[37] The twenty-minute interview ended when the monarch informed his *Capo del Governo* that in view of the Council vote he had decided to appoint Marshal Badoglio in his stead. The rejected *Duce* remonstrated in vain; finally he murmured repeatedly, "Then everything is finished." Before Mussolini left the room, the King promised him and his family personal protection.[38] As the *Duce* stepped out of the villa, a *Carabiniere* captain approached him and suggested he climb into a waiting police ambulance rather than his own car in order to avoid a "hostile crowd." Falling into this trap like a child, Mussolini was driven to a near-by police barracks, not yet aware that he was really under arrest.[39]

At 10:45 p.m. the Italian radio announced tersely the replacement of Mussolini by Marshal Badoglio and then it broadcast two proclamations—one signed by the King, the other (though drafted by Orlando) signed by Badoglio. The latter declared:

"Italians! By order of His Majesty the King and Emperor, I assume the military government of the country with plenary powers. The war continues. Italy, heavily struck in the invaded provinces, in its destroyed cities, maintains faith in its plighted word, jealous custodian of its thousand-year-long traditions. Let all ranks close around His Majesty the King and Emperor, who is the living image of the Fatherland and an example to everyone.

"The trust received is clear and precise. It will be scrupulously executed, and whoever deludes himself of being able to impede its normal development, or attempts to disturb the public order will be inexorably struck." [40]

[37] Benedetto Croce, *Per la nuova vita dell'Italia: scritti e discorsi, 1943–1944* (Naples, 1944), pp. 28–37.
[38] Bolla, *Colloqui con Vittorio Emanuele III*, pp. 123–124. Cf. versions of Mussolini, *Storia di un anno*, pp. 89–91; Badoglio, *Italy in the Second World War*, pp. 41–42; and Attilio Tamaro, *Due anni di storia, 1943–1945* (3 vols.; Rome, 1948–1950), I, 26–33.
[39] Monelli, *Mussolini*, pp. 217–218; Jò di Benigno, *Occasioni mancate. Roma in un diario segreto, 1943–1944* (Rome, 1946), pp. 78–81.
[40] Quoted in Bonomi, *Diario di un anno*, pp. 35–37, and Badoglio, *Italy in the Second World War*, p. 43.

The conspirators had the double intention of removing Mussolini from power and Italy from the war; events quickly revealed, however, that they had no rational plan for co-ordinating the two problems. They had achieved the first without making coherent preparations for the latter. Instead of clear-eyed and stout-hearted statesmen Italy had only mediocre and superannuated Machiavellians: 72-year-old Badoglio and 74-year-old Victor Emmanuel III. Had the aged Savoyard foreseen the tribulations he was to face in the next few months and abdicated right then, instead of waiting till May 9, 1946, possibly he could have preserved the Monarchy; as it turned out, the vacillations of the binomial government during these first weeks fatally undermined it.

Royal-military dictatorship

At the outset of their royal-military dictatorship, supported by the same oligarchic groups who had flanked the Fascists, the King and Marshal Badoglio were afraid (unduly so, it turned out) of trouble from both sides—from Fascist diehards and from politicians and factory workers supposedly bent on revolution.

Fear of the Right

With respect to the first, arrangements had been made for Senise's police to occupy strategic communication centers in the capital, and instructions were issued to maintain public order and curfews and prohibit mass meetings. The government did not immediately abolish the Fascist Militia but simply enrolled it in the armed forces. The new leaders sought out a few "really dangerous Fascists," but their basic policy was to "go slow," lest "any violent program arouse the Germans and make the Fascists desperate." [41] Actually, most PNF officials had long been hypo-

[41] Senise, *Quando ero Capo della Polizia*, pp. 213–217; Badoglio, *Italy in the Second World War*, pp. 57–59, 61.

Among the few to be arrested at once was Germanophile ex-Chief of Staff Marshal Cavallero. PNF Secretary Scorza remained free for a while, but in August police hauled him in along with his predecessors, Achille Starace and Ettore Muti. Others eventually to be nabbed were Tringali-Casanova, President of the Special Tribunal; Guido Buffarini-Guidi, Undersecretary for Internal Affairs; Attilio Teruzzi, Minister for East Africa; and General Enzo Galbiati, Militia Chief of Staff.

Bottai was arrested but later fled from Italy. He enrolled in the French Foreign Legion to fight the Germans in France as "Private Battaglia," and later

critical and were anxious to save their pelts by sidling into the new ruling class.

Meanwhile, Badoglio had to decide what to do with Mussolini, as the original plans had included no long-term provision for him. A few hours after his arrest the ex-*Duce* received a polite note from Badoglio asking where he would like to go.[42] With patent obsequiousness, Mussolini penned a reply, suggesting his own crumbling castle of Rocca delle Caminate (near Predappio, above Forlì). Badoglio did not concur, though he permitted the family to proceed there. On the evening of the 27th he had the prisoner escorted to Gaeta, and thence to Ventotene. When his guardians discovered there was a German garrison there, they transferred him to Ponza. By this time the discharged demagogue no longer nourished illusions; he felt sure he was going to be handed over to the Anglo-Americans. Rumors of a German plot to rescue him caused the guards to transfer Mussolini on the night of August 7 to LaMaddalena, off northeastern Sardinia. On the evening of the 20th a German plane flew low over that islet. Fearing that the pilot might have recognized the ex-dictator, the guards flew him on the 28th to the resort hotel of Campo Imperatore atop Gran Sasso, tallest peak in central Italy. He perched on that crag until a few days after the armistice, almost

---

to fight as a sergeant in Indo-China. Thus he escaped the death sentence imposed in the autumn of 1943 by Mussolini's neo-Fascist Verona court, and he was unavailable when an anti-Fascist court handed him *in absentia* a life sentence. In 1948 he returned and was cleared by a purge court; the same year he published his memoirs; he died in 1959.

Farinacci and Alessandro Pavolini, director of Rome *Messaggero*, escaped by air to Berlin on July 26 with the help of German Embassy officials. In 1945 they both died at the hands of the Italian partisans.

Grandi secured a passport, flew to Portugal, and eventually went into business in São Paolo, Brazil. When Ciano requested a passport for himself and family, Badoglio told him this was unnecessary because the King wished him to stay at his Vatican post. Ciano insisted upon resigning. He obtained an Argentine passport with which he planned to travel to Spain, but for some reason he could not go direct from Italy. An airplane to Berlin was placed at his disposal; foolishly, he went that route and was taken into custody by the Nazis. That autumn they turned him over to Mussolini's puppet northern Italian Social Republic (RSI), which tried and convicted him of "betrayal" of the Axis. See Eugen Dollmann, *Roma nazista* (Milan, 1951), pp. 169–171; Hoettl, *The Secret Front*, pp. 265–278.

On the broad subject of de-Fascistization see U.S., OSS, Research & Analysis Branch Document No. 2688, "Treatment of Former Fascists by the Italian Government: An Analysis of the Process of De-Fascistization in Italy from July 1943 to March 1945," Washington, 17 March 1945, pp. 1–9.

[42] Quoted in Mussolini, *Storia di un anno*, pp. 92–93.

forgotten by the royal government during its frantic escape from Rome on September 8.[43]

Fear of the Left

Contrary to the fears of some of the new leaders, Italians greeted news of the *coup d'état* with undisguised exuberance, even though they were perplexed by Badoglio's phrase, "The war continues." For a day or two spontaneous demonstrations broke out in Rome, Milan, and elsewhere, with people surging up and down flag-draped streets, singing patriotic songs, and shouting, "Down with Fascism!" Some of them coursed into the deserted courtyard of Palazzo Venezia, as well as into the old PNF headquarters and *Popolo d'Italia* plant. Wherever Mussolini's picture had not already been timely removed, it was torn from the walls. Though Romans occasionally heard the chatter of small-arms fire, scarcely anyone was injured. Exultation and relief, mixed with hope for a quick end to the war, characterized the popular mood.[44] Bonomi struck a responsive chord in an impromptu speech to a crowd in Piazza Colonna: "After twenty years of Fascist domination I can speak freely in a Rome piazza. After waiting so long, my heart exults, as does yours. Italy has freed herself! Italy is restored to the Italians! Let us respect order. Freedom must be born out of order. . . . The hour is grave. All Italians who wish to reinstate freedom must remain united in a spirit of firm decision. Long live free Italy!" [45]

The clandestine parties quickly put out special editions of their papers, hailing the overturn of Fascism and calling for peace. *Il Mondo*, published by Labor Democrat Ruini, blazoned photographs of the martyrs Amendola and Matteotti. A crowd ejected the arch-Fascist propagandist Virginio Gayda from Rome's *Giornale d'Italia* and replaced him with its previous Liberal editor, Senator Alberto Bergamini. Corrado Alvaro, another eminent opposition journalist, took over *Popolo di Roma*,[46] while in Milan Ettore Janni resumed the post he had held in 1925 on the staff of *Corriere della sera*.

[43] *Ibid.*, pp. 93–105; Admiral Franco Maugeri, *From the Ashes of Disgrace*, ed. Victor Rosen (New York, 1948), pp. 125–153.

[44] Graphic eye-witness accounts of the scene in Rome may be found in Monelli, *Roma, 1943*, pp. 131–136.

[45] Printed in *Il Mondo* that day and republished in Bonomi, *Diario*, pp. 39–40.

[46] Cf. Corrado Alvaro, *Quasi una vita: giornale di uno scrittore* (Milan, 1950).

A general strike with manifestly political aims erupted in Milan between July 26 and 28. In some parts of the city hammer-and-sickle banners flew and workers' councils, analogous to the Russian soviets of 1917, appeared.[47] There was little if any violence, however, because of the restraining influence of the moderate wing of the opposition as well as because of the repressive measures of the government.[48]

The royal-military dictatorship intended to tolerate no disturbances. Through an order issued by General Mario Roatta, Chief of Army General Staff, it proclaimed a virtual state of siege on the 27th.[49] Indeed, in Bari on the 26th, police already had fired on demonstrators, killing twenty-three, including a son of Tommaso Fiore, the provincial Pd'A leader.[50]

Badoglio's first actions

On July 26 Marshal Badoglio announced the formation of his cabinet. His earlier understanding with Bonomi (whereby the latter, Casati, Soleri, Bergamini, and Einaudi would be appointed) went by the board. "You must have a ministry of experts who will carry out your orders efficiently," the King told Badoglio. "Here is a list of the new ministers." Badoglio did not object strenuously.[51] All those appointed came from the upper echelons of the civil service, magistracy, and military; only two had any link with traditional liberalism: Leopoldo Piccardi, Minister of Corporations, and Dr. Leonardo Severi, Minister of Education.[52]

[47] *Cf.* clandestine reports reaching London, in T. L. Gardini, *Towards the New Italy* (London, 1943), pp. 108–110.
[48] Longo, *Un popolo alla macchia*, p. 48.
[49] "In the present situation, any disturbance of public order, even the slightest . . . will constitute treason, and can lead if not repressed to extremely grave consequences. Every movement must inexorably be cut short at its origin; . . . the troops must proceed in combat formation, opening fire . . . without warning, as if they were proceeding against the enemy; . . . whoever—even if acting alone—creates acts of violence against the armed forces will be shot at once; any soldier employed in tasks of maintaining public order who makes the slightest gesture of solidarity with the demonstrators and who does not obey his orders will be shot immediately." Quoted in *ibid.*, pp. 46–47.
[50] Ragghianti, *Disegno della liberazione italiana*, p. 288.
[51] Badoglio, *Italy in the Second World War*, pp. 42–43.
[52] Raffaele Guariglia, ambassador to Turkey, became Foreign Minister. The portfolio of War was assigned to General Antonio Sorice; Navy to Admiral Raffaele de Courten; Aviation to General Renato Sandalli; War Production to General Carlo Favagrossa; Internal Affairs to an ex-Prefect Bruno Fornaciari,

The cabinet's first session took place on the 27th in the Viminal Palace. Ironically it made use of Fascism's own system of "decree-laws" to liquidate the regime. Thus by fiat it dissolved the PNF and various paraparty organizations; eradicated the Fascist Grand Council, Special Tribunal for Defense of the State, Chamber of Fasci and Corporations; emancipated certain categories of political prisoners; and abrogated laws restricting rights of bachelors. One important decision made was to delay election of a Chamber of Deputies until four months after hostilities. This seemed to mean that the nation would return to the pre-Fascist political system without the opportunity of reform by a Constituent Assembly. Meanwhile, the binomial dictatorship would prevail; the King would resume command of the armed forces and exercise martial law; and political parties would be forbidden to function overtly for the duration of the war.[53]

Only partially aware of these developments, the anti-Fascist juntos in Rome and Milan [54] discussed their plan of action. Finally they instructed Bonomi to confer with Badoglio and advise him to approve quickly four recommendations which had been pushed through by the leftist parties: (1) dissolution of the PNF, Militia, and Special Tribunal; (2) liberation of political prisoners and abolition of all racial decrees; (3) complete freedom of the press; and (4) formation of a government composed of representatives of all the parties that expressed the "national will." [55]

Quite likely the underground leaders were sure that the fourth demand would be rejected, for it is doubtful they really wished to assume governmental responsibilities prior to an armistice.

---

and later to Umberto Ricci; Finance to Inspector-General Domenico Bartolini; Justice to Gaetano Azzariti; Popular Culture to Guido Rocco; Public Works to Domenico Romano; Agriculture to Alessandro Brizi; and Communications to General Federico Amoroso. S/M, *Sdf*, pp. 951–952.

[53] Royal Decree-Laws Nos. 704, 705, 706, Aug. 2, 1943, in *Gazzetta Ufficiale*, Aug. 5, 1943, cited in Howard M. Smyth, "Italy: From Fascism to the Republic," *The Western Political Quarterly*, 1 (1948), 208; cf. S/M, *Sdf*, p. 952.

[54] The Milan Anti-Fascist Committee had met on July 26 in the law offices of Adolfo Tino (Pd'A) in Via Monte di Pietà. Participants included Stefano Jacini (DC); G. Arpesani and Tommaso Gallarati-Scotti (PLI); Lelio Basso and L. Luzzatto (MUP); and G. Grilli (PCI). The committee met almost daily thereafter. Franco Catalano, *Storia del CLNAI* (Bari, 1956), pp. 34–35.

[55] A fifth recommendation, calling for an immediate armistice, was not stressed. Catalano, *Storia del CLNAI*, pp. 35–37; Pd'A (Rome) *L'Italia Libera*, July 27, 1943.

Indeed, DeGasperi, the gaunt, unrhetorical captain of Christian Democracy, had expressed the consensus of the Rome committee when he observed that two things must be done: Fascism must be liquidated and an armistice with the Anglo-Americans negotiated. Those who accomplished the first would win the country's plaudits, he explained, whereas those who took the onus for the latter would face criticism from every side; for a humiliated, defeated nation inevitably will berate the men who have to take the rap. Consequently, DeGasperi reasoned, it would be a blunder for the anti-Fascists to join the Badoglio government in any show of "national unity" before it negotiated a cease-fire. Persuaded by DeGasperi's reasoning, the group decided to await further developments before offering support.[56] The Pd'A insisted, however, that there was no need to mull over the problem, because neither the King nor Badoglio was a true anti-Fascist or fit company at any time for the underground elite. The Actionists predicted that the new dictatorship would not permit a Constituent Assembly to meet after the war to determine the fate of the Monarchy but would, instead, reinstate the Chamber of Deputies—which would mean no sharp repudiation of the pre-Fascist political pattern. (Badoglio's announcement of the 27th proved the accuracy of their prediction.) [57]

On the 28th Bonomi presented the resolutions of the Rome and Milan committees to Badoglio, who informed him that action already had been taken on the first point. As for the second, he promised that political prisoners not already scheduled for trial would be freed, while those condemned to prison terms would have their cases reviewed with the possibility of executive clemency in mind. Bonomi argued that a general amnesty would be preferable. As it turned out, the Communists and Anarchists (a conveniently broad category) were the very last to be released in August.[58] Badoglio promised to inform leaders of the Jewish community that although the government did not yet dare annul anti-Semitic decrees because of the presence of the Germans, it would not enforce them.[59]

[56] Bonomi, *Diario di un anno*, pp. 34–35.
[57] *Ibid.*; Bruno Visentini, *Due anni di politica italiana* (1943–1945) (Vicenza, 1945), pp. 5–6.
[58] Senise, *Quando ero Capo della Polizia*, p. 216.
[59] Badoglio, *Italy in the Second World War*, pp. 61–62.

Turning to the third resolution, Bonomi emphasized that the Ministry of Popular Culture and Enlightenment was a public disgrace: 98 per cent of its paid propagandists were rabid Fascists. He asked Badoglio to disband it at once and requested that the press be placed under the premier's direct supervision. Though Badoglio appeared annoyed, he promised to study this problem.[60] The ministry survived, however, until after the armistice and it rigorously censored the press. It stifled the resurrected *Il Mondo* and *La Riscossa* and reprimanded *Corriere della sera* for its purportedly communistic tone; afterward large empty spaces marked "censored" blanked the latter's pages.[61]

With respect to Bonomi's final demand, Badoglio explained what his cabinet had decided, *viz.*, election of a new Chamber of Deputies to take place within four months after the war, with political parties remaining illegal so long as the war lasted. Badoglio made no effort to quash Bonomi's committee, to be sure, but he permitted no formal party meetings.[62]

Italo-German relations

Though Badoglio was not sure how to go about the problem, he hoped to negotiate a bargain with the Anglo-Americans whereby Italy would not appear as an abject petitioner for "unconditional surrender" but as a prospective partner in the Allied war effort, and whereby she could assure herself of their military support before breaking her ties with Germany. To gain time he had announced that "the war continues"; but this only bewildered the Italians, and it did not fool many Germans for more than a few hours. In the final reckoning, the very situation

[60] Bonomi, *Diario di un anno*, p. 36 ff.

[61] Marian Taylor Abbagnano, "The Collapse of Fascism in Italy," *Forum*, CXII (1949), p. 13.

[62] The spirit of the new dictatorship was revealed in a policy memorandum dated August 16 that Badoglio inadvertently left in his desk when he fled from Rome on September 8: "The present government must conserve and maintain . . . its same characteristics of 'military government' as announced in the proclamation of July 25 . . . , exclusively technical experts in all the ministries. The facing of political problems must be postponed to a later date and to a subsequent reorganization of the government when the climate is quite different and more tranquil. . . . No party must be permitted to organize itself openly and to manifest itself with publications and labels. . . ." Seized by the Germans, the document was turned over to Mussolini, who published it in his *Storia di un anno*, pp. 111–113. On the King's general attitude see also Livio Pivano, *Meditazioni nella tormenta* ([Modena], 1947), a valuable source on events in Piedmont during this period.

that Badoglio had hoped to prevent took place—unconditional surrender to the Allies, German seizure of most of the peninsula, and popular discrediting of the Monarchy.

The Germans had anticipated some trouble in Italy; nevertheless, the actual *coup* caught them by surprise. When word of it reached Hitler the evening of July 25 he exploded with fury. He had never liked Victor Emmanuel III, and he now referred to Badoglio as "our most bitter enemy." "Although that so-and-so declared immediately that the war would be continued, that won't make any difference. They have to say that, but it remains treason. But we'll play the same game while preparing everything to take over the whole crew with one stroke, to capture all of that rif-raff." [63] Though he recognized that Italy as an ally had become a liability to him, he was determined to keep her as a vassal, for possession of the Mediterranean "boot" would keep the Anglo-Americans farther from the Reich and assure it access to valuable food supplies and some industrial resources. He ordered additional divisions (which had been denied to Mussolini at Feltre) to move at once over the Brenner Pass, and measures taken to cope with any defection by Italy. [64]

Hitler flatly rejected Badoglio's early suggestion that the *Fuehrer* meet with the Italian King. But a few days later Ribbentrop proposed a conference between the two Axis Foreign Ministers and the Chiefs of Staff. Before this took place on August 6 in the frontier town of Tarvisio, the Germans seriously debated the feasibility of arresting the King, Badoglio, and the Prince, liberating and reinstating Mussolini, seizing the Italian Navy, and occupying the whole peninsula. As early as July 27 SS agents discussed with embassy officials in Rome plans for such a *Putsch*, including a foray into Vatican City. According to Eugen Dollmann, an embassy attaché, they envisaged a veritable "night of St. Bartholomew." On the 26th Ambassador Hans von Mackensen and Field Marshal Albert Kesselring talked with Badoglio and the King, who temporarily convinced them of the good faith of the new government as well as of the futility of trying to reinstate the unpopular *Duce*. Kesselring flew to Hitler's headquarters and so reported the next day. The intuitions of both

[63] Germany, Wehrmacht, Oberkommando, *Hitler Directs his War*, ed. Felix Gilbert (New York, 1950), p. 50.
[64] *Nazi Conspiracy and Aggression* (Washington, 1946), VII, 930–935.

the *Fuehrer* and Goebbels told them the contrary, but on the advice of Kesselring and Rommel (the new Commander-in-Chief of German Armed Forces in Italy), they decided to suspend plans for a *Putsch*, while accelerating concentration of German troops in the peninsula. After all, they lacked tangible proof of peace negotiations, and Mussolini's whereabouts remained a mystery.[65]

In Tarvisio on August 6 Foreign Ministers Ribbentrop and Guariglia met, as did the two Axis Chiefs of Staff, Generals Keitel and Ambrosio. Hoping to find out what the Italians were up to, Ribbentrop made it clear that the new government could not expect the degree of faith from Germany that the Blackshirt regime had enjoyed, but intimated that the Reich was ready to extend military aid within the limits of its possibilities. With as straight a face as he could muster Guariglia assured his colleague that Italy would stay loyal to the alliance and prevent any domestic leftist disturbances. Guariglia departed with the impression that tension had been lessened and precious time gained.[66]

If the diplomats' talks were at least correct, those of the Chiefs of Staff were hardly so. Sparks flew when the Italian officers complained about mysterious German troop movements. Their efforts to get permission to pull back their own forces from the Balkans "to defend Italy from the Allies" were abortive, though in a later conference in Bologna on August 15 Generals Rossi and Roatta met Rommel and Jodl and arranged for repatriation of three divisions of the Italian Fourth Army in France.[67]

Italo-Allied relations

During the weeks after the *coup* both the Allies and Italians suffered from tragic mutual ignorance of each other's intentions

[65] *Hitler Directs his War*, pp. 47–71; Lochner (ed.), *The Goebbels Diaries*, pp. 402–421; Bullock, *Hitler: A Study in Tyranny*, pp. 648–650; Field Marshal Albert Kesselring, *The Memoirs of Field-Marshal Kesselring* (London, 1953), pp. 169–171; Dollmann, *Roma nazista*, Ch. 7; Von Rintelen, *Mussolini als Bundesgenosse*, pp. 223–254; E. F. Moellhausen, *La carta perdente: memorie diplomatiche 25 luglio 1943–2 maggio 1945* (Rome, 1948), pp. 38–39; Von Hassell, *The Von Hassell Diaries, 1938–1944*, p. 284; and Hoettl, *The Secret Front*, pp. 224–229.

[66] Guariglia, *Ricordi, 1922–1946*, pp. 616–630.

[67] Howard McGaw Smyth's manuscript on the Italian armistice, cited in Herbert Feis, *Roosevelt, Churchill, Stalin: The War They Fought and the Peace They Sought* (Princeton, 1957), p. 161; General Francesco Rossi, *Come arrivammo all'armistizio* (Rome, 1946), pp. 385–401.

and strength. The Italian leaders hoped that the Anglo-Americans would forget "unconditional surrender" and agree to a negotiated *volte-face* which would enable them to escape German revenge. The Allies still estimated Italy to be stronger than she really was; yet they were relatively uninterested in gaining her military assistance. For psychological and strategic reasons the Allies were anxious to force Italy's surrender and gain control of at least the southern portion of the peninsula. Such an invasion would provide bases for the bombardment of Germany and possible operations in the Balkans; furthermore, it would pull a substantial number of German units south of the Brenner, and divert them from the Channel coast and from the Russian front.[68]

Suspicious of Italian duplicity and lacking trustworthy information regarding conditions in the country, the Allies were cautious. Having expected a peace feeler, they were puzzled by the phrase, "The war continues." Within a few hours the American Office of War Information broadcast an analysis of the situation in which it referred to "the moronic little King" and "the Fascist King," and to Badoglio as a "high-ranking Fascist." [69] When Churchill and Roosevelt learned of this they were irritated, for they did not wish to hamper any Italian approach. Though OWI promised to avoid such epithets, another broadcast from Algiers a few days later intimated that if the Italians surrendered "honorably," their prisoners-of-war would be restored at once—a promise manifestly impossible to fulfill. Churchill was so "furious . . . he cabled Hopkins expressing his views on the 'anonymous and unauthoritative low-level propaganda pumped out by the machines.' " [70] Churchill quickly made it clear to Commons on the 27th that "unconditional surrender" was still the policy: "My advice . . . at this juncture [is that the] Italians [should] 'stew in their own juice' for a bit . . . until we obtain from their Government, or whoever possesses the necessary authority, all the indispensable requirements we demand for carrying on the

[68] See Norman Kogan, *Italy and the Allies* (Cambridge, 1956), pp. 22–25 ff., for a discussion of Allied policy.

[69] *NYT*, July 28, 1943, 1:3.

[70] Robert E. Sherwood, *Roosevelt and Hopkins, an Intimate History* (New York, 1948), p. 744; *cf.* Churchill's paper of July 26, 1943, expressing his "thoughts on the fall of Mussolini," in his *The Second World War*, Vol. v: *Closing the Ring* (Boston, 1951), pp. 55–59.

war against our prime and capital foe, which is not Italy, but Germany." [71] Next day the President in a broadcast referred to "Mussolini and his Fascist gang" and promised that they "will be punished for their crimes against humanity." [72]

As early as July 28 the *New York Times* reported rumors of Italian armistice soundings in Bern and Istanbul, but the first significant gambit occurred the night of the 30th when Guariglia arrived from Istanbul and sought out Cardinal Maglione, Vatican Foreign Secretary. To his distress, Guariglia learned that neither the British nor American representative to the Holy See had a code secure from the Germans. Other approaches quickly followed. Consul-General Alberto Berio traveled to Tangier, while Lanza d'Ajeta, godson of Sumner Welles and Counselor of the Italian Embassy to the Holy See, flew to Lisbon, where he spoke to the British ambassador on August 4. Both ran up against a stone wall on the issue of unconditional surrender.[73]

Criticism from the underground

Unaware of these developments, the clandestine United Freedom Front met on July 31 with Bonomi. He reported that General Giacomo Carboni, commander of a motorized army corps near Rome, had told him that the Germans were rapidly augmenting their forces. Some 120,000 troops had been observed in the Trentino, and a "potential fifth column" of 6,000 German civilians was reputedly in Rome. Bonomi was greatly worried lest Badoglio allow the war to drag on to the stage where the people became completely demoralized. A split between the government and the masses conceivably might facilitate a resurgence of Fascism.

Long discussions followed, during which the Actionists reiterated their firm refusal to collaborate in any way with Badoglio. But at last the covert politicos renewed their confidence in Bonomi and instructed him to tell the Marshal that if he assumed a strong anti-German posture, he had their enthusiastic support.[74] Accordingly, Bonomi visited Badoglio on August 2 and

[71] Quoted in *NYT*, July 28, 1943.
[72] *Ibid.*, July 29, 1943.
[73] Guariglia, *Ricordi*, pp. 586–587, 601–605; Alberto Berio, *Missione segreta (Tangeri: agosto 1943)* (Milan, 1946); Churchill, *Closing the Ring*, pp. 101–103; and Harry C. Butcher, *My Three Years with Eisenhower* (New York, 1946), pp. 378–379.
[74] Bonomi, *Diario di un anno*, pp. 46–49.

expressed his group's concern about German troop movements and reminded him that the people expected him to bring them peace. This irritated the veteran commander, who interrupted with asperity, "I have deluded no one; I wrote in my proclamation that 'the war continues'; therefore I have spoken quite clearly." [75] None the less, he admitted that he too was worried, and he mentioned the imminence of a meeting of the Foreign Ministers and Chiefs of Staff. This news greatly alarmed Bonomi, who felt sure the Allies would misconstrue it. For that reason he inquired if armistice negotiations were under way. Badoglio replied that it was hard enough to make peace when just two parties were involved and incomparably more so when three had to be considered. He conceded that thus far all efforts had failed. Downcast, Bonomi wrote, "There is no strong will on the part of the Badoglio government; it is drifting." [76]

After the United Freedom Front heard Bonomi's report it voted unanimously to "impose" on Badoglio the "national will" to end the war, even if this should lead to hostilities with Germany. The PCI and PSIUP were especially insistent upon this breach, come what might; Buozzi asserted that "all the Italian proletariat would come forth with arms to defend the country." [77] But the Actionists were somewhat worried lest such popular unity in an anti-German war enable the "prostituted" Monarchy to "re-establish its virginity." [78]

Bonomi's committee visited Badoglio on the 3rd. He was not at all anxious to receive them, and did so only after lengthy persuasion by Bonomi. "He does not understand democratic necessities," the latter wrote afterward. Badoglio read the committee's resolution but refused to discuss it. He did promise, however, to give it serious attention and to show it to the King.[79]

The period from the August 6 Tarvisio conference of the Foreign Ministers until the 12th was quiet, the Allies having all but halted their bombardments of Italy. Optimistic that D'Ajeta's mission to Tangier would bear fruit, Guariglia made no attempt either to break relations with Germany or to agree to "uncondi-

[75] *Ibid.*, p. 51.
[76] *Ibid.*, pp. 50–52; *cf.* Badoglio, *Italy in the Second World War*, p. 51.
[77] Bonomi, *Diario di un anno*, pp. 53–54; Monelli, *Roma, 1943*, p. 203.
[78] Bonomi, *Diario di un anno*, p. 54.
[79] *Ibid.*, pp. 55–56; Monelli, *Roma, 1943*, p. 203. The delegation consisted of Bonomi, Casati, DeGasperi, Ruini, Salvatorelli, Buozzi, and Amendola.

tional surrender." Later he defended this policy on the grounds that: (1) Italy needed time to repatriate her forces from France, Yugoslavia, and elsewhere; (2) she had insufficient gasoline to supply her armed forces in the event of premature hostilities with Germany; and (3) she needed time to make the Allies appreciate her peril and synchronize Allied and Italian military actions.[80]

In Milan the party leaders moved into clear-cut opposition to Badoglio on the 7th, when spokesmen of the Pd'A, PCI, and PSIUP signed a joint declaration which became the basis of their policy till June 1944. They agreed to act within the larger Milanese body as a "permanent committee for vigilance and defense of freedom and peace for the Italian people." Their specific demands upon the government won the approval of even the rightist currents.[81]

Milan's insistence upon agitation to compel Badoglio to sign an armistice was conveyed quickly to the Rome committee, whose sessions of August 11 and 12 in the law offices of Spataro (DC) were attended by an unusually large number of people. They heard Actionist LaMalfa bitterly accuse Badoglio's regime of being "the faithful executor of premeditated plans of the Monarchy, which, through feigned liberalism on occasion, wishes to save itself and the plutocratic, reactionary currents of Fascism." Despite warnings by Bonomi and DeGasperi that demonstrations should be staged only after the Allies landed and were able to help the Italians defend themselves against the Germans,[82] the meeting approved a revised resolution by Ruini calling for condemnation of the government's procrastination in ending the war, in purging Fascists, and in bestowing freedom of the press. The Milanese and Roman committees obviously had reached a turning point in their relations with Badoglio.[83]

[80] Guariglia, *Ricordi*, p. 642 ff.

[81] Ragghianti, *Disegno della liberazione italiana*, pp. 19–20, 31. See Tupini, *I Democratici Cristiani*, pp. 93–105, for data regarding development of the DC in this period. A photograph of the "August 7 Deliberation" is printed in Tamaro, *Due anni di storia, 1943–45*, I, 101.

[82] Meanwhile, on the 11th Bonomi heard Crown Prince Humbert, in command of armed forces in the South, report that rumors of troop demoralization there were quite true. The Prince predicted that the Allies would invade the mainland as easily as they had Sicily. He agreed that Badoglio must contact the Allies at once, and he was hopeful of an early breach with Germany. Bonomi, *Diario di un anno*, pp. 57–58, 69–70.

[83] Ragghianti, *Disegno della liberazione italiana*, pp. 32–33; Bonomi, *Diario*, pp. 71–73.

Lisbon parleys

On August 12 the Anglo-Americans heavily bombarded Milan, Foggia, and other industrial and transportation centers. These devastating raids, worse than anything before, helped convince the government of the need for immediate talks, as did renewed pressure from the anti-Fascist committees and peace demonstrations in Milan in the form of ten-minute daily work stoppages. D'Ajeta's report that further diplomatic approaches were futile and that a military officer must be dispatched to talk to the Allies also carried weight.

Badoglio, Guariglia, and Ambrosio thereupon decided to send to Lisbon General Castellano, who had been at the hub of the conspiracy to unseat Mussolini, and who was thought to be friendly to the Anglo-Americans. Traveling in mufti with a false passport, he left Rome on the 12th in a diplomatic train en route to Lisbon to escort home some overseas attachés.[84] In a stopover in Madrid on the 15th he saw the British ambassador, who notified Churchill and Roosevelt, then in Quebec, of his mission. Arriving in Lisbon the next day he presented himself to the British minister. On the 19th General Eisenhower dispatched to Lisbon his tough-fibred American Chief of Staff, Major General Walter Bedell Smith, and British Brigadier Kenneth W. D. Strong, Assistant Chief of Staff, G-2. They were instructed to make no advance promises; once the Italian government agreed to surrender unconditionally it must simply trust the Allies' sense of justice. After all, Allied Headquarters had little trustworthy intelligence regarding the Italian people's true feelings. They knew that among the hundreds of thousands of PW's in North Africa apathy rather than anti-Germanism predominated, and that in Tunisia most of the 100,000 Italian residents had long backed Vichy. Throughout North Africa Italian troops had fought the Allies vigorously, and in Sicily, though many surrendered, none had turned upon the Germans.[85]

Thus Smith and Strong opened their talks with Castellano by reading off a list of terms (later called the Short Armistice) to which he was to answer "yes" or "no." One of the major articles required Italy to accept political, economic, and financial con-

---

[84] Guariglia, *Ricordi*, p. 645; Castellano, *Come firmai l'armistizio*, p. 77 ff.
[85] Salvadori, *SRI*, p. 121; Salvadori, *Resistenza ed azione*, pp. 209–220.

ditions that would be disclosed at a later time (in the Long Armistice). Another called for the Italian Navy, merchant marine, and Air Force to proceed to Allied bases.[86]

To all of this Castellano replied that he had no authority to negotiate an armistice. His task, he explained, was to clarify Italy's military situation to the Allies, to offer the participation of her armed forces in the struggle against the Germans, and to agree upon methods for making such collaboration effective. Italy could not dissociate herself from Germany without Allied help, and this should consist preferably of two landings—one to the north of Rome; the other to the north of Rimini on the Adriatic. Thus the Germans would withdraw toward the Alps, leaving Rome and central Italy safe. Obviously what Castellano hoped to do was to facilitate Italy's change of sides without actually capitulating.[87]

Smith thereupon made it clear that unconditional surrender was imperative. But he reassured Castellano that the Allies would help those Italian forces which in any way fought the Germans. At this point he handed Castellano an aide-memoir drafted by Churchill and Roosevelt in Quebec which indicated how Italy could "work her passage back." [88] During the rest of the conference Castellano presented the Allies with considerable data regarding the extent of German and Italian military forces in the

[86] Castellano, Come firmai l'armistizio, p. 98 ff.; cf. Howard McGaw Smyth, "The Armistice of Cassibile," Military Affairs, xII (1948), pp. 12–35, for an authoritative account of the Allied side of negotiations; his "Some Recent Italian Publications regarding World War II," ibid., xI (Winter 1947), pp. 245–253; Feis, Churchill, Roosevelt, Stalin, pp. 153–166; Kogan, Italy and the Allies, pp. 31–41; Paul Kecskemeti, Strategic Surrender: The Politics of Victory and Defeat (Stanford, 1958), pp. 71–118; and the accounts in the memoirs of Churchill, Eisenhower, and Butcher.

[87] Castellano, Come firmai l'armistizio, p. 105.

[88] Text in Documenti relativi ai rapporti tra l'Italia e le Nazioni Unite (Rome, 1945), I, 23–25, quoted in Kogan, Italy and the Allies, p. 34. When the Italian expressed concern over the naval terms and warned that the sailors might scuttle their ships rather than surrender them, Smith reassured Castellano that the Quebec memoir appeared to "tone down" the clause calling for naval disarmament. Though he could put nothing in writing, Smith promised that the Italian flag would continue to fly over the vessels. This commitment became the basis of the nonsurrender of the Italian Navy. Ibid., p. 34.

Castellano was also concerned about possible extension of Allied Military Government (AMG) to the mainland. This would mean a derogation of Italian sovereignty, he insisted, and would make it hard to conserve the King's authority in the difficult period ahead. As this clearly was a political issue, Smith could make no change.

peninsula. Understandably, the Allied delegates were not equally frank.

Finally they agreed (since Castellano had no power to conclude an armistice) that the Italians would inform the British envoy to the Vatican of their response to the terms. Castellano returned to Rome on the 27th, a day later than he had promised Smith and Strong. Fifteen precious days had elapsed since he started on his mission, and in that interval the Germans had greatly buttressed their positions.[89]

Italian labor emancipates itself

Meanwhile in mid-August northern labor leaders threatened a wave of strikes, largely because of stepped-up Allied bombardments and lack of evidence that Badoglio was seeking an armistice.[90] They demanded not only immediate peace but release of *all* political prisoners, removal of all Fascists and military personnel from industry, and restoration of elective "internal commissions" such as had existed between 1919 and 1922.[91] During the crisis the northern workers insisted they would discuss their goals only with the government, not with management.

Consequently, Badoglio was forced to turn to Leopoldo Piccardi, a bona fide Liberal who was his Minister of Corporations. The latter appealed to several of the labor spokesmen for support and in time was able to promote a minor crisis within their ranks. Most of them decided to give him limited co-operation, so long as this did not imply endorsement of other governmental policies. Before the PSIUP and PCI would agree they insisted upon dissolution of remaining Fascist organs and amnesties for all political prisoners.[92] At last Piccardi named an informal committee of labor commissioners made up of knowledgeable and

[89] During the long silence that enveloped the Lisbon talks, Badoglio became more worried than ever; without consulting Guariglia, he dispatched to Lisbon and Algiers another agent, General Giacomo Zanussi, Chief of Staff to General Mario Roatta. The Allies at last presented Zanussi with a copy of the Long Armistice terms. Castellano, *Come firmai l'armistizio*, pp. 107–118; Zanussi, *Guerra e catastrofe d'Italia*, II, 150 ff.; Guariglia, *Ricordi*, pp. 674–677; and Churchill, *Closing the Ring*, pp. 107–109.

[90] See Giorgio Vaccarino, "Il movimento operaio a Torino nei primi mesi della crisi italiana (luglio 1943–marzo 1944)," *MLI*, No. 19 (July 1952), pp. 3–47; and No. 20 (Sept. 1952), pp. 3–43.

[91] Catalano, *Storia del CLNAI*, p. 44.

[92] Federico Comandini, *Breve storia di cinque mesi* (Rome, 1944), pp. 26–27, 85; Longo, *Un popolo alla macchia*, p. 49.

competent men: the veteran Socialist Buozzi (who before the dictatorship had been secretary of the Turin Metallurgical Workers Federation); the Communist Giovanni Roveda (who once had headed the Turin Chamber of Labor); two Christian Democrats, Achille Grandi and Giovanni Quarello; and an Actionist, Professor DeRuggiero.

Accompanied by Buozzi and Roveda, Piccardi hurried to Turin on August 20. By assuring the workers that their status would be improved and elected internal commissions legalized, he persuaded them to call off the stoppages. Yet the trouble continued. On August 27 and 28 the Communists, perhaps irritated by the extent of co-operation offered Piccardi by the other groups, provoked a new crisis. After more negotiations, however, their hostility ceased and on September 2 final agreement was achieved. A joint statement promised that the pre-Fascist kind of internal commissions, elected by direct, secret ballot, would be established in concerns collaborating with the new labor organization. Excited by such prospects but often differing greatly in their conception of the proper role of such agencies, many northern workers prepared for the elections. Thus during Badoglio's "45 days" Italian labor, chiefly by its own determination, began to enjoy once more the right of democratic self-control.[93]

In Rome steps already had been taken on August 16 to reestablish the powerful pre-Fascist national labor organizations. What finally emerged was the Italian General Confederation of Labor (CGIL), a fusion of the old Socialist CGL and the Catholic Confederation of Italian Laborers. Collaborating in this signal accomplishment were the PCI delegates, Roveda and DiVittorio; the revisionist Socialists Buozzi and Lizzadri; and the Christian Democrats Grandi and Quarello. The Pd'A was not represented (it had held out for a more decentralized type of organization, representing all types of employees, including technicians and white-collar workers).[94] Buozzi became CGIL Commissar; he held the post until the spring of 1944 when the Nazis captured and executed him.

[93] Vaccarino, MLI, No. 19 (July 1952), p. 44; cf. Gardini, Towards the New Italy, pp. 140–141; and Piccardi, "Colpo di stato e Movimento di Liberazione," MLI, No. 34/35 (1955), pp. 120–124.

[94] Vaccarino, MLI, No. 19 (July 1952), pp. 45–46; Rome L'Italia Libera, Aug. 10, 21, 1943.

After Rome's liberation in June 1944 the nature of the new CGIL was fully revealed. DiVittorio, Grandi, and Lizzadri, representing the three *partiti di massa,* served in the original secretariat, each enjoying ostensibly equal power. Almost immediately, though, the Communists, backed by the Socialists, dominated the puissant labor organization.[95]

Opposition rumblings

During the period from August 12 to 24 the Rome United Freedom Front of Bonomi did not meet as often as before, though its chairman kept up his talks with influential people and learned from Guariglia on the 20th that secret armistice negotiations were under way. Among the Milan underground, on the other hand, frequent conferences produced stiffer hostility than ever to Badoglio. A resolution of the 23rd stoutly condemned the regime and called for a brand-new "political" government. It ended with the warning that this new government must realize that the nation, and especially the working classes, was determined to resort to direct action of the most extreme type in order to gain its ends. This resolution was indeed a harbinger of the partisan warfare soon to erupt in the North. The tenor of the declaration was relayed to the Rome committee by the Communist G. Grilli and Christian Democrat G. Malavasi.[96]

Pressed by the Milanese politicians and disturbed by rumors of an attempted Nazi-Fascist *Putsch* in the capital the night before, Bonomi's bloc on August 24 and 25 drafted a vigorous declaration calling for establishment of a truly democratic government reflecting the country's will. It denounced Badoglio for "not knowing how" to prevent the Germans from overrunning Italy, "thereby assuming a grave responsibility," and called for "mobilization of the Italian spirit to prepare it for an anti-German crusade." Bonomi, it seems, did not deliver this resolution to Badoglio until September 1.[97]

On the 30th the Central Committee of a covert tripartite Na-

[95] Giulio Trevisani, "Italia (CGL)," *Piccola enciclopedia del socialismo e del comunismo,* pp. 221–222.

[96] Catalano, *Storia del CLNAI,* pp. 47–48; cf. G. Grilli, *Due generazioni. Dalla settimana rossa alla guerra di liberazione* (Rome, 1953), pp. 219–222.

[97] Bonomi, *Diario di un anno,* pp. 77–85; Catalano, *Storia del CLNAI,* pp. 48–49.

tional Front held a very important meeting at which it decided to establish liaison with similar local committees, with all known organizations of the working masses, "with the Army and the other armed forces in order to be sure of their support in the carrying out of direct action." A manifesto was drafted in this sense. Present at the session were Longo, Scoccimarro, and Amendola of the PCI; Lussu, LaMalfa, and Bauer of the Pd'A; and Nenni and Saragat of the PSI. These men decided to form a "military junta" composed of Longo, Bauer, and Pertini. Already these men had approached General Giacomo Carboni, who had been charged with the defense of Rome. None of them knew that the armistice would be declared on September 8; they assumed, instead, that it would be the 12th.[98]

In Milan on August 27 another significant meeting took place —the first convention of what was to become the Italian section of the Movimento Federalista Europeo (MFE; "European Federalist Movement"). A score of men and women who had emerged from Ventotene (including Altiero Spinelli and Ernesto Rossi)[99] and clandestinity rendezvoused secretly in the home of Mario Alberto Rollier. At least three of the group (Eugenio Colorni, Leone Ginzburg, and Guglielmo Jervis) were to die in the ensuing war of liberation. The group approved a six-point declaration that stressed, first, the need for armed resistance against Nazism. With what proved to be excessive optimism, it emphasized, next, the importance of winning the battle of federalism during the revolutionary upheavals that presumably would occur right after the war (just as they had in 1918). Spinelli argued that the war had "disqualified" most of the nationalist diehards, and that key decisions in favor of federation could be taken by only a few hundred enlightened politicians.[100] The declaration stressed that the European citizenry, not the states, must directly control the executive, legislative, and judiciary organs of the new Federation of Europe. Though the Milan conferees did not explicitly debar any group fighting against

[98] Pietro Secchia, "La Resistenza: organizzazione o spontaneità?" MLI, No. 55 (1959), pp. 58-81.
[99] See supra, Ch. v, Proposed military intervention.
[100] See especially his arguments in "Le vie della politica estera italiana," written in September 1944 and printed in A. Spinelli, Dagli Stati sovrani agli Stati Uniti (Florence, 1951), pp. 158-159.

Fascism, they made a veiled reference to Soviet Communism when they observed "that a federalist orientation excludes any form of totalitarianism and excludes also those forms of unity that are either hegemonic or only superficially federalist and really subject to the iron control of totalitarian bodies of whatever type." [101]

Before adjourning, the Milan federalist conclave instructed a provisional committee to keep in touch with similar groups in other countries. The MFE published in Milan eight clandestine issues of the newspaper *L'Unità Europea*, edited first by Colorni and then by Rollier. Allusions to European federation could be found in almost all of the party programs drafted in this period except the PCI. Federalist propaganda even infiltrated the PSIUP, despite that party's "unity of action" pact with the PCI. This came about through the adroitness of Colorni, editor of the Rome edition of *Avanti!* during the Nazi occupation. It should be observed, however, that none of the underground parties regarded these preliminary declarations as binding.[102]

During the last days before announcement of the armistice, the Partito d'Azione convened its first congress furtively in Florence (September 3–6). Parri issued the summons. Though some of the delegates guessed that an armistice was imminent, this consideration did not lessen their hostility to Badoglio. Indeed, Bauer and LaMalfa voiced a demand for an open breach with the Marshal on the grounds that he was doing nothing while the Germans were taking over the country.[103]

Completion of the armistice

After Rome's weak radio signal notified Algiers of the return of General Castellano on August 27, the Italian government heads, instead of agreeing to capitulate, spent hours debating a course of action. An atmosphere of near hysteria enveloped Rome; government offices resounded with confusion and recriminations.[104] Castellano's clear-cut offer to fight alongside the Allies

[101] See clandestine [Milan] *L'Unità Europea: Voce del Movimento Federalista Europeo*, No. 5 (July–Aug. 1944), p. 1.
[102] Altiero Spinelli, "Il Federalismo Europeo in Italia: Nascita del Movimento," typewritten copy of lecture delivered in February 1952, p. 5.
[103] Ragghianti, *Disegno della liberazione italiana*, pp. 67–82 ff.; Catalano, *Storia del CLNAI*, p. 50.
[104] Caviglia, *Diario*, pp. 431–432, and *passim*.

greatly irked Guariglia, who would have preferred to negotiate that issue later, with compensations for Italy.[105]

At last the government decided that Italy must be allowed to transfer her Navy to LaMaddalena instead of to Allied ports. Most important, at least fifteen Allied divisions (more than the Anglo-Americans had available for the entire invasion!) must be landed in order for Italy to be secure from the Germans. An air-borne division must be dropped north of Rome near Civitavecchia in order to safeguard the capital. Finally, Italy must know the date of the Allied debarkation in order to co-ordinate the proclamation of the armistice, which must be announced only *after* the actual landing. Armed with these instructions, Castellano set off for Sicily to talk to the Allied delegates a second time.[106]

There in a Cassibile olive grove south of Syracuse, Generals Smith and Strong received him on the 31st. Smith was impatient when he learned that Castellano still lacked authority to sign an armistice. He rejected both the proposal that the fleet go to LaMaddalena and the effort to get the timing of the armistice proclamation modified to depend upon actual landings north of Rome. (By this time the Anglo-Americans had decided, for better or worse, on a large-scale invasion scheduled for September 9, with the Salerno beaches the target, but with an earlier and smaller debarkation in Calabria across the Straits of Messina on the 3rd. All this was kept secret from the Italians.) Smith did concede, however, that amphibious and air-borne landings might be arranged to increase Rome's security, and agreed to send an air-borne division if the Italians could provide and control the airfields. Castellano and Zanussi (whom the Anglo-Americans brought with them) flew back to Rome the same evening, carrying with them the Allied demand that Italy accept the terms not later than midnight, September 3.[107]

After listening to different suggestions from his frightened advisers, Badoglio went to the King on the afternoon of September

[105] Guariglia, *Ricordi*, p. 669; Castellano, *Come firmai l'armistizio*, pp. 125–127.
[106] *Ibid.*, pp. 125–132; Guariglia, *Ricordi*, pp. 671–674; Monelli, *Roma, 1943*, pp. 243–246.
[107] Castellano, *Come firmai l'armistizio*, pp. 136–145, 161, and 219–223; Smyth, *Military Affairs*, xii (1948), pp. 12–35.

1 and secured his approval of the surrender. Next day he dispatched Castellano to Cassibile for the final time. There in a field tent at 5:15 p.m. he and General Smith signed the Short Armistice, the strictly military terms of which omitted the vexing phrase "unconditional surrender." Later in the evening Castellano was provided with a copy of the Long Armistice,[108] but the latter was not signed until September 29 when Marshal Badoglio met General Eisenhower at Malta.[109]

Final imbroglio

General Castellano remained in Sicily to work out details of the Allied air-borne and amphibious landings near Rome. In the capital on the 6th, Army Chief of Staff Roatta learned to his dismay that the aerial landing was to consist of but one division while the main invasion would be much farther to the south. Quickly he decided that his own poorly supplied forces near Rome were incapable of carrying out the plan for securing the air bases.[110] According to a well-informed American military historian, this was the essential fact that explained the Italian government's incoherent behavior during the next forty-eight hours. "All along the King and the group associated with him had been unwilling to run any risks but insisted on being rescued by the Allies." [111]

On the evening of the 7th, U.S. Brigadier General Maxwell D. Taylor and Colonel William T. Gardiner arrived in Rome on a risky mission to verify the local situation. They discovered that it was entirely different from what they had been led to expect. The Italian generals, for their part, found the Allied timing different from what they had convinced themselves it would be.[112]

[108] When Castellano protested the term "surrender unconditionally," Smith countered that since Zanussi already knew of this, so did Badoglio. Smith agreed to send a qualifying note to Badoglio to the effect that the "additional clauses have only a relative value insofar as Italy collaborates in the war against the Germans." Castellano, *Come firmai l'armistizio,* p. 161.

[109] Texts of both armistices are in U.S. Dept. of State, *United States and Italy, 1936–1946: Documentary Record* (Washington, 1946), European Series No. 17, Publ. No. 2669, pp. 51–64.

[110] Mario Roatta, *Otto milioni di baionette* (Milan, 1946), pp. 304–307.

[111] Smyth, *Military Affairs,* XII (1948), pp. 29–30.

[112] General Castellano had surmised, by a curious computation, that the invasion would not take place till the 12th. It had been arranged that the cease-fire

Knowing that the invasion forces were due to hit the Salerno beaches at dawn the 9th, Taylor and Gardiner insisted on seeing Army Deputy Chief of Staff General Rossi, as well as General Carboni, commander of the troops in the Rome zone. To their dismay they learned that his Motorized Army Corps (consisting of the divisions "Granatieri," "Piave," "Centaura," and "Ariete") could not secure the airfields, since the Germans already (it was alleged) had taken them. Carboni argued that the original plan was unworkable in any event, and that the armistice announcement must be postponed a few days while a new plan for defense of the capital was prepared.[113]

Knowing the impossibility of this, Taylor interrupted and demanded to see Badoglio. Accompanied by Carboni, he found him at his home about midnight. Carboni first talked alone with the Marshal and apparently swung him to support his view, for Badoglio dumbfounded the two Americans by calling for cancellation of the air-borne landings and delay in the armistice announcement.[114] In Algiers Eisenhower was shocked when he received word of the cancellation at noon on September 8. In a stern radio message he warned the dictator that the armistice would be proclaimed at the hour already fixed. Eisenhower proclaimed the armistice at 6:30 p.m. while the invasion flotilla was under way.[115]

When Badoglio and his counselors heard of this they were almost hysterical; but there was no alternative but to proclaim the armistice to the Italian people. This the *Capo del Governo* did at 7:45 p.m. in a broadcast which was less than crystal clear in its instructions to military commanders: "[Thus] all hostilities by the Italian armed forces against the British and American forces must now cease. They will, however, repel attacks from whatever quarter they may come." [116] When the Marshal went to bed Carboni's intelligence was reporting methodical withdrawal of Germans to the north of Rome. Actually, they were

would be announced simultaneously by radio by Eisenhower and Badoglio on "D-Day," the date of which would be made known to Badoglio a few hours ahead of time by an Allied broadcast consisting of music by Verdi. This broadcast occurred at the proper time on the 7th, but no Italian monitors reported it.

[113] Smyth, *Military Affairs*, XII (1948), p. 32.
[114] *Ibid.*, pp. 33–34.
[115] Eisenhower, *Crusade in Europe*, p. 186.
[116] Quoted in Badoglio, *Italy in the Second World War*, pp. 74–75.

doing the opposite; by midnight they were overrunning Italian soldiers stationed near the capital.

The bankruptcy of the armistice policy of the royal-military dictatorship rapidly became clear. The anti-Fascists were to spend many hours "second-guessing" the problem. Their denunciation of the way the armistice negotiations were conducted has been epitomized by General Rossi, Deputy Army Chief of Staff. Arguing with the advantage of hindsight, he has contended:

"The armistice declarations would have been very opportune on July 25. On that date four German divisions were tied up in Sicily, and with the aid of [our] Navy they could have been prevented from passing to the mainland. There remained almost two armored divisions in the South, and the noted Third Panzer Grenadiers (composed only of 12 to 15,000 men) in the zone of Lake Bolsena—a situation much easier than that which existed on September 8. . . .

"We declared the armistice on September 8 . . . the worst moment. The German forces on the mainland had been notably strengthened following the overthrow of Mussolini—there were sixteen divisions including the Sicilian veterans instead of three —and they were extremely suspicious and vigilant, so that it was no longer materially feasible to put into effect any preventive measures necessary to oppose the invasion.

". . . [If we had gotten out of the war on July 25] we would have been able to avoid requesting any armistice of the Allies; to prepare in time and secretly both psychologically and militarily a resistance against the Germans; and then to inform the Allies of our detachment [from the Axis], in order that the advantages of the Italian action might be utilized both by the Allies and by ourselves. . . ." [117]

What actually would have happened had Italy broken away from Germany on July 25 can only be speculated, but it is most doubtful that the Allies would have been content with anything short of unconditional surrender. Whatever the merits of the arguments over Badoglio's armistice negotiations, there can be

[117] F. Rossi, *Come arrivammo all'armistizio*, pp. 293–294, quoted by kind permission of the publisher, Aldo Garzanti Editore, Milan. For more or less similar arguments, cf. Soleri, *Memorie*, p. 261; Castellano, *Come firmai l'armistizio*, pp. 194, 204; and C. Cavallero, *Il dramma del Maresciallo Cavallero* (Milan, 1952), pp. 157–158.

no doubt they were bumbling and needlessly protracted. Thus there was ample ground for criticisms by the anti-Fascists, and they did not delay in hurling them.

The botches thus far committed were soon worse compounded. At 4 a.m. on the 9th Badoglio was awakened and another conference hastily called, attended by a few officials. In the meantime the King and Queen had moved from the Quirinal Palace to the War Ministry. They agreed with Badoglio that the capital no longer could be defended and that they should escape at once in order to join the Allies in the South, preserve the validity of the armistice, and (not least) save themselves.

Granted that their departure was advisable, the panic-stricken way in which it took place and left Rome undefended produced enormous political repercussions and permanently tarnished the Savoyard escutcheon. When Badoglio pinpointed the Adriatic port of Pescara as the rendezvous for the fleeing government, he allegedly ordered that all his ministers be notified so that they might go too; yet only a handful of officials (many of whom did not dare sleep in their own homes) received the word.[118] He failed to leave clear orders as to who should take charge of the abandoned capital and armed forces, nor did he even take time to clear his desk of many important documents that soon were to fall into the hands of the Germans. During the dash across the Apennines, however, he repeatedly assured the King that he had done so—a point which later led to no little ill-feeling between them.[119]

The auto caravan bearing the bedraggled Badoglio, King, Queen, Crown Prince, and several other members of the royal family and of the government reached Pescara the afternoon of September 9. After several hours' delay, during which time it was decided not to risk an airplane flight, most of the entourage was picked up at near-by Ortona by the corvette *Baionetta*, which transported them to Brindisi.

[118] Badoglio, *Italy in the Second World War*, pp. 79–86. Among the many left behind was Foreign Minister Guariglia. Badoglio's son Mario stayed in the capital and was active in the Armed Resistance there until his arrest by the Germans on Easter Monday in 1944. During the rest of the war he was interned at Mauthausen and Dachau.

[119] Bolla (ed.), *Colloqui con Umberto II; colloqui con Vittorio Emanuele III*, pp. 15–16, 20, 135–136.

PART II
THE ARMED RESISTANCE
SEPTEMBER 8, 1943 – APRIL 25, 1945

CHAPTER VII · THE PARTISAN MOVEMENT

September 8, 1943 – January 1944

SEPTEMBER 8, 1943, marked the birth of the Resistenza Armata in the half of Italy under the German heel. The void left in Rome and the North by the fugitive royal-military government and the disintegrating Italian armies in the face of ruthless German attack, followed by the shocking news of Mussolini's rescue, helped induce thousands of Italian patriots to join the partisan movement. This struggle, undertaken against heavy odds, climaxed two decades of clandestine opposition to Fascism and in no small degree helped to redeem Italy's all-but-shattered moral and military reputation.

The Resistenza Armata was not only the militant phase of anti-Fascism but the start of a new political movement—that of the Committees of National Liberation. Henceforth anti-Fascism's artillery aimed not just at the *Duce* and *Fuehrer* (whose fate, almost everyone sensed, was sealed) but also at the frightened King and his fumbling prime minister in the South. The anti-Fascists' barrage seldom slackened till they achieved their objectives—partially in the spring of 1944 when they deposed Victor Emmanuel III and Pietro Badoglio, and finally in June 1946 when they disposed of the Monarchy itself.

Neo-Fascist Italian Social Republic

At the time of the September 8 armistice imbroglio, Mussolini was still a prisoner atop Gran Sasso. Marshal Badoglio's Chief of Police Senise originally had instructed the *Carabinieri* to shoot their prize if he tried to escape, but on the morning of the 12th Senise changed his mind, apparently fearful of German reprisals in the "open city" of Rome, wired the guards to behave "with utmost prudence." [1] That same day Hitler's redoubtable Captain Otto Skorzény, accompanied by ninety Nazi paratroopers in "Stork" gliders, swooped down to rescue Mussolini like a second Andromeda. [2]

---

[1] Senise, *Quando ero Capo della Polizia*, pp. 251, 259.
[2] Otto Skorzény, *Secret Missions: War Memoirs* (New York, 1950); Mussolini, *Storia di un anno*, pp. 147–156; Giovanni Dolfin, *Con Mussolini nella tragedia: diario del capo della segreteria particolare del Duce, 1943–1944* (Milan, 1949), p. 250; and Ermanno Amicucci, *I 600 giorni di Mussolini (dal Gran Sasso a Dongo)* (Rome, 1947), pp. 9–14.

Skorzény first flew the flabby Fascist to an airport near Rome in order to transfer him to a larger plane which would carry him to Hitler's headquarters, where in humiliation he confronted the *Fuehrer*. The old Axis relationship was dead. So far as Hitler and Goebbels were concerned, Mussolini was little more than a pawn.[3] When the *Duce* intimated that he thought his own career had run its course, Hitler snapped that if he wished to return to Italy he must head a new pro-Nazi government, place the "traitors of July 25" on trial, and agree to German occupation of several border provinces. Had Mussolini refused, Hitler probably would have selected the even more Germanophile Farinacci to be his marionette.[4] Powerless, the *Duce* listened apathetically to the harangue and acquiesced in his new role. Later Hitler sought to cheer him by alluding to novel "secret weapons" that would assure ultimate victory. And he referred him to his own quack physician, Dr. Morell, for medical treatment. The latter, according to Goebbels, found Mussolini suffering from circulatory trouble and disordered bowels—"the typical ailment of a modern revolutionary politician." [5]

Quickly Hitler shunted Mussolini to Munich to broadcast a message to his fellow countrymen. Somehow the old phrasemaker mustered the requisite quota of bombast on September 18. He appealed to "faithful Blackshirts" to renew Axis solidarity, regroup Italian armed forces around the Fascist Militia, purge the "royalist betrayers" of the regime, and destroy the "parasitical plutocracy" so that labor manifested in the peasants, factory workers, and white-collar categories could now become the "indestructible basis of the state." [6]

Meanwhile, the new Partito Fascista Repubblicano (PFR; "Fascist Republican Party") secretary Alessandro Pavolini—who with Farinacci and Vittorio Mussolini had fled to Germany

[3] Goebbels, *Diaries*, pp. 453, 468, and *passim*.

[4] Other possible choices were Giovanni Preziosi, Renato Tassinari, and Guido Buffarini-Guidi. Felice Bellotti, *La repubblica di Mussolini, 26 luglio 1943–25 aprile 1945* (Milan, 1947), p. 56; Tamaro, *Due anni di storia, 1943–1945*, I, 566.

[5] Goebbels, *Diaries*, p. 470. On the conference see *ibid.*, pp. 450–471; Bullock, *Hitler*, pp. 652–653; Monelli, *Mussolini*, p. 230; *cf.* Mussolini's own account to Mezzasoma, Minister of Popular Culture, cited in Dombrowski, *Mussolini*, pp. 80–84.

[6] Printed in Tamaro, *Due anni di storia*, I, 590–593. On the 19th Badoglio replied in a broadcast from Bari; *cf. ibid.*, I, 593–595.

earlier and was a fanatic advocate of a bloody purge of all "traitors"—was sent on a mission to Rome to see what luck he would have recruiting ministers and military men for a reanimated satellite state. No more than fifteen people in Rome responded to Pavolini's initial appeal for a new Militia, Goebbels has revealed.[7]

When Pavolini returned, Mussolini announced on September 23 the formation of a leftist-oriented neo-Fascist Italian Social Republic (RSI; "Repubblica Sociale Italiana") and the appointment of a Council of Ministers in anticipation of a Constituent Assembly.[8] Other protagonists in the "new order" included Pavolini; Buffarini-Guidi, the heavy-jowled, constantly intriguing Minister of Interior; Fernando Mezzasoma, a zealous, impassioned youth leader who now became propaganda designer in the Ministry of Popular Culture; and Renato Ricci, ex-head of the ONB youth movement and now leader of the Fascist Militia.[9] Among Mussolini's other confidants in the sordid final phase of Fascism were ex-Communist Nicola Bombacci, a vigorous proponent of his neo-socialism, and Renato Tassinari, his personal secretary and quondam agricultural expert.

On the 27th SS General Karl Wolff escorted Mussolini back to his private castle at Rocca delle Caminate in the Apennines. It was there that the RSI Council of Ministers held its first meeting and took up the problem of where to locate the seat of government. Actually it had little choice, for the Germans had made

---

[7] Goebbels, *Diaries*, p. 479.

[8] A point of departure for study of the RSI may be found in the last sections of S/M, *Sdf*; the works of Bellotti, Monelli, Tamaro, Dombrowski, Dolfin, and Amicucci cited above; Giacomo Perticone, *La Repubblica di Salò* (Rome, 1947); Cione, *Storia della RSI*; Alberto Mellini Ponce-de Leon, *Guerra diplomatica a Salò* (*ottobre 1943–aprile 1945*) (Bologna, 1950); Luigi Villari, *Affari esteri, 1943–1945* (Rome, 1948); Filippo Anfuso, *Roma, Berlino, Salò* (*1936–1945*) (Milan, 1950); Stanis Ruinas, *Pioggia sulla Repubblica* (Rome, 1946); Ugo Manunta, *La caduta degli angeli: storia intima della RSI* (Rome, 1947); Carlo Silvestri, *Mussolini, Graziani, e l'antifascismo* (*1943–1945*) (Milan, 1949); Franz Turchi, *Prefetto con Mussolini* (Rome, 1950); and the final volume of Pini and Susmel, *Mussolini: l'uomo e l'opera*, Vol. IV, *Dall' Impero alla Repubblica* (*1938–1945*). A study by F. W. Deakin, *The Brutal Friendship: The Fall of Mussolini*, will appear in 1961.

[9] The new cabinet also included Count Serafino Mazzolini (Foreign Affairs); Tringali-Casanova (Justice); Domenico Pellegrini (Finance); Marshal Rodolfo Graziani (Defense); Silvio Gai (Corporative Economy); Edoardo Moroni (Agriculture); Carlo Alberto Biggini (National Education); Giuseppe Poverelli (Communications); and Francesco Maria Barracù (Undersecretary of the Presidency of the Council). S/M, *Sdf*, pp. 966–967.

it clear that the capital must be adjacent to their line of communications over the Brenner Pass.[10] Thus it was that Salò, a resort on the western shore of Lake Garda not far from Verona, became the capital of Mussolini's quisling *repubblichetta*, as many contemptuously dubbed it. The President of the RSI, his wife, and some of their children occupied the ugly but habitable Villa Feltrinelli; a few miles away Signorina Claretta Petacci ensconced herself. The *Duce*'s offices were in a *palazzo* not far from his residence, but many of the ministries remained scattered in Rome, Milan, and elsewhere, which added to the confusion. Bureaucrats in Rome were especially loath to leave that seductive city, and were amazingly successful in postponing transfers.

Mussolini's every move was watched by Wolff and the new German ambassador, Dr. Rudolf Rahn, who established his embassy at near-by Fasano. Marshal Kesselring's headquarters were far away at Monte Soratte, north of Rome, the first winter. Kesselring slowly came to believe that Germany could have fought the peninsular war more effectively had there been no intermediary, "unpopular" Salò regime.[11]

The *Fuehrer* insisted upon hanging on to vassal Italy in order to keep his foes far from the Reich and to exploit Italian manpower and economic resources. Furthermore, he determined to annex the northern border zones of Trent and the South Tyrol as well as the northeastern region of Trieste and Venezia Giulia.[12] This he did in October 1943, not even bothering to ask the *Duce*'s leave but subtly intimating that they had agreed upon the matter.[13] Mussolini dispatched a letter of protest but got no reply. Unquestionably Mussolini was chagrined that his regime, which had battened so long on the theme of irredentist national-

[10] The Vatican was also anxious that Rome be free of military and political headquarters; but this was of less importance in motivating the German decision. The Vatican scrupulously avoided any form of diplomatic recognition of the RSI and maintained its recognition of the Kingdom of Italy.

[11] Kesselring, *Memoirs*, p. 190.

[12] Goebbels, *Diaries*, pp. 433, 444, and *passim*.

[13] *Gauleiter* Franz Hofer took command of the Trentino (Alpenvorland); *Gauleiter* F. Reiner took over Venezia Giulia (Gau Küstenland). Zara was turned over to the puppet state of Croatia. Regarding the Trentino in this period, see Conrad F. Latour, *Germany, Italy and the South Tyrol, 1939–1945*, Ph.D. dissertation, American University, 1955; and Antonino Radice, *La Resistenza nel Trentino, 1943–1945* (Rovereto, 1960).

ism, could not even hang on to what Italians had won in World War I. Though he sometimes grumbled to close friends, he prudently avoided further correspondence with Hitler about the humiliating matter. Nothing revealed more clearly his passive servility.

Military recruitment

Decreeing that the Royal Armed Forces had ceased to exist on September 9 and that new Republican formations would take their place, RSI officials worked hard to raise a military force to aid the Germans. On September 23 Mussolini appointed Marshal Rodolfo Graziani, a bitter rival of Badoglio and veteran of the Ethiopian War and other colonial assignments, Commander of the new Armed Forces as well as Minister of National Defense and Chief of the General Staff. Graziani owed his appointment partly to his own peculiar conception of military loyalty and partly to German pressure. He hastened to Hitler's headquarters to draw up plans for the new fighting forces.

Most German strategists were diffident about the new Italian Army. Certainly they did not wish to see any autonomous force controlled solely by the RSI, and they insisted that the new units must be trained in Germany and that they be fresh recruits, not the defeatist ones "of Badoglio." The Italian generals naturally objected to training in Germany, for they sensed the people's growing hostility toward their Teutonic overlords; moreover, they did not want their forces to be employed elsewhere than in Italy. Nevertheless, in the protocol signed at last on October 16, they agreed to arm and train in Germany four divisions, half of whom would be new recruits and the remainder volunteers enrolled from Italian soldiers interned in Germany.[14]

The whole process moved very slowly (as did an analogous program in the Allied-controlled South), partly because of Italian apathy and partly because the Germans (like the Allies) really had very little desire for Italian soldiers but great need for labor

[14] As it turned out, however, very few of the more than 600,000 Italian military and civilian internees in Germany were willing to take an oath of loyalty to the RSI. Only 1.03 per cent took such an oath, and only 5 per cent agreed to become voluntary workers. Statistics cited by Giorgio Vaccarino, "La resistenza al fascismo," MLI, No. 54 (Jan.–Mar. 1959), p. 33; cf. S/M, Sdf, pp. 967–968.

battalions. On October 15 orders were issued for remaining officers and men of the class of 1924, all those of 1925, and all parachutists to report for duty by November 15. Much propaganda was composed on the themes of "honor" and "resentment against Badoglio." It was claimed by RSI authorities that 82 per cent of the 18-year-old class of 1925 responded. Even if this is correct (which seems unlikely), many who reported quickly deserted, often taking with them whatever meagre equipment they had been issued. By February 19, 1944, the neo-Fascists issued a "final" decree, ordering renitents of the classes of 1923–1924–1925 to appear by March 8—a decree which induced many to flock, instead, into the guerrilla Resistenza forces in the mountains.[15]

Though formidable enough, the RSI armed forces never attained their intended strength. Instead of a single army imbued with national feeling, a congeries of autonomous and rival organizations emerged as the result of the initiative of individual commanders and adventurers. One such body was the Fascist Republican National Guard (GNR; "Guardia Nazionale Repubblicana"), raised by Ricci. Offspring of the old Fascist Militia, this force was integrated in December 1944 with the Army, where it assumed a position analogous to that of the *Carabinieri* in normal times. Eventually the GNR numbered some 150,000 and consisted in large measure of antiaircraft units.[16]

Another force was the Tenth Torpedo-boat Flotilla (X^{ma} MAS; "Decima Flottiglia Motoscafi Anti-Sommergibile"). Its nucleus consisted of several hundred marines, dislocated at the LaSpezia naval base on September 8 and devoted to Prince Junio Valerio Borghese, a dashing young officer who had won several decorations for raids against British naval units and was absolutely dedicated to the Axis alliance.[17] Unable to persuade the German Navy to outfit his group for sea duty, Borghese got permission and supplies to convert his X^{ma} MAS into a "comando" land unit. Technically it was under Graziani's com-

---

[15] Renato Carli-Ballola, *Storia della Resistenza* (hereafter cited as Carli-Ballola, *Sdr*) (Milan-Rome, 1957), pp. 118–119; S/M, *Sdf*, p. 968.

[16] Moellhausen, *La carta perdente*, pp. 400–402.

[17] Junio Valerio Borghese, *Decima Flottiglia Mas* (Milan, 1950), *passim*; Moellhausen, *La carta perdente*, pp. 402–409; Turchi, *Prefetto con Mussolini*, pp. 30–39.

mand, but Borghese's headquarters were established in Milan. The X^ma MAS soon became noted and feared for its fanaticism. Eventually it was ordered to direct its operations chiefly against the guerrillas, who had good reason to hate it during the numerous offensives launched against them.[18] Ironically, some of these RSI warriors still sported royalist emblems.[19]

Mussolini also made use of the Autonomous Police, organized by Interior Minister Buffarini-Guidi. They employed the same brutal methods of interrogation that the OVRA and Gestapo had popularized. Perhaps the most notorious Fascist police were the Milanese "Muti" band and the agents of Lieutenant Koch, an Italian sadist who had affected a Teutonic surname;[20] but every large city had its quota of blackguards.

Finally, there were the Black Brigades ("Brigate Nere"), organized in the summer of 1944 by Party Secretary Pavolini and deployed chiefly against the partisans. Their brutality greatly augmented popular hatred of the regime.[21]

Radical orientation of the RSI

Having lost the love of most of the middle class, Mussolini oriented his new RSI to the left, hopeful of ingratiating himself with the northern populace. To this end, he bent every effort to blame latter-day corruption on profiteering "plutocrats" and minions of the Monarchy.

At the first (and only) PFR Congress in Verona on November 15, 1943, he unwrapped a radical eighteen-point socialistic manifesto which, in some respects, harked back to his pre-World War I Marxian views and to the 1919 edition of Fascism. Composed by a small band of Blackshirt adventurers and *déclassés* and approved by their Nazi masters, the Verona Manifesto set forth a demagogic program that supposedly would be translated into

[18] On Feb. 18, 1949, an Italian tribunal found Borghese guilty of collaboration with the Germans during the war. He was sentenced to twelve years' imprisonment, but because of amnesty legislation this was reduced to four. As a matter of fact, he was released just ten days later. NYT, Feb. 18, 28, 1949. By that time Borghese was one of the directors of the intensely neo-Fascist postwar Italian Social Movement (MSI; "Movimento Sociale Italiano").

[19] Battaglia, SRI, p. 164.

[20] Gianpietro Pogliani, Guglielmo Gislandi, Nardini Alessandro, "Alcuni documenti sull'attività della banda Koch," MLI, No. 8 (1950), pp. 17–49; Luigi Pestalozza (ed.), Il processo alla "Muti" (Milan, 1956).

[21] Amicucci, I 600 giorni di Mussolini, pp. 215–218; Moellhausen, La carta perdente, pp. 338–344; Cione, Storia della RSI, p. 227.

practice by a Constituent Assembly. This "sovereign power of popular origin" would be composed of representatives of syndical associations, administrative divisions, soldiers, prisoners of war, Italians abroad, magistrates, and universities, the first four points of the document explained. The Constituent Assembly would not be elected in democratic fashion by everyone; instead, nomination of officials would come partly from above in hierarchical fashion and partly from below. But all of this was left conveniently vague. Point number five set forth the principle of a strictly elitist Fascist Republican Party, an "order of fighters and believers . . . absolutely pure [and] worthy of being the custodian of the revolutionary idea"; yet membership in it would not be necessary for officeholders.

Problems of foreign policy were discussed in the eighth point, which was replete with Nazi-like slogans demanding "integrity" for the fatherland, "living space," elimination from the Continent of "century-long British intrigues," abolition of plutocracy, respect for the Moslems, and development of Africa.

The Manifesto's last ten points took up social policy. Labor was proclaimed the basis of the Social Republic. In hopes of pleasing all groups, the charter announced a dual system of private and public property: private property that was the fruit of labor and of savings would be guaranteed so long as it did not lead to exploitation of others' labor; everything of collective interest in the economy would be socialized. In all factories delegates of the workers and technicians would help determine wages and profits. Uncultivated and badly run farms would be expropriated in favor of day laborers (*"braccianti"*) and cooperatives. Everyone would have the right to property in the form of "people's housing" (*"case del popolo"*), to be promoted by a state agency. Membership in syndicates would be mandatory for all laborers, and there would be a single General Confederation of Labor and Technicians; however, there would be no strikes.[22] Black-market speculators could expect the death penalty. Magistrates were to be independent, and citizens could not be detained more than a week without order of judiciary authorities. Roman Catholicism would be the religion of the RSI; other cults would be respected. Members of the Jewish race, however,

---

[22] *Cf.* Francesco Galanti, *Socializzazione e sindacalismo nella RSI* (Rome, 1949).

would be regarded as foreigners and enemies for the duration of the war.[23]

Two months later (January 13, 1944) the government issued a Fundamental Premise, further explicating the new economy. Socialization would occur wherever necessary for national self-sufficiency and in those sectors concerned with production of raw materials, energy, and indispensable services. In these the state would be financier and administrator, issuing bonds to reimburse the present investors. Workers would share in the management of both nationalized and private enterprises. Publicly financed ones would be run by a management council elected by all the workers, clerks (*"impiegati"*), and technicians; privately financed enterprises would be run by councils in which the workers would be equally represented with the stockholders. In private shops, or where there was a single boss with at least fifty workers, a three-member advisory council of workers, clerks, and technicians would be instituted. Additional regulations explained responsibilities of the factory head and methods for his removal.[24]

Among other things, the neo-Fascists sought to preserve and utilize the factory "internal commissions" (which Communists and Socialists had re-established during Badoglio's interregnum) but to put their own men in control of them. The PCI and PSIUP quickly disavowed the perverted commissions and organized in their stead secret factory "agitation committees." [25]

As a matter of fact, the RSI was as unsuccessful in achieving its socio-economic as it was its military goals. Actual socialization never got beyond a few delayed beginnings, and the much bruited Constituent Assembly never convened. In myriad ways most people made it clear they were surfeited with Mussolini's opportunistic rhetoric.

Verona purge trial (January 8–10, 1944)

When Hitler let Mussolini return home he stipulated that the "traitorous" hierarchs must be punished and he insisted that the Italians handle this job themselves. Mussolini probably welcomed

[23] S/M, *Sdf*, pp. 969–970; Battaglia, *SRI*, pp. 163–166; and F. W. Deakin, "Le congrès de Vérone," *Revue d'histoire de la deuxième guerre mondiale*, No. 26 (1957), pp. 59–66.
[24] S/M, *Sdf*, pp. 970–971.
[25] See *infra*, Ch. VII, Agitation in the factories.

the chance to deal sternly with most of the accused, though there is reason to think he was reluctant to see his son-in-law Ciano executed, as they had achieved a partial reconciliation while in Germany. As late as November 9, 1943, Goebbels wrote in his diary that he did not think the *Duce* would dare to kill his ex-Foreign Minister. Farinacci and Buffarini-Guidi, however, exerted great pressure on Mussolini to punish Ciano with death, and he knew that Ribbentrop and Goebbels (both of whom detested Ciano) were waiting to see how he handled this case.[26]

Ciano was hauled back to Italy late in 1943. Somewhat to his surprise, he found himself included in the "traitors list." The "treachery" obviously was to Mussolini's regime alone, for all of the Fascist Grand Councillors had expressed loyalty to the King and State in their resolutions of July 24. Only six of the accused were actually held by the RSI authorities in the cloister of the Scalzi in Verona, now transformed into a prison, when the Fascist Special Tribunal met in that city January 8–10, 1944.[27] The accused argued that they had dutifully sought to remedy the crisis of the regime within the framework of its institutions. But after two days the court ruled that the hierarchs' vote had been a deliberation, not a view, and that it had "tended toward the elimination of Fascism and its *Duce* as well as toward peace and national surrender"—the very antithesis of the Fascist idea. The judges ordered all except Cianetti (sentenced to thirty years because of his timely recantation) to be shot in the back. On the morning of January 11 the victims were strapped to the chairs and the sentence executed.

For weeks Edda Ciano had pleaded desperately with her father to spare her husband. She even involved herself in a bizarre, futile plot with a German SD agent to utilize her husband's hidden diaries and records of conversations as bargaining counters with the Germans. When it finally became apparent there was

[26] Goebbels, *Diaries*, p. 472 ff.; Hoettl, *Secret Front*, pp. 274–278; Renzo Montagna, *Mussolini e il processo di Verona* (Milan, 1949); Domenico Mayer, *La verità sul processo di Verona* (Verona, 1945); Dombrowski, *Mussolini*, pp. 102–113.

[27] They were Ciano; 78-year-old Emilio DeBono, Minister of Colonies from 1925 to 1935 and Commander of Expeditionary Forces in the Ethiopian War; Giovanni Marinelli, long-time Party Administrative Secretary; Tullio Cianetti, ex-Undersecretary and finally Minister of Corporations (1939–1943); Carlo Pareschi, ex-Minister of Agriculture (1941–1943); and Luciano Gottardi, formerly of the Confederation of Industrial Workers.

no chance of saving him, Edda fled to Switzerland to join her children. She took some of the diaries dealing with the 1939–1943 era with her, hiding them beneath a belt in her skirt; these she later made available to an American journalist.[28]

Mussolini's execution of Ciano demonstrated again that the *Duce* had linked himself inseparably to Hitler. No doubt his sometime fascination for the *Fuehrer* was shifting to hatred; yet he made no effort to escape from the fate he had forged for himself in the Axis. Though the aging demagogue continued to dream of Germany's "secret weapons" and deceive himself as to his postwar role, such conjurations seldom served to rouse him from his torpor. Leaving most decisions to his ministers, who for their part intrigued incessantly, he made fewer and fewer public appearances. Ennuied of family life, he turned ever more for solace to Claretta Petacci, his faithful camp follower to the end.

Committees of National Liberation:
Rome CLN

When Ivanoe Bonomi's Anti-Fascist Committee, meeting in a house on Via Adda early in the morning of September 9, 1943, heard the news of the royal-military government's hegira, it sought to fill the political void. At the suggestion of Labor Democrat Ruini, it voted that afternoon to rename itself the Committee of National Liberation (CLN), in the style of the French CLN that had been organized in Algiers a few months earlier. Later, the Rome body often called itself the Central CLN (CCLN), to distinguish itself from sister agencies that sprang up in Milan, Turin, Florence, and elsewhere, and to suggest its somewhat greater prestige. It consisted of the same hexarchy (PCI, PSIUP, Pd'A, DC, DL, PLI) that had been collaborating on a basis of parity in previous weeks.[29]

Bonomi was the CCLN's unanimous choice for president. To

---

[28] Hoettl, *Secret Front*, pp. 265–278; *cf.* Dombrowski, *Mussolini*, pp. 102–134; Monelli, *Mussolini*, pp. 236–243; S/M, *Sdf*, pp. 972–973.

[29] The renascent Italian Republican Party (PRI) decided to stay clear of the CLN, preferring to keep its inflexibly republican creed unsullied by any compromise the CLN might conceivably make with the House of Savoy.

After Rome's liberation the PRI republished all of the articles that had appeared clandestinely in its newspaper. Giovanni Conti (ed.), *"La Voce Repubblicana" clandestina: 1 agosto 1943–5 giugno 1944* (Rome, 1945).

be sure, his royalist proclivities scarcely made him the enthusiastic choice of the leftists, but they could not afford to overlook his prestige as a former premier and his manifest knack for facilitating compromises—qualities, they sensed, that might favorably impress the Allies. Though personally identified with the minuscule current of Labor Democracy, Bonomi sought to maintain a neutral stance as CCLN chairman. Sergio Fenoaltea, a Pd'A attorney, was elected secretary.

Because of the obvious hazards of underground life, the spokesmen of the six parties in Rome often changed. After November a special effort was made to create a "reserve" string. In one or the other of these teams Mauro Scoccimarro and Giorgio Amendola usually represented the PCI. The PSIUP, previously piloted in Rome by Giuseppe Romita, now was steered by Pietro Nenni (freed from Ponza about the time Mussolini was taken there) and, on occasion, by Giuseppe Saragat and Sandro Pertini. The latter two, however, were captured on October 15 and imprisoned first in the infamous police station on Via Tasso and then in Regina Coeli penitentiary, whence they were liberated by party comrades in a daring *coup de main* on January 22, 1944.[30] The Pd'A was represented in the furtive conclaves by the impassioned Ugo LaMalfa, Riccardo Bauer, and Fenoaltea. Alcide DeGasperi was, of course, the Christian Democrats' undisputed champion, though on occasion Giovanni Gronchi, Avv. Giuseppe Spataro, and Avv. Adone Zoli substituted for him. Meuccio Ruini was the usual delegate of Labor Democracy. The Liberals mandated Alessandro Casati and Niccolò Carandini. The constant peril of police raids often forced the CCLN to shift its meeting places. On September 11 and 12 it convened in the Via del Gesù apartment of the Crocean historicist, Professor Carlo Antoni. The residence of Monsignor Pietro Barbieri at Via Cernaia 14 was another favorite rendezvous, and on not a few occasions members took shelter in the Lateran Seminary and other extraterritorial buildings of the Holy See—an experience that probably helped to cement warmer personal friendships between many Catholics and anticlericals than modern Italy had ever known.[31]

[30] Carli-Ballola, *Sdr*, p. 88.
[31] Bonomi, *Diario di un anno, passim*; his introduction to Pietro Barbieri, *Il travaglio della democrazia italiana, 1943-1947* (Rome, 1948), pp. vii–x; and Tupini, *I Democratici Cristiani*, p. 74.

At its initial convocation on the 9th the CCLN summoned "all Italians to the struggle and to the Resistance, and to reconquer for Italy the place it deserves in the community of free nations." [32] Two days later a headline of the Pd'A covert *L'Italia Libera* boasted, "The anti-Fascist parties have constituted themselves into a Committee of National Liberation, whereas the Monarchy and the Government have revealed their total incapacity." [33]

Military debacle in Rome and elsewhere

Of that "incapacity" there could be little doubt. The headlong flight of the King, his premier, and their entourage in the dawn of September 9 had left the capital in anarchy. Just before his own departure Army Chief of Staff General Roatta allegedly dictated instructions to General Carboni, commander of the four divisions stationed around the city; but these were scarcely practical. Defenders of Badoglio have insisted that at the last minute he orally instructed War Minister Sorice to telephone Interior Minister Ricci to take charge of the city. Whatever the truth, no one stepped into the breach effectively. The military and civilian chain of command dissolved; no one seemed to have the vaguest idea of who was in control or what should or could be done. Whether Rome really was capable of being defended at the time remains a moot point. At least some generals, including Giacomo Carboni and Raffaele Cadorna, have contended that it could have been held successfully had proper and timely measures been taken.[34]

At Porta San Paolo and a few other places on the periphery resistance to the Germans was improvised—for example, by the

---

[32] Bonomi, *Diario di un anno*, p. 100; cf. Ragghianti, *Disegno della liberazione italiana*, p. 40 ff.

[33] Rome *L'Italia Libera*, Sept. 11, 1943.

[34] The failure to defend Rome adequately became the subject of prolonged official inquiries. A pamphlet by Republican Avv. Federico Comandini in 1943, *Breve storia di cinque mesi*, launched the attack on General Carboni who (with Roatta, Ambrosio, Badoglio, and the King) has come in for heavy condemnation. Most of the principals have composed their apologias: Carboni, *L'Italia tradita dall'armistizio alla pace* (Rome, 1947); *L'armistizio e la difesa di Roma: verità e menzogne* (Rome, 1948); *Più che il dovere* (Rome, 1952), reprinted in 1956 as *Memorie segrete*; Mario Roatta, *Otto milioni di baionette*; Badoglio, *Italy in the Second World War*, pp. 79–86. Cf. A. Carona, *La verità sul 9 settembre* (Rome, 1945); Monelli, *Roma, 1943*, pp. 272–311, 217–229; Tamaro, *Due anni di storia, 1943–1945*, I, 403–432, 441–446; Carli-Ballola, *Sdr*, pp. 12–18.

"Ariete" armored division of General Cadorna,[35] and by some 2,000 civilians who were hastily armed (after some hesitation on the part of General Carboni's staff) by an anti-Fascist Military Junta that was created soon after an important CCLN meeting on August 30. The junta was headed by recently liberated stalwarts of the leftist parties: Luigi Longo (PCI), Sandro Pertini (PSIUP), and Riccardo Bauer (Pd'A).[36] They transported fighters to strategic centers and distributed three truckloads of arms from various barracks. Longo had his command post in the apartment of F. Onofri; the Actionists had theirs in Via Leone IV. But impromptu street fighting of the 1848 sort could not stave off the mechanized German units that smashed into the city. Salvation could have come only from the regular armies; unhappily, most of their commanders proved unequal to the task.[37] Longo and his like had no alternative but to try again farther north.

Meantime, on the 9th, Field Marshal Kesselring had issued an ultimatum, threatening to send 700 planes to bombard the capital and destroy its water and gas supplies if the defenders did not capitulate by 4:30 p.m. the next day. On his own initiative, therefore, elderly Marshal Caviglia, the highest ranking officer at hand, signed (with General Carboni's acquiescence) an armistice accord which provided that Rome's center should remain unoccupied by the Germans and be designated an "open city" ("città aperta").[38] The King's son-in-law, General Calvi di Bergolo, took command of it. He was permitted to have at his disposal the police force and the "Piave" infantry division, bivouacked in the Villa Borghese. But General Calvi and his token force were little more than prisoners of the local German commandant. During the fortnight of "open city" status, Romans once more were subjected to martial law, tight censorship, and prohibition of any strikes or disturbances, while prominent Fas-

[35] Cadorna, La Riscossa, pp. 23–28, and his La difesa di Roma (Rome, 1953).
[36] Other combatant leaders were the painter Antonello Trombadori (PCI); Oreste Lizzadri, Peppino Gracceva, and Giuliano Vassalli (PSIUP); and Emilio Lussu and Baldazzi (Pd'A). See PCI, Per la libertà e l'indipendenza d'Italia, p. 179; Carboni, Più che il dovere and Memorie segrete.
[37] Longo, Un popolo alla macchia, pp. 52–59; Battaglia, SRI, pp. 91, 101; Antonello Trombadori, "Esercito e popolo nella battaglia di Roma," in Milan and Vighi (eds.), La Resistenza al fascismo, pp. 73–76.
[38] Caviglia, Diario, pp. 435–456.

cists who had been immobilized during the "45 days" regained their freedom.[39]

Rome's "open city" status came to an abrupt halt on September 23, when the German commandant, General Stahel, announced a visit to General Calvi. Escorted by two companies of paratroopers who blocked off adjacent streets, he entered the War Ministry. Informing the Italian staff that the radio shortly would announce the advent of Mussolini's new government, he demanded their collaboration. When General Calvi, General Maraffa, and the commandant of the "Piave" declined this invitation, the Germans arrested and deported them over the Alps. A few days later they surprised 1,500 *Carabinieri* in their barracks and deported them too.

During the Germans' visit to the War Ministry, one young officer, Colonel Giuseppe di Montezemolo—a stanch royalist who had long detested Fascism and who had served for a while in the interregnum as Badoglio's secretary until he resigned because of the delays in the armistice talks [40]—calmly changed into civilian clothing in an office adjacent to that in which the Germans were talking and then walked out unchallenged by the guards. Falsifying his name and affecting a disguise, he quickly organized a Centro Militare with the help of Colonel DeMichelis, Colonel Croci, and others. He put up much of his own money to create a covert intelligence network and to recruit bands composed chiefly of ex-Army personnel and *Carabinieri*.[41] By mid-November his information service was in touch with both Milan and Bologna; Milan, in turn, had a feeder outpost in Varese, while Bologna had links with Verona, Venice, Treviso, and Bolzano.[42] Montezemolo's organization seldom if ever collaborated with Bauer's rival underground military apparatus attached to the Rome CLN, and Montezemolo's men, it has been charged, did not find it easy to adapt themselves to the exigencies of conspiratorial life. On December 10 the Brindisi government designated Colonel di Montezemolo Head Liaison Officer be-

[39] Monelli, *Roma, 1943*, pp. 280–336; Kesselring, *Memoirs*, pp. 178–179.
[40] Allason, *Memorie di un'antifascista*, p. 91.
[41] Gabrio Lombardi, *Montezemolo e il fronte militare clandestina* (Rome, 1947); Salvadori, *SRI*, pp. 139–143.
[42] Vincenzo Fornari, *Il servizio informazioni nella lotta clandestina: "Gruppo Montezemolo"* (Milan, 1946), pp. 17–19.

tween the Italian Military High Command [43] and all underground units working with it.[44] Scarcely a month later the enemy arrested him and most of his collaborators (January 17–18, 1944) and brutally killed them in the Ardeatine Caves massacre.[45]

The Germans, meanwhile, were busily confiscating gold reserves in the banks of Rome and mulcting the local Jewish community (which then numbered some 12,000). The Vatican circumspectly helped the Jews to meet these levies. But money was not the only thing the Germans desired; they imposed a blood tax as well. On October 16 Nazi police, headed by the hated Herbert Kappler, systematically rounded up hundreds of Jews as well as some other noncollaborators.[46] They did not even respect the extraterritoriality of Vatican convents in which many of these refugees were hiding.

The women of Rome did their best to help their menfolk evade forced labor and military service. Their cleverness was attested to by the German commandant, who noted wryly that telephone censors were reporting almost no conversations either by or about men because women were referring to them only under feminine pseudonyms. Hospitals burgeoned with "bed patients" suffering from what the Germans sarcastically termed "Kesselring's disease." At least 200,000 hid from the Nazis in other people's homes,[47] and to outwit the enemy the under-

[43] Cadorna, La Riscossa, pp. 84–87.

[44] One such Badoglio-sponsored mission was landed on the Ligurian coast early in November 1943. Colonel E. Simbula and Naval Captain J. Kulszjcki tried to recruit disbanded military personnel in the region into a "Corpo Volontari Armati Italiani" (VAI) and to compete with Professor Ottorino Balduzzi's "Otto" group (cf. infra, Ch. vii, Early Allied liaison with the Resistance). But most of the leaders were caught in March 1944 by the Germans. Renzo Baccino, Contributo alla storia della Resistenza di Genova (Genoa, 1955), p. 39.

[45] Cf. infra, Ch. ix.

[46] According to the Centre de Documentation Juive Contemporaine, Les Juifs en Europe (Paris, 1949), pp. 43–46, some 10,000 Jews were deported from Italy, and of these only 605 returned alive. Regarding the fate of Italian Jews deported to Auschwitz after October 1943, see Miriam Novicht (ed.), "Documenti sulla persecuzione degli ebrei italiani," MLI, No. 49 (1957), pp. 60–66.

[47] Fulvia Ripa di Meano, Roma clandestina (Rome, 1944); Moellhausen, La carta perdente, pp. 102–129, 142–169; Monelli, Roma, 1943, pp. 331–341, and passim; Ezio Bacino, Roma prima e dopo (Rome, 1945); Armando Troisio, Roma sotto il terrore nazi-fascista (8 settembre–4 giugno 1944) (Rome, 1944); Jane Scrivener, Inside Rome with the Germans (New York, 1945); M. de Wyss, Rome under the Terror (London, 1945); Carlo Trabucco, La prigionia di Roma (Rome, 1945).

ground furnished quantities of false documents, including 3,000 Todt labor-service cards, 15,000 residence permits, and 50,000 regular identity cards.[48]

By September 10 commanders of the Italian armed forces in Turin, Milan, and most other places had capitulated to the Germans with scarcely a pretense of resistance. Altogether in the Mediterranean basin the Germans took prisoner some 640,000 Italians. Most of these were herded northward over the Alps to internment camps until their fate could be decided.[49] Only a tiny fraction of these opted to fight for Mussolini's refurbished regime.[50] Some 30,000 died in the fearsome German laagers.[51]

In a few places Italian military discipline did not completely break down on September 8 and some imaginative officers (usually junior ones) correctly interpreted Badoglio's obscure bid to put up some resistance. Thus Italian garrisons in Cuneo, Savona, Ascoli Piceno, and Treviso fell only in the face of overwhelming pressure. In Apulia sparse contingents safeguarded the port of Bari and several airdromes. In Sardinia and Corsica the "Cremona" and "Friuli" divisions helped expel German units and then fraternized almost to a man with the Allied forces which soon debarked. Whereas in Venezia Giulia, Dalmatia, Croatia, and Bosnia-Herzegovina most of the disintegrating Italian corps were taken prisoner, in Montenegro two divisions (the "Taurinense" and "Venezia"), learning of Communist Party directives, reorganized themselves in December as the "Garibaldi Partisan Division." Under a Communist political commissar, they fought alongside Josip Broz Tito's IX Yugoslav Corps and gave a good military account of themselves. When Belgrade was liberated ten months later (October 1944), additional Italian prisoners of war joined Tito's Partisans. More than 35,000 were

[48] Longo, Un popolo alla macchia, p. 223.
[49] Edoardo Scala, La riscossa dell'esercito (Rome, 1948), p. 319 ff.
[50] Cf. supra, n. 14; Carli-Ballola, Sdr, pp. 18–20.
[51] Salvadori, SRI, p. 67. Regarding internment of Italians in Germany, see M.B., "Voci della Resistenza nei campi di concentramento militari in Germania," MLI, (Jan. 1951), p. 5 ff.; Adler Raffaelli, Fronte senza eroi (Vicenza, 1956), describing the peregrinations of the prisoners; Piero Caleffi, Si fa presto a dire fame (Milan, 1954), another prize-winning account by a Ligurian Actionist. Also of interest are Enea Fergnani, Un uomo e tre numeri (Milan, 1955); Enrico Piccaluga, "Testimonianze sui campi di concentramento—una fuga da Dachau," MLI, No. 38/39 (1955), pp. 46–70.

thus enrolled. In March 1945 some units were repatriated via Bari.[52]

Meanwhile, in Greece and Albania, though entire divisions melted away (many either to be massacred by the local populace or taken captive by the Germans), some escaped and joined local guerrillas.[53] On Cephalonia the Italian "Acqui" garrison of some 8,400 men fought fiercely for a week until amost the entire defending force was finally butchered by the German invaders.[54] In France numerous Italians joined the *maquis*.

Northern CLN's

Milan's clandestine counterpart to Bonomi's CCLN met in the office of Avv. Arpesani (PLI) soon after news of the September 8 armistice. Nenni arrived from Rome to tell of the street fighting that had taken place in the capital and of the decision of the Rome committee to transform itself into a CLN. The Milanese decided at once to do likewise. By virtue of its location and capable leaders, the Milan CLN rapidly became the most prestigious underground agency in the North.[55] In mid-winter it was to create a still higher body, the CLNAI (CLN dell'Alta Italia; "CLN of Upper Italy"), which had more or less parallel status with the Rome CCLN.

At its charter meeting the Milan CLN discussed the nature of the emergent guerrilla warfare, thus far limited in the Lombard sector to a few officers and soldiers of the collapsing Army who had refused to lay down their weapons and to some unusually ardent young men who had thrown in their lot with the new political parties and named themselves a "National Guard." [56] Many in the CLN were uncertain about the prospects for underground warfare. When Nenni asked Parri if he were ready to

[52] G. Maras and Others, *Fratellanza italo-jugoslava nella lotta di liberazione* (Rome, 1950); "La resistenza italiana all'estero," Bollettino del Comitato Nazionale ANPI, IV, No. 23 (1952).

[53] Captain Mario Fantacci, "Un Italiano in Albania," *MLI*, No. 40 (1956), pp. 29–52, No. 41 (1957), pp. 37–50, and No. 42 (1956), pp. 9–38; M. Marsato, "A fianco dell'ELAS," and N. Bassi, "Da Smirne a Firenze," *Società*, No. 6 (1946), pp. 415–443.

[54] R. Formato, *Eccidio di Cefalonia* (Rome, 1943); F. Ferrari, *Cefalonia, settembre 1943* (Parma, 1954); Battaglia, SRI, pp. 102–123.

[55] Initial members of the Milan CLN included Arpesani, Collino Pansa, and Casagrande (PLI); A. Casò, Enrico Falck (DC); V. Albasini-Scrosati, F. Parri (Pd'A); Roberto Veratti, Viotto (PSIUP); and G. LiCausi (PCI). Catalano, *Storia del CLNAI*, p. 62.

[56] *Ibid.*, pp. 56–57; Valiani, *Tutte le strade conducono a Roma*, p. 101.

accept the command of fighting forces, Parri replied that it seemed a bit premature to establish a military headquarters until more was known about the confused situation. The conferees did agree, however, to hasten the recruitment of partisan bands and antisabotage squads; to raise funds to support them; to resist the Todt labor draft; and to wage a relentless propaganda war against the neo-Fascists.[57]

In Turin the Committee of the Opposition that had existed since early in 1943 relabeled itself the CPLN ("Comitato Piemontese di Liberazione Nazionale"). In addition to its executive committee,[58] it had sections looking after military, financial, supply, and propaganda problems. Like all the clandestine CLN's, it operated amid utmost secrecy. Its conventicles were kept as restricted as possible, outsiders being admitted only if there was unanimous consent. Some early meetings took place in Hotel Canelli, a Socialist haunt on Via San Dalmazzo in old Turin; others in various law offices, for in that city a signal number of magistrates and lawyers manned posts in the underground; still others in students' rooms or in shopkeepers' back offices. Gatherings out of doors preferably were restricted to two or three persons and were confined usually to outlying streets. While walking, the conspirators might exchange a few important documents, though a basic rule was to keep written material at a minimum and in code whenever feasible.

The Tuscan CLN (CTLN) boasted an early birth in Florence. Professor Gaetano Pieraccini (PSIUP) was its first chairman.[59] In Genoa, Bologna, Padua, Trent, and Trieste other municipal and provincial committees mushroomed. On a much smaller

---

[57] Catalano, *Storia del CLNAI*, pp. 62–63.

[58] Initial members included Osvaldo Negarville (PCI); Rag. Piero Passoni (PSIUP); Mario Andreis (Pd'A); Andrea Guglielminetti (DC); and Guido Verzone (PLI). See Mario Giovana, "Ricerche sulla storia del CLN piemontese," *MLI*, No. 34/35 (1955), pp. 69–74, and "L'inizio della Resistenza in Piemonte e la costituzione del CLN Regionale Piemontese," *ibid.*, No. 38/39 (1955), pp. 3–30; Irene di Collegno-Rignon, *I Nostri: vita clandestina in Piemonte* (Turin, 1947), pp. 14–15; Battaglia, *SRI*, p. 203. For a broad survey of the Armed Resistance in Piedmont, see *Aspetti della Resistenza in Piemonte*, ed. Istituto Storico della Resistenza in Piemonte, a cura di I. Cotta, P. Serini, and G. Vaccarino (Turin, 1950).

[59] Also in the CTLN were Avv. Adone Zoli (DC), who was jailed in November-December 1943 and who was to become Italian premier in 1957–1958; Aldobrando Medici-Tornaquinci, Vittorio Fossombroni, Marino Mari, Eugenio Artom (PLI); Avv. Luigi Boniforti, Carlo Furno, Enzo Enriques-Agnoletti, Cesare Gnudi, Cesare Fasola, Carlo Ragghianti (Pd'A); Arturo Bruni, Diego Giurati, Alfredo Bruzzichelli, Foscolo Lombardi (PSIUP); Giulio Montelatici and Gian-

scale, CLN's made their debut in the liberated *Mezzogiorno*, the one in Naples being the most influential.[60]

Some CLN divergencies

Unlike their French prototypes (which were friendly to the British-backed DeGaulle government), the Italian CLN's emerged as foes of the British-backed Badoglio government.[61] And in contrast to Tito's Communist-dominated Anti-Fascist Council for the National Liberation of Yugoslavia (AVNOJ), the Italian committees insisted upon the principle of hexpartite [62] parity and tried to pursue a program acceptable to all. To be sure, some of the CLN's in the Po valley demanded on occasion but a simple majority, but in Florence and Rome the committees made every effort to achieve unanimity. The Tuscan Actionist leader, Carlo Ragghianti, justified this on the grounds that "the CLN was not an organ elected by the people. Only elections, free elections, can justify and legitimize majority rule. Unanimity was therefore both the expression and guarantee of the *provisional* function of the CLN, of the pledge that power assumed in the name of the people would be reconsigned to the people as soon as the CLN had finished its particular task, which was

---

franco Musco (PCI). Contini-Bonacossi and Ragghianti-Collobbi (eds.), *Una lotta nel suo corso*, p. 3, n. 1; pp. 8–9, n. 8.

[60] Regarding the Naples CLN, see *infra*, Ch. VIII.

[61] Italy's Resistenza Armata also originated differently from France's. There was no single military leader in Italy to issue a clarion call in the way General DeGaulle did from London on June 22, 1940. Furthermore, the French Résistance (at least initially) was chiefly a military, moral, and national movement that arose in the wake of the breakdown of the multiparty Third Republic. The Italian Resistenza Armata, on the other hand, had more of a political complexion; it stemmed from twenty years of undercover anti-Fascism and the excitement that surrounded the rebirth of a multiparty system after the collapse of Mussolini's totalitarianism. Comparisons cannot easily be made, but one writer with firsthand knowledge of both movements has rated the Italian Resistance as more widespread and aggressive: Tasca, *In Francia nella bufera*, pp. 176–177; *cf.* E. Enriques-Agnoletti in preface to Piero Malvezzi and Giovanni Pirelli (eds.), *Lettere di condannati a morte della Resistenza italiana* (8 settembre 1943–25 aprile 1945) (Turin, 1952), pp. 13–15; and E. Enriques-Agnoletti, "Francia," *Il Ponte*, xiv (1958), pp. 652–657.

[62] There were six parties in Rome and the South. In the North, however, there were but five, as DL had no following there. Later in the struggle the PCI sought to bring into the CLN's parapolitical groups like labor unions, women's groups, and guerrilla forces which they controlled. Miniature CLN's were also organized in some factories later in the war.

that of liberating the national territory and of establishing harmoniously the basis for a free National Constituent Assembly." [63] In Rome and Milan Presidents Bonomi (DL) and Pizzoni (PLI) sought to keep their own political biases in the background and let others in their own parties lead the debates; in Florence, however, the presidency rotated regularly among the parties and the incumbents made no effort to camouflage their own views. The northern committees were much more concerned than the Rome and southern ones in the problems posed by Mussolini's pseudo-socialistic RSI and by the Resistenza Armata; consequently they found themselves often interfering with their respective military headquarters. The Rome CCLN, on the other hand, managed to keep its eyes focused chiefly on the political problems raised by the hegira of the royal government.[64]

Emigration to Switzerland

When the enemy captured forty-two men in the Milan PSIUP headquarters on September 12, 1943, it was apparent that those anti-Fascists who had dared to raise their heads too high during Badoglio's interregnum must go into hiding.[65] Many decided forthwith to flee to Lugano, where they joined several thousand other refugees, some of whom (like Ignazio Silone) had been in Switzerland since the fall of France or before.[66]

In Switzerland they had to compete politically with Princess Maria José, Ambassador Magistrati, and consular representatives of the Brindisi government, as well as an assortment of refugee industrialists and financiers. The militant left wing thought it would be unwise to form a foreign-based CLN lest the moderate DC and PLI parties dominate it to their disadvantage; but underground leaders in Milan thought otherwise, particularly after Togliatti's return to Italy in April 1944. Thus later that spring Lugano's anti-Fascist community established a "Delegation" of the Milan CLN, an offshoot that performed much useful liaison

[63] Ragghianti, Disegno della liberazione italiana, p. 41.
[64] Ibid., pp. 40–66.
[65] On November 25, 1943, the SS captured the covert headquarters of the PSIUP in Via Borgonuovo, Milan. Those who escaped made their way to Switzerland. Marcello Cirenei of Genoa was summoned to replace the deceased Roberto Veratti as PSIUP northern secretary. He held the post until June 1944 when Sandro Pertini and Giorgio Marzola took it over. Carli-Ballola, Sdr, pp. 88–89.
[66] See supra, Ch. v.

work.[67] Leftist refugee circles also formed the Comitato Italiano di Cultura Sociale to provide political education for Italian youths interned in Switzerland.

The mountainous republic also became the base of operations of those Italian advocates of European federation who had formed the MFE in Milan late in August 1943.[68] Altiero Spinelli, Ernesto Rossi, and Professor Luigi Einaudi, to name but the most prominent figures, spent the rest of the war working indefatigably in Switzerland for the cause of a United States of Europe. Many of their articles were smuggled to Milan to be printed in the clandestine *Unità Europea*, which influenced especially the Pd'A and PSIUP. The most ambitious publication was a long pamphlet by Rossi (who employed the pseudonym "Thelos"), *L'Europe de demain*. It was printed in ten thousand copies on very thin paper and sent covertly in May 1944 into Nazi-occupied France.[69] The Italian refugees quickly learned of the existence of parallel groups in foreign resistance movements. They worked hard to co-ordinate these currents and were greatly assisted by the Rev. Dr. Willem Visser 't Hooft, the Dutch Secretary-General of the World Council of Churches. They held their own version of a Dumbarton Oaks Conference in his Geneva home from March until May 1944. At the end of that time a group representing undergrounds of eight countries [70]

[67] Early members included Tommaso Gallarati-Scotti and Casagrande (PLI); Piero Malvestiti and Stefano Jacini (DC); Cipriano Facchinetti (PRI); Adolfo Tino, A. Zanotti, and A. Damiani (Pd'A); F. Targetti and Rodolfo Morandi, the latter just released from a ten-year sentence imposed in 1937 (PSIUP); and Massarenti (PCI). Damiani handled most of the military problems till April 1944; G. Bacciagaluppi, Stucchi, and Pezzotta did so later. Catalano, *Storia del CLNAI*, pp. 56–57, n. 6.

[68] See *supra*, Ch. vi, Opposition rumblings.

[69] In January 1945 it was reprinted by the Geneva Centre d'Action pour la Fédération Européenne in a volume with other federalist documents: *L'Europe de demain* (Neuchâtel).

Rossi also collaborated with the Comitato Italiano di Cultura Sociale and wrote the chapter "La Nazione nel mondo," which appeared in a volume, *Uomo e cittadino*, published by this body. He also penned the sections dealing with federalism in a little political dictionary that accompanied the volume, and he prepared eight periodicals of the MFE which circulated in mimeographed form and included writings by Roepke, Layton, Beveridge, and Wootton. Finally, he was responsible for publication of four pamphlets by the "Nuove edizioni di Capolago," including Einaudi's *I problemi economici della federazione europea* (Lugano, 1944) and his own (signed "Storeno") *Gli Stati Uniti d'Europa*.

[70] France, Italy, Netherlands, Norway, Poland, Czechoslovakia, Yugoslavia, and Germany.

signed a memorable International Federalist Declaration, edited by the Italians, which emphasized the need for all the European resistance movements to engage at once in a common struggle for European federal union. This declaration was sent covertly into the countries still under occupation and also to England.[71]

Partisan warfare

The Armed Resistance occurred mainly in northern and central Italy. Yet in the *Mezzogiorno* there was a somewhat analogous uprising that deserved attention, even though it attained neither the degree of political purpose nor mass support that characterized the struggle in the North.

The "quattro giornate" of Naples

The South's spontaneous fighting took place in Naples between September 27 and 30, 1943. After Badoglio's announcement of the armistice, the Germans, though inferior numerically, had quickly subdued Italian forces near the great seaport. A committee of the anti-Fascist parties had already been formed; in due course it became the Naples CLN, but it was unable to organize military volunteers, because of the traditional political apathy of the Neapolitans and the lack of support from Army officers.[72] After the Germans took command of the city on September 12 they began to conscript men from the age of 18 to 33 for compulsory labor service and threatened reprisals at the ratio of 100-to-1 if any of their own soldiers were hurt. Popular anger mounted rapidly when German soldiers set fire to part of the University of Naples and executed a sailor as retaliation for the killing of one of their men. In Piazza della Borsa four other Italians were executed for illegal possession of pistols, while next day in near-by Aversa the Germans shot fourteen *Carabinieri* for resisting destruction of the telephone exchange. Meanwhile, the populace suffered from food and water shortages as well as from repeated Allied aerial bombardments. As the Anglo-Americans approached the city the Germans forcibly evacuated many denizens from the water-front section.

[71] See *L'Unità Europea*, No. 5 (July–Aug. 1944), 1, and *ibid.*, No. 8 (Jan.–Feb. 1945), 4, for text; also reprinted in *L'Europe de demain*, pp. 68–75.
[72] Corrado Barbagallo, *Napoli contro il terrore nazista (8 settembre–ottobre 1943)* (Naples, 1944), p. 17 ff.

At last, on the 27th violence erupted in Vomero Vecchio where the Germans, in requital for the death of one of their motorcyclists, shot five and imprisoned fifty Italians in the Campo Sportivo. From that epicenter the revolt spread rapidly but disjointedly through the twisting and often easily barricaded streets. In the forefront were young boys aided in some cases by a few Navy and Army officers. Yet almost no trace of organization or premeditated action was apparent during Naples' *quattro giornate* (the "four glorious days," as the uprising came to be dubbed, in allusion to Milan's "five" in March 1848). Nor was there evidence of any clearly defined political objective on the part of the fighters. Even when the rebels, capturing some armored cars, liberated the athletic field and got the German commander to raise the white flag at the Hotel Parker (perhaps the first such instance in modern Italo-German relations), they were satisfied to let him evacuate the city on the night of the 29–30th with the help of an armed escort. Some of the enraged Germans before they retreated set fire to many precious documents in the Naples Archivio Storico at San Paolo Belsito.

The Neapolitan revolt was not true partisan warfare. Spontaneity, improvisation, and the immediate objective of self-defense characterized the uprising. Yet it is noteworthy that, unlike the 1799 anti-French insurrection, Naples' rebellious *lazzaroni* and *bourgeoisie* this time fought shoulder to shoulder. Moreover, they unwittingly demonstrated to the rest of their countrymen that the *Wehrmacht*, hitherto deemed invincible, might under favorable circumstances (an imminent Allied juncture) be driven out by the Italian people's own efforts.[73] Northern patriots did not delay in emulating and expanding the examples of popular revolt which the Neapolitans and the other Southerners [74] had furnished.

[73] *Cf. ibid.*; Mario Martelli, "Le quattro giornate napoletane," *Il Ponte*, XII (1956), pp. 1917–1926; Antonio Tarsia in Curia, *La verità sulle "quattro giornate" di Napoli* (Naples, 1950); Angelo Raffaele Jervolino, "Le 'quattro giornate' di Napoli," *Civitas*, VI (1953), pp. 82–84; Alfredo Parente, "Le 'quattro giornate' di Napoli," in Milan and Vighi (eds.), *La Resistenza al fascismo*, pp. 77–80; Aldo DeJaco, *La città insorge* (Rome, 1956); Longo, *Un popolo alla macchia*, pp. 87–101; Battaglia, SRI, pp. 123–134; Carli-Ballola, *Sdr*, pp. 30–34; and delayed dispatches of Herbert L. Matthews from Naples in NYT, Oct. 6, 7, 10, 12, 1943.

[74] In a few other places in the South (Irpinia, Caserta, Matera, Rionero in Vulture, and in the Abruzzi-Molise) the populace engaged in small-scale fighting.

Northern "partigianeria"

The militant *partigianeria* emerged chiefly in the mountainous arc that flanks the Po valley and in the Apennines of central Italy. To carry out an offensive, partisan bands had to be in range of enemy strongholds. At the same time, they needed reasonably impregnable wooded terrain or mountainous retreats with relatively few access roads; yet forests and the absence of access roads were precisely the desiderata that Italy lacked, in comparison to a country so admirably designed for partisan warfare as Yugoslavia. Of necessity, bands tended to emerge fastest wherever they could draw recruits from near-by population centers, and logistics restricted their range of operations to zones where supplies might readily be acquired. Food and clothing had to be "scrounged" from towns and farms where sympathetic people dwelt. Weapons had to be seized in many cases in swift, nocturnal raids on isolated military supply depots and enemy outposts.

Italy did not possess much of a tradition of guerrilla warfare, though in the South there had been the early nineteenth-century brigands, to be sure, and Giuseppe Garibaldi's Redshirts and others had engaged in irregular combat.[75] Impetus for the Resistenza Armata of World War II came less from such distant memories than from the experience of the preceding two decades of undercover opposition to Fascism and from the peculiar circumstances of the military debacle of 1943. Certainly the PCI, PSIUP, and Pd'A leaders had vivid impressions of what guerrillas had been able to do during the Spanish Civil War and in the Resistance movements in France, Yugoslavia, and eastern Europe. A lively debate has arisen among Resistance chroniclers as to whether the Italian struggle was spontaneous or the result of premeditated organization. Doubtless there was a good measure of spontaneity;

See Corrado Colacito, "La Resistenza in Abruzzo (1943–1944)," *MLI*, No. 30 (1954), pp. 3–19; Francesco Nitti, "Le giornate di Matera (sett. 1943)," *ibid.*, pp. 20–30; F. Nitti, "Sulla resistenza a Nola," *ibid.*, pp. 31–34; F. Nitti, "Cronache dell'occupazione in Lucania: le giornate di Rionero in Vulture (sett. 1943)," *ibid.*, pp. 51–59; and Corrado Graziadei, "La Resistenza in Terra di Lavoro," in Milan and Vighi (eds.), *La Resistenza al fascismo*, pp. 81–84.

[75] Professor Raffaele Ciasca has discerned some forerunners in popular revolts of the late eighteenth century: "Moti di popolo nella storia d'Italia," *Civitas*, VI (1955), pp. 92–102.

yet premeditation must not be minimized.[76] For example, in broadcasts from Moscow Togliatti had been exhorting Italians to gird themselves for an underground struggle. In the Fascist prison centers PCI leaders took this advice seriously and busily studied whatever relevant literature they could find pertaining to guerrilla warfare. The proper moment for action presented itself when Badoglio's breach with Germany was announced and the Allies landed on the peninsula; yet the Communists in Rome had anticipated the task as early as August 30, 1943. And the Pd'A in its Florence congress of September 3–5, 1943, had also made some precise military plans.[77] To comprehend the readiness of many Italians to enter the *macchia* [78] one must also keep in mind that they were confident that the Allies, resolutely committed to unconditional surrender, would not halt their offensive and would soon reach the Po valley. Under such circumstances guerrilla warfare did not seem hopelessly romantic.

Most of the *partigiani* who chose to "go to the mountains" were actuated by the same kind of motives that induced unpretentious men and women in France, Yugoslavia, and other Nazi-held countries to rebel against their brutal foreign masters— *viz.*, a mixture of patriotic, ideological, idealistic reasons, intertwined with self-interest.

Doubtless many ex-Army men joined the Armed Resistance out of a sense of loyalty to their oaths and a feeling that the war soon would be over. This was especially true in Piedmont and the Veneto. In the former area, for example, a significant proportion of the earliest patriot fighters came directly from the disbanded Italian Fourth Army, which had been called back from France during Badoglio's "45 days" and concentrated near Cuneo. They, of course, knew something firsthand about the French *maquis*. Unlike the German commanders in the Cuneo

[76] Pietro Secchia, "La Resistenza: organizzazione o spontaneità?" *MLI*, No. 55 (1959), pp. 58–81, which refutes the "spontaneity" thesis of Raimondo Luraghi in his review (*MLI*, No. 51 [1958]) of Pietro Secchia and Cino Moscatelli, *Il Monte Rosa è sceso a Milano*; cf. Ragghianti, *Disegno della Liberazione*, pp. 80–83; Carli-Ballola, *Sdr*, pp. 69–72; Battaglia, *SRI*, pp. 183–184; and Leo Valiani, "Antifascismo e Resistenza," *MLI*, No. 54 (1959), pp. 39–43.

[77] Cf. *supra*, Ch. vi, Opposition rumblings.

[78] *Macchia* (like the French word *maqui*) meant "dense underbrush" and was synonymous for "the underground."

sector, the Italian ones did not anticipate Badoglio's armistice proclamation. In the ensuing confusion a good many officers and men contended unheroically that they had been duped on all sides and struck out for home to buy up whatever scarce articles of civilian clothing they could find to camouflage their military status. A certain number of others argued that "military honor" demanded that they stay loyal to the Axis in spite of Badoglio's severance of that tie. Opposed to these were several hundred officers and men who were determined to uphold their oath of fidelity to the King and to fight for his government as best they could, confident that the Allies soon would drive into the Po valley. It was such *sbandati* ("disbanded soldiers") who speedily organized themselves into the so-called "autonomous" patriot bands, usually retaining their previous military ranks. Field Marshal Kesselring later blamed Erwin Rommel, his top general in the North, for allowing the Italians to desert en masse into these bands.[79] These Autonomi professed to be apolitical with respect to the new parties emerging; they preferred to delay until war's end all talk of constitutional reforms. Though most of the officers were royalist-inclined, this was not necessarily true of their men.[80] For the rest of the war a dichotomy persisted between the Autonomi (also nicknamed "Badogliani" by their rivals) [81] and the unabashedly "political" bands mustered by the leftist parties of the CLN's. This was attenuated somewhat after April 1944 when Premier Badoglio finally reformed his cabinet to include CLN spokesmen.

While anti-Germanism and patriotism may have outweighed the ideological motives of anti-Fascism and of Communism in the case of the ordinary recruits (particularly those from the Army), ideological considerations predominated among the leaders of the political formations and in a substantial number of their rank-and-file. It would have been risky in the extreme for the many politicos who had dared to come out into the open

[79] Kesselring, *Memoirs*, p. 185.

[80] Gen. Alessandro Trabucchi, *I vinti hanno sempre torto* (Turin, 1947), pp. 13–46; Enrico Martini, *Con la libertà e per la libertà* (Turin, 1947), pp. 10–18 ff.; *cf.* exchange of letters regarding G. Salvemini's review of Dante Livio Bianco, *Guerra partigiana: raccolta di scritti*, ed. Giorgio Agosti and Franco Venturi (Turin, 1954) appearing in Rome *Il Mondo*, Feb. 1, 22, and Mar. 1, 1955.

[81] Bianco, *Guerra partigiana*, pp. 19–25.

during the "45 days" to remain in their usual abodes after September 8; [82] yet it was not just for personal safety that they hurried to the foothills. Most of them believed sincerely that by fighting in the *macchia* for a Democratic Republic, for Socialism, or for Communism, as the case might be, they could amass enough pressure to bring about a radical renovation of Italy's social and political structure. To be sure, Communists generally acted upon orders. Pietro Secchia has revealed that the PCI issued orders to all of its organizations to "send 15 per cent of its card-carrying members and 10 per cent of its cadres into the partisan formations" (and later the number was increased).[83] In their own self-interest many of the other parties felt obliged to compete with the Communists. But it is also true that many in the underground sincerely believed that if the common people participated vigorously in the liberation struggle, they could redeem the dismal record left by the royalist government on September 8 and even persuade the Allies to regard Italy as a meritorious partner instead of as a defeated, abject enemy. If Italians did not "work their passage back," they felt that they could expect neither moral nor political status in the new world being forged in the war's crucible.

Manifestly, great numbers of those in the age brackets liable to conscription by either Mussolini's or Hitler's officials (especially after the early spring of 1944) flocked into the foothill forces for personal safety. Still others signed up out of youthful exuberance and a sense of personal emancipation after years of regimentation. Doubtless a few joined for motives of revenge and plunder; but this category was often purged by the others, and in any case tended to lose heart during the arduous moments and to desert at the first sign of an enemy "comb-out." During the final phase of the Resistenza Armata in 1945 there was, of course, a vast influx of "Johnny-come-latelies," many of them disreputable opportunists.

Still, the historian cannot deny the presence of a substantial measure of tough-fibred idealism and discipline among the underground fighters if he is to explain satisfactorily the readiness of the hard core of volunteers to face up month after month to the

[82] Parri, *MLI*, No. 34/35 (1955), pp. 16–25; Ada Gobetti, *Diario partigiano*, pp. 17–25.
[83] Secchia, *MLI*, No. 55 (1959), p. 63.

handicaps of that kind of warfare and the cruel tortures, if not death itself, that almost certainly became their lot when captured. The idealism of this elite can be discerned in many of the "last letters" composed by those who were taken prisoner by the Germans and condemned to death. In them one finds ample evidence of a sense of political vision and of calm, moral fortitude—qualities that had been all too frequently missing in much of Italy's modern history. For example, before his execution "Duccio" Galimberti (Pd'A) of Cuneo wrote to his loved ones, "I acted with good intentions for an ideal: for this I am serene, and so must you also be." [84] No doubt some of the victims shared the judgment of the young PCI poet and critic Giaime Pintor [85] that the Armed Resistance offered the chance of another glorious Risorgimento. Like many other intellectuals in Italy's highly stratified and fairly rigid social structure, Pintor had gone through no little mental agony before deciding to "rough it." His final letter, written in the winter of 1943 before he crossed enemy lines from Naples to Rome only to be captured and executed, ended: "Today the possibilities of the Risorgimento are reopened for the Italians: no gesture is useless provided it does not become an end in itself. As for me, I assure you that the idea of going to be a partisan in this season gives me very little pleasure; I have never appreciated as now the comforts of civilized life and I feel sure that I would become an excellent translator and a good diplomat, but according to every likelihood a mediocre partisan. Nevertheless, it is the only possibility open and I accept it." [86]

Recalling that era, Professor Calamandrei of Florence (a man who has been dubbed the "cantor" of the Resistance and who has interpreted it as a struggle for the defense of the "dignity of

---

[84] Piero Malvezzi and Giovanni Pirelli (eds.), *Lettere di condannati a morte della Resistenza italiana* (8 settembre 1943–25 aprile 1945) (Turin, 1953), p. 96. The same editors have compiled a companion volume, *Lettere di condannati a morte della Resistenza europea* (Turin, 1954). Cf. Franco Antonicelli, "Per una storia spirituale della Guerra di Liberazione: 'Lettere di condannati a morte della Resistenza Italiana (1943–1945),'" *MLI*, No. 17/18 (1952), pp. 3–19.

[85] See Arnaldo Bocelli, *Giaime Pintor e la letteratura della Resistenza* (Caltanissetta, 1958).

[86] Giaime Pintor, *Il sangue d'Europa* (Turin, 1950), pp. 245–248; Aldo Garosci, "Un mese e mezzo con Giaime Pintor," *Mercurio* (*anche l'Italia ha vinto*), No. 16 (Dec. 1945), pp. 98–106; Bianca Ceva, "A proposito di Giaime Pintor e la letteratura della Resistenza," *MLI*, No. 58 (1960), pp. 72–77.

man") phrased the issue succinctly: "The hour to resist had arrived; the hour to be men—to die like men, and to live like men." [87]

Political wing of Armed Resistance

The political bands differed from the autonomous ones chiefly in their leadership, which came more often than not from party activists. Their rank-and-file were mostly obscure men—a minority from civilian life but the majority either from the dispersed armies or from the age groups that stood to be drafted by the Nazi-Fascists.[88] In the long run, the political bands outnumbered the Autonomi. A careful Allied liaison officer and investigator has estimated that in the North (including upper Tuscany) political bands accounted for three fourths of the guerrillas, and in central Italy about two thirds.[89]

The PCI Garibaldini were by far the most numerous and widely distributed of all the political bands; indeed, they constituted almost two fifths of the whole movement. During the early phase of the struggle they usually acted quite independently, but their efficient organization often served as a paragon for other groups. Each unit had its political commissar in addition to a military commander—a system of dual control that was later copied by some of the other parties. Not all Garibaldini were Communists (for there was always a very strong tendency for men to join whatever band was closest, and only a fraction of the young men who volunteered the first autumn subscribed to coherent political creeds); but to rise to a post of leadership in the Garibaldi brigades, one had to be a Communist. As would be expected, the political commissars made every effort to indoctrinate their men and the surrounding population.

[87] Piero Calamandrei, *Uomini e città della Resistenza* (Bari, 1955), p. 13. Too well known an oppositionist to stay in Florence after September 8, Calamandrei took refuge in the Umbrian town of Collicello. There he prepared for publication a new edition of Beccaria, *Crime and Punishments*, which he found a timely subject. *Cf.* special issue of *Il Ponte*, xiv (Nov. 1958), p. 67 (issue entitled "Piero Calamandrei").

[88] Reviewing Secchia and Moscatelli's *Il Monte Rosa è sceso a Milano*, R. Luraghi notes in *MLI*, No. 51 (1958), pp. 80–84, that a large number of officers in the Garibaldi formations came from the dispersed armies.

[89] Salvadori, *SRI*, pp. 85 and 90. Ragghianti has discussed the role of some CLN parties in providing cadres for these bands: "Le premesse del Movimento di Liberazione," *MLI*, No. 23 (1953), pp. 54–55.

Luigi Longo and Pietro Secchia had barely gained their freedom from Ventotene in August 1943 when they transmitted to their comrades instructions from Togliatti in Moscow that all Communist activity henceforth must be viewed with respect to the way in which it would help drive out the Germans, because "the entire Italian situation is now dominated by the German occupation." The whole party must mobilize itself to this end. Domestic politics must be subordinated to this all-important task of helping the Soviet Union in its titanic struggle against Nazi Germany.[90] Longo busied himself first in the nigh-impossible defense of Rome; thereafter he hurried north. So did Secchia.

The Garibaldini were the first to erect a central military headquarters, organizing their Supreme Command in Milan early in November. Longo ("Gallo") became Supreme Commander; Secchia, Commissar-General; Roasio, chief organizer for Venetia and Emilia; and Francesco Scotti, for Piedmont, Liguria, and Lombardy. These and others took every conspiratorial precaution; indeed, not a single one of the top PCI chieftains was to be caught during the war.[91] Vincenzo ("Cino") Moscatelli, the Moscow-trained mechanic whose agitation in 1930 had landed him in prison until 1936, was the most renowned Garibaldi commander in the field. His men concentrated themselves in the industrialized and strategic Biellese, Valsesia, and Val d'Ossola northwest of Novara. Starting out with a mere thirty-six men, Moscatelli's forces had expanded by war's end to 3,600. His almost legendary military reputation helped win him a seat in the Senate of the postwar Italian Republic.

Next to the Communists in strength were the fighting forces of the Pd'A, whose groundwork had been laid by the covert congress in Florence (September 3–5, 1943). On that occasion Bauer was sent back to Rome to organize military resistance; Ragghianti was to do the same in Florence; and Parri was to supervise the program in Milan.[92] Actionists accounted for perhaps one fourth the underground combatants, but they were not

---

[90] Longo has published a collection of PCI directives which appeared in the clandestine press from 1943 to 1945: *Sulla via dell'insurrezione nazionale* (Rome, 1954), pp. 5–7; cf. P. Secchia's article in *La nostra lotta* (Dec. 1943), reprinted in *I Comunisti e l'insurrezione* (Rome, 1954), pp. 47–48, 64.
[91] Magnani and Cucchi, *Crisi di una generazione*, p. 35; Battaglia, *SRI*, p. 196.
[92] Ragghianti, *Disegno della liberazione*, p. 97.

so evenly distributed as the Garibaldini. Piedmont was their stronghold, just as it had been for Carlo Rosselli's Giustizia e Libertà movement after 1929. Their ideological descent was recalled in the labeling of the fighting contingents: "GL," "Italia Libera," and "Rosselli." In the northern cities the Actionists probably took pride of place in attracting non-Communist guerrillas, and they shared honors with the PCI in the publication and dissemination of propaganda. Though the Giellisti did not have the rigorous hierarchical discipline of the Garibaldini, they possessed a deep-seated sense of self-control. Radical idealists and unyielding republicans, they never hid their distrust of career military officers, whose sympathies, they firmly suspected, lay with the dynasty. Like the Garibaldini, the Giellisti appointed political commissars, but they often called them euphemistically "CLN representatives" or "civilian delegates." By early 1944 GL had imitated the PCI in setting up military headquarters in Milan.

Professor Parri became top commander of the Giellisti and served as one of the directors of the eventual supreme headquarters of the Armed Resistance (the CG/CVL). He had gained his military experience as a staff officer in World War I and had helped plan the final victory of Vittorio Veneto. With unflagging zeal Parri sought to endue the Resistenza with moral fervor, and he was warmly loved by his men, who nicknamed him "Zio Maurizio." Communists, however, made fun of Parri's "romantic idealization" of the people who supposedly could be animated and guided simply by example; they argued, instead, that the Resistance chieftains must look upon the people with no Mazzinian illusions and provide them with sturdy leadership.[93]

The most vaunted local GL commander was Tancredi ("Duccio") Galimberti, an idealistic lawyer from Cuneo in southwestern Piedmont. Immediately after announcement of the July 25 *coup d'état* he addressed his fellow townsmen from his office balcony on the central square, urging war against Germany. In September he recruited a civilian partisan force which won an enviable reputation during the next fifteen months and served

---

[93] Catalano, *Storia del CLNAI*, pp. 77–81; Battaglia, *SRI*, p. 192; Valiani, *Tutte le strade conducono a Roma*, pp. 113–115. *Cf.* F. Parri, "Il CLN e la guerra partigiana," in *Lezioni sull'antifascismo*, p. 215 ff.

as a matrix for other GL formations in the region. Galimberti's close friend, Avv. Dante Livio Bianco, a skilled Alpinist, was another crack GL field officer; his men also fought in the Cuneese. Livio Bianco was one of the first Resistance veterans to pen a coherent, incisive historical account of the partisan movement in his sector.[94] Closely associated with these men in initiating the *partigianeria* was a Celliniesque personality, the doughty Carrarese sculptor, Lieutenant Nardo Dunchi, who has written a sprightly personal account of the heroic phase of the Resistance.[95] The distinguished young historian and ex-*fuoruscito*, Franco Venturi, was another politico-military director in Piedmont. Filippo Beltrami, a sensitive architect and Army captain from Milan, went into the Lake Orta-Omegna zone above Novara to rival Moscatelli in exploits. Beltrami was one of the first commanders to die on the field of battle (February 12, 1944). By that time his group of 70 had grown to some 700. His personal politics were divided between the Pd'A and PLI.[96]

From the accounts of certain Communist and Actionist writers, one might suppose that the other political parties were scarcely represented in the *macchia*. That would be an inaccurate supposition; what is true is that the other CLN parties entered the Armed Resistance on a considerably smaller scale except in some localized sectors where they possessed sturdy roots. Both the Christian Democrats and the Liberals at first preferred to buttress the existing Autonomi rather than institute separate units of their own. A substantial proportion of the Autonomi were sincere Catholics who eventually took out DC party cards. The Christian Democrats' close links with the Church often enabled them to gain the use of convents and other suitable places for succoring the wounded and ill and for hiding refugee Jews and PW's. The DC tried (not too successfully) to introduce military chaplains into all of the covert fighting forces.

---

[94] *Cf.* his autobiographical "Venti mesi di guerra partigiana nel Cuneese," first published in *Nuovi Quaderni di Giustizia e Libertà*, Nos. 5–6 (Jan.–Aug. 1945), pp. 13–98, and reprinted in his *Guerra partigiana*, edited posthumously by Agosti and Venturi. Bianco died in a mountaineering accident in 1953.

[95] Nardo Dunchi, *Memorie partigiane* (Florence, 1957).

[96] *Cf.* biography by his widow, Giuliana Beltrami, *Il Capitano* (Milan, 1946); A. Marchetti, *Ribelli* (Milan, 1947), p. 9 ff.; *La Resistenza a Omegna* (Novara, 1953).

In the course of 1944 and 1945 the Christian Democrats found it expedient in certain areas to sponsor their own fighting units, often with the help of ex-Army men. Their "Fiamma Verde" brigades were to be found especially in Lombardy, the three Venetias, and to some extent in Emilia. In Val d'Ossola, northwest of Milan, the Christian Democrats built up the plucky "Di Dio" divisional group that played a stellar role during the autumn of 1944 when that sector enjoyed a few weeks of independence. From the Milanese headquarters of the Armed Resistance, Enrico Mattei co-ordinated the military efforts of the DC. He claimed to have some 65,000 men under his command prior to the great influx at the moment of final insurrection.[97]

The Liberals, like the Christian Democrats, concentrated first on augmenting the numerous Autonomi formations, especially in the Langhe sector of southeastern Piedmont. There Major Enrico Martini ("Mauri") commanded some 6,000 patriots and for a long time held undisputed sway over that strategic zone leading to Genoa.[98] In Lombardy, Edgardo Sogno ("Franchi") was a fighter to be reckoned with; he was in radio communication with the Allies and controlled a nerve center in the Resistenza Supreme Military Command after the spring of 1944.[99]

The Socialists generally entered the *macchia* late. Finding it difficult to compete with the Garibaldini and Giellisti for scarce manpower in the hills, they bent their efforts toward mobilizing urban fighting groups (together with the PCI, with whom they had renewed their "unity of action" pact on September 28, 1943) and recruiting factory workers for the domestic politico-economic "class struggles" to come. They obviously felt more at home in this kind of task. Yet on occasion they canvassed the countryside and rounded up enough "left-overs" to outfit "Matteotti" brigades that were congregated chiefly in the Lombard and Piedmontese uplands. The first such PSIUP force was

[97] Enrico Mattei, *L'apporto delle forze partigiane DC alla guerra di liberazione* (Milan, 1946), portions of which are also cited in Tupini, *I Democratici Cristiani*, pp. 95–105; Achille Marazza, "I Cattolici e la Resistenza," *MLI*, No. 43 (1956), pp. 3–15; *Donne cristiane nella Resistenza: Testimonianze e documentazioni sul contributo femminile alla lotta partigiana in Lombardia*, ed. Mov. femminile della DC di Milano (Milan, 1956).

[98] See his memoirs, *Con la libertà e per la libertà*.

[99] See his memoirs, *Guerra senza bandiera* (Milan, 1950).

fielded in the autumn of 1943 near Asti by Renato Martorelli, while in the Val d'Ossola hydroelectric center other contingents were amassed by Professor Tibaldi, Mario and Corrado Bonfantini.[100]

Though the Italian Republican Party (formally reconstituted in March 1944) almost never joined the CLN's, it sponsored some fighting groups in the Marches and Romagna, and a "Mazzini" unit in Lombardy. Finally, some Anarcho-Syndicalists near Carrara and Leghorn manned a few libertarian "Schirru" and "Malatesta" cadres which were tied in with the "Matteotti" formations.[101]

Social composition

Italy's "Second Risorgimento" was characterized by much greater popular participation than her original one, even though the resistants numbered but a small fraction of the total population.[102] Accurate statistics about the social composition of the underground are difficult to compile. Proportions varied in accordance with the geography of the zone, political complexion of the covert groups, and the season. Some analyses of limited areas are suggestive, however. In Piedmont (where about one third of the partisans were concentrated) one investigator found that the patriot personnel consisted of 30.50 per cent laborers, 13.62 per cent artisans, 20.39 per cent farmers, 29.89 per cent middle class, and 5.6 per cent well-to-do; but his criteria for making these distinctions are not very clear.[103] A survey of 6,181 members of certain GL formations in Piedmont revealed 1,859 workers; 1,283 peasant farmers; 738 artisans; 707 students; 541 clerks;

[100] Carli-Ballola, Sdr, pp. 47–50, 85–89, and passim. His study is the most complete Socialist interpretation of the epopee.

[101] Ibid., pp. 92–93.

[102] Professor Ettore Passerin d'Entrèves has traced interesting similarities between the ethical and religious impulses of the Risorgimento and those of the Armed Resistance in an article, "Risorgimento e Resistenza," Civitas, VI (1955), pp. 85–91. So has Franco Salvi, "Valori morali della Resistenza," ibid., pp. 9–14; and Paolo Emilio Taviani, "Il significato della Resistenza," ibid., pp. 3–8; and Elizabeth Wiskemann, "Italian Resistance Movement," in Arnold and Veronica Toynbee (eds.), Hitler's Europe (London, 1954), p. 331. Luigi Bulferetti in his "Risorgimento e Resistenza—gli Artom," MLI, No. 34/35 (1955), pp. 44–55, (and others too) has suggested caution in making facile comparisons of the two superficially similar historical movements.

[103] Cited in article by M. Niccoli, "Resistenza Italiana," Enciclopedia Italiana, Seconda Appendice, 1938–1948, I–Z, 687.

331 professionalists; 259 businessmen; 103 domestic servants; 102 state employees; 90 *Carabinieri* and Finance Guards; 72 officials of the Società Piemontese Elettrica; 54 tank men and truck drivers; 38 industrialists; and 4 priests.[104]

An indication of the age level (and also, to some extent, of the previous military experience) of the fighters can be derived from the fact that men of the military classes of 1920–1925 (who were subject to military conscription in this period) comprised 46.3 per cent of the total; those of the classes of 1910–1919 and of 1926–1927 (subject only to labor service) were 40.8 per cent; and those of other military classes were 12.9 per cent.[105] One should also recall the presence, especially in the initial period, of several thousand Allied prisoners of war, particularly in Lombardy, Tuscany, the Abruzzi, and the Marches. Most, but not all, preferred to be evacuated as soon as this was feasible.[106]

The number of fighters directly involved in the Armed Resistance fluctuated widely. During the fall of 1943 several thousand volunteered, but the harsh winter and the enemy comb-outs reduced them to 9,000 or 10,000 in the North by the end of January 1944. Thereafter the number rose rapidly, approaching 100,-000 by midsummer when the forces were becoming unified. During the winter of 1944–1945 it declined again, but increased once more after February until, swelled by eleventh-hour converts, it reached perhaps 150,000 by the April 1945 insurrection.[107] Perhaps two or three times that number could be classified as sympathizers who stayed home, covertly furnishing their friends and relatives in the bands money, supplies, and medicines.[108]

Though the hard core of resistants remained relatively small, this does not mean that most of the population was hostile to their cause. Quite the contrary. After July 25, 1943, there were

[104] Mario Giovana, "La composizione sociale delle formazioni 'GL' in Piemonte," *MLI*, No. 10 (1951), pp. 20–29.

[105] Niccoli, *Enciclopedia Italiana, Seconda Appendice*, 1938–1948, I–Z, 687.

[106] See *infra*, Ch. vii, Early Allied liaison with the Resistance.

[107] Massimo Salvadori-Paleotti, "The Patriot Movement in Italy," *Foreign Affairs*, xxiv (1946), pp. 545–546; *cf.* his *SRI*, p. 86, and *passim*; Battaglia, *SRI*, pp. 337–338, and *passim*. These figures include both overt bands in the hills and covert ones in the towns and open countryside. They coincide basically with estimates made by OSS, Research and Analysis Branch Study No. 2993, *The Contribution of the Italian Partisans to the Allied War Effort* (Washington, March 31, 1945), pp. 3–4. *Cf.* F. Parri, "Relazione introduttiva" al III Convegno di Studi sulla Storia del Movimento di Liberazione, *MLI*, No. 52/53 (1958), 9 ff.

[108] Salvadori, *SRI*, p. 95.

few genuine Fascists left in the North. Those industrialists and businessmen who lost their enthusiasm for the dictatorship when World War II began had still less use for Mussolini's RSI.[109] Upper- and middle-class groups who formerly favored Fascism for selfish motives quietly withdrew their support. Though they hesitated to show open hostility, there was no doubt that erstwhile "half-Fascists" (to use Salvadori's epithet) were becoming at least "passive anti-Fascists." To be sure, they often saw in the Social-Communist wing a danger of leftist totalitarianism, but they were willing to go along with the moderate Liberals and Christian Democrats and extend secret financial help to them. As a matter of fact, many bankers became indispensable friends of the patriots, and two of the nation's biggest financial institutions (Credito Italiano and Banca Commerciale Italiana) eventually channeled most of the money that the Allies were to make available to the underground.[110] Many industrialists in Turin and the Valsesia and Biellese sectors subsidized local bands—and not necessarily as a means of "insurance." Such facts helped to explain why a large segment of the banking and industrial community escaped arrest or execution at the hands of the insurgents during the turbulent days of the Liberation.[111]

Traditionally, Italian peasants and farmers have been less interested in politics than urbanites; nevertheless, they were hospitable to the partisans as well as to the many ex-PW's who sought shelter.[112] After all, many of them asked themselves, were not these renitents also *figli di mamma* ("mothers' sons")? When the Germans launched their counteroffensives at the end of 1943 they tried to destroy this feeling of solidarity between peasants and patriots. And sometimes they succeeded. Most peasants did not relish the risk of harboring guerrillas who un-

[109] Even Fascist writers have conceded this. *Cf.* Dolfin, *Con Mussolini nella tragedia*, p. 120.

[110] See *infra*, Ch. IX. As early as September and October 1943 Dr. Alfredo Pizzoni of Credito Italiano and head of the Milan CLN finance subcommittee amassed 8,000,000 lire, three fourths of which was spent aiding the evacuation of thousands of ex-PW's and Jewish internees. A. Pizzoni, "Il finanziamento della Resistenza," *MLI*, No. 24 (May 1953), p. 49 ff.

[111] Salvadori-Paleotti, *Foreign Affairs*, xxiv (1946), p. 548; *cf.* Giorgio Vaccarino, "Alcuni documenti delle gerarchie di Salò sull'industria italiana e sulla classe industriale del Nord," *MLI*, No. 11 (1951), p. 41; Carli-Ballola, *Sdr*, pp. 74–76.

[112] Illustrative of this social characteristic is the diary kept in Tuscany by Iris Origo, *War in Val d'Orcia* (London, 1947; 1956).

wittingly often left behind compromising evidence of their stay. Furthermore, they resented the way some bands in the poorer areas lived off the land. Still, most peasants succored the covert fighters. Their growing appreciation was revealed by their tendency to substitute the affirmative labels "patriots" and "partisans" for the negative one "rebels" (which had been so common during the initial weeks of the Armed Resistance).[113]

During the winter many patriots (especially the Garibaldini) romantically identified themselves with their rural surroundings, affecting such prosopopoeias of the animal world as Volpe ("Fox"), Lupo ("Wolf"), Corvo ("Crow"), Struzzo ("Ostrich"), and Pecora ("Sheep"). Legendary heroes suggested several common names: Rolando, Rinaldo, and Guerrino. Some chose epithets describing natural phenomena: Terremoto ("Earthquake"), Fulmine ("Lightning"), Saetta ("Thunderbolt"), Tempesta ("Storm"), and Turbine ("Whirlwind"). Such revolutionary heroes as Gracco, Spartaco, and Robespierre were also re-evoked. Even the American comic strips registered an impact, noticeable in names like Tarzan and Gordon. Partisans from the South usually preferred to go by the name of their home town.[114]

Available evidence suggests that most parish priests (especially in Piedmont and in the Friuli region, but less so in anticlerical Emilia) were sympathetic to the guerrillas, though they naturally aspired to keep violence to a minimum. After all, the lower clergy usually came from and knew intimately the common people. Among the higher clergy there was more ambiguity of attitude, more *attesismo* ("watchful waiting"), and in some cases unconcealed aversion for the Armed Resistance.[115]

First fighting

The first evidence of partisan warfare in Piedmont was in mid-September 1943 at the village of Boves, south of Cuneo. There a German officer was killed by one of the Autonomi led

[113] Bianco, *Guerra partigiana*, pp. 35–37; Carli-Ballola, *Sdr*, pp. 70–74.
[114] Battaglia, *SRI*, pp. 208–211.
[115] Mattei, *L'apporto delle forze partigiane DC alla guerra di liberazione*, cited in Tupini, *I Democratici Cristiani*, pp. 96–97; Bianco, *Guerra partigiana*, pp. 36–37; G. Rovero, "Il clero piemontese della Resistenza," in *Aspetti della Resistenza in Piemonte*, pp. 41–67; Battaglia, *SRI*, pp. 293–298; Ragghianti, *Disegno della liberazione italiana*, p. 115; Carli-Ballola, *Sdr*, p. 74.

by Lieutenant Ignazio Vian. On the 19th the Germans inflicted a fearful reprisal, killing twenty-four civilians (including the local priest) and burning the village.[116] Vian and his men kept up the struggle, and on Christmas Eve blew up the viaduct on the Cuneo-Ventimiglia railway line. By the following July the Germans had caught the fervently religious young officer and hanged him from a tree in Turin.[117] Meantime, news of the butchery at Boves helped to speed recruitments in both the autonomous and political bands. Within a few weeks rival groups were guarding jealously such sectors as the Valsesia, Biellese, Chisone-Sangone, Cuneese, and especially the Langhe-Monferrato (dominated by the Autonomi of Enrico Martini ["Mauri"]). Eventually there were fifteen autonomous divisions in Piedmont.

In central Italy, Teramo, nestling in the Abruzzi highlands northeast of Gran Sasso, stood out as an early rallying point of the Autonomi. There several hundred disbanded components of the "Legnano" division quickly reassembled in September as the "Banda di Bosco Martese" and carried out some missions until the enemy dispersed them after three days' hard fighting (September 25–27).[118] In Umbria and the Marches some Slavic ex-PW's provided impetus for guerrilla bands.[119] Another epicenter of fighting was Latium, where in December a "Centro Militare" was established and over one hundred detachments operated, especially in the Castelli Romani. Not attempting to capture entire valleys, they infiltrated strategic zones and kept up constant harassment, hopeful that the Allies soon would arrive. With anarchistic ingenuity they did their best to attack enemy vehicles with incendiary bombs, ambush isolated detachments, and raid inadequately guarded supply dumps. Everywhere they strewed sharp-pointed polyhedrons along the roadway to puncture the enemy's tires. They paid careful attention to dynamiting

[116] Vittorio E. Giuntella, *Un capo della Resistenza in Piemonte, Ignazio Vian, il difensore di Boves* (Rome, 1954).

[117] B. Giuliano, "Vita della Banda di Boves," *Il Ponte*, I (1945), pp. 520–530. Earlier in December they seized brief control of the border town of Vinadio. Cf. Bianco, *Guerra partigiana*, pp. 15–16; *Aspetti della Resistenza in Piemonte*, pp. 155–181; Carli-Ballola, *Sdr*, pp. 39–41; and Battaglia, *SRI*, p. 140.

[118] Pio Costantini, "La Resistenza a Chieti," *Il Ponte*, XIII (1957), pp. 382–389; Battaglia, *SRI*, pp. 140–141, 185.

[119] Roberto Battaglia, *Un uomo, un partigiano* (Florence, 1945), pp. 23–42, 163–168. The author was commander of the "Lunense" division and fought in Massa and Carrara.

bridges and railroads. Perhaps the most audacious such explosion in central Italy was the mining of a bridge and stretch of track on the Rome-Cassino line on December 20, which resulted in derailing a troop train and the explosion of another train loaded with munitions and gasoline.[120]

Elsewhere in central Italy the partisan movement developed slowly during the first autumn. Generally speaking, it was less organic and political south of Florence than in the North. In Rome (after the abortive resistance put up by the clandestine anti-Fascist Military Junta and units of the Army at the moment of the armistice proclamation) it depended largely on stalwarts like Colonel di Montezemolo, many of whom were brought into liaison with the Brindisi government. Perhaps there simply was not enough time to create in central Italy the kind of "free state within enemy territory" that often was staked out in the North. Moreover, the social structure of much of middle Italy rested on the agrarian *mezzadria*; such people were not nearly so politically advanced as those in the more industrialized North.[121]

Near Genoa, Ottorino ("Nullo") Balduzzi ("Otto"), a medical professor, headed an efficient covert intelligence service, which was in radio contact with the Allies from October 1943 until its collapse in March 1944.[122] To the east and inland from LaSpezia in the Garfagnana mountains other compact bands existed.[123]

In Milan and other cities small, Communist-sponsored terroristic groups soon appeared;[124] but in the exposed Lombard plain irregular warfare was not very feasible. In the uplands, however, occurred one of the first direct military encounters between partisans (the "Pisacane" group) and the enemy. This skirmish took place at Pizzo d'Erna, near Lecco to the north of Milan, on October 17-20. The patriots' lack of success against 1,000 Germans who were equipped with light artillery[125] led some right-wing anti-Fascists to advocate a more cautious policy,

[120] P. Levi-Cavaglione, *Guerriglia nei Castelli Romani* (*diario di un partigiano dal 3 ottobre 1943 al 4 marzo 1944*) (Rome, 1945), pp. 91-96; Comando Raggrupamento Bande Partigiane Italia Centrale, *Attività delle bande* (Rome, 1945), p. 27.
[121] Salvadori, SRI, pp. 75-76; Battaglia, SRI, p. 224.
[122] See *infra*, Ch. vii, Early Allied liaison with the Resistance.
[123] Baccino, *Contributo alla storia della Resistenza di Genova*, p. 67.
[124] See *infra*, Ch. vii, Gappisti.
[125] The partisans lost seven dead and ten wounded; the Germans, some thirty killed and wounded. M. DeMicheli, *Uomini sui monti* (Rome, 1953), p. 48.

pejoratively called *attendismo* or *attesismo* ("watchful waiting"), until the approach of the Allies, in the hope of avoiding needless reprisals against the civilians. Static *attesismo* became rather common that first fall when hopes were still high for an early arrival of the Anglo-Americans. Before long, though, certain left-wingers perceived that *attesismo* might endanger their political goals. Thus Pietro Secchia, PCI Political Commissar-General in the North, published in November a predicatory article in the covert *La nostra lotta* denouncing "watchful waiting" and advocating an all-out fight.[126] The much-abused term *attesismo* came often to be hurled against one's rivals in defamatory fashion.[127] During this period of rising polemics, Christian Democratic *Fiamme Verdi* ("Green Flames") combat units emerged in the mountains above Bergamo and Brescia. Their political orientation was not much different from that of the Autonomi.[128] GL's First Alpine Division saw action in the Valtellina near Sondrio.[129]

Because of inadequate supplies and support, very few bands could be armed in the Emilian Apennines during the first winter. This was also the case in the Trentino and Alto Adige, straddling the enemy communication lines over the Brenner. The Germans had firm control of the latter zones; indeed, they had annexed and relabeled them. In view of the heavy enemy concentrations, patriots there worked amid great handicaps.[130]

But in northern Venetia, where the peasantry was anti-German by tradition, the patriot movement quickly gained momentum. In fact, conditions there most nearly approximated those in Piedmont, thanks partly to the favorable terrain and partly to the disintegration of the Italian Second Army, many of whose *sbandati* flocked into guerrilla units.[131] The Pre-Alpine Belluno zone (incorporated by the Germans into the South

---

[126] Cf. *supra*, n. 90; reprinted in Secchia, *I Comunisti e l'insurrezione*.

[127] See discussion in Rome *Il Mondo*, Feb. 1, 22, and Mar. 1, 1955.

[128] Alfonso Vajana, *Bergamo nel "ventennio" e nella Resistenza* (2 vols.; Bergamo, 1957).

[129] Ideale Cannella, "La prima divisione alpina nella Resistenza in Valtellina," *MLI*, No. 40 (1956), pp. 3–17.

[130] Antonio Radice, *La Resistenza nel Trentino, 1943–1945* (Rovereto, 1960); Antonio Radice, "La Resistenza trentina ed il problema istituzionale," *MLI*, No. 52/53 (1958), pp. 136–145; Bice Rizzi (ed.), "La correspondenza clandestina fra Giannantonio Manci e Gigino Battisti tra la fine del '43 e il maggio del '44," *MLI*, No. 37 (1955), pp. 32–43.

[131] F. Parri, "Gli inizi della Resistenza," *MLI*, No. 34/35 (1955), p. 19.

Tyrol) above Vicenza and Padua became a patriot stronghold very early. One of the Garibaldi forces in this area was the redoubtable "Nino Nannetti" division, which had moved en masse from the less defensible Apennines above Bologna, and which was christened for a PCI martyr in the Spanish Civil War.[132]

The Friuli uplands of the Isonzo and Tagliamento rivers farther east above Udine were other patriot bastions. Some officers of the Alpine regiments of the "Tridentina" division organized autonomous units which came to be styled the "Osoppo-Friuli," taking their name from an ancient fort that for centuries had protected the Venetian Republic from northern invaders. Interestingly, the Pd'A joined the DC in backing these Autonomi, doubtless thinking that this was the best way to checkmate PCI Garibaldi units in the stanchly Catholic region. Thus the Friuli was one of the first zones to support more or less permanently integrated partisan formations. In ensuing months bitter rivalry between the Osoppo and Garibaldini ended in bloody victory for the latter. Harbingers of future trouble with Tito's Partisans were discernible in certain operational accords effected late in September by Ing. Fermo Solari ("Somma"), the Pd'A political commissar, with Slavic guerrilla forces at San Leonardo del Natisone.[133]

The University of Padua served as a Resistenza base throughout the German occupation. Professor Concetto Marchesi, the Communist Latinist who had been named rector by the Badoglio government, opened the academic year in November 1943 not in the name of the King but of the "workers, artists, and scientists." He had scarcely finished his prolusion when uniformed militiamen of the RSI pushed him off the stage. Within a few days Marchesi fled to Switzerland, leaving behind an "Appeal to the Students," dated December 1. Professor Egidio Meneghetti next took over the direction of the academic refractories who

---

[132] M. DeMicheli, 7ma GAP (Rome, 1954), p. 49; Arcangelo Bortolotto, "Ricordi sulla costituzione delle forze di resistenza delle bande armate alpine venete nelle Alpi e Prealpi bellunesi e feltrine nel 1943," MLI, No. 34/35 (1955), pp. 37–43.

[133] Fermo Solari, "Le origini della Resistenza Friulana e la prima formazione GL," MLI, No. 34/35 (1955), pp. 128–133; R. Trabucchi, "Il primo convegno di studi sulla Resistenza nel Veneto," ibid., No. 37 (1955), pp. 48–50; Salvadori, SRI, p. 82; Teodolfo Tessari, Le origine della resistenza nel Veneto (sett. 1943–aprile 1944) (Venice, 1959).

enterprisingly produced explosives in the university's chemistry institute. Later Meneghetti headed the Venetian CLN, and in free moments he composed verses extolling the underground struggle.[134]

For a few weeks during the autumn and winter of 1943 the Venetian Resistenza was also spearheaded by the Giellista, Silvio Trentin, the eminent professor of constitutional law who had returned in September from years of exile in Toulouse. Trentin had barely found shelter in his native region when, by almost unanimous agreement, he was accorded a pivotal post in the underground. After a few weeks the enemy learned his true identity and was about to arrest him when he suddenly died of a heart ailment on March 12, 1944, in Treviso. Pd'A sympathizers christened one of their brigades in the region in his honor; all of its leaders eventually lost their lives.[135]

In September 1943 Tito's men gained temporary control of the Istrian peninsula. Within a few weeks, however, the Germans expelled them and annexed most of the region. Throughout the remaining struggle this area, with its mixed ethnic groups, bedeviled the Italian patriots with thorny political problems. Despite the handicaps, some partisan groups were recruited in the shipyards of Monfalcone, the University of Trieste, and elsewhere in Venezia Giulia.[136]

The first of the systematic *rastrellamenti* (*Anglice*, "rakings" or "comb-outs") against the partisans was launched on December 31, 1943, against the Boves band in southwestern Piedmont. After three days the band was dispersed. On January 12, 1944, the enemy turned on Galimberti's men in Val Grana; a month later they attacked the remnants of Vian and those of Martini

[134] Prof. Egidio Meneghetti, "Cronaca dell'Università di Padova," *Mercurio* (*Anche l'Italia ha vinto*) (Dec. 1945), pp. 179–180; E. Meneghetti, *La partigiana nuda e altre cante* (Milan-Rome, 1958), pp. 1–73; Anonymous, *L'Università di Padova durante l'occupazione tedesca* (Padua, 1946), p. 68; Battaglia, SRI, pp. 177–178. The "Appeal" is reprinted in Milan and Vighi (eds.), *La Resistenza al fascismo*, pp. 113–115. For a collection of Professor Marchesi's political writings, see *Scritti politici di Concetto Marchesi*, ed. Maria Todaro-Faranda (Rome, 1958).
[135] Gavagnin, *Vent'anni di resistenza al fascismo*, pp. 432–444; Norberto Bobbio, *Ricordo di Silvio Trentin* (Venice, 1955).
[136] Parri, MLI, No. 34/35 (1955), 19; Antonio Luksich-Jamini, "La lotta nell'Istria e a Fiume dall'8 settembre al 15 novembre 1943," *ibid.*, No. 49 (1957), pp. 30–47.

in the Monregalese. Soon it was the turn of Beltrami (who was killed) and of Moscatelli. It took time for the partisans to learn the value of fluid defense rather than rigid, futile efforts to hang on to territory.[137]

Gappisti

The Resistenza Armata was not restricted just to the hills and countryside. As early as the fall of 1943 the Communists (and sometimes the Socialists too) organized tightly knit bands of young terrorists called Gappisti (GAP; "Gruppi di Azione Popolare"). Three or four boys in their teens, led by a PCI activist, constituted a group, which worked in absolute secrecy and made use of the party's efficient intelligence network. According to Secchia, there were never more than forty to fifty Gappisti at work in the large industrial cities at any one time; but because of high casualties the turnover was great. Their conspiratorial techniques were borrowed largely from the French Résistance by Ilio Barontini, a one-time Tuscan railway worker and veteran of the Spanish Civil War who eventually became commander of the PCI partisan formations in Emilia. Giovanni Pesce ("Visone"), who had also seen service with the international brigades in Spain, was a pivotal organizer in Turin and Milan, as was Giacomo Buranello in Genoa.[138]

Blowing up command posts, assassinating Fascist bigwigs, killing enemy sentinels—indeed, almost any mission that lent itself to audacious hit-and-run, cloak-and-dagger tactics—were the kind of thing in which the Gappisti gloried. The PCI, at least, felt that the resultant danger of reprisals was worth the price if it imbued the city folk with the spirit of recklessness necessary for a successful insurrection.

Agitation in the factories

It is no exaggeration to say that in Turin and certain other industrial cities "agitation committees" forged ahead of both the partisan bands and CLN's in offering resistance to the enemy.

---

[137] Bianco, *Guerra partigiana*, pp. 38–45; Giovanni Monaco, *Pietà l'è morta* (Milan, 1955), pp. 48–61; Martini, *Con la libertà e per la libertà*, pp. 58–61.

[138] Secchia, *MLI*, No. 55 (1959), 63; Longo, *Un popolo alla macchia*, pp. 177–180; DeMicheli, 7ma GAP, *passim*; Carli-Ballola, *Sdr*, pp. 94–96; Giovanni Pesce, *Soldati senza uniforme* (Rome, 1950).

These agitation committees dated from September 1943, when it became apparent that the "internal commissions," in process of development in the factories during Badoglio's "45 days," were going to be subverted by the neo-Fascists. The Communists thereupon seized the initiative and converted them into secret agitation committees. Unlike the multiparty CLN's, these factory agencies remained strictly Red strongholds.[139] They were responsible for most of the political overtones that surrounded the wave of strikes of November and December 1943 and those of the ensuing March. In addition, there were "clandestine syndical committees," established outside the factories by the CLN to counterbalance the neo-Fascist syndicates. In them the three *partiti di massa* enjoyed equal representation.[140]

It was not difficult to stir up the workers in view of the hardships caused by Allied bombings, layoffs with consequent peril of being conscripted by the Germans, ever-mounting inflation, and shortages of fuel and rationed goods. The incident that triggered the first work stoppage in Turin on November 16 was an Allied raid which caused the death of many workers in a factory whose doors had been barricaded. Metallurgical workers were in the vanguard of demonstrators. Mussolini's officials conceded some wage demands but would not reinstate the internal commissions. Although a German colonel threatened punishment to anyone who interfered with war production, the trouble did not cease. Communists called a new strike on December 1—prematurely, it proved, for only one other party (Pd'A) in the Turin CLN was ready to support the gambit. Nevertheless, production came to a near standstill for nine days. Other strikes occurred in Milan and were perhaps more effective than Turin's, despite German seizure of hostages. In the Communist bastion of Genoa, where shipyard workers were seething, a strike began in mid-December and spread to near-by Savona. Thus from mid-November until Christmas many northern plants faced one stoppage after another; the underground had made a start in checkmating Mussolini's pseudosocialistic propaganda.

On balance, however, these winter strikes were not nearly so

[139] Vaccarino, "Il movimento operaio a Torino nei primi mesi della crisi italiana," *MLI*, No. 20 (1952), pp. 42–43.
[140] Carli-Ballola, *Sdr*, pp. 96–100.

effective as those of either March 1943 or March 1944. They demonstrated clearly the need for better co-ordination of the Armed Resistance, and thus provided one of the incentives that led to the establishment of the autonomous CLNAI (CLN for Upper Italy) in Milan on January 31, 1944.[141]

Early Allied liaison with the Resistance: SF and OSS

From the very first, militants in the Armed Resistance were more aware of the Anglo-Americans in the South than vice versa. But in time a few Allied leaders learned a little about the behind-the-lines Resistenza and, despite considerable initial diffidence, gradually came to appreciate its usefulness and to discard many clichés about Italy's being an enemy country peopled by fine fiddlers and barbers but few first-rate fighters. Reliable intelligence made it clear that not only were the great majority of "Eye-ties" in the North pro-Allied but that many were anxious to fight. If the Allies, who were handicapped by their own numerical inferiority in the Mediterranean theater of operations, could make use of the northern patriots, the latter might help them speed their advance up the rugged peninsula. Liaison with the partisans thus became urgent.

Allied communication with the underground was effected chiefly through such "combined operation" (*i.e.*, joint land, sea, and air force) agencies as the British Special Operations Executive (SOE), better known in Italy as Special Forces (SF), and the American Office of Strategic Services (OSS). The British wisely tried to keep their SOE (which was organized early in the war and reorganized in the fall of 1943 after a fiasco in Holland) distinct from their Intelligence Service. The former was not concerned with espionage but with encouraging long-term resistance behind the lines through the dispatch of liaison officers and supplies. More than 500 SOE agents were sent out in three years, their "useful life" before "expenditure" being estimated as six months.[142]

[141] Vaccarino, MLI, No. 20 (1952), pp. 10–29; Secchia, *I Comunisti e l'insurrezione*, pp. 77–87; Longo, *Sulla via dell'insurrezione*, pp. 87–126; Longo, *Un popolo alla macchia*, pp. 141–147; Valiani, *Tutte le strade conducono a Roma*, pp. 123–124, 154–155; Battaglia, *SRI*, pp. 167–173; Carli-Ballola, *Sdr*, pp. 100–104; Catalano, *Storia del CLNAI*, pp. 90–97.
[142] See lecture of General Sir Colin Gubbins, top commander of SOE during the final two years of the war, in *Journal of the Royal United Service Institution*, XCIII (April 1948).

In 1941 the SOE laid down basic policy for dealing with European underground movements. It called for reconciling disparate resistance factions in order "to bring them effectively under the common authority of a British Command." Movements should be restrained "from activities which would lead to their premature destruction. Their role [should rather be] to organize a common front, and secretly to build up a disciplined force whose operations could be connected at a later stage directly with those of the Allies." [143] For a mixture of military, security, and political reasons, SOE did not seek to promote large underground armies to which they would have to divulge "classified" information regarding impending strategy. Instead, SOE encouraged specific types of sabotage and subversion. Thus in June 1943, Lieutenant General F. E. Morgan, British Chief of Staff to the Supreme Allied Command, remarked that "the assistance of the [French Résistance] groups should . . . be treated as a bonus rather than an essential part of the [Allied invasion] plan." His successors continued this policy, though some changes in practice had to be made as a result of the vast expansion of the *maquis* in 1943 and early 1944 and General DeGaulle's augmented strength in the interior. Alterations also had to be made in strife-torn Yugoslavia during the same period.[144] According to SF-man Massimo Salvadori (who eventually became liaison officer in Milan between the Allied Fifteenth Army Group and the Armed Resistance headquarters), General Bernard Montgomery had very little confidence in guerrilla warfare and was therefore unwilling to furnish much material assistance.[145]

At the time of the Salerno invasion British Colonel Alp supervised the Special Forces section for Italy from his operational headquarters in Blida, near Algiers. After a few weeks Navy Captain Gery Holdsworth replaced him. Not till the spring of 1944 were headquarters transferred to Bari.

In addition to SF and OSS men there were British Intelligence

---

[143] John Ehrman, *Grand Strategy*, v, August 1943–September 1944 (London, 1956), p. 77 ff. Ehrman's six volumes form a part of the *History of the Second World War, United Kingdom Military Series*, ed. James R. M. Butler (London, 1956–1957). *Cf.* F. Deakin, "Great Britain and the European Resistance," and N. Kogan, "American Policies toward European Resistance Movements," II International Congress on the History of the Resistance, Milan, March 26–29, 1961.

[144] *Ibid.*, pp. 76–83, 270–278, for a discussion of SOE shifts regarding the Yugoslav Resistance; and pp. 321–331 regarding the French Resistance.

[145] Salvadori, *Resistenza ed azione*, p. 214.

Service agents and "A-Force" missions operating behind the lines, often in overlapping and rival fashion, to the bewilderment of Italians who worked with them. The A-Force missions sought to help Allied PW's escape from enemy territory. They had plenty of work in Italy, where thousands of such prisoners suddenly found themselves emancipated on September 8, only to be in danger of recapture by the Germans. Many of the prisoners gravitated into the Resistenza Armata during its initial weeks (as many as one fourth of the original resistants in Lombardy were reputed to be ex-PW's), but most desired to get back to their own side of the lines as soon as possible.[146] Of some "80,000 of these men, conspicuously clothed in battle-dress and in the main with little knowledge of the language or geography of the country, at least ten thousand," according to Prime Minister Churchill, "mostly succoured by the local population with civilian clothes, were guided to safety, thanks to the risks taken by members of the Italian Resistance and the simple people of the countryside." [147] This furtive activity continued throughout the war but reached its peak in November 1943. Though dozens of escape routes were used, most PW's passed through Milan en route to Switzerland. The partisans and the Milan CLN offered indispensable aid in this work, paying most of the costs (some six of the 8,000,000 lire total) out of their own limited funds.[148] Most of the Allied personnel who escaped in this way were enthusiastic about the Italian partisans and peasants, reported a Second New Zealand Division intelligence officer.[149]

In the fall of 1943, OSS in Italy was being reorganized more or less along the British pattern, though it did not make so neat a differentiation between intelligence gathering and Resistance stimulation. As a matter of fact, most OSS missions concerned themselves only secondarily with the latter.[150] Apart from the more-or-less overt Research and Analysis Branch (headed by the young Harvard-trained historian, H. Stuart Hughes), OSS had three major covert sections. The first of these was Secret Intelli-

[146] Catalano, *Storia del CLNAI*, p. 61; Salvadori, *SRI*, p. 117; *cf.* Gordon Lett, *Rossano (An Adventure of the Italian Resistance)* (London, 1955).

[147] Winston S. Churchill, *Closing the Ring* (Boston, 1951), pp. 187–188.

[148] G. Bacciagaluppi, "Rapporto finale sull'attività svolta dal CLN Alta Italia in favore di ex-prigionieri di guerra alleata," *MLI*, No. 33 (1954), pp. 3–31.

[149] Geoffrey Cox, *The Road to Trieste* (London, 1947), pp. 152–153.

[150] Salvadori, *RSI*, pp. 113–114, 118.

gence (SI), the real espionage groups behind the lines who ferreted out all sorts of information useful to military commanders. In addition, there were Special Operations (SO) units, consisting of up to five men dressed in full military uniform. These men were skilled in the techniques of sabotage and demolition. After being dropped a short distance behind the lines to blow up communications systems, radio stations, gasoline and ammunition dumps, bridges, and other targets, they would go into hiding and await the arrival of their fellow combat troops. Lastly, there were Operational Groups (OG), comprised of some thirty experts in weapons, demolition work, and guerrilla warfare. The latter were dropped in American uniform far behind the enemy lines in order to arm and encourage partisan bands. OSS made greater use of foreign-born personnel than did SF, which remained predominantly British despite frequent commissioning of refugee nationals of other countries. In supreme command of OSS was the late General William ("Wild Bill") Donovan, a New York friend of President Roosevelt. Algiers and later Caserta were the headquarters for the Italian sector, under the command of Colonel William Eddy and later of Colonel Edward Glavin. Skeletal air bases were maintained near Algiers for months after transfer of most echelons to the Caserta, Bari, and (later) Siena sectors. In the American Legation in Berne, Allen W. Dulles was to become a pivotal figure in OSS contacts with the Italian and German undergrounds.[151]

During the Salerno invasion four SF officers (including Major Malcolm Munthe, son of the Swedish novelist Axel Munthe, and Captain Salvadori ["Sylvester"]) plus British noncommissioned personnel landed near Paestum and were attached to the American Fifth Army. They were quickly joined by Tarchiani, Cianca, Garosci, Valiani, Gentili, Pierleoni, and some other unmistakably anti-Fascist *fuorusciti* whom the Allies had helped return to stimulate the liberation movement.[152] OSS also sent in key personnel.

One of their first tasks was to escort Benedetto Croce from his

[151] NYT, Sept. 18, 1945, 8:1; A. Icardi, *Aldo Icardi: American Master Spy* (New York, 1956), pp. 6–8; A. W. Dulles, *Germany's Underground* (New York, 1947).
[152] Salvadori, *RSI*, pp. 113–114, 118; Salvadori, *Resistenza ed azione*, pp. 200–208; Valiani, *Tutte le strade conducono a Roma*, Chs. 1 and 2; Dino Gentili, *Italia ignorata: documenti* (Naples, 1943).

summer residence in Sorrento to the greater security of Capri, lest he be nabbed by the retreating Germans. In the course of conversations with OSS General Donovan, Croce and Tarchiani made it clear that in their opinion a good number of Italians were reluctant to volunteer to fight for the wobbly King but would join military units if they did not have to take an oath of loyalty to the Monarchy. Croce remained personally attached to the royal form of government but he sensed the unpopularity of the incumbent monarch. Thus he and Tarchiani, along with some others, suggested to Donovan that there be a volunteer corps, pledging allegiance to the Italian nation rather than to Victor Emmanuel III and fighting under the direct command of the Allies.

The idea spread quickly, so that on September 24 (two days after the birth of Naples' sexpartite CLN) Croce, Tarchiani, Cianca, and Raimondo Craveri (Croce's eldest son-in-law and a native of Piedmont) decided to form a National Liberation Front to promote recruitments for such a volunteer corps to be commanded by General Giuseppe Pavone, a rather aged southern supporter of the Pd'A. Unfortunately, the propelling force behind this plan was confined to just two parties (Pd'A and PLI), though the young PCI writer Pintor also backed the gambit at a certain point.

During the critical fighting of September and for a few weeks thereafter, this suggestion was given serious thought by Colonel Ellery C. Huntington, Jr., OSS commander attached to the Fifth Army, and by Major Munthe and other British SF officers attached to the Fifth Army. The Americans were inclined to be favorable, and, after the launching of an appeal on October 10, several hundred volunteers rallied to the Gruppi Combattenti Italia which General Pavone was recruiting in Naples. But the idea speedily stirred the fierce hostility of royalists in Brindisi, especially after the King got around to declaring war on Germany on October 13. It also worried British advisers in Italy, who feared its political implications. Thus they first limited the size of the enterprise to 510 men, who would be scattered into small operating units rather than fielded as a solid republican contingent. Then a few days later (November 9) the Allied Control Commission, acting mainly for political reasons, decided in favor of the monarchist foes of the Pavone corps and published orders to disband it.[153] Henceforth, almost all of the limited number of Italians who marched to the front from the South did so under the aegis of the royal government.

Some of the personnel who had been rounded up for Pavone, however, were taken over by Craveri for the ORI ("Organizzazione della Resistenza Italiana"), which he recruited in behalf of OSS after he was approached on Capri in September by General Donovan. Helping him was a Neapolitan scientist, Dr. Enzo Boeri, whose political sympathies (like Craveri's) oscillated between the Pd'A and PLI. Co-ordinated by OSS, the ORI often worked more closely with the CLN's and political parties than did the British SF.[154]

As early as September ORI helped dispatch the first Allied ("Law") mission to the North. Transported by submarine, its destination was Lavagna in Liguria. Headed by a nephew of Matteotti, Guglielmo ("Mino") Steiner, it included Fausto Bazzi and Guido DeFerrari. The mission sought out Piero Caleffi of the Genoa Pd'A and others and hired Giuseppe Cirillo to be radio-telegraphist; later Cirillo set up shop in the Milanese nerve center of the Resistenza.[155]

By October Craveri's ORI established radio communication with a clandestine intelligence service, the "Otto," just organized in Genoa by Ottorino Balduzzi, who was then a supporter of Pd'A. The "Otto" had decided that the best way to approach the Allies and prove to them the existence of determined partisans behind the lines was to dispatch some ex-PW's. To this end,

[153] Benedetto Croce, *Quando l'Italia era tagliata in due: estratto di un diario* (*luglio 1943–giugno 1944*) (Bari, 1948), pp. 12–31, 145–156 [trans. by Sylvia Sprigge as *Croce, the King, and the Allies* (New York, 1950)]; Claudio Pavone, "I Gruppi Combattenti Italia," *MLI*, No. 34/35 (1955), pp. 80–119; Salvadori, *Resistenza ed azione*, pp. 225–234; Salvadori, *SRI*, pp. 99, 231; Valiani, *Tutte le strade conducono a Roma*, p. 46; Garosci, "Un mese con Giaime Pintor," *Mercurio*, 1 (Dec. 1944), pp. 101–102; Agostino degli Espinosa, *Il Regno del Sud* (Rome, 1946), pp. 133–147; F. Caracciolo, "Il Governo di Salerno," *MLI*, No. 7 (1950), p. 7 ff.; G. Vaccarino, "I rapporti con gli alleati e la missione al sud," *MLI*, No. 52/53 (1958), pp. 56–57; Battaglia, *SRI*, p. 179.

[154] Enzo Boeri, "Intervento," *MLI*, No. 52/53 (1958), pp. 173–174; Raimondo Craveri, "Un servizio segreto," *Mercurio* (*Anche l'Italia ha vinto*), II, No. 16 (Dec. 1945), pp. 104–110.

[155] Baccino, *Contributo alla storia della Resistenza di Genova*, pp. 38–39; Caleffi, *Si fa presto a dire fame*, p. 17 ff.

Balduzzi had helped British Colonel Gore make his way to Corsica.[156] Within a short time Parri was able to make frequent use of its services and communicate with the Allies until March 1944, when the enemy smashed "Otto." Both ORI and SF were in regular communication with the successor "Franchi" intelligence service, established by Edgardo Sogno and other Autonomi.[157]

Meanwhile, in October 1943, SF had dispatched Valiani and Pierleoni across the fluid front to Rome. Pierleoni stayed there to help organize resistance, while Valiani (who was joined in Rome by his wife) hastened north to collaborate with Parri and the Milan CLN. Soon after he found Parri (in the wake of the Pizzo d'Erna skirmish) the two men slipped across the Swiss frontier to confer with Allied intelligence officers in the hope of selling them the idea of massive support of behind-the-lines warfare. In a villa in Certenago on November 2 they talked with Allen W. Dulles ("Arturo") of the American Legation and with John McCaffery ("Rossi"), assistant press attaché in the British Legation. Fortunately for the Italians, both of these Allied officers were deeply impressed by what the underground was doing to help ex-PW's escape via Switzerland.[158]

Parri assured his interlocutors that nothing would halt the work of the partisans, and he outlined plans for large-scale military formations, which he obviously hoped would serve as a political counterpoise to whatever regular-Army units the Allies could muster from Badoglio. Dulles and McCaffery were manifestly taken aback by Parri's insistence upon open warfare by partisan "armies," as well as by his implacable hostility to the binomial royal government (which, incidentally, maintained a diplomatic mission in Berne that sought to deprecate Parri's movement). Doing his best to play off the Allied spokesmen, Parri persuaded them to furnish air drops to guerrilla units in the hills and financial subsidization via Switzerland to the "patriot movement" (as the British preferred to call the underground, eschewing the Communist-tainted label "partisan").[159]

---

[156] Cf. supra, n. 44; Baccino, Contributo alla storia della Resistenza di Genova, pp. 39, 65–73; M. Zino, Più duri del carcere, pp. 214–216; Salvadori, SRI, p. 117.
[157] Sogno, Guerra senza bandiera, passim.
[158] Valiani, Tutte le strade conducono a Roma, pp. 75–91 ff.
[159] Parri, "L'Italia partigiana," Mercurio (Anche l'Italia ha vinto), II, No. 16

In the long run Allied aid was to make possible organization of an Armed Resistance much larger than the Anglo-Americans had anticipated. Yet during the first autumn and winter help was meagre and slow—a fact which aroused speculation among the resistants about the Allies' real intentions.

As a matter of fact, for reasons that will be seen, the commander of SF in Italy decided in mid-November that liaison with the Resistance should be conducted through pro-Badoglio channels. According to royalist officials in the Brindisi rump government, the northern Resistance was being organized almost exclusively by disbanded regular-Army personnel with whom Brindisi had established a Military Information Service (SIM) in October. SIM contributed, incidentally, not a few of the personnel for OSS missions. Naturally it preferred to collaborate with the Autonomi, most of whose leaders (though not all their men) tended to be monarchist. And it was in close touch with Colonel Giuseppe di Montezemolo's covert group in Rome. Indeed, on December 10, 1943, the Brindisi government designated Montezemolo to be Head Liaison Officer between the Italian Military High Command and all underground units working with it.[160]

Insofar as the limited data available in November permitted, Captain Salvadori did his best to correct his SF superior, Colonel Alp, regarding the true composition of the underground; and he pointed out that an Information Service was not the same thing as Armed Resistance.[161] Though unconvinced, Colonel Alp agreed to let Major Munthe's unit in Naples try to establish contact with the Rome CLN. (It should be noted that Salvadori's sister, Signora Joyce Lussu, had crossed the lines on foot with a message from the CCLN asking the Allies for radio and military equipment.) Early in December Munthe attempted to para-

---

(Dec. 1945), pp. 9–19; Parri, "Il movimento di liberazione e gli alleati," *MLI*, No. 1 (1949), pp. 7–24; Parri, "Relazione introduttiva" [al III Convegno di studi sulla storia del Movimento di Liberazione], *MLI*, No. 52/53 (1958), pp. 16–17; Valiani, *Tutte le strade conducono a Roma*, pp. 108–115; McCaffery's letter to Parri on Aug. 16, 1944, reprinted in Catalano, *Storia del CLNAI*, p. 279; and Valiani, "La resistenza e la questione istituzionale," *MLI*, No. 52/53 (1958), pp. 32–33.

[160] Cadorna, *La Riscossa*, p. 84; Battaglia, SRI, p. 237; *cf. supra*, Ch. VII, Military debacle in Rome and elsewhere.

[161] Salvadori, *Resistenza ed azione*, pp. 225–237.

chute supplies to the CCLN's Military Command, which was headed by Bauer (Pd'A) and Antonio Colombi (PCI) and had outposts as far north as Ancona and just short of Leghorn. But these drops somehow failed to reach their destination. Munthe also held on to some of the volunteers amassed in Naples for Pavone and arranged for them to receive parachute training so that they could eventually be flown north.

Meanwhile, Salvadori flew to Sardinia in December to see if he could persuade some of the regular-Army personnel dislocated there to go north and join the Resistance. To his chagrin, he met with disappointing co-operation from the officers in command. His gloom deepened on Christmas Eve when higher-ups notified Munthe that henceforth only OSS would work with the Rome underground. SF, for the present, would confine its operations to the Adriatic sector, with Monopoli as its forward base. "We are liquidated," commented Munthe sadly.[162]

[162] *Ibid.*, pp. 237–240; Salvadori, *Brief History of the Patriot Movement in Italy, 1943–1945*, pp. 58–59; Joyce Lussu, *Fronti e frontiere, passim*; and Bonomi, *Diario di un anno*, p. 100 ff.

CHAPTER VIII · CONFUSION IN "KING'S ITALY"

September 9, 1943 – June 4, 1944

Royal government in Brindisi

AT THE southeastern port of Brindisi at 2 p.m., September 10, 1943, King Victor Emmanuel III, Marshal Pietro Badoglio, and their retinue stepped ashore from the corvette *Baionetta* which had borne them on the last half of their escape from Rome. The royal family appropriated the quarters of the local ranking admiral; the prime minister and others moved into small barracks belonging to submarine crews. There they anxiously awaited news of the outcome of the battle of Salerno and the arrival of Field Marshal Montgomery's Eighth Army, pushing up the heel of the Italian boot.[1]

As soon as he had established skeletal headquarters (for days he possessed not even a typewriter),[2] Marshal Badoglio radioed General Eisenhower in Algiers by means of the apparatus the Allies had provided him. The American Supreme Commander in the Mediterranean assured him that an Advisory Commission, headed by Lieutenant General Sir Frank Noel Mason-Macfarlane (ex-military attaché in Berlin and military governor of Gibraltar), would soon be dispatched. And he relayed a message from Prime Minister Churchill and President Roosevelt: "March forward with your American and British friends in the great world movement toward freedom, justice, and peace!"[3] On September 11, while British contingents were entering Brindisi, Victor Emmanuel III broadcast to his subjects that he had moved south "for the salvation of the capital and in order to carry out fully my duties as King. . . . Italians! I trust confidently in you for every event, as you can count even on the last sacrifice by your King."[4] At the same time, Badoglio issued orders to the Italian troops to regard the Germans as enemies, and in a broadcast on the 13th

[1] Degli Espinosa, *Il Regno del Sud*, pp. 1–13.
[2] Charles R. S. Harris, *Allied Administration of Italy, 1943–1945* (London, 1957), p. 108, n. 1; a volume in the "History of the Second World War, United Kingdom Military Series," ed. J. R. M. Butler.
[3] Badoglio, *Italy in the Second World War*, pp. 87–90.
[4] Quoted in Ugo Maraldi, *Storia della seconda guerra mondiale* (Milan, 1946), p. 367.

exhorted his people to resist German domination in every way.[5]

For days the military struggle hung in the balance until at last, after heavy losses, Allied troops secured the Salerno beachhead. Yet through most of September the Germans remained dug in at the port of Naples and the airfields between Bari and Foggia.[6] In Brindisi the rump government helped Allied authorities prepare port and railway facilities for the many hard battles to come.

The King and his prime minister, meanwhile, sought to clarify Italy's legal status. To them it seemed reasonable that she should now be regarded as one of the Allies. Victor Emmanuel communicated such a petition to President Roosevelt and King George VI, but was soon informed that fulfillment of this entreaty was out of the question. The Savoyard's chagrin was compounded by word that his writ extended only over the four Apulian provinces of Taranto, Lecce, Brindisi, and Bari. In months to come that region (subsequently expanded) was popularly known as "King's Italy" or "Kingdom of the South." In those southeastern provinces Allied officers served in a strictly liaison and supervisory capacity with the Italian bureaucracy, whereas elsewhere in the liberated peninsula Allied Military Government (AMG) temporarily ruled supreme.

With no little difficulty Roosevelt persuaded Churchill on September 21 to agree to recognize Italy as a co-belligerent if she declared war upon Germany. This meant that Italy could not sit at the peace conference on the victors' side but would have the opportunity of reducing the severity of her eventual punishment to the extent that she redeemed herself on the battlefield, or, as Churchill phrased it, "worked her passage." The Allies would recognize the right of the Italian people to choose freely at war's end the form of government they wished. Premier Stalin quickly gave his assent to this formula.[7] Next day Secretary of State Hull informed Eisenhower of the co-belligerency possibility and stressed the importance of getting Victor Emmanuel to declare war on Germany. He hoped this would infuse new vigor

[5] Roatta, *Otto milioni di baionette*, pp. 338–339; Kogan, *Italy and the Allies*, p. 42.

[6] U.S. War Department, Dept. of Military Art and Engineering, *Operations in Sicily and Italy (July 1943 to May 1945)* (West Point, 1945), p. 15 ff.

[7] USSR, Ministry of Foreign Affairs, *Stalin's Correspondence with Churchill, Attlee, Roosevelt and Truman, 1941–45* (2 vols.; Moscow, 1957; New York, 1958), I, 163–164, 169–170 (Docs. Nos. 194, 195, 200, 201).

into the torpid southern populace and at the same time encourage the northern Italians to boycott Mussolini's RSI.[8]

For several reasons the King preferred not to issue such a declaration until after Rome could be emancipated. Not only did he fear German vengeance on two thirds of the peninsula; he also objected to the vagueness of "co-belligerency," the probable limitation of Italian fighting forces, the minuscule extent of his realm, and the political risks which he and the very monarchical institution itself faced in view of mounting domestic and Allied pressure on him to gamble his throne in a postwar election—especially when they were simultaneously urging him to broaden his cabinet and include men whom he regarded as unfriendly.[9]

The thorny problem of the so-called Long Armistice also played a capital role. It will be recalled that the Short Armistice, signed in Cassibile on September 3, omitted reference to "unconditional surrender" and restricted itself to military clauses. The Long Armistice contained political and economic strictures, and in its original version mentioned "unconditional surrender." After remonstrances from Badoglio (and also from Croce on September 18), the Anglo-Americans eventually agreed to modify some of the phraseology to bring it more into line with the spirit of the September 3 instrument. Tactfully Eisenhower handed Badoglio a clarifying letter when the Marshal affixed his signature to the Long Armistice aboard H.M.S. *Nelson* at Malta on September 29. Later additional changes were made, and a new protocol on November 9 deleted the term "unconditionally" after the word "surrender" in Article 1, only to reinsert it in paragraph 6: "These terms . . . have been accepted unconditionally by Marshal Pietro Badoglio. . . ." Despite these recondite maneuvers, there was no doubt that the Allies controlled the destiny of the Italian people in the liberated zones after September 29.[10] As matters

[8] Valiani, *Tutte le strade conducono a Roma*, pp. 25–27.

[9] Badoglio, *Italy in the Second World War*, p. 96; Churchill, *Closing the Ring*, pp. 200–201; Kogan, *Italy and the Allies*, pp. 44–45; Harris, *Allied Administration in Italy, 1943–1945*, Ch. v; Feis, *Churchill, Roosevelt, Stalin*, pp. 176–182.

[10] Even the Navy, which technically had not yet surrendered, was obliged to do so on November 17, in the wake of pressure from Soviet Russia and Britain after the October conference in Moscow of the Big Three Foreign Ministers. At the ensuing Teheran conference in November, Churchill and Roosevelt agreed to Stalin's demand for division of the Italian fleet. Early in 1944 the Anglo-Americans persuaded Stalin for reasons of politico-military expediency to delay any immediate seizure of such naval units, and to accept temporarily in their

turned out, several clauses of the Long Armistice never took effect and some others were rendered of slight import. Yet many misunderstandings continued, and there were enough highhanded Allied deeds to persuade many Italians to credit the wildest rumors about Allied intentions.

Co-belligerency in practice

Pricked by his own premier and blandished by the Allies who promised that his realm would be broadened as more soil was freed, the weak-kneed King at last consented to declare war on October 13. The same day the Allies recognized Italy as a co-belligerent.

The next problem they faced was how best to utilize the Italians. Badoglio was anxious to march combat troops to the front, in order to improve his country's bargaining position at the peace table. According to his calculations, Italian land forces dislocated in the liberated provinces and islands soon after the armistice consisted of nine mobile divisions; twelve divisions for coastal defense; some small motorized units; and territorial organizations and services, functioning efficiently in Apulia but seriously disorganized or even nonexistent elsewhere. All told, there were 430,000 men, of whom half were in Sardinia. He conceded that they possessed limited means of transport and were not adequately equipped for modern warfare. Nevertheless, they had resisted the Germans bravely till September 20, at which time the Allied Military Mission had issued instructions to halt fighting.[11]

In broad terms, the American State Department favored using Italian military personnel to the greatest practicable extent. On September 22 Hull cabled Eisenhower "to permit the Italians to wage war against Germany within the limit of their capacities . . . , [to] encourage the vigorous use of Italian armed forces."[12] Eisenhower was agreeable, but most of the British and

stead a loan of Anglo-American vessels. *Cf. Stalin's Correspondence with Churchill* . . . , I, 186–198; U.S. Dept. of State, *United States and Italy, 1936–1946*, pp. 51–80; Kogan, *Italy and the Allies*, pp. 46–49; Malbone W. Graham, "Two Armistices and a Surrender," *The American Journal of International Law*, XL (1945), pp. 148–155.

[11] Badoglio, *Italy in the Second World War*, pp. 177–178.

[12] Cordell Hull, *The Memoirs of Cordell Hull* (New York, 1948), II, 1550–1551.

not a few American military men on the scene were less than lukewarm about such a policy. Indeed, General Mason-Macfarlane, after speedily surveying the grim picture in Brindisi, had radioed Algiers on September 15 with brutal frankness that, apart from the Italian fleet, "we have virtually nothing to gain . . . from the Army, except as the soldiers may be used as slave labor at ports and on our line of communication." [13] Field Marshal Montgomery soon doused more cold water: he doubted the "ability of the Italians seriously to influence events in the way it was hoped." [14]

It was quite understandable that these officers should form a low opinion of the bedraggled and dazed Italian troops, equipped mainly with 1918 armor and short of almost everything. Under existing conditions such men would be more useful behind the lines on fatigue duty than as a combat force. Moreover, there were political considerations for the British. They refused to forget that until recently "Eye-ties" had fired on them in the desert and in Sicily and that Mussolini had elected to plunge his dagger into their ribs at the very moment of Dunkirk. As for the thousands of PW's held by the British all around the globe, there would be difficulty in diverting precious shipping to send them home; and, in any case, the British needed them for farm labor.[15] Finally the British reasoned that "the greater the concessions now made . . . , the more difficult would it be to impose such sanctions as the Allies might wish . . . at the end of the war." [16]

The Italians themselves were not agreed as to how best they might buttress the joint cause; for them the problem was inextricably linked to the political one revolving about the King and Badoglio, as has been seen in the case of the abortive effort to create a nonroyalist volunteer corps under General Pavone.[17]

At the very time the Allies were pondering the Pavone proposal, they agreed (September 28) to permit the First Italian

[13] Butcher. *My Three Years with Eisenhower*, p. 420.
[14] Field Marshal the Viscount Montgomery of Alamein, *El Alamein to the River Sangro* (London, 1948), p. 106; and *The Memoirs of Field-Marshal the Viscount Montgomery of Alamein, K.G.* (Cleveland, 1958), pp. 173–178 ff.
[15] Churchill, *Closing the Ring*, p. 199; Harris, *Allied Administration in Italy, 1943–1945*, pp. 151–153.
[16] Hull, *Memoirs*, ii, 1559.
[17] Cf. *supra*, Ch. vii, Early Allied liaison with the Resistance.

Motorized Group, led by General Utili and composed of soldiers in the royal Army, to prepare for front-line duty.[18] Equipped entirely with Italian matériel, this motorized group eventually consisted of 5,000 men: there were infantry and artillery regiments, an antiaircraft battery, an antitank battalion, and supporting units. In December this motorized group entered the fray at Montelungo near Cassino and won plaudits from Fifth Army's General Mark Clark. But after a week or more of fighting and heavy (320) casualties, it had to pull back for reorganization. By April 1944 its men were ready to go back into action as part of the Corps of Italian Liberation (CIL). This corps fought valiantly halfway up the peninsula alongside the Allies. In September it was reorganized and continued the liberation struggle into the Po valley.[19]

Apart from the First Italian Motorized Group enterprise, Allied strategists were reluctant in 1943 to employ Italians at the front. Badoglio's request at Malta on September 30 for use of at least seven divisions that could be brought back from the islands got no response, as did most of his other plans which he submitted almost weekly. Particularly discouraging was a memorandum submitted by General Taylor four days after Italy's declaration of war: "For the moment we do not intend to use any Italian troops for military operations except the motorized contingent. We propose to employ ten Italian divisions for the defence of the lines of communication in the peninsula and the Islands, some anti-aircraft batteries, and some engineer units. The Italian Air Force will be used exclusively in the Balkan theatre." [20]

The Allies made faster use of the Italian Navy and Air Force.

[18] General Eisenhower also intimated to Badoglio that vaunted Alpine troops would be employed in the mountains farther north and that Italian forces would help occupy Rome. He authorized training of one Italian division, the "Legnano," for service at the front, and to be equipped with Italian matériel. As things turned out, the Allies commandeered so much of the equipment for Tito that the "Legnano" could not be fielded. General Alexander cut it to one Alpine group. Badoglio, Italy in the Second World War, pp. 184–186.
[19] See infra, Ch. x; Scala, La riscossa dell'esercito, pp. 202–242; Badoglio, Italy in the Second World War, pp. 100–103, 177–178; G. Lombardi, Il Corpo Italiano di Liberazione (Rome, 1945); General Taddeo Orlando, Vittoria di un popolo (Rome, 1946); Arturo Scattini, "La partecipazione dell'esercito italiano alla Guerra di Liberazione," Civitas, VI (1955), pp. 41–59.
[20] Badoglio, Italy in the Second World War, pp. 178–184.

The Navy, still in fairly good shape in September 1943, consisted of: 5 battleships; 9 cruisers; 11 destroyers; 37 submarines; 40 torpedo boats and corvettes; 30 motor torpedo boats (MAS); and auxiliary vessels. In accordance with the armistice, some of the battleships and cruisers (minus the flagship *Roma*, bombed and sunk by German planes en route to Malta, with the loss of 1,500 men) had been transferred to Allied bases; others were in ports in Free Italy. In addition, the Navy was in control of the important arsenal of Taranto and efficient dockyards and services in the South and in Sardinia.

Badoglio's government had no great complaints about Allied utilization of Italian sea power, although there was some feeling that two new battleships, the *Vittorio Veneto* and the *Italia*, interned in Egypt with reduced crews and breechblocks removed, ought to have been repaired and put into service. From September 8, 1943, to April 30, 1944, the Italian Navy reported total ship movements amounting to 1,889 units and covering 646,370 miles. Operations involved: (1) bombardments of the Adriatic coast; (2) patrol activity throughout the Adriatic; (3) transport of Allied personnel from Albania and Greece; (4) numerous missions by submarines and MAS for transport of Italian and Allied saboteurs and agents; (5) supplies carried by submarines and destroyers for troops in Aegean islands; and (6) sweeps by destroyers and torpedo boats to intercept German naval forces and for protection of Italian positions in the Ionian isles, Sardinia, and Corsica. Losses for that period amounted to: 1 battleship (the *Roma*); 4 destroyers; 5 torpedo boats; 1 corvette; 3 auxiliary cruisers; 1 submarine; and 14 MAS. Casualties included: 733 killed; 6,369 missing; 748 wounded. From September 1943 until the end of the war the Navy escorted 1,621 convoys.[21]

The Navy contributed directly to the Resistenza Armata in several places. For example, most of the personnel cut off in Rome, Venice, LaSpezia, and Milan rallied to the underground struggle. In Rome Admiral Ferreri headed the covert work. Admiral Maugeri, chief of Navy secret service, also kept busy there. Several of their aides were executed by the Germans. Three patriot bands of naval personnel operated in Tuscany, Carnia,

[21] *Ibid.*, pp. 186–189; Ministero della Marina, *La Marina italiana nella lotta per la liberazione* (Rome, 1945), pp. 3–22.

and the Apennines. The "San Marco" marine regiment fought in the Corps of Italian Liberation from April 1944 until V-E Day. And it was an underground naval unit near Rome that prevented the Germans in June 1944 from carrying out their plans to blow up the important radio communications center and supply base at Santa Rosa. All told, some 8,000 men and 450 officers took an active part in the Resistenza; about 700 men and 34 officers paid with their lives.[22]

The Air Force was in sad shape at the time of the armistice. The Brindisi government counted: 115 fighters; 90 bombers and transport planes; 50 seaplanes; and 50 miscellaneous craft, for a total of 305. Ground organization, still satisfactory in Apulia and Sardinia, was nonexistent elsewhere. What was worse, all industrial plants for construction and maintenance of the planes were in the North. Badoglio complained of the lack of freedom of action for the Air Force, which was used exclusively to sustain partisan warfare in the Balkans. The government argued that if proper equipment were provided for the available personnel, some 1,100 aircraft could have been manned, and if 500 skilled PW's were released, a total of 1,500 airplanes could have been equipped. As it was, the Air Force between September 8, 1943, and April 15, 1944, clocked 12,500 flight hours; flew 350,000 miles; carried out 9,444 sorties; dropped 40,000 bombs; fired 100,000 rounds; dropped 150,000 kilograms of supplies; transported 119 wounded personnel; and carried 900,000 kilograms of mail and matériel. Virtually all of the matériel used was of Italian provenance. Casualties numbered 80 killed and 46 missing.[23]

Institutional crisis

All of the military frustrations formed but one aspect of a much larger problem—the fate of the House of Savoy. Washington and London differed substantially in their attitudes toward the abstract merits of kingship. Churchill, whose opinion usually

[22] Commander Marc'Antonio Bragadin, *The Italian Navy in World War II* (Annapolis, 1957), pp. 349–353.
[23] Badoglio, *Italy in the Second World War*, pp. 189–191. See also Badoglio's private memorandum prepared after his resignation as premier in June 1944 and detailing his grievances with the Allies: "L'Armistizio, gli alleati ed il governo Badoglio," MLI, No. 54, 55, 56, 58 (1959–1960).

counted most in the Mediterranean, intended unquestionably to uphold the royal binomial of Victor Emmanuel and Badoglio. He argued that the men who had signed the armistice must guarantee its execution; any political upheaval might aggravate the critical military situation and endanger collaboration by the Italian Navy. While conceding to the Americans that a search for competent men to increase the "leftward emphasis" of the government ought to continue, Churchill was fearful of any radical renovation until Rome was taken. "In Rome lie the title-deeds of Italy and of the Roman Catholic Church," he advised Harold Macmillan, his political adviser to Allied Force Headquarters in Algiers, on October 23: "Badoglio and the King reinstated there will have a far better chance of rallying such elements of Italian strength as exist. There is the place for us to make our deal and for them to issue their prospectus. In the meanwhile, be careful that nothing is done to make the King and Badoglio weaker than they are. On the contrary, we must hold them up and carry them forward with our armies." [24]

For a time Churchill was able to get Roosevelt's acquiescence and also that of Stalin, who quoted approvingly an old Russian proverb, "You may always walk with the Devil till you get to the end of the bridge." [25] Yet there was recurrent controversy with the State Department (still smarting from domestic criticism of its pro-Darlan "expediency" in North Africa), and of course much more with the Italian anti-Fascists. "I myself was not at all sympathetic to the idea of keeping King Victor Emmanuel on the throne," Hull has explained. "He had, to all intents and purposes, gone along with Mussolini. We had hoped that the King would keep Mussolini from going to war, but he had done nothing, possibly because he could do nothing. . . . As for Badoglio, he was the appointee of a King with whom we had no sympathy. He was adequate for the purpose of signing the terms of surrender, but I did not consider him adequate for the purpose of governing Italy. I felt that, as soon as feasible, the people of Italy, represented by the parties in opposition to Fascism, should be permitted to express their choice of the form and personnel

[24] Churchill, *Closing the Ring*, p. 201.
[25] *Ibid.*, p. 188.

of the Government they wanted. . . . I found that [the President] was fully of the same opinion." [26]

Indeed, among the conditions for recognition of Italy as a cobelligerent was that the cabinet be broadened to include spokesmen of the anti-Fascist parties. Badoglio promised to do this shortly, "leaving unchanged the principle, already enunciated, that once the war is finished the Italian people will be free to choose, by elections, the Government [*"governo"*] they wish." [27] The rub was that so long as the King and the Marshal headed the executive branch, most of the anti-Fascist leaders refused to serve under them. Furthermore, as Bonomi, Salvemini, and others quickly noted, there was ambiguity in Badoglio's use of the term *governo*. In ordinary parlance the word simply meant "cabinet" rather than the form or institutions of government. Republican tribunes would accept nothing less than reform of the latter.[28]

Naples was the pintle of the South's anti-Fascism. There a sexpartite CLN had emerged by September 22, regarding itself as a sister of the septentrional committees. In much the same manner as the northern juntos, two of the parties (Pd'A and PLI) tried to field a volunteer antiroyalist corps, but confronted by Allied reticence they had to back down.[29] No one could be sure how much grass-roots support the CLN parties really enjoyed in the *Mezzogiorno*; the British were inclined to minimize it. Traditionally, the indigent southern masses had been apathetic and susceptible to clerico-royalist propaganda; and in chaotic 1943 they were almost exclusively concerned with eking out a bare living. But among property owners and professionalists there was considerable political interest, focusing especially on the PLI, historically puissant in the South. To that party's good fortune, its most respected mentor, Croce, lived in Naples.

[26] Hull, *Memoirs*, II, 1550.

[27] Cited in Smyth, "Italy: From Fascism to the Republic," *The Western Political Quarterly*, I (1948), p. 210.

[28] *Ibid.*; Norman Kogan, "The Action Party and the Institutional Question," *The Western Political Quarterly*, VI (1953), p. 276; Bonomi, *Diario di un anno*, p. 125; Gaetano Salvemini, "Program for Italy," *New Republic*, XIX, No. 20 (Nov. 15, 1943), pp. 679–680.

[29] Conspicuous figures in the southern CLN included Croce, V. Arangio-Ruiz, and Enrico DeNicola (PLI); Ciccio Cerabona (DL); Giulio Rodinò, Angelo R. Jervolino (DC); Prof. Adolfo Omodeo, Prof. Alfredo Parente, Alberto Cianca, and Michele Cifarelli (Pd'A); Pietro Mancini (PSIUP); Egidio Reale and Velio Spano (PCI). After his return in April 1944 Togliatti became undisputed PCI leader. Tarchiani and Sforza were friendly to the Pd'A but not members.

By mid-September Croce decided to campaign against Victor Emmanuel's retention of the throne. His decision was reinforced by news of the Rome CLN's attitude, brought to him on October 5 by Joyce Lussu. The Savoyard's "clear will to make use of institutions and men of Fascism, his long delay in declaring war on Germany, made necessary his retirement," Croce explained after the war.[30] He did not wish Crown Prince Humbert to take the throne because he too had been closely identified with Fascism. (A year later, however, Croce formed a more favorable estimate of Humbert.) The philosopher-historian advocated a temporary regency for the 6-year-old grandson, the Prince of Naples, to be followed by a postwar Constituent Assembly and plebiscite which could settle the Monarchy's fate. Croce was willing to keep Badoglio, in view of his anti-Germanism and military experience, and conveyed these thoughts to him by way of Leopoldo Piccardi.[31]

Pressed by the Allies, the Naples CLN indicated on October 19 that it would enter a cabinet under the King and Badoglio if all six parties were included.[32] This decision was not carried out, though, partly because of Carlo Sforza's actions after his return to Italy on the 23rd and partly because of recalcitrance from the northern CLN's.

After years of exile—the most recent having been in the United States, where Sforza enjoyed vast prestige—the veteran diplomat had gained permission late in September from Assistant Secretary of State Berle to return home as a private citizen. As his part of the bargain, Sforza had signed a letter drafted by the State Department wherein he promised to support "the man who would eventually destroy any remaining vestiges of Fascism"— meaning Badoglio or any other premier acceptable to the United Nations.[33] Yet, in a news conference in New York, Sforza criticized the idea of using Victor Emmanuel III as a rallying point and called, instead, for a "Cromwellian army" of Italians.[34] When he stopped off in London to lunch with Churchill, the latter sought to persuade him to support the old monarch.

[30] Benedetto Croce, "Ricordi," Milan *Corriere della sera*, April 6, 1949.
[31] Croce, *Quando l'Italia era tagliata in due*, pp. 20–39.
[32] Kogan, *Italy and the Allies*, p. 51.
[33] H. L. Matthews in NYT, Dec. 12, 1944, 7:1; Hull, *Memoirs*, ii, 1551–1552.
[34] NYT, Oct. 1, 1943, 1:7.

Sforza's answer was a bit opaque, but Churchill thought he had secured a promise of co-operation with Badoglio. Sforza then flew on to Algiers and finally reached Bari. As soon as he had a chance to judge the situation firsthand, he balked at accepting the posts of deputy prime minister and foreign minister in a Badoglio government so long as Victor Emmanuel stayed on the throne—a development which stirred Churchill's wrath for months to come.[35] Sforza indicated, however, that he would co-operate if a regency were established in behalf of the young grandson.[36]

Any such plan horrified the King, who on October 21 had prepared for the Allies a letter expressing his views. In addition to retaining his crown, he insisted upon keeping his present cabinet till Rome was freed, at which time a broad government resting on all the parties could be formed. The institutional question would be set aside until an elected parliament (the Chamber of Deputies to be chosen within four months after the war) should decide the matter.[37] His views were not readily made known to the oppositionists.

On October 22 the Big Three Foreign Ministers issued from Moscow an important declaration calling for "negative and positive" measures to stimulate the growth of Italian democracy. On the negative side, they called for a rigorous purge ("epurazione") of Fascist personnel and procedures; positively, they demanded democratic organs of local government and a strengthening of the democratic character of the national government by inclusion of prominent foes of Fascism. Freedom of speech, press, assembly, religion, and political beliefs must be restored and organization of anti-Fascist political parties permitted. Because of British pressure, no mention at all was made about the status of the Monarchy.[38]

Before October's end the Naples CLN had to withdraw its hint of readiness to enter the royal government. This change, as has been observed, resulted partly from pressure from the Rome

[35] Churchill, Closing the Ring, pp. 197-199.
[36] Letter of Sforza to Bari Gazzetta del Mezzogiorno, Dec. 14, 1943, cited by Kogan, Italy and the Allies, p. 51; Badoglio, Italy in the Second World War, pp. 108-109.
[37] Bolla, Colloqui con Vittorio Emanuele III.
[38] Harris, Allied Military Administration of Italy, 1943-1945, p. 131.

CCLN. From the outset the latter group had found themselves split on the institutional question. The three rightist currents were disposed to effect a *modus vivendi* with the Monarchy for the duration of the war and in anticipation of a referendum. The leftist parties (though the PCI was a bit more hesitant than either the PSIUP or Pd'A) were determined to force the King to abdicate at once and to set up an "extraordinary government" with full constitutional powers (after the manner of the French Revolution's Committee of Public Safety).[39]

President Bonomi offered a compromise on October 16 that called for creation of an anti-Fascist cabinet solemnly pledged to let the people decide the institutional issue after the war. Until such a plebiscite the "extraordinary government" would wield full constitutional powers, with the Monarchy remaining in nominal existence (though suspended for all practical purposes) to assure the Allies of fulfillment of the armistice terms. This proposal was rejected by the Pd'A, which balked at the slightest concession to royalism. Actionists would agree, however, to a DC compromise formula drafted by Gronchi whereby the "extraordinary government," representing "those political forces that have constantly fought against the Fascist dictatorship and since September 1939 have been arrayed against the Nazi war," would "assume *all* the constitutional powers of the State, avoiding, however, any attitude that might compromise national harmony and prejudice the future popular decision." This pledge of all the parties for an "extraordinary government" was of great importance. Disputes inevitably arose over its meaning.[40]

When news of the Rome CCLN resolution filtered south (Parri and Valiani transmitted it via the Lugano CLN, which they visited briefly on November 2) the members of the Naples CLN quickly got into step. Most of them interpreted the resolu-

[39] Bonomi, *Diario di un anno*, pp. xii–xv; Ragghianti, *Disegno della liberazione*, pp. 43–57 ff.; Riccardo Bauer, "L'attività del CLN in Roma nel maggio 1944 in una relazione di Riccardo Bauer," *MLI*, No. 50 (1958), pp. 57–85.

[40] Bonomi, *Diario di un anno*, pp. 117–124; Ragghianti, *Disegno della liberazione*, pp. 55–56; Valiani, "I partiti antifascisti nel 1943," *MLI*, No. 34/35 (1955), 134–137. So adamantly republican was Lussu (Pd'A) that in November he sought to merge his party with certain Socialists and create an autonomous group outside the CLN that would shun unpalatable compromises. His efforts failed as a result of LaMalfa's quick work in preserving precarious unity. Valiani, *Tutte le strade conducono a Roma*, pp. 132–139; Rome *L'Italia libera*, Nov. 11, 1943.

tion to mean a Constituent Assembly, abdication of the King, and formation of a civilian Regency Council made up of leading democrats. Henceforth, there was a real imbroglio: the King refused to abdicate; Churchill backed him and Badoglio; Roosevelt, upon the advice of Eisenhower, recommended a regency but was willing to acquiesce in the existing arrangement until the liberation of Rome, then thought to be imminent. Unhappily, however, the Allied drive bogged down in November at Cassino.

The Italians found themselves in no less a deadlock. So long as the King refused to budge, the CLN would have no truck with the government. After all, most leftists viewed the institutional struggle as an integral part of their renovation of Italy's socio-political structure; in their estimation, the House of Savoy, like the Church, was too closely identified with tradition, order, and Fascism. If the Allies really wished to extirpate Fascism root and branch, they argued, then the Monarchy too must go—or at least its present protagonists. Meeting in Naples on November 9, the Liberals called for Victor Emmanuel's abdication—though, to be sure, some Liberals, Christian Democrats, and others were willing to accept a regency for the young Prince of Naples. Some who were sympathetic to the royal institution reasoned that such a compromise might "purify" the dynasty and improve its chances of survival. But most of the unwavering republicans, and especially those in the North, feared the scheme for the same reason. Indeed, the Rome CCLN on November 16 passed a resolution that the institutional question must not be prejudiced by substitution of any other person for the incumbent sovereign. It dispatched a delegate across the lines to convey this news to the Naples CLN.[41]

Badoglio's government of undersecretaries

That same day Badoglio, utterly frustrated in his efforts to entice CLN spokesmen into his government, named a new cabinet of "technical experts" as undersecretaries.[42] But this body

[41] Bonomi, *Diario di un anno*, p. 133.
[42] They included Dr. Vito Reale, Interior; Dr. Giuseppe DeSanctis, Grace and Justice; Guido Jung, Finance; General Taddeo Orlando, War; Admiral Pietro Barone, Merchant Marine; Prof. Giovanni Cuomo, National Education; Prof. Raffaele DeCaro, Public Works; Prof. Tommaso Siciliani, Agriculture and Forests;

had almost no effective power, because, in accordance with un-conditional surrender and the decision of the Moscow Foreign Ministers' conference, General Eisenhower announced the establishment in Brindisi on November 10 of the Allied Control Commission (ACC) for Italy.

The ACC carried out most of its tasks far to the rear of the battle lines, whereas in forward zones Allied Military Government (AMG) operated under the direct command of the local Army Headquarters.[43] As the Allies slowly pushed northward, ACC replaced AMG in the administration of the intermediate areas, and meanwhile relinquished direct control of the southern-most provinces to "King's Italy." In one way or another, ACC exercised a broad measure of control over the Italian government until the peace settlement, albeit the word "Control" was erased from the Commission's title in October 1944. Brilliance seldom attired its work. The war was in its final phase before very coherent directives emerged regarding restoration of economic life, purge of Fascist institutions, maintenance of public security, and guidance of the political parties and the Armed Resistance.[44]

Prof. Epicarmio Corbino, Industry, Commerce and Labor; General Giovanni di Raimondo, Railways and Transport; Prof. Mario Fano, Posts and Telegraphs; and General Giovanni Messe, Chief of the General Staff.

[43] Harris, Allied Military Administration of Italy, Ch. IV; Thomas R. Fisher, "Allied Military Government in Italy," Annals of the American Academy of Political and Social Sciences, CCLXVII (January 1950), pp. 114–122; Robert W. Kromer, "The Establishment of Allied Control in Italy," Military Affairs, XIII (Spring 1949), pp. 20–28.

[44] Top ACC personnel changed often. U.S. Major General Kenyon W. Joyce headed the agency briefly. He was replaced by British General Noel Mason-Macfarlane, who had already been sent to Brindisi as Chief of the Allied Mission; but ill health and political considerations forced him to retire after the collapse of Badoglio's government at the gates of Rome in June 1944. Thereafter a conservative businessman, Commodore Ellery Stone of the U.S. Navy, became Chief Commissioner. He was flanked after November by Churchill's confidant, Harold Macmillan, who assumed the title of Acting President. Most of the subcommissions were headed by Britishers, who tended to outrank the Americans in the Mediterranean after Eisenhower's transfer from the theater at the end of 1943. Cf. citations in n. 43; Carl J. Friedrich, et al, American Experiences in Military Government in World War II (New York, 1948), Ch. VI; Hajo Holborn, American Military Government, its organization and policies (Washington, 1947), Ch. IV; Henry M. Adams, "Allied Military Government in Sicily, 1943," Military Affairs, XV (Fall 1951), pp. 157–165; Feis, Churchill, Roosevelt, Stalin, pp. 182–188, 324–331; Badoglio, Italy in the Second World War, pp. 138–140, 172–176; Kogan, Italy and the Allies, passim. For very hostile Italian appraisals, cf. Tamaro, Due anni di storia, 1943–1945, and Luigi Villari, The Liberation of Italy, 1943–1947 (Appleton, Wisc., 1959).

During November 1943 the political attack on the diminutive King continued, with Anglo-American journalists like Cecil Sprigge and Herbert L. Matthews daily informing the democratic world of it. At the University of Naples on the 28th both Croce and Sforza made highly critical speeches, though carefully distinguishing between the royal institution and the incumbent monarch. The crowd was more radical, often interrupting them with shouts: "Down with the Monarchy!" "Away with all the Savoyards!" "Republic!" Two weeks later in a broadcast Croce again berated the King for failing to abdicate.[45] And, in Rome, Niccolò Carandini announced early in December that the PLI favored not only Victor Emmanuel's abdication but convocation of a Constituent Assembly after the war to decide the institutional dispute. Apparently he thought that the Monarchy could survive, once the unpopular ruler was gone.[46]

Late in December rumors reached Croce and Sforza that Victor Emmanuel might indeed abdicate, but only in favor of the Crown Prince. That would not be enough, they were convinced. On the 30th they conferred with an illustrious Neapolitan jurist, Enrico DeNicola, who had served as the last president of the free Chamber of Deputies. He proposed a compromise—a Lieutenant-Generalship of the Realm. Such a *combinazione* presumably would gain readier approval from both the King and country than would a regency. In the past it had been used occasionally when the monarch was abroad or with the Army. Rather than abdicate, the King would simply "retire" to private life, naming a Lieutenant-General of the Realm. DeNicola thought that the latter should be one of the princes, but he wished to exclude Humbert from consideration and also the Duke of Aosta and "King" Tomislav of the satellite-state of Croatia. This apparently would leave only the elderly Count of Turin, untainted by Fascism but deaf and not overly bright. Croce and Sforza, though not committing themselves, suggested that DeNicola present the plan to the King. This he did, only to see him reject it out of hand. The approach had been made in complete secrecy so that the Naples CLN was unaware of it. Thus that body con-

---

[45] Croce, *Quando l'Italia era tagliata in due*, p. 36; Croce, *Per la nuova vita d'Italia (scritti e discorsi, 1943-1944)* (Naples, 1944), pp. 30-31.
[46] Bonomi, *Diario di un anno*, p. 137.

tinued its stubborn stand, and now Sforza and Croce resumed theirs.[47]

Bari Congress of CLN's (January 28–29, 1944)

The Naples CLN had scheduled a conclave of anti-Fascist leaders in that city on December 20, 1943, when suddenly the Allies forbade it, alleging reasons of "military security." The cancellation apparently resulted from royalist pressure on the British. The CLN was unwilling to accept the prohibition without a fight. With the help of Croce, it drafted a protest resolution, copies of which were cabled to Churchill, Roosevelt, and Stalin. The Milan CLN also sent a protest on the 26th.[48]

Considerably embarrassed, the Anglo-Americans reconsidered their action. This time they allowed the Congress of Anti-Fascist Leaders to assemble in the Adriatic city of Bari, January 28, 1944 —a week after the landings at Anzio. Nevertheless, they circumscribed the congress with many restrictions, limiting the number who might attend, forbidding any broadcasts, and not allowing spectators or Allied military personnel to attend. Military police cordoned off the Piccinni Theater where the congress met. Some people wondered if the Allies feared a revolution.[49]

The Bari Congress was historic for several reasons, the most significant being that it was the first democratic assembly to meet openly in Europe since the Nazis overran the Continent. In Italy it was the first such conclave in almost two decades. Of the ninety delegates, about twenty had bravely crossed the lines from German-held territory.[50] Each party was permitted one representative per province. Alberto Cianca, Amendola's old journalistic collaborator, back from exile, acted as presiding officer together with Tito Zaniboni, the ex-*confinato* Socialist deputy who had been accused of trying to assassinate Mussolini

[47] Croce, *Quando l'Italia era tagliata in due*, pp. 51–59; Degli Espinosa, *Il Regno del Sud*, pp. 304–313.
[48] Catalano, *Storia del CLNAI*, p. 104; Croce, *Quando l'Italia era tagliata in due*, p. 45.
[49] Ibid., p. 69; Harris, *Allied Military Administration of Italy*, pp. 136–137. In near-by Taranto the Allies permitted an unblushingly royalist congress of the Democratic Liberal Party to meet with no such restrictions. Some months later this faction fused with the PLI.
[50] Paolo Treves, "Bari Conference: Symbol of a New Start," *Italy's Struggle for Liberation* (London, 1944), pp. 23–25.

in 1925.[51] At least one future premier, Antonio Segni (DC) of Sardinia, was among the delegates. The congress did not, of course, mark the birth or rebirth of free political parties, but it signaled their first dramatic bow on the public stage. Exhilarated by the Anzio landing, most delegates thought Rome's redemption near.

Croce delivered the prolusion, which reached its climax with a challenge to the Allies: "As long as the present King remains head of the State, we feel that Fascism is not finished, that it remains attached to us, that it continues to corrode us and to weaken us, that it will resurge more or less camouflaged; and to sum up, this way we cannot breathe and live." [52] Supporting Croce's charges, Sforza turned his thoughts to the future peace conference, hammering home the argument that if Italians got rid of the "supremely guilty" King they could "go to the peace negotiations with heads high. . . . If . . . we can present ourselves without the dead weight of a horrible past, I assure you of the strong possibility of coming out with honor." [53]

None of the other delegates knew of DeNicola's secret talks with the King about a Lieutenant-Generalcy. Socialist delegate Oreste Lizzadri, speaking for the Rome CCLN and the Milan CLN, presented a copy of the Rome underground resolution of October 16. He called upon the congress to transform itself into an "extraordinary government" with all constitutional powers, pending final popular referendum.[54] This was rejected by the Southerners as vague and impractical, as was another resolution of the three leftist parties calling for an indictment of the King and transformation of the congress into a "representative assembly of liberated Italy" which should thereupon form an "executive junta" to govern the South until Rome was freed.[55] Croce denounced this as "idiotic," observing with asperity that such a "government" could not "wield powers that it does not have." For without Allied acquiescence Italians could not hope

---

[51] See *supra*, Ch. I, Zaniboni affair and the attack on Freemasonry.

[52] B. Croce, *La libertà italiana nella libertà del mondo* (Bari, 1944), p. 8; reprinted also in C. Buonanno and O. Valentini, *Gli atti del Congresso di Bari* (Bari, 1944), p. 21.

[53] *Ibid.*, pp. 80–81; Sforza, *L'Italia dal 1914 al 1944 quale io la vidi*, p. 193 ff.

[54] Degli Espinosa, *Il Regno del Sud*, p. 257; Bonomi, *Diario di un anno*, p. 174; Catalano, *Storia del CLNAI*, pp. 108–110.

[55] Buonanno and Valentini, *Gli atti del Congresso di Bari*, pp. 32, 44, 54.

to organize an impromptu government to supersede that of the incumbent team. *Coups d'état* were out of the question; until the King had legally stepped aside, the Allies would not recognize such a government.[56]

At last a compromise DC resolution, battered out by Rodinò and Sforza, was accepted. It called merely for abdication of the King and referral of the institutional problem to popular referendum after the war. This compromise was feasible because the southern PCI, engaged at the moment in a furtive flirtation with Badoglio,[57] failed to give vigorous support to the leftists' resolution.[58] To achieve the new goal, the Bari Congress before adjourning on January 29 appointed an Executive Junta, composed of one representative from each of the six parties. It was instructed to keep in touch with Sforza, Croce, and other leaders. On February 9 it addressed a letter to the King, beseeching him to abdicate in view of the congressional resolution. This got no result, so on the 16th it sent a circular to various Italian civilian and military officials, inviting them not to support the stubborn monarch, and appealed to the masses to sign a petition demanding a plebiscite.[59]

The Bari Congress had brought the southern oppositionists into a fair degree of harmony with their clandestine brethren in the North, but the institutional question remained far from set-

---

[56] *Ibid.*, pp. 56–87; Croce, *Quando l'Italia era tagliata in due*, pp. 68–71.

[57] Southern PCI leaders seemed disposed in January to shelve the vexing issue in order to dedicate their energies exclusively to expulsion of the Germans from Italy. Rumors had it that the PCI (and perhaps the PSIUP too) might even decide to join a government of Badoglio and the King. According to Croce, the PCI failed to do so only because Badoglio refused to assign them a majority of portfolios. The coquetry of the southern Communists did not meet with favor among their compatriots in the North. Croce, *Quando l'Italia era tagliata in due*, pp. 63–69; Vaccarino, "Il movimento operaio a Torino nei primi mesi della crisi italiana," *MLI*, No. 19 (1952), pp. 16–19; PCI, *Relazione della Direzione del PCI al V° Congresso*, pp. 53–62; PCI, Federazione Campagna, *Che cosa vuole oggi il Partito Comunista Italiano?* (Naples, [1944]), printed in OSS, Research and Analysis Branch, No. 2081.2, "Italian Political Documents, Part II: Anti-Fascist Parties and Royal Government (July 1943–March 1944)," (Washington, May 13, 1944), pp. 10–11, 27–29.

[58] Psychological Warfare Branch, D Section, "Report on Conditions in Liberated Italy," Feb. 1, 1944, cited by Kogan, *Italy and the Allies*, p. 56.

[59] The official chronological summary of action taken at its meetings may be found in "La Giunta Esecutiva dei partiti antifascisti nel Sud," *MLI*, No. 28/29 (1954), pp. 41–121. Members were Arangio-Ruiz (PLI), Cerabona (DL), Jervolino (DC), Lizzadri (PSIUP), Calace (Pd'A), Spano (PCI), and Filippo Caracciolo (Secretary).

tled.[60] The King and Badoglio still could not form a government representative of the CLN hexarchy. Victor Emmanuel's position was weaker than ever.

The northern wings of the PSIUP and Pd'A were disappointed at the Bari Congress's failure to indicate exactly what would happen once Victor Emmanuel abdicated. Nenni made it clear in Rome on February 9 that a regency would not satisfy his party; the King must be ousted irrevocably, and the Constituent Assembly must proclaim a republic. As a result, bitter crisis engulfed the underground CCLN during the next weeks. The PSIUP won the support of the Pd'A, while the PCI wobbled on the issue. The PLI, DL, and DC showed a growing inclination to postpone this plan, if not to reject it altogether. As a matter of fact, Bonomi got word to the King to delay any change of cabinet until Rome was liberated (then thought to be imminent), at which time a CLN government would be installed, with the understanding that a Constituent Assembly would be called after the war.[61]

Meantime, Churchill dug himself in to uphold the King— Bari Congress or no. His cables to Roosevelt re-echoed all his past arguments in favor of hanging on to men who had signed the armistice and commanded the armed forces; the perils of changing governments in the midst of military difficulties; and the better opportunities for leisurely surveying the roster of suitable ministers once the Eternal City had been freed. On February 10 Roosevelt agreed to his request that he make no unilateral decisions, and ordered the State Department "to insure that no effort is made . . . to effect any change in the existing Government of Italy at the present time, and until our military situation in the Italian campaign is sufficiently improved to warrant risking disaffection of those Italians who are now assisting the Allied armies." [62] In a cable to Churchill, however, he added, "I think, though, that you and I should regard this only as a temporary reprieve for the two old gentlemen." [63]

On February 11 the seat of the royal government (though not

[60] Ragghianti, *Disegno della liberazione*, pp. 59–60, 117–119.
[61] Bonomi, *Diario di un anno*, pp. xiii–xv, 160–181; Valiani, *MLI*, No. 52/53 (1958), pp. 36, 41–43.
[62] Hull, *Memoirs*, II, 1552–1554.
[63] Churchill, *Closing the Ring*, p. 497.

all its scattered ministries) was shifted from Brindisi to Salerno, the King taking up his residence in Ravello. Simultaneously his realm was enlarged by the Allies, who handed over to his administration all provinces south of Naples and Foggia.[64] Of these, Sicily proved most troublesome, due to resurgence of a long-existent separatist movement, now spearheaded by Finocchiaro Aprile. The Salerno government appointed a none-too-capable High Commissioner and dispatched two divisions to the unruly island.[65]

By February 16, Harold Caccia and Samuel Reber, key Anglo-American officials of the ACC Political Section, decided that the monarchical dilemma must be resolved. Their thoughts reflected in considerable degree the arguments that Adlai Stevenson (who had headed an Economic Survey Mission in Naples for some weeks at the turn of the year) had cogently presented to the State Department upon his return.[66] Approaching the new Executive Junta, they asked it for a concrete proposal, and two days later received it. The plan called for Victor Emmanuel to abdicate unconditionally in favor of Humbert, who thereafter would surrender his authority to a collegial Lieutenant-Generalcy and a political government with full powers until general elections could be held after emancipation of the whole peninsula. Approved by the ACC and by General Henry Maitland Wilson at Allied Force Headquarters in Algiers, this formula was bucked up to the Combined Chiefs of Staff.[67]

The ACC endorsement of the scheme made it imperative for the King to decide whether to abdicate or seek some other exit. Next day (February 19) he told DeNicola in confidence that he would accept his original proposal and, without abdicating, simply retire in favor of Crown Prince Humbert as Lieutenant-General. The old monarch insisted that the actual transfer of power must await the liberation of Rome, to which he desired to return with more glory than had graced his departure.[68]

[64] Harris, *Allied Military Administration of Italy*, pp. 144–145.

[65] *Ibid.*, pp. 59–60, and *passim*; Badoglio, *Italy in the Second World War*, pp. 122–123, 136–142.

[66] Norman Kogan, "Intervento," *MLI*, No. 52/53 (1958), p. 181.

[67] Minutes of February 16, 18, 1944, meetings, in "Attività della Giunta Esecutiva del Congresso di Bari," *MLI*, No. 28/29 (1954), pp. 67–76; Harris, *Allied Military Administration of Italy*, p. 139.

[68] Croce, *Quando l'Italia era tagliata in due*, pp. 79–82.

At this critical point (the 22nd) Churchill rose in Commons to champion the cause of the King and Badoglio.[69] The CLN reaction to Churchill's pronunciamento was as melancholy as the King's was jubilant. The anti-Fascist politicians especially resented the Briton's implication that they would not possess enough authority over the armed forces to prosecute the war effort. The three leftist parties hoped to call a ten-minute protest strike. This the Allies forbade, but allowed them to hold a public meeting. In Washington there was resentment too, and both Hull and Roosevelt renewed (March 13) their pressure on Churchill to accept the Junta proposal. But on the 15th the unyielding prime minister, after consulting his War Cabinet, again declined to make any changes before the emancipation of Rome.[70]

Togliatti's PCI "svolta"

While these messages warmed the trans-Atlantic cables, Moscow announced that it was exchanging diplomatic representatives with the Italian royal government. Hitherto none of the United Nations had established normal relations with the "Kingdom of the South." Understandably, the Anglo-Americans, who had not been consulted, were indignant.[71] In Italy General Mason-Macfarlane accused Badoglio of bad faith. The latter insisted, however, that he previously had told American General Joyce, quondam ACC head,[72] of the Soviet approach, which had occurred in December 1943 [73] when Andrei Vyshinsky, Soviet delegate to the ACC, informed him that Moscow would welcome direct diplomatic communication with Brindisi. Badoglio had replied that he would be equally happy. From his point of view,

[69] Winston S. Churchill, *The Dawn of Liberation* (*War Speeches*) (Boston, 1945), pp. 17–19.

[70] Harris, *Allied Military Administration of Italy*, p. 140; Hull, *Memoirs*, II, 1555–1558; Churchill, *Closing the Ring*, pp. 501–505; Kogan, *Italy and the Allies*, pp. 57, 188–189; Degli Espinosa, *Il Regno del Sud*, pp. 283–284; Croce, *Quando l'Italia era tagliata in due*, pp. 83–84.

[71] Hull, *Memoirs*, II, 1555–1556.

[72] Joyce apparently did not grasp the import of Badoglio's casual tip at dinner. In any case, Badoglio did not consult the ACC in ensuing developments. Harris, *Allied Military Administration of Italy*, pp. 141–142; Badoglio, *Italy in the Second World War*, pp. 121, 128–133.

[73] An earlier one occurred in Algiers late in October when Alexander Bogomolov, Soviet ambassador to the French CLN, sounded out Count Prunas, the ex-Italian ambassador to Portugal who was then en route to Brindisi. Raimondo Luraghi, "I rapporti diplomatici Italiani-URSS nel 1944," *MLI*, No. 52/53 (1958), pp. 116–118.

such recognition would improve the kingdom's status vis à vis the Anglo-Americans; from the Kremlin's, such a gambit would strengthen the Soviet position in an almost exclusively Western-controlled theater. Vyshinsky later was summoned to Moscow and was replaced by Alexander Bogomolov, who reminded Badoglio of the conversation. They agreed to carry out the idea. Thus on March 13 the USSR appointed Mihail Kostylev its envoy to Italy, and the latter eventually named Pietro Quaroni of the Italian Legation in Afghanistan to be its representative.

Despite angry orders from the Allied Supreme Commander that the royal government not communicate directly with any state, either Allied or neutral, except through the ACC, the Italo-Soviet bargain was not entirely cancelled. For various reasons, including the Polish crisis, the Anglo-Americans did not wish to make too much of the matter, but they did get the Kremlin to reduce *de jure* to *de facto* recognition, implying exchange of "direct representatives" rather than "ambassadors." After a few weeks, the British somewhat grudgingly followed suit, designating Sir Noel Charles their High Commissioner to Italy. Later the United States did likewise, naming Alexander Kirk. These men were not accredited to the Italian government, and neither London nor Washington permitted Italy to send representatives to them. Ironically enough, Badoglio soon became annoyed by Kostylev's presence and complained about him to the Anglo-Americans.[74]

Meanwhile (March 15), DeNicola reported to Croce that the King desired the precise formula of the proclamation in which he would announce his decision to name Prince Humbert Lieutenant-General. DeNicola felt it best to delay two or three weeks, lest the appearance be given that the decision was influenced by a leftist demonstration that had taken place in Naples on the 12th. He feared that the PCI might claim credit and even provide Badoglio with a pretext to propose a government solely of Social-Communists.[75] But DeNicola and Croce could not procrastinate, for news of the King's decision began to leak.[76]

[74] Badoglio, *Italy in the Second World War*, pp. 131–132; Kogan, *Italy and the Allies*, p. 59; Feis, *Churchill, Roosevelt, Stalin*, pp. 326–328.
[75] He did not seem to understand that such a radical move would have been checked immediately by the Anglo-Americans.
[76] Croce, *Quando l'Italia era tagliata in due*, p. 92.

337

In the underground northern CLN's the monarchical issue had come to a boil. On March 17 the Pd'A pushed through the Milan CLNAI the most scorching antiroyalist declaration yet. But in Rome the hexpartite CCLN split evenly, and, because of the impasse, Bonomi tendered his resignation as president on the 23rd. He argued that the leftists were seeking a "government of public safety" in violation of the joint pledge of October 16 not to jeopardize national unity before the end of the war.[77]

Into all this tinder the Communists dropped a match. Moscow's *Izvestia* published an editorial on March 30, the gist of which was repeated to the PCI National Council in Naples on April 1 by the Kremlin's *longa manus*, Togliatti, who four days earlier had returned to his homeland.[78] To the consternation of most of the PCI and especially its northern wing, Togliatti indicated that he had no objection (provided the other anti-Fascist parties went along) to collaborating with Premier Badoglio, regardless of whether Victor Emmanuel III stayed on the throne. The all-important problem was successful prosecution of the war against the Nazi-Fascists; the dispute over the Monarchy was subsidiary. The King, after all, was an "institution," not a person, and it had already been agreed that final solution of the "institutional question" should await a postwar Constituent Assembly.[79] Despite the warning of the PCI coryphaeus that his party would campaign for a republic after the war, Victor Emmanuel was delighted; to a journalist he confided, "Togliatti . . . has spoken as an Italian. . . . At this moment the Communist leader is sincere. . . . The world is moving to the left. . . ."[80] A "veritable Lohengrin to the rescue" of Badoglio, was Bonomi's

[77] Catalano, *Storia del CLNAI*, pp. 153–154; Valiani, *Tutte le strade conducono a Roma*, pp. 217–218; Contini-Bonacossi (ed.), *Una lotta nel suo corso*, pp. 109–111; Bonomi, *Diario di un anno*, pp. 162–166; Valiani, MLI, No. 52/53 (1958), pp. 42–43.

[78] The Anglo-Americans had permitted the royal government in January to approve the return of "Ercole." The trip required several weeks and took him through the Persian Gulf, Egypt, and Algiers.

[79] PCI resolution of April 1, 1944, printed in Naples *Risorgimento*, April 2, 1944, and included in OSS, Research and Analysis Branch, No. 2081.3, "Italian Political Documents, Part III: April 1944" (Washington, May 30, 1944), pp. 1–2. *Cf.* Vincenzo Calace, "I Comunisti e la monarchia nel 1943–1944," *Il Ponte*, VII (1951), pp. 17–23; and correspondence between Salvemini and Togliatti in *Belfagor*, Nos. 1 and 2 (1950).

[80] Bolla, *Colloqui con Vittorio Emanuele III*, p. 128.

comment. The difference between the stanch Leninist Togliatti and the previous Communist leadership in the South was like that between St. Ignatius Loyola and St. Francis, it has been said.[81]

The PCI *svolta,* later rationalized by Togliatti as an original twist to the Popular Front line of Spanish Civil War days,[82] was a very adroit Soviet thrust to counter Anglo-American hegemony in Italy.[83] The British and Americans now faced the possibility of a hybrid undemocratic government composed only of the extreme Right and Left, since the moderates were still unready to compromise.[84] Togliatti's action undermined the whole CLN program erected since Bari. Clearly the Executive Junta's demand for unconditional abdication was a lost cause. The Pd'A and PSIUP who just three weeks before had joined the PCI in a public protest in Naples against Churchill's speech were bowled over by the "Herculean" maneuver. In the northern CLN's a propaganda battle was fought for a couple of weeks between Actionists and Communists over the merits of the *svolta:* when the PCI produced resolutions of support from "factory committees," the Pd'A denounced them as forgeries; the PCI, in turn, decried Actionist "sectarianism." [85]

Lieutenant-Generalcy of the Realm

Against this backdrop Croce unveiled the contents of De-Nicola's talks with Victor Emmanuel, hoping thereby to force the King to carry out his promise to name a Lieutenant-General. On April 6 he read to the Executive Junta a document that DeNicola, Sforza, and he had prepared for the King's signature. It called for his retirement but not abdication, and for appoint-

---

[81] Salvadori, *Resistenza ed azione,* p. 248 (April 16, 1944).

[82] Palmiro Togliatti, *Linea d'una politica* (Milan, 1948), p. 27.

[83] For a discussion of some hypotheses regarding Soviet motives, see Kogan, *Italy and the Allies,* pp. 62–65.

[84] On April 4 and 5 the PLI, DC, and DL repeated their refusal to join a Badoglio cabinet.

[85] Valiani, *Tutte le strade conducono a Roma,* p. 237; OSS, Research and Analysis Branch, No. 2081.3, "Italian Political Documents, Part III: April 1944," pp. 13–14; *cf.* Contini-Bonacossi (ed.), *Una lotta nel suo corso,* p. 111 ff. The PSIUP's reluctant adherence to the new PCI line was explained in a long statement by the Rome Directorate on May 1; it is printed in Carli-Ballola, *Sdr,* pp. 321–332.

ment of Prince Humbert as Lieutenant-General of the Realm. Actual transfer of powers would await Rome's liberation.[86] Gritting their teeth, all the politicians (including Togliatti) agreed to DeNicola's *combinazione* (which still required Allied placet).[87] The Pd'A objected to Badoglio's presence in a new government and would greatly have preferred a "civil lieutenancy" under Croce, Orlando, and Sforza.[88] The PSIUP demanded revision of the armistice terms (in vain, of course).

By this time the Americans grasped what had happened and convinced the British that there was no choice but to push the King into immediate retirement so that all the CLN parties could enter a cabinet headed by Badoglio. On April 10 the Anglo-American strategists Mason-Macfarlane, Macmillan, and Murphy obtained an audience with the King, ostensibly to present Sir Noel Charles, the newly named British High Commissioner. As soon as that formality was over, they insisted without periphrasis upon immediate publication of the document transferring power to Humbert. Victor Emmanuel was taken aback by their "suggestion," presented (in Badoglio's metaphor) "with a pistol pointed at the King's head," for it was not customary to bring up other topics than the specific one that occasioned the audience. The King was heartbroken that he must announce his retirement before Rome was taken, but he had no alternative. He insisted upon waiting a day before making his decision and then coldly concluded, "Now I must ask you gentlemen to withdraw, as your presence has annoyed me sufficiently." [89] Next day (the 12th) the penultimate Savoyard published his act of devolution: ". . . Giving effect to what has already been communicated to the Allied authorities and to my Government, I have decided to withdraw from public life, appointing as Lieutenant-General my son, the Prince of Piedmont. This appointment will take effect by means of the official transfer of powers the same day on which

[86] Technically he did not abdicate until May 1946, a month before the national referendum on the institutional question. His abdication then was designed to aid the royalist cause. After the republican victory at the polls in June 1946, "King of the May" Humbert II also abdicated.

[87] Croce, *Quando l'Italia era tagliata in due*, pp. 98–101; Croce, *Per la nuova vita d'Italia*, pp. 71–72.

[88] Emilio Lussu, "Intervento," *MLI*, No. 52/53 (1958), p. 187.

[89] Degli Espinosa, *Il Regno del Sud*, pp. 333–334; Badoglio, *Italy in the Second World War*, pp. 145–147; Bolla, *Colloqui con Umberto II*, pp. 46–47; Hull, *Memoirs*, II, 1558; Feis, *Roosevelt, Churchill, Stalin*, pp. 330–331.

the Allied troops enter Rome. This, my decision, which I am firmly convinced will facilitate national unity, is definitive and irrevocable." [90] Two days later the Allies informed Badoglio that in view of the King's action they "consider[ed] the institutional changes concluded until that time when, with the liberation of the national territory, the Italian people will be able freely to render their decision." [91]

Badoglio's CLN government

The way was now clear for a new political cabinet that would embrace all six parties in the CLN's. In vain the Pd'A tried to persuade either Croce or DeNicola rather than Badoglio to head such a government. Badoglio visited Croce in Sorrento on April 14 and discussed with him suitable candidates. The PLI mandarin assured him of his party's support; Rodinò did the same for the DC. Badoglio already could count upon Togliatti, and of course the PSIUP was linked to the PCI. He was told that the DL would also back him. Only the Pd'A remained aloof.

Badoglio got over one hurdle by promising equal representation to the five parties who thus far had agreed to join. But assigning specific posts was not easy—especially the Ministry of Interior, which everyone aspired to in a time of flux. Finally he devised a system of checks and balances that proved acceptable. Most ingenious was his strategy of creating "ministries without portfolio" to mollify rival sensibilities. In the past it had been customary to name to such posts eminent people whose presence would bolster a government. For that reason, Badoglio decided to name Croce, honored by everyone yet too old to take on the hard and drab day-to-day supervision of a department. But Sforza (whom Badoglio had assumed would become Foreign Minister —until Churchill interposed his veto) [92] wished to have a ministry without portfolio just like Croce. And when Rodinò heard of Sforza's move, he pointed out with equal immodesty that since he had been a minister several times and Sforza but once, he

[90] Quoted in Maraldi, *Storia della seconda guerra mondiale*, p. 411.
[91] Smyth, "Italy: From Fascism to the Republic," *The Western Political Quarterly*, 1 (1948), p. 213.
[92] No love was lost between them since Sforza had referred to Churchill as a *testa di passerotto* ("sparrow-head"). Croce, *Quando l'Italia era tagliata in due*, p. 108. By 1948 the two old gentlemen had patched up their relationship and sipped tea together in London.

must have a similar honor. Next the PSIUP and PCI demanded parity, so the names of Professor Pietro Mancini and Togliatti were added to the roster of "super-ministers." Despite the top-heaviness of the cabinet, Badoglio professed to see an advantage in having some ministers unburdened by detailed work and available to study special problems. Each ministry had an under-secretary belonging to a different party from the head man.[93]

At last, on the evening of the 21st, Professor Adolfo Omodeo and Alberto Tarchiani, leaders of the Pd'A in the South, swallowed their misgivings and adhered. Arguments by Croce and Allied promises of increased economic aid and aerial drops to the Armed Resistance helped influence their decision.[94] The Actionists were somewhat miffed not to have their pick of cabinet posts but rationalized their lack of a ministry without portfolio on the grounds that they wished to emphasize they were associating with Badoglio only because of wartime urgency. When the Pd'A moguls in Rome (LaMalfa and Lussu) learned what had happened, they wished to read Omodeo and Tarchiani out of their ranks, but farther north calmer counsel prevailed (primarily, as Parri has explained, because they did not care to risk the disaffection of numerous guerrilla commanders). On the 30th the Tuscan CLN, after much soul-searching by the Pd'A, accepted a face-saving resolution by Ragghianti recognizing the new government as "the expression of the CLN" and answerable to it. It asserted that the CLN was "the sole representative of the Italian people in the liberation struggle" and the nucleus around which the future Constituent Assembly would be built.[95]

In Rome, meanwhile, the bitter fight that had split the Central CLN for weeks slowly came to an end.[96] On May 10 Bonomi resumed his chairmanship and set forth three objectives: (1) a precise and unequivocable legislative pledge for popular consultation regarding the institutional question; (2) a new formula

[93] Badoglio, *Italy and the Second World War*, pp. 148–149.

[94] Valiani, MLI, No. 52/53 (1958), p. 41; Kogan, *Italy and the Allies*, p. 60; Salvadori, SRI, p. 100.

[95] Valiani, *Tutte le strade conducono a Roma*, pp. 238–240; Valiani, MLI, No. 52/53 (1958), pp. 43–44; Parri in *ibid.*, 190–193; E. Enriques-Agnoletti in *ibid.*, 175–179; Catalano, *Storia del CLNAI*, pp. 158–161; Ragghianti, *Disegno della liberazione*, pp. 122, 138–140, 162–172; Contini-Bonacossi (ed.), *Una lotta nel suo corso*, pp. 111–140, 156–163; Rome *L'Italia libera*, April 19, 1944.

[96] Bauer, "L'attività del CLN in Roma nel maggio 1944," MLI, No. 50 (1958), pp. 57–85.

for the oath, in order to permit republican parties to take an honorable place in the government; and (3) consolidation of the legislative and executive powers so that the government will be "the extraordinary instrument for an extraordinary crisis." [97]

In Salerno the new Badoglio cabinet was sworn in on April 24.[98] The oath to the monarch was administered on the basis of a compromise formula concocted by Tarchiani: "Your Majesty, I have the honour to present the members of the new Government. They belong to every party, and while not abandoning their party allegiances, they are ready at this grave moment to subordinate these to the need for agreement, which is indispensable for the salvation of the country." [99] In addition, the cabinet pledged the Allies not to try to upset the Lieutenant-Generalcy for the duration of the war and to accept the armistice obligations—no small promises.[100]

Premier Badoglio issued a long statement of policy, to which by implication his cabinet was bound. In some instances this involved very great concessions by the three leftist currents, as when they swallowed his remarks that radical political and economic reforms must be avoided "while Italy is divided into two parts, the larger portion being still occupied by the enemy." Badoglio promised, however, that the new government "at the appropriate moment" would draft the necessary electoral law to let the people choose by universal suffrage a Constituent Assembly. Meantime, the government, "working in collaboration with the Committees of Liberation," would create as a "symbol of the nonexistent Parliament, a Consultative Council ["Consulta Nazionale"] to which it will report at intervals on its activities." [101] Critics at once objected that all this was a policy

[97] Bonomi, *Diario di un anno*, pp. xvii, 163–181.
[98] The final roster included Croce, Sforza, Rodinò, Mancini, and Togliatti as Ministers without Portfolio; Badoglio as both Prime and Foreign Minister; Dr. Salvatore Aldisio (DC), Interior; Prof. Vincenzo Arangio-Ruiz (PLI), Justice; Quinto Quintieri (nonparty banker), Finance; General Taddeo Orlando, War; Admiral Raffaele de Courten, Marine; General Renato Sandalli, Air; Prof. Adolfo Omodeo (Pd'A), Education; Alberto Tarchiani (Pd'A), Public Works; Dr. Fausto Gullo (PCI), Agriculture and Forests; Dr. Francesco Cerabona (DL), Communications; Dr. Attilio di Napoli (PSIUP), Industry, Commerce and Labor. It will be noted that the heads of the military departments remained the same as before.
[99] Badoglio, *Italy in the Second World War*, p. 149.
[100] Kogan, *Italy and the Allies*, pp. 60–62.
[101] Badoglio, *Italy in the Second World War*, pp. 151–156.

declaration and not a legal obligation. The Consulta, really excogitated by Croce, was the only novel facet of Badoglio's program. The ministers without portfolio were instructed to adumbrate its functions; as events worked out, the Consulta was not set up until September 1945.

Badoglio announced that expurgation (*"epurazione"*) would be continued "by just and energetic measures . . . to a successful conclusion as soon as possible." [102] To implement this, the government reshuffled de-Fascistization organs. Sforza and Avv. Mario Berlinguer, an ex-parliamentary associate of Amendola, were named, respectively, Commissioner and Assistant Commissioner of the High Commission of Expurgation, apparently to the dismay of the British.[103] They replaced Tito Zaniboni, who now took over the care of refugees. In practice, Sforza's agency watched over the trials of Fascist criminals; another body, the Commission for De-Fascistization, headed by Professor Omodeo (Pd'A), superintended the pruning of Fascists from the bureaucracy.[104] The new government continued to use the decree-law system to dismantle remnants of totalitarianism. Thus on May 16 it abolished the Mussolinian title *Capo del Governo*, in favor of "Prime Minister, Secretary of State." [105]

In his inaugural address Badoglio declared that economic restoration, re-establishment of taxation, and filling of the vacuum in public administration all required immediate attention.[106] But foremost in his list of urgent tasks was winning the "War for Liberation." He predicted that "with a new democratic Government and freed from the feeling of frustration," the fighting men would be united and animated by a new spirit. He pledged to do all in his power to support the underground patriots.

[102] *Ibid.*, p. 155.

[103] Ragghianti, *Disegno della liberazione italiana*, p. 163.

[104] OSS, Research and Analysis Branch, No. 2688, "Treatment of Former Fascists by the Italian Government: An Analysis of the process of defascistization in Italy from July 1943 to March 1945," (Washington, March 17, 1945), pp. 1–9; *cf.* Harris, *Allied Administration of Italy*, pp. 147–150.

[105] Smyth, *The Western Political Quarterly*, 1 (1948), p. 213. For a discussion of some of the legislation promulgated at Brindisi and Salerno, see Harris, *Allied Military Administration of Italy*, pp. 146–150.

[106] In at least one of these fields a significant measure was introduced. The PCI Agricultural Minister Gullo proposed on June 3 a law proroguing contracts between small tenant farmers and large landowners, thereby giving temporary relief to thousands of peasants.

"Whatever party they represent they are all at one in the determination to free Italy and defeat the Germany of Hitler." [107]

The Allies responded favorably to the new program. Within a few days Churchill announced the return of three Italian cruisers and dispatch of five squadrons of British-manufactured aircraft. The size of the Italian fighting forces at the front was increased slightly in April to 14,100 and this figure was doubled the following month, but efforts by the anti-Fascist currents to permit volunteer contingents to be inserted in these forces failed.[108]

Badoglio made a renewed effort to win "allied" status, reminding Roosevelt of the latter's promise in January 1944 to reexamine the problem once Italy settled the institutional question, created a broad democratic government, and maximized the war effort. Though he won American sympathy, Badoglio ran up against a stone wall of opposition from the British, French, Greeks, and Yugoslavs.[109]

Politics in the South moved along fairly serenely until the contents of an inept press interview granted in April by Prince Humbert to a correspondent of the *London Times* became known. In the interview he had imprudently observed that his father had approved the June 1940 war declaration because "any other course was out of the question"; failure to do so "would have brought the Germans down upon us." "Moreover, there was no sign that the nation wanted it otherwise. No single voice was raised in protest. No demand was made for summoning Parliament. Ostensibly Mussolini had the country with him." [110]

This interview stirred the CLN leaders to fury. They pointed out that no one could register opposition in June 1940 because of the absence of a free Parliament and a free press. Incensed by Humbert's effort to absolve the House of Savoy of responsibility,

---

[107] Badoglio, *Italy in the Second World War*, p. 154.

[108] Probably the chief explanation for the increase of Italian forces lay in the Allies' need to find replacements for their own troops being shifted to other theaters. But political considerations were not entirely absent. Kogan, *Italy and the Allies*, p. 100; Badoglio, *Italy in the Second World War*, p. 157; OSS, Research and Analysis Branch, No. 2081.3, "Italian Political Documents, Part III: April 1944," 14–18.

[109] Hull, *Memoirs*, II, 1554–1559; Kogan, *Italy and the Allies*, pp. 66–67; Feis, *Roosevelt, Churchill, Stalin*, p. 331.

[110] *London Times*, April 20, 1944, printed in OSS, Research and Analysis Branch, No. 2081.3, pp. 24–26. The same arguments were often set forth by Victor Emmanuel III; cf. Bolla, *Colloqui con Vittorio Emanuele III*, pp. 118, 123.

the Salerno government rebuked him on May 11 for speaking "not in consonance with the ideas and policy of the Government, [which] unanimously repudiates any accusation against the Italian people concerning its responsibility for the Fascist war." [111]

Prince Humbert thereupon denied that his remarks should have been so construed. He was astounded when the Pd'A demanded that he renounce his claim to the Lieutenant-Generalship. But the Actionists blundered in delaying their demand till the eve of Rome's liberation; they should have acted at the moment the Prince made the statement if they wished to reap advantage. As events turned out, they were constrained to withdraw their demand.

[111] OWI Italian News Bulletin, May 12, 1944, printed in OSS, Research and Analysis Branch, No. 2081.3, p. 26.

CHAPTER IX · UNDERGROUND
RESURGENCE

January – June 1944

WHILE the shadow Kingdom of the South wrestled with the institutional question during the winter, underground fighters in Mussolini's marionette Italian Social Republic concentrated on the difficult tasks of surviving the bitter cold and mounting enemy assaults upon them. Probably not more than 10,000 were left in their lairs after the ruthless *rastrellamenti* of late December, January, and February—rakings that were especially thorough in Piedmont and Venetia.

Some partisan commanders concluded that their narrow valleys were untenable against such comb-outs and advocated limiting guerrilla warfare to small, terroristic bands. This the guardian spirits of the Armed Resistance's left flank would not consider, for they needed large-scale military operations to facilitate the attainment of their political goal of outstripping the royal government.[1]

Internal discipline

Almost everyone agreed, however, that tighter discipline and co-ordination of the Resistenza Armata was imperative. Thus during the winter saluting became fashionable, even among the Giellisti who during the autumn had bridled at anything smacking of "spit and polish." In these early months Communist guerrillas used the clenched-fist greeting; and when entering or leaving a room they pronounced the ritualistic slogan "Death to the Fascists!" ("*Morte ai Fascisti!*"), to which the usual antistrophe was "Freedom for the people!" ("*Libertà ai popoli!*").[2] More systematic patterns of organization and dress also emerged. Though still lacking real uniforms, partisans often wore something distinctive—a flame on the jacket lapel, a red or blue neckerchief, or a red star on the beret.[3] But after the consolidation of the Resistenza into a "national movement" later in the

---

[1] Battaglia, *SRI*, pp. 200–202.
[2] See memoirs of a British liaison officer with a PCI brigade in Venetia: H. W. Tilman, *When Men and Mountains Meet* (Cambridge, 1946), p. 169.
[3] Salvadori, *SRI*, p. 86.

war, Communist protocol formulators deemed it expedient to minimize such affectations.[4]

Many units sponsored special police corps in their intelligence sections to ferret out troublemakers and maintain order in their mountain strongholds; they punished those who harmed the peasants without cause; and they systematized the "requisitions" from the local populace. Punishment for breaches of discipline generally was intended to be exemplary and ranged from temporary suspension of the tobacco ration to doubling of guard turns, expulsion from the band, or even execution—the latter, however, requiring authorization of a military tribunal.

Formal courts-martial were impossible because of the dearth of properly trained officers; instead, drumhead tribunals prevailed. At first they dispensed a rough sort of justice and functioned under conveniently flexible rules; but eventually greater standardization of procedure developed. Ordinarily the unit commander would preside, a vice-commissar or other designated official would present charges, while a small jury would hand down the verdict.[5] Inevitably such trials elicited sardonic comments, and in some Piedmontese Garibaldi units partisans nodded knowingly when they heard the jingle, *"Andar in val di Viù vuol dire non tornar più!"* ("To go to Val di Viù [Val di Lanzo] means you don't come again to view!").[6]

Political commissars played a capital role in instilling and maintaining discipline. Employment of such officials was a hotly debated question during the early phase of the Resistance, and the military commanders usually resented these applicators of the party line. The Communists had used commissars at different times in the Russian Red Army, the international brigades of the Spanish Civil War, and the Balkan partisan movements. It was not surprising, therefore, that they introduced the system on a broad scale in the Garibaldi units early in the winter, naming Pietro Secchia Commissar-General. With some reluctance, and perhaps in self-defense, certain other formations also adopted the system. Usually they did not call such officials "commissars"; they preferred, instead, such circumlocutions as "civil-

[4] Fabrizio Alvesi, *La ribellione degli Italiani* (Rome, 1956), p. 179.

[5] Bianco, *Guerra partigiana*, p. 52 ff.; Longo, *Un popolo alla macchia*, pp. 373–376.

[6] Trabucchi, *I vinti hanno sempre torto*, p. 114.

ian representatives of the CLN," but usually they carried out the kind of tasks recommended for such officers by the PCI. It should be noted that the Communists did their best to infiltrate their own trusted men into other formations as such "delegates." [7]

The Garibaldini had one political commissar for each detachment (*i.e.*, for every forty to fifty men in the early period), whereas the Giellisti limited themselves to one for an entire brigade (which at that stage meant any unit exceeding one hundred men).[8] They specified certain hours almost daily for political lectures and discussions. Some impression of the PCI system may be derived from a 1944 party directive: "Wherever Communists find themselves—in factories, villages, offices, partisan formations—they have the duty to organize themselves and carry on activity. In the absence of this, they cease for practical purpose to function in the party. There is weakness and lack of discipline wherever Communists are not present, and the Communists are an element of force only if they are organized." In every unit one person had to be responsible for PCI work and report to the "federal committee" in each province, which assumed responsibility for the operations of cells in the patriot bands in that province; where such cells did not exist, party members in the unit immediately had to form them; they were required to work together on all general problems of a political, economic, and military nature, and had to exercise local authority and initiative in accepting new members and removing inefficient ones.[9]

The instructions of the Pd'A to one of its Piedmontese political commissars in March 1944 provide similar enlightenment:

1) Fix well in the mind of each partisan that he is a soldier of a NEW AND REVOLUTIONARY army, the Army of National Liberation, which is not identical with, nor even the successor of the old Royal army, which failed so miserably;

2) Explain what the CLN is—*viz.*, the only organ which, after the flight of the King, his courtesans and ministers, has raised the banner of active resistance against the Nazi-Fascists and has promised, in-

[7] Longo, *Un popolo alla macchia*, pp. 119–120; Battaglia, *SRI*, p. 197; *cf. supra*, Ch. VII, Political wing of the Armed Resistance.

[8] Mario Giovana, "La composizione sociale delle formazioni 'G.L.' in Piemonte," *MLI*, No. 10 (1951), p. 26.

[9] Quoted in Cadorna, *La Riscossa*, pp. 307–309.

spired, sustained, and continued this struggle. It is substantially the TRUE AND AUTHENTIC NATIONAL GOVERNMENT OF INVADED ITALY, and only from this Government, and not from that of Badoglio, may the partisan formations receive orders and directives;

3) Illustrate . . . clearly that the soldiers of this Army of National Liberation are not so much . . . the champions of a generic patriotism . . . as they are the arm and the resolute advance guard of a revolutionary process . . . which . . . must make of Italy . . . once more a free, democratic, and civil nation;

4) Consequently, avoid hackneyed patriotic rhetoric, and insist that each man personally understand the aims of the partisan struggle, which, more than the mere expulsion of the Germans from Italy, seeks the radical destruction of Nazism and Fascism in all its manifestations, however camouflaged . . . ;

5) Use every method and occasion to eliminate the rather widespread notion that the partisan formations are a kind of "beneficiary society" . . . protecting . . . renitents and deserters [from being] interned in Germany or sent to the battlefield;

6) . . . The partisan must conceive his service like he would a vocation, being ready to carry it out TO THE VERY END, facing discomforts, privations, and sacrifices, including that of life itself, for the triumph of a higher civic ideal which finds its insuperable expression in the formula: "GIUSTIZIA E LIBERTÀ." [10]

Unlike the apolitical Autonomi, GL officers usually did not swear fealty to the King, and in general they tolerated within their bands a wide range of political views. In the Cuneo zone the GL fighter obligated himself in these terms:

I, the undersigned . . . , obligate myself—confirming my duty with the oath of a gentleman—to serve in the bands, *Italia Libera*, which are promoted by the Action Party and embraced in the CLN, in order to take part actively in the struggle against the Germans and Fascists, and to pursue the realization of the ideals of social justice and democratic freedom.

I obligate myself to observe strictly the military discipline of the band, and to execute faithfully all orders which the headquarters of the band may give me, and to follow unswervingly the service I have voluntarily assumed, until the anti-German and anti-Fascist struggle is finished with the installation in Italy of a political and social regime worthy of a free and civilized country.

I recognize that from this moment any transgression on my part of

[10] Quoted in Bianco, *Guerra partigiana*, pp. 62–63. Reprinted by kind permission of Giulio Einaudi Editore, Turin.

the obligations above assumed may constitute an act of treason and baseness, and expose me to the gravest sanctions, including the loss of my very life.[11]

Clandestine press and songs

To help sustain morale and clarify the ideals of the Resistenza, almost all of the fighting groups (and the parties that stood behind them) engendered a luxuriant clandestine press. Despite manifest difficulties, they either printed or mimeographed dozens of newspapers, innumerable bulletins, maps, resolutions, and other documents. At first patriots usually had their newspapers printed in the cities, but sometimes mastheads bore the romantic elucidation, "It appears wherever and whenever it can."

The earliest journals tended to resemble World War I trench papers. Instinctively they eschewed rhetoric and sentimentality, and did not at first display much humor; obviously their chief aim was to shed political and military enlightenment. Some of the papers affected a didactic, propagandistic tone and sought with scant subtlety to "orient" the reader.[12]

At a later stage (September 13, 1944) Supreme Headquarters of the Resistance issued a decree exhorting the fighting units to grind out mimeographed papers and offered them suggestions on how best to prepare them. Political commissars should take the lead, it advised, but more than one man should write; "generic rhetoric" and "romanticism" should be avoided; articles should take up topics of local interest, and be educative and critical of concrete things—"concepts of discipline, democracy, brotherhood toward other formations and the people;" writers should shun Latin phrases and unfamiliar words; and they should inject some humor. Commissars, it recommended, should also learn to make use of bulletin boards.[13]

The PCI and Pd'A, for whose directors this kind of work was

[11] Quoted in *ibid.*, p. 55. Reprinted by kind permission of Giulio Einaudi Editore, Turin.

[12] On the broad subject see S. Tomaselli, *Storia della stampa clandestina* (Rome, 1951); Laura Conti, "La stampa clandestina della Resistenza in una raccolta documentaria," *MLI*, No. 58 (1960), pp. 3–23. Carli-Ballola, *Sdr*, pp. 163–165; Battaglia, *SRI*, pp. 403–407.

[13] Italy, Presidenza del Consiglio, Ufficio Storico per la Guerra di Liberazione, *Atti del Comando Generale Corpo Volontari della Libertà dalla sua costituzione all'insurrezione nazionale (giugno 1944–aprile 1945)* (Rome, 1946), Decree No. 59 (Sept. 13, 1944), pp. 102–106. Hereafter cited as *Atti del CG/CVL*.

an old story, gave birth to the largest number of publications; the PSIUP probably ranked next. Their publications were in two broad categories: (1) regular covert papers in Rome and Milan (and certain other cities) and high-brow reviews; and (2) publications belonging to the guerrilla formations. The PCI line could best be untangled in the theoretical review *La nostra lotta*, and in the sundry editions of *L'Unità*. The Socialists set forth their positions in Rodolfo Morandi's *Politica di classe*, and in municipal editions of *Avanti!* The Pd'A published *L'Italia libera* in Rome and Milan, while in the North historian Franco Venturi (aided by Valiani, Riccardo Lombardi, Mario Dal Pra, and Domenico Boffito) edited the massive *Nuovi Quaderni di Giustizia e Libertà*, some of whose numbers reached a remarkable thickness of 200 pages. Among the many martyrs in the editorial ranks three were pre-eminent: Leone Ginzburg, of the Rome *L'Italia libera*; Eugenio Colorni, of the Rome *Avanti!*; and Eugenio Curiel, of the Milan *L'Unità*.

In the Piedmontese partisan formations perhaps *Il Partigiano Alpino* was the best-known GL publication. It first appeared in February 1944 and later came out in a Lombard edition as well; by the end of the war it attained a circulation of some 20,000 copies. Its masthead showed an Alpine soldier defending his homeland. The first issue explained the problems of the Resistance and discussed agrarian reform. In order to broaden its appeal, references to the Pd'A were eliminated at a later time. Other GL papers in Piedmont included *Quelli della montagna*, *Giustizia e Libertà*, and *Il Pioniere*. *La Stella alpina* and *Voci d'officina* also enjoyed popularity.[14] Unfortunately, data regarding the many short-lived papers are far from complete.

In addition to running off newspapers and pamphlets, the patriots composed songs, poems, and doggerel verse, often satirical in tone and couched in the local dialects.[15] Some tunes and

[14] Emilio Castellani, "La stampa partigiana delle GL piemontesi," *Nuovi Quaderni di Giustizia e Libertà*, No. 5/6 (1945), pp. 193–197; Mario Dal Pra, "Venti mesi di stampa clandestina," *Mercurio* (*Anche l'Italia ha vinto*), II, No. 16 (Dec. 1945), pp. 227–232. Other regions had their own journals. For the Venetian press, see G. Gaddi, *Saggio sulla stampa clandestina della Resistenza veneta* (Bologna, 1955).
[15] Several of these have been collected and printed since the war: Elio Filippo Accrocca and Valerio Volpini (eds.), *Antologia poetica della Resistenza italiana* (Florence, 1955); Alvesi, *La ribellione degli Italiani*, Ch. x, "Canti, giornali e manifesti"; Maria Donadio, *I canti clandestini* (Milan, 1950); *Canti della Resistenza* (Turin, 1961); and Antonio Russi, "Significato della poesia della Resistenza," *Il Ponte*, XI (1955), pp. 673–681.

themes harked back to the Risorgimento and World War I; others were inspired by international Communism (*e.g.*, "Red Banner," "Hymn of the Workers," "Sons of the Factory"). In Emilia, where there was some chance that class strife might overshadow patriotic solidarity, some leftists sought to write poetry that would combine the two themes.[16] Piedmont, with its ingrained military tradition, probably produced the greatest number of war tunes, with the Friuli sector of the Veneto taking second honors. *"Pietà l'è morta!"* (a bitterly anti-German song of the GL First Alpine Division) and the *"Badoglieide"* (a ribald lampoon of Badoglio and the King, "fattened on the *fascio littorio*," and set to one of the ditties of the operetta *Il Boccaccio*) were perhaps the most popular songs among the Giellisti from Cuneo. But the air which attained widest popularity was *"Fischia il vento, urla la bufera"* ("The wind whistles, the storm howls"), written by Felice Cascione, a Garibaldino of Liguria, and set to the Red Army tune of *"Katiuscia."* [17]

For a time in March and April 1945 Moscatelli's Garibaldini in Piedmont made use of a portable radio transmitter that they somehow had acquired; they broadcast a series of musical and propagandistic programs.[18]

As one might suspect, the epiclike Armed Resistance has registered a notable impact upon postwar Italian literature (Elio Vittorini, Cesare Pavese, Vasco Pratolini, and others),[19] upon

---

[16] Battaglia, *SRI*, pp. 409–418.

[17] *Cf.* diary of Giovanni Monaco, *Pietà l'è morta* (Milan, 1955), p. 4; Dante Livio Bianco, *Il Ponte*, v (1949), p. 1067.

[18] Secchia and Moscatelli, *Il Monte Rosa è sceso a Milano*, pp. 425–428.

[19] Vittorini, for example, has written *Uomini e no* (Milan, 1949); Pavese, *La casa in collina; Il carcere;* and *Prima che il gallo canti* (Turin, 1949); Pratolini, *Il Quartiere* (Florence, 1947) [English version: *The Naked Streets* (New York, 1952)].

Other competent writers include Arrigo Benedetti, *Paura dell'alba* (Rome, 1945); Guglielmo Petroni, *Il mondo è una prigione* (Milan, 1949); Bonaventura Tecchi, *Un'estate in campagna (diario 1943)* (Florence, 1945). For the pre-1943 period of the Resistance one must certainly include the novels of Ignazio Silone, Carlo Levi, and the posthumously published *Il sangue d'Europa, 1939–1943* (Turin, 1950) of young Giaime Pintor.

Cf. Valerio Volpini, "Note intorno alla letteratura sulla Resistenza," *Civitas*, VI (1955), pp. 103–112, for a bibliographical survey of forty-five Italian writers on Resistance themes. According to him, Italy lacked a "Vercors" but had many capable poets and novelists, of whom Salvatore Quasimodo, Alfonso Gatto, Italo Calvino, Silone, Vittorini, and Pavese have been the best known. *Cf.* Aristide Marchetti and Guido Tassinari (eds.), *La Resistenza nella letteratura* (Milan, 1955); Angelo Paoluzzi, *La letteratura della Resistenza* (Rome, 1956); and Arnaldo Bocelli, "Resistenza e letteratura," Rome *Il Mondo*, April 23, 1957, p. 8.

the "neo-realistic" school of cinematography, and upon composers of serious music.[20] But a discussion of these artistic and cultural trends cannot be undertaken here; in any case, they deserve judgment from a longer perspective.

CLN for Upper Italy (CLNAI)

The first winter of the Armed Resistance revealed that tighter CLN direction in the North was imperative. A vexing financial squabble that involved General Piero Operti of the disbanded Fourth Army in Piedmont brought the problem to a head in January 1944.

General Operti preserved a large portion of the funds of the ill-fated Fourth Army; for this very practical reason he was viewed at first with favor by everyone in the Turin CLN except the Communists. In return for his making the money available, that committee had assigned to him in October 1943 sole direction of a "united command" ("comando unico") for recruiting partisans in Piedmont. Operti apparently hoped to become commander of all these patriots; with the money he possessed he thought he could keep 20,000 in the field for ten months. By December he had frunished the CPLN with 190,114,769 French francs and 11,830,000 Italian lire to finance operations in Piedmont.[21] But from November until January 1944 the CPLN was rocked by charges and countercharges involving the general. Few of his foes denied that he was a sincere patriot, but they accused him of being too friendly to the House of Savoy and too generous to the Autonomi. PCI delegate Celeste Negarville went farther and presented evidence designed to show that Operti advocated the "heresy" of static attesismo and unrealistic bureaucratization

[20] See Franco Valobra, "Filmografia sulla Resistenza italiana," *MLI*, No. 36 (1955), pp. 51–58, for a list and discussion of the chief motion picture films and documentaries dealing with the Resistance. These included in 1945: "Due lettere anonime"; "Giorni di gloria"; "'O sole mio"; "Roma città aperta!" In 1946 appeared "Il corriere di ferro"; "Davanti a lui tremava tutta Roma"; "Felicità perduta"; "Un giorno nella vita"; "Paisà"; "Pian delle stelle"; "Il sole sorge ancora." In 1947–1948 appeared "Anni difficili"; "Gli uomini sono nemici"; while in 1951 "Achtung, Banditi!" was brought out. Documentaries included "L'Italia s'è desta" (1946); "La nostra guerra" (1946); "Lettere dei condannati a morte della Resistenza italiana" (1953); "San Miniato, Luglio '44" (1954); and "Il Generale della Rovere" (1959). An unsympathetic treatment of the Resistance was "Nessuno ha tradito." See also Luigi Pestalozza, "Musica ispirata alla Resistenza," *Il Ponte*, xi (1955), pp. 687–695.

[21] General Piero Operti, *Il tesoro della 4ᵗᵃ Armata* (Turin, 1946), pp. 25–26, 142–147, 207–208, 219–221, 239–240, 263–266, and *passim*.

of the underground fighting arm. So implacable was the leftists' hostility that the general was dismissed by the CPLN early in January, soon to be replaced by General Perotti, who had been in charge of resistants within the city of Turin.[22]

Meantime, other northern patriots were demanding to be cut in on what was left of Fourth Army funds—apparently still equivalent to some 50,000,000 lire. Who should make the apportionment? The CPLN? The Milan CLN? Both committees were unblushingly ambitious, and each dispatched envoys to Rome to persuade the Central CLN to assign supreme authority to it. They argued cogently that the CCLN was too far down the peninsula to handle efficiently matters involving the North; that Mussolini's shrewd propaganda in behalf of socialization and his skillful attempts to turn rightist resistants against the Communists needed to be countered more effectively and at closer range; and that the Allied debarkation at Anzio on January 22 suggested that Rome might soon be freed and thus cut off from direct contact with the northern CLN leaders.

For these manifold reasons, the sexpartite Rome CCLN agreed to turn over its reins in the North to the Milanese pentarchy. Thus on January 31 it issued a long letter, bestowing the status of "Extraordinary Government of the North" upon a new "CLN for Upper Italy" (CLNAI), with headquarters in Milan. "One intent alone must guide you in drawing into the struggle all strata of the population," the directive declared. "Strike the enemy at once by every means. . . . The struggle must have as its final result general insurrection against the occupant. . . . Defend against every attack your solidarity, which is the essential condition for effective action by the Italian people. . . ." This last sentence revealed clearly the ascendancy of the three leftist currents in the hitherto evenly balanced hexarchy of the CCLN and their (temporary) triumph over *attesismo*.[23]

By sheer arithmetical preponderance the leftist triad overawed

---

[22] Trabucchi, *I vinti hanno sempre torto*, pp. 48–50, 66–69; Valiani, *Tutte le strade conducono a Roma*, pp. 141–153; Longo, *Un popolo alla macchia*, pp. 204–206; Battaglia, *SRI*, pp. 203–205; Mario Giovana, "L'inizio della Resistenza in Piemonte e la costituzione del CLN Regionale Piemontese," *MLI*, No. 38/39 (1955), pp. 3–30, and "Il Comitato Militare del CLN Regionale Piemontese nei primi mesi del 1944," *ibid.*, No. 41 (1956), 3–36; and "Ricerche sulla storia del CLN Piemontese," *ibid.*, No. 34/35 (1955), pp. 69–74.

[23] Catalano, *Storia del CLNAI*, pp. 113–114 ff.

the DC and PLI from the beginning. (In the Po valley it was not so customary as in Rome to seek unanimity in CLN voting.) It is not surprising therefore that the CLNAI quickly approved a PCI resolution: "There will be no place tomorrow among us for a reactionary regime, however masked, nor for a limp democracy. The new political, social, and economic system will not be other than a clear and effective democracy. The CLN of today is a prefiguration of the Government of tomorrow. In tomorrow's Government this is certain: workers, peasants, artisans, all the popular classes will have a determining weight, and a place adequate to this weight; and a place adequate to this weight will be held by the parties which represent them. Among these is the Communist Party, which is included in the CLN on a plane of perfect parity with the other parties, with equal fulness of authority today and of power tomorrow. . . . Against the affirmations of anti-Communist proposals . . . we must reaffirm the unity . . . that links the five parties. Whoever works against this union of them works against the Nation. We direct this warning especially to certain industrial and financial circles." [24]

The PCI mandataries to the CLNAI were Longo ("Gallo") and the Bolognese Giuseppe Dozza. The latter was surrogated in the winter of 1944–1945 by Emilio Sereni, who had been ruminating for some five years in Fascist prisons. Momentarily emancipated in the summer of 1943, Sereni was re-arrested after the September armistice and consigned to the Germans who, fortunately for him, did not know his Jewish descent, so that somehow he managed to escape their execution list. An expert on agrarian problems, Sereni served as president of the Lombard CLN before taking on the important CLNAI post. Incapable of relaxation, he was always a driving force within his party.[25]

The PSIUP was successively represented by the Genoese Marcello Cirenei,[26] Avv. Giorgio Marzola, Sandro Pertini, and Rodolfo Morandi. Pertini, veteran of years of conspiratorial action, had been in clandestine Rome during much of the first winter, and after the erection of the Bonomi government in

[24] PCI, *Per la libertà e l'indipendenza d'Italia*, p. 91.
[25] Valiani, *Tutte le strade conducono a Roma*, p. 285.
[26] Marcello Cirenei, "Contributo socialista al resistenza: Il primo Comitato di Liberazione Alta Italia ed il problema istituzionale," *MLI*, No. 52/53 (1958), pp. 105–108; Carli-Ballola, *Sdr*, pp. 89, 134.

June 1944 he served as a CLNAI liaison man with it; he returned to Milan in November. Lelio Basso was another signal conspirator in the septentrional PSIUP. Though the party maintained its "unity of action" pact with the PCI, it often resented some of the latter's *faits accomplis* and consequently cultivated ties with the Pd'A.

Parri ("Maurizio") was the idealistic paladin of the latter party in the CLNAI. Another Pd'A delegate was Avv. Vittorio Albasini-Scrosati, to be replaced during the last year of the struggle by the party's indefatigable northern secretary, Valiani (who, with Allied blessing, had crossed the lines). Other key Actionists in the CLNAI (or at least in reasonably close communication with it) were Altiero Spinelli (like Valiani an ex-Communist and a firm advocate of European federation); Riccardo Lombardi, an industrial engineer; and Vittorio Foà, advocate and writer. All of them hoped that after the insurrection the CLNAI and its dependent network would become the cornerstone for the nation's new administrative system. Their views on this point were resisted somewhat by the more conservative Albasini-Scrosati and Mario Paggi.[27]

The DC and the PLI tended to vote as a bloc within the CLNAI in order to gain a modicum of respect from the preponderant leftist parties. They did their best to utilize the Autonomi as leverage for their cause, and the Liberals recalled proudly their Risorgimento record, while the Christian Democrats emphasized their descent from the once-puissant Popular Party. Ing. Enrico Casò, alternating with the industrialist Giovanni Falck, and later Avv. Achille Marazza were the DC delegates to the CLNAI; and Marazza served also as his party's northern secretary.[28] The PLI was represented by Avv. Giustino Arpesani, alternating with Dr. Coda.[29]

Though nominally a Liberal, CLNAI President Alfredo Pizzoni ("Longhi"), a 50-year-old banker, preferred to assume a neutral stance. A high officer of the Credito Italiano and an ex-lieutenant colonel of the *Bersaglieri*, he was chosen chairman be-

---

[27] Valiani, *Tutte le strade conducono a Roma*, pp. 231–234.

[28] Achille Marazza, "La Democrazia cristiana nella lotta," *Mercurio* (*Anche l'Italia ha vinto*), ii, No. 16 (Dec. 1945), pp. 252–254, and his "La Democrazia cristiana come forza politica nella Resistenza," *Civitas*, vi (1955), pp. 15–29.

[29] Cadorna, *La Riscossa*, p. 129.

cause of his financial ability, widespread acquaintances, bravery and tactfulness, all of which won him the trust of the underground leaders and the Allies too, with whose emissaries in Switzerland he was in frequent contact in order to solve many knotty problems of Resistance finance. G. L. Balzarotti ("Cecconi") served as CLNAI secretary-general. His work was parlous in the extreme, for he received couriers and guarded the archives; necessarily his address was widely known.[30]

From its inception the CLNAI behaved almost as if it were an independent government, acting as a foil and a challenge both to the RSI and to the Kingdom of the South, and often undertaking negotiations with Tito's Partisans and the French De-Gaullists. Almost daily it denounced decrees issued by Mussolini's minions. Often the effects of such oppugnancy seemed scant (for example, people continued to pay with resignation their taxes to the RSI); but on not a few occasions the CLNAI scored some successes. Early in 1944, for example, when it sought to dissuade civil servants from subscribing to an oath of loyalty to the neo-Fascist regime, the *Duce* was compelled repeatedly to postpone the deadline, and after a year of frustrations gave up the attempt.[31] As for the King and the Marshal's meridional government, CLNAI conspirators could agree that in one degree or another they were unhappy with it; but they usually did not spend so much time arguing its merits as did their cousins in liberated Italy, perhaps chiefly because they faced more pressing problems closer to home.

One of these problems was to establish a secure communications system, independent of the PCI's highly elaborate network, which hitherto had been almost the sole means of sending quick messages. The CLNAI came to employ on a vast scale individual couriers, many of them women. During the final months it also made much use of radios, especially when communicating with the Allies. There was also the bedeviling problem of apportion-

---

[30] Valiani, *Tutte le strade conducono a Roma*, pp. 279–283; Massimo Salvadori-Paleotti, "The Last Hours: In Milan with the Resistance," *The Commonweal*, XLIII (1946), p. 614.
[31] For diametrically opposed judgments of the efficacy of CLNAI appeals, *cf.* the neo-Fascist verdict of Tamaro, *Due anni di storia*, 1943–1945, III, pp. 15–18, and the anti-Fascist one of Valiani, *Tutte le strade conducono a Roma*, p. 216, and *passim*, and Catalano, *Storia del CLNAI, passim*.

ing funds, supplied at first by the Operti group and certain northern industrialists, and later by the Allies.

Intensified "partigianeria" in central Italy

Prior to the Anzio landing on January 22, some one hundred
patriot detachments were roaming the hills of Latium and central Italy. Steadily they had harassed the enemy, experimenting
with simultaneous attacks from different directions but not seeking to take permanent control of territory. Their main type of
work was sabotage of communication lines. Most of them were in
communication with the secret nerve center of Colonel Montezemolo in Rome, until late in January when the Germans captured
him and most of his aides.[32] Scared by the Anzio landings, the
Germans increased their strength in Latium and crushed the
partisan bands.

Allied hopes of freeing Rome had quickened during the early
days of the Anzio gamble. In January their specialized units
transported to Monte Gennaro three eminent anti-Fascists—
Aldo Garosci, Corrado Alvaro, and Guido DeRuggiero—who
sneaked into the city to work with the Central CLN. SF Major
Munthe and Captain Salvadori, together with Alberto Tarchiani,
landed with the invasion forces at Anzio, hoping to make their
way to the metropolis. Injuries soon hospitalized the first two
for more than a month,[33] but, in any case, they could not easily
have slipped through because of the furious German counter-
attack.

Soon it became clear that, instead of a wildcat hurled on the
Anzio short, all the Allies had got was a stranded whale, as
Churchill has tartly put it.[34] Guerrilla activities consequently
shifted northeastward. The zones where the partisans could fight
most effectively were restricted chiefly to the Apennines from the
Maiella to Spoleto, to the hilly sectors of Umbria and the
Marches, and to isolated parts of the desolate Maremma in
southern Tuscany.[35] The most renowned partisan groups were

[32] Salvadori, Brief History of the Patriot Movement in Italy, pp. 58–60; Battaglia, SRI, pp. 224–226, 237.
[33] Salvadori, Resistenza ed azione, pp. 240–251; Alberto Tarchiani, Il mio
diario di Anzio (Milan, 1947).
[34] Churchill, Closing the Ring, p. 488.
[35] Salvadori, SRI, pp. 141–142; Battaglia, SRI, p. 199.

the "Maiella," led by Avv. Ettore Troilo, which fought all the way from the Sangro River to Pesaro between January and September. This contingent established a high reputation for itself with the Allies; indeed, it soon was to be integrated into the Eighth Army (the first guerrilla unit so to be).[36] Unlike the "Maiella," most formations in central Italy confined their fighting to specific zones. In general there was less solidarity between them and urban CLN's than was true of the patriot movement farther north.[37]

In this same area the Italian Corps of Liberation (CIL)—i.e., the regular-Army force that had been fielded in the South— returned to action in April after several months spent in reorganization and training. During the next few months it campaigned through the Abruzzi and Marches from Monte Marrone to the Gothic Line and helped liberate Chieti, Teramo, Ascoli Piceno, Macerata, and Urbino.[38]

Such collaboration helped to open the eyes of many hitherto-diffident Allied commanders, so that by late spring they showed much greater interest in the potentialities of both the underground and the thousands of Italian troops moldering in the South. Of course, logistical needs also helped bring about the new outlook: many Allied units were being transferred to Britain for the forthcoming invasion of France, and the gaps in Italy would have to be filled by increasingly polyglot forces. Thus in April the size of the Italian combat forces at the front was augmented slightly to 14,100, and in May this figure was doubled to 28,000.[39]

Upsurge in the North

If the Anzio operation helped to stimulate the *partigianeria* in much of central Italy, it was chiefly Mussolini's peremptory mobilization decrees of February 14 and 19, in conjunction with the mounting German drafts of Italian manpower (which incidentally worked at cross-purposes with Mussolini's task),[40] that

[36] Nicolo Troilo, "La storia del 'Maiella,'" *MLI*, No. 50 (1958), pp. 16–51.
[37] Battaglia, *SRI*, pp. 224–226, 259–267.
[38] See *supra*, Ch. viii, Co-belligerency in practice.
[39] See *supra*, Ch. viii, Badoglio's CLN government; *cf.* Salvadori, *Resistenza ed azione*, pp. 245–251.
[40] By the beginning of April 1944 the Germans had ordered Marshal Graziani to

impelled many renitents in the specified age brackets to take their chances in the ranks of the Armed Resistance.

For several weeks the Resistenza leaders found themselves overwhelmed with recruits whom they could not properly equip. The influx was truly a liability for a time, but the guerrilla chieftains could not morally reject such volunteers and leave them to the vengeance of Mussolini's army mobilizers.[41] Consequently, they did their best to split up existing bands and "seed" new ones in other valleys, all the while seeking to commandeer scarce weapons and equipment.[42]

By late March the underground had mustered twenty to thirty thousand men. Large-scale brigades had superseded the initial small detachments. Generalizations are hazardous in describing so fluid and diverse a phenomenon as the *movimento partigiano*, but by late spring the following pattern of organization was taking shape: on the lowest echelons were "nuclei" of five or six fighters; two "nuclei" made a "squad"; three, four, or five "squads" comprised a "detachment" (40 to 50 men); three of the latter, a "battalion"; and three of these, a "brigade." The average strength of a "brigade" (which usually was concentrated in a single narrow valley) was about 450 men. Three "brigades" formed a "division." By April hardly a zone on the military maps lacked a red pin to mark the epicenter of a guerrilla unit.[43]

Several brigades were scattered through the mountains between Florence and Bologna. To the west in Emilia others held the rugged terrain between Modena and the Garfagnana above Massa and Carrara; the sector between Parma and LaSpezia;

---

supply them with 27,000 Italians for the German Navy; 8,000 for chemical warfare units in Germany; 16,000 for Kesselring's disposition; 150,000 to be sent to Goering; and 1,000,000 for the labor battalions of Sauckel. These were in addition to the 118,000 men already furnished to Kesselring and Richthofen for various purposes. *Cf.* telegram of Graziani to von Keitel, April 2, 1944, in which Graziani pleaded to reduce these figures so that the RSI could augment its own forces to comb out the "rebels." Longo, *Un popolo alla macchia*, pp. 201–203.

[41] Mussolini threatened to impose the death penalty upon those who failed to respond to the February 14 decree that called up the maritime class of 1924, and to the February 19 decree that set March 8 as the deadline for presentation of the recalcitrants of the classes of 1923, 1924, and 1925. Carli-Ballola, *Sdr*, p. 147.

[42] Bianco, *Guerra partigiana*, pp. 42–66.

[43] *Ibid.*, p. 52; Longo, *Un popolo alla macchia*, pp. 189–191; Valiani, *Tutte le strade conducono a Roma*, pp. 194–195; Battaglia, *SRI*, p. 307; Alvesi, *La ribellione degli Italiani*, pp. 167–177.

and that between Piacenza and Genoa. Many of the villages were under patriot fiat.

Along the Apennines separating coastal Liguria from Piedmont numerous brigades occupied the depressions between Savona and Acqui, Imperia and Mondovì, as well as in the Langhe and Monferrato zones. An arc of bands stretched clockwise from the Cuneo sector of southwestern Piedmont across the tributaries of the upper Po west of Turin, through Val d'Aosta on the slopes of Mont Blanc, to the Val d'Ossola northwest of Milan.

In the Lombard lake region and the Valtellina to the northeast of Lake Como, still other brigades were fighting efficiently in the spring. In the Trentino, astride the well-guarded German communications line across the Brenner, there was perforce less activity. The story was different in the Venetian Pre-Alps, where the pugnacious "Nino Nanetti" Garibaldi division gained predominance in the Belluno area. Above Udine in the Friuli, a "Garibaldi" and an "Osoppo" battalion (the latter starting out under Pd'A aegis and winding up mostly under DC sponsorship) won enviable reputations—but unfortunately they also became very jealous of each other.[44] Along the enemy's major lines of communication in the Veneto acts of sabotage were common. Anti-Fascists also slowed down ship repairs in the Venice Arsenal.[45]

The partisans did not necessarily confine themselves to the mountains. In the marshes around Ravenna and the Valli di Comacchio near the Adriatic, ebullient and valorous groups lashed out with a great deal of vigor. This sector, incidentally, provided the setting for one of the better literary works (winner of the 1949 "Premio Viareggio") to come out of the Resistance: *L'Agnese va a morire* (Turin, 1949), written by the Communist journalist Renata Viganò.

Liaison with the Allies

After Parri and Valiani visited Dulles and McCaffery in Switzerland in November 1943 and won their promises of Allied subsidization and supply of certain kinds of patriot forces, hope

[44] Battaglia, *SRI*, pp. 143–145.
[45] Gavagnin, *Vent'anni di resistenza al fascismo*, pp. 445–451.

of speedy assistance soared among the underground leaders. But the Allies' *deus ex machina* could not be quickly rigged up that first winter. To be sure, as early as September 1943 the British SF and American OSS dispatched some missions across enemy lines, and the first successful drops to the northern guerrillas took place just before Christmas. But these were restricted almost entirely to items designed to support sabotage and transmit intelligence rather than to facilitate formation of big underground armies such as Parri and Valiani contemplated.[46]

Naturally, the patriots did not know that, as of December 1943, the Anglo-Americans were committed only to an advance in Italy as far as the Pisa-Rimini line,[47] and that most Allied commanders continued to take a dim view of the military value of guerrilla warfare, in contrast to the arguments of most SF and OSS men. Nor did they know that the British had launched their aerial support of patriot operations in southern France and Italy in the autumn with only four bombers available, as compared with thirty-two on hand for the succor of Tito, sixteen for Western Europe's *maquis*, and six for Central Europe's underground. (Later, of course, the number of craft increased considerably, thanks especially to American production.) [48]

Not till late spring, 1944, did liaison operations with the Italian Armed Resistance proceed with much regularity. One obvious early handicap had been the distance from Allied air bases, most of which were not moved from Algeria to the heel of the Italian boot until spring. Supply lines from British and American production centers were long and already heavily taxed. The SF and OSS had to compete with other fighting services for their small share of the total supplies and aircraft. Moreover, there were priority commitments to underground forces in Yugoslavia (and in 1944 also in France), to be honored partly at the expense of the Italians.[49]

Allied missions behind the lines consisted sometimes of a

[46] See *supra*, Ch. vii, Early Allied liaison with the Resistance; Catalano, *Storia del CLNAI*, p. 100; Badoglio, *Italy in the Second World War*, pp. 192–194.
[47] Ehrman, *Grand Strategy*, v, 273–274, 588.
[48] On the general topic of American aerial support of the Italian underground, see U.S. Office of Air Force History, *Europe: Argument to V-E Day, January 1944 to May 1945*, Vol. iii of *The Army Air Forces in World War II*, ed. Wesley Frank Craven and James Lea Cate (Chicago, 1949–1951), pp. 493–524.
[49] Ehrman, *Grand Strategy*, v, 321–322.

single person (often nicknamed "Joe" or "Jane" by the Allied personnel who flew in these "mystery men") able to speak the local dialect fluently and trained in the operation of a radio transmitter. On other occasions there was a mission head, accompanied by a radio operator and a guide. The mission might be composed exclusively of British or of American personnel, or of foreign volunteers, or it might be a mixed group. If the front was fluid, as it still was in the autumn of 1943, missions might be dispatched on foot. Usually, though, it was advisable to land them by submarine, motor torpedo boat, or parachute. Casualties were not infrequent. As soon as he reached his destination, the mission head (usually attired in standard uniform) became liaison officer with the Resistance and sought: (1) to assure regular contact between the patriot organization and the base; (2) to interpret Allied decisions to the patriots and convey their needs and ideas to the Allies; and (3) to take the necessary steps to arrange for delivery of supplies and their proper distribution.[50]

Such tasks demanded much of the liaison officers, whose experiences were often more harrowing than those of soldiers at the front. The anonymous agents (usually young volunteers) had to be willing to forego for months at a time the morale-sustaining effects of association with fellow nationals. Playing a constant cat-and-mouse game with a foe who would probably show them very little mercy if he caught them, they had to rely almost entirely upon their own judgment and resources. Often they had to put up with suspiciousness on the part of the patriot groups to which they were assigned, whose members seldom were fully satisfied with the drops that, luck being with them, they might persuade Allied authorities in the South to send.[51]

As an ex-SF man has explained, officers who hailed from nations where freedom was deeply ingrained found it hard to fathom the political passions and rivalries unleashed by totalitarianism. Many did not readily understand why the patriots

[50] Salvadori, SRI, pp. 115-116, 124.

[51] Though it should be read with caution as it is self-serving, some parts of the memoirs of Lieutenant Aldo Icardi, a highly controversial OSS officer behind the lines, give an impression of the difficulties: Aldo Icardi: American Master Spy. Of interest too are the memoirs of Roy Farran, who headed a mixed contingent dropped behind the lines above Modena and Reggio Emilia in the spring of 1945: Winged Dagger: Adventures on Special Service (London, 1948), pp. 261-340. Cf. Tilman, When Men and Mountains Meet.

were not content merely to carry out sabotage assignments and report intelligence. The political goals of the leftist parties transcended strictly military operations, of course, but sometimes these remained a riddle to Allied personnel, who understandably could be confused by the intricacies of Italian multiparty politics. And even if they grasped the political ramifications of the underground, liaison officers might well be tempted to reflect either the prejudices of the group with which they worked most closely or of the group whose program most nearly coincided with their own politico-economic predilections, as was the case of Laborite Major MacDonald, who worked at "Cherokee" with Moscatelli's Garibaldini during most of 1944.[52]

Whatever the composition of the liaison mission, it usually took months to erect behind the lines such reliable intelligence centers as the "Otto" in Genoa, "Franchi" in the Piedmontese Langhe, and the "CoRa" in Florence.[53] Even then, messages often were garbled, due to poor atmospheric conditions or other factors. To minimize possible detection by enemy radio detection-finders (DF's), the underground operators had to limit their broadcasts to as few as fifteen minutes a day, which often resulted in backlogs. Patriots who sought to reach the Allies on foot to pass on information might be caught, while those who had dispatched them remained ignorant and impatient.[54]

Compounding the frustrations were the major disasters that all too often bedeviled the patriots. Sometimes these were caused by the indiscretion of the Allied officer, his partisan associates, or the infiltration of enemy agents. One of the worst catastrophes happened in Genoa on March 29, 1944, when the "Otto," whose radio and maritime links with Sardinia and the South had brought tangible Allied support to patriot units within a radius of more than 100 miles, was captured along with its codes and plans. Edgardo Sogno, the young Italian Army officer whom the British and SIM had parachuted into the Langhe in December

[52] Salvadori, SRI, pp. 130–131; Secchia and Moscatelli, Il Monte Rosa è sceso a Milano, pp. 469–473.

[53] The vicissitudes in organizing and operating the "CoRa" link between Florence and the South are mentioned in Bonacossi and Ragghianti-Collobi (eds.), Una lotta nel suo corso, pp. 313–318. See Sogno, Guerra senza bandiera, p. 30 ff., for the story of the "Franchi."

[54] Salvadori, SRI, pp. 124–125; Battaglia, SRI, p. 179; Icardi, American Master Spy, pp. 30–33, 43–44.

to direct the "Franchi" communications organization, was also arrested in the roundup but managed to escape.[55]

Even when contacts were solidly established, Allied agencies often lacked the kind of supplies needed at a particular moment, and sea- and air-borne missions might have to be delayed for weeks if the skies were overcast (as during the autumn and winter they often were in the North). Under the best of circumstances errors were numerous and unavoidable; at night one valley looked much like another to a pilot delivering supplies.

To be sure, partisans would light signal fires at the drop zone (DZ)—which preferably was 300 to 400 yards wide and far from inhabited places or enemy garrisons—in accordance with prearranged radio signals. To indicate that a drop was en route, the Allies would announce from one of their radio stations a "positive" signal (e.g., "Grass grows in summer") to complement a "negative" one (e.g., "Bees give honey"). Recipients were also supposed to flash a light from the field in Morse code, repeating the first letter of the negative message. But often the enemy— or rival groups—would light decoy fires, to the confusion of the pilots and exasperation of the rightful recipients. If the partisans controlled an area with a radius of twenty kilometers from the DZ, then drops could also be pitched in daylight, with white drapes (or, in snow-covered terrain, red- or black-colored drapes) instead of lights for signals.[56] In any case, the bombing planes needed a place free from peaks where they could make a run safely at 1,000 feet or less—not always an easy thing to do. Another hazard was provided by parachutes that failed to open properly. It was no wonder, therefore, that liaison men calculated two or three operations for every successful one. Indeed, when the final statistics for the Italian campaign were tallied in 1945, it was found that "Allied special-duty aircraft had completed 2,646 of 4,268 attempted sorties to Italian targets and had dropped more than 6,490 short tons of supplies. The [American] Army Air Forces flew 70 per cent of the completed sorties and dropped 68 per cent of the tonnage." [57]

[55] Sogno, Guerra senza bandiera, pp. 30–168, and passim.
[56] Regarding Allied instructions for preparations of "drop zones," see Atti del CG/CVL, No. 27 (July 26, 1944), pp. 55–57, and No. 36 (Aug. 11, 1944), pp. 72–73.
[57] U.S. Office of Air Force History, The Army Air Forces in World War II, III, 517.

The preceding figures embraced the entire period from September 1943 until May 1945. Up to May 1944, according to statistics released by Badoglio's government, 26 missions were sent to occupied territory, of which 22 were provided with radio equipment and 4 were to carry out special acts of sabotage. More or less permanent radio liaison was established with 54 patriot groups. By the end of May, 129 landing fields had been covertly prepared for aerial drops. The first deliveries had taken place in January. Usually a single plane could haul, in special containers, a ton and a half of matériel needed for sabotage and incendiary purposes, hand grenades, provisions, clothes, medicines, and comforts. During April the first machine guns were landed by parachute. In May, 99 flights went out to drop 174 tons. The partisan groups known to Badoglio's Army High Command counted during the winter of 1943–1944 some 100 armed encounters with the enemy and 155 deeds of sabotage.[58]

Understandably enough, the partisans seldom appreciated all of these difficulties, and they were easily inclined to accuse the Allies (especially the British) of deliberate procrastination and malevolence toward their particular group. Charges of Allied preference for royalist patriots were common. Many Piedmontese republican patriots, for example, were sure that Sogno's liberal-monarchist "Franchi" group in the Langhe was better supplied than they. And in Rome there was jealousy between the CCLN Military Command of Bauer and the royalist one of Montezemolo. No doubt there was some validity to these charges, particularly in the spring of 1944 before tight military co-ordination of the entire clandestine movement was achieved; yet Salvadori, who occupied a delicate post in SF, has cautioned that most of these complaints were exaggerated and that over a period of time favoritisms cancelled out.

Allied policy in Italy during the first year was quite different from that pursued in Yugoslavia, he has also observed. Across the Adriatic, the British late in 1943 (seconded soon by the Americans) had switched their support from the royalist Draža Mihailović's Serbian Četniks to the Communist Josip Tito's Croatian Partisans in the hope (forlorn, it proved) of bettering the chances of King Peter's return.[59] In Italy there was, of course,

[58] Badoglio, *Italy in the Second World War*, pp. 192–194.

[59] Salvadori, *SRI*, pp. 129–131; for the official British interpretation of this switch, see Ehrman, *Grand Strategy*, v, 76–83, 270–278.

no blinking the fact that the British preferred the Monarchy and Badoglio, whereas the Americans were anything but enthusiastic about them. Perhaps because of this point, instructions from London and Washington to SF and OSS were to aid any formation to the extent that it carried out positive action against the Germans or their neo-Fascist collaborators. As a result, all bands —be they royalist, republican, or Red—shared in the distribution of Allied supplies. Indeed, by the eve of the 1945 insurrection, Communist brigades were receiving more than 40 per cent of the funds, the Actionists a little less than 30 per cent, and the others the remainder.[60]

Though the Anglo-Americans were manifestly unenthusiastic about Parri's proposal of November 1943 for great secret "armies in the field" whose chief purpose would be to augment the political prestige of the northern Resistance, they did not stop him and the others from going ahead with their ambitious plans (which were to culminate in the remarkable liberation of many northern cities in April 1945).[61] Insofar as the Allies intervened politically during the first year of operations it was chiefly in order to achieve a balance among the medley of patriot groups and thus minimize the likelihood of such internecine strife as had bedeviled other underground movements. To be sure, it was easier to issue such orders than to carry them out with complete impartiality. Most liaison officers continued to show preference for the units to which they were assigned.[62]

Military unification

To reduce such inequities, the Allies urged the patriots to establish a more cohesive underground headquarters so that responsibility for distribution of supplies would come to rest chiefly upon the Italians.[63]

Creation of the CLNAI on January 31, 1944, had been a great step forward in the political systematization of the Resistenza Armata. Yet it had not fully solved the problem of co-ordinating the military side of the struggle. The PCI and Pd'A, it is true, had

[60] Letter of Professor Salvadori to Professor Salvemini, Sept. 10, 1945, cited in Kogan, *Italy and the Allies*, pp. 110–111.

[61] Parri, "L'Italia partigiana," *Mercurio*, II, No. 16 (1945), pp. 9–19; Parri, "Il movimento di liberazione e gli alleati," *MLI*, No. 1 (1949), pp. 7–24.

[62] Salvadori, *Resistenza ed azione*, p. 268.

[63] Salvadori, *SRI*, pp. 129–131.

organized efficient command structures throughout the North; but there was no over-all headquarters for the fighting forces of the other CLN parties and the Autonomi. The desirability of such an arrangement was perceived by a growing number of patriots—more, at first, by the rightist and centrist currents and by the Allies than by the leftists. Quite frankly, the PLI and DC hoped to reduce the radical overtones of the Resistance by integrating it more closely with Allied plans.[64]

Parri seemed a likely choice to be supreme military co-ordinator of the Armed Resistance. He possessed an exemplary political background as well as military experience; he had negotiated the original compact with the Allies for support of the patriot movement; he had won considerable praise for his fair apportionment of funds obtained from General Operti; furthermore, he had many well-placed friends in Milanese financial and industrial circles. Quite likely most non-Communists would have settled for "Zio Maurizio," but the Communists for many weeks in February and March were loath to concede any such preferential status to the white-haired Actionist prophet. Perhaps they felt that their own numerical superiority in the field made them potential masters of the situation so that they could afford to wait until the other parties agreed to accept one of the Garibaldini.[65]

Because of this impasse CLNAI President Pizzoni slipped across the frontier into Switzerland to confer with McCaffery and Dulles on March 27. He talked chiefly to the former, who seemed to display somewhat more solicitude for the aims of the rightist parties than did his American colleague. The competent banker evidently made a favorable impression upon the Anglo-American officials, to judge by the largesse he secured. This came via Switzerland until May, at which time the Germans succeeded in halting Swiss collaboration. After that, Pizzoni turned to the Italian banks for help in transferring Allied funds. These included the Banca Lombarda di Depositi, whose manager was to become paymaster of the Patriot Military Headquarters; Pizzoni's own Credito Italiano; and the Banca Commerciale. Some 35,000,000 lire were also raised in fictitious loans made to the

[64] Sogno, *Guerra senza bandiera*, p. 223.
[65] Catalano, *Storia del CLNAI*, pp. 146–147.

Edison, Falck, and Pirelli companies, whose directors signed the receipts.[66]

As the season for renewed offensives approached, sentiment in favor of military consolidation of the Resistance spiraled. A particularly strong push was given by Togliatti upon his return to Italy at the end of March.[67] Laying down the line to the PCI (and to any who would listen) that all political considerations must be subordinated to the central task of "winning the war," [68] he entered Badoglio's government. Quickly seeing the light, northern Communists began to preach piously the virtues of military integration.[69] In issuing such an appeal on May 10, the PCI Military Command pointedly included the Autonomi.[70]

On June 9, just after the liberation of Rome and the Normandy invasion, the CLNAI approved a specific plan, drafted by Parri and Longo, for the erection of a Supreme Military Command of the Corps of Freedom Volunteers (CG/CVL; "Comando Generale del Corpo Volontari della Libertà"), also sometimes called the CMAI ("Comando Militare Alta Italia"), in which all the military formations were to be represented.[71] Parri has judged the event to be of "great political significance, representing a political moment of great importance and of extreme interest," for henceforth the Armed Resistance's complex ties with Rome and the Allies became ever more solid.[72]

General strikes of March 1944

Soon after its birth on January 31, 1944, the CLNAI busied itself with blueprints for a gigantic general strike with political

[66] *Ibid.*; Pizzoni, "Il finanziamento," *Mercurio* (*Anche l'Italia ha vinto*), II, No. 16 (Dec. 1945), pp. 83–86; Pizzoni, "Il finanziamento della Resistenza in una nota di A. Pizzoni," *MLI*, No. 24 (1953), pp. 49–54.

[67] See *supra*, Ch. VIII, Togliatti's PCI "svolta."

[68] The PCI official history admits that hitherto the party had "busied itself more with the leadership of the armed forces than with achieving first of all the unification of all sincerely patriotic forces." PCI, *Relazione della Direzione del PCI al V° Congresso*, p. 96.

[69] Valiani, *Tutte le strade conducono a Roma*, p. 237; OSS, Research and Analysis Branch, No. 2081.3, "Italian Political Documents: Part III: April 1944" (Washington, May 30, 1944), 13–14.

[70] Longo, *Un popolo alla macchia*, p. 211; Longo, *Sulla via dell'insurrezione*, pp. 213–214; Catalano, *Storia del CLNAI*, p. 163.

[71] Final approval was given by the CLNAI on June 19. See *Atti del CG/CVL*, pp. 1–5; Catalano, *Storia del CLNAI*, pp. 163–164.

[72] Parri, "Relazione introduttiva," *MLI*, No. 52/53 (1958), p. 12.

goals superimposed on economic ones. The impetus for this daring work stoppage came from the PCI factory agitation committees, which had forged ahead of the mountain-based partisans in audacity during the winter. PCI strategists argued that a great general strike would demonstrate the political potential of the Resistenza better than anything else, and at the same time incite the masses to new endeavors. Their escalating minds reasoned that such a strike would slow down war production, prevent the dismantling of machinery, and halt the deportations of workers to Germany—though just how they deduced the last two points was far from clear. Winning warm support from their PSIUP partners and no objections from the other CLNAI parties, the PCI began to sound out labor leaders in the major factories. Much careful planning was imperative, and it could hardly be kept entirely secret. More than once the date of the strike had to be delayed to achieve better synchronization of demonstrations in Turin, Milan, Genoa, Florence, Bologna, Venice, and elsewhere.[73]

At last, on March 1 at 10 a.m. several hundred thousand workers either folded their arms or walked away from their benches and tools in the northern cities. Some Communist agitators claimed that as many as 1,200,000 struck; neo-Fascist officials insisted that it was only 208,549 out of a total of some 5,000,000 workers in the North; and of these 119,800 in Milan, 32,600 in Turin (with 21,000 at the Fiat-Mirafiori alone), 12,860 in Florence, et cetera.[74] Doubtless the true number was somewhere between these extremes; whatever the figure, it was impressive. For a week virtually all production came to a standstill, especially in Milan and to a lesser degree in Turin. In the Lombard metropolis not only factory laborers but tram workers struck, to the immense disruption of urban life. *Corriere della sera* failed to appear for three days. Strikers were able to distribute their own

[73] Longo, *Un popolo alla macchia*, pp. 135–158; Valiani, *Tutte le strade conducono a Roma*, pp. 158–173; Battaglia, *SRI*, pp. 213–214; Vaccarino, *Il movimento operaio a Torino nei primi mesi della crisi italiana* (*luglio 1943–marzo 1944*); Catalano, *Storia del CLNAI*, pp. 135–143; Carli-Ballola, *Sdr*, pp. 122–125; Riccardo Levi, "L'Azione economica e sociale dei CLN dell'Alta Italia," *Il Ponte*, III (1947), pp. 994–1000.

[74] Dolfin, *Con Mussolini nella tragedia*, p. 272; Turchi, *Prefetto con Mussolini*, p. 125; Amicucci, *I 600 giorni*, pp. 148–149; Carli-Ballola, *Sdr*, pp. 128–129; Tamaro, *Due anni di storia, 1943–1945*, II, 507–516.

clandestine leaflets, however. German General Zimmermann proclaimed a state of siege and threatened to send a list of workers to Germany and to punish industrialists who agreed to pay the strikers for the days they were off the job. Despite such warnings, numerous industrialists quietly promised to reimburse their employees as soon as the war ended.

Elsewhere the strike ended sooner, and its efficacy varied considerably. In Bologna peasant demonstrations occurred in conjunction with the industrial ones, and in Florence strikers burned one of the Fascist headquarters. But in Venice the *sciopero* was less extensive, and in such cities as Trieste, Genoa, and Biella it was a failure, partly because of prior wage boosts, fear, and hastily called "preventive holidays" ascribed to alleged "electric power shortages." In its diligent "self-criticism," the PCI pointed out that some workers mistakenly conceived the goal to be insurrection, while others blundered in evacuating factories so that it was hard to keep them disciplined. The chief weaknesses were attributed to the lack of participation by most employees of the public services—railroads, streetcars, electric and gas plants, telephones, and newspapers.[75] Some Resistance leaders also berated the Allies for not sending in military and economic aid and giving the strike better propaganda coverage.[76] The latter complaint was a bit unfair, for the *New York Times* of March 9 had commented that there could be no doubt that the strike was the most widespread of any yet in Hitler's *Festung Europa*. Just as the strikes of the previous March had helped spark the plots that unseated Mussolini, so this one signaled the onset of greater popular hostility to neo-Fascism and helped to instill solidarity among the renitents.[77]

Yet the Armed Resistance paid a heavy toll. Perhaps as many as 2,000 workers, and especially their syndical and Social-Communist leaders, were seized by neo-Fascist and German security forces and hauled off to Mauthausen, Buchenwald, Dachau, and Auschwitz.[78] And it may well have disillusioned some workers and caused them to lapse into a mood of *attesismo*.

[75] Longo, *Sulla via dell'insurrezione nazionale*, pp. 91–126, 140–202; Battaglia, *SRI*, pp. 221–223.
[76] Catalano, *Storia del CLNAI*, pp. 142–143.
[77] Valiani, *Tutte le strade conducono a Roma*, p. 215; Vaccarino, *Il movimento operaio a Torino*, pp. 32–34.
[78] Carli-Ballola, *Sdr*, pp. 125–132.

Gappisti and the Ardeatine Cave massacre

In the early spring the Communist GAP became increasingly daring in the major cities. Terrorism spread rapidly, with PFR bosses the prime targets. In Bologna the local commissioner of the Fascist Federation was murdered; whereupon PFR Secretary Pavolini hastened to the "red citadel" and had ten men arrested and tried for complicity in the affair. Mussolini pardoned one, but nine were executed—a "serious and unnecessary mistake," according to a neo-Fascist chronicler.[79]

The most widely publicized (and criticized) assassination was that of Giovanni Gentile, Fascism's well-known idealist-philosopher of education and an ex-collaborator of Croce. Four unidentified youths shot the corpulent old man (who never took precaution) as he walked down a Florence street on April 15. Most of the non-Communist parties deplored this deed, whose repercussions, they feared, would only be deleterious to the anti-Fascist cause. Gentile's sons urgently requested the Italian and German authorities in Florence not to carry out reprisals, and none were in this case.[80]

Adverse repercussions certainly had ensued from the most audacious GAP *coup* of the entire Resistance a few weeks earlier in Rome. There the PCI was anxious to combat *attesismo*, reputedly more popular than ever in Rome after the Allied debarkation at Anzio, and to stir up the citizenry. They therefore launched a new wave of violence that reached its crest on the afternoon of March 23 (the anniversary of the foundation of the Fascist movement) with an attack upon a detachment of German security police which regularly marched toward the Viminale along Via Rasella (between the Quattro Fontane and Via del Traforo) in the heart of the city. A squad of young GAP students executed the deed, though this fact was not immediately known. One of them disguised himself as a street cleaner, filled his rubbish cart with explosives, ignited it, and sent it hurtling down the incline upon the marchers, while simultaneously his hidden companions opened fire, killing thirty-three and injuring others.[81]

---

[79] Villari, *The Liberation of Italy*, pp. 102, 120.

[80] Ragghianti. *Disegno della liberazione*, pp. 130–133; Villari, *The Liberation of Italy*, pp. 119–120.

[81] Battaglia, *SRI*, pp. 227–230; Carli-Ballola, *Sdr*, pp. 141–143.

In a frenzy and fearful of general insurrection, the Germans decided upon reprisals. But how many victims should their St. Bartholomew's Night claim? Settlement of that question brought into the picture most of the key German military and diplomatic officials in Italy. Marshal Kesselring's headquarters telephoned Hitler. According to Eugen Dollmann (*SS Standartenführer* and liaison man between Kesselring and SS General Wolff in northern Italy), Hitler's reaction was one of fulminating rage. He first recommended blowing up an entire section of the city and shooting from 30 to 50 Italians for each German policeman killed. Officials in Rome eventually calmed him to the point where he set this ratio at 10-to-1.[82] Kesselring was advised by Kappler of the SS in Rome that he had available for this purpose men already condemned to death. But there were not enough in that category; moreover, in the excitement of rounding up the men, the quota of 330 was exceeded by five. Jews accounted for 176 and Army personnel for 47 of the total. A high Italian police official, Pietro Caruso, helped select the hostages from the cells of Regina Coeli and Via Tasso, as well as from the neighborhood of the crime. Colonel Montezemolo was among the victims; so were Generals Simoni (a World War I hero) and Fenulli (one-time vice-commandant of the "Ariete" division); and of course numerous undercover party workers. The night of the 24–25th Kappler quickly hauled the hostages in trucks out Via Ardeatine to a cave on the edge of town. The Germans shot the victims in the neck five at a time and then mined and sealed the cave entrance.[83]

No doubt Hitler was responsible in the final reckoning, but the others carried out his only slightly attenuated orders with the blind discipline characteristic of the Nazis. Mussolini was aware of the measures, yet he made no attempt to intervene. On November 30, 1946, a British court-martial in Rome handed down

[82] Dollmann, *Roma nazista*, pp. 241–255. Heinrich Himmler, police chief in Berlin, was even more furibund; he advocated rounding up all men from 18 to 45 in those quarters of Rome suspected of Communist leanings and deporting them. In the face of objections about the difficulty of carrying out such an order and its probable backfiring results, Himmler allowed himself to be dissuaded. S/M, *Sdf*, p. 980.

[83] Attilio Ascarelli, *Le fosse Ardeatine* (Rome, 1945); Moellhausen, *La carta perdente*, pp. 213–242; S/M, *Sdf*, pp. 979–980; Troisio, *Roma sotto il terrore nazifascista*, pp. 74–94; Battaglia, *SRI*, pp. 252–258; Tamaro, *Due anni di storia*. II, 533–542.

death sentences for Colonel General Eberhard von Mackensen, ex-Commander of the Fourteenth Army in Italy, and Lieutenant General Kurt Maelzer, ex-Commander of the Rome Garrison; [84] later these were commuted (July 4, 1947) to life imprisonment.[85] On May 6, 1947, a second British court-martial, sitting in Venice, convicted Kesselring, the top *Wehrmacht* commander, of over-all responsibility. His death sentence was also commuted (July 4, 1947) to life imprisonment, still later cut to 21 years, and finally cancelled altogether (October 1952), to the chagrin of many Italians.[86]

Though the Ardeatine massacre broadened the breach between the RSI and a large section of public opinion in Rome,[87] it also aggravated the very *attesismo* the PCI had sought to combat. And within the CCLN it heightened the tension and recriminations that already had caused President Bonomi to tender his resignation as chairman on the very day of the bombing,[88] so that henceforth the leftist parties were on the defensive in the Rome committee.[89] The PCI, however, did its best to put a good face on the Via Rasella attack, contending that: (1) it had not known the Germans would react so brutally; (2) the Germans did not dare to repeat in Florence or Bologna such acts of vengeance as those displayed at the Ardeatine Caves; and (3) the only way to check German violence was to intensify the underground struggle.[90]

Spring tribulations

The rapid resurgence of the *partigianeria* after February alarmed both the German military leaders and the neo-Fascists. They especially resented the rebels' nibbling at their communication lines to southern France, where invasion by the Allies was a constant danger.

Knowing that the patriots were in radio communication with the Allies, the Nazi-Fascists assigned high priority to knocking out their wireless centers. They met with initial success, as

[84] *NYT*, Dec. 1, 1946, 1:3.
[85] *Ibid.*, July 5, 1947, 2:7.
[86] *Ibid.*, May 7, 1947, 10:4; Oct. 24, 25, 26, 27, 1952.
[87] Carlo Silvestri, *Mussolini, Graziani, e gli antifascisti* (Milan, 1949), p. 107 ff.
[88] See *supra*, Ch. VIII, Togliatti's PCI "svolta."
[89] Carli-Ballola, *Sdr*, p. 143.
[90] Longo, *Un popolo alla macchia*, pp. 201–203; Battaglia, *SRI*, pp. 252–258.

has been seen, on March 29 when they smashed the Genoese "Otto." [91]

The day before, in Turin, the enemy captured virtually the entire Regional Military Command headed by General Perotti and consisting of representatives of all five CLN parties. Under torture one member of the group blurted out enough information to enable the neo-Fascists to ferret out his colleagues from their hide-out in the cathedral sacristy. Hauled before the Turin Court of Assize on April 2, they bore themselves with great dignity. Interior Minister Buffarini-Guidi supervised their summary trial and saw to it that they were shot at dawn on April 5.[92] Some of the victims' last letters, preserved and published after the war, bore eloquent testimony to Resistance idealism.[93] Two months elapsed before a new clandestine military headquarters could be built in Piedmont.

Still another shattering disaster occurred during that star-crossed week. In the hills above Genoa the "3ª Brigata Liguria" and the "Gruppo Odino," which menaced the enemy's lines leading into the Po valley, were attacked by German and neo-Fascist contingents based upon Alessandria. Though these *rastrellamenti* failed to capture most of the "Liguria," they did pull in a group of 100 as-yet-unarmed draft evaders whom the "Odino" had concealed in a half-destroyed monastery on Benedicta hill near Voltaggio. Surprising the hapless youths on April 7, the Nazi-Fascists butchered the lot, throwing their bodies into a common grave. In addition, they dragged some 200 prisoners from the zone to trans-Alpine concentration camps.[94]

The devastating series of spring *rastrellamenti*, launched as early as March in some valleys, reaped their biggest harvest in Piedmont and Venetia in April. At first the Germans supervised most of these combings. Only after April did they assign most of the arduous task to Marshal Graziani's neo-Fascist forces

[91] See *supra*, Ch. IX, Liaison with the Allies.
[92] M. Giovana, "Il Comitato Militare del CLN Regionale Piemontese nei primi mesi del 1944," *MLI*, No. 41 (1956), pp. 3–36; Battaglia, *SRI*, pp. 268–283; Trabucchi, *I vinti hanno sempre torto*, pp. 74–75; Valiani, *Tutte le strade conducono a Roma*, p. 219 ff.; Catalano, *Storia del CLNAI*, pp. 148–150; Bonacossi and Ragghianti-Collobi (eds.), *Una lotta nel suo corso*, p. 120.
[93] Malvezzi and Pirelli (eds.), *Lettere di condannati a morte della resistenza italiana*, pp. 40–43, 48–49, 53–55, 102–104, 105–109, and 173–175.
[94] Baccino, *Contributo alla storia della resistenza di Genova*, pp. 45–46.

(and to various satellite conscripts, including Cossacks), while they themselves concentrated on repelling the Allied push toward Rome.

In coping with the "rebels" the Germans introduced new raking techniques, often with stunning results. In southwestern Piedmont, for instance, they employed an entire division for the combings and blocked off whole valleys with the goal of either destroying or dispersing the troublesome partisans. Several motorized columns would advance from the valley floor in an encircling fashion toward a cul-de-sac. They experimented with such techniques in Valli Corsaglia and Casotto in March, and with even greater results in April in the Valli Varaita. In the case of Val Maira, however, the enemy reverted to an older tactic of spearhead offensives designed to catch by surprise a partisan position; this was not so successful, and the Giellisti and Garibaldini defenders managed to pull back relatively intact.

At dawn on April 20 the Germans lashed out against patriot strongholds in the Valli Vermenagna, Gesso, Stura, and Grana. Partisans in the first two escaped just in time, but those in the latter pair of valleys had to fight a bloody rear-guard action for more than a week. During that time they learned the hard way to give up the outmoded transversal defense tactics and adopted, instead, what Bianco has described as a "multiple defense system in depth along only one side of the valley and based fairly high up it," using also numerous and complex road blocks. Some of these skirmishes took place at elevations of 7,500 feet.[95]

Perforce the partisans began to experiment with many kinds of defensive and counteroffensive measures. Increasing flexibility became the rule. Some units dispatched "flying squads" down onto the plain on swift assault missions against certain vulnerable spots in the enemy's communication and supply lines.[96] But the most common tactic in the face of overwhelming power was to fall back to higher elevations to regroup. Some Piedmontese units even found themselves pushed back over the crest of the Maritime Alps into France. There they faced new trials.[97]

Meantime, Marshal Graziani sought to augment his neo-

[95] Bianco, *Guerra partigiana*, pp. 66–70.
[96] Longo, *Un popolo alla macchia*, pp. 165–170; Carli-Ballola, *Sdr*, pp. 127–128, 148–151.
[97] See *infra*, Ch. ix, Armed Resistance diplomacy: France.

Fascist armed forces, which often had to compete disadvantageously with the Germans for Italian manpower.[98] On April 25 Mussolini's government issued a stern decree promising death on the spot to all "rebels" found with arms in their hands but at the same time promised an amnesty for those who turned in their arms and themselves by May 25. It proclaimed, further, that any soldier or civilian who joined or abetted the "armed bands" could be shot in the back. Pavolini and Farinacci objected to Mussolini's "softness" in granting a period of grace. In due course, the Salò government alleged that "44,145 sbandati" had responded—a figure that seems excessive.[99] Of course, some hundreds of guerrillas did succumb to the blandishments and threats, but most ignored them contemptuously. Possibly a few joined the neo-Fascists on orders from the underground, the better to subvert Graziani's forces.[100]

In the midst of the spring crescendo of combat Mussolini and Graziani visited Hitler (April 21–22) in the beautiful eighteenth-century Klessheim Palace near Salzburg, where they had conferred a year before. The *Duce* suggested that the 600,000 Italian soldiers in Germany should stay there long enough to get adequate training, and he timidly brought to Hitler's attention the fate of the thousands of Italian workers deported to Germany. Obsessed with faith in ultimate victory, the charismatic *Fuehrer* was uninterested in such trivialities; in his usual monologue fashion he asserted that the workers were getting along fine and that the soldiers would get adequate training. He was most concerned about seeing sterner defense measures taken in Italy.[101]

In northern Bavaria Mussolini reviewed his troops who were training there under iron-fisted German instructors. Four divisions ("Italia," "San Marco," "Monterosa," and "Littorio," composed largely of the classes of 1924–1925 drafted by the RSI in Italy, because very, very few of the Italian soldiers previously

[98] See *supra*, Ch. IX, n. 40.
[99] Tamaro, *Due anni di storia, 1943–1945*, III, 14–15, 69; Longo, *Un popolo alla macchia*, pp. 199–203; Rodolfo Graziani, *Processo Graziani* (Rome, 1950), I, 359–361.
[100] Carli-Ballola, *Sdr*, p. 154.
[101] See the German account published in U.S. State Department *Bulletin*, XV, No. 388, p. 1040 ff., and tr. in Italian in Tamaro, *Due anni di storia, 1943–1945*, III, 58–69; cf. *ibid.*, pp. 23–30.

interned in Germany were willing to serve) [102] were almost ready to be redeployed across the Brenner to fight the "rebels" and the Allies. Soon after returning to Salò, Mussolini, pressed by Fritz Sauckel, called up several military classes for obligatory labor with the Germans. This was a clamorous failure, Graziani has admitted, for many of the would-be draftees fled to swell the ranks of the partisans.[103] Certainly in this enterprise the CLNAI propaganda was effective, as even neo-Fascist writers have conceded.[104]

Despite the *rastrellamenti* and other heartbreaking disasters, the number of armed patriots mounted speedily during these weeks. Italians anticipated a quick end of the war, once the Allies broke through the Cassino bottleneck. Thus by May there were more than 70,000 guerrillas (as compared to the 10,000 at the beginning of the year). These were deployed in some thirty northern zones of operations; everywhere new units proliferated. According to General Harold Alexander, Supreme Commander of the Allied Armies in Italy, these patriots were "holding check" on six German divisions by May 22. The next month the patriot enrollment was estimated to have climbed to 90,000.[105]

Yet the majority of people in the RSI apathetically went ahead with their business in the face of the brutal German occupation and the devastating, unceasing Allied air raids and interruptions of communications. As neo-Fascists liked to point out, food conditions in the North, though difficult, were better than in Liberated Italy (they always had been!); public services still functioned fairly regularly; inflation was not nearly so rampant as in the South, and only Italian currency circulated.[106]

Armed Resistance diplomacy: France

Among the Piedmontese forces whom the enemy drove across the summit of the Maritime Alps into southeastern France in the spring were the Giellisti of the Valle Maira. In France they

[102] See *supra*, Ch. vii, Military recruitment.

[103] Graziani, *Processo Graziani*, p. 463.

[104] Tamaro, *Due anni di storia, 1943–1945*, iii, 30–32.

[105] Carli-Ballola, *Sdr*, pp. 154–158; Battaglia, *SRI*, pp. 196, 307; Cadorna, *La Riscossa*, p. 150.

[106] Villari, *The Liberation of Italy*, p. 121.

found it expedient to work out accords with the local *maquis*. On May 12 some of the GL officers held initial discussions with officials of the French Résistance at Colle Sautron, high in the Maritime Alps. Parri has called the event one of the signal developments of the underground struggle, for it marked the "insertion of the Italian Resistenza into the cadre of the international Resistance"—most notably with that in France and in Yugoslavia, but to a limited degree with the Czech and even the German underground (via Dulles in Switzerland).[107]

On May 22 a meeting was held near Barcelonette. The GL warrior-lawyer, "Duccio" Galimberti, headed the Italian delegation which reached the high village after a hard all-day hike. The French were represented by a vice-commander of their Southeastern Zone, a delegate from Algiers, and others. Eventually the conferees signed an agreement: (1) to intensify by radio and other means liaison between the adjacent valleys; (2) to appoint an officer from a French unit and one from an Italian to establish permanent collaboration; (3) to exchange war matériel; and (4) to place at the disposal of the two Resistance movements all means of communication which either might have with the Allies.[108]

On May 29–30 there was a third conference at Saretto in the upper reaches of Valle del Maira. The French politico-military head of "R-2" (the second of the twelve regions of the French Résistance), his adjutant, and an Italian delegate (Dante Livio Bianco of the Pd'A) from the Piedmont CLN took part. With romantic, almost utopian optimism, their written agreement dismissed any reason for resentment by either over previous misunderstandings between the two clandestine movements. Mutual auguries of republican and democratic governments of social justice were put in writing. No one even mentioned possible boundary problems.

These accords did not bring about important military results, though they facilitated the exchange of some supplies. It was in the political sense that they were most significant, even though they were localized agreements between neighboring units. The

---

[107] Parri, "Relazione introduttiva," *MLI*, No. 52/53 (1958), pp. 13–14.
[108] Bianco, *Guerra partigiana*, pp. 75–76.

Italian delegates made it clear that they did not pretend to represent the "old" Italy, and at least temporarily they found a friendly response from like-minded Frenchmen.[109]

Armed Resistance diplomacy: Yugoslavia

From the outset the fate of Trieste and the northeastern border zone of Venezia Giulia loomed high on the list of urgent problems facing the CLNAI. That polyglot gateway to the Italian peninsula was the scene of a three-way struggle involving Tito's guerrillas, the Germans, and the Italians (with the latter split in their attitude). The Germans detached the region from Mussolini's RSI in October 1943, forming out of it the "Gau Kustenland" ("Litorale Adriatico"), ruled by Dr. F. Reiner and his corps of Viennese officials. That same autumn a Communist-dominated, strongly nationalistic Slavic Resistance current, the "Osvobodilna Fronta" ("Liberation Front"), came to life in the hinterland and especially in Istria. It was succored by Tito, who was rapidly building up strength in the wake of the Italian debacle and Churchill's recent assignment of British aid to him instead of to Mihailovič's Serbian Royalists.

As for the Italian population, some attorned to the Germans and neo-Fascists,[110] while a few (chiefly Communists) collaborated with the Yugoslavs (who often repaid manifoldly the ill-treatment which in the past had been meted out to them by Italian Blackshirts; [111] but probably the majority simply hoped desperately for an early landing by Anglo-American forces that might end the uncertainty of the region's status. A determined minority sought to create a local wing of the Italian Resistenza Armata, thinking this the best way of insuring a restoration of Italian title to the disputed area. They speedily organized a CLN

[109] *Ibid.*, pp. 76–79; G. Vaccarino, "I rapporti con gli Alleati e la missione del Sud," *MLI*, No. 52/53 (1958), p. 63; Italy, Presidenza del Consiglio, Ufficio Storico per la Guerra di Liberazione, Virgilio Ricci (ed.), *Il Contributo della Valle d'Aosta alla Guerra di Liberazione* (Rome, 1946), pp. 31–34.

[110] Regarding Italo-German relations, see Bruno Coceani (prefect of Trieste), *Mussolini, Hitler, Tito alle porte orientali d'Italia* (Rocca S. Casciano, 1948); G. Esposito, *Trieste e la sua odissea* (Rome, 1952); an anonymous, embittered Fascist's "Un anno di amministrazione germanica in Venezia Giulia (8 settembre 1943–31 dicembre 1944," *MLI*, No. 17/18 (1952), pp. 70–82.

[111] See Pro-Slav Comitato cittadino dell'Unione Antifascista Italo-Slavo, *Trieste nella lotta per la democrazia* (Trieste, 1945).

in Trieste, only to see it collapse in November 1943 when most of its leaders were hustled off to Dachau. Undaunted, they patched together a second committee in the spring.[112]

The PCI in Venezia Giulia found itself faced with an awkward problem: should it collaborate with Tito's OF or identify itself strictly with the Italian underground? Some weeks prior to the armistice, the PCI had made agreements with Yugoslav leaders to join forces against the common foe and postpone all territorial discussions till the end of the war, at which time they would be solved "on the basis of national rights of all peoples and according to the necessity of fraternity and collaboration among neighboring peoples." [113] Neither Tito nor the PCI adhered faithfully to this.

By early 1944 the CLNAI was urgently seeking some means whereby all the Triestians might be united in the struggle against Germany and at the same time not compromise the future territorial status of the region. Hoping to persuade the Yugoslavs to mitigate their nationalistic ambitions, the Pd'A (true to its federalistic approach to European problems) suggested that the Italians offer to internationalize the port facilities of Trieste. This proposal was turned down resolutely by most of the other anti-Fascists in Trieste. The Pd'A then decided that greater Italian participation in joint Italo-Slav guerrilla operations in the region was necessary in order to improve Italy's bargaining

[112] Regarding the complex history of the underground in this sector, see especially Edvino Taucer's documented "La ripresa antifascista dopo l'8 settembre nella regione giuliana," *MLI*, No. 51 (1958), pp. 3–19; and his "Il secondo CLN ed i rapporti italo-slavi," *MLI*, No. 51 (1958), pp. 20–37; Enzo Collotti, "Antifascismo e resistenza nella Venezia Giulia all'alba della lotta di liberazione," *MLI*, No. 34/35 (1955), pp. 59–68; Roberto Cessi, "Comitati di liberazione e brigate del popolo delle provincie del Veneto Orientale," *MLI*, No. 34/35 (1955), pp. 56–58; Ercole Miani, "La Resistenza nella Venezia Giulia," *Il Ponte*, III (1948), pp. 339–345; the Actionist Giovanni Paladin, *La lotta clandestina di Trieste* (Trieste, 1954); Bruno Steffé (of Venezia Giulia CLN), *Le mouvement italien de la Résistance dans la Vénetie Julienne* (n.p., n.d.); Vittorio Furlani, "La realtà di Trieste," *Nuova antologia*, XCI (1956), pp. 209–222; Partito Socialista della Venezia Giulia, *Il Socialismo triestino nella lotta antifascista e nella difesa dell'italianità* (1942–1948) (Trieste, 1948); Franco Ventura, "La stampa clandestina a Trieste dal luglio 1943 al 1 maggio 1945," *MLI*, No. 46 (1957), pp. 3–28; Carlo Ventura, "La stampa clandestina a Trieste dal 1 maggio 1945 all'inizio dell'amministrazione alleata," *MLI*, No. 47 (1957), pp. 3–12; Valiani, *Tutte le strade conducono a Roma*, pp. 177–178, 186–187; and Battaglia, SRI, pp. 143–144.

[113] Longo, "I Comunisti hanno sempre difeso l'italianità di Trieste," *Rinascita*, X (1953), pp. 651–653.

position. Not all party members agreed; the older ones stoutly opposed anything smacking of collaboration with Tito, while younger Actionists were more sanguine about the possibility of fruitful understanding emerging from effective co-operation.[114]

The easiest way to achieve contact with Tito was through the PCI, whose apparatus in Trieste was manipulated by the veteran conspirator Luigi Frausin (until the Germans arrested him in September 1944). Negotiations were slow and arduous because the Yugoslavs insisted that the Italians should regard Tito as head of an "Allied power" possessing the same right as Britain or the United States to liberate and occupy the region. During the talks the Slavs indicated their willingness to back the general strike the CLNAI planned for March.[115]

On February 7 the CLNAI set forth its position in writing. It drafted its declaration only after personal visits to Trieste by the Actionist Valiani (a native of Fiume) and President Pizzoni (formerly a resident of Trieste). It was transmitted to the Slav leaders by the PCI and Trieste CLN. The CLNAI declared that the Italians were anxious to fight alongside the Slovenes and Croats against the Nazi-Fascists for the common end of achieving national freedom and unity on the basis of the democratic principle of popular self-determination. The CLNAI appealed to Italians of Friuli-Venezia Giulia, and especially of Trieste, to intensify the armed struggle in collaboration with Slavic groups. The declaration affirmed, furthermore, that the CLNAI had decided to stabilize relations with the Slovenian and Croatian CLN's for the purpose of mutual aid and co-ordination, certain that fraternal understanding would flow therefrom.[116] This declaration was the very first CLNAI document to have true diplomatic significance.

On March 27 the CLNAI (again at the behest of the PCI) dispatched another message to Tito, advocating co-ordination of military operations. The CLNAI declared that after the war Venezia Giulia should be permitted to decide freely its own status. For a while it seemed as if this friendly gesture would

[114] Valiani, *Tutte le strade conducono a Roma*, pp. 177–178, 187; Catalano, *Storia del CLNAI*, pp. 128–130.

[115] Valiani, *Tutte le strade conducono a Roma*, pp. 188–190.

[116] *Ibid.*, p. 192; Catalano, *Storia del CLNAI*, p. 130; Longo, *Rinascita*, x (1953), 654; L. Valiani, "Alfredo Pizzoni," *MLI*, No. 49 (1957), pp. 92–93.

lead to an entente; and, indeed, a military accord was worked out on May 7 between headquarters of the Garibaldi brigades and IX Army Corps Command of the NOVJ, recognizing formation "on territory of the Slovene littoral" of the "Trieste" Garibaldi Assault Brigade and its right to recruit members in "Italian centers of population." [117]

A much more sweeping agreement was signed the same day between delegates of the Garibaldi "Friuli" brigade and the Slovenian "Briski-Beneski-Odred," taking up the boundary problem. It left this question open, noting that it would depend upon the "general situation" in Europe and especially in Yugoslavia and Italy at the end of the war. Tito obviously would be influenced by the degree to which Italy collaborated with Yugoslavia during the struggle and fought against the common enemy. The agreement implied, however, that "national aspirations of the Italian people" should be satisfied. Both the March 27 and May 7 agreements were approved on July 17 in Milan by the new Italian CG/CVL.[118] Nevertheless, Yugoslav-Italian relations did not long remain on this seemingly happy course.

Liberation of Rome

Frustrated for months at Cassino and Anzio, the Allies at last were ready on May 12 to hurl forth the offensive that had as its goal the emancipation of Rome. Though the battle lines stretched all the way from the Tyrrhenian to the Adriatic, the chief line of attack was in the West. Included in the Allied array were four French divisions under General Alphonse Juin.

During the first ten days, the victory-hungry troops cleared the mountainous slopes of the Aurunca and captured Minturno. The campaign's second phase saw the capture of Terracina and the juncture with forces at Anzio and Nettuno. Meanwhile, Eighth Army drove up the valley of the Liri behind Cassino, and the Germans fell back to the Alban hills southeast of Rome. On the 28th Bari Radio broadcast to the patriots in central Italy an order to "impede German military movements southward

[117] Longo, Rinascita, x (1953), 654; Catalano, Storia del CLNAI, pp. 131–134; and Valiani, Tutte le strade conducono a Roma, pp. 259–260.
[118] Atti CG/CVL, pp. 33–38; Valiani, Tutte le strade conducono a Roma, pp. 260–262; Catalano, Storia del CLNAI, pp. 193–194; Longo, Rinascita, x (1953), p. 654; and Battaglia, SRI, pp. 319–322.

along the west coast" and to keep the Allies informed of German activities from the Tiber to the Arno. "Although the hour for mass movement has not yet struck, it will be opportune to intensify action against the Nazis and Fascists whenever possible without coming out too much into the open." [119]

The Germans made no effort to fight for Rome, despite orders from Hitler to defend the city until the last German had left it and to blow up the bridges across the Tiber. Marshal Kesselring saw no valid military reason for trying to retain possession of the city and he decided as early as May 16 not to blow up the bridges. Because there had been very few German combat troops in the city since the previous autumn, he faced no great danger in evacuating the few who were there.[120]

The absence of an insurrection in Rome like those in the North has occasioned comment among chroniclers of the Resistenza. Several factors help to explain its nonoccurrence. In the first place, Rome's social structure was quite different from that of Milan and Turin. Instead of having a large and volatile industrial working class, it was populated mainly by churchmen and a bureaucratic *bourgeoisie* identified with political traditionalism. Whatever the other virtues of that kind of people, they were scarcely the type to lash out in bloody insurrection. This was truer than ever after the Germans' slaughter of 335 victims in the Ardeatine Caves on March 24–25. Fear of new terror stabbed deeply into the hearts of most Romans. The enemy, moreover, managed to drive most of the covert leaders into hiding during the last weeks of the occupation. Most of the CCLN politicians were concealed in a Lateran convent; the majority of officers in Bauer's CCLN Military Center were under arrest during the final days; the federalist-minded editor Eugenio Colorni of the Socialist *Avanti!* was killed on May 27; and, in the midst of the German withdrawal, PSIUP syndical leader Bruno Buozzi (who had just negotiated the tripartite Pact of Rome [121] with the PCI and DC

---

[119] NYT, May 29, 1944, 3:8.

[120] S/M, *Sdf*, pp. 993–995.

[121] It is printed in Carli-Ballola, *Sdr*, pp. 332–334. Buozzi had worked furtively with Giuseppe DiVittorio (PCI) and Achille Grandi (DC). Emilio Canevari signed for the captured Buozzi. In the CGIL which emerged publicly in June as soon as Rome was freed, these three *partiti di massa* were represented equally. The three original secretaries were DiVittorio, Grandi, and Lizzadri (PSIUP). The three parties were similarly balanced in the provincial labor federations and

for a new Italian General Confederation of Labor—CGIL) was assassinated.[122]

Furthermore, the CCLN was badly split, both as to the institutional issue and the role of its Military Center.[123] Indeed, President Bonomi had tendered his resignation on March 23; he did not withdraw it till May 10 after the Togliatti *svolta* and the reconstruction of Badoglio's government in the South.[124] Bonomi and the conservative wing of the underground dreaded any anarchy or leftist insurrection occurring at the moment of Rome's freedom. So did the Vatican, which favored collaboration with the Allies and encouragement of the DC as Italy's best hope; and the Vatican's voice carried much weight among the beleaguered Romans. Certainly Premier Badoglio (and perhaps Togliatti, who shared a key post in his government) desired to enter Rome unhampered by popular disturbances, in the hope that with Allied backing his cabinet could endure. And, finally, the Allies also desired no unseemly commotion in the Eternal City. Thus *attesismo* was the order of the day.[125]

After Colonel Montezemolo had been captured in January, Badoglio's government had sought to persuade General Raffaele Cadorna in Rome to become Head Liaison Officer of the scattered resistants and caretaker of Rome at the moment of German withdrawal. Cadorna was a son of the distinguished World War I commander and had himself led the "Ariete" division which had acquitted itself better than most units in Rome's suburbs on September 9, 1943. Though he had been working with the underground in Rome since that fateful day (and had recommended Montezemolo's appointment as Head Liaison Officer), he declined Badoglio's invitation, his reason being that he understood full well the attitude of the CCLN toward the royal gov-

chambers of labor. The tripartite arrangement survived until July 15, 1948. By 1950 the Catholics had organized a rival CISL, while rightist Socialists countered with a UIL. S/M, *Sdf*, p. 1001; Tupini, *I Democratici cristiani*, pp. 80–83; and G. Candeloro, *Il movimento sindacale in Italia* (Rome, 1950).

[122] The Germans had snatched him and fourteen others from a jail and shot them at LaStorta along the Cassian Way.

[123] Tupini, *I Democratici cristiani*, pp. 74–76, provides some data about DC covert politico-military activities in Rome and its environs.

[124] See *supra*, Ch. viii, Togliatti's PCI "svolta."

[125] R. Bauer in preface to Salvadori, *SRI*, pp. 15–16; Battaglia, *SRI*, pp. 227–235, 251, 257–258, 299–304; Iò di Benigno, *Occasioni mancate*; Bonomi, *Diario di un anno, passim.*

ernment. He had a premonition of the difficulties which he would encounter in winning the confidence of the political wing of the Armed Resistance. Cadorna preferred to bide his time till the CLN should initiate a request for a professional soldier to co-ordinate patriot resistance.[126]

Following Cadorna's demurral, Premier Badoglio designated General Quirino Armellini to act as Military Commandant in Rome at the moment of deliverance. Because of his past admiration for Fascism and his connection with Blackshirt groups during the "45 days," however, Armellini was *persona non grata* to the CCLN, which suggested, instead, General Roberto Bencivenga, an anti-Fascist royalist who once had been in *confino*. After prolonged bickering, Badoglio agreed to let Bencivenga assume a parallel position with Armellini—the former to handle civilian affairs, the latter military administration of Rome during the interregnum. Whereupon Armellini became disgusted and withdrew from the scene in March. Not long afterward, Bencivenga let it be known that he did not recognize the CCLN's authority; meanwhile, Bonomi had quit in a huff.[127] Such was the unedifying acrimony that permeated the Roman underground.

In view of all these circumstances, it was scarcely surprising that the Allied High Command issued orders that armed squads in Rome should await explicit signals before acting, in order not to upset Allied operational plans (and because they were not sure what the political repercussions might be). Nor was it very surprising that this signal never came. Learning that the Vatican was negotiating with the Germans for the peaceful evacuation of the city, the Allies were willing that the papal authorities keep General Bencivenga immobilized in his Lateran hide-out (as a matter of fact, he had accidentally slipped and fractured his pelvis), and apparently Bonomi and CCLN rightists were just as willing. There was no one to replace him, for most of the Military Command were already under arrest. (General Caruso, who headed the secret network of *Carabinieri*, had managed to escape the fate of his colleagues by swallowing the address list

[126] Cadorna, *La Riscossa*, p. 84.
[127] Bonomi, *Diario di un anno*, pp. 187–188; Benigno, *Occasioni mancate*, pp. 298, 305, 362.

of his men and standing firm against brutal blows.) [128] Meanwhile, Allied deliverance came too unexpectedly for any of the lower echelons of the underground to take matters into their own hands and try to seize the Quirinal Palace, Campidoglio, or Palazzo Venezia.[129]

As Germans pulled back from the Porta Pia, Americans descended into Piazza Venezia in the late afternoon of June 4, the first invaders in fourteen centuries to enter from the south.[130] The populace greeted them with delirious joy and gratitude. Soon at least a quarter of a million flocked to St. Peter's Square to thank Pope Pius XII for his tireless efforts to spare bloodshed in the Eternal City. Socialists and Communists were among the vast throng, and for the first time the Red flag dipped in salute before the Pope's window. Throughout the Allied world headlines hailed the liberation of the first "enemy" capital. Two days later other headlines proclaimed the successful invasion of Normandy.

[128] Andreotti, *DeGasperi e il suo tempo*, p. 140; Carli-Ballola, *Sdr*, pp. 145–146.

[129] So reported SF Captain Salvadori, who entered Rome by jeep at dawn on the 5th and quickly established contact with his colleague Renato Pierleoni (who for eight months since crossing the lines had worked with Rome's GAP) and other politicians in the underground. *Resistenza ed azione*, pp. 249–251.

[130] Early in the morning of the 5th, Lieutenant General Mark Clark, accompanied by Brigadier General Edgar Erskine Hume, arrived at Rome's Campidoglio, where they were met by General Bencivenga, and set up AMG. Harris, *Allied Military Administration of Italy*, pp. 163–164.

CHAPTER X · CLN'S IN THE ASCENDANT

June 5 – November 13, 1944

Rome conference of CCLN and Badoglio

WHEN the Allies forced the Nazis out of Rome, they kept King Victor Emmanuel III from returning to the old capital lest he renege on his retirement pledge. At Ravello on June 5 ACC Chief Commissioner Mason-Macfarlane constrained him to sign the decree transferring power to his "beloved son," Prince Humbert of Savoy, now Lieutenant-General of the Realm. Simultaneously Premier Badoglio tendered his resignation to Humbert, who quickly invited him to form a new cabinet including CLN leaders from Rome and other liberated areas. On the next day, Mason-Macfarlane, Badoglio, and southern spokesmen of the six parties flew to Rome to confront the CCLN directorate.[1] On the 8th Humbert also put in a brief appearance in the emancipated metropolis.

As soon as the southern delegation sat down with the CCLN in Rome's Grand Hotel, it was clear that Badoglio could not form a government that would win CCLN approval. The PSIUP and Pd'A insisted unswervingly that Badoglio was out of the running, that the new cabinet must consist solely of representatives of the CLN hexarchy, and that no oath of allegiance would be taken to the Monarchy.[2] Quickly Badoglio talked to Togliatti, who (with the British) hitherto had been his mainstay. To his dismay he learned that the Red, though cordial, intended to go along with the majority of the CLN directors. Standing erect, the old Piedmontese army officer shook hands with his erstwhile

---

[1] Present from the South were Badoglio, Sforza (Ind.), Rodinò (DC), Mancini (PSIUP), Cerabona (DL), Togliatti (PCI), and Cianca (Pd'A). Croce was unable to go. The Rome CCLN was represented by President Bonomi and Secretary Fenoaltea, DeGasperi (DC), Casati (PLI), Ruini (DL), Nenni (PSIUP), LaMalfa (Pd'A), and Scoccimarro (PCI). Elder Statesman Orlando also sat in, as did Anglo-American political advisers.

General Maitland Wilson and Harold Macmillan would have preferred to bring the Rome committee to Salerno, but Noel Charles had recommended the contrary and London approved. Field Marshal Lord Wilson of Libya, *Eight Years Overseas, 1939–1947* (London, 1950), p. 210.

[2] P. Nenni, "The Rebirth of Italy," *The Nation*, Sept. 23, 1944, p. 352; R. Bauer, "L'attività del CLN in Roma nel maggio 1944," *MLI*, No. 50 (1958), pp. 57–85.

Communist ally, and then with heavy sarcasm told the assembled Rome politicos that it was "not because of any action on your part that you have met round this table in Rome; you were in hiding or living safely with friars in convents. The man who has done the work, who has shouldered the heaviest responsibilities, is that soldier who, as Ruini has said, does not belong to any party." [3] Whereupon he took his leave, meditated on his memoirs, and finally faded away in 1956.

Bonomi's "Concerto for Six Parties"

The CCLN did not give Prince Humbert a chance to take the initiative in seeking a new premier; instead, it notified him that Ivanoe Bonomi was its choice. This 71-year-old quondam prime minister and CCLN president accepted the official invitation on three conditions: that a decree could be issued calling for a Constituent Assembly to settle the institutional dispute at war's end and draft a new constitution; that the oath of allegiance be revised to avoid objectionable obeisance to the dynasty; and that the cabinet have exclusive power to issue decrees until new parliamentary institutions came into existence.[4] Agreeing to these, Humbert authorized Bonomi to proceed—much to the ire of the royalists and the British, who fought a delaying action for a fortnight, trying to get Badoglio back into power.

Indeed, Mason-Macfarlane made it known that the new government must have Allied placet, and that each minister must sign a pledge of loyalty to the armistice clauses (something not explicitly demanded of individual members of Badoglio's cabinet in April).[5] He also notified Bonomi that Sforza could not be Foreign Minister. Though he asserted that he spoke for both Allied governments, this was not true, for Secretary Hull quickly protested that Sforza was entirely acceptable to Washington.[6] But no change occurred, and on the 10th Mason-Macfarlane, acting on his own authority, publicly approved Bonomi's *concerto a sei voci*.[7] Bonomi retained for himself the Foreign Affairs

[3] Badoglio, *Italy in the Second World War*, pp. 165–166.
[4] Bonomi, *Diario di un anno*, pp. 197–198.
[5] Badoglio, *Italy in the Second World War*, pp. 166–168.
[6] Hull, *Memoirs*, II, 1563.
[7] The epithet was coined by Giulio Andreotti, author of an account of the political crisis of the sexpartite Bonomi government, *Concerto a sei voci* (Rome, 1945).

and Interior ministries but named seven distinguished "ministers without portfolio" to placate the jealous parties: Croce (PLI), who soon resigned and was succeeded by N. Carandini (PLI); DeGasperi (DC); Ruini (DL); Cianca (Pd'A); Saragat (PSIUP); Togliatti (PCI); and Sforza (Ind.). The latter also kept the thankless post of High Commissioner of Sanctions against Fascism. Bonomi chose all civilians except for Admiral DeCourten (Minister of Navy) and General Piacentini (Minister of Air), and he gave equal weight to all parties and regions.[8] He pledged not to reopen the institutional question "without the prior consent of the Allied governments until all Italy is liberated and the Italian people have the opportunity themselves to choose the form of government." [9]

At this point Churchill, who had been away for a few days observing the Normandy invasion, exploded angrily at Badoglio's replacement by a "cluster of aged and hungry politicians." Cabling Roosevelt and Stalin, he insisted that it was his understanding that Badoglio was to carry on at least until the "democratic North" could be consulted and a thoroughly sound government formed; he was "unaware" that the Allies had given the Italians the right to set up, without reference to the victorious powers, any cabinet they chose. Stalin's reply of the 11th was most solicitous: "To me, too, [Badoglio's] resignation came as a surprise. I thought that without the consent of the Allies—the British and Americans—that Badoglio could not be removed and replaced by Bonomi. However, it appears from your message that this has happened against the will of the Allies. It is to be expected that certain Italian circles will try to change the armistice terms in their favour. Be that as it may, if circumstances suggest to you and the Americans that Italy should have a Government different from that of Bonomi, you may rest assured that the Soviet side will raise no obstacles." [10] Stalin acquiesced in sub-

[8] To the PLI was assigned Treasury (Marcello Soleri) and War (Alessandro Casati); to DL, Communications (Francesco Cerabona); to DC, Industry, Commerce and Labor (Giovanni Gronchi) and Grace and Justice (Umberto Tupini); to Pd'A, Finance (Stefano Siglienti) and Public Instruction (Guido DeRuggiero); to PSIUP, Public Works (Pietro Mancini); and to PCI, Agriculture (Fausto Gullo).
[9] Revealed by Nenni in March 1946; text in New York Il Mondo (April 1946), p. 17, cited in Kogan, Italy and the Allies, p. 77.
[10] Ministry of Foreign Affairs of the USSR, Stalin's Correspondence with Churchill, Attlee, Roosevelt and Truman, 1941–1945, I, 227–228 (Doc. No. 279).

sequent British moves that month, perhaps expecting analogous support from the West when he pushed into eastern Europe.

But Roosevelt, after checking with American observers, stood his ground. Replying to Churchill that it would be a grave mistake not to permit prompt installation of Bonomi's cabinet, he predicted that the new government would prove helpful. Eventually Churchill gave in, but the ailing Mason-Macfarlane was made something of a scapegoat and resigned as ACC Chief Commissioner, while Macmillan and General Maitland Wilson also felt Churchill's wrath.[11] Captain (soon Commodore) Ellery Stone of the U.S. Navy replaced Mason-Macfarlane as Acting Chief Commissioner.

Two weeks later the cabinet was installed, not in Rome but in Salerno, which remained the capital till July 15. At the ceremony each minister read the armistice terms (they remained veiled from the public until November 6, 1945) and agreed to them. All but Bonomi swore "on their honor to exercise their functions in the supreme interest of the nation and not to commit, before the calling of the Constituent Assembly, any action which might in any way prejudice the solution of the institutional question." Two concessions were made to mollify Churchill: Bonomi personally took the traditional oath of allegiance to the King (significant because as Head of the Government, Bonomi alone was responsible for the governance of the nation); and the monarchist Admiral DeCourten remained Minister of Navy.[12] A provisional constitution (to last till the Constituent Assembly could draft a permanent one after the war) was announced on June 25 in the guise of Decree-Law No. 151.[13] It gave the cabinet power to issue decree-laws in the name of the

[11] Wilson, *Eight Years Overseas*, 1939–1947, p. 210; Hull, *Memoirs*, II, 1564–1565; Harris, *Allied Military Administration of Italy*, 1943–1945, pp. 201–204; Barbara Barclay Carter, *Italy Speaks* (London, 1947), p. 96; Matthews in *NYT*, June 19, 20, and July 2, 1944.

[12] Grindrod, *The New Italy*, p. 24; Kogan, *Italy and the Allies*, pp. 78–79.

[13] Though this decree appeared to repudiate the 1848 *Statuto*, Bonomi tried within a month to re-establish one of the signal features of the old regime—consultation with the President of the Chamber of Deputies and the President of the Senate in all cabinet crises. Thus he named (with British encouragement) to these posts the venerable PLI royalists, Orlando and Marchese della Torretta. Republicans protested loudly, since a Chamber of Deputies did not yet exist—and, even if it did, it must elect its own president. The translated decree-law is printed in part in Smyth, "Italy: From Fascism to the Republic," *Western Political Quarterly*, I (1948), pp. 214–217.

Lieutenant-General, calling for convocation of a postwar Constituent Assembly to be elected by universal, direct, and secret ballot, and confirmed dissolution of the old Fascist parliamentary bodies. Thus women gained at last the right to vote in the new Italy. Because of the "bloodless revolution," effective political power lay in the hands of the CCLN rather than of Humbert, at least so long as the ACC did not intervene (for, of course, that omnicompetent body was always in the wings). Henceforth the political issue no longer was *whether* the Italian people would have the right to choose freely between a monarchy and a republic but *how* this would be done. Regarding this question, the Pd'A, PSIUP, and PCI insisted that the Constituent Assembly (which they presumed would be susceptible to their own party organizations) have the power, Jacobin style, to abolish the Monarchy; royalists in the PLI, DC, and DL tended to favor, instead, a referendum (expecting the conservative southern peasants to uphold the Monarchy).[14]

Political freedom was as refreshing as Frascati wine to the new popular tribunes and they were all thirsty. In a spirit of exuberance the parties busily spent the summer redefining their positions through either congresses or pronunciamentos of their directorates. The Pd'A, as long in leadership as it was short in support, began to agitate not just for any republic but for a "social republic," hoping thereby to proselyte right-wingers from the PSIUP—an indispensable move if it aspired seriously to first-rank status. Its alternative was to cultivate the moderates, and in Rome LaMalfa tried to do so. While he elicited some sympathy from Pacciardi's Mazzinian Republican Party (which still steered clear of the CLN's for fear the latter would compromise with monarchism), he was rebuffed by rightist Socialists, Labor Democrats, and Christian Democrats. At the Pd'A Second Congress, which foregathered in distant Cosenza from August 4 to 7, Lussu rammed through a maximalist, Jacobinic prospectus; yet in the next breath the congress insisted that the party was resolutely antitotalitarian. Meanwhile, in the North, Valiani, Riccardo Lombardi, and Vittorio Foà tried to galvanize the Actionists into a semirevolutionary mood and achieve greater leftist

---

[14] *Ibid.; cf.* L. Valiani, "La battaglia per la sovranità della Costituente," *Il Ponte*, xiv (special supplement to Nov. 1958 issue; dedicated to Piero Calamandrei), pp. 80–94.

solidarity.[15] But this latter effort was in vain. About all that Pd'A radicalism accomplished was to frighten many of the middle class into either the Liberal or Christian Democratic ranks.[16]

On July 9 Togliatti declared that the PCI favored respect for the institutional "truce"; all-out prosecution of the "war of liberation"; implacable hostility to the return to power of any groups tainted by Fascism; and reaffirmation of the "unity of action" pact with Nenni's Socialists. Insisting that his party respected Catholicism, Togliatti invited the DC to collaborate economically and politically with his bloc.[17] Obviously Togliatti dreamed of a government by the three *partiti di massa*. Talk of proletarian dictatorship was deliberately played down in favor of patriotic unity.

Nenni favored "unity of action" with the Communists because of his deep-seated conviction that Mussolini's triumph in 1922 was facilitated by the schism in the Socialist movement. On August 8 he and Togliatti renewed the agreement.[18] For the same reasons as the Communists, Nenni also minimized the traditional revolutionary slogans; moreover, he recognized that he could not afford to ride roughshod over Saragat's democratic and revisionist group, reinforced by the arrival on October 14 of Silone and Modigliani from long exile in Switzerland.[19] The "unity of action" pact, however, did not keep Nenni from hurling anathemas against the Monarchy and ridiculing the fiction of parity in the CLN hexarchy. Farther north in the Po valley the underground wing of the PSIUP, piloted by Pertini and Rodolfo Morandi, steadily expanded its membership, as did its burgeoning Communist partner (the PCI in the North increased its number of card carriers from 5,000 to 100,000 between 1943 and 1944).[20]

---

[15] Battaglia, *SRI*, pp. 380–381.

[16] Francesco Compagna, *La lotta politica italiana nel secondo dopoguerra e il Mezzogiorno* (Bari, 1950), pp. 33–43; Dipiero, *Storia critica dei partiti politici*, p. 232; Valiani, *Tutte le strade conducono a Roma*, p. 309. See pamphlet series, "Quaderni del Partito d'Azione" (Rome, 1944–1946) for significant programmatic articles by E. Lussu, F. Comandini, C. Bandi, F. Fancello, U. LaMalfa, M. Rossi-Doria, A. Garosci, *et al*. See Riccardo Bauer, *Alla ricerca della libertà* (Milan, 1957), for a collection of articles he wrote after 1944 on the Action Party and Socialism and on problems of national reconstruction.

[17] PCI, *Relazione della Direzione del PCI al V° Congresso*, p. 72.

[18] It is published in PCI, *Orientamenti* (Rome), Jan. 19, 1948, pp. 5–6.

[19] *NYT*, Oct. 15, 1944, 17:1.

[20] Giancarlo Pajetta, "Intervento," *MLI*, No. 52/53 (1958), p. 202; P. Nenni, *Una battaglia vinta* (Rome, 1946), pp. 3–20; Battaglia, *SRI*, pp. 383–384; *NYT*, Sept. 5, 1944, 3:4.

Guided by DeGasperi, the Christian Democrats pursued a cautious tack during the summer. They spurned Togliatti's advances, fearful of any more intimacies with the Reds than they already were experiencing within the CLN and CGIL. At the DC Second Inter-Regional Convention in Naples on July 29–30 DeGasperi stressed that his was a "party of order and law," that reconstruction was above all a moral problem, and that social reform must respect the supreme rights of the individual.[21] The Christian Democrats were sure that the course of events would enable them to dominate the center of the national stage. On the institutional question they could not yet speak as one: if in the South most seemed to be royalist, this was not so in the North.[22] The best they could do, therefore, was to defer any stand until their first postwar congress.

The laic Labor Democrats, heirs of the pre-Fascist radical Left, depended for their prestige almost solely upon the personalities of Bonomi and Ruini. Outside Rome and some southern cities they attracted no adherents. Since their status in the CLN was quite unrealistic, they desperately sought to pool their limited strength with the PLI and DC, hoping to maintain a rough balance of power within the CLN and on the institutional question.

The PLI also turned more conservative, especially in the *Mezzogiorno*. A handful of progressives (like Carandini and Brosio) fell back in confusion before the octogenarian Orlando, darling of the royalists and potential surrogate for Bonomi. Croce himself provided further proof of the party's shift to the right: whereas in 1943 he had co-captained the fight against Victor Emmanuel III, he was developing genuine admiration for Prince Humbert by mid-1944.[23]

While Italy's political cauldron steamed in the sticky summer heat, Churchill flew in for a three-week sojourn in August, partly to watch the Allied assaults upon the Gothic Line and the French Riviera, but also to confer with Tito and Italian politicos.

[21] Tupini, *I Democratici cristiani*, pp. 84–89. The "Quaderni della Democrazia Cristiana" (Rome, 1946) contain several of DeGasperi's speeches and papers of this era.

[22] Battaglia, *SRI*, pp. 285–286.

[23] Compagna, *La lotta politica italiana nel secondo dopoguerra e il Mezzogiorno*, pp. 25–32. A trenchant analysis of the parties' attitudes toward the Monarchy may be found in OSS, R. & A. Branch, Report No. 2687, "Attitudes of the Italian Political Parties on the Monarchical Question," Jan. 1, 1945, pp. 1–15.

Many Italians saw in his visit an augury of their country's return to grace. While the doughty Briton gained a better appreciation of the nation's desire to work with the Allies, he did not hesitate to lecture the chief figures "in the debris of Italian politics" on freedom's responsibilities. Decrying "political excitement and the clash of many parties," he called upon the citizenry to rid their soil of the "foul German taint." "Hard work, a strong resolve, high inspirations, and above all true unity will all be needed if Italy is to . . . resume her place among the leading Powers [and] recapture the ideals of freedom which inspired the Risorgimento." On the 23rd Churchill lunched with Prince Humbert. His "powerful and engaging personality [and] grasp of the whole situation . . . were refreshing, and gave one a more lively feeling of confidence than I had experienced in my talks with the politicians," Churchill has written. "I certainly hoped he would play his part in building up a constitutional monarchy in a free, strong, united Italy." [24]

Meantime, President Roosevelt, soliciting Italo-American votes in his campaign for re-election, offered (against Anglo-French wishes) augmented relief supplies and dollar credits equivalent to the lire issued to American troops in Italy. And on August 15 the Allies relinquished Rome, Littoria, and Frosinone provinces to "King's Italy." Next month they erased the detested word "Control" from the ACC title, while the British High Commissioner assumed the additional appellative of Ambassador, a dignity which the American representative already enjoyed. They invited Rome to name envoys to Washington and London. Such gambits increased Bonomi's prestige somewhat until delays in implementation caused renewed disillusionment. [25]

Indeed, by the last week of September a new cabinet crisis shaped up. The causes were not new: demands for expanded socio-economic reforms, a more thorough purge of Fascist officials, and clarification of the status of the CLN. [26] The first centered on the breakup of southern *latifondi*, advocated by landless

[24] Churchill, *Triumph and Tragedy*, pp. 115–116, 126–127; Churchill, *The Dawn of Liberation*, pp. 218–220; NYT, Aug. 26, 1944, 1:4; Aug. 29, 6:4.

[25] Hull, *Memoirs*, II, 1565–1568; Leahy, *I Was There*, pp. 264–265; Harris, *Allied Military Administration of Italy*, Chs. VII, VIII, IX; Kogan, *Italy and the Allies*, pp. 80–89, 43.

[26] Other causes included Sicilian separatism and the official inquiry into the

day laborers and opposed by property owners.[27] Vexatious too was the problem of amassing grain in the new "granaries of the people."

Even more exasperating was the Augean problem of de-Fascistization. On July 29 the so-called "Sforza decree" (No. 159) for retroactive "sanctions against Fascism" wiped out the previous welter of decrees.[28] Though not so strict as the blueprint under which AMG Regional Commissioner Charles Poletti had been operating in Rome, it was more akin to Italian legal tradition and temperament.[29] Its administration was entrusted to a High Commissariat, headed by Sforza and four assistants, each in charge of a major field of investigation.[30]

Though the "Sforza decree" was perhaps an improvement over previous measures, it was still difficult to prove Fascist activity.

---

failure to defend Rome after the armistice. The latter was finally postponed for expediency's sake while Army officers retrained for service at the front with the CIL. See Harris and Kogan's studies for details.

[27] Kogan, *Italy and the Allies*, pp. 90–92; Harris, *Allied Military Administration of Italy*, pp. 59–60; S/M, *Sdf*, p. 999.

[28] See Tommaso Fortunio, *La legislazione definitiva sulle sanzioni contro il fascismo: delitti fascisti, epurazione, avvocazione: commento, dottrina, giurisprudenza* (Rome, 1946).

[29] NYT, Aug. 1, 1944, 7:4.

[30] Avv. Mario Berlinguer (then in Pd'A) took over the first category—punishment of crimes committed by Fascists and German collaborators. Fascist sponsors of the 1922 "March on Rome," *squadristi*, promoters of the *coup d'état* of January 3, 1925, those who had accepted or, worse still, had bought a *sciarpa Littorio* (Fascism's highest political decoration), and virtually all others who had contributed with relevant acts to maintain the dictatorship were liable. (On the latter grounds, most of the senators, including Badoglio, in due course lost their seats.) Anyone who deliberately abetted the Nazis after September 7, 1943, was subject to judicial trial. Punishment was entrusted to one of the following: a High Court of Justice appointed politically by the cabinet; ordinary criminal tribunals; military courts; or provincial commissions. Possible penalties included life imprisonment and death.

Scoccimarro (PCI) supervised the *epurazione* of Fascists from the administration. Here local and ministerial commissions were to function, with the accused having the right to appeal to the central commission. Actual removal was to be decreed by regular authorities normally entrusted with such tasks.

The third category under the Sforza decree provided for forfeiture of profits made during Fascism. It was under the control of Mario Cingolani (DC). Special sections of the provincial tax commissions were to handle such forfeitures, provision being made for appeal to the Central Tax Commission. Liquidation of Fascist property was entrusted to Pier Felice Stangoni (DL), aided by the Financial Administration of the State. OSS, R. & A. Branch, No. 2688, "Treatment of Former Fascists by the Italian Government: An analysis of the process of de-Fascistization in Italy from July 1943 to March 1945," Washington, Mar. 17, 1945, 9–11.

At least one fourth of the population at one time or another had belonged to the PNF or its collateral agencies, and at least half a million civil servants had been active members. It was generally agreed that not all ex-Fascists could or should be punished, since membership in the PNF had often been *"per necessità familiare."* Lenience for the "small fry" but remorselessness for the "fat fish" was Sforza's rule of thumb. Still, border-line cases were hard to decide, and the bureaucracy tried to protect its own people, while Allied officials often slowed the purge to protect "indispensable technicians." Scoccimarro and other leftists who cried for wider purges of "big bankers" and "private concerns" aroused much uneasiness; to many, this seemed the harbinger of a Red onslaught against the profit system and private property.[31] The usual wartime difficulties of travel and communication led to further procrastination.

In mid-September Sforza reported that some 2,000 persons accused of Fascist crimes were in jail and that 750 trials were scheduled. First of the major criminals to come up for trial was Pietro Caruso, Rome's chief of police during the Nazi occupation. He was accused of having turned over to the Germans more than fifty of the hostages who were shot in the Ardeatine Cave atrocity. On September 18, the day before his scheduled trial, relatives of the victims joined by an angry mob that swelled to 7,000 sought to wrest him from the judicial authorities and lynch him. Foiled, the mob turned upon an innocent prosecution witness, Donato Carretta, vice-director of the Regina Coeli prison, who had actually helped political prisoners (including Saragat) escape from the penitentiary. They mauled him brutally before the Palace of Justice while 200 policemen watched helplessly. Half dead, he was thrown into the Tiber and prevented from getting out of the water. Every Rome newspaper except the PCI *L'Unità* deplored the murder.[32] Occurring in the midst of mounting criticism of the purge, it demonstrated the government's weakness and was a major cause of the crisis that erupted in November.[33]

[31] *Ibid.*, pp. 11–13; Andreotti, *Concerto a sei voci*, pp. 12–16; Harris, *Allied Military Administration of Italy*, pp. 206–209; Friedrich, *et al*, *American Experience in Military Government*, pp. 124–125.
[32] See eye-witness account of Matthews, *Education of a Journalist*, pp. 473–481, and his dispatches to *NYT*, Sept. 19, 1:6; Sept. 22, 1944, 8:4.
[33] OSS, R. & A. Branch, No. 2688, pp. 13–20. The court's condemnation of

398

When Scoccimarro late in November demanded elimination of certain finance and maritime officials, this was too much for Treasury Minister Soleri (PLI) and Navy Minister Admiral DeCourten, who promptly tendered their resignations. There is evidence that the British encouraged conservatives within and without the government to demand its reorganization.[34] Bonomi refused to accept the retirement of Soleri and DeCourten and demanded, instead, that the CLN dissolve the High Commission for Sanctions against Fascism. A first-rate crisis was at hand;[35] and it was to coincide with an equally severe one for the Resistenza Armata.

Upsurge of northern Resistance: Bonomi versus CLNAI

In the wake of Rome's liberation and the advent of Bonomi's first CLN government, there was greater harmony within the Milanese CLNAI than at any other period. Advocates of closer co-operation with the extreme left pushed forward in all the clandestine parties.[36] Some predicted a new order resting on a pyramid of CLN's; indeed, on June 2 the CLNAI issued a blueprint of the future relationship of provincial, municipal, and local committees to the CLNAI. It envisioned additional CLN's on the level of urban wards ("*rioni*"), factories, and villages, and stressed the importance of having such local bodies collaborate with groups of agitators, students, youth, and women. Implementation of most of these schemes had to await a later period, but it was noteworthy that they were officially recommended as early as June.[37]

Many CLNAI members eagerly expected Premier Bonomi to assign them full political power in occupied Italy, in line with the January 31 proclamation that had created the northern agency. Such thoughts were quickened by the creation in June of the CG/CVL (General Headquarters of the Corps of Volunteers of Freedom), which marked a forward step in unifying

---

Caruso to death on September 21 was an anticlimax. On October 14 the High Court of Justice sentenced to thirty years' imprisonment Dr. Vincenzo Azzolini, ex-Governor of the Bank of Italy, for turning over the entire stock of gold to the Germans; ultimately, on appeal, the charge was proved unfounded.

[34] Hughes, *The United States and Italy*, p. 136.
[35] Soleri, *Memorie*, p. 300; Kogan, *Italy and the Allies*, pp. 94–95.
[36] Battaglia, *SRI*, pp. 379–386.
[37] Catalano, *Storia del CLNAI*, pp. 173–176.

and co-ordinating the military side of the Resistenza. At that time scarcely anyone foresaw the bitter squabbling that would beset it.

On the question of CLNAI status the leftists were to be disappointed, because Bonomi, taking his cue from the Allies, simply charged the northern committee with "direction of the war of the patriots against the Germans in Upper Italy." [38] Undaunted, the CLNAI went ahead on June 10 to announce confidently that it had assumed the functions and duties of the Central CLN for all sections of Italy still under German occupation. And on the 14th it issued a proclamation for the national insurrection, which many then deemed imminent (in view of the Allied push northward from Rome, to say nothing of the Normandy invasion and the Russian drive beyond the 1939 frontiers).[39]

Bemused by these campaigns, the CLNAI impetuously issued vigorously phrased new legislation condemning "enemies of the fatherland" and setting forth rigid reprisals and economic norms to be applied at the moment of insurrection. These were forwarded to Rome in the hope that Bonomi would underwrite them.[40]

When it seemed that an Allied descent into the Po valley was at hand, Premier Bonomi got around to acting on the CLNAI's repeated requests for clarification of its legal status. Bonomi's first message was a personal letter of August 6, in which rather cautiously (he could never escape the ACC's imprimatur) he remarked that he considered the CLNAI the "delegation of the Italian Government for the purpose of the national struggle in the territory where the German armies and final betrayers of the fatherland are encamped." [41] Then on August 25, following Churchill's Roman holiday, Bonomi sent a more formal document to the CLNAI, recognizing it as the "co-ordinating authority" of all political and military activities of the Resistance

---

[38] *Atti del CG/CVL*, pp. 1–5; Catalano, *Storia del CLNAI*, p. 207; Valiani, *Tutte le strade conducono a Roma*, p. 254; Parri in Bonacossi and Ragghianti-Collobi (eds.), *Una lotta nel suo corso*, pp. 232–233.

[39] Catalano, *Storia del CLNAI*, p. 177; Battaglia, *SRI*, p. 387.

[40] Longo, *Sulla via dell'insurrezione*, p. xxxviii; Catalano, *Storia del CLNAI*, pp. 179–185, 208–211.

[41] Archivio CLNAI, Milan, xix/13.

in occupied Italy, authorizing it to "issue all instructions and orders" necessary for "disciplining the Resistance of the entire country, for making uniform the criteria and directives which, taking into account the different local situations," seem most opportune. He further conferred upon it the power to apply laws pertaining to the Resistance, to provide for the discipline and relief of the populace until such time as it would be feasible to establish contacts with the Allied Commands and legitimate Italian authorities. Bonomi concluded his mandate with an appeal to the Northerners to collaborate to the maximum with the CLNAI.[42]

From Rome to Florence

By June 1944 the number of men in the Resistenza Armata had jumped sharply, as statistics compiled by Mussolini's own army staff on the 15th revealed. These estimated a total of about 82,000 "rebels"—an increase of some 27,000 over the preceding season.[43] The Salò regime calculated (fairly accurately) the regional distribution to be: Piedmont, 25,000 (an increase of 15,000); Liguria, 14,200 (an increase of 7,000); Venezia Giulia, 16,000 (stable); Emilia and Tuscany, 17,000 (an increase of 4,000); Venezia Euganea, 5,600; and Lombardy, 5,000 (an increase of 2,000). All told, the figure was about equivalent to the 93,000 men (half of these being service troops) then comprising the Republican National Guard (GNR). The Fascist staff officers ascribed the patriot build-up to general aversion to Fascism and the Germans, a desire to bring the war to a quick end, conscription of new classes, the inefficacy of the rastrellamenti, certain abuses committed during these combings, and lack of effective government in some valleys. The report went on to list 1,942 "rebel" actions in April; 2,035 in May; and 2,200 in June. In the last month attacks were even reported against army barracks and munitions deposits. The number of instances of railway sabotage jumped from 189 in April to 241 in May and 344 in June.

[42] Archivio CLNAI, xix/16.
[43] See "Situazione ribelli alla data del 15 giugno 1944," prepared by Stato Maggiore Esercito, reprinted in Battaglia, SRI, pp. 338–340. Resistance leaders regarded the figures as approximately correct; General Cadorna estimated about 90,000 for this period. La Riscossa, p. 150.

Mussolini and his cohorts Pavolini (PFR Secretary) and Farinacci became increasingly concerned over the Lernean hydra of the Resistance. Every week brought the fighting closer to them, making it clearer than ever that neither they nor their German patrons could regain the southern provinces. In this mounting crisis, Pavolini argued that the PFR must become an elite and intransigent combat organization; he persuaded the *Duce* to proclaim a drastic new program on June 21.[44]

Beginning July 1, this announcement declared, the PFR's political structure would be strictly military. All PFR members between the ages of 18 and 60 who did not already serve in one of the RSI armed forces would be drafted into an auxiliary Blackshirt corps composed of *squadre d'azione*. On their shirts they would wear the party emblem. The "action squads" would be the cellular base for the new fighting arm: three squads would form a company; three of these, a battalion; and three of the latter, a *Brigata Nera* ("Black Brigade"). Most of the supplies would come from the German SS, commanded in Italy by General Karl Wolff. Pavolini would assume charge of the new program and personally command the Black Brigades in Piedmont. Elsewhere provincial PFR officials would exercise military control over the corps, which was supposed to be subject to the wartime code of military discipline. Thus Mussolini's regime in its last, sordid phase sought to preserve itself by an amalgam of conscription and *squadrismo*.[45]

The Black Brigades were ordered to ferret out partisan "bandits and outlaws" and "enemy parachutists." They were also supposed to maintain "public and revolutionary order." Actually their brutality served only to intensify popular hatred of the regime, as several neo-Fascist chroniclers have frankly conceded.[46] As a matter of fact, toward the end of the war when Wolff was engaged in armistice soundings in Switzerland, he considered the Black Brigades a liability and cut off most of their supplies.[47]

During July the *Duce* set forth on still another pilgrimage

[44] Filippo Anfuso, *Rom-Berlin in diplomatischem Spiegel* (Munich, 1951), p. 293.
[45] S/M, *Sdf*, p. 1006.
[46] Cione, *Storia della RSI*, p. 227.
[47] Moellhausen, *La carta perdente*, pp. 342-343.

to Hitler's Reich. He reviewed Italian troops training there and urged them to imitate the *Wehrmacht*. Next he traveled to Hitler's headquarters in distant East Prussia, arriving a few hours after the German Army's abortive "July 20" plot. Understandably, Hitler was in no mood to listen to his decrepit Italian partner. The latter sat speechless as the *Fuehrer* poured forth an hysterical tirade about his plans for ruthlessly crushing the German traitors. Mussolini returned to Lake Garda more shaken than ever. But the game had to go on, and on August 2 Marshal Graziani was assigned command of an Italo-German army on the Italian front, operating under Kesselring's supreme control.[48]

Meanwhile in mid-June Kesselring candidly acknowledged the danger presented by the partisans, especially those in the central Apennines. During that summer German trucks could seldom move safely through this area unless in convoy. "The fight against the partisans must be carried on with . . . the utmost severity," Kesselring ordered; "I will protect any commander who exceeds our usual restraint in the choice of severity of the methods he adopts." The German commandant still regarded the partisans as "illegitimate combatants" who were not entitled to be treated like regular PW's.[49] The CLNAI, on the other hand, insisted on June 23 that the partisans were "legitimate belligerents," because they respected even the conditions set down by the Fascists' own law of warfare of July 8, 1938, which held that the Militia and Volunteer Corps were fully covered if they had a responsible commander, wore a uniform, and carried arms openly. All these requirements were met by the partisans in June, for both the CLNAI and CG/CVL had been created and the Allies had accorded them legal status.[50]

On June 7 General Alexander, Commander of Allied Armies in Italy, broadcast a message urging the patriots to rise against the enemy, sabotage his communication lines, and hinder his efforts to withdraw from Rome. "The liberation of Italy is

---

[48] S/M, *Sdf*, p. 1005; Battaglia, *SRI*, p. 342; Catalano, *Storia del CLNAI*, p. 236.

[49] *Nuremberg Trial Proceedings* (London, 1946–1947), Part IX, p. 53 ff.; Albert Kesselring, *The Memoirs of Field-Marshal Kesselring* (London, 1953), pp. 224–233; E. Canevari, *Graziani mi ha detto* (Rome, 1947), pp. 327–328.

[50] Catalano, *Storia del CLNAI*, pp. 167–169.

well under way. In less than a month the strength of the German armies has been broken," Alexander confidently asserted.[51] Backed up by Churchill, he and General Wilson were anxious to push on to the Po valley that summer. To their chagrin, American strategists overruled them on June 14 and insisted upon diverting substantial forces from Italy to southern France by mid-August in order to help Eisenhower's campaign in Normandy. Reluctantly and with clear resolve to reopen the question, Churchill agreed to the more limited goal of a line from Pisa to Rimini in the rugged Apennines.[52] The Italian theater of operations was rapidly shrinking to second-rate status; but this could not be revealed to the patriots behind the lines, whose expectations during these weeks remained at fever pitch. Unhappily for all concerned, the Allies required three months to reach even the Pisa-Rimini line.

As the Allies pushed north from Rome they ran into "guerrilla bands in large numbers for the first time," according to the official historian of the Fifth Army: "Though not as highly organized as resistance groups in the Po valley or in France the bands south of the Arno performed valuable service on many occasions. The partisans identified themselves by red-white-and-green armbands and carried a great assortment of weapons; some groups were led by escaped Allied prisoners of war." [53] Combat officers who dealt directly with these fighters were usually favorably impressed, a New Zealand intelligence officer has written. Yet there was a legacy of distaste and diffidence that hindered policy at many stages; no one apparently "had contemplated that, if the Italians were to 'work their passage,' the crews would come aboard in red shirts, flaunting revolutionary banners. The military mind preferred the grey-green of the reformed Italian Army, even if it had been the uniform of Mussolini." [54] According to this observer, the "Fifth Army had greeted many of the partisan bands in the Apennines by putting them in concentration camps.

[51] AP dispatch, June 7, 1944, Allied Headquarters, Caserta, in NYT, June 8, 1944.
[52] Ehrman, Grand Strategy, v, 345–358, 606.
[53] Lt. Col. Chester G. Starr (ed.), From Salerno to the Alps: A History of the Fifth Army, 1943–1945 (Washington, 1948), pp. 275–276.
[54] Cox, The Road to Trieste, p. 148.

The Poles, inflamed by the undoubtedly anti-Soviet feelings of those rank and file who had been in Russian prison camps between 1939 and 1941, were liable to arrest anyone wearing a red scarf. The Brazilians, it is true, found them most useful allies, and often used them as a forward screen. But many other formations looked on them as did our troops, as excitable bands of adolescents who might be more of a nuisance than help.

"This policy, however, gradually changed under the impact of events. The official attitude grew warmer. Field-Marshal Alexander had early laid down a policy of full co-operation, which was in the later months of 1944 interpreted more generously." [55]

Colonel Starr reported that "occasionally the partisans joined Army units and fought alongside our soldiers; at other times they fought by themselves. Generally, however, the partisans proved themselves of most value to us as internal police in areas occupied by our troops before the Allied Military Government (AMG) could be set up and *Carabinieri* brought in to enforce the laws. . . . [They] also ferreted out numbers of German soldiers who had donned civilian clothes and frequently brought in other stragglers who had been by-passed by our forces. As information gatherers and as guides the partisans were especially useful; in these respects the support of the Italian populace proved very helpful to Fifth Army throughout the Italian campaign." [56]

There can be no doubt that both partisan bands and the Italian Corps of Liberation (CIL) helped the Allies significantly in the often difficult fighting from Rome northward. The CIL, which had come back into the fray in April after receiving new equipment and training, fought valiantly in May in Campania, Latium, and the southern Abruzzi. In June the Allies transferred it to the Adriatic sector northeast of the Maiella, where it operated within the framework of the Eighth Army and helped liberate Chieti, L'Aquila, and Teramo. At the latter town the partisan "Gramsci" brigade acquitted itself bravely, while throughout the Abruzzi peasants did their bit for the patriotic

[55] *Ibid.*, pp. 148–149; cf. Harris, *Allied Military Administration of Italy*, pp. 277–278.
[56] Starr, *From Salerno to the Alps*, p. 276.

cause by concealing their cattle from the retreating enemy. By the end of June the CIL fought its way into the Marches, with Ancona its objective. A few weeks later it reached the German defense line north of the Metauro River. On August 31, after three months at the front, it was called back for reorganization into two large combat groups, the "Legnano" and "Folgore," destined to serve later on the Emilia-Romagna front. By August the Allies had found it imperative to enlarge the CIL, in view of the transfer of some seven Allied divisions to France. General Alexander, who had thus been left with only about 153,000 men, was authorized to make use of five Italian combat groups totaling 45,000 men (equivalent to about three Allied divisions).[57] These formations were equipped and trained by British Major General Langley Browning and integrated piecemeal into Eighth Army. With typical Anglo-Saxon self-esteem, he boasted in November, "The rank and file are of first-rate quality. Give me two years with British officers and NCO's . . . and we'd have an army as good as any in Europe." [58]

On the western side of the peninsula Fifth Army troops forced their way into Umbria and southern Tuscany in mid-summer. For a time the Germans sought unsuccessfully to erect a defense line along Lake Trasimeno.[59] As a rule, German resistance was less resolute here than along the Adriatic. Partisan bands, swelled by half-grown boys, flocked down from the highlands and headed for the cities as soon as an area was reasonably clear. Thus the "Spartaco Lavagnini" rushed into Siena a few hours before Allied troops entered.[60] In Arezzo,[61] Leghorn, and Pisa patriots played a helpful role. German reprisals against hostages were widespread; hundreds of civilians were slaughtered. Yet most Italians could agree with the English-born Marchesa Iris Origo who wrote

[57] Hull, Memoirs, II, 1565; Kogan, Italy and the Allies, pp. 72, 79–80; Lombardi, Il Corpo Italiano di Liberazione, passim; Scala, La riscossa dell'esercito, pp. 224–242; C. Primieri, "La Resistenza: il contributo delle Forze Armate alla guerra di Liberazione," in Il Secondo Risorgimento, pp. 181–261; and Battaglia, SRI, pp. 327–328, 333–334.

[58] Allied Commission, Weekly Bulletin, Nov. 26, 1944.

[59] Kesselring, Memoirs, pp. 207–209.

[60] Salvadori, Resistenza ed azione, p. 255; S/M, Sdf, p. 1003; cf. Smeraldo Amidei, Infamia e gloria in terra di Siena durante il nazifascismo (Siena, 1945); and General Domenico Angelica, Come si è salvata Siena (Siena, 1945).

[61] See Antonio Curina, Fuochi sui monti dell'Appennino Toscano (Arezzo, 1957).

in her diary of this phase of the liberation, "[though] destruction and death have visited us, . . . now there is hope in the air." [62]

"War in a museum"

Historic Florence, astride the main highway leading from Rome to the Po, was the next Allied target. Here the Germans were determined to resist block by block. Throughout the German occupation Mussolini's officials had experienced trouble with the Florentine underground; [63] indeed, since the beginning of the dictatorship this Tuscan city had been a hotbed of political extremism, both of the right and of the left. At the end of July PFR Secretary Pavolini tried to make a bargain with some of the Resistance leaders whereby all political prisoners would be freed if the *partigiani* permitted the Germans to withdraw unhampered and promised not to take reprisals against the Fascists. Word also got around that the Germans planned to proclaim the Tuscan capital an "open city" if the partisans left them alone; but the patriots stoutly refused to deal with Pavolini and warned the citizenry not to be taken in by the German promise. There was to be no "open city." Fortunately, most portable works of art had been taken long since from the city.

Tension mounted to the breaking point as three fifths of the urban workers went on strike, some of them joining local Gappisti. In the hills several partisan units congregated and took up combat stations. Their over-all strategy called for saving the bridges and attacking German forces in the city center at the moment of their withdrawal, pursuing them into the outskirts on the right bank of the Arno.[64]

[62] *War in Val d'Orcia: A Diary of Civilian Life in Wartime Italy* (Harmondsworth, 1947; 1956), p. 221.
[63] For a record of clandestine Florence in the PCI press, see Orazio Barbieri, *Un anno di lotta contro il fascismo e il nazismo (dall'8 settembre 1943 alla liberazione di Firenze), documentato attraverso la stampa clandestina della Federazione Comunista Fiorentina* (Rome, 1944). On the work of the Pd'A, see especially Ragghianti, *Disegno della liberazione;* Contini-Bonacossi (ed.), *Una lotta nel suo corso;* and P. Calamandrei, *Uomini e città della resistenza.* See also Sylvia Lombroso, *No Time for Silence* (New York, 1945).
[64] On the broad subject see Nicolas Petresco Comnène, *Firenze, città aperta* (Florence, 1945); the articles in *Il Ponte*, 1 (1945), pp. 414–455, on the first anniversary of the Liberation; Enzo Enriques Agnoletti, "La politica del Comitato Toscano di Liberazione Nazionale"; Alberto Predieri, "La battaglia partigiana per la liberazione di Firenze"; Vittore Branca, "La stampa clandestina in Toscana." See also N. Niccoli, "La liberazione di Firenze (5 agosta–7 settembre 1944),"

On July 31 the Germans, some 75,000 strong in this sector, issued an ultimatum to the 50,000 residents along the Arno, giving them twelve hours to evacuate. Three days later they proclaimed a state of emergency and forbade people to leave their residences. Bombarded constantly from two sides, the city soon was without electricity, water, or bread, and was threatened with serious epidemics. After a thorough preparation lasting five days, early on the morning of the 4th the Germans blew up all the bridges except the Ponte Vecchio, which, however, was rendered temporarily untraversable by the blowing up of medieval palaces at both ends. Bitter fighting continued for another week. Though the Germans ordered all Italian men except Fascist combatants to stay indoors, GAP and other covert formations persistently kept up their sniping against Nazi-Fascists. Some 300 patriots lost their lives in the street fights.

While there were many heroes, the exploits of 30-year-old Aligi Barducci ("Potente"), an aggressive Communist commander who was killed in action on the 8th, came to be specially extolled.[65] It appeared that he helped free the southern bank of the Arno before the Allies reached it on the 6th, whereafter he managed to cross over into the northern sector and join a GL "Rosselli" brigade and others in further sniping at the enemy.

The insurrection proper in Florence began with the tolling of the bell in Palazzo Vecchio at 6 a.m., August 11. It antedated a few days the deliverance of Paris (23rd) and the invasion of southern France (15th). Florence's insurrection differed from Naples' in that it was carefully directed and politically coordinated by the local CLN, which transferred its meeting place on the morning of the 11th from an apartment on Via della Condotta to Palazzo Riccardi. It was marked off from the subsequent northern insurrections by the fact that there was not yet clear evidence that the war would soon end. Florence's uprising lasted the longest of any in Italy. During the first day the Ger-

MLI, No. 16 (1952), pp. 17-25, and Nos. 17/18 (1952), pp. 50-69. See also the collection of articles by P. Calamandrei, E. Enriques Agnoletti, C. Levi, C. Sprigge, and others published on the tenth anniversary: "La battaglia di Firenze," Il Ponte, x (1954), pp. 1312-1480. Cf. Battaglia, SRI, pp. 363-364; and Salvadori, SRI, pp. 144-145.

[65] See the almost hagiographic biography by Orazio Barbieri, Ponti sull'Arno (Rome, 1958).

mans evacuated the northern sector of the city, so that by the morning of the 12th Allied units could cross the river unopposed. Small-arms fire continued for several days, however. Not till the 22nd did the Germans pull back into the Tuscan hills to the north; for still another ten days fighting persisted in the city's outskirts.[66]

Allied leaders qualified their praise of the Florentine partisans. General Mark Clark asserted later that though the *partigiani* in the environs were courageous, they were not so effective as those who rose up later in the Po valley, chiefly because their coordination with the Allied Forces was deficient.[67] General Alexander thought the partisans blundered in making no adequate attempt to safeguard the bridges. *New York Times* correspondent Matthews criticized this too, calling it the "worst failure" of the partisans "in the whole war." Only after the bridges were destroyed, he went on, did the Florentines rise up in anger.[68] This criticism, understandably, became a subject of debate for months to come.[69]

For the nonce, however, the squabble over military strategy gave way to a more important one involving politics. The Tuscan CLN, headed by art historian Carlo Ragghianti (Pd'A) and ensconced in Palazzo Riccardi, was strong-willed. Nevertheless, its attitude toward the Allies at first was amicable, and it provided them with a *fait accompli* of key administrators, beginning with 83-year-old Professor Gaetano Pieraccini, an ex-Socialist deputy, as Mayor of Florence. All went well enough until Premier Bonomi sent in a "reactionary" career prefect (Paternò), who

---

[66] Battaglia, *SRI*, pp. 363–364; Salvadori, *SRI*, pp. 144–145.

[67] General Mark W. Clark, *Calculated Risk* (New York, 1950), p. 381; Harris, *Allied Military Administration of Italy*, p. 187.

On the matter of liaison, it should be noted that an especially daring *coup* was executed right under the noses of the Germans on August 5, when Enrico Fischer, a local Giellista commander, slipped through the corridor in the Ponte Vecchio that connected the Uffizi Gallery with the Palazzo Pitti. He was soon followed by Ragghianti, head of the CTLN, and Nello Niccoli, in charge of the CTLN Military Command. They established telephonic communication with the Allied Command on the left bank of the Arno. Contini-Bonacossi, *Una lotta nel suo corso*, p. 242.

[68] H. L. Matthews, *NYT*, Aug. 4, 1944, 6:2; Aug. 5, 1:7; Aug. 11, 4:6; Aug. 13, 1:4; Aug. 14, 1:4; Sept. 1, 1.7, and also in his later book, *Education of a Correspondent*, pp. 472–473.

[69] See particularly the rebuttal of E. Enriques Agnoletti, "Perchè i ponti di Firenze non furono difesi?" *Il Ponte*, 1 (1945), pp. 58–63.

evidently had no use for the CLN philosophy and supported other people for urban and regional posts. The CTLN declined to back down. For a month there was much tension, and at one juncture the CTLN sent a delegation to Rome, while Togliatti and other stalwarts from the capital visited Florence. The Tuscan capital gave AMG more headaches than any other liberated city in Italy.

Eventually a compromise was announced on October 21 by the ACC Civil Affairs Section. It advised its officials that while the CLN's had no official standing in the conduct of affairs within the province and though its members must not be permitted to assume any executive function, CLN officials were to be treated courteously, and the Allied Provincial Commissioner and the Italian Prefect "may" seek their advice. What they would then do with such advice was up to them.[70] Thus the superior power of the Allies and of the Rome government was brought to bear on the fractious Tuscans; but in actual practice, as one CTLN officer has noted, "the Allies discovered that they needed the collaboration of the Liberation Committees. . . . They entered the town unprepared to collaborate with and recognize the Committees; they left it prepared to do so as a normal practice." [71] Florence thus did its best to establish a precedent for Allied recognition of CLN's farther north.

Allied policy regarding patriots

During the early summer the ACC established a Patriots Branch in Rome to draw up plans for either demobilizing or re-employing the guerrillas after liberation of territory. In due course the authorities defined "patriots" as "persons in the ranks of genuine bands who have carried arms against the enemy, engaged in sabotage or secured important military information for the benefit of the Allied war effort." [72] Heading the Patriots Branch at first was British Colonel C. D. McCarthy, and subse-

---

[70] Harris, *Allied Military Administration of Italy*, p. 187; NYT, Sept. 2, 1944, 5:1.
[71] E. Enriques Agnoletti, "Dopo dieci anni," *Il Ponte*, x (1954), p. 1312 ff.; cf. his "La politica del CTLN," *ibid.*, 1 (1945), pp. 424–429, and his "Intervento," MLI, No. 52/53 (1958), pp. 175–179; Contini-Bonacossi, *Una lotta nel suo corso*, p. 229 and *passim*; Ragghianti's essay, "Il Comitato di Liberazione Nazionale Toscano come Governo provvisorio ed i suoi atti," in *Disegno della liberazione*, pp. 235–271; Catalano, *Storia del CLNAI*, pp. 215–217; Kogan, *Italy and the Allies*, p. 94.
[72] NYT, July 22, 1944, 4:4.

quently two other British colonels, R. G. B. Spicer and F. Craig. Assisting them during 1944 were Major B. L. Drage, Major P. Magnus, and Captain Max Salvadori (the latter on "detached service" from SF). The Land Forces Sub-Commission (MMIA) also worked on the problem.

The Bonomi government established a bureaucratic counterpart, the Patriot Office, composed of Lieutenant Colonel Siro Bernabò (of the Badoglio wing of the Resistenza in central Italy), Riccardo Bauer (of the Rome CLN wing), and Colonel Guido Fava, acting as liaison officer with the ACC. Branches were soon established in Florence, Perugia, Ancona, L'Aquila, and Naples. Above this executive agency stood the advisory Italian National Patriots Commission, made up of the prime minister, Colonel Bernabò, General Oddone (secretary), and spokesmen of the six CLN parties: Palermo, Fenoaltea, Garosci, Spataro, Brosio, and DiPietro. These agencies prepared records of patriot activities, supervised distribution of pay and awards, and provided other information to Patriots Branch.[73]

Almost everyone conceded that there were real problems to solve. The number of patriots was soaring rapidly, and the false ones seemed to proliferate fastest. For example, the Allies first assumed that there were some 400 genuine guerrillas in Naples' insurrection, but a year later 4,900 certificates had been issued and they could still be bought for a price.[74] Until local governments were revamped by AMG and Rome, patriots often had to be left in charge of certain police functions; but this policy could not be allowed to continue indefinitely, if for no other reason than that some "of the sturdy elements were not without less reputable attachments,"[75] behaving improperly and looking upon themselves as above the law—in some ways not unlike the behavior of Fascist *Arditi* after World War I.

Consequently, ACC looked upon the reintegration of daredevil patriots into "normal" patterns of life as "civilian priority No. 1" in the summer.[76] It called for their speedy identification by apposite communal committees and their disarmament as

[73] Salvadori, *Resistenza ed azione*, pp. 253–256; Harris, *Allied Military Administration of Italy*, p. 226.
[74] H. L. Matthews, "Can Italy Slay the Fascist Dragon?" NYT *Magazine*, Oct. 1, 1944, p. 13 ff.
[75] Harris, *Allied Military Administration of Italy*, p. 179.
[76] *Ibid.*, p. 178 ff.

soon as their emergency role in local government terminated. (In Rome when the AMG in June quickly persuaded the CCLN to disband the local partisans and turn in their arms, all except the Communists co-operated; it took a police raid on party headquarters to bring them into line. The arms turned in by partisans near Florence on September 7 seemed sparse to Allied observers.) [77] The veterans were to receive Allied certificates of recognition and be helped either to join the regular Army or to find employment. To obviate the bitterness that would result if brusque orders to disarm were issued, it was planned to emphasize that the surrendered weapons would be shipped to other patriots farther north. What was of chief concern to Allied planners, however, was getting the arms out of the hands of "unruly" elements who might wish to use them for political ends.[78]

"Separation centers" thus became imperative. There the veterans could be brought together for as long as a month, fed Italian Army rations, and receive essential clothing and hospitalization. And, of course, their arms could be collected. During the late summer and autumn such camps were established in Florence, Pescia, Ravenna, and Forlì. Soon the Allies sensed that it was impolitic for their own men to disarm the *partigiani*, and to use the *Carabinieri* would be even worse. Instead, they arranged for Italian Military Patriot Representatives (IMPR) from the Italian Army to work in each zone and act as buffers between AMG and partisan officers. Even so, the underground survivors tended to be "thin-skinned" and resented the "bureaucratic mentality" and "lack of moral recognition" they sensed in the camps (notably those in Tuscany).[79] The whole experience was reminiscent of the highhanded way Cavour treated Giuseppe Garibaldi's guerrillas after their conquest of Sicily and Naples in 1860.[80]

Authentic patriots could be encouraged to enlist individually in the regular Army or be recruited for behind-the-lines service

[77] *Ibid.*, pp. 164, 182-184, 197-199.
[78] NYT, July 22, 1944, 4:4. On July 30 Togliatti published in *L'Unità* an article denouncing "reactionary" officials who were seeking to minimize the role of the partisans and make life difficult for them.
[79] Harris, *Allied Military Administration of Italy*, pp. 180-184, 197-200.
[80] Regarding 1860, see Denis Mack Smith, *Italy: A Modern History*, p. 54.

with Lieutenant Colonel Wladimir Peniakoff's SF group ("Popski's Army"),[81] but care was to be taken to avoid unnecessary proliferation of Communist cells in the Army. Thus it was thought that most veterans should be encouraged to return to "normal" employment. "For the colonel [McCarthy] the problem is terribly complex," Captain Salvadori noted with some asperity on September 5. "He feels it is necessary at every moment to arrange a meeting with the head of the Allied Commission, with the generals of Fifth and Eighth Armies, with members of the Government, the Minister of War, etc." [82]

Headquarters of the 15th Army Group, however, gave much discretion to the generals of each division in handling the patriots. By summer's end they took advantage of this to muster several of the best bands into their armies. Thus the "Maiella," which had chalked up a brilliant record along the Adriatic, was assigned to the Eighth Army,[83] and the bands of the lower Arno were integrated into the Fifth Army.[84] Yet most guerrillas who wished to continue fighting had to sign up individually in the new CIL, expanding rapidly at last and being fitted with modern technical resources. A minority did so enlist.[85] A big step forward occurred in February 1945 when five patriot "reconnaissance companies" were admitted intact into CIL. By the end of March, 3,000 had thus enlisted.[86]

General Cadorna and the CG/CVL

When the CG/CVL came into existence on June 9 all the CLNAI parties agreed upon the desirability of having Premier Bonomi dispatch a professional officer to act as "military counselor" to the CG/CVL (and, not least, serve as a kind of buffer between Longo and Parri). In due course they requested General Raffaele Cadorna, who, apart from merits already men-

[81] Wladimir Peniakoff ("Popski"), *Private Army* (London, 1950), pp. 449–460.
[82] Salvadori, *Resistenza ed azione*, pp. 254–256.
[83] Ettore Troilo, "I partigiani della Maiella," *MLI*, No. 38/39 (1955), pp. 71–89.
[84] Salvadori, *Resistenza ed azione*, pp. 254–256. According to Harris, in December 1944, the Eighth Army was empowered to employ in the field up to 1,200 patriots; the Fifth Army, up to 200. *Allied Military Administration of Italy*, p. 197.
[85] Starr, *From Salerno to the Alps*, p. 276.
[86] Harris, *Allied Military Administration of Italy*, pp. 198–199.

tioned, knew personally several Resistance spokesmen and felt quite at home in the North.

Since the CLNAI indicated that it had "full faith" in Cadorna, his appointment as Military Adviser won the speedy approval of the Allies and the Italian Ministry of War, both of whom had long been urging such a move.[87] After an accelerated course in parachute jumping at the SF base in Monopoli, Cadorna (who henceforth went by the *nom de guerre* "Valenti") was transported in mid-August by an SF plane to Val Cavallina near Bergamo. Despite his age, he made the jump safely and quickly reached Milan.[88] He was accompanied by a British SF officer, Major Oliver Churchill ("Peters"), no relative of the prime minister.

When they arrived, the precarious unity among the parties was dissolving. A long series of misunderstandings and recriminations ensued before General Cadorna and the CLNAI agreed upon what were his duties and prerogatives. Accustomed to traditional military tactics, the general argued that he could not serve very helpfully as a "technical consultant" in irregular guerrilla warfare; what he hoped to do was transform the Resistenza Armata into an efficient fighting force that would be loyal to the government in Rome and have no political overtones of its own. It was his understanding that the Allied Supreme Headquarters wished him to take over direction of the northern military forces, and he had reason to believe they might suspend financial subsidization if political rivalries hampered the Resistance's military efficacy.[89]

Soon it became evident that Cadorna enjoyed the full faith of only the PLI, DC, and the Autonomi commanders. The three leftist parties regarded him with misgivings, especially because

[87] Somewhat earlier in July, however, the Allies and Bonomi, fearing a Communist plot to gain tight control of the northern Resistance, rejected a move by Communist Undersecretary of War Palermo to gain recognition of the northern partisans as members of the Italian Army. Palermo had also suggested sending an Italian general from liberated Italy to direct their operations, and desired that the Italian government be consulted before the dropping of arms. Harris, *Allied Military Administration of Italy*, p. 226.

[88] Cadorna, *La Riscossa*, pp. 113-115.

[89] *Ibid.*, pp. 130-138; *cf.* his letter of April 23, 1954 (in rebuttal to a statement by Longo) in *MLI*, No. 28/29 (1954), pp. 122-124; Sogno, *Guerra senza bandiera*, p. 223 ff.; Valiani, *Tutte le strade conducono a Roma*, pp. 256-257; Catalano, *Storia del CLNAI*, pp. 219-225; Raffaele Cadorna, "Organizzazione della lotta partigiana," *Civitas*, vi (1955), pp. 30-34; and Aurelio Fernando, "I Volontari della Libertà," *ibid.*, pp. 35-40.

of the openly anti-CLNAI attitude of his British companion, Major Churchill.[90] They feared that if Cadorna became military commander of all the septentrional forces, royalist officers would infiltrate CVL headquarters and compromise the political autonomy of the entire underground. Thus the PCI and PSIUP (as well as the Pd'A to a slightly lesser degree) resisted Cadorna's ambitions.[91]

Cadorna sensed the dearth of enthusiasm and discretely decided for the present to "maintain the functions of military consultant for which [he] had been freely chosen, and . . . profit by [his] nonpolitical attitude with the [CG/CVL] to exert an equilibrating and mediating force." [92] Nevertheless, a variety of developments prevented him from being an effective peacemaker. Indeed, the controversy grew ever more acrimonious.

Liberation of northern "republics"

During the early summer of 1944 Piedmontese patriots achieved their greatest successes of the underground struggle. On July 27 the headquarters of General Alexander radioed the CPLN in Turin that the Piedmontese underground could expect an Allied signal very soon, at which time it should launch "violent and sustained" operations against the enemy which would greatly assist Allied military operations (the nature of which Alexander, of course, could not reveal). He promised to dispatch more supplies and a liaison officer to co-ordinate plans. General Trabucchi erroneously inferred from all of this that the Allies intended to drive into the Po valley (really they were headed for the French Riviera) and ordered his forces to move down from the mountainous zones.[93]

Already the patriots had gained control of most of the Alpine passes along the French frontier and established autonomous "republics" in several defiles, ranging from Aosta (freed May 2)

[90] According to a fellow SF officer, the major was "just as courageous as he was limited in mentality." Salvadori, *Resistenza ed azione*, p. 257. Upon CLNAI insistence, the British later recalled Churchill.

[91] Valiani, *Tutte le strade conducono a Roma*, pp. 256–257; Catalano, *Storia del CLNAI*, pp. 226–227.

[92] Valiani, *Tutte le strade conducono a Roma*, pp. 256–257.

[93] Trabucchi, *I vinti hanno sempre torto*, pp. 103–104, 249. Regarding summer partisan operations in Piedmont, see especially Mario Giovana, "Le operazioni partigiane dell'estate-autunno 1944 in Piemonte," *MLI*, No. 44/45 (1956), pp. 3–19.

and Valsesia (June 11) in the north to the Cuneese in the south-west.[94] In Valsesia (north of Vercelli) fluid guerrilla warfare was the watchword of Moscatelli's Garibaldi, whose headquarters was constantly on the move. In Val Chisone (above Pinerolo), on the other hand, the resistants continued to fight along more or less rigid defense lines and employed artillery. In much of Piedmont there was a tendency to transfer commands farther down the valleys. The Langhe, near Mondovì, was liberated chiefly by Autonomi who made skillful use of offensive maneuvers and reserves of regular troops.[95]

In the latter zone a significant political accord was negotiated on August 7 between the Cuneo Giellisti led by Avv. Dante Livio Bianco and the royalist Autonomi of Enrico Martini ("Mauri"). It marked a victory by the republican wing of the Resistenza. The Autonomi conceded that the "partisan forces do not represent the survival and continuation of the old Italian military organism but are the expression of an autonomous movement, of free popular initiative." Much to Bianco's distress, however, the Autonomi later renounced this "great opportunity." [96]

All told, some fifteen northern "oases of freedom" were staked out during the summer for periods ranging from a few days to a few weeks.[97] They included the Venetian Cansiglio plateau and parts of the Friuli; the Piedmontese valleys of the Sesia, Varaita, Maira, Stura, Gesso, Lanzo, Langhe, and Astigiano; the southern Lombard hills of the Oltrepò Pavese; the much publicized Ligurian "Republic of Torriglia" between Genoa and Piacenza;[98] the Ligurian hinterland between Savona and San Remo; and several extremely barren Apennine valleys in western Emilia between Parma-Piacenza and LaSpezia. In view of the denuded terrain, these latter cul-de-sacs afforded scant concealment to the guerrillas and were consequently unsuitable for fighting a mechanized foe.[99] The Germans warned their troops of the existence of the

[94] Bianco, *Guerra partigiana*, pp. 80–91, 98–101.
[95] Battaglia, *SRI*, pp. 343–348; cf. Enrico Martini, *Con la libertà e per la libertà* (Turin, 1947); and Angela Trabucco, *Partigiani di Val Chisone, 1943–1945*, with preface by Ferruccio Parri (Torre Pellice, 1959).
[96] Quoted in Bianco, *Guerra partigiana*, pp. 102–104.
[97] Longo, *Un popolo alla macchia*, pp. 271–299; Battaglia, *SRI*, pp. 395–396.
[98] See especially G. B. Canepa ("Marzo"), *La Repubblica di Torriglia*, ed. A.N.P.I. of Genoa (Genoa, 1956).
[99] Salvadori, *SRI*, pp. 153–154.

partisan strongholds by erecting signs, *"Banden Gebiete,"* along the roads in the vicinity.

When partisan brigades liberated valleys their general instructions called for as rapid enlargement of them as possible. Occupation of towns was not a primary goal, unless these could serve as bases from which to attack the enemy more effectively. On the basis of the Yugoslav Partisans' experience, the CVL recommended that there be parallel forces wherever feasible—one mobile and available for attack; the other an administrative presidio unit. Seldom were there enough forces to permit such luxury, however. Nor did the Italian terrain, covered at best with scrub *macchia,* lend itself to such a system as well as Yugoslavia's heavily timbered mountains. Imbued with the mistaken notion that general liberation was imminent in the late summer, Italian patriots often blundered in defending their republics *à outrance.*[100]

Wherever these partisan republics emerged, the local inhabitants gained their first experience in partial self-government in more than two decades. Urgent socio-economic and administrative problems had to be faced, complicated at times by bitter rivalries between Communists and non-Communists.[101]

Near-by CLN's, or perhaps the liberating band, laid the basis for local "popular administrative juntas" (*"giunte popolari amministrative"*) to supersede the military rule. The Pd'A was more sincerely democratic in these gestures than the PCI, which always insisted that nothing important could take place except by PCI initiative. The Garibaldi brigades naturally found it expedient to dissociate this missionary work from that of their own political commissars. They would turn it over to "civil delegates" with no military duties. These officers, aided perhaps by the village elders and priest, would prepare for elections. The administrative junta was designed to represent social classes as they actually existed in the locale. Thus, in selecting candidates, the majority of seats "was assured to the poorest classes who were in the majority in the countryside," a Communist historian has explained. Because of the primitive and precarious conditions,

---

[100] Battaglia, *SRI,* pp. 391–395.
[101] Fredino and Giulio, "Nascono i Comitati della Resistenza," *Nuovi Quaderni di Giustizia e Libertà,* No. 5/6, pp. 199–202.

use of printed ballots generally was out of the question; voting by show of hands was the rule. For one with a "purely formal" conception of democracy, all this "may be difficult to digest," this same historian has conceded.[102] In these "popular progressive democracies" the junta usually named the mayor ("*sindaco*").[103]

The administrative agencies handled distribution of food, fixed prices, and issued commercial licenses. Since the economy of most of the liberated zones was primarily agricultural and was greatly disrupted by the war, it was imperative to give the peasants incentives to produce and turn in grain, which would thereby reduce the "black market." Usually this was achieved by paying more for the grain—part of the supplementary price to the peasant being in the form of bonds. No price increase was passed on to the consumer. Taxes, which the patriots hitherto had exhorted the people to stop paying to the Nazi-Fascists, now had to be collected by the new popular juntas. The old imposts were usually reinstated, with the exception of such obnoxious ones as those on bachelors. Only in Carnia, far to the northeast, was there any attempt to overhaul the whole system. There a progressive inheritance tax was announced. No tax was levied on a valuation of less than 200,000 lire; 2 per cent from 200,000 to 300,000 lire; a maximum of 8 per cent up to 1,000,000. Property of Fascist sympathizers was sometimes expropriated.[104] In a few places currency ("*buoni di liberazione*") was issued, most notably by the GL units in the Piedmontese Canavese late in 1944.[105]

Sometimes the CLN's and juntas requisitioned supplies needed by the patriots, arranged train schedules, ordered road blocks and antiaircraft defenses. They also organized courts, revived labor unions, established hospitals, took charge of schools, and printed newspapers.

[102] Battaglia, *SRI*, p. 397.
[103] Longo, *Un popolo alla macchia*, pp. 279–287. For a documentary study of the subject see Italy, Presidenza del Consiglio, Ufficio Storico per la Guerra di Liberazione, Documenti No. 8, *Costituzione ed attività degli organi del potere democratico nelle zone liberate* (Rome, 1946), pp. 71–72, and *passim*. Cf. Carli-Ballola, *Sdr*, pp. 182–188.
[104] Longo, *Un popolo alla macchia*, pp. 287–296; Battaglia, *SRI*, pp. 399–401; Emilio Sereni, "La politica economica dei CLN nelle zone liberate dai partigiani," *Rinascita*, xii (April 1955), pp. 260–267. This issue was dedicated to the tenth anniversary of the Liberation.
[105] Mario Bendiscioli, "A proposito di emissioni monetarie della Resistenza," *MLI*, No. 48 (1957), pp. 73–76.

Bloody battles

The biggest open-field battles of the Italian Resistenza took place at Montefiorino above Modena on the upper Secchia River from July 31 until August 3. The Germans had perceived the importance of the area faster than the Allies and were determined to regain it. The partisans, hitherto inadequately armed for such open warfare, belatedly obtained reinforcements from the Fifth Army, which dropped a battalion of Italian parachutists. But the objective proved too much for the partisans. The Germans, resolved not to lose this critical nerve center in the Apennines, tightened a circle around the patriot units and brought in no fewer than three divisions with artillery, mortars, armored units, and flame throwers. Casualties were heavy on both sides: the partisans counted 250 dead and 70 wounded; they claimed that the enemy suffered some 1,400 casualties. Most of the patriots sought to escape over the rugged mountains into Tuscany, where they could join the Allies.[106]

In the flatlands of Emilia-Romagna and Lombardy [107] appeared a new patriot fighting force during the summer: the Sappisti (*"Squadre d'Azione Patriottica"*; sometimes also known as *"Squadre Protezioni Aziendi"*). Sponsored by the Communists, these were, at first, chiefly rural groups who roamed furtively up and down the Po valley, fighting the so-called "battle of grain" —i.e., seeking to hide the harvest from the enemy, or, failing that, to destroy it. Later the Sappisti moved into the cities as a kind of rival and supplementary force to the Gappisti. Their activities henceforth were not dissimilar, though the Sappisti perhaps concentrated more on safeguarding factory installations from sabotage than in attacking the enemy. In sum, the Sappisti were another useful "capillary organ" of the underground.[108]

Audacious prison raids provided excitement for numerous Venetian patriots in the summer. In Verona, for example, on the evening of July 17 a group rescued a key PCI labor organizer, Giovanni Roveda, from the Scalzi prison, while in near-by Belluno other patriots successfully effected the liberation of seventy-three prisoners.[109]

[106] Carli-Ballola, *Sdr*, pp. 188–189; Battaglia, *SRI*, pp. 355–357.
[107] A somewhat-analogous development occurred in Piedmont too.
[108] Longo, *Un popolo alla macchia*, pp. 233–236; F. Ferro, *I nostri sappisti nella liberazione di Torino* (Turin, n.d.), p. 26 ff.; Battaglia, *SRI*, pp. 350–351.
[109] Giuseppe Silvestri, *Albergo agli Scalzi* (Milan, 1946), pp. 193–194; Berto

419

Everywhere in the Veneto the *partigianeria* gained momentum during the summer. Venetian peasants were anti-German (or, more precisely, anti-Austrian) by tradition; their tempers were further inflamed by recent draft calls of hitherto-exempt classes and the mounting reprisals against not only guerrilla captives but hundreds of Jews (the city of Venice was a focal point of Italian Jewry) and others innocent of any act of sabotage.[110] In the Friuli, Communist guerrillas regrouped into two vigorous divisions, the "Natisone" and "Nino Nanetti," the latter consisting of some nine brigades and five thousand men.[111] Non-Communists flocked to the Osoppo Friuli brigades. Deciding that he could not tolerate a patriot build-up so close to the Austrian frontier, the enemy unleashed in August one attack after another on the Carnia-Cadore sector. Soon he secured that border zone and, turning upon the near-by "Nino Nanetti," inflicted heavy losses.[112]

When the northern patriots got word of the August liberation of Florence and of successful Allied landings in southern France, they felt sure their own deliverance was at hand. Many expected parallel Allied debarkations on the Italian Riviera. Anticipating such a move, Piedmontese fighters tightened their grip on the highlands above Genoa and on Tenda Pass (connecting Cuneo with Nice). The enemy lost no time in ordering a counteroffensive to preclude any Allied invasion from France that could outflank his Gothic Line. As a result he ordered vicious *rastrellamenti* against the Piedmontese partisans in mid-August. So massive did his mechanized attacks become that the partisans were driven out of Val Chisone, Maddalena, Tenda, and other narrow defiles—but not until it was too late for the Germans to prevent the Allies from securing their beachheads in southern France.[113]

Perotti, "L'assalto agli Scalzi del luglio '44 alla luce di nuove rievocazioni e testimonianze," *MLI*, No. 47 (1957), pp. 61–66; Attilio Dabini, *Dos muertos en un automóvil* (Buenos Aires, 1956).

[110] For some of the high lights of the Resistance in the Veneto in this period see Gavagnin, *Vent'anni di resistenza*, pp. 452–511.

[111] Battaglia, *SRI*, pp. 358–362.

[112] *Ibid.*, pp. 368–376.

[113] *Ibid.*, pp. 343–348; Bianco, *Guerra partigiana*, pp. 102–110; Paolo Gobetti, "Le formazioni partigiani della Val Susa," and Carlo Mussa and Giorgio Rolli, "I partigiani della Val Pellice," in *Nuovi Quaderni di Giustizia e Libertà*, No. 5/6, pp. 177–178, 144–146; Ada Gobetti, *Diario partigiano*, pp. 259–364; Giovanni Monaco, *Pietà l'è morta*, pp. 113–133 ff.

One of the GL brigades of the Cuneese—the Rosselli of Valle Stura di Demonte—was forced to fall back in perfect order into France. There, in Valle Tinée and Valle Vésubie, it underwent a host of novel experiences. At first the American Seventh Army supplied it as generously as its own units. But when the French took over the region, they sought either to disband the Rosselli or to enroll it in their armed forces. It was unfortunate for the Italian Resistance that nationalistic DeGaullists gained power in Paris after its liberation. They ignored the amicable pacts signed in May between the French and Italian resistants on the frontier. French troops (and certain Italians as well) began to voice the desire that France annex Aosta and other border zones, partly for linguistic and historic reasons and partly as punishment for Mussolini's knifing in 1940. Because of this, the Italian partisans who sought haven in France felt less and less at home there. Finally, in the face of considerable Anglo-American pressure, the Rosselli brigade was allowed to sojourn intact on foreign soil until the spring of 1945, when more auspicious conditions permitted it to return in time to share in the final deliverance of Piedmont.[114]

In the vicious *rastrellamenti* of the late summer, the enemy employed Italian troops who had finished their training in Germany as well as Pavolini's Black Brigades and other neo-Fascist forces. Unable to spare their own crack troops, the Germans also assigned Ukrainian and Mongol defectors to the sordid struggle against the "rebel bandits." These vassals enjoyed the right of plunder. Terrorism, reprisals, and massacres became the order of the day, exacerbating the hatreds already displayed by both sides. The enemy, for example, shot forty-three partisans in cold blood after a June "raking" in the Verbano mountains, while on the night of July 12–13 he massacred sixty-two prisoners at Fossoli. When the Germans in Italy learned of their own generals' abortive plot to assassinate Hitler on July 20, their sternness increased. On August 14 the German Command ordered fifteen partisan hostages shot in Milan's Piazzale Loreto in reprisal for the death of two Germans. (Nine months later the cadavers of Mussolini,

---

[114] Bianco, *Guerra partigiana*, pp. 111–114; Giorgio Bocca, *Partigiani della montagna: vita delle divisioni "Giustizia e Libertà" del Cuneese* (Borgo S. Dalmazzo, 1945), pp. 61–64, 80–81; Catalano, *Storia del CLNAI*, pp. 259–261; Ricci (ed.), *Il contributo della valle d'Aosta alla guerra di liberazione, passim*; and *Aspetti della resistenza in Piemonte*, p. 132.

his mistress, and several henchmen filled the same square.) Some kind of a record was set on August 12 when SS troops surrounded the village of Sant'Anna di Stazzema above Lucca in the Alpi Apuane and machinegunned (so it is asserted) 560 inhabitants, including the aged and children. Religious leaders issued protest after protest, and public indignation mounted steadily; yet the butchery of partisans, hostages, and civilians simply increased.[115]

On rare occasions the patriots arranged brief truces with the enemy. The Rutto and DiDio formations in Val d'Ossola did this with the Germans on August 10. This was repudiated by the CG/CVL, however, when it learned of it later that month. In general, the patriots steadfastly shunned such deals.[116]

The rising incidence of bloody requitals brought about a new patriot policy involving military prisoners. Till the spring of 1944 partisans had often handed back their prisoners to prevent the Germans from carrying out threats to kill civilian hostages. They discovered, however, that the Nazis then began to seize hostages in advance, threatening to shoot them if the guerrillas attacked. Sensing that this sort of thing could undermine the Resistenza, Piedmontese chieftains intervened, declaring that restitution of German prisoners could be permitted only in exchange for captured partisans and never in order to free civilians held by the foe. If the enemy shot civilian pawns, the partisans would counter by shooting German prisoners; and if he extended his reprisal list, the partisans would execute enemy prisoners held in other zones. This was indeed a Hammurabic policy; but at least in some places it produced salutary results.[117]

Tension between partisans and Allies

The amount of arms and equipment dropped to patriots from July through September was less than that parachuted during May and June.[118] Many partisans inferred from this that the Allies (particularly the British) were deliberately withholding

[115] S/M, Sdf, p. 1012; Valiani, Tutte le strade conducono a Roma, pp. 264–266; Catalano, Storia del CLNAI, p. 234; Longo, Un popolo alla macchia, pp. 343–344; Battaglia, SRI, p. 450.

[116] Ibid., p. 388; Cadorna, La Riscossa, pp. 152–153; Atti CG/CVL, No. 48 (Aug. 30), pp. 89–90.

[117] Trabucchi, I vinti hanno sempre torto, p. 105.

[118] Army Air Forces in World War II, III, 515; Craveri, "Un servizio segreto," Mercurio (Anche l'Italia ha vinto), II, No. 16 (1945), pp. 104–111; cf. McCaffery report of Aug. 14, 1944, in Cadorna, La Riscossa, pp. 150 ff. and 175 ff.

supplies for fear of augmenting Communist and antiroyalist forces. Though this consideration was not entirely absent, the underground overlooked several less Machiavellian factors.

Foremost was the Allied decision of June 14 (in the face of Churchill's persistent objections) to push in Italy for the moment only as far as the Pisa-Rimini line (assumed, mistakenly, to be quickly attainable), and to launch the "Anvil-Dragoon" invasion of the French Riviera by August 15 in order to strengthen Eisenhower's right flank and provide his forces with the major supply port of Marseille. France and northwestern Europe, regarded by the Americans as the fastest way to Berlin, thus took precedence over Churchill's strategy of a drive through Trieste and the Ljubljana Gap into Vienna ahead of the Russians and their Red Army-borne ideology.[119] For the Riviera operation more than seven Allied divisions and supporting units had to be bled out of Italy. Perforce, Italy henceforth was a second- or third-rate theater of operations. Its role was limited to pinning down as many Germans as possible. Even so, the Germans found it possible to shift four divisions from Italy to France.[120]

While Allied ships, planes, and manpower were tied up with the "Anvil-Dragoon" operation, aerial supply of the Italian partisans "was of necessity neglected." Only in early September did the 88th Bombardment Squadron of the U.S. Army Air Force become available for new assignments to support the underground. From Algiers it flew its first mission to northern Italy on the night of September 9–10, and in less than two weeks made thirty-six sorties and dropped fifty-nine tons "in the Po valley." The squadron then transferred its base to Brindisi. During the last week of September it completed nine more sorties to the same Italian locales as well as some daylight missions to the Balkans.[121]

---

[119] Samuel Eliot Morison, *Strategy and Compromise* (Boston, 1958), pp. 54–60. American strategists contended that the tortuous Ljubljana Gap with its innumerable railway tunnels would be a tactical cul-de-sac and, in any event, would not enable the Western Allies to beat the Russians to Vienna; moreover, they would be hard put to explain to Generals Patch and de Lattre de Tassigny why American and French soldiers were being sent on a "Balkan safari" rather than on the invasion of Provence and the direct support of "Ike."

[120] Churchill, *Triumph and Tragedy*, p. 96.

[121] *Army Air Forces in World War II*, III, 515; Ehrman, *Grand Strategy*, v, 370–376; Salvadori, SRI, pp. 126–128.

Not long before the Allied invasion of the Riviera, Parri displayed unmistakable annoyance at the slow-down in Allied deliveries to the rapidly expanding northern patriot movement. He even considered forwarding a sharp protest to Anglo-American leaders, charging them with bad faith. Mr. McCaffery of the British SF in Switzerland got wind of Parri's disgruntlement and addressed a friendly but candid letter to him on August 16. The document shed light on Allied thinking:

". . . Because of our extremely difficult but successful operations, you have been able to have a *coup d'état*. That it did not go well is due in considerable measure to the lack of preparation and to the lack of reciprocal trust among the favorable elements [in the South]. The writer knows something about it.

"Now you have had the opportunity of finding yourselves again and ending up alongside those countries to which Italy caused such grave damage. No one is happier than we over this possibility; no one readier to help you. But, for heaven's sake, don't you pretend now to direct military operations instead of Eisenhower or Alexander.

"A long time ago I said that the greatest military contribution that you could bring to the Allied cause was continuous sabotage, spread out on a vast scale. You wanted bands. I supported your desire for them, because I recognized the moral value of them for Italy. The bands have worked well. We know it. But you wanted to organize armies. Who asked you to do that? Not we. You did it for political motives, and precisely in order to reintegrate Italy. No one will blame you for this idea. But don't blame our generals if they work, at least essentially, upon the basis of military considerations. And especially don't try to accuse us of political intrigue because these military considerations don't fully conform with your own political ones.

"I don't wish to say more. One last word of advice. You have friends. Don't try to lose them." [122]

Apart from the priorities held by the French Forces of the Interior and Tito's Partisans, there was still another consideration that greatly reduced the Allies' ability to deliver supplies to northern Italy at this stage. General Bor-Komorowski's non-Communist Polish Home Army had risen up against the Germans in Warsaw on August 1 in a heroic if tragic struggle that

[122] Re-translated from the Italian version in Archivio CLNAI, Milan, vIII/57.

continued in the sewers and rubble till October 2, while Russian forces a few miles across the Vistula River offered almost no aid until after September 14. SF men in Italy, meantime, were ordered to do everything possible to fly in supplies to the beleaguered Polish patriots. Many heavy bombers and Allied personnel, operating from bases near Foggia 1,400 miles away, were lost in this arduous and futile relief mission, which reached its culmination in a mass flight on September 18 of 104 bombers over Warsaw.[123]

Despite the American victory over the British in siphoning off Allied divisions from Italy, the indomitable Churchill refused to discard his scheme for an autumn offensive that could drive the Germans from the lower Po by Christmas and enable the Allies to push into Istria and Trieste (perhaps with amphibious landings) and on through the Ljubljana Gap to Vienna.[124] He argued that this was not an absurdity in view of the war of movement that had prevailed since the breakthrough at Cassino. Eighth Army men had almost clawed their way out of the mountains south of Rimini, he noted. Moreover he was anxious to checkmate Stalin's likely dominance of east-central Europe.

Meanwhile, in the west, Paris was delivered on August 25–26, and by early September Allied forces had pushed into Belgium, Luxemburg, and Metz. In Italy General Alexander decided to hurl a heavy offensive across the Metauro River in the east on August 26. All told, 23 Allied divisions could be pitted against 27 German and elements of 6 Italian ones, though only 18 enemy divisions were immediately available to defend the Gothic Line.[125] The chief objective was Rimini, gateway to the northern plain. In the center after September 10, the Fifth Army would try to push over the mountains toward Bologna and other towns lying between it and Rimini. With high hopes, Churchill personally watched the kickoff on the Adriatic front.[126]

[123] Ehrman, *Grand Strategy*, v, 370–376; Salvadori, *SRI*, pp. 126–128; Churchill, *Triumph and Tragedy*, pp. 128–145; Craveri, *Mercurio* (*Anche l'Italia ha vinto*), II, No. 16 (1945), pp. 104–111.

[124] Churchill, *Triumph and Tragedy*, pp. 100–101, 120, 122, 158–159; Ehrman, *Grand Strategy*, v, 345–367.

[125] Churchill, *Triumph and Tragedy*, p. 104; Starr, *From Salerno to the Alps*, pp. 299–300. Mussolini, incidentally, visited the Gothic Line in August. Monelli, *Mussolini*, p. 245.

[126] Churchill, *Triumph and Tragedy*, pp. 118–122; Starr, *From Salerno to the Alps*, pp. 301–364.

Despite Kesselring's brilliant defense, some headway was made.[127] In the west, the Tuscan cities of Pisa, Lucca, and Pistoia were emancipated, partly with the aid of Garibaldi and Rosselli underground formations.[128] The Gothic Line was pushed back beyond Forte dei Marmi, short of Massa. In the rugged center, the Fifth Army slugged its way by September 18 somewhat beyond the watershed on the road from Florence to Faenza, and ten days later on the parallel road to Bologna. Along the Adriatic, the Eighth Army finally reached Rimini on September 20 and was in a position to drive on to the Marecchia River. As the northern flatlands stretched out before them, Allied spirits soared.

Imminent liberation?

The clandestine fighters were also exhilarated by dreams of imminent liberation, even though General Clark and other Allied strategists had largely ignored any specific military role for them.[129] The partisans believed the moment of insurrection in the Romagna was at hand.

Anticipating such a development for weeks, the CLNAI had been meeting almost daily, girding itself for the assumption of interim political power.[130] As early as August 9 and 10 it issued decrees forbidding any accords with either the foe or northern industrialists that might preclude a vigorous insurrection.[131] On the 16th it outlined plans for courts of assize, purge commissions, and organs of civil administration. During the next two months it clarified these blueprints and designated various people to take charge.[132]

On August 30 it took an important step to broaden the scope of the CLN's. Since factory workers alone were not enough to

[127] Kesselring, *Memoirs*, pp. 212-213.
[128] Salvadori, *SRI*, p. 145; cf. [Manrico Ducceschi], "Relazioni sull'attività militare svolta dalle formazioni patriottiche operanti alle dipendenze del Comando XI Zona dell'Esercito di Liberazione Nazionale," *MLI*, No. 44/45 (1956), pp. 39-94, and No. 46 (1957), pp. 29-68.
[129] Battaglia, "La Resistenza e gli Alleati," *MLI*, No. 52/53 (1958), pp. 167-168.
[130] Leo Valiani, "Ricordi personali," *Il Ponte*, XI (1955), pp. 470-483.
[131] Catalano, *Storia del CLNAI*, p. 238.
[132] *Ibid.*, pp. 237, 297-299; Battaglia, *SRI*, pp. 388-389. In Rome about this time it was announced that Colonel Poletti would become Regional AC Commissioner in Milan as soon as the industrial heart of Italy was liberated. *NYT*, Sept. 7, 1944, 6:6.

carry out a successful insurrection, shopkeepers, professional men, and farmers must also be organized and brought into the movement. Prodded by the Communists, the CLNAI agreed to promote professional, municipal, and rural CLN's as well as Youth Fronts (*"Fronti della Gioventù"*) and Groups for Defense of Women (*"Gruppi di Difesa della Donna"*).[133] The Pd'A acquiesced in this program, but the rightist parties and even the PSIUP feared that the PCI would simply proselyte groups ordinarily unsusceptible to Red propaganda. The hesitance of the right-wing Socialists was overcome by the arguments of Rodolfo Morandi, who had just returned to Milan for convalescence after seven years of imprisonment.[134] Though there was some basis for all these fears, the risk eventually was taken, and on October 16 the CLNAI invited the regional and provincial CLN's to incorporate the youth and women's groups. It appropriated 100,000 lire for their organization and propaganda.[135]

Meanwhile, the CLNAI kept up a drumbeat of denunciation of Mussolini's regime. On September 11 it exhorted citizens to refuse to pay taxes, decreed special war loans, and prepared CLNAI currency.[136] On the 14th it decided that instead of denouncing the Salò decrees one by one, it would declare "all the legislative norms issued by the Fascist Republican Government, as well as all the sentences, decrees, and ordinances . . . null and void." [137]

One of the weightiest decisions in the fall concerned establishment of central and regional Economic Commissions to study the problems of purging industrialists and financiers and restoring normal production and distribution after the war. Much of the initial discussion was abstract and premature; moveover, meetings in which all five parties were present were difficult to schedule because of the underground life and reluctance of some rightists. Thus the talks went on from mid-September till early February 1945. Much discord arose over the question whether such peripheral bodies as the Chambers of Labor should

[133] CLNAI, *Documenti ufficiali del CLNAI* (Milan, 1945), pp. 44–47; Archivio CLNAI, Milano, IV/9, cited in Catalano, *Storia del CLNAI*, pp. 240–244.
[134] Valiani, *Tutte le strade conducono a Roma*, pp. 279–283.
[135] Catalano, *Storia del CLNAI*, p. 296.
[136] CLNAI, *Documenti ufficiali del CLNAI*, pp. 11–15.
[137] Battaglia, *SRI*, p. 387.

be included in these Economic Commissions. While the PCI, PSIUP, and Pd'A backed this move, the other two parties objected on grounds that the leftists would gain an unfair majority. The DC and PLI preferred to confine the Economic Commissions to strictly technical tasks. Eventually, on February 5, 1945, they worked out a compromise: the leftists could bring in a Chamber of Labor representative and the DC a representative of the peasants at the time of liberation, with the CLNAI reserving the right to establish their prerogatives. Provincial commissions would be delayed till the Liberation, but the central and regional commissions would start work at once. The Central Economic Commission was located in Milan: Dr. Cesare Merzagora (PLI), a banker and industrialist, presided; other members included the industrialist Ivan Matteo Lombardo (PSIUP); the banker Domenico Boffito (Pd'A); and half a dozen technicians. By early February it was submitting to the Rome Ministry of Finance valuable data regarding economic conditions.[138]

In September the CLNAI took up the problem of an early insurrection, especially in Milan. It thought that it could profit from the recent experiences of Florence, Paris, and Warsaw. In both the CLNAI and CVL there was much hesitancy among rightists about the advisability of an early insurrection. Even many left-wingers (especially Parri) sensed the difficulties involved. The Pd'A titan noted that, because of disastrous *rastrellamenti*, Milanese patriots would have to rely chiefly on their own manpower. Supplies there were totally inadequate, he continued. Longo observed that the prime source of weakness in Milan was the lack of combat experience among the factory squads who would have to be the nerve center of any uprising; he proposed that the citizenry might gain at least some experience through small daily acts of sabotage. This they agreed to.[139]

Meanwhile, in the Romagna deeds not words characterized the underground's work. When the Allies fired their way into

[138] Ferruccio Parri, "Politica economica del CLNAI," *MLI*, No. 48 (1957), pp. 42-51; Catalano, *Storia del CLNAI*, pp. 373-378; Valiani, *Tutte le strade conducono a Roma*, p. 284; Cesare Merzagora, *I pavidi (dalla cospirazione alla Costituente)* (Milan, 1946), p. viii, and *passim*; Domenico Boffito, *Scritti raccolti e pubblicati a cura degli amici per il decimo anniversario della sua morte*, with preface by F. Parri (Milan, 1956); and "Documenti della Commissione Economica del CLNAI," *MLI*, No. 49 (1957), pp. 56-59.
[139] Catalano, *Storia del CLNAI*, p. 247.

Rimini on September 20, the CLNAI issued a call for insurrection throughout Romagna and preparations for the same elsewhere. Gappisti and partisans from Bologna to Ravenna rose in fierce combat, while a series of GAP raids on jails freed several prisoners in Bologna. Though the uprising failed to achieve general deliverance in the face of stubborn German defense and torrential rains, hundreds of enemy troops were knocked out of combat and many supplies were either destroyed or captured.[140] German broadcasts conceded that patriot-sponsored "hold-ups and acts of sabotage in the center of Bologna temporarily were the order of the day" and that at times partisans shelled German concentrations in the city.[141]

In the midst of this holocaust the Germans inflicted the worst massacres of the entire Italian campaign. By way of punishment for the local peasantry's succor of the Red Star partisans of "Lupo" (Mario Musolesi), the German SS engaged in vicious reprisals between September 28 and 30 in the village of Marzabotto, south of Bologna. They slaughtered at least 1,830 civilians, including the local priest, and continued the butchery for more than a week in the countryside. In the first post-Liberation census the town was listed as "inhabited nucleus that has disappeared." President Luigi Einaudi of the Italian Republic brought the *Medaglia d'Oro* decoration to the *gonfalone* of Marzabotto on September 30, 1949, which only then was beginning to resume its life. The poet Salvatore Quasimodo composed an epigraph for the occasion. Several years after the war Walter Reder, the Austrian SS major in the area who annihilated the "Lupo" partisans (and who was also suspected of complicity in the assassination of Chancellor Engelbert Dollfuss), was handed over to the Italians for a war-crimes trial. He was found guilty of several of the charges and sentenced to life imprisonment in October 1951.[142]

---

[140] Longo, *Un popolo alla macchia*, pp. 299–328.

[141] *NYT*, Oct. 28, 1944, 7:2.

[142] Renato Giorgi, *Le stragi di Marzabotto* (Bologna, 1954) and *Marzabotto parla* (Milan-Rome, 1955); Longo, *Un popolo alla macchia*, pp. 344–345. The complicity of Major Reder in the massacre has been questioned unconvincingly by certain neo-Fascist writers. *Cf.* F. J. P. Veale, *Crimes Discreetly Veiled* (London, 1958), Ch. v; Villari, *The Liberation of Italy*, pp. 147–151; and the rebuttal of P.P., "La strage di Marzabotto: una favola," *Il Ponte*, xvi (1960), pp. 1162–1163.

Ossola Republic

While the Allies jabbed at the lower rim of the Po valley, patriots in the North achieved two sensational triumphs. Between September 8 and 10 they seized control of the strategic Val d'Ossola to the northwest of Milan. Two weeks later other partisans announced the advent of the Republic of Carnia in the uplands of northeastern Venetia. The liberation of Carnia (consisting of some 160 communes and 2,500 square kilometers) did not result from one quick *coup* as in Ossola, but was the outgrowth of a summer of heavy fighting. And it survived more than two months (into December), whereas the much more industrialized and hence more valuable Ossola held out five weeks. In Carnia there was less bickering than in Ossola for the simple reason that Communists in the CLN were the propelling force from the outset. They quickly broadened the CLN base to include "youth fronts," "defense of women groups," and other fringe "mass" agencies. Radical *epurazione*, with numerous "popular tribunals," characterized patriot rule in Carnia.[143]

The Piedmontese Val d'Ossola, located just west of Lake Maggiore on the Swiss frontier, contained 32 towns and a population of 85,000. Through it passed the main railway from Milan over the Simplon to Lausanne. It was also a key hydroelectric center. Since July the Allies had stressed the importance of this valley as a strategic route through which the Germans might retreat.[144]

To everyone's surprise, the Catholic "Valtoce" patriots (led by Captain Alfredo DiDio), the Autonomous "Valdossola" (commanded by Ettore Superti, an ex-Army officer), the Autonomous "Piave" and "Beltrami," and Moscatelli's 2nd and 8th "Garibaldi" gained control of the thinly garrisoned valley between September 8 and 10. Some of the patriots regarded Ossola as an admirable strongpoint from which, bolstered by Allied supply drops, they could support an eventual insurrection in Milan.[145] Others (particularly with hindsight's wisdom) sus-

[143] Carli-Ballola, *Sdr*, pp. 206–207; Battaglia, *SRI*, pp. 428–434.
[144] Parri, "Il movimento di liberazione e gli alleati," *MLI*, No. 1 (1949), pp. 15–16; B. Ceva, "Documenti relativi all'attività politica e militare del rappresentante del Pd'A nei suoi rapporti con gli Alleati," *ibid.*, No. 27 (1953), p. 4.
[145] On the general topic see Anita Azzari, *L'Ossola nella resistenza italiana*

pected that it was a military mistake for guerrillas to try to hold on permanently to a large zone that did not lend itself easily to defense.[146]

At first, Superti tried to fill the administrative vacuum in Val d'Ossola. Because the original CLN had long since fled to Switzerland, he named a brand-new Provisional Junta, headed by Dr. Ettore Tibaldi, a Socialist physician who had returned from Lugano; otherwise it consisted mostly of men with moderate views. Certain leftists in the Lugano CLN refused to accept Superti's nominees, objecting both to their appointment "from above" and to their reputedly royalist proclivities. At this point, two PCI top-echelon men, Giancarlo Pajetta and Umberto Terracini, rushed into the valley; the DC countered by dispatching Augusto DeGasperi (brother of Alcide) and Piero Malvestiti posthaste via Switzerland; and the PSIUP, not to be outmaneuvered, sent in Corrado and Mario Bonfantini. Rightist groups were more than a bit annoyed by the influx of these eager politicians. In Milan the CLNAI busied itself for a month with the increasingly bitter wrangle.[147] Swiss authorities, meanwhile, announced their "recognition" of the provisional government, and Gigino Battisti, a Trentine exile, and the veteran Republican conspirator, Cipriano Facchinetti, served as "ambassadors" to the Helvetic Republic.[148]

In due course the anti-Fascists achieved a political compromise, broadening the Ossola Provisional Junta into a CLN which promised to co-ordinate "democratically" all aspects of public life. The usual Red-sponsored "youth fronts," "unions for defense of women," and peripheral economic bodies were conjured. Courts and purge commissions were deemed imperative and were rapidly established. These agencies corresponded extensively with the CLNAI regarding proper procedures. It is

---

(Domodossola, 1954); T. L., "La liberazione dell'Ossola in alcuni documenti inediti," *MLI*, No. 12/13 (1951), pp. 3–87; Secchia and Moscatelli, *Il Monte Rosa è sceso a Milano*, pp. 378–416; Mario Bonfantini, "Breve storia dell'Ossola," *Mercurio* (*Anche l'Italia ha vinto*), II, No. 16 (1945), pp. 201–207.

[146] Valiani, *Tutte le strade conducono a Roma*, pp. 375–376.

[147] *Ibid.*, pp. 290–291; Carli-Ballola, *Sdr*, pp. 201–210; Cadorna, *La Riscossa*, pp. 160–164; Catalano, *Storia del CLNAI*, pp. 266–282; Salvadori, *SRI*, pp. 156–157; Battaglia, *SRI*, pp. 428–434; Longo, *Un popolo alla macchia*, pp. 277–286; and Ferruccio Lanfranchi, *La resa degli ottocentomila* (Milan, 1948), pp. 48–49.

[148] *NYT*, Oct. 2, 1944, 6:2.

noteworthy that they decided against capital punishment and were content to intern a goodly number.

Despite efforts by General Cadorna to mediate, acrimonious disputes continued between Moscatelli's Garibaldini and the non-Communist brigades of DiDio and others over possession of the infrequent Allied supply drops.[149] Well aware of Churchill's negative attitude toward the northern CLN's, the leftist currents suspected the Allies of deliberately leaving them to their fate in Ossola. To be sure, there were some political misgivings regarding the future behavior of the Communists developing in the minds of Churchill and other British officials (and some American ones too) in Italy, especially as a result of events in Poland, Greece, and elsewhere in eastern Europe; [150] but these were not yet decisive factors in Allied policy in Italy. Indeed, at this juncture in September, Churchill and the British were doing everything possible to make their offensive into the lower Po valley succeed. The last thing they wished to see at this stage was a halt to the mighty war effort against the Gothic Line. The principal reasons for the Allied failure to supply the defenders of Ossola adequately were simply the unusually foggy and inclement weather and the prior commitments of planes and supplies to succor underground forces in Warsaw, France, and Yugoslavia.[151] The British and the Americans knew well that the war had yet to be won, and that the covert northern fighters could be most helpful, especially if properly balanced and co-ordinated by Allied missions.

New Anglo-American missions

In September, when it seemed quite likely that the Allies would break through into the Po valley, Brigadier M. Lush, second-in-command of the AC, drew up plans to have SF drop three AMG and three PWB officers into the Milan area to "advise" the Allied officers attached to CLNAI and CG/CVL; but this proposal was not accepted by AFHQ. Instead, SF pre-

[149] Cadorna, La Riscossa, pp. 160–164; Atti CG/CVL, No. 70 (Oct. 8, 1944), p. 117; Anita Azzari, "I rapporti tra l'Ossola e gli alleati nell'autunno 1944," MLI, No. 52/53 (1958), pp. 95–99; Secchia and Moscatelli, Il Monte Rosa è sceso a Milano, pp. 378–416, 469–473; and G. Zandano, La lotta di liberazione nella provincia di Vercelli, 1943–1945 (Vercelli, 1958), passim.
[150] See infra, Ch. XI.
[151] See supra, Ch. x. Tension between partisans and Allies.

pared to parachute Major Max Salvadori into Lombardy to serve as Chief of Mission and Liaison Officer between the Fifteenth Army Group (consisting of Fifth and Eighth armies and CIL) and the Milan CLNAI and its CG/CVL. Some fifteen other officers and enlisted specialists would accompany him. Salvadori's principal tasks would be to occupy the major provincial cities with the help of the partisans—or, better, accompany them when they occupied these places. As soon as his group reached Lombardy it was to request arms, medicines, and clothing, and to lay plans for maintenance of public order and protection of industrial plants. At first it was planned to drop the mission into the Bergamo foothills (where General Cadorna and Major Churchill had jumped in August), but unfortunately the Germans seized this DZ at the critical moment. Next it was planned to have the mission jump over the Langhe. Because of the collapse of the Allied offensive and other factors, however, all these plans were indefinitely postponed in October.[152]

Instead, American OSS got the nod to be first in establishing direct liaison between the Fifteenth Army Group and CLNAI.[153] On September 26, a fortnight after the sudden liberation of Val d'Ossola, OSS dropped the "Mangosteen-Chrysler Mission" into the adjacent Lake Orta zone—a wretched operation whose melodrama produced many sensational headlines after the war. The mission was apparently a last-minute fusion of two that had been contemplated: Special Intelligence's "Mangosteen" and Operational Group's "Chrysler." [154] "Mangosteen" was to establish contact with the CLNAI and then remain under cover till the Germans evacuated Milan (which OSS thought could happen quickly), at which time it would move into Milan, set up its radio, and relay instructions from Allied Headquarters to the patriot leaders. The "Chrysler" aspect of the mission was to work closely with the partisans in the Ossola region, reporting

---

[152] Harris, *Allied Military Administration of Italy*, pp. 274–275; Salvadori, *Resistenza ed azione*, pp. 257–262; Salvadori, *Brief History of the Patriot Movement*, p. 54. By September SF had 37 British and 17 Italian missions behind the lines.
[153] According to Dr. Enzo Boeri, ORI liaison man at Parri's headquarters, the CLNAI had asked for a helpful American mission in order to counterbalance pro-royalist maneuvers of British Captain "Peters" (Churchill), who had arrived in August with General Cadorna. Boeri, "Intervento," *MLI*, No. 52/53 (1958), pp. 173–174.
[154] Regarding OSS terminology, see *supra*, Ch. VII.

on relative strength of Communist and non-Communist patriots and recommending which should get priority in supply drops and monetary assistance. Overcast skies twelve times delayed the landing of "Chrysler"; hence its consolidation with "Mangosteen." [155]

To command the mission, General Donovan and Major William Suhling, his new director of Italian operations, selected husky, unmarried, 40-year-old Major William V. Holohan, a newcomer to Italy in August. A Harvard-trained lawyer, Holohan spoke some French but no Italian—an obvious handicap in this kind of mission. He was quickly promoted to major in order to enjoy greater prestige in his mission. Second in command was First Lieutenant Victor Giannino, an American of Italian extraction who already had served behind the lines. The third officer was 23-year-old Second Lieutenant Aldo Icardi, a quick-witted University of Pittsburgh graduate. Also of Italian parentage, he spoke the language fluently and even had an Astigiano accent, which would be advantageous in the near-by Orta zone. Icardi had been in OSS Special Intelligence work in southern Italy since his arrival late in 1943. Technical Sergeant Arthur Ciarmicola was Giannino's Operational Group demolition expert. Staff Sergeant Carl LoDolce, an ex-factory worker of Sicilian descent, was the radio operator; he had been with Lieutenant Giannino on some earlier perilous assignments.

Major Holohan and his companions carried with them a sum of money variously estimated to have been between $14,000 and $16,000. According to Icardi, it consisted of about $10,000 worth of Italian currency for day-to-day expenses; $2,000 in Swiss francs and $1,000 in U.S. currency for transactions with Italian businessmen; and an additional $3,000 in the form of gold coins known as French Louis d'Ors, to be used as last-resort "blood money" to bribe an enemy captor. Icardi has declared that Giannino carried an additional $4,000. Just before the group took off from Maison Blanche near Algiers, they were joined by Captain "Landi" (Tullio Lussi), a young Italian who was to join OSS's Special Intelligence "Augusta" radio team on the Mottarone heights between Lake Orta and Lake Maggiore—a team that worked in conjunction with Dr. Enzo Boeri's "Salem" unit in

[155] Icardi, *Icardi: American Master Spy*, pp. 10–11.

Milan's CG/CVL; his radio operator; and a third Italian, who worked with Special Operations and had separate orders.[156]

A few days after they parachuted safely near the village of Coiromonte on the Mottarone, Holohan and Icardi were met by Parri and Dr. Boeri ("Cremona"). The Americans told Parri of the plan to move the mission into Milan at the moment of enemy surrender, and they inquired of Parri how effectively the CLNAI could control the patriots at that time. According to both Icardi and Boeri, they achieved complete understanding. Temporarily this ended the "Mangosteen" phase of the mission. Later Holohan wrote a letter to Parri proposing that supply drops for the Ossola-Orta zone be consigned to a special command, appointed by the CLNAI, which should take responsibility for apportionment to rival patriot forces.[157]

The beleaguered Ossola Republic, meantime, neared its final crisis. Neo-Fascist Black Brigadesmen, militiamen of the GNR, parachutists of the "Folgore," plus German troops with tanks and artillery, were preparing to attack in force on October 9. Captain DiDio, commander of the best-armed "Valtoce" Catholic division, came to see Holohan twice—ten days after the mission's arrival and again on October 8. He pleaded for supply drops, which he claimed the Swiss office of OSS had promised. He also explained his plan to capture the town of Gravellona at the southern exit of Ossola valley to prevent the enemy's penetration. Holohan ordered Lieutenant Giannino and Sergeant Ciarmicola to go with DiDio to the Ossola on the 8th to prepare defenses. (After the Republic fell, these two Americans escaped to Switzerland.) About this time OSS signaled Holohan to prepare for a daylight drop, but this never arrived. Rainy weather hampered any such operation.[158]

By this time the enemy, which outnumbered the patriots 12,000 to 3,000, was attacking in strength. During the desperate defense a makeshift "unified headquarters" was belatedly erected by Socialist Avv. G. B. Stucchi ("Colonel Federici") and his Communist political commissar, Paolo Scarpone. (The redoubtable Communist chieftain, Moscatelli, who had sought the latter position, was excluded by DiDio's pressure.) But it was in vain.

[156] *Ibid.*, pp. 11–14, 42–46.
[157] *Ibid.*, pp. 17–18, 206; Boeri, *MLI*, No. 52/53 (1958), p. 174.
[158] *American Air Forces in World War II*, III, 515; Battaglia, *SRI*, p. 440.

Patriot resistance collapsed soon after DiDio was killed in action on the 14th. In the ensuing debacle some contingents managed to escape into Switzerland, surrendering their arms to border guards. Moscatelli's forces chose to retreat in a twenty-day "long march" westward to Valsesia and Val Strone, where they reorganized in late October and November.[159] Some of the Catholic partisans accused them, perhaps unfairly, of leaving them in the lurch.[160] The internecine strife certainly complicated the defense of Ossola; yet it is doubtful if the guerrillas (separated from the Allies by more than 100 miles) could have held out for long against the massive enemy offensive, even had they been harmoniously united.

Holohan mystery

According to Icardi (whose self-vindicatory account is to be read with caution), Major Holohan decided in mid-November that the war was going to drag on through the winter; consequently he should make the mission more useful by seeking additional drops, thereby raising its prestige with the local forces and the CLNAI.[161] Thus he revived, it is asserted, the idea envisaged in October of a drop on the Mottarone. This drop was to go chiefly to remnants of the DiDio Catholic brigade at "Blueberry" pinpoint.[162] On December 2 "Blueberry" drop took place: 30 Sten sub-machine guns and 14 Bren machine guns and much ammunition hit the ground. The drop occurred, according to Icardi, the very same night that Holohan and he paid their first visit to Moscatelli a few miles away. Holohan offered Moscatelli drops, it is claimed, if the Communist provided information regarding his strength, present equipment, needs, and military plans. Moscatelli promised this but seemed skeptical of the

[159] Ibid., pp. 439–442; Cadorna, La Riscossa, p. 163; Secchia and Moscatelli, Il Monte Rosa è sceso a Milano, pp. 413–416; Zandano, Lotta di liberazione nella provincia di Vercelli, 1943–1945, passim.

[160] Icardi, Icardi: American Master Spy, p. 51.

[161] On November 13 General Alexander broadcast a message to the patriots calling for a halt of "large-scale military operations" and saving of munitions. See infra, Ch. XI.

[162] It should be noted that the mission's chief intelligence reporter since September had been Aminto Migliari ("Giorgio"), an officer of DiDio's group and a bitter foe of Moscatelli.

Americans' willingness to produce.[163] Soon he got what he desired.[164]

In the wake of the Ossola comb-outs, the Americans and their partisan associates—"Giorgio" and his handymen, the cook Gualtiero Tozzini ("Pupo") and Giuseppe Manini ("Manin")—fled from lair to lair, fearful of enemy capture. "Giorgio" stayed with them only after the Americans allegedly offered him substantial monetary inducement, to be transferred through a most peculiar "partnership" arrangement between Icardi and himself in a "wood-working toy factory" in a near-by village. (This "factory," according to Icardi, went bankrupt soon after the war.) [165]

On December 14 Icardi and LoDolce radioed their Siena headquarters that Major Holohan had "disappeared" the night of December 6. They "surmised" that he had been killed in an "ambush" that purportedly took place in the darkness at their Orta lake-shore hide-out, the 22-room Villa Castelnuovo, at the moment they were moving out of it.[166]

That same month General Cadorna's CG/CVL was busy reestablishing (partly at Holohan's insistence, it seems) the short-lived Unified Ossola Command that had collapsed with the "republic." It would supervise apportionment of drops to the different brigades in that region. Shortly after Christmas, Colonel "Delle Torri" (Curreno di Santa Maddalena) took command.[167] He and Icardi, it appears, arranged with OSS for a large daylight drop on January 18, 1945, at the Alpine village of Quarna. At

[163] Icardi, *Icardi: American Master Spy*, pp. 40–52.

[164] According to Icardi, another drop fell unexpectedly at "Blueberry" on the Mottarone on December 15—by mistake, for it was supposed to have gone to the British "Cherokee" mission (with Moscatelli) to the southwest. When Garibaldini seized some of these supplies without authorization, Icardi allegedly protested. *Ibid.*, pp. 60–62.

According to Moscatelli's memoirs, in mid-December as a result of his increased pressure, the British "Cherokee" mission finally brought 18 planeloads of Bren and Sten guns, mortars, heavy machine guns, and Italian '91 rifles to Baldicati DZ near Soprana, east of Biella. "The Garibaldini, loaded like mules, wended their way towards their bases satisfied with the arms that had finally rained from the sky." Secchia and Moscatelli, *Il Monte Rosa è sceso a Milano*, pp. 471–473.

[165] Icardi, *Icardi: American Master Spy*, pp. 18–30.

[166] *Ibid.*, pp. 53–77, and *passim*.

[167] *Ibid.*, pp. 206–207; Cadorna, *La Riscossa*, pp. 160–164; *Atti del CG/CVL*, No. 105 (Dec. 21, 1944), No. 110 (Dec. 20), No. 111 (Jan. 2, 1945), No. 115 (Jan. 20), No. 125 (Feb. 9), No. 130 (Mar. 2), pp. 172–230; *cf.* Battaglia, *SRI*, pp. 442–444.

that time some twenty-four tons of arms were distributed fairly, according to Icardi, who has freely admitted that he also requested supplies on numerous occasions for both Communist and non-Communist formations in the Valsesia and Varese-Alto-Milanese zones, in accordance with general wartime Allied policy.[168]

A few days later OSS instructed him and his remaining personnel (now attired in civilian clothing) to undertake such military espionage as radioing reports of train movements. Icardi, LoDolce, and others continued this type of work in Piedmont and Lombardy until the eve of the insurrection.[169]

At intervals between 1945 and 1947 U.S. Army investigators interrogated Icardi regarding Holohan's disappearance. Though Icardi gained the impression that the matter was closed, the Army remained unconvinced of the veracity of his story. On August 15, 1951, learning that the journalist Michael Stern, on the basis of interviews with Italian guerrillas, was about to publish in *True Magazine* (September 1951) an exposé of the "murder" plot, the Department of Defense decided to reveal its own version of the bizarre story, implicating Icardi and LoDolce. (Much of the original press release was a verbatim copy of Stern's account.) The government's statement was based chiefly upon a series of incriminating depositions by two of the ex-partisans (Manini and Tozzini) who accused the Americans of plotting the murder of Holohan, and upon the August 1950 "confession," later repudiated, by LoDolce to the U.S. Army's Criminal Investigations Division. In June 1950 a partially decomposed corpse had been pulled up from frigid Lake Orta by *Carabiniere* Lieutenant Elio Albieri. Two 9 mm. bullets were found in the skull and traces of cyanide in the intestines. Two Italians who had seen Holohan five and a half years before vouched for the fact that the body was his. Later the alleged lethal weapon, a Beretta pistol which had been sold by Manini to a third party (Maulini), was recovered. According to the prosecution, Icardi and LoDolce arranged for potassium cyanide to be included in Holohan's soup the evening of December 6, 1944; when he became ill, they shot him twice in the head (LoDolce acting as

---

[168] Icardi, *Icardi: American Master Spy*, p. 207, and *passim*.
[169] *Ibid.*, pp. 81–188, and *passim*.

"trigger man"), after which they embezzled the funds he carried. The prosecution charged that they and the three Italians dumped Holohan's body, tied in a sleeping bag, into thirty feet of water. Holohan, the prosecution further explained, had opposed granting financial support and aerial supply drops to Moscatelli's Garibaldini and others to the extent desired by Icardi and LoDolce, who for their part feared for their lives at the hands of the guerrillas if such a "discriminatory" policy persisted. Prior to December 6, it was pointedly observed, the mission had asked for but one aerial drop, whereas during the next four months some fifty, involving about 600 tons, were requested by Icardi and delivered.[170]

Complex and often seemingly haphazard court proceedings dragged on from 1951 until 1956. In the judges' minds there seemed to be little doubt that Icardi and LoDolce were guilty. Nevertheless, technicalities finally caused the prosecution to give up the case.[171]

[170] NYT, Aug. 16, 17, 18, 19, 22; Sept. 1, 25; Oct. 24; and Dec. 20, 1951. Icardi contended that Holohan asked for four and received two drops while he was in command, and that in the last nine months of the war forty-four supply drops were received on request. *Icardi: American Master Spy*, p. 212, and *passim*.

[171] Since Icardi and LoDolce no longer were in the U.S. Army, they were not subject to court-martial. The Italian courts attempted to extradite them for trial in that country, but U.S. Federal Judge John Knight in Buffalo ruled "reluctantly" on August 12, 1952, that the Italian government had not exercised physical control over the Ossola zone at the time of the alleged crime. He expressed his own conviction that the accused were guilty of plotting the crime.

In the autumn of 1953 an Italian court in Novara tried Icardi and LoDolce *in absentia*, their three Italian "accomplices" (Manini, Tozzini, and Migliari), and the Italian (Maulini) who was caught in possession of the gun. On November 5, 1953, Judge Sicher acquitted the three accomplices; sentenced Maulini to four months' imprisonment and a 10,000-lire fine; sentenced Icardi to life, and LoDolce to seventeen years' imprisonment. Neither of the latter sentences would become effective unless the Americans returned to Italy. An Italian appeals court upheld the sentences.

Then in August–September 1955 a Federal grand jury in Washington, D.C., indicted Icardi on eight charges of perjury in his March 26, 1953, testimony before a House Subcommittee on Armed Services investigating the Holohan slaying. (For some reason LoDolce was not called before the committee.)

At last, on April 20, 1956, Federal Judge Keech acquitted Icardi of perjury, on the technical grounds that the charges had grown out of an unconstitutional "legislative trial" by the House Subcommittee, whose chairman was W. Sterling Cole of New York. Seemingly this has brought an end to the complex litigation.

See NYT, April 15 through 22, 1956; Jesse Gordon, "The Holohan Case: A Pentagon Snafu," *The Nation*, CLXXXI (Sept. 10, 1955), pp. 217–219; "Strange Case of a Slain Major," *U.S. News and World Report*, XXXIX (Sept. 16, 1955), pp. 37–38; and Icardi's documentary version in *Icardi: American Master Spy*, pp. 191–275.

Clarification of General Cadorna's status

In the midst of the Ossola crisis the CLNAI held a lengthy session on September 27, 1944, to take up the problem of General Cadorna's proper functions.[172] Sogno ("Franchi"), who recently had visited Allied Headquarters, was also invited to attend. At the conference Longo declared that he would accept General Cadorna as Supreme Commander of the CG/CVL only if he himself were given equal powers as Political Commissar and the right to countersign all orders. Parri and the PSIUP delegate ostensibly supported Longo but insisted also upon parallel status for themselves. Longo, it quickly appeared, was ready to concede such parity only to Parri. For his part, Cadorna rejected the idea of any political commissar holding a veto over his decisions. He reminded the CLNAI that all five parties had expressed "full confidence" in him when they asked him to come. He went on to declare that he would accept the command only if his appointment were accompanied by serious guarantees from Longo, Parri, and their men to collaborate unreservedly with him. The dispute rumbled on.[173]

The CLNAI sought to resolve the impasse by returning to the arrangement that had prevailed before Cadorna came. By a majority vote of the three leftist parties, the committee sent to Rome a message recommending that Cadorna's nomination be cancelled and that the former kind of headquarters be restored. Cadorna at this point declared that he too would inform Rome of the true situation. Meanwhile, on September 26 Premier Bonomi had forwarded a message which said that anything the CLNAI did to improve co-ordination and standardization of the work of the patriot forces had his full support.[174]

On October 3 Longo tried to win credit for the PCI by slashing the Gordian knot; he proposed a new organization of the CG/CVL which, in appearance at least, seemed to satisfy Cadorna. Probably he did so because of the heavy Allied pressure to uphold Cadorna and the risk of jeopardizing subsidies and supply drops for PCI units. Longo's plan called for "a structure

---

[172] See *supra*, Ch. x, General Cadorna and the CG/CVL.

[173] Cadorna, *La Riscossa*, p. 141; Catalano, *Storia del CLNAI*, pp. 227-228; Valiani, *Tutte le strade conducono a Roma*, pp. 256-257.

[174] Archivio CLNAI, xxvi/32, cited in Catalano, *Storia del CLNAI*, p. 229.

of a purely Military Command which therefore would be acceptable to General 'Valenti' [Cadorna], as well as to the Allied Headquarters, and which would assure the best collaboration of the Italian political forces to common ends. For such purposes [the PCI] propose a Command composed of General 'Valenti' as Commander; 'Italo' [Longo] as Vice-Commander; 'Maurizio' [Parri] as Chief of Staff. This Command will function with the collaboration of a college of the representatives of the parties of the CLN." [175] To Longo's chagrin, however, the PCI proposal aborted in the face of intense PSIUP resentment at being passed up in the Command.

Later in October a CLNAI mission composed of President Pizzoni, Valiani, and Sogno met in Lugano with Anglo-American agents, who received them courteously. They discussed various hypotheses regarding the final phases of the war, including the possibility of Allied occupation of the Veneto during the pursuit of the enemy, who presumably would fall back across the Brenner Pass. Should that be the case, Allied intelligence officers wished to know if the CLNAI had enough prestige to control northwestern Italy temporarily. If so, they suggested that Cadorna be assigned command over Liguria, Piedmont, and Lombardy. The conferees agreed at last to terminate the Cadorna squabble and dispatch a mission from both the CLNAI and CG/CVL to Allied Force Headquarters in Caserta, where they could systematize plans for the temporary administration of the three northwestern industrial compartments. [176]

On October 31 Valiani (in the presence of Parri and Longo) presented this news to the CG/CVL, with the suggestion that the problem of the Supreme Commander of the CVL be discussed and settled once for all. Three days later, just prior to Parri's departure for Caserta, he informed General Cadorna that his status had been settled. Cadorna was to become Supreme Commander; Longo and Parri would both become Vice-Commanders. This time a PSIUP member was also given recognition and assigned the post of Chief of Staff. At first Avv. Mosna and

[175] Archivio CLNAI, ix bis/99, cited in *ibid.*, p. 230, and in Cadorna, *La Riscossa*, p. 142.
[176] Valiani, *Tutte le strade conducono a Roma*, pp. 201–202, 257, 293–300; Catalano, *Storia del CLNAI*, pp. 230–231; Harris, *Allied Military Administration of Italy*, p. 265 ff.

later Sandro Pertini and Corrado Bonfantini represented the PSIUP in the CG/CVL; during the last weeks of the war Avv. G. B. Stucchi ("Noris") held the position of Chief of Staff. Major Mario Argenton (PLI) and Enrico Mattei ("Este") (DC), a young industrialist, were added to the headquarters as Vice-Chiefs of Staff. The CG would meet weekly; all decisions would be collegial; if the voting resulted in a tie, the question would be referred to the CLNAI. Cadorna indicated that he would agree to all this as soon as he received written confirmation as well as a definition of his duties. Actually, several months transpired before such confirmation was delivered to him.[177]

Despite its difficult birth, the CG/CVL was a distinct improvement over the previous Military Committee of the CLNAI. It assumed the usual responsibilities of a military headquarters and tried to standardize procedure.[178] Unlike regular Army practice, duties were assigned to those whose parties most fully engaged in the Resistenza Armata. Thus "in practice the . . . Actionists and Communists had preponderance," Cadorna has explained. "First of all, their authority derived from . . . Parri and Longo, who participated simultaneously in the CLNAI and CG"; they "could influence decisions in the CLNAI, or even pay little attention to it when it did not seem favorable to them." Secondly, the Operations Section, always of paramount importance, was assigned to the same two men. Assisted by Cadorna, they convened this body twice a week, whereas meetings of the entire headquarters occurred but once a week. Sessions of the Operations Section often merely confirmed what already had been decided and executed by Longo and Parri. Because of the excellent intelligence apparatus of the PCI, Longo at first did most of the Operations Section's paper work. Longo and Parri's pre-eminence was further assured by the untimely arrests and other mishaps which often paralyzed the work of delegates of the PLI, DC, and PSIUP.[179]

Parri took charge of the Operations Section's important Office

[177] Cadorna, La Riscossa, pp. 142–143; Sogno, Guerra senza bandiera, p. 279.

[178] See decrees giving advice about hierarchical tables of organization, insignia, regional headquarters, political commissars, courts-martial, treatment of PW's, et cetera, in Atti del CG/CVL, passim.

[179] Cadorna, La Riscossa, p. 132; Valiani, Tutte le strade conducono a Roma, pp. 248–249.

of Information, Liaison with Allied Missions in Switzerland, Assistance to Victims of the Resistance Struggle, and the Finance Office. He was fortunate to have assigned to CVL the old "Montezemolo Group" which had functioned covertly in Rome. Dr. Enzo Boeri, in radio communication with OSS, co-ordinated the "Salem" intelligence service. In the Finance Office Parri was aided by Ing. F. Solari ("Somma") in distributing funds.[180]

Cadorna tried to organize his own personal staff, key members of which included Lieutenant Colonel Palombo of the Italian Army General Staff and Major Argenton, PLI representative. Cadorna's efforts to obtain additional regular Army officers from the South were futile. Hoping to free himself from dependence upon PCI couriers, he sought to create his own liaison network, and in this he was encouraged by Sogno, who headed the "Franchi" radio communications system. Sogno had been rather widely criticized by the leftists for his cordial ties with Anglo-Americans. Cadorna agreed to have Sogno financed and controlled directly by CG/CVL in order to reduce such causes for criticism. In January Sogno superseded Argenton as PLI representative in the CG/CVL.[181] Next month both Sogno and Palombo were captured. Thereafter it was necessary for Cadorna to use the CG/CVL as it had previously existed, "leaving to representatives of the parties the more delicate tasks." Cadorna stubbornly tried to maintain his role as an "equilibrator" among the five parties.[182]

The CG/CVL's chain of command presented a neat chart on paper.[183] Under it were, first, the half dozen regional commands: Piedmont, Liguria, Lombardy, Venetia, Emilia-Romagna, and North Emilia. Except in Piedmont, however, the line of command was tenuous. Too often information from Venetia and Romagna was meagre and delayed. In Emilia the politico-military situation became so complicated that the regional adminis-

---

[180] Boeri, "Radio, informazioni, controspionnagio," *Mercurio* (*Anche l'Italia ha vinto*), II, No. 16 (Dec. 1945), pp. 159–164; Boeri, "Vicende di un servizio informazioni: relazione del dott. Enzo Boeri alla organizzazione OSS sulla sua missione nel Nord Italia (17 marzo 1944–10 maggio 1945)," *MLI*, No. 12/13 (1951), pp. 88–117; Fornaro, *Il Servizio informazioni nella lotta clandestina: "Gruppo Montezemolo,"* p. 24 ff.

[181] Sogno, *Guerra senza bandiera*, pp. 304–306.

[182] Cadorna, *La Riscossa*, pp. 148–149.

[183] See chart in *Atti del CG/CVL*.

tration had to be subdivided. Parma and Modena were removed from the jurisdiction of Bologna, a PCI stronghold under Ilio Barontini,[184] and put under a new North Emilia Headquarters in Piacenza. North Emilia and the strategic Valsesia and Val d'Ossola were the only areas indisputably under the aegis of the CG/CVL.[185]

From the regional headquarters depended the rural "zone commands" and "piazza commands," with various echelons under them. For example, under the "zone commands" were the organic partisan units (divisions, brigades, battalions, detachments) as well as GAP and SAP squads; while under the "piazza commands" were "service" and GAP and SAP units. All of these subsidiary headquarters differed somewhat, but the usual model was the PCI "unified command," with a commander flanked by a political commissar, one or more vice-commanders, and a chief of staff. These posts were distributed proportionately among the political currents, although the Garibaldini and Giellisti often tried to superimpose themselves on posts already assigned to others. The Operations Committee did its best to iron out such ceaseless squabbles.[186]

Relations with the Yugoslavs

Venezia Giulia continued to worry the Italian Resistance leaders. The non-Communist underground resented the behavior of the Garibaldini in the Trieste sector, where they repeatedly co-ordinated their activities with Tito's Ninth Army Corps.[187] By early June 1944 the PCI persuaded Tito to send to Milan an official mission headed by Dr. Vratusa ("Prof. Umberto Urban"), a functionary in the Press Office of the Trieste Prefecture and one of the pivotal figures in the central OF (Slovenian Titoist Front), and Franz Štoka ("Rado"), who was one of the chief organizers of Slovenian workers in Trieste and Venezia Giulia. Persuaded by a day-long discussion with the Slavic dele-

---

[184] Aldo Cucchi, who with Valdo Magnani in 1951 was to lead a Titoist secession movement from the PCI, was a vice-commandant of the PCI "Bologna" division.

[185] Battaglia, SRI, p. 391.

[186] Cadorna, La Riscossa, pp. 132-160.

[187] See supra, Ch. ix.

gation, on June 10 the CLNAI issued orders to the Italian resistants in Venezia Giulia to organize forthwith mixed Italo-Slovene and Italo-Croat CLN's.[188]

Soon certain non-Communist currents in Trieste (notably the DC and Pd'A) raised objections to what they felt was an unduly conciliatory policy by the CLNAI and emphasized the need to safeguard Trieste's *italianità* and to look out for Italian minority rights in Dalmatia as well. Because of all this, a delegation of the Trieste CLN (Don Marzoni [DC]; Giuliano Gaeta [Pd'A]; Luigi Frausin [PCI]) was called to Milan for consultations in mid-July, as were the Venetian CLN and a delegation from the Friuli.[189] They met in a residence on Via Malpighi with President Pizzoni, Arpesani (PLI), Marazza (DC), G. Marzola (PSIUP), Valiani (Pd'A), Dozza (PCI), and "Cecconi" (Balzarotti) as secretary. On the 16th they were joined by Dr. Vratusa and Štoka. At last on the 19th the CLNAI signed the so-called Milan Pacts with the POOF (Inter-Regional Committee of the National Front for the Slovene Littoral). The Slovenes, it should be noted, declined to speak for the Croats in Fiume and Zara. A spirit of goodwill and mutual faith seemed to exude from the pacts, which followed hard on the June 16 *rapprochement* of Tito and Premier Šubašič of the Yugoslav government-in-exile. The CG/CVL dispatched a congratulatory message to Tito.[190]

The Milan Pacts set forth the principle of self-determination of peoples after the Liberation and expressed the importance of achieving concrete co-ordination of efforts during the war to eliminate national intolerance. Specifically they recommended that both Italians and Slovenes combat chauvinistic and imperialistic propaganda; that the two Resistance organizations give each other technical aid; that mixed CLN's be set up in bilingual zones; that factory "committees of worker unity" be created irrespective of nationality; that two representatives of the Italian and Slovenian CLN's form a common Anti-Fascist Co-ordination Committee; that a bilingual *Lotta/Borba* news-

[188] Catalano, *Storia del CLNAI*, pp. 194–197.
[189] E. Taucer, "Il secondo CLN ed i rapporti Italo-Slavi," *MLI*, No. 51 (1958), pp. 25–37; Catalano, *Storia del CLNAI*, pp. 194–197; G. Gaeta, *La lotta del Comitato di Liberazione Nazionale di Trieste* (Trieste, 1949), pp. 5–11.
[190] *Atti del CG/CVL*, No. 18/19 (July 17 and 19, 1944), pp. 33–38.

paper be published in Trieste; that the CLNAI do its best to unify its partisan forces in order to facilitate military collaboration with the Slavs; and that the CG/CVL work out "the necessary agreements with the Ninth Army Corps of the NOVJ for collaboration and mutual support on the basis of the agreements already signed by the Garibaldi Assault Brigades." [191]

When the Slovenian delegation was not present the PCI raised some mild objections to the CLNAI attitude, particularly the tendency to think the Italians were getting nothing in return. The PCI contended that it was enough for the CLNAI to gain the right to be treated on an equal standing with the Yugoslav representatives and to work out accords without any veto from the Anglo-Americans. This remained the PCI line with respect to the disputed border zone until February 1945 and the bloody encounter between Garibaldini and non-Communist Osoppo guerrillas at Malga Porzus.[192]

In ensuing weeks the Italians dispatched some partisan formations to co-operate with the Slavs, and the Italian underground press lauded Tito's men. To demonstrate its solidarity, the CLNAI "lent" the Slovene POOF 3,000,000 lire (equivalent to considerably more than $30,000). The funds were raised and transmitted to Dr. Vratusa by Enrico Falck, an Italian steel industrialist who was treasurer of the covert DC and who held a seat in the CLNAI.[193] This meant no little sacrifice. Dr. Vratusa handed over the funds to his superiors; yet on August 30 (two weeks after Tito's conference in southern Italy with Churchill) [194] he insisted that he had no authority to bring the negotiations to an effective conclusion unless Italy recognized in writing that the Slovene Littoral would be included in Yugoslavia's

[191] Archivio CLNAI, xx/12, cited in Catalano, *Storia del CLNAI*, pp. 197–203; Taucer, *MLI*, No. 51 (1958), pp. 27–33.

[192] *Ibid.*, pp. 33–37; Catalano, *Storia del CLNAI*, p. 204.

[193] Parri's preface to Michele U. Buonafine, "Note sulla resistenza a Dongo," *MLI*, No. 38/39 (1955), pp. 31–45.

[194] General Wilson told Tito at that time that AMG would be erected over the whole territory of Venezia Giulia which before the war had been under Italian rule, pending its ultimate disposition, thus automatically suspending Italian sovereignty. The Yugoslavs agreed in principle that the Supreme Allied Commander should exercise general operational control throughout the region in order to protect communication lines to Austria, but the Yugoslavs intimated they would demand a share in the local civil and military administration. Harris, *Allied Military Administration of Italy*, pp. 328–330; Churchill, *Triumph and Tragedy*, pp. 81–82 ff.

borders. He disclaimed, however, any desire to annex Trieste itself in view of that seaport's *italianità*.[195]

This intelligence thoroughly angered most of the CLNAI, for it meant a complete repudiation of the principle of popular self-determination set forth in the Milan Pacts. The CLNAI learned at this juncture that as far back as November 29, 1943, Tito had decreed the return to Yugoslavia of certain territories "subjugated by the Italian imperialists." [196] Why this had not been mentioned to them earlier was not explained. On September 14, 1944, Tito, in a broadcast honoring the second anniversary of the Dalmatian Brigade, announced Yugoslavia's demands for Istria, Trieste, the hinterland, and the entire Dalmatian coast.[197] Quite likely Tito felt that his hand was strengthened by the Red Army's push into Rumania, Bulgaria, and Hungary, and almost certainly he was worried about a possible Anglo-American drive through the Ljubljana Gap. The whole problem of spheres of influence in east-central Europe was then coming to a head, with Churchill about to fly to Moscow for talks with Stalin.

Thus Italo-Yugoslav relations were greatly strained after September. The dream of collaboration for the duration of the war dissolved, except among some thoroughly disciplined Italian Communists. Dr. Vratusa and his colleagues quit Milan, promising to ask their superiors for further instructions; yet none came. On the 27th the CLNAI sent an urgent message to Premier Bonomi, outlining its fears and expressing the belief that only an entente on the diplomatic level with Tito could safeguard Italian interests in Venezia Giulia. The frontier problem henceforth was of cardinal importance.[198]

[195] Valiani, *Tutte le strade conducono a Roma*, pp. 259–262.
[196] Archivio CLNAI, xx/31, cited in Catalano, *Storia del CLNAI*, pp. 261–262.
[197] *NYT*, Sept. 15, 1944, 5:8; Sept. 17, 24:1.
[198] Valiani, *Tutte le strade conducono a Roma*, pp. 259–262; Catalano, *Storia del CLNAI*, pp. 262–266.

November 1944 – March 1945

Collapse of the Allied campaign

THE Allied drive in Italy that Prime Minister Churchill launched so confidently in August 1944 bogged down after the capture of Rimini on September 20. Not till October 19 could the Eighth Army take Cesena. The climax of the campaign occurred between the 20th and 24th of that month, when the Fifth Army reached a point southeast of Bologna only four miles from the Imola road and very nearly succeeded in cutting in behind the enemy facing the Eighth Army.[1] Thereafter, in General Alexander's bitter words, "assisted by torrential rains and winds of gale force, and the Fifth Army's exhaustion, the German line held firm."[2]

Chief cause for the failure of the "battle of the Apennines" was the previous sapping of seven Allied divisions for the invasion of southern France. To a lesser degree the failure resulted from diversion of additional British units to Greece in October, where they quickly ran into bitter strife with the Communist-led EAM/ELAS.[3]

By the last week of October wintry weather brought an end to operations in the mountainous center of the Gothic Line. They continued for a while on the foggy Romagnole plain, now a virtual quagmire, where the crossing of each stream meant a major operation. On November 9, supported by patriot actions, the Eighth Army advanced from Cesena to Forlì, a highway junction connecting with Florence.[4] No longer was a major offensive feasible, though General Alexander ordered a modest one in the east on the 28th, which resulted in the deliverance of Ravenna [5]

---

[1] On the 23rd Marshal Kesselring was badly injured in a motor accident on this front. He was out of action until March, at which time Hitler transferred him to the Western Front. Kesselring, *Memoirs*, p. 218.

[2] Quoted by Churchill, *Triumph and Tragedy*, p. 222; see map in *ibid.*, p. 119. Cf. Kesselring, *Memoirs*, p. 213; Starr, *From Salerno to the Alps*, p. 365.

[3] Churchill, *Triumph and Tragedy*, pp. 283–325; Ehrman, *Grand Strategy*, VI, 37–40, 47–56.

[4] *NYT*, Nov. 13, 1944, 4:1.

[5] Regarding partisan operations there by Arrigo Boldrini ("Bülow") and others, see Gianni Giadresco, *Ravenna zona operazioni, 1944–1945* (Ravenna, 1955) and Guido Nozzoli, *Quelli di Bülow* (Rome, 1957); cf. Peniakoff ("Popski"), *Private Army, passim*. Thanks to all of them, Ravenna's art treasures were saved.

and Faenza on December 4–5 and 16, respectively. After that, the Gothic Line remained almost unchanged till the final Allied push in April. During the rest of the winter the chief task of the Allied armies in Italy was simply to pin down the bulk of the German forces there.[6]

Churchill's recurrent dream of a quick thrust through the Ljubljana Gap to Vienna was shattered; all he could do now was to hope that Stalin would abide by his Moscow bargain of October 9 regarding the sharing of Anglo-Russian political influence in Yugoslavia, Hungary, Greece, Bulgaria, and Rumania.[7]

Intensified rakings

When it became clear that the Allied offensive had lost its punch, the enemy hurled all-out attacks against the partisans in the liberated "republics." Practically all of Mussolini's neo-Fascist troops were deployed in these cruelest of all the *rastrellamenti*, as were some five or six German divisions, including armored equipment. Numerous Cossack and Mongol troops were also employed. Scarcely a sector of septentrional Italy escaped the enemy's scourge. In village after village the SS and their neo-Fascist collaborators strung up partisans, leaving their corpses on the trees and lamp posts to intimidate the others.

In the wake of the Ossola disaster and in the face of an impending one in Val d'Aosta,[8] the Turin Regional Military Command appealed urgently to the CG/CVL (October 14): "In order for formations to obey [us] they must first *be* aided. Up to now, aid has been almost purely on paper and on faith. . . . Unless one wishes to see the Resistance degenerate into an association of simple renitents, we must have money, arms, means for liaison, and pressure on the French to respect agreements freely undertaken. . . ."[9]

---

[6] Starr, *From Salerno to the Alps*, p. 368.

[7] Stalin's pencilled tick to Churchill's jottings on the back of an envelope gave the British 50/50 parity in Yugoslavia and Hungary; 90 per cent of the "say" in Greece; 25 per cent in Bulgaria; and 10 per cent in Rumania. Neither Italy nor Austria was mentioned. The United States technically was not a party to the accord. Churchill, *Triumph and Tragedy*, pp. 226–227; on the broad subject *cf.* the present author's chapter, "Russian Power in East-Central Europe," in John L. Snell (ed.), *The Meaning of Yalta: Big Three Diplomacy and the New Balance of Power* (Baton Rouge, 1956).

[8] Ossola was recaptured by mid-October; Aosta, between October 27 and 31.

[9] Arch. Ist. Storico della Resistenza in Piemonte, Dossier: AM/B-II—Cartella:

Meanwhile, in the Veneto the enemy struck 30,000 strong at the Monte Grappa bastion. After ten days of bloodshed he eliminated that redoubt on September 28. Next he attacked the crack "Osoppo" and "Natisone" in the Friuli; from the north he drove into the "Republic of Carnia." The battle continued almost without surcease until the republic was wiped out in mid-December. Allied aerial aid was too little and too late. Horrible massacres took place, just as they had in the Bologna and Carrara [10] sectors a few weeks before. The enemy lost 3,000 men in the Veneto.[11]

In the Piedmontese Langhe sector the foe's pincer offensives made the region untenable for Martini's Autonomi, who bravely held out for forty days (November 12 to December 20) against greatly superior forces. Disasters also befell patriots in Liguria, the Astigiano,[12] and Bergamesco.[13] In Bologna from November 7 to 15 Gappisti and Sappisti indulged in intermittent but futile street fighting—the only major instance of urban combat apart from the climactic final insurrection.[14]

Partisan commands collapsed in several sectors, and the foe captured and killed many of the best underground officers. At the end of November he seized the entire Piedmontese GL Command and brutally slayed "Duccio" Galimberti, the valiant Cuneese Giellista. The enemy captured the Regional Commands in Venetia and Liguria. Later in the winter he nabbed most of

---

OM/B-II, cited by Mario Giovana, "La campagna invernale '44–'45," *MLI*, No. 48 (1957), p. 5.

[10] See Nardo Dunchi, *Memorie partigiane* (Florence, 1957); Battaglia, *Un uomo, un partigiano*, p. 144.

[11] Pietro Ferraro, "La disperata lotta nelle prealpi venete," *Mercurio* (*Anche l'Italia ha vinto*), II, No. 16 (Dec. 1945), pp. 51–66. Ferraro was a GL leader in this region. His statistics of casualties suffered by partisans in the twenty-month struggle in the Venetian Pre-Alps show that of some 350,000 male inhabitants of all ages, the Garibaldi "Friuli" and the "Osoppo" together accounted for 22,000 patriots, of whom 1,585 died in combat, 1,200 were wounded, 450 scattered, and 315 condemned to death. All told, the Friuli and Carnia zones suffered 6,000 partisans interned and 15,000 arrested. Reprisals destroyed 7 communes. Refugees numbered 15,000. The Grappa units, numbering 1,700 men, suffered 264 condemned to death. In Belluno province, out of 97,000 males, there were 7,000 partisans, 7,000 internees, and 1,667 political deportees. Salvadori, *SRI*, pp. 158, 160, 169.

[12] Raimondo Luraghi, "La zona libera del Basso Astigiano nei documenti dell'Archivio Storico della Resistenza di Torino," *MLI*, No. 48 (1957), pp. 31–41.

[13] Battaglia, *SRI*, pp. 434–449.

[14] *Ibid.*, p. 467.

the military technicians of the CVL, stole the plans for the Milanese insurrection, and executed Sergio Kasman, Giellista underground commandant of the Milan Piazza.[15]

General Alexander's message

Amid these unparalleled calamities, the OWI Radio "Italia Combatte" broadcast on November 13 a message by General Alexander to the patriots. His much maligned and often mis-interpreted proclamation suggested that in view of the "seasonal barrier," they "halt large-scale military operations," "save their munitions and matériel until further orders," and "prepare for a new phase of the struggle, against a new enemy, winter." [16] Probably the Allied Commander intended thereby to prevent unnecessary loss of life, since the Allies could not advance much farther "in the rains and mud." He recognized many of the hardships that would face the partisans during the months when overcast skies would make it still more difficult for the Allies to fly in supplies with any regularity. On the other hand, he did not preclude the possibility of small-scale actions, intelligence-gathering, and even large-scale operations if the Germans should be forced into general retreat. In the calmer postwar period Parri was able to take a rather charitable view of the Allied recommendation, attributing it not to any subversive aim but rather to an inability by the Allied commanders to appreciate what would be its repercussions. Rightly he has cautioned that there was never just "one" Allied policy toward the Resistenza Armata but many competing ones operating on different levels.[17]

Quite likely General Alexander did not foresee that his infelicitously phrased announcement of the halt of major Allied operations would in effect give the enemy a "go-ahead" to annihilate the patriots. Certainly in the face of such onslaughts it was impossible for them to hibernate and conserve their ammunition as Alexander had recommended; and if they went "home," almost surely they would be spotted and arrested.[18]

[15] Pestalozza (ed.), *Il processo alla "Muti,"* p. 37 ff.

[16] See text in "Il proclama Alexander e l'atteggiamento della Resistenza all'inizio dell'inverno 1944–45," *MLI*, No. 26 (1953), pp. 25–26; printed also in Catalano, *Storia del CLNAI*, pp. 284–285; cf. *NYT*, Nov. 14, 1944, 10:1–2.

[17] Parri, "Intervento," *MLI*, No. 51/52 (1958), pp. 195–196.

[18] *NYT*, Nov. 18, 1944, 8:6; Nov. 19, 11:4; Nov. 20, 8:2; Nov. 23, 22:1; Nov. 26, 23:5.

With these thoughts in mind, editors of such Rome party organs as *Italia Libera* and *Unità* dashed off protest after protest. Many expressed the view that the British, suddenly involved in a serious crisis with the Greek underground EAM/ELAS, deliberately intended to sabotage the political goals of the Italian leftists. Such censurers noted that Alexander had omitted any mention either of the CLNAI or CVL in the broadcast. That this could have been a simple oversight seemed incredible to Italians who knew something of the bureaucratic procedure pursued in drafting significant Allied policy papers.

By November the Anglo-Americans thought they had good reason to be fearful of the intentions of the Communists everywhere in Europe; conversely, the left wing of the Resistenza had reason to suspect that the Allies (especially the British) were being less than candid in their public utterances. Churchill and many high Allied officials were deeply disturbed by the Soviet attitude during the tragic uprising of the Polish Home Army in Warsaw between August and October and by the Kremlin's continuing support of the Communistic Lublin Committee against the British-recognized Polish Government-in-Exile. They were concerned too by evidence of Soviet highhandedness in Rumania and Bulgaria; by Tito's sudden flight in October to Moscow without prior notice to the British; by the behavior of certain Resistance factions in liberated France and Belgium; and, most disturbing of all, by the failure of the Communist-dominated EAM/ELAS to disarm after the British landed in Greece in October—a crisis that erupted into bitter fighting by December 3.[19]

As Major Salvadori of SF has explained apropos of this period, many British leaders had come to the conclusion that they them-

---

[19] Two mutinies by Greek military forces in Egypt had led the British late in the summer of 1944 to cut sharply their supplies to the antiroyalist, Communist-dominated EAM/ELAS. Instead, the British decided to throw their chief support to the King's government-in-exile. On September 26 the "Caserta Agreement" was signed by the British, Premier Papandreou, and representatives of the rival ELAS and Nationalist underground forces, whereby all guerrilla groups would place themselves under the orders of the Greek government, which in turn would be under the orders of British General Scobie. Yet just a few weeks after the British landed in October, EAM/ELAS rebelled, and by December it was engaged in full-scale civil war with royalist elements and with the British. Churchill, *Triumph and Tragedy*, pp. 108–114, 283–325; Ehrman, *Grand Strategy*, v, 86–87, 386; vi, 53–55, 57–64.

selves had contributed to Communist strength in Greece and Yugoslavia by listening to the glowing reports of their own liaison officers; thus they greatly feared that at war's end power in northern Italy "would fall probably into the hands, not of those who were supported by the majority of the population, but of those who had at their disposal rifles and machine guns." [20] Harold Caccia's advice to the AC, printed in the Commission's *Weekly Bulletin* of October 15, suggested the new policy: "Publicity on Patriot activities would now be definitely played down particularly behind the Allied lines." News releases should, instead, give more coverage to the expanding Italian Corps of Liberation.[21]

Against this backdrop of depressing events, quite a number of partisans from Emilia-Romagna, still attired in summer shorts and shoes, slipped across the lines at the rate of fifty or sixty a night to join the Allies near Florence; but most of the hungry and ill-clad fighters—many suffering from rheumatism and respiratory ailments—had no such possibility. Shortage of funds and matériel was so grave in Piedmont that there was serious discussion of furloughing many resistants: the PLI, DC, PSIUP, and General Trabucchi leaned toward this action, but the PCI and Pd'A were oppugnant.[22] In many sections Mussolini's amnesty bids, reiterated regularly between October 28 and November 10, caused defections; fear of reprisals produced others. By December desertions for one cause or another had reduced total Resistenza enrollment to some 80,000. Thus the underground faced its supreme crisis. There was even danger that it might collapse altogether. That it did not was proof of the stubbornness of its hard core.[23]

Seeking to stave off a debacle, the PCI held in Milan a secret national conference of its insurrectional triumvirate in order to assess the year's labors and future objectives; and at the end of November Longo went so far as to issue his own "clarification" of Alexander's message, declaring that it did not mean cessation of activity for the whole winter but just till the onset of a hard

[20] Salvadori, *Resistenza ed azione*, p. 263; Salvadori, SRI, p. 129; Harris, *Allied Military Administration of Italy*, p. 274 ff.; Catalano, *Storia del CLNAI*, p. 336.
[21] Cited by Kogan, *Italy and the Allies*, p. 106.
[22] Giovana, "La campagna invernale '44–'45," MLI, No. 48 (1957), pp. 8–12.
[23] Vittorio Foà, "La crisi della Resistenza prima della Liberazione," *Il Ponte*, VII (1947), p. 986; Amicucci, *I 600 giorni di Mussolini*, p. 224.

freeze.[24] The new order-of-the-day became "Struggle against the cold, hunger, and terror!" In Emilia civilians competed in gathering clothing and equipment for the patriots during "Partisans' Week" in November.[25] When the first snow fell, Resistance chieftains ordered their men to descend from the mountains wherever these were "inhospitable" and to regroup in smaller but connected units near small villages on the plain. This *pianurizzazione* of the Resistance was one of the noteworthy tactical innovations of the war. During the winter new-type brigades were organized on the flat lands, and with great mobility they carried out flank attacks, ambushes, and sabotage.[26]

To add to the complications, some German truce-feelers (soon to increase) reached the CLNAI late in October and November. These suggested that the patriots refrain from any collective action which might impede their withdrawal; in return, the Germans would limit property destruction to railway lines.[27] Though this sounded good to many, CLNAI leftists bitterly denounced it. Some of them wished to go further and liquidate industrialists doing business with the foe, impose a "war levy" upon all businessmen in order to subsidize the hard-pressed underground, embark upon a rigorous purge of thousands of bureaucrats, and convert the CLNAI into an "Extraordinary Secret Government." For a few weeks it seemed as if the radicals might prevail.[28]

Despite the foul weather and depressing tone of General Alexander's message, the Allies hoped to keep up pressure on the Italian front. A new directive from the Combined Chiefs of Staff

[24] Longo, *Sulla via dell'insurrezione nazionale*, pp. 297–338; Secchia, *I Comunisti e l'insurrezione*, pp. 285–318; "Il proclama Alexander e l'attegiamento della Resistenza all'inizio dell'inverno 1944–45," MLI, No. 26 (1953), pp. 28–50; Cadorna's comments in *ibid.*, No. 28/29 (1954), 122–124; *Atti del CG/CVL*, No. 100 (Dec. 27), pp. 154–160; Carli-Ballola, *Sdr*, pp. 263–265.

[25] Longo, *Un popolo alla macchia*, p. 352.

[26] *Atti del CG/CVL*, No. 69 (Oct. 8) and No. 82 (Oct. 28), pp. 116, 130–131; Giovana, "La campagna invernale '44–'45," MLI, No. 48 (1957), pp. 12–13; Catalano, *Storia del CLNAI*, p. 324; Carli-Ballola, *Sdr*, pp. 253–256; Battaglia, *SRI*, pp. 467–473.

[27] *Ibid.*, p. 462; Rudolf Rahn, *Ambasciatore di Hitler a Vichy e a Salò* (Milan, 1950), p. 329; Ildefonso Cardinale Schuster, *Gli ultimi tempi di un regime* (Milan, 1946), pp. 86, 92, 108–113; Lanfranchi, *La resa degli ottocentomila*, pp. 24–27, 59 ff.; Carli-Ballola, *Sdr*, pp. 239–240, 267–270; Catalano, *Storia del CLNAI*, pp. 316–319, 370–371.

[28] *Ibid.*, pp. 300–302, 322–323; Valiani, *Tutte le strade conducono a Roma*, pp. 309–310.

to the Supreme Commander in the Mediterranean Theater on December 2, rejecting any major Balkan operation, declared the "immediate objective should be to capture Bologna, then to secure the general line Ravenna-Bologna-Spezia and thereafter continue operations with a view to containing Kesselring's army." [29] This "offensive-defensive" policy was essentially successful. Kesselring had to keep as many men in Italy in January 1945 as he had had there in November.[30]

Meanwhile, Allied drops to the patriots reached new records in November and December as a result of the transfer to Tuscany of two American Troop Carrier Groups (62nd and 64th) and the 859th Bombardment Squadron from England. Between November 22 and January 9 the 62nd dropped 494 short tons in northwestern Italy. The Polish 301st Squadron and the RAF 205th Bombardment Group and 148th Squadron helped significantly, but it was AAF units which "delivered practically all of the air-borne supplies reaching the Italian Partisans after November 1944." Throughout the entire Italian campaign Americans flew 70 per cent of the completed sorties and dropped 68 per cent of the tonnage; they completed 2,646 of 4,268 attempted sorties to Italian targets and dropped 6,490 short tons of supplies. Deliveries to Yugoslavia continued to be far greater than those to northern Italy, though the discrepancy lessened steadily. In the last weeks of 1944 supply drops were concentrated in the Ligurian and Maritime Alps and especially west of Modena and north of Pisa, Lucca, and Pistoia, where officials estimated that partisans kept some 40,000 second- and third-rate enemy troops on police duty.[31] When the foe triggered a major offensive at year's end in the Garfagnana mountains and threatened Lucca and Tuscany, some 7,000 patriots, reinforced by supply drops and liaison personnel, resisted doggedly and eventually regrouped northwest of LaSpezia.[32] Target "Lifton," some twenty-five miles north of LaSpezia, received special attention in those days, but

[29] Cited in Ehrman, *Grand Strategy*, vi, 56.
[30] *Ibid.*, pp. 83–84.
[31] "Air Support for the Underground," *The Army Air Forces in World War II*, iii, 515–517.
[32] Battaglia, *SRI*, p. 466. In this sector British Major Gordon Lett, an ex-PW, led a polyglot partisan group; cf. his *Rossano* (*An Adventure of the Italian Resistance*).

bad weather and enemy interference prevented the planes from dropping more than sixteen tons. At year's end activity increased greatly in the Veneto.[33]

CLNAI mission to the South

For months Parri had been anxious to persuade top Allied officials to recognize the CLNAI formally as the only truly effective political authority behind the lines; to obtain desperately needed funds for the nearly bankrupt patriot movement (funds of the disbanded Fourth Army had run out in July); and to maximize the military effort of the Italian patriots in conjunction with the Allies.[34] Hitherto Allied authorities had refused to accord any form of political recognition to the CLNAI on grounds that to do so would make more difficult the establishment of AMG when northern Italy eventually was freed. By autumn, however, the CLNAI obviously was expanding its prestige and power; moreover, Allied liaison officers had begun to work with many of the patriot brigades, and it seemed clearer that these were fairly well co-ordinated by the CLNAI. Thus the CLNAI considered the moment propitious to renew the request.

Early in October 1944 it decided to send Parri to Allied Force Headquarters. Partly because of the squabble over General Cadorna's status in the CG/CVL, rightists tried to send, instead, the CLNAI banker-president Pizzoni. Allied agents in Switzerland helped settle this dispute in a preliminary conference with Pizzoni and Valiani on October 25.[35] These officers suggested that the mission include both Pizzoni and Parri, and also Sogno ("Franchi"). The latter, of course, was not a member of the CLNAI but he was a vigorous spokesman for the Autonomi and was trusted by the Allies. The CLNAI agreed to this but also added Communist Giancarlo Pajetta ("Mare"), substituting for Longo. The intelligence officers did not seem overjoyed at this but did not cavil inasmuch as the Garibaldini were the largest segment of the underground; in any case, they did not wish to

[33] *Army Air Forces in World War II*, III, 516.

[34] Parri, "Intervento," *MLI*, No. 52/53 (1958), pp. 193-194.

[35] This was the conference that suggested terminating the Cadorna imbroglio so that the CVL could take over temporary command of northwestern Italy in case of a successful Allied drive into Venetia that autumn. *Cf. supra*, Ch. x, Clarification of General Cadorna's status; Valiani, *Tutte le strade conducono a Roma*, pp. 201-202, 257, 293-300.

jeopardize anti-Fascist solidarity. The DC and PLI did not complain about their exclusion, but the PSIUP was miffed.[36]

In mid-November the four delegates rendezvoused in Lugano and Berne. Thence they were "transported by a delicate, precise and secret mechanism"[37] via Geneva, Annemasse, and Lyon to Naples. They experienced immediate disillusionment. The Neapolitans seemed blissfully unconcerned about the northern struggle; the local prefect told them his chief problem was getting streetcar service restored. In Rome Premier Bonomi received the emissaries "with somewhat formal courtesy"; he seemed to be preoccupied with the emergent political crisis of his government and stressed its impotence in the face of the Allied Commission. The Northerners were left to carry on alone their talks with Anglo-American leaders.[38]

On November 23 they had their first meeting with British General H. Maitland Wilson, Supreme Allied Commander, MTO. Others present included Commander Holdsworth, Chief of British SF Operations in Italy; American Major General Stawell, in charge of subversive operations in the Mediterranean Theater (SOMTO), who had drawn up a long policy paper as a basis for discussion; and a stenographer.[39] The conference was amicable and almost every kind of question was discussed. To the delegation's request that the CLNAI be recognized as the co-ordinating agency and promoter of the liberation struggle and assured adequate financial support, General Wilson promised that the AC would soon suggest to the Italian government that the time had come to recognize the CLNAI officially. He seemed to react favorably to Pizzoni's suggestion that because of inflation the subsidy be increased to at least 160,000,000 lire per month instead of 100,000,000—the figure mentioned in Stawell's paper.[40] At that time, it should be recalled, the official exchange

---

[36] Sogno, *Guerra senza bandiera*, pp. 264–279; Parri, *MLI*, No. 1 (1949), pp. 18–19; Cadorna, *La Riscossa*, pp. 179–180; Archivio CLNAI, xxiv/5 and Archivio CVL, xxx/8, cited by Catalano, *Storia del CLNAI*, pp. 326–329; Giorgio Vaccarino, "I rapporti con gli alleati e la missione al sud (1943–1944)," *MLI*, No. 52/53 (1958), pp. 50–71.

[37] Parri, *MLI*, No. 1 (1949), p. 18.

[38] *Ibid.*, pp. 18–19; Sogno, *Guerra senza bandiera*, pp. 279–286; Catalano, *Storia del CLNAI*, pp. 329–330; and Catalano, "La missione del CLNAI al Sud," *MLI*, No. 36 (1955), pp. 3–43.

[39] Harris, *Allied Military Administration of Italy*, pp. 275–276.

[40] Pizzoni, "Il finanziamento della Resistenza," *MLI*, No. 24 (1953), p. 53.

rate in the South was 100 lire to the dollar. Allied officials estimated that the cost per month of maintaining one partisan away from his home district rose from 1,000 to 3,000 lire between June and December 1944.[41]

In view of the redeployment of so many Allied troops to France and of Alexander's broadcast, Parri could not hope to maximize the military effort at this juncture. General Wilson assured him that he intended to aid the patriots to the limit of his ability in order to keep them busy during the winter. But at the same time he recommended that because of the practical factors of bad weather and shortage of planes and supplies, they organize chiefly for action at the moment the Germans evacuated the peninsula. Commander Holdsworth professed unhappiness over the wording of Alexander's broadcast of the 13th and agreed that it was impractical "to put brakes on" patriots who operated far from their homes. Uninterrupted operations were imperative, he agreed. The Resistance leaders were pleased by much of the discussion but were disturbed by Allied insistence upon quick disarmament of the patriots after liberation.[42]

With Stawell's encouragement,[43] the delegation decided to launch parallel discussions with Premier Bonomi in the hope of persuading his cabinet to recognize officially and in the broadest possible form the CLNAI and CVL, and thus achieve a triangular agreement. Parri was anxious to have the Bonomi government take action even before the Allies did. Such recognition would facilitate granting status to the patriots comparable to that enjoyed by members of the Italian Armed Forces. The delegation submitted a memorandum expressing its desires. It was clear, though, that Bonomi was unenthusiastic.[44] To make matters worse, Rome's long-simmering political crisis boiled over, with the aged premier tendering his resignation on the 25th. This weakened the Northerners' bargaining position. Knowing they held the trumps, the Allied officials thereafter ponderously drafted a document defining their relationship with the CLNAI in a way that would satisfy their own requirements for "security."

[41] OSS, R. & A. Branch, No. 2993, "The Contributions of the Italian Partisans to the Allied War Effort," p. 6; cf. Agosti's estimates in Cadorna, La Riscossa, pp. 321-341.
[42] Archivio CLNAI, xxv/11.
[43] Harris, Allied Military Administration of Italy, p. 276.
[44] The memorandum is cited in Catalano, Storia del CLNAI, pp. 332-336.

Fall of Bonomi's government

The collapse of the Bonomi government was precipitated not only by British maneuvers and the imbroglio over Scoccimarro's attempt to broaden the purge [45] but by the vexing problem of the Monarchy's relationship to the CLN's. Spearheaded by Nenni, the leftists sought to have the local CLN's rather than the Rome government name prefects, mayors, police chiefs, and communal councils—something already being done on a limited scale by the covert northern CLN's. Obviously an entire philosophy of government was at stake. The issue had been graphically posed in Florence in the early autumn when the Tuscan CLN had objected vehemently to a provincial prefect named by Rome.[46]

Compounding the difficulties was the revelation in Italy that Prince Humbert had granted an audience on October 31 to *New York Times* correspondent Herbert L. Matthews, who reported him as saying that "monarchy, like all political institutions in postwar Europe, should move to the left." The Prince, who spoke fluent English, implied that Italy ought to have a liberal, democratic monarchy such as in Britain or Scandinavia. His solution to the institutional question "would be to have a plebiscite in accordance with the principles of the Atlantic Charter. . . . The Prince . . . believes that if there is a plebiscite it should represent a straight choice of republic or monarchy. Then there would be a constituent assembly to decide the exact form that the republic or monarchy would take. . . ." [47]

According to tradition, the Italian Crown was not supposed to express personal opinions. Thus when republicans learned that Premier Bonomi had approved the Prince's interview, apparently in the hope of enhancing the royalist cause, the crisis came to a head. On November 7 the cabinet proceeded to slap down both the Prince and Bonomi by reaffirming "its solemn pledge to decide the constitutional issue through the vote of a constituent assembly established by state law." [48]

Meanwhile, the aged ex-Premier Orlando came out of the shadows on the 4th to deliver a thumping royalist oration in

[45] See *supra*, Ch. x, Bonomi's "concerto for six parties."
[46] See *supra*, Ch. x, "War in a museum."
[47] NYT, Nov. 1, 1944, 1:6–7.
[48] *Ibid.*, Nov. 8, 1944.

Rome's Quirinal theater.[49] Nenni dumped more fuel on the conflagration when he appeared with Togliatti on the same platform on the 12th before an impressive, orderly crowd of 80,000 in the ruined Domitian Stadium on the Palatine and bitterly denounced the Monarchy. While Nenni cried, "All power to the CLN's!" Togliatti limited himself to more oblique references to the throne. The crowd cheered both. Afterward Nenni told correspondent Matthews to inform Humbert that "instead of going to the left . . . he is going out of Italy!" [50]

Premier Bonomi tendered his resignation on the 25th, not to the CCLN but to the Lieutenant-General of the Realm; this move enabled Prince Humbert to regain the political freedom of initiative he had lost in June. To anguished cries of the PSIUP and Pd'A that the CCLN had "designated" him for the premiership in June whereas the Lieutenant-General had merely "invested" him, Bonomi replied that he was submitting his resignation to the man who had charged him with forming a government; he contended that it would be absurd to submit the letter to himself as President of the CCLN. Bonomi patently was dissociating himself from any conception of a new political order based on supremacy of the CLN over the old state apparatus. He argued that since he now represented the nation and not just the parties, he was responsible to the Head of the State. The PLI backed him up. That same night Prince Humbert held his first consultations regarding a successor. Pointedly he talked first with Orlando and Della Torretta, "heads" of the nonexistent Parliament, rather than with any CLN official.[51]

The CCLN met on the 26th to search for a formula on which to base a new cabinet. The three leftist parties demanded that this cabinet "be the emanation of the CLN"; the PLI desired only that it "have the support of the CLN." When the DC and DL threw their weight behind the leftists, the PLI at last gave in and Bonomi indicated his approval. Thus the CCLN preserved its *de facto* position.

The next problem was composition of the cabinet. The Pd'A and PSIUP got the CCLN to suggest Sforza for premier or, at

---

[49] *Ibid.*, Nov. 5, 1944.
[50] Matthews, *Education of a Correspondent*, pp. 488–489; NYT, Nov. 13, 1944, 1:4.
[51] Benedetto Croce, *Pagine politiche (luglio–dicembre 1944)* (Bari, 1945), p. 80; Kogan, *Italy and the Allies*, pp. 92–93.

the very least, foreign minister. As in June, Churchill blocked Sforza from access to such curule chairs—this time publicly, and again without prior consultation with Washington.[52] In Commons, Eden asserted that Sforza had worked against the Bonomi government (a charge that Bonomi quickly scotched), and he went on to say it was "easy" to be an exile. Such ill-considered words made Sforza a hero-martyr in Italy and angered the American State Department, which had accepted Sforza as Italian ambassador-delegate. Explaining his stand, Churchill cabled Washington on December 4 that Sforza had not only been intriguing against the Monarchy but was a mischief-maker in general. Next day the new Secretary of State Edward R. Stettinius, Jr., issued a public announcement that Washington was not opposed to Sforza and expected Italians to "work out their problems of government along democratic lines without influence from the outside."[53] Americans voiced similar criticism of current British intervention in Greek and Belgian political crises. Churchill remained obdurate; in Parliament on December 8 he declared, "We do not trust the man [Sforza], we do not think he is a true and trustworthy man, nor do we put the slightest confidence in any Government of which he is a dominating member."[54] Under the circumstances, Sforza's candidacy had to be shelved, much to the chagrin of the Pd'A and PSIUP.

The three rightist currents were now quite willing to back "England's man," Bonomi, in a new government. Suddenly Togliatti's Communists joined them. The Kremlin's factor thus repeated with the same ductility the maneuver he had used to save Premier Badoglio eight months before. Doubtless Togliatti appreciated Bonomi's tactful approach to the PCI as a *partito di massa* with "special responsibility," but probably the chief reason behind his decision was that Stalin would be disturbed by any move that might reduce the war effort against Germany. Italian Communism's best interests could be served by keeping a strategic position within the government. Having done the British a favor in Italy, Stalin could hope too for Western acceptance of his protégé governments in eastern Europe.

A *combinazione* was now possible. Bonomi promised to base

[52] Hull, *Memoirs*, II, 1568.
[53] Edward R. Stettinius, Jr., *Roosevelt and the Russians: The Yalta Conference* (Garden City, 1949), p. 51; NYT, Dec. 6, 1944, 1:1.
[54] Churchill, *The Dawn of Liberation*, p. 360.

his new cabinet on the CLN program but rejected a Socialist demand that he present his resignation to the CCLN. He also resigned the presidency of the latter body, to be surrogated there by Sforza. The PSIUP was left in a crisis. Despite the "unity of action" pact with the PCI, Nenni hesitated to follow Togliatti's move, while Saragat and Silone of the reformist wing adamantly fought any dilution of CLN primacy and got the Party Executive Committee to vote against joining the new government.[55] The Pd'A, which had stoutly pushed Sforza, also boycotted the new government, though Valiani and Spinelli in the North both favored participation in order to checkmate the PCI.[56] While both the PSIUP and Pd'A remained in the CCLN, their absence from the government was an ill-omen of what was to happen to Italy's democratic left in the postwar era. Ever more frustrated in their attempts to renovate the Italian state, leftist leaders reverted to politics in its least attractive form, ceaselessly disputing among themselves and spinning their ideological gossamers. In the liberated provinces the public merely yawned.[57]

The center of gravity of the new quadripartite government shifted perceptibly to the right. The atmosphere of the capital took on the redolence of the Giolittian age. Humbert's position was strengthened; the CLN's weakened. The oath formula remained the same as in June. Premier Bonomi kept the key Interior Ministry but relinquished the Foreign Office to the escalating Alcide DeGasperi (DC). Togliatti (PCI) and the 72-year-old Neapolitan Giulio Rodinò (DC) became Vice-Premiers. The latter had been a Minister of Justice and of War in pre-Mussolini days. Another new personality was Manlio Brosio (PLI General Secretary from Turin), assigned a Ministry without Portfolio. He had served on a special committee in 1924 to investigate Matteotti's murder. One signal innovation was a Ministry of Occupied Italy, with military, economic, and public welfare subsections. This strategic post went to Mauro Scoccimarro (PCI), who explained its functions as, first, to promote unity

[55] Between October and November important changes occurred in the PSIUP's vice-secretariat. Pertini had been seized by the Germans, and Andreoni resigned because of his opposition to close partnership with the PCI. Nenni thereupon replaced them with Giuliano Vassalli and Oreste Lizzadri, the latter a stout advocate of "fusion" with the PCI. Emiliani, *Dieci anni perduti*, p. 23, n. 20.
[56] Catalano, *Storia del CLNAI*, pp. 310–311.
[57] Hughes, *The United States and Italy*, p. 137; NYT, Dec. 9, 1944, 6:2.

among all resistants under General Cadorna, and, second, to serve as intermediary between the CLNAI and the Allies in matters pertaining to prosecution of the war and treatment of partisans and local CLN's. After a rather slow start it began a program of publicity for the Resistenza. Since many communications with the North were discussed in this ministry, the Pd'A and PSIUP often found themselves at a disadvantage during the crucial last months of the war. In time, many of their leaders came to realize they had blundered in staying out of the new cabinet; they had difficulty explaining their "moral" issue. Others in the cabinet included the Neapolitan lawyer-educator, Vincenzo Arangio-Ruiz (PLI), Minister of Education; Francesco Cerabona (DL), Minister of Transportation; Meuccio Ruini (DL), Minister of Public Works; Mario Cevolotto (DL), Minister of Posts and Telegraphs; Carlo Scialoia (DL), Minister of Air; and Antonio Pesenti (PCI), Minister of Finance.[58]

In view of Churchill's personal attacks, Sforza soon resigned as High Commissioner of Expurgation, declined an appointment as the ambassador to the United States, and sought to "clarify" the record regarding Churchill's allegations.[59] Though Scoccimarro was succeeded by another Communist (Ruggiero Grieco) and four new Assistant High Commissioners were named to work directly under Premier Bonomi, the purge program ground to a near halt by year's end. The conservatives had triumphed; the purge machinery ceased to be a political weapon and was turned over to the jurists who, understandably, were reluctant to apply *ex post facto* legislation.[60]

CLNAI-Allied agreement of December 7, 1944

The cabinet crisis stiffened the Allied attitude toward the CLNAI delegation. So did the rapidly expanding clash between the British and Greek EAM/ELAS underground. "The actions

[58] Harris, *Allied Military Administration of Italy*, pp. 214–216; Kogan, *Italy and the Allies*, pp. 96–97; Kogan, "The Action Party and the Institutional Question," *Western Political Quarterly*, VI (1953), pp. 275–295; Andreotti, *Concerto a sei voci*, pp. 26–28; OSS, R. & A. Branch, No. 2993, "The Contribution of the Italian Partisans to the Allied War Effort," pp. 16–17; Cesare Moscone, *La legislazione partigiana* (Turin, 1947), pp. 5–6.

[59] NYT, Dec. 12, 1944, 7:1.

[60] Kogan, *Italy and the Allies*, p. 97.

involving the ELAS in Greece bore down upon us like an incubus," Parri has recalled.[61] Major Salvadori of SF helped prepare the first draft of the Allied-CLNAI accord, a version that was somewhat more palatable to the Northerners than the ultimate one.[62] As the bureaucratic processing dragged on, the Allies put more stress upon getting ironclad assurances. They insisted that the patriots must abide by all of the 1943 armistice clauses (which were revealed to them), obey all orders issued by the Allies, stay in the struggle in full force to the very end, concentrate upon safeguarding the country's economic resources, and agree to rapid disarmament after liberation. The Allies purposely excluded any kind of political recognition of the CLNAI and specifically insisted that the latter must agree to recognize AMG as the postwar governing authority in the North.[63]

On December 7 in Rome's Grand Hotel the Allies presented the CLNAI with the final version of the document. "On one side, imposing, majestic as a proconsul, Sir Maitland Wilson, on the other we four," Parri has reminisced; "a glass of something, a few words, a handshake: then the signature. . . . At one point we asked ourselves if we should sign. But we signed. What we had obtained was too great, too important to be jeopardized by other considerations." [64]

Indeed, the subsidies alone, totalling eventually some 1,100,-000,000 lire, justified it. In addition, the Allies were to deliver by air and water several thousand tons of food, clothing, arms, and ammunition between January 1 and May 2, 1945.[65] Dr. Pizzoni, who had been manager for years of Credito Italiano, arranged for the Allies to turn over the money to the Rome branches of his institution and the Banca Commerciale Italiana. Only their top personnel had any inkling of what Pizzoni was up to. Later, after his circuitous return, he told the directors of the Milanese

---

[61] Parri, "Gli inizi della Resistenza," *MLI*, No. 34/35 (1955), p. 24; Ehrman, *Grand Strategy*, VI, 57–64.

[62] Salvadori, *Resistenza ed azione*, p. 263.

[63] Harris, *Allied Military Administration of Italy*, pp. 276–277.

[64] Parri, *MLI*, No. 1 (1949), pp. 23–24; Parri, *MLI*, No. 52/53 (1958), pp. 193–196; Sogno, *Guerra senza bandiera*, p. 288.

[65] Allied Forces, Mediterranean Theatre, *The Italian Campaign, 12th December 1944 to 2nd May 1945: A Report to the Combined Chiefs of Staff by the Supreme Allied Commander Mediterranean, Field-Marshal the Viscount Alexander of Tunis* (London, 1951), p. 19.

offices of these same houses about the deposits and requested permission to draw checks for similar amounts. They took him at his word and handed over the huge sums. The Germans became suspicious and sent their own auditors into the banks. By expert juggling of the books, however, the Milanese banks offered plausible reasons for having released the sums. In the long run, of course, the funds furnished to the patriots by the Allies were added to the general occupation costs for which Italy was liable as a defeated power.[66]

The full text of the important secret agreement of December 7 read: [67]

1. The Supreme Allied Commander wishes the utmost military cooperation to be established and maintained among the elements which are active in the resistance movement. The CLNAI will establish and maintain such cooperation as will bring together all active elements in the resistance movement whether they belong to the CLNAI anti-fascist parties or to other anti-fascist organizations.

2. During the period of enemy occupation the GENERAL COMMAND OF THE VOLUNTEERS OF LIBERTY (being the military command of the CLNAI) will, on behalf of the CLNAI, carry out all instructions of the Commander-in-Chief, AAI., acting under the authority of the Supreme Allied Commander. It is in general the wish of the SUPREME ALLIED COMMANDER that particular care should be given to all measures which will safeguard the economic resources of the territory against scorching, demolitions and like depradations by the enemy.

3. The Military Head of the General Command of the Volunteers of Liberty (being the military command of the CLNAI) must be an officer acceptable to the Commander-in-Chief, AAI., acting under the authority of the Supreme Allied Commander.

4. When the enemy withdraws from territory occupied by them the CLNAI will exercise its best endeavours to maintain law and order and to continue the safeguarding of the economic resources of the country until such time as Allied Military Government is established. Immediately upon the establishment of Allied Military Government, CLNAI will recognize Allied Military Government and

---

[66] Pizzoni, "Il finanziamento della Resistenza," *MLI*, No. 24 (1953), p. 53 ff.; *NYT*, Jan. 5, 1958, "Alfredo Pizzoni, Banker, Dead."

[67] A photostatic copy is printed in Mario Niccoli's article, "Resistenza," *Enciclopedia Italiana, 1938–1948, Appendice II, I–Z*, p. 686. Quoted by kind permission of the editor-in-chief of the Istituto della Enciclopedia Italiana fondata da Giovanni Treccani, Rome.

will hand over to that Government all authority and powers of local government and administration previously assumed. As the enemy withdraws all components of the GENERAL COMMAND OF THE VOLUNTEERS OF LIBERTY in liberated territory will come under direct command of the Commander-in-Chief, AAI., acting under the authority of the Supreme Allied Commander, and will obey any order issued by him or by Allied Military Government on his behalf, including such orders to disband and surrender their arms, when required to do so.

5. During the period of enemy occupation in Northern Italy the utmost assistance will be given to the CLNAI in common with all other anti-fascist organizations, to meet the needs of their members who are engaged in opposing the enemy in occupied territory; a monthly contribution not exceeding 160 million lire will be made on the authority of the Supreme Allied Commander to meet the expenses of the CLNAI and all other anti-fascist organizations.

Subject to the general control of the Commander-in-Chief, AAI., acting under the authority of the Supreme Allied Commander, this sum will be apportioned to the following areas in the following ratio for the support of all anti-fascist organizations in those areas:—

LIGURIA	20
PIEDMONTE	60
LOMBARDIA	25
EMILIA	20
VENETO	35

The above sum and allocations will be subject to variations according to the requirements of the military situation: the maximum sum will be reduced proportionately as and when Provinces are liberated.

6. Allied Missions attached to the CLNAI[,] to the General Command of the Volunteers of Liberty, or to any of their components, will be consulted by them in all matters relating to armed resistance, anti-scorch and maintenance of order. Orders issued by the Commander-in-Chief, AAI., under the authority of the Supreme Allied Commander and transmitted through the missions concerned will be carried out by CLNAI, the General Command of the Volunteers of Liberty and their components.

SUPREME ALLIED COMMANDER
MEDITERRANEAN THEATRE OF OPERATIONS
[signed] H. Maitland Wilson
. . . .
General

FOR THE COMMITTEE OF NATIONAL
LIBERATION FOR NORTHERN ITALY

[signed] Pietro Longhi [Alfredo Pizzoni]
....
[signed] Maurizio   [Ferruccio Parri]
....
[signed] Mare   [Gian Carlo Pajetta]
....
[signed] E. Sogno   [Edgardo Sogno]
....

On the same day, General Wilson wrote an official letter to the CLNAI: [68]

Referring to the agreement which we have signed this day, I am pleased to note that the C.L.N.A.I. has appointed General Valenti [Cadorna] as the military head of the General Command of the Volunteers of Liberty and that Messrs Mauritzio [Parri] and Gallo [Longo] have been appointed as his joint deputy commanders.

I sincerely appreciate the excellent work which has been accomplished by the C.L.N.A.I. and its military command the Volunteers of Liberty. I hope that when the present crisis in the Italian Government is resolved early considerations may be given to the recognition of the C.L.N.A.I. as the agent of the Government in enemy occupied Italy.

Appreciating as I do the fighting qualities of the Volunteers of Liberty, I am pleased to be able to inform you that steps have been taken to enlist into the Italian Armed Forces as many suitable volunteers of high medical category as the existing ceiling for the Italian Armed Forces will allow.

I hope that these Volunteers will continue to fight with the Allies until final victory is achieved.

I have issued instructions that all Allied Missions, receiving orders from the Commander-in-Chief, A.A.I., on my behalf, will at all times act in the closest cooperation and consultation with those formations of the Volunteers of Liberty to whom they are accredited. Only in this way can our common aim be achieved.

I am glad to have had the opportunity to discuss with you so many problems of common interest, and hope the decisions reached will make our cooperation closer.

I wish you a safe return to your posts and every success in the tasks which lie ahead.

[signed] H. Maitland Wilson
GENERAL
SUPREME ALLIED COMMANDER

[68] A photostatic copy is printed in *ibid.*, p. 690; quoted by kind permission of the editor-in-chief of the Istituto della Enciclopedia Italiana fondata da Giovanni

Thus the CVL obtained recognition as the military executor of orders of the Allied Commander in Chief. Consequently, it acquired a certain official status, as did the CLNAI. About the same time the CLNAI delegation and Allied officials reached a further understanding whereby AMG, when it assumed power after liberation, would approve all appointments of prefects, mayors, councillors, et cetera, made by the CLNAI except in the case of men who failed to pass the normal security investigation. To be sure, the Allies talked disconcertingly of the advisability of naming "career" vice-prefects to avoid errors in bureaucratic procedure. Yet, all in all, the *combinazione* was as good as could be expected by the underground leaders.[69]

The latter still hoped to expand this into a tripartite accord that would bind the new Bonomi government to recognize the CLNAI in the broadest possible way. (General Wilson's accompanying letter of December 7 had not ruled this out.) The Northerners hoped that by pooling their bargaining power with that of the Rome politicians they could persuade the Allies to modify some of the Long Armistice clauses and water down the role of AMG. Unhappily for them, a welter of political developments in Athens, London, and Rome made such a triangular compact unfeasible.[70] Instead, Premier Bonomi agreed at last to sign (December 26) a bilateral accord with Pajetta (PCI), who stayed in Rome longer than Parri and the others:

"The Italian Government recognizes the Committee of National Liberation in Upper Italy (CLNAI) as the organ of the anti-Fascist parties in enemy-occupied territory.

"The Italian Government delegates the CLNAI to represent it in the struggle which the patriots have launched against the Fascists and the Germans in that part of Italy not yet liberated.

"The CLNAI agrees to act for such purpose as the delegate of the Italian Government, which is recognized by the Allied Governments as the successor of the Government which signed the armistice conditions, and is the sole legitimate authority in

Treccani, Rome. On December 12 Sir Harold Alexander, promoted to Field Marshal status, succeeded General Wilson as Supreme Allied Commander, MTO.

[69] Archivio CLNAI, xxv bis/37, report of Pizzoni, Dec. 27, 1944; *cf.* Kogan, *Italy and the Allies*, p. 107; Harris, *Allied Military Administration of Italy*, pp. 281–283 ff.

[70] Catalano, *Storia del CLNAI*, pp. 341–342.

that part of Italy which has already been, or will subsequently be, restored to the Italian Government by the Allied Military Government." [71] The CLNAI made good use of this pact.

Northern responses

In December Piedmontese underground leaders learned first-hand about some new Allied policies. British Colonel John M. Stevens was parachuted in during the first half of that month to replace Major Temple, the liaison officer who had been killed during a recent *rastrellamento*. With scant concern for the practicalities of the situation, Stevens peremptorily advised the CPLN on the 20th that he intended to "reorganize" their underground to make it "more efficient than before." In an attempt to cut the power of leftist groups, he announced his intention to reassign functions in the "Provisional Government" so that the PLI and DC would have charge of public order and schools; the PSIUP and PCI of economic affairs; and the Pd'A of administration of justice and supervision of public health. In the military field he proposed to divide Piedmont into two independent sectors (centered, respectively, in the Biellese and Langhe), each under a mission head and organized as "bases" for sabotage and troop-carrying planes. Political commissars would be relegated to the role of intelligence reporters and recruiters of local rural guides. The colonel claimed the untrammeled right to judge leaders and subalterns without explanations to anyone. He insisted that the CPLN decide upon his plan before the 28th.

Such behavior by a foreigner naturally aroused hostility, and Stevens was challenged by both the Garibaldini and Autonomi in the Langhe. Finally, the CPLN tactfully but firmly rejected his effort to break up their political solidarity. All that he could obtain was a promise that a single commander for the underground would be nominated—a problem which had long oc-

[71] The AC insisted upon adding the long clause in the third paragraph. Archivio CLNAI, xxiv/8; Parri, "I protocolli di Roma," *MLI*, No. 1 (1949), p. 27; Kogan, *Italy and the Allies*, p. 107.

In a somewhat embarrassing footnote to these actions, the Allies ordered the Bonomi government to issue a press release on December 30 clarifying an erroneous earlier statement by Scoccimarro that the Allies had "recognized" the CLNAI as the "organ representing all anti-Fascist parties" in enemy-occupied territory. *NYT*, Dec. 31, 1944, 11:1; Harris, *Allied Military Administration of Italy*, p. 277.

cupied the CLNAI, and which was closely connected with unification of the clandestine forces.[72]

Meanwhile, Parri, Pizzoni, and Sogno had left Allied Headquarters. They stopped off in Lyon and Upper Savoy between December 17 and 20. Taking advantage of their layover, they talked at some length with French and Anglo-American officials and sought to smooth over some of the difficulties that had arisen regarding the status of Val d'Aosta and of Italian units dislocated across the border. They succeeded in paving the way for the repatriation of those forces and agreed that the historian Professor Federico Chabod (PLI), who had made his way to Grenoble,[73] should head the Aosta CLN. Unfortunately, only a few dozen tons of military supplies from France actually were moved overland to the Italian patriots that winter.[74]

While passing through Switzerland the Resistance leaders were warned by SF and OSS that the Germans knew of their absence and had increased surveillance of the border. Pizzoni made his way back to Milan safely just before Christmas, while on Christmas Day Parri and Sogno hiked across the high Limidario Pass—no easy task for an older man like Parri—into Val Cannobina, held by patriots of the Ossola Command. Crossing Lake Maggiore in a small boat, they caught a train, Parri proceeding to Milan, Sogno to Novara.[75]

The CLNAI assembled quickly to hear the delegates' report. Its initial reaction seemed favorable, but by January 12, 1945, Pertini and Marzola (PSIUP) were denouncing Sogno's courtesy call in Rome upon the Lieutenant-General of the Realm and the delegation's failure to co-ordinate its negotiations with the Rome CCLN. Furthermore, they objected to the delegation's acquiescence in the armistice clauses. The other committeemen at last persuaded the PSIUP not to publicize these objections lest they jeopardize Allied subsidization.[76]

[72] Giovana, MLI, No. 48 (1957), pp. 23–30; regarding Stevens, see Farran, Winged Dagger, pp. 261, 278, 292, 300, 310.
[73] A. and E. Passerin d'Entrèves, "Federico Chabod e la valle d'Aosta," Rivista storica italiana, LXXII (1960), pp. 793–809.
[74] Catalano, Storia del CLNAI, pp. 344–348; Harris, Allied Military Administration of Italy, p. 317.
[75] Sogno, Guerra senza bandiera, pp. 289–294.
[76] Catalano, Storia del CLNAI, pp. 348–350; Valiani, Tutte le strade conducono a Roma, pp. 313–314; Carli-Ballola, Sdr, p. 246.

A few weeks later the Socialists and Actionists voiced louder dismay when they learned the nature of the Bonomi-Pajetta agreement of December 26. The Allied-imposed phraseology implying inferiority of the CLNAI as a mere "delegate" of the Rome government greatly displeased them, though they conceded that Pajetta had been in an unenviable bargaining position. On February 12 the CLNAI decided that, in view of the displeasure with the form of Bonomi's delegation of authority to them, they would give their own interpretation to the document.[77]

Parri had scarcely returned to Milan when, on December 31, he was arrested as he left his lodging at Via Monti 92. His capture was a first-rate calamity because so many activities revolved about him. The Germans treated Parri with special consideration, for they sensed the possibility of using him as a pawn in eventual armistice negotiations. The GL patriarch remained a prisoner in Milan and Verona until March 1945.[78] Sogno and some other patriots endeavored to rescue Parri, only to be nabbed themselves.[79] Solari ("Somma") acted as Parri's replacement in the CG/CVL. Others in the CG/CVL to fall afoul of the enemy during the midwinter included Mattei (DC), Colonel Palombo, and seven staff members—a loss that was partially counterbalanced by the escape of Major Argenton and Mattei. Nevertheless, the CG/CVL remained in a serious predicament during the first months of 1945.[80]

Another calamity was reported from Genoa. There, on February 6, Luciano Bolis, the Pd'A secretary and GL regional inspector, was arrested. After enduring brutal tortures he cut his own wrists in a vain attempt at suicide. Eventually he was res-

[77] Catalano, *Storia del CLNAI*, pp. 343–344.

[78] In 1953 the neo-fascistic MSI (Italian Social Movement) accused Parri of "betraying" the partisans to the Germans while he was a prisoner. These patently ridiculous charges resulted in a curious trial at which Italians of all political beliefs as well as German SS General Wolff offered testimony. After fifteen sessions the court decided it lacked territorial jurisdiction. That such defamation of an ex-premier whose whole life had been dedicated to anti-Fascism could be taken half seriously was in itself a commentary on the involution that characterized this phase of Italian political life. For details of the trial, see Renato Carli-Ballola, *1953, Processo Parri* (Milan, 1954).

[79] Sogno, *Guerra senza bandiera*, pp. 307–328 ff.; Valiani, *Tutte le strade conducono a Roma*, p. 315.

[80] Cadorna, *La Riscossa*, pp. 196–198; Valiani, *Tutte le strade conducono a Roma*, pp. 314–316.

cued, and out of his experiences came one of the most unusual autobiographies of the Armed Resistance—*Il mio granello di sabbia* (Genoa, 1947).

Neo-Fascist upswing

Because of the mired-down Allied offensive, the seemingly indiscriminate aerial bombardments by what Mussolini called the "Anglo-assassins," and the melancholy message of General Alexander in November, the Nazi-Fascists in Italy experienced a temporary upswing in their fortunes during the winter.[81]

Mussolini left his Lake Garda headquarters long enough in mid-December to deliver a speech in Milan. Unable to use the bomb-scarred LaScala, he spoke for fifty-five minutes to several thousand people in the Lirico Theater on Saturday the 16th.[82] The speech was broadcast. It turned out to be one of the *Duce's* best oratorical performances, and he got a surprisingly enthusiastic reception in Milan, much to the chagrin of the underground. Mussolini declared that at least 786,000 Italians were engaged as workers or soldiers on Germany's side, but he conceded some "moral inertia that events have produced in many classes of people." Hinting that powerful new German arms would insure victory over the "plutocratic" Anglo-Americans, he went on to speak of the RSI's Verona Manifesto. The Constituent Assembly of the RSI would be convened at war's end, he assured his auditors. The "single party" upon which the state was founded must be preserved, but alongside it might exist other groups with the right of responsible, constructive criticism within the framework of the new regime. Thus the master demagogue veered back toward a kind of "sacred union" policy of collaboration with elements that were not strictly Fascist. It was a shrewd move to placate the moderate "fellow travelers" of the so-called "national socialist republican group," some of whom seemed willing to cry out, "A plague o' both your houses!" to the contending foreign armies in Italy.[83]

During the winter Mussolini also inaugurated a series of social measures designed to meet pressing economic problems and win

[81] *NYT*, Dec. 18, 1944, 3:1.
[82] It was the anniversary of the assassination of the Fascist Commissioner of Milan Province.
[83] S/M, *Sdf*, p. 1007; Battaglia, *SRI*, pp. 460–462; *NYT*, Dec. 17, 1944, 8:2.

mass support. These sought to translate into action the socialization of productive enterprises, cut inflation, speculation, and the black market, and assure the people basic necessities. He announced the establishment of collective mess halls and communal consumers' co-operatives, the requisitioning of warehouses of food wholesalers, and the requisitioning of farm produce by special workers' committees and soldier details, and the assignment of workers to check on the distribution of merchandise. On January 19 he approved a series of decrees designed to bring hoarded money into the state's coffers, reduce the amount of currency in circulation, update the tax assessment rates, increase taxes on farm income, inheritances, and capital transfers, reduce salaries of civil servants, and regulate transportation more efficiently.[84]

The foregoing were largely necessitated by the economic crisis. In addition, the *Duce* sought to carry out his "socialization" in the hope of pointing up the differences between the septentrional Social Republic and the meridional capitalistic Kingdom, subservient to Allied "plutocracies." He made no effort, however, to resurrect corporativism. Mussolini's suddenly renewed interest in the proletariat met with much skepticism. Most of the workers knew well that the Fascist economic program of the past two decades had been geared far more to the well-being of property owners than to that of themselves. The first socialization of large industrial enterprises of national importance took place in February. In March the program was extended to many steel, chemical, paper, and printing establishments. Fiat, Montecatini, Alfa Romeo, and Acciaierie Lombarde were among the plants affected.[85] As late as April 14 Mussolini, in a talk with SS General Wolff, mentioned the possibility of using the threat of further socialization as a bargaining lever with the Anglo-Americans. He reasoned that, since Allied investors had considerable money tied up in these plants, they would not wish to see them nationalized.[86]

Resistance leaders quickly warned factory workers of the "co-

[84] S/M, *Sdf*, pp. 1007–1010.

[85] *Ibid.*, p. 1010; Francesco Galanti, *Socializzazione e sindacalismo nella RSI* (Rome, 1949), pp. 80–91.

[86] Gen. Karl Wolff, "Ecco la verità," *Il Tempo* (Rome), Nos. 5–11 (1951), cited in Battaglia, *SRI*, pp. 562–563.

lossal fraud" of socialization and achieved resounding success. For example, when 32,676 Fiat employees in Turin were asked to vote in March on nominations for "internal commissions" and "management councils," 31,450 abstained. There were 547 blank ballots, and 274 were nullified. Only 405 were valid.[87] In Turin the program never got under way.

Taking his cue from Mussolini's December 16 speech which had opened the door slightly to a "loyal opposition," Edmondo Cione (long a follower of Croce and a latter-day convert to neo-Fascism) pressed the *Duce* to let him publish a daily newspaper, *L'Italia del popolo*, which would offer "constructive criticism." Considerable time elapsed before the first issue appeared on March 28. Though most of the editorials were innocuous, even this mild criticism disturbed ultra-Fascists like Farinacci who were unaccustomed to any public censure. They managed to quash Cione's paper on April 10 after thirteen issues had come out.[88] Though of limited importance, the curious experiment was symptomatic of the almost hysterical efforts of certain desperate Fascists to ingratiate themselves with the increasingly radical-minded public.

About this time, the RSI decided to get rid of some of the most brutal personnel in its heterogeneous police forces, partly as a result of pressure from the clergy and also in the hope of facilitating timely armistice accords that could cut the ground from under any popular insurrection. But it was too late to make the people forget the nature of the old totalitarian apparatus. A somewhat similar move was announced on March 31, when Marshal Graziani (then in charge of units in Liguria) took command of all the RSI armed forces, including such *condottiere*-led groups as the Black Brigades and National Guard. Insurrection and liberation occurred before the reshuffling of the neo-Fascist fighters could be finished.[89]

"Open letter" debate

Between November 1944 and February 1945 a significant debate arose among the clandestine parties in Milan and Turin over

[87] Raimondo Luraghi, *Il movimento operaio torinese durante la resistenza* (Turin, 1958), pp. 268–270.
[88] Cione, *Storia della RSI*, pp. 384–388.
[89] Bellotti, *La Repubblica di Mussolini*, pp. 125–126; G. Silvestri, *Albergo agli Scalzi* (Brescia, 1946), pp. 50, 210–212; Cione, *Storia della RSI*, p. 284; NYT, Nov. 22, 1944, 8:6.

the political goals of the Resistenza.[90] Some of the moderately conservative groups feared that an insurrection coinciding with the final Allied drive might result in a revolutionary government challenging the existing form of the state.

Conservatives had cause to be concerned. In mid-November some Actionists (Valiani and Riccardo Lombardi) circulated a letter expressing their dismay at Premier Bonomi's temporizing with the old system. They set forth their own plans to transform the CLNAI into an Extraordinary Secret Government which would proclaim a republican, socialistic program at the moment of insurrection. The *coup de main* would occur during the interregnum that presumably would prevail for a few days before the arrival of Allied troops. In that hiatus they hoped to purge leading Fascists and confiscate the war profits of big industrialists. They anticipated that the workers would seize and occupy the factories, though they did not expect to complete socialization of industry in the brief time available. The revolutionary interlude would see the expansion of the CLN's to include labor and "mass" organizations and would culminate in convocation by the insurrectional juntas of a Constituent Assembly wherein the "people" would choose the new form of the state.

The dispute over this ambitious scheme proceeded in the form of "open letters," deposited in the CLNAI archives. Communists were the first to answer (November 26). While agreeing with some of the Pd'A ideas, they felt that Valiani and Lombardi paid insufficient attention to current problems. The Communists suggested *immediate* expansion of the CLNAI to embrace mass agencies like the Fronte della Gioventù and the Gruppi di Difesa della Donna, as well as the CVL. They wished the CLNAI to serve as a parliament. If it succeeded in levying and collecting war taxes, mobilizing the people, and achieving national security, it would then deserve to be the "Secret Government of Occupied Italy." [91]

The other three parties waited until January and February to formulate their positions. The PSIUP's counsels were divided; the party favored some modest reform of the CLN's to include

[90] Valiani, *Tutte le strade conducono a Roma*, pp. 201–202, 309, 323; Catalano, *Storia del CLNAI*, pp. 300–301; "Carlo Inverno" [V. Foà], "Commento al programma del Pd'A," *Nuovi Quaderni di Giustizia e Libertà*, No. 4 (Sept.–Dec. 1944), pp. 131–140; Giovana, "La campagna invernale '44–'45," *MLI*, No. 48 (1957), pp. 14–23; Carli-Ballola, *Sdr*, pp. 247–251; Battaglia, *SRI*, pp. 517–519, 458–460.
[91] *Ibid.*, pp. 519–521; Catalano, *Storia del CLNAI*, pp. 302–303.

labor commissions and secretariats but did not welcome the Pd'A idea of a "Secret Government" or heterogeneous representation of peripheral groups. The latter should enjoy only an advisory role in the CLNAI.[92]

On January 12 the DC declared its approval of the Pd'A idea of regional autonomies but strongly opposed anything minimizing the traditional role of parties or free elections. In February the PLI denounced as "authoritarian" the Pd'A proposal and nostalgically re-evoked pre-Fascist liberalism. The Liberals could see no sense in the northern "delegate" (CLNAI) attacking the "delegator" (Rome). They favored only bureaucratic reform of the CLN. Obviously both the PLI and DC objected to any fundamental change of state apparatus.[93]

Since the PCI found itself alone in favoring immediate broadening of the CLNAI, it prudently held its fire and called, instead, for buttressing existing unity in preparation for the insurrection. As a result, even the special wartime tax [94] decreed on December 4 became a dead letter. Clearly, the PCI had begun to appreciate the unlikelihood of radical political changes in the face of the entrenched conservatism of most Italians and the omnipresence of the Allied forces. Instead of pushing toward *coups de main* with the Pd'A, it sidled toward a closer entente with the other *partiti di massa* (DC and PSIUP). It would use the Resistance role as a means of augmenting its popularity with the voters rather than seizing power or forcibly altering the structure of state.[95]

Further evidence of the desire of the northern CLN pentarchy to maintain superficial harmony vis-à-vis the Allies was shown in February, when after much talk the parties tentatively assigned pivotal post-Liberation administrative posts in Milan, Turin, Genoa, Venice, and Bologna. They apportioned the spoils with due consideration for local political complexions. In general, the leftists fared well.[96]

[92] Carli-Ballola, *Sdr*, pp. 248–249.
[93] Battaglia, *SRI*, pp. 521–525; Catalano, *Storia del CLNAI*, pp. 313–315.
[94] Printed in *ibid.*, pp. 322–323.
[95] The new PCI strategy was to become quite apparent in Togliatti's speech of April 8, 1945, to the Party National Council. Dipiero, *Storia critica dei partiti italiani*, pp. 194–196; Mario Niccoli, "Resistenza," *Enciclopedia Italiana*, Appendice II, I–Z, p. 689; Giorgio Amendola, "L'insurrezione di aprile," *Rinascita*, v (Aug. 1948); Battaglia, *SRI*, pp. 525–526.
[96] See chart in Catalano, *Storia del CLNAI*, pp. 379–382. Prudently they re-

Second Bonomi government

Premier Bonomi's second government gave Prime Minister Churchill an excuse to sound off in Commons once more on Italian politics (January 18):

"We have the Bonomi Government, which has been trying to do its best under extraordinary difficulties, but which, of course, has no electoral authority behind it. . . .

"But now at any time . . . the cities of Turin and Milan and other centers of industry and activity [will be freed]. A large population of all kinds of political views, but containing great numbers of violent and vehement politicians in touch with brave men who have been fighting in maintaining a guerrilla war in the Alps, all these will be thrown . . . hungry upon the fragile structure of the Italian Government in Rome, with consequences which cannot be accurately foreseen and certainly not measured. . . .

"Let me say once and for all that we have no political combinations in Europe and elsewhere in respect of which we need Italy as a party. We need Italy no more than we need Spain, because we have no designs which require the support of such powers." [97]

Churchill's blunt coupling of the new Italy with Franco's authoritarian regime struck many Italians as a rude insult.[98]

On February 1 Premier Bonomi announced that postwar elections would be conducted on the basis of a completely democratic suffrage—even women would at last have the vote. It was chiefly the prompting of the Allied Commission that brought this to pass, but the women's role in the underground, as well as the growing influence of the leftist and DC parties, made the move possible with scarcely a protest.[99]

The government also saw fit to manifest greater public interest in the Armed Resistance. On February 18, the anniversary of the first meeting of the Parliament in Turin after the proclamation of the Kingdom of Italy in 1861, the government proclaimed

---

frained from spotting Communists as either prefects or vice-prefects, or police questores, but the PCI was granted the mayorships in Turin and Bologna and vice-mayors elsewhere.

[97] *NYT*, Jan. 20, 1945, 5:8.
[98] *NYT*, Jan. 24, 1945, 4:1.
[99] Harris, *Allied Military Administration of Italy*, p. 383; Smyth, "Italy: From Fascism to the Republic," *Western Political Quarterly*, 1 (1948), pp. 217–218.

"Day of the Partisan and the Soldier." In Rome's Piazza del Popolo, Bonomi, Scoccimarro, and Minister of War Casati addressed the crowd on the virtues of "unity, independence, and freedom" and conferred decorations upon many patriot heroes.[100] Three days earlier a decree bestowed the *Medaglia d'Oro* upon the banner of the CVL.[101] Meantime, the Allied Commission kept pressing Bonomi to find means for paying demobilized Freedom Volunteers.

After five months' delay, the Allies on February 24 fulfilled the promise made at Quebec and abolished the Political Section of the AC. They withdrew their regional commissioners from "King's Italy," and AMG came to a halt in the middle provinces. The Allies also relinquished their right to veto decrees and appointments (even Sforza's!) except in the northern AMG bailiwicks. They permitted Italy to send envoys to friendly and neutral countries and dispatch uncensored diplomatic correspondence. On the other hand, in the wake of the Yalta Conference (February), the Big Three did not grant Italy a seat in the imminent San Francisco Conference that would frame the United Nations Charter.[102] This was a disappointment that caused the honored Catholic *émigré*, Sturzo, to remark sadly, "The rebirth of Italy is hard in itself but it is harder because of the incomprehension of the Allies and their uncertain and incoherent policy." [103]

Despite several positive accomplishments, the second Bonomi government was vulnerable to criticism regarding de-Fascistization. On March 5 General Mario Roatta, arrested in November 1944 on charges of complicity in numerous Fascist misdeeds as well as of inadequately defending Rome at the moment of the armistice, escaped from a hospital in the capital; he was never recaptured.[104] Outraged mobs thereupon invaded the Viminale

[100] Ministero dell'Italia Occupata, 18 *Febbraio: Giornata del partigiano e del soldato* (Rome, 1945), pp. 1-31.
[101] Catalano, *Storia del CLNAI*, p. 391.
[102] Kogan, *Italy and the Allies*, pp. 112-113; Parri, "I rapporti con gli Alleati nel 1945 in un pro-memoria di Harold Macmillan," *MLI*, No. 50 (1958), pp. 52-56.
[103] Sturzo, *Italy and the Coming World*, p. 249.
[104] In hiding, Roatta found time to write his memoirs: *Otto milioni di baionette: l'esercito italiano in guerra dal 1940 al 1944* (Verona, 1946). Roatta was tried *in absentia* and sentenced to some seven years' imprisonment. After absconding, he never appeared again on the public scene, even after revision of the trial and cancellation of the sentence.

Palace, threatening to burn it and kill both Premier Bonomi and his Undersecretary of the Interior. Deplorable as it was, the incident produced some good, for it revealed to the politicians the need for reorganizing the purge, now entrusted to a four-man commission consisting of Scoccimarro, Brosio, Cevolotto, and Tupini.[105] It also caused the government to pledge itself to convoke the *Consulta* ("Consultative Assembly"), which would advise the cabinet until general elections were held. The pledge was not put into effect, however, until several weeks after the war.[106]

The Allies and the Armed Resistance in late winter

By the turn of the year the Italian patriots were being aerially "supplied on a scale never before attempted." The AAF 64th Troop Carrier Group, recently transferred from England and based at Rosignano in Tuscany, began its air life on January 11. From then until the surrender it completed more than 1,000 sorties and dropped some 1,800 short tons of supplies. During the same period 2641st Special Group (Prov.) dropped almost 1,260 tons. Its B-24's delivered to patriots in the distant Alps from Piedmont to Venetia. Most of its missions were flown in daylight; failures were due not to enemy attacks but chiefly to weather and signal difficulties at the drop zones.[107]

Meanwhile, the British SF organized "on its own" between January and May some 856 drops, of which 551 were successful. Altogether 1,228 tons of SF matériel reached the patriots during those months: 666 tons of arms and ammunition, 291 tons of material for sabotage, and 272 tons of other equipment. "It was not as much as was needed, but it was the maximum that [SF] could do." [108]

Clothing was always dispatched in substantial amounts, as were antitank weapons, booby traps, and explosives useful for sabotage. Sten sub-machine guns, excellent for *coups de main*, were dropped in considerable number all along, but large-scale delivery of rifles of the Italian '91 type, as well as old Greek and French models, small arms, and ammunition, was generally withheld for prudent political reasons until the very last days of the war, in accordance

[105] NYT, Mar. 8, 1945, 6:5.
[106] Smyth, *Western Political Quarterly*, 1 (1948), pp. 218–220.
[107] *Army Air Forces in World War II*, III, 516–517.
[108] Salvadori, *Brief History of the Patriot Movement in Italy*, p. 53.

with an Allied directive issued early in February 1945.[109] During the final frenzied days partisans near enemy communication lines were able to capture large stores, thus freeing themselves from heavy dependence upon air lifts.[110]

The cold weather which had set in early also ended early. By late January new possibilities were open for both the Resistance and the Allies. On the 23rd the latter dispatched two messages to the Rome government "for the orientation" of the CG/CVL. The first requested the patriots to prevent at all costs the destruction of dikes and bridges that could result in flooding the Po valley, particularly those dikes near Argenta and Lake Comacchio —no mean undertaking. The latter called upon the underground to initiate the "battle of the communication-lines" in co-ordination with Allied air power.[111] "Stay united and compact," it exhorted, "and organize for the day in which you will be ordered to carry out operations in grand style." [112] The tone of this message was distinctly brighter than that of Alexander's in November.

With the advent of the new year SF hastened to infiltrate liaison officers to link the regional underground commands with the Allied Fifteenth Army Group, as well as to replace the officers behind the lines who had been captured or killed. Some of these missions had been originally scheduled for the previous autumn but had had to be postponed.[113] By December, however, Colonel John Stevens had reached Piedmont, and in mid-January Major Basil Davidson, transferred from liaison duty in Yugoslavia, was dropped into the Langhe zone. He was followed by Colonel Mac-Mullen, designated to serve as Chief of the Ligurian Mission. Max Salvadori (soon to be promoted to lieutenant colonel) was ordered to prepare to go north as Chief of Mission in Milan, where he was to work with the CG/CVL and CLNAI as well as with the Lombard CLN and Military Command.[114]

Late in January Salvadori requested his superiors to clarify cer-

[109] Battaglia, SRI, pp. 495–496.
[110] Army Air Forces in World War II, III, 517–518.
[111] Allied air power met with "magnificent" success after mid-January in hampering enemy communications over the Brenner and northeastern passes, according to Field Marshal Alexander, The Italian Campaign, 12th December 1944 to 2nd May 1945, pp. 26–27.
[112] Atti del CG/CVL, "Istruzione del Quartiere Generale Alleato e dell'Alto Comando Italiano," 23 gennaio 1945, pp. 201–202.
[113] See supra, Ch. x, New Anglo-American missions.
[114] Basil Davidson, "Con i partigiani in Liguria," Il Mese, No. 23 (London, 1945), p. 513; Salvadori, Resistenza ed azione, pp. 253–267.

tain points regarding his duties. "Combining the instructions received from 15th Army Group Headquarters with decisions that I am authorized to make on my own," Salvadori has written, "I have decided upon a program in which there are seven principal points:

(1) Co-ordinate insofar as possible the activities of the partisans and Gappisti with Allied military operations;

(2) Arrange for the delivery of maximum supplies to the CVL without distinction as to the political complexion of the units;

(3) Encourage the CLNAI to form in every province an organization capable of assuming administrative responsibilities during the interim period between enemy withdrawal and Allied arrival;

(4) Warn the CLNAI and CVL to make sure their peripheral agencies take the necessary steps to protect industrial plants and power stations;

(5) Prevent any kind of agreements whatever between the CLNAI and CVL and the Germans;

(6) Keep watch over the situation both on the eastern and western borders to prevent Yugoslav or French infiltrations;

(7) Do everything possible to maintain a spirit of harmony among the component groups in the CLNAI.

The first four of these corresponded to written instructions from headquarters, Salvadori has clarified. The second point, especially that part calling for impartial deliveries, would have to become a reality, for hitherto most SF officers had tended to favor whichever group they lived with. Salvadori decided that as soon as he could get accurate information in Milan about the effective strength of the formations, he would arrange for equitable distribution of supplies. Regarding the fifth stipulation, Salvadori explained that the Germans were often offering seemingly advantageous conditions. Whenever patriot leaders had sought advice from Allied Headquarters the answers had been evasive, ostensibly to avoid the impression of seeking to control the groups, but more likely because the Allies wished to keep a free hand and be able eventually to dissociate themselves from the patriots with the pretext that the latter had negotiated with the enemy. For himself, Salvadori decided that, apart from purely military activity, his function should be simply to offer "suggestions" but never "orders," because "the CLNAI must act as a sovereign body and not as the executor of the will of others." [115]

[115] *Ibid.*, pp. 267–269.

A few days later (February 4) AFHQ ordered British SF, in the light of the Greek experience and of reports of internecine patriot fighting in northeastern Italy contrary to the spirit of the December 7 accord, to send a directive to its liaison officers advising them to: "(1) discourage any indiscriminate expansion of armed contingents; (2) encourage organized acts of sabotage, complementary to operations foreseen, and acts of countersabotage; (3) increase nonmilitary supplies to sustain morale of partisans." [116] Caution was to be exercised in issuing arms, and these were to be confined to carefully controlled units. This was issued a day after the Combined Chiefs of Staff, meeting in Malta en route to Yalta, sent a new directive to Field Marshal Alexander. The Italian front would be "bled" of five divisions and two fighter groups which would go to the Western front. Nevertheless, continued the directive, the existing front should be held solidly: "You should do your utmost, by means of such limited offensive action as may be possible and by the skilful use of cover and deception plans, to contain the German forces now in Italy and prevent their withdrawal to other fronts. You should, in any case, remain prepared to take immediate advantage of any weakening or withdrawal of the German forces." [117]

Early in February Salvadori, accompanied by an Irish captain and a sergeant radiotelegrapher, took off from Rosignano and jumped into the western Langhe between Cuneo and Savona.[118] Because of rastrellamenti, bad weather, and transportation difficulties, over a month transpired before Salvadori could complete the hazardous journey from southern Piedmont to Milan. He had to change into civilian clothes and use false documents made out in his true name; his companions, who were unable to pass for Italians, hoped to reach patriot units in the lower Monferrato near the Po and set up their radio, but unfortunately they could not make it function. En route, Salvadori visited Colonel Stevens east of Cuneo, and noted how much trouble he was having with the leftist CLN parties as a result of his partiality

[116] Quoted in "Il contributo della Resistenza italiana in una relazione sull'attività del n. 1° Special Force," MLI, No. 4 (1950), p. 20; cf. Niccoli, "Resistenza," Enciclopedia Italiana, Seconda Appendice, I–Z, 689.

[117] Ehrman, Grand Strategy, vi, 94–95.

[118] Another mission, destined to go to the Alessandria zone, jumped from the same plane; two of its three members were to be killed.

for the Autonomi.[119] Salvadori decided that for his own part he would let the CLNAI exercise as much self-government as possible and not try to play off factions within it. In Turin he visited briefly with General Trabucchi and Franco Venturi, Pd'A political commissar. He reached Milan early in March.[120]

The hope expressed by certain British policy planners in February that "indiscriminate expansion" of the Armed Resistance could be discouraged was doomed to failure. During that month the partisans' ranks filled out again almost as if there had been no winter hiatus; everyone seemed sure that spring would see the end of the war. According to reliable estimates, the number of active guerrillas reached 100,000 by the end of February.[121] In the Allied distribution of funds in the spring the PCI brigades received more than 40 per cent, the Pd'A ones slightly less than 30 per cent, and the others the remainder.[122] As the underground combatants regrouped, their chieftains based them more on the lowlands than the mountains. In anticipation of the insurrection, they devoted more thought to logistics (always a weak point) and the perfection of medical and police forces. Meanwhile, General Clark warned on February 15: "The moment of final attack is approaching, and for you the moment of insurrection. Prepare yourselves, listen to us carefully. When the time has come we will give you the signal. To those in northern Lombardy: Remain united better to provide for the equipment and armament of your men. Do not permit the enemy to waste your strength with large-scale offensives." [123]

One of the urgent problems needing solution in Milan was General Cadorna's status in the CG/CVL. Encouraged by Sogno (who had replaced Major Argenton in the CG on January 11), Cadorna decided to find out once for all whether he was "supreme commander" in the "politico-military field" or simply commander in respect of "technico-military" affairs and subject to collegial decisions by the CLNAI on all "politico-military" matters. On

---

[119] Regarding the trouble see Trabucchi, *I vinti hanno sempre torto, passim,* and Bianco, *Guerra partigiana, passim.*

[120] Salvadori, *Resistenza ed azione,* pp. 269–280.

[121] *Ibid.,* p. 170.

[122] Letter of Salvadori to G. Salvemini, Sept. 10, 1945, cited in Kogan, *Italy and the Allies,* pp. 110–111.

[123] NYT, Feb. 16, 1945, 8:5.

January 23 he wrote the CLNAI, asking which was correct.[124]

While this crisis shaped up, the PCI and Pd'A drafted plans to unify the Armed Resistance. The Pd'A clearly wished to solidify the underground in order to strengthen its bargaining power with the Allies and southern rightists; the PCI sought unification perhaps chiefly to get the partisans incorporated into the postwar Army. The PCI plan seemed to call for a more gradual approach than the Pd'A. The PLI and DC appeared to be rather indifferent in January but accepted the unification principle. Though bridling at any integration of partisans into a "tainted" royal Army, the PSIUP went along with the broad plan. Both Italian and Allied officials in the South happily encouraged the consolidation. On February 5 the CLNAI appointed a committee composed of Cadorna and representatives of the PCI and Pd'A to draft a specific plan.[125]

Trouble began almost at once. The Pd'A suggested "political inspectors" for all brigades, including the erstwhile Autonomi. Cadorna disapproved strenuously and submitted a counterproposal on the 14th; he insisted that his views must prevail, since a "political inspectorate" was essentially a "technico-military" problem. Heated discussions ensued. Then on the 21st the CLNAI replied to Cadorna's inquiry of January 23 regarding his status. The CG/CVL, the answer made it clear, was a "working section of the CLNAI. It is evident, therefore, that where the Command must take decisions and issue orders having political character, it is impossible to proceed except through the collegial consultation of all its members who at that moment represent the CLNAI, which is the body from which their power derives. . . ." [126]

"Taking advantage of the favorable occasion, which he had been waiting for for some time," Cadorna on the 22nd submitted his resignation as CVL Commander.[127] Probably his chief motive was to block the leftists' unification scheme, for this was the most

[124] Sogno, *Guerra senza bandiera*, pp. 305–306; Cadorna, *La Riscossa*, pp. 201–202.
[125] Archivio CLNAI, 1/10, 1/11, cited in Catalano, *Storia del CLNAI*, pp. 354–356; Allied Commission, *Weekly Bulletin*, Jan. 13, 1945, cited in Kogan, *Italy and the Allies*, p. 107.
[126] Quoted in Cadorna, *La Riscossa*, p. 211.
[127] *Ibid.*, p. 212.

important topic of the day.[128] In his letter Cadorna indicated implacable hostility to the "political inspectorates" but was willing to accept most of the other ideas in the leftist blueprint. He went on to argue that "collegial operation of the CG did not permit him to carry out the task of commander, even in strictly technico-military matters." [129]

Next day the CLNAI met. The PSIUP wished to fire Cadorna, but Longo was ready to pour oil on the troubled waters. He attributed the crisis to Cadorna's "typically military temperament" and inability to understand government drawing its power "from the bottom up." Those who analyzed the problem with a measure of calmness soon realized that they could not force the Allies to appoint a new commander at this late hour; instead, they must devise a "face-saving" compromise with Cadorna. A committee composed of Pizzoni and Valiani was thus instructed to confer with him and persuade him to appear personally before the CLNAI to explain his resignation. They found the general packing his valise, preparing to depart for Val d'Ossola to fight alongside patriots in that zone. After listening to them, Cadorna insisted that the affair be resolved in writing. Prolonged discussions ensued. Everyone agreed not to communicate the nature of the dispute either to the Bonomi government or to Allied Headquarters, at least until it was all settled.[130]

The CLNAI was impelled to speed the search for a *combinazione* by a message that came (by coincidence?) on February 27 from Allied agents in Switzerland, requesting a meeting with both Cadorna and Valiani. On the 28th in a conference with CLNAI spokesmen, Cadorna turned down the Pd'A compromise proposal and, with PLI help, drafted one of his own, which won the approval of the DC and Pd'A and thereafter of the PCI and PSIUP. In essence, Cadorna recognized the CLNAI as his superior so long as he was not given directives which conflicted with orders received from the Allies or the Rome government.[131]

---

[128] Catalano, *Storia del CLNAI*, pp. 357–360. Unification did not take place until March 29; cf. *infra*, Ch. xii.

[129] Cadorna, *La Riscossa*, p. 212.

[130] *Ibid.*, pp. 213–217.

[131] The text read: "General *Valenti* [Cadorna] confirms that his authority as Commander of the CVL depends from the CLNAI, which, as delegate of the Italian Government for the struggle against the Nazi-Fascists in Occupied Italy,

While Cadorna was in Switzerland and later in southern Italy, the Milanese directorate reverted more or less to their previous pattern of operations. His long absence prevented him from sharing in most of the decisions that laid the basis for the final insurrection.[132]

Plan "E-27"

Perhaps the most far-reaching of the early plans for insurrection was the one drawn up, or rather re-elaborated, on January 30 by the Piedmont Regional Command. Labeled "Plan E-27," it was a modernized version of a plan prepared the previous summer when hopes were high for liberation. Its guiding assumption was that the Germans would withdraw from Piedmont when the Allies launched their drive into Venetia. It anticipated more or less tenacious fighting by Fascist volunteers but not by the conscripts. It assigned specific countersabotage tasks and liberating missions to various patriot units, and it called for partisan "war tribunals" to be organized at each divisional headquarters as well as in provincial centers to determine the guilt of captured soldiers and Fascist officials. All Fascist ministers, undersecretaries of state, prefects, and provincial party secretaries who had held office since

has requested him of the Italian Government, and has conferred upon him the title and function of Commandant.

"He holds that such relation of dependence from the CLN cannot alter the fact that his position as Italian General would prevent him from holding this post should disharmony manifest itself regarding the directives between, on the one hand, the delegating Italian Government and the Allies who control the work of it on the basis of the Armistice conditions, and, on the other hand, the CLNAI, which is delegated by the said Government.

"Whenever, according to his judgment, such disagreement should reveal itself, he will refer it to the CLNAI in order that unity of directives may be re-established, reserving the right, in case of lack of agreement, to reassume his freedom and to return to the CLN the mandate he has received.

"General Valenti declares that the political conduct of the war depends from the CLN, from which he demands precise directives.

"On the other hand, he considers the military conduct of the said war to pertain to himself. Wherever a conflict arises over the evaluation of the politico-organizational character, and not the military character, of a decision taken by the Commander, the members of the Command who represent the various parties of the CLN have the right to appeal to the CLN, which shall decide the matter either in plenary session, or create within itself a permanent sub-committee to which shall be assigned the tasks of holding more frequent contacts with the said Commander." Quoted in Cadorna, La Riscossa, pp. 218–222; cf. Valiani, Tutte le strade conducono a Roma, p. 319; L. Longo, "Note e discussioni," MLI, No. 30 (1954), pp. 49–51.
[132] Cadorna, La Riscossa, p. 223 ff.

September 8, 1943, would be deemed *ipso facto* to have aided the enemy and would be subject at once to the death penalty without right of appeal; the only necessary preliminary would be accurate identification. The same would be true for all who bore arms in a Fascist volunteer unit after September 8. Conscripted troops, on the other hand, except for officers, would be freed, provided they promised not to bear arms against the CLN.[133]

Undeniably the directive was stern. "Errors may be made," conceded General Trabucchi, "but they will be justified so long as they are not errors of inertia." [134] In mid-February the enemy captured copies of "E-27," which necessitated the preparation of a new but essentially similar plan on February 20.[135]

The Piedmontese provisions for punishment of Fascist volunteers were more severe than those agreed upon in Milan by the CG/CVL and recommended by the Allies. Consequently Longo informed Turin on March 28 that "these do not correspond to the position which we must assume in this problem—a position which is specified in our directive: 'Whoever surrenders himself must have his life preserved, provided he is not guilty of particular crimes. Every Fascist captured with arms on his person must be shot.' " [136] According to Cadorna, this warning did not entirely repair the grave effects of the radical Piedmontese instruction.

When the Germans read the captured document their first reaction was to intensify punishment of partisans they seized, but soon they reversed their policy, apparently sensing the imminence of defeat and deeming it expedient not to antagonize the patriots unduly. The latter, for their part, let it be known that German prisoners in their hands would be treated less severely than Italian ones and hinted that drafted enemy troops would receive better treatment than volunteers. Thus they helped foment ill feeling between Italians and Germans as well as between conscripts and volunteers.[137]

Resistance planners believed that in Genoa, long an anti-Fas-

[133] Mario Giovana, "La ripresa partigiana in Piemonte nel 1945: l'unificazione delle formazioni," *MLI*, No. 49 (1957), pp. 3–29.

[134] Trabucchi, *I vinti hanno sempre torto*, pp. 156–157.

[135] *Atti del CG/CVL*, No. 148, pp. 246–254; Battaglia, *SRI*, pp. 533–535; Cadorna, *La Riscossa*, p. 248.

[136] Quoted in Cadorna, *La Riscossa*, loc. cit.

[137] Trabucchi, *I vinti hanno sempre torto*, pp. 171–180.

cist bastion, 3,000 local partisans would be enough to defend the port and utilities against sabotage by the German garrison of 4,000.

In Milan a much larger number would be required. Though the Lombard metropolis was militarily important to the foe only in terms of east-west communications, presumably he would be anxious to hang on to it for political motives, since the Resistance "capital" was there. In view of the enthusiastic reception which had greeted Mussolini as recently as December 16, the Milanese underground was not anxious to launch a premature insurrection. This should not be sparked until "Allied troops have definitely taken Pavia and Lodi and are headed decisively toward Milan," they decided. Partisan forces must undertake measures to prevent or hamper a German withdrawal to the east via Bergamo or Brescia. Patriots in Val d'Ossola and Valsesia, under the direct control of the CG/CVL, should disrupt any enemy retreat via Lake Como and then hasten to Milan. The plans envisaged the use of some 32,000 partisans in the Milan area.[138] In addition, there would be the well-armed Finance Guard, with whose commanders the CLNAI had been secretly negotiating for weeks. (It was to be the Finance Guards who occupied the Milan prefecture at the decisive moment on April 25.) [139]

On March 10 the CG/CVL announced certain individual assignments for the coming insurrection. Longo was put in charge of the all-important secretariat. He was assisted by Solari (Pd'A) in this liaison with Allied officials and partisan formations. The new PSIUP mandatary, Stucchi, was given authority over distribution of air drops and dissemination of false identity cards; DC delegate Mattei was charged with financial and medical services; and PLI representative Argenton with management of the intelligence service.[140]

On March 11-12 an enlarged covert PCI Directorate listened to Longo's political report [141] and Secchia's organizational one,[142]

---

[138] An earlier plan was prepared by Valiani and Egidio Liberti (Pd'A) on February 19; some of its suggestions were embodied in the final instructions. Valiani, "Un memoriale del Partito d'Azione sull'insurrezione di Milano," *MLI*, No. 47 (1957), pp. 53–60; Battaglia, *SRI*, pp. 535–537.

[139] A. Maugeri, *L'occupazione di Milano e la liberazione* (Milan, 1947), p. 89 ff.

[140] *Atti del CG/CVL*, No. 138, pp. 235–236.

[141] Longo, *Sulla via dell'insurrezione nazionale*, pp. 395–444.

[142] Secchia, *I Comunisti e l'insurrezione*, pp. 389–438.

containing a series of basic directives for the imminent insurrection. Then it issued an ultimatum to the enemy: "Surrender or perish!"

Soon partisans recaptured several zones lost the previous autumn, including the "Republic of Torriglia" above Genoa and the Oltrepò Pavese. In a three-day struggle in the Lombard pass of Mortirolo, between Val Camonica and Valtellina, they decisively repulsed Mussolini's "Val Tagliamento" division which had inflicted harsh treatment on Venetian patriots a few weeks before.[143]

Yugoslav troubles again

The final winter of the struggle produced a recrudescence of several of the squabbles that intermittently had plagued the Resistenza. Perhaps the worst of these was the problem of Tito's forces in Venezia Giulia.

After *rastrellamenti* destroyed the Carnia "republic" in the Friuli uplands in late 1944, some of the local Garibaldini switched their allegiance to Tito's Ninth Corps. Rival "Osoppo" formations, composed of Christian Democrats and Giellisti, protested bitterly. In due course the problem came before the CLNAI. The Garibaldini sent a memorandum to Milan on December 22 explaining that they had taken their action because they were fighting in what was "widely known to be a Yugoslav zone of operations." The populace spoke Slovene; moreover, Tito's combatants were worthy of support because they were the first "People's Army" to fight the foe. Militarily it was advantageous, the Communists argued, to unite with the nearest Allied army. They further asserted that they would have joined either the Anglo-American or Soviet forces had they been closer. Denouncing the "calumnies" hurled against them by the "Osoppo," they stoutly insisted that their action was not traitorous. They warned the "Osoppo" not to fight any more in the zone unless they took orders from the Ninth Corps.[144]

Longo insisted that everything had been properly approved by the Venetian Regional Command as well as by the CG/CVL.[145]

---

[143] Battaglia, *SRI*, pp. 500–507.
[144] Protocol No. 211, cited in Cadorna, *La Riscossa*, pp. 202–203.
[145] Longo, *Rinascita*, x (Dec. 1953), pp. 654–655.

His interpretation was not accepted by most of the other currents in Milan, many of whom hotly accused the PCI of presenting a *fait accompli*. There seemed to be nothing that the CLNAI could do to change the situation.

That the Garibaldi threats were not to be dismissed lightly was proved on February 7, 1945, when a shock unit of the PCI "Natisone" brigade murdered twenty top leaders of the "Osoppo" at Porzus in the mountains above Udine. The news was most alarming to Allied Headquarters. Seven years after the war the Porzus affair came before the Italian courts, which adjudged many of the accused guilty.[146]

The wartime disputes among the Resistance forces in the strategic border region were harbingers of the violence that characterized much of postwar Italo-Yugoslav relations. They also evidenced the ambiguous attitude of the PCI toward Trieste. In the early months of 1945 moderate currents in the northern CLN's warned the Anglo-Americans through their liaison officers to prepare for trouble in Venezia Giulia and suggested that troops be dispatched there quickly at the moment of the final offensive. The Allies did not need such warnings, for Tito's Foreign Minister Josip Smodlaka had publicly demanded in London on January 7 that Trieste and Fiume be given to Yugoslavia.[147]

At the Yalta Conference the Anglo-Americans unsuccessfully tried to get clear-cut agreement that AMG would assume authority in Venezia Giulia up to the 1939 frontier. In a talk with Field Marshal Alexander in Belgrade late in February, Tito promised to subordinate his claim to rule all of Venezia Giulia, indicating that he would accept AMG over-all administrative responsibility, provided Yugoslav authorities in *de facto* control were allowed to function unhampered, and that this would not prejudice the ultimate disposition of the region. Yet in the course

[146] In the spring of 1952 in Lucca, fifty-two members of the "Natisone" brigade accused of murder and treason were tried. Seventeen were acquitted; the remainder were convicted of murder and sentenced to terms ranging from twelve to thirty years. The three ringleaders, among whom was the PCI Secretary in Udine, received thirty years each, but they and six others were sentenced *in absentia*, as they could not be found in Italy. The court disallowed the treason charges. The PCI press in 1952 almost ignored the trial of the party members, inasmuch as the PCI, after the Cominform denunciation of Tito in 1948, no longer favored Yugoslav claims to Trieste. See *Manchester Guardian*, April 8, 1952; cf. Carli-Ballola, *Sdr*, p. 243; Battaglia, *SRI*, p. 465, n. 10.

[147] NYT, Jan. 9, 1945, 9:4.

of March it became clear that Tito was not going to abide by this arrangement.[148]

Franco-Italian relations

At least a slight improvement could be noted in the relationships between the "new Italy" and liberated France in these months. At Christmas it was announced that the French Provisional Government had sent a delegation to Rome to talk over such problems as diplomatic relations, termination of old Italian privileges in Tunisia already abrogated by the Allies, clarification of Marshal Badoglio's 1943 denunciation of the 1940 Franco-Italian armistice, and protection of interests of French-speaking groups in Val d'Aosta. General DeGaulle's envoy, M. Couve de Murville, was accompanied to Rome by 68-year-old Dr. Domenico Russo, a distinguished Christian Democratic *émigré* who had edited *Italie libre* since 1941 and presided over the Italian CLN in Paris for a year. (It consisted of the same six parties as in southern Italy and claimed 40,000 adherents.) [149] After several weeks substantial agreements were reached. Diplomatic relations were not yet formally resumed but "delegates" were to be exchanged.[150]

Closer ties with the French Résistance in this era were also forged by the clandestine Italian wing of the European Federalist Movement, whose chief bases of operations were in Milan and Switzerland.[151] A copy of the MFE's "Milan theses" of August 1943 reached like-minded people in Lyon, who followed it almost to the letter in a declaration they issued in June 1944.[152] When the French Committee for European Federation learned that the Dumbarton Oaks proposals for the charter of the United Nations did not rest on federalist principles,[153] it recommended convening an international conclave of federalists in Paris. With the help

---

[148] Feis, *Roosevelt, Churchill, Stalin*, pp. 545–546, 627–628; Ehrman, *Grand Strategy*, VI, 129–130.

[149] Some 200,000 Italians dwelt in Paris and about 800,000 in all of France. *NYT*, Dec. 10, 1944, 13:1; Dec. 27, 7:4.

[150] *Ibid.*, Mar. 1, 1945, 8:6.

[151] See *supra*, Ch. VI, Opposition rumblings.

[152] Printed in *L'Europe de demain*, pp. 75–78, and also in the covert [Milan] *L'Unità Europea*, No. 6 (Sept.–Oct. 1944), p. 4.

[153] The pessimism with which the federalists greeted the Dumbarton Oaks plan can be discerned in the article, "Dopo Dumbarton Oaks: 'Le Nazioni Unite' e il Federalismo Europeo," in *L'Unità Europea*, No. 6 (Sept.–Oct. 1944), pp. 3–4.

of the "Mouvement de Libération National" and "Combat," this Paris conference took place March 22-25, 1945, a month after the Big Three left Yalta.[154] Italy's leading advocate of European federation, Altiero Spinelli (accompanied by his wife), attended the Paris meeting. Other participants included George Orwell, Spanish Republican exiles, Frenchmen, Swiss, Austrians, Germans, and Greeks. The resolution, drafted by Spinelli, called not for new parties but for "establishment of close international agreements among all (existing) movements, parties, and states who advocate a European federalist policy, with the hope of developing a common and co-ordinated action." [155] Thus idealists in the Italian anti-Fascist underground made another substantial contribution to the planning of a better postwar international order.

[154] For the MFE reaction to UN plans announced at Yalta and reaction to Italian exclusion from the San Francisco Conference, see "San Francisco e l'Italia," in *ibid.*, No. 8 (Jan.–Feb. 1945), pp. 1–2. The article argued that Italy's exclusion was understandable, since "only a small minority of Italians have really thrown themselves into the war of expiation." "Italian expiation must proceed beyond the partisan struggle—from the Constituent Assembly to the radical institutional renovation of the state."

[155] See *ibid.*, No. 9 (April 29, 1945), pp. 3–4, for Spinelli's report of the work of the Paris congress.

CHAPTER XII · THE INSURRECTION

March – May 2, 1945

Ultimate underground crisis

WHEN it was the Italian front's turn to come to life the first week of April, the Nazi-Fascists had available some twenty-three German and four Italian divisions against an Allied array of seventeen divisions, four Italian combat groups, six armored brigades, and four infantry ones.[1] The Allies enjoyed unquestioned superiority in air power, artillery, tanks, and supplies.

Field Marshal Alexander's plans no longer called for an all-out assault against the fortress of Bologna. Instead, most elements of the Eighth and Fifth Armies would bypass it to the northeast and west, respectively. They would advance as rapidly as possible from Argenta and Ferrara to the Po and do their best to defeat the Germans south of the river. The bulk of the Fifth Army would push to the Po and on to Verona, gateway to the Brenner Pass, while on the Ligurian coast a wing of the Fifth Army would drive through LaSpezia toward Genoa and Piedmont. As soon as Piedmont and Lombardy were occupied, the Fifth Army would offer support to the Eighth Army in the Veneto, where the Germans had amassed their heaviest concentrations and had at least five potential defense lines. Trieste and the roads to Austria would be the prime objectives; Venezia Giulia would be occupied as far as the 1939 frontier.[2]

This strategy called for giant forward lunges, accompanied by full-scale aerial attacks against the enemy's lines of retreat. The patriots' role, according to Allied plans shaping up since autumn, would be restricted chiefly to "antiscorch" (safeguarding industrial plants and power stations from enemy sabotage), harassment of enemy movements, and eventual elimination of pockets of resistance—assignments the patriots could carry out by themselves without help from parachute troops.[3] Clearly most Allied policy

[1] Alexander, *The Italian Campaign, 12th December 1944 to 2nd May 1945*, p. 39.
[2] *Ibid.*, pp. 32–37.
[3] In London in the autumn the Allies had assembled experts to study the best ways of organizing countersabotage. Many instructions subsequently were dropped to the underground. Inconsistently, however, the Allies themselves dropped bombs on the Monfalcone shipyards a month before the end of the war. Giorgio Vacca-

493

makers were unenthusiastic about the idea of CLN-instigated uprisings that might present them and the royal government with all sorts of political headaches. The Allies rushed plans to dispatch AMG personnel to the northwest at the earliest possible moment.[4]

The very nature of these Allied plans produced one last crisis in the ranks of the Armed Resistance. Among the more or less conservative factions many leaned once more toward a policy of *attesismo*. After all, they asked themselves, did the Allies really need the partisans' military support? Did not the Anglo-Americans have preponderance? Was not Hitler's defeat inevitable regardless of what the underground did? Were not the Germans showing signs of willingness in March and April to chaffer, leaving industries intact if the patriots winked at their withdrawal over the Alps? Were not the neo-Fascists evincing some desire to transfer peacefully their power to the CLNAI? In the face of such queries, it was not easy for the radical-minded echelon of the Resistenza to carry through its determination to launch furious insurrections hours or even days ahead of the Allied arrival—uprisings that were indispensable for the effectuation of the leftists' political program.

Enemy efforts to stave off insurrections

Though unconcerned about their own units' élan (it scarcely flagged at all),[5] several German commanders were worried about the possibility of partisan insurrections handicapping their eventual retreat into the Reich. Understandably, such anxiety was even more acute among Italian Fascists. Ecclesiastical circles were worried too, but more for humanitarian reasons.

It was not surprising, therefore, that Milan's Archbishop Ilde-

---

rino, "Il contributo della resistenza italiana in un documento alleato," *MLI*, No. 3 (1949), pp. 3–23, and No. 4 (1950), pp. 3–23; S. Bellone, "La salvezza degli impianti industriali," *Rinascita* (April 1955); and Carli-Ballola, *Sdr*, pp. 289–293.

[4] For details of Allied planning for administration in the North, see Harris, *Allied Military Administration of Italy*, Ch. x, and map of the military districts, p. 270. No. 2 District consisted of Piedmont, Liguria, and Lombardy; No. 1 District comprised Venezia Euganea, Romagna, Marches, Tuscany, and Umbria; Peninsular Base Section comprised the corridor extending from the Brenner Pass down through Verona, Bologna, and the Leghorn coastal strip as far as Naples. No. 3 District included most of the South.

[5] Alexander, *The Italian Campaign*, p. 40.

fonso Cardinal Schuster (himself once an ardent admirer of Fascism) found himself chosen to serve as a "go-between" in the frenzied series of negotiations that occurred between the hard-pressed Nazi-Fascists and the Armed Resistance. The Germans and neo-Fascist Italians persistently betrayed one another during these unedifying gambits. *Wehrmacht* leaders transmitted their first feeler to the CLNAI via Schuster in November 1944, offering to leave factories and utilities intact if the patriots would promise to let their troops pull back unmolested at the proper time. CLNAI spokesmen rejected such bids more or less summarily during the last weeks of the war. They could at last perceive some advantage for themselves by invoking the Allies' "unconditional surrender" policy—something that they had often maligned in previous months. On March 13 the *Duce*'s son Vittorio asked the Cardinal to propose armistice negotiations between the Allies and the RSI with the understanding that the latter could survive as a "bulwark of public order" against Communism. The Allies rejected this offer out of hand.[6]

Meanwhile, in February, unbeknownst to Mussolini, Karl Wolff (senior SS General and Police Commander in Italy and Plenipotentiary-General of the *Wehrmacht*'s rear areas as well as Chief Liaison Officer with the RSI) established secret contact with Allen Dulles, the top OSS officer in Switzerland. Wolff's intermediary was Baron Luigi Parilli, an Italian industrialist. Reiterating the Casablanca formula of surrender, Dulles also insisted upon the release of Parri before any further talks could be entertained. To this Wolff complied. Dressed in civilian clothes, the German general arrived in Switzerland on March 8 by automobile, accompanied by blindfolded Parri and another Italian Resistance hostage. Conferring with Dulles in Zurich, Wolff expressed the hope of working out an arrangement whereby northern Italy would be taken over by the Allies without needless bloodshed and destruction. He suggested that the Germans would be willing to forego demolition of industries and public works if

[6] See Schuster, *Gli ultimi tempi di un regime*, pp. 104–105, 135–137; certain rectifications regarding same by Riccardo Lombardi, "Il 'libro bianco' del cardinale Schuster," *Il Ponte*, II (1946), pp. 1053–1061; Archivio CLNAI, xxv/47 and Archivio CVL, GE xxx/12, cited by Catalano, *Storia del CLNAI*, p. 317; Valiani, "Intervento," *MLI*, No. 52/53 (1958), pp. 209–210; Valiani, *Tutte le strade conducono a Roma*, p. 320; Cadorna, *La Riscossa*, pp. 248–249; Salvadori, *Resistenza ed azione*, p. 289.

the partisans would renounce the underground warfare. He insisted that the Allies (not the patriots) must accept the eventual German surrender and guarantee security to prisoners and hostages.

On March 19 Field Marshal Alexander's American Deputy Chief of Staff General Lemnitzer and British Assistant Chief of Staff General Airey, who traveled to Switzerland incognito to explore this so-called "Operation Sunshine," talked to Wolff at the border town of Ascona. They insisted upon the signature of the German commander-in-chief in Italy showing his approval of these talks before any more serious discussions could take place. They also decided that Wolff should first visit Marshal Kesselring (recently transferred to command the Western Front) and seek his acquiescence before approaching Colonel General Heinrich von Vietinghoff, Kesselring's successor as *Wehrmacht* Commander-in-Chief of Army Group Southwest in Italy. If Vietinghoff could be persuaded, qualified envoys could be dispatched to Switzerland and thence, under Allied escort, to Caserta to work out military technicalities and sign the surrender instrument. Late in March, however, Heinrich Himmler of the SS, involved in armistice soundings of his own, forbade any further contacts in Switzerland until he personally could talk to Wolff. These two conferred later in the month but came to no decision. Himmler, it seems, went so far as to order Wolff's family taken into custody as a security measure against any independent action. While Wolff's contacts with Dulles were temporarily severed, the Allies hurled forth their final offensive on April 5.[7]

---

[7] Parenthetically, it may be noted that although President Roosevelt had kept Premier Stalin fully informed of the German approaches ever since March 12, the suspicious Soviet dictator and Molotov raised extremely bitter and unfair protests against alleged "talks behind the backs of the Soviet Union." Stalin unwarrantedly accused the Anglo-Americans of working out a deal with the Germans to "open up" the Western Front so that the Anglo-Americans could drive farther east than had been envisaged. These acrimonious charges and replies troubled the President's last days (he died on April 12) and probably delayed the final surrender in Italy.

Regarding the tortuous armistice negotiations, see especially Herbert Feis's account, based on Allen Dulles' papers, in his *Roosevelt, Churchill, Stalin*, pp. 583–596; Field Marshal Alexander, *The Italian Campaign*, pp. 62–66; Admiral Leahy, *I Was There*, pp. 330–335; Churchill, *Triumph and Tragedy*, pp. 440–454; Ministry of Foreign Affairs of the USSR, *Stalin's Correspondence with Churchill, Attlee, Roosevelt, and Truman, 1941–1945*, I, 311–313, and II, 198–214; Ehrman, *Grand Strategy*, VI, 122–128; Dollmann, *Roma nazista*, pp. 454–

Cadorna and Valiani's talks with the Allies

Early in March General Cadorna and Valiani (Pd'A) were summoned to Berne for talks with Allied representatives. After conferring with Dulles and McCaffery, they crossed the frontier for talks with Lemnitzer, Airey, and British Colonel Rosebery in Lyon. These officers were anxious to learn "what was the real strength" of the Communists in the North and whether insurrections might lead to a repetition of the Greek tragedy. They desired an end to the recriminations within the CG/CVL, and were therefore gratified by news of the compromise solution regarding Cadorna's status. They could suggest little more in the way of a practical solution, but explained to Cadorna that although Allied Supreme Headquarters must find the CVL Commander acceptable, he was to be selected and nominated by the CLNAI. Allied Headquarters would transmit directives to CLNAI with copies to CG/CVL; but in urgent cases, it might reverse this procedure. The Commander of CVL would provide CLNAI with an "information copy" of all reports sent to Allied Headquarters. In case of dispute over interpretation of directives from the South, the CVL Commander and CLNAI must make every effort to reach agreement.[8]

Cadorna was aware that SS General Wolff desired an accord with the partisans along the lines already mentioned. He was inclined to favor such a pact, since he doubted the ability of the Italian Volunteers of Liberty to safeguard industries and utilities if the Germans really set out to sabotage them;[9] nevertheless, he had rejected Wolff's feelers in view of the adamant unconditional surrender terms of the Allies. When the matter came up in Lyon, Allied officials reiterated their opposition to any such pacts. Later Cadorna urged Rome to discuss this further with the Allies and CLNAI.[10]

Venezia Giulia and Val d'Aosta were two other problems discussed. Both the Italians and the Allies feared that these territories

---

496; Moellhausen, *La carta perdente*, pp. 439–480; Lanfranchi, *La resa degli ottocentomila*, pp. 291–297 ff.; NYT, Sept. 18, 1945, 8:1.

[8] Cadorna, *La Riscossa*, pp. 225–227; Valiani, "La Resistenza e la questione istituzionale," MLI, No. 52/53 (1958), p. 34.

[9] Cadorna, *La Riscossa*, p. 239.

[10] *Ibid.*, pp. 228–229; Valiani, *Tutte le strade conducono a Roma*, p. 323.

might be seized by *revanche*-minded Yugoslavs and French. Cadorna learned that the Allies intended to occupy Venezia Giulia up to the prewar frontier until its status could be defined in the peace settlement. He was also told that efforts were being made to re-equip and send back to Italy those partisan units (like the "Rosselli" brigade) which were still dislocated in France.[11]

After the Lyon talks Cadorna and Valiani repaired to Berne for more instructions. Because of reports of increased enemy surveillance of the Italo-Swiss frontier, Dulles and McCaffery advised Cadorna to stay in Switzerland a few days longer, but they let Valiani return to Milan at once. Upon his arrival there (March 15) Valiani reported to CLNAI and CG/CVL that Allied plans did not conflict with those for national insurrection which the underground was drafting.[12]

In Switzerland on the 23rd Cadorna experienced a welcome surprise when he was greeted by Parri in Dulles' home.[13] The snowy-haired patriot leader seemed to be little the worse for wear after more than nine weeks of captivity. Doubtless Parri and Cadorna had some inkling of the complications arising from the Wolff-Dulles talks when, on the 27th, they received instructions to proceed to AFHQ in Caserta. Nevertheless, Cadorna was suspicious at first, thinking there must be some plot to keep him away from Milan. He and Parri obeyed, however, and arrived in Naples and Caserta by the first of April.[14]

New Allied spokesmen come north

During February and March two competent interpreters of emergent Allied policies were parachuted behind the lines: British Lieutenant Colonel Max Salvadori and Aldobrando Medici-Tornaquinci, Undersecretary of the Ministry of Occupied Territories.

Dispatched by Headquarters Fifteenth Army Group to serve as Liaison Officer with CLNAI and CG/CVL as well as with the Lombard CLN and its Military Command, Salvadori was also to be responsible for Val d'Ossola and Valsesia. He finally reached

[11] Cadorna, *La Riscossa*, p. 228.
[12] Valiani, "Intervento," *MLI*, No. 52/53 (1958), p. 210.
[13] Cadorna, *La Riscossa*, p. 229.
[14] *Ibid.*, p. 230.

Milan early in March.[15] Its atmosphere he found much less siege-like than Turin's; its stores and factories were running more or less as usual; its streets and piazzas were filled with civilians. Quickly he obtained secret lodging on Via Visconti di Modrone and made (or in some cases renewed) the acquaintance of pivotal underground leaders. His rendezvous with but one person could be held fairly safely outdoors; with a group, however, it was preferable to meet in a convent. Prudently he avoided public places, trams, and the city center. His nerves he soothed with camomile tea.[16]

Salvadori's rapid and expert appraisal of the military side of the Resistenza revealed that the partisans and Gappisti were better organized and disciplined than southern intelligence officers had supposed. Within the CVL, he judged, the Garibaldini accounted for 40 per cent of the fighting force; Giellisti, 25 per cent; Liberals, Catholics, and Socialists, the remainder. Initially one fifth of the patriots had been Autonomi and had held aloof from the CLN's, he learned, but by 1945 most of these groups had become political-minded and had gravitated toward either the PLI or DC. Socialists, whose strength traditionally centered in the factories, were still the least well-organized military movement in the rural zones, though belatedly they had fielded some units. According to the best estimates he could get, the Germans had had to assign at least one third of their troops to "contain" the Resistenza Armata. Erstwhile "flankers of Fascism" (*"fiancheggiatori"*) had mostly deserted Mussolini, Salvadori observed; only a few fanatics were still faithful to the semisenile *Duce*. Most industrialists and financiers (whom Salvadori found far less enlightened than their American counterparts) were now collaborating with the Resistance, some joyfully, others reluctantly. In any case, their plants produced as little as possible for the Germans. Almost everyone in the countryside and cities seemed willing to aid the underground insofar as it was prudent. Yet a mood of uncertainty hung over the Lombard capital. To Salvadori's question as to how many people the patriots could count on in Milan in case of insurrection, the answer was "600 if there's no hope; 60,000 if all goes well." [17]

[15] See *supra*, Ch. XI, The Allies and the Armed Resistance in the late winter.
[16] Salvadori, *Resistenza ed azione*, pp. 279–280, 290.
[17] *Ibid.*, pp. 282–283, 285–287.

Since the political facet of the Resistance was more important in Milan than its purely military side, Salvadori made it a point to become well acquainted with the principal politicians, labor leaders, industrialists, and bankers. The PLI and DC were divided on the questions of the Monarchy and the proper degree of governmental intervention in the postwar economy, he learned. Evidence was overwhelming that the Catholics would become a mighty political force that laics could ignore only at their own risk; already the DC ranked in third place (behind the PCI and PSIUP) in mobilizing factory workers. Salvadori found the Actionists inspired (just as the old Giellisti had been) more by a dream than by a program and sometimes unwilling to face up to the philosophical problem of individual freedom. His talks with left-wingers in the split Socialist organization revealed that they thought Italy's future could only be collectivist; but they were less ready than the Communists to use force to achieve their goal. Right-wing Socialists, Salvadori was pleased to learn, were quite tolerant and pragmatic in their view of collectivism. The Communists he found to be compactly regimented and ready to sacrifice everything for their party's cause. Agreement among such a disparate array was never easy; yet almost every clandestine conclave he attended ended in a fair degree of harmony. "Three or four years of this firmness and this moderation and the Italians will have faith in these their new leaders and will be able to govern themselves freely," Salvadori estimated.[18] Perhaps he underrated the fact that it was chiefly the common threat of Nazi-Fascism that kept them from fighting among themselves.

Salvadori often dispatched his reports (usually prepared over week-ends) via Valiani's feminine couriers to SF agents in Switzerland, but he also had access to several radio transmitters belonging to different services.[19] He signaled the patriots' inquiries to the Allies, offered advice as to where missions should be spotted

---

[18] Ibid., pp. 282–288.

[19] Unfortunately, the British sergeant who was to have been his radio operator never made it from the landing field in Piedmont to the lower Monferrato zone nearer Milan, as he had orginally planned. Salvadori had access to an American radio used by "Somma," who substituted for Parri in these weeks; another apparatus near Brescia; a third in the Oltrepò Pavese, controlled by MacMullen, the British liaison officer in Liguria; and a fourth in the Canavese. Missions that were dropped later in the Bergamasco and Valtellina further simplified the communications problem. Ibid., pp. 280–282.

and certain military units should proceed, made recommendations about future AMG administration, and passed on news of the underground's relations with Titoists and Gaullists. In line with the seven-point program he had set for himself, Salvadori gave "suggestions," never "orders," and succeeded in winning and keeping the friendly co-operation of all political currents. Frequently he was asked to clarify Allied policies regarding priorities in supply drops, co-ordination of military actions, establishment of security forces, administration of justice, and safeguarding of industries and utilities. He took special pains to explicate Allied policy with respect to negotiations with the enemy. He was called upon to advise his own headquarters about the significance of Wolff's peace-feelers in Switzerland.[20]

The other high official to arrive from the South in March was Medici-Tornaquinci. He came to explain the Bonomi government's prospectus for the patriots in the postwar period and to arrange for harmonizing the work of the northern CLN's with AMG. Regarding the latter point there was no doubt that most Allied officials and conservative Italian bureaucrats wished to pare down the CLN's to merely advisory entities (as had been demonstrated during the November cabinet crisis).[21] The Undersecretary of Occupied Territories visited Turin first, perhaps because Piedmont was the chief military stronghold of the underground and because he wished to gain its support before going on to Milan. His discussions with the CPLN took place on March 26, 27, and 28. Somewhat peremptorily Medici-Tornaquinci told them: "I come under orders of the Allied Supreme Command

---

[20] *Ibid.*, pp. 288–290. Salvadori's attitude toward the CLN's was more or less shared by Charles Poletti, the outgoing military governor of Latium and Umbria, who was preparing to go to Lombardy as AMG regional commissioner. (He got there before the troops on April 29.) In an interview with a *NYT* correspondent in Rome in mid-March, Poletti declared that he intended to work closely with the partisans. "I don't know what they'll ask for, but unless their demands are completely unreasonable—" A shrug completed the sentence. The partisans he regarded as an alert, active, hard-hitting group that "must be respected," for they were expunging Italy's sense of guilt. Poletti declared that he hoped to give them preference in jobs and to use some in the police force; others would be demobilized. He further stated that he would regard as a Fascist anyone who held office in the party organization, and promised that he would remove him at once from the government. *NYT*, Mar. 19, 1945, 4:7–8; *cf.* comments about Poletti by Prof. Thomas R. Fisher, "Allied Military Government in Italy," *Annals of the American Academy*, cclxvii (Jan. 1950), p. 120.
[21] Catalano, *Storia del CLNAI*, p. 389.

and the Italian Government to tell you what they intend to do as soon as they get to Piedmont. . . . I don't believe that they will agree to any request that the CLNAI may make of a substantial character, small or large. They do not intend to accept modifications of their plans. . . . We must remember that we are a nation liberated by them, not an ally, and therefore we must face the situation as it really is. . . ." [22] The Allies, he explained, wished the CLN's to appoint advisory committees and sundry technical experts to work alongside their opposite numbers in AMG. Describing the nature of Allied agencies and their ponderous procedures, he illustrated his talk with examples of CLN-Allied relations in liberated Florence, of which he had personal knowledge (he had been PLI delegate in the CTLN when it had fought the prefect appointed by the Rome government).[23]

Though dismayed by much of what they heard, the CPLN decided to accept Medici-Tornaquinci's instructions on the assumption that he was doing his level best to save as much status as possible for the CLN's. General Trabucchi noted wryly, however, that the emissary from the South seemed more enthusiastic about plans for corralling partisans into demobilization camps after the war than in dispatching supply drops that could hasten the day of liberation. Right after this conference, incidentally, the enemy captured Trabucchi and kept him in a Milan prison till the eve of the insurrection.[24]

The Florentine Undersecretary next proceeded to Milan for a conference with the CLNAI on the 29th. This meeting (the first full-dress one to be held in several weeks, because of Parri's arrest and stepped-up enemy surveillance) took place in a convent; Salvadori was present. The CLNAI moguls were even less disposed to accept Rome's plans supinely than had been their Piedmontese partners. In a rather stormy session they informed Medici that several revisions were necessary. Some of the Actionists and Socialists even made it clear that they thought the Bonomi government (in which they were not then represented) was in-

[22] Amedeo Ugolini (ed.), "Resistenza e Governo italiano nella missioni Medici-Tornaquinci," *MLI*, No. 25 (1953), pp. 40–41. This is the verbatim report of the Turin conference. The first part is in *MLI*, No. 24, pp. 3–38; the remainder, in No. 25, pp. 25–59.
[23] See *supra*, Ch. x, "War in a museum."
[24] Trabucchi, *I vinti hanno sempre torto*, pp. 182–183; cf. Gobetti, *Diario partigiano* (Mar. 28, 1945), pp. 379–380.

triguing against them. Hours later a revised document was drawn up. It emphasized, as Medici insisted, that the CLN's would rule in accordance with the 1915 Local Government Law; but the Northerners made it clear that they would: (1) retain full power over the purge; (2) stress the need for a uniform policy for all of Upper Italy in CLN-Allied relations; and (3) insist upon the right of the CLN's to name the men who would serve as advisers to Allied agencies.[25] The Bonomi government neither condoned nor ratified these revisions. Technically, therefore, they were invalid; but, as might have been expected, the CLNAI ruled according to its own best judgment during the first emotion-charged days after the insurrection.[26]

Military unification of the Resistance

The fast changing politico-military picture which Medici-Tornaquinci had sketched induced the CLNAI to announce at last (March 29) its approval "in principle" of the long-debated military unification plan.[27] (In the Ossola sector, Oltrepò Pavese, and Piedmont unification already had been achieved.) [28] During the next two weeks several amendments were added. These clarified the nature of military tribunals, the internal structure of the General Command, and accounting procedures, but did not alter the basic blueprint.[29] Affected by the unification were some 43 military zones, 104 divisions (effectives of a patriot division varying from 800 to 1,500 men), and 52 autonomous mountain brigades.[30]

The preamble of the decree indicated that its purpose was to

[25] The text of the CLNAI version of the document is printed in *Documenti ufficiali del CLNAI* (Milan, 1945), p. 41 ff.; also in Catalano, *Storia del CLNAI*, pp. 391–393; cf. Harris, *Allied Military Administration of Italy*, p. 282; Salvadori, *Resistenza ed azione*, p. 287.

[26] Regarding the Milan meeting see also Valiani, "Sul partito della democrazia," *Nuovi Quaderni di Giustizia e Libertà*, No. 5/6 (Jan.–Aug. 1945), pp. 248–249; Valiani, "Ricordi personali e documenti sul CLNAI e l'insurrezione di Milano," *Il Ponte*, XI (1955), 475–477.

[27] See *supra*, Ch. XI, The Allies and the Armed Resistance in the late winter.

[28] Mario Giovana, "La ripresa partigiana in Piemonte nel 1945; l'unificazione delle formazioni," *MLI*, No. 49 (1957), pp. 18–29.

[29] Archivio CLNAI, XXVI/53, cited in Catalano, *Storia del CLNAI*, pp. 363–368; also printed in *Atti del CG/CVL*, No. 151 (Mar. 29), pp. 256–261; Cadorna, *La Riscossa*, pp. 294–299. On April 18 an additional decree clarified CVL internal structure; cf. *ibid.*, pp. 300–306.

[30] Valiani, *Tutte le strade conducono a Roma*, p. 330.

make the Corps of Volunteers of Liberty more efficient and to open the way for its recognition as an integral part of the Italian Armed Forces. Henceforth all fighting groups would take orders from the CG/CVL. The old headquarters erected by political parties would be scrapped, as would such labels as "Garibaldi," "Giustizia e Libertà," "Matteotti," "Autonome," "Fiamma Verde," and "Julia." Detachments, battalions, brigades, and divisions were to be distinguished by both a number and the name of some Resistenza martyr. Brigades would be assigned numbers extending progressively through the entire CVL; divisions would be labelled numerically by region. The new CVL emblem would be the tricolor flag and five-pointed star of Italy, with the CLN seal superimposed. Battalions would normally be commanded by a first lieutenant, and brigades by a major or a lieutenant colonel.[31]

A second section clarified CVL structure. The CG/CVL was to work directly under CLNAI, "which is officially charged with representing the Italian Government in the struggle which the patriots have undertaken against the Fascists and the Germans in unliberated Italy and which for that purpose acts as delegate of the Italian Government." A third subsection discussed the nature of central, regional, zone, and piazza headquarters. On the top echelon would be one commandant, two vice-commandants, one chief of staff, and two attachés. Appointments to the *Comandi Regionali* would be made by the *Comando Generale* upon the recommendation of the regional CLN's. Both the *Comando Generale* and the *Comandi Regionali* "may [italics the author's] organize Corps of Inspectors and any other organisms deemed necessary for the better functioning and strengthening of their command duties. Zone and Piazza Commands, on the other hand, *must* [italics the author's] be composed of a commandant and a commissar, assisted respectively when necessary and opportune by a vice-commandant and vice-commissar and chief of staff. Commandant and commissar must be considered to have equal rank and must collaborate closely, since they are jointly responsible for the military and political behavior of the units as-

[31] Despite ostensible cancellation of political rubrics, many units continued to show their preferences by wearing colored neckerchiefs (blue for the Autonomi, red for the Garibaldi, and green or red for the Giellisti). Battaglia, *SRI*, pp. 508–510.

signed to them, even if the commandant has special care for the military training and direction of the formations and the commissar the political and moral training and leadership of the men, as well as good relations with the population."

Another part of the decree discussed problems of military justice, police, and finance. Military tribunals, to be organized only at the divisional level, would have competence to adjudicate acts committed by enemy civilians and military personnel that were harmful to the interests of the partisan organizations and to the struggle for national liberation. They could also adjudge crimes committed by partisans either on or off duty. In cases involving minor offenses not subject to the death penalty, higher headquarters could suspend trial and sentencing until after the war, at which time the subsequent behavior of the accused would be given due consideration. Military police sections would be formed at divisional headquarters and eventually at the brigade level. Financing of the CVL would be carried out by the CLNAI.

The fifth subsection took up criteria to be followed in military consolidation. These included standardization of various command echelons. For all problems of military operations the headquarters would function according to the normal chain of command; but in matters of political organization (*e.g.*, appointment and dismissal of commanders and commissars and regrouping of units) the headquarters would function in collegial fashion. Secretariats, liaison offices, transportation, and supplies belonging to the myriad political formations would all be placed at the disposal of the CVL commands. In so doing, the latter were not to jeopardize conspiratorial security, which, it was explained, depended not only upon unified direction but upon multiple "sealed compartments."

Finally, the decree enjoined (though with adequate loopholes!) the Freedom Volunteers to don the patriotic hue of the CVL and to shed all political factionalism. Officials of the units were not to participate (in their official capacity) in meetings of the parties but only in manifestations organized on the "political, unitary, and national basis of the CLN." This, however, would not preclude any volunteer from belonging to the anti-Fascist party of his choice and entering into its work insofar as his military duties permitted. CVL units were to assure the broadest freedom of assembly and press for all parties and currents of the CLN. The different headquarters were urged to publish newspapers for the politico-military education of the fighters. These publications should reflect the "line" of national unity in the liberation campaign and shun all "sectarian" polemics. They must circulate freely everywhere.

Parri and Cadorna learn of Allied plans

Early in April Parri and Cadorna reported to Field Marshal Alexander, Supreme Commander of the Mediterranean Theater of Operations, at AFHQ in Caserta. They discussed at length with him topics they had previously explored in Berne and Lyon and reassured him that the Allies would face no such trouble as they had in Greece.[32]

Leaving Caserta, they proceeded to OSS headquarters in Siena, where they examined closely the Franco-Italian frontier disputes. Allied officials indicated that they were ready to permit French forces to penetrate into northwestern Italy in order to tie up a number of German divisions at the moment of the Allied jump-off from the South, but they promised that this French incursion would be limited to twenty kilometers and that no French presidio would be established in Turin. Any French occupation of Piedmontese territory would be controlled by Anglo-American missions. Meanwhile, Italian patriot refugees from disputed border zones would be returned speedily to their homeland to avoid unpleasant incidents. Parri and Cadorna sought to impress the Allies with the need to back up the CLN's position regarding the *italianità* of Val d'Aosta.[33]

On April 4 they called at the Florence headquarters of General Clark, now in command of the Fifteenth Army Group (Fifth and Eighth Armies and CIL). After talking over the plans for administration of the North and for patriot demobilization, they returned to Siena. Two days later they were back in Rome, where Cadorna received his promotion to "general of the division" and conferred with Scoccimarro, Minister of Occupied Territories, about demobilization plans.[34] On the 9th Cadorna and Parri pro-

---

[32] Cadorna, *La Riscossa*, pp. 230–233.
[33] *Ibid.*, pp. 233–235; cf. Harris, *Allied Military Administration of Italy*, p. 318.
[34] Cadorna, *La Riscossa*, p. 235.

ceeded to Caserta to arrange for their transportation back to Milan. Their departure was delayed in order for them to discuss Allied subsidization of the CLNAI with Pizzoni, who had just come from Milan.[35] After these parleys Cadorna and Parri departed by air on the 12th for Lyon and Switzerland. At last they reached Milan on the 19th, one week ahead of the Liberation.[36]

In his full report to the CLNAI on the 19th, Parri explained that the Allies intended to handle all armistice discussions. Though the Allies had reaffirmed the unconditional-surrender formula and intended that, broadly speaking, German troops should surrender and consign their weapons only to Allied troops, they had intimated that local accords between Germans and Freedom Volunteers might be permissible, so long as Allied officers were present when they were made. Units of the Fascist Republican Regular Army should be treated like German ones, the Allies had explained, as should the X[ma] MAS, Republican National Guard, and Black Brigades. Parri reported that he and Cadorna had objected in vain to this arrangement. The Allies, it seemed, wished to avoid any chance of the patriots' using the arms of the defeated foe for their own ends. Parri went on to note that the Allies had underlined the importance of preventing any "scorch" of power plants and industries, or the escape of any Fascists across the frontiers.

The Anglo-Americans were greatly concerned (as always), he continued, lest the CLNAI seek to repudiate the authority of the Rome government after liberation. He and Cadorna had sought to allay these fears by assuring them there would be no trouble, provided there was a full measure of mutual respect. He had promised to furnish the Allies a list of clandestine leaders who could be assigned in an advisory capacity alongside their opposite numbers in AMG regional commissions in Milan, Turin, Genoa, Bologna, Venice, and Padua.[37] The Allies were also desirous, he explained, of up-to-date information about the economic needs of northern industry, so that a unified plan might be worked out

[35] The CLNAI was disturbed by the Allies' continuing practice of sending funds directly to regional CLN's and guerrilla units instead of clearing through the Milan directorate. Some feared this was new evidence of Allied distrust of the CLNAI. Catalano, *Storia del CLNAI*, p. 395.

[36] Cadorna, *La Riscossa*, p. 236.

[37] Harris, *Allied Military Administration of Italy*, pp. 282–283.

for national economic rehabilitation.[38] They had promised supplies of food to forestall disorders that might arise from such shortages. With respect to subsidization of the Armed Resistance, the Allies had sought reassurance that funds were reaching their proper destinations. Concluding his long report, Parri set forth briefly what he had learned about the plans for handling the patriots after the emancipation. He was frank to say that he and Cadorna were not entirely happy about these schemes, and had emphasized the importance of the Allies' avoiding *"decisioni brusche, autoritarie ed unilaterali."* [39]

The demobilization projects, it will be recalled, had been gestating since the liberation of Rome and had been the subject of discussion by the AC Patriots Branch, the Italian Patriots Office, and almost every echelon of the Allied and Italian bureaucracies.[40] Doubtless many of these plans were well intended and useful, but they often bogged down into a tangle of overlapping jurisdictions. A Patriots Office, established in December 1944 under the Presidency of the Italian Council of Ministers and headed by Lieutenant Colonel Siro Bernabò, began to prepare systematic records of bona fide clandestine patriots and plan for their demobilization. After February 2, 1945, this task was taken over (for northern Italy) by the new Ministry for Occupied Italy (created in December 1944); but its Communist minister, Scoccimarro, was not always trusted by his Allied opposite numbers and was not allowed to proceed to the Po valley until several days after the final liberation.[41] Meanwhile, in March Premier Bonomi created another agency, the High Commissariat for Veterans, to look after demobilized patriots (chiefly in central Italy) who no longer fell under the jurisdiction of the Ministries of Occupied Italy and of War. From the outset this agency proved to be a "fifth wheel." By July 1945 the High Commissariat and the Ministry of Occupied Italy merged to form the Ministry of Postwar Assistance. Henceforth all problems affecting the patriots were referred to it. Into this labyrinth crept also (April 5, 1945) an

[38] Of interest here was the planning directive prepared in Rome in April 1945 by the Ministry of Industry and Commerce, reprinted in *MLI*, No. 42 (1956), pp. 3–8.
[39] Report cited in Cadorna, *La Riscossa*, pp. 237–244.
[40] See *supra*, Ch. x, Allied policy regarding the patriots.
[41] Cadorna, *La Riscossa*, p. 236.

unofficial veterans' organization: the ANPI (National Italian Partisans' Association), whose purpose was to help the patriots in the way that the National Combatants Association defended regular Army veterans. ANPI was Communist-controlled from its birth, much to the dismay of democratic resistants.[42]

Shortly before the final Allied drive, Headquarters Fifteenth Army Group issued an operational instruction over the signature of General Alfred M. Gruenther. It assigned responsibility for disarming the Freedom Volunteers to headquarters of the Fifth and Eighth Armies and of IV Corps, with local responsibility being charged to AMG, "with whom the local military commanders will be required to co-operate." [43] Plans called for "stand-down parades," replete with flags and bands, at the end of which the patriots should turn in their weapons. Such ceremonies should appear to be the result of patriot initiative, and Allied commanders were exhorted to bend every effort to win the trust of the partisans, and to be present in the reviewing stands alongside suitable Italian officials. If more than one fifth of the patriots failed to turn in their arms, they should be threatened with punishment after a certain deadline. It was sensed that it would be tactless to hold these parades immediately after the enemy's surrender; and in any case, the partisans and Gappisti probably would have to perform emergency police duties for a few days. It was believed, however, that the ceremonies could be scheduled within a week or ten days after the liberation of each major city.

By spring AC Local Governments Subcommission and Patriots Branch had agreed that guerrilla veterans should enter separation centers as soon as they could be released from temporary police duties. To hasten such discharge, they drew up plans to import several thousand *Carabinieri* from the South.[44] Scoccimarro, it may be noted, decried this move, warning that the *Carabinieri*, traditionally loyal to the King, would be unpopular in the republican North. In supervision of each of the thirty or forty patriot centers would be commissions composed of one Allied officer and

[42] Cesare Moscone, *La legislazione partigiana* (Turin, 1947), pp. 5–9 ff.; C. Moscone, *Leggi sulla Resistenza e suoi partigiani* (Turin, 1949); R. Battaglia, "Il riconoscimento dei partigiani," *Il Ponte*, III (1947), pp. 1001–1014; and unpublished ms. in Hoover Library, Stanford University, *L'attività dell'ufficio patrioti della Lombardia dal 1º maggio al 15 settembre 1945*.

[43] Harris, *Allied Military Administration of Italy*, p. 278.

[44] *Ibid.*, pp. 285–288.

509

an Italian Military Patriots Representative, responsible to the AMG Regional Commissioner. In some cases there might also be a local CLN delegate. Discipline should be maintained by a patriot officer. Veterans should remain in these centers no longer than two to four weeks, it was hoped, at the end of which time they could choose one of three courses. A substantial minority might be permitted to enroll individually in the regular Army insofar as its quota permitted.[45] Some others might be recruited to work for AMG in sundry labor and reconstruction projects (Scoccimarro suggested using them for mine clearance); but probably most should be encouraged to return home quickly to a "normal" life.

It was planned that in the patriot centers the veterans would receive food on the Italian Army scale if the Combined Chiefs of Staff approved and it was available. (Unhappily, this was not always possible.) In case of need, they should be given a few basic articles of clothing out of surplus, to be dyed distinctively and stamped with a yellow "V." If available, they should receive up to eighty cigarettes a week, and should have hospitalization in Italian military hospitals on the same basis as regular Army personnel. They definitely should receive a mustering-out certificate signed by Field Marshal Alexander and attesting to their patriotic services. And, not least, there should be separation pay. This latter problem necessitated even more negotiations than the others. The initial plans in mid-February 1945 called for but 500 lire for patriots with more than three months' service; 5,000 for wounded veterans; and 10,000 for families of patriots killed in action. (The official exchange rate in the South at this juncture was 100 lire to the dollar.) Then on March 24 Scoccimarro raised these sums to one, five, and ten thousand lire respectively. After a new tussle in the post-liberation weeks this was further elevated in June to five, ten, and twenty thousand lire, respectively. In the final summation of accounts, the Italian government was responsible

[45] In mid-February the army had 48,000 vacancies; ex-partisans, it was then surmised, could fill about 10,000 of these. Scoccimarro would have preferred enrollment of units en bloc into the Army. The possibility was foreseen of various reconnaissance companies of about 500 each from patriot bands to be employed with the five Italian combat groups in the CIL. For Mauro Scoccimarro's political program, see his *Nuova democrazia*, ed. Bruzio Manzocchi (Rome, 1958).

for the funds, just as it had to bear most of the other costs of occupation.[46]

Final liberation drive

On March 28 General Clark warned the partisans by radio that large-scale action was impending. He advised them to "consolidate and perfect their present organizations" rather than take on new personnel. If necessary, they should "weed out" inefficient recruits. "When the Germans retreat, leaving Fascist troops to cover their rear," the patriots should "harry their retreat." Clark promised more arms to the patriots in the central Apennines, as they doubtless would be first to fight. He issued special instructions to certain units and entreated everyone to avoid political discord.[47]

At last on April 5 the Allies kicked off their final offensive with a diversionary attack by the Fifth Army along the Ligurian coast. During the next six days elements of that army captured Massa and "with the aid of Italian partisans the town of Carrara." [48] On the 9th the Eighth Army delivered the major thrust—a stunning blow in the flooded Lake Comacchio region; then they moved forward toward Argenta and Ferrara, in the hope of outflanking Bologna and pushing toward Padua.

While this drive was in progress General Clark broadcast yet another special message (April 13) to the patriots: "You are prepared to fight, but the time for your concerted action has not yet come. Certain bands have been given special instructions. Other bands will concentrate on preserving their districts and towns from destruction when the enemy is forced to withdraw. . . . To those bands not given specific tasks for the immediate future: you are to nurse your strength and be ready for the call. Do not play into the hands of the enemy by acting before the

[46] Cadorna, *La Riscossa*, pp. 235–244; Harris, *Allied Military Administration of Italy*, pp. 279–282 ff.; talks of Scoccimarro with Col. Cripps, Director of Local Governments Subcommission of AC, and with Lt. Col. Craig of AC Patriots Branch on March 7, 27, April 11, 26, 27, 1945; Ugolini (ed.), "Resistenza e Governo italiano nella missione Medici-Tornaquinci," *MLI*, No. 24 (1953), pp. 8–9; Moscone, *Leggi sulla Resistenza, passim*.

[47] *NYT*, Mar. 29, 1945, 9:2.

[48] Clark, *Calculated Risk*, p. 429. Regarding the Carrara sector, see memoirs of GL commandant Nardo Dunchi, *Memorie partigiane* (Florence, 1956).

time chosen for you. Do not squander your strength. Do not be tempted to premature action. When the time comes, one and all will be called upon to play his or her part in liberating Italy and in destroying the hated enemy." [49] There is little doubt that Clark hoped the patriots would refrain from attempting any insurrection, lest it open a Pandora's box of political imponderables.

The northern underground strategists, however, were not inclined to be so patient and self-effacing as General Clark would have liked them to be. On April 10 PCI headquarters in Milan issued Directive No. 16, one of the capital documents of the Resistenza Armata. Laying the basis for the final insurrection and eliminating any chance of *attesismo* or dissuasion by Allied military missions, it summarized under three headings the role of the people in the uprising:

(1) *Procedure.* Partisan formations will attack and eliminate Nazi-Fascist headquarters and effect the liberation of cities, towns, and villages. Gappists and Sappists will break up road-blocks and wipe out Nazi-Fascist command posts. The appropriate organizations will proclaim a general strike whose character must be clearly and unmistakably defined—*i.e.*, it must be made plain from the first that this strike is not a mere popular demonstration of anger, but that it is the culmination of the people's long campaign for freedom and the expression of their unshakable determination.

(2) *Disintegration of the enemy.* The enemy will be faced with the following alternatives: "Surrender or Die."

(3) *The struggle against attesismo.* The Gordian knot of *attesismo* must be cut without delay. On no account whatsoever must our comrades in military or civil organizations accept any proposal or advice or consider any plan designed to limit, prevent, or obstruct the national uprising. . . . A combination of firmness, tact and skill must be employed in all discussions with Allied Military Missions which have elected to be the mouthpiece of the *attendisti*, and are therefore inclined to attach too little importance to our urgent requests for the arms and ammunition needed to ensure the success of the insurrection. . . . In the circumstances, we must be prepared to face the fact that the Allies may decide, for one reason or another, to withhold their support, instead of making the contributions for which we have asked.[50]

[49] Clark, *Calculated Risk*, p. 430; NYT, April 14, 1945, 16:6.

[50] Excerpts from the long document may be found in Longo, *Un popolo alla macchia*, p. 413; Secchia, *I Comunisti e l'insurrezione*, pp. 486–489; Battaglia, *SRI*, pp. 543–545; and in abbreviated English translation (cited above) in Battaglia, *Story of the Italian Resistance*, tr. and ed. by P. D. Cummins (London:

The PCI directive provided the frame of reference for more detailed ones to be issued by the CLNAI in the next few days.

On the 12th, for example, the CLNAI denounced as war criminals all members of the Fascist directorate. On the 13th it decreed the following regulations for the patriot formations to observe toward those Nazi-Fascists who surrendered:

(1) The struggle undertaken against the Nazi-Fascist military formations will be continued until their unconditional surrender. At the moment of surrender, the Nazi-Fascist formations must consign, in addition to their arms, all other means and matériel which they possess.

(2) Without exception, all the armed formations that have served the so-called "Italian Social Republic" must be dissolved and disarmed. Under no pretext—even if they should declare themselves ready to pass to the service of the CLN—may such formations be employed for services of any kind whatsoever. The individuals formerly belonging to the Fascist military formations who, after the dissolution of these, are captured while still bearing arms, shall be executed.

(3) The military personnel of the Fascist army (except for officers and noncommissioned officers) who have served because of conscription and who surrender on the basis of Article 1 shall be given their freedom. If they are responsible for crimes prescribed under existing dispositions, they must be interned. Officers and noncommissioned officers will be interned.

(4) Everyone without exception—officers, noncommissioned officers and soldiers belonging to voluntary Fascist military formations (Black Brigades, Muti, GNR, X^{ma} MAS, Police Corps, etc.)—shall as soon as they are disarmed be interned, it being necessary to ascertain their responsibility. The custody of these groups shall be very rigorous and carried out with sufficient personnel to prevent escape or mass liberation.

(5) German officers and soldiers who surrender, in accordance with what has been set forth in Article 1, shall be treated as prisoners of war and consigned to the Allies as soon as possible.[51]

On the 19th the CLNAI assembled for a session of great importance. After listening to Parri report on Allied plans, it issued a proclamation giving "formal" notice to the German and Fas-

Odhams Press, 1957), pp. 260–261. Quoted by kind permission of the publishers.

[51] Printed in Documenti ufficiali del CLNAI, pp. 19–20, and in Catalano, Storia del CLNAI, pp. 403–404. Quoted by kind permission of the publishers: Gius. Laterza & Figli Casa Editrice, Bari.

cist armed forces, civil officials of the Fascist Republic and of the German occupation apparatus to "surrender or perish." [52]

Later that day it took up the problem of the CLNAI presidency. In view of the growing evidence that the Allies and Southerners hoped to whittle down the CLN's to purely advisory status, the three leftist parties advocated measures to intensify the political complexion of the CLNAI and enable it to hold its own in the coming showdown. Hitherto, Pizzoni, the highly respected banker who had negotiated the financial accords with the Allies in December 1944 and who at this moment was in Caserta on a similar mission, had held the presidency on an ostensibly nonpartisan basis, though his personal sympathies tended in the direction of the PLI. For some weeks Pertini (PSIUP) and other hotspurs had been talking of the need for a CLNAI chairman who would "stand up" to the Allies at the Liberation. Pertini naturally favored a Socialist. Marazza (DC) argued, on the other hand, that someone from his party deserved the post if Pizzoni were to be cashiered (which he did not favor in any case). Both could make out a good case for greater recognition of the weight of their parties in the CLNAI in order to counterbalance the practical predominance of the PCI and Pd'A in the CVL. Valiani (Pd'A) also wanted the group to discuss the question of who should become President of the Council of Ministers and Minister of Interior. The others considered this premature. Consequently, the talks were restricted to the problem of the CLNAI presidency. The leftists agreed upon the candidacy of Rodolfo Morandi, who hitherto had represented the PSIUP in the Piedmontese CLN. As there was reluctance on the part of the DC and PLI to agree in Pizzoni's absence, however, the decision was postponed until the eve of the insurrection of April 25, at which time the need for quick action forced all to accept Morandi.[53] The Allies continued to invite Pizzoni to formal functions, "thus ignoring his successor," Cadorna has related.[54]

[52] *Documenti ufficiali del CLNAI*, pp. 82–84; Archivio CLNAI, IV/17, cited in Catalano, *Storia del CLNAI*, pp. 406–407.

[53] Valiani, "Ricordi personali sul CLNAI e l'insurrezione di Milano," *Il Ponte*, XI (1955), pp. 477–478; Catalano, *Storia del CLNAI*, pp. 394–398; Salvadori, *Resistenza ed azione*, pp. 294–295. For the writings of Morandi during the underground era, see his multivolume *Opere* (Turin, 1958 ff.). Cf. also *supra*, Ch. IV, n. 99.

[54] Cadorna, *La Riscossa*, p. 258.

As the hour for insurrection neared, the CLNAI dispatched (the 21st) an "emergency circular" to the local CLN's and military headquarters ordering them to violate the curfew in order to halt any Nazi-Fascist patrols in circulation lest they sabotage factories and utilities.[55] At PLI instigation on the 23rd, the CLNAI declared that anyone found guilty of destroying means of communication and any kind of industrial establishment would be considered a war criminal.[56] Another decree on the 23rd announced appointment of a committee made up of Sereni, Pizzoni, and others to take into custody the official archives of the scattered RSI ministries.[57] Finally, on the 24th the CLNAI fired a warning to the enemy to stop maltreating Jews imprisoned in San Vittore.[58]

Allied troops and Freedom Volunteers, meanwhile, pressed their offensive. During the first few days of April Piedmontese patriots repossessed Alba, Val Pellice, the Pinerolese, and some other sectors evacuated by the foe.[59] But the most violent action took place in Emilia-Romagna, in the center of the Allied push. On the 14-15th Fifth Army, supported by tremendous artillery barrages and many fighter-bombers, blasted its way into the corridor below Bologna. Insurrection broke out in Imola on the 14th, with the result that the city was in patriot hands when Polish elements of the Eighth Army entered next day. The Poles began shelling Bologna on the 18th. To the north, Argenta fell that day. The road to Ferrara lay open.[60]

Caught in a pincers by the Fifth and Eighth Armies, Bologna could no longer hold out. As early as the evening of the 19th some of its inhabitants rose up; within a few hours, volunteers led by Communists Barontini ("Dario"), Cavazzuti, and Aldo Cucchi gained control of parts of the city. Quiet efficiency characterized these operations. Most of the partisans were not derisive of the German prisoners they managed to take; rather, they were proud and scornful. At dawn on the 21st, Allied troops (among them the Italian "Legnano" Combat Group) entered Bologna.

[55] Archivio CLNAI, iii/18, cited in Catalano, Storia del CLNAI, p. 408.
[56] Archivio CLNAI, ii/27, cited in ibid., p. 409.
[57] Cited in ibid., pp. 409–410.
[58] Archivio CLNAI, v/34, cited in ibid., p. 410.
[59] Valiani, Tutte le strade conducono a Roma, p. 331.
[60] Clark, Calculated Risk, pp. 431–432.

The "Red citadel" gave the liberators a sober, mature reception which differed markedly from anything they had yet experienced in Italy. Quickly the CLN elected Giuseppe Dozza (PCI) mayor. He greeted the American Senior Civil Affairs Officer for the II Corps upon his arrival, and the latter decided to keep him in office. The smooth co-operation between patriots and Allies in Bologna set a good precedent. On the 25th Bologna held its "stand-down" parade of 15,000 in the presence of Prince Humbert (who got a surprisingly warm reception) and Generals Clark and Hume. Not more than 4,000 weapons were turned in, however, and these were mostly old rifles.[61]

Having descended onto terrain where their armored units could operate effectively, the Allies raced toward the Po. Hitler unwittingly helped them, for he had ordered his commanders to hold the entire basin rather than retreat to either the Po or Adige rivers where strong defensive positions could have been erected.[62] "Everywhere in the Po Valley there was action and movement— the enemy struggling to get out of the plain, but disorganized in command and smashed by our ranging planes; our forces moving here and there in seeming confusion, but actually carrying out a masterful plan to hem the enemy into ever narrowing pockets," historian Starr has written.[63]

The partisans offered close combat to the retreating foe in Modena and freed it on April 21–22, just before the Fifth Army entered. Helping out in the operation was a hard-hitting mixed-nationality SF contingent led by Roy Farran and dropped behind the lines in the Secchia valley in March.[64] The patriots, it was claimed, killed some 200 Germans and took 500 prisoners.[65] Modena followed Bologna's precedent in installing a Communist mayor (Alfeo Corassori, an ex-construction worker). Again, as in Bologna, the partisans displayed "cold scorn and contempt" for the Germans.[66] When the "stand-down" parade of 9,000 men

[61] Ibid., pp. 433–434; Longo, Un popolo alla macchia, p. 429; Starr, From Salerno to the Alps, p. 418; Harris, Allied Military Administration of Italy, pp. 297–300; NYT, April 27, 1945, 5:7.
[62] Clark, Calculated Risk, pp. 434–435, 441.
[63] Starr, From Salerno to the Alps, p. 429.
[64] Farran, Winged Dagger: Adventures on Special Service, pp. 261–340.
[65] Battaglia, SRI, pp. 570–572.
[66] Milton Bracker in NYT, April 25, 1945, 3:8.

took place in Modena, somewhat more arms were turned in pro-portionately than in Bologna, however.[67]

To the northeast, Ferrara also experienced heavy casualties in guerrilla combat. Eighth Army units reached it on the 23rd and got to the south bank of the Po next day. Everywhere they came upon partisans. Most of the foreign liberators formed a much higher opinion of the patriots than before: "These guys are good," remarked the intelligence officer of the 2nd New Zealand Division.[68]

In the center of the valley the Fifth Army fanned out to the north and northwest. On the 24th the American 10th Mountain Division, heading for Verona, Salò, and Trent, was the first Allied unit to cross the Po at San Benedetto Po. The crossing generally was the signal for patriot uprisings in the northwest. Together with the 85th and 88th Mountain Infantry Divisions of II Corps, the 10th Mountain Division reached Verona on the 26th and then pushed toward Lake Garda. In Verona the II Corps Civil Affairs Chief confirmed Socialist Aldo Fedeli as mayor; he represented the local CLN in its third transfiguration.[69]

Striking northwestward along Via Emilia on the right bank of the Po, the 1st Armored Division, followed by Brazilian troops, moved into Reggio Emilia on the 24th, Parma the 25th, and reached Piacenza the next day. Everywhere partisan operations were of real help in liberating these cities and clearing the mountains to the south. In Piacenza an enemy garrison of Italian SS and German troops held off the Americans and Brazilians until the 28–29th. The American 34th Division blocked off the Piacenza escape route to the northwest, while other Allied forces crushed a strong enemy pocket in the Cremona zone to the northeast.

Along the Ligurian coastal highway the exceptionally distinguished Japanese-American 442nd Battalion from Hawaii and other Allied units made headway, capturing LaSpezia naval base on the 23rd. Early the 27th they reached Genoa, only to find that the German garrison had surrendered the day before to the patriots. Indeed, prior to the juncture of Allied forces in Italy's

[67] Harris, *Allied Military Administration of Italy*, p. 298.
[68] Cox, *Road to Trieste*, p. 153.
[69] Bracker in *NYT*, April 27, 1945, 5:1.

"industrial triangle," successful insurrections had occurred in Genoa, Milan, and Turin.

German negotiations in Switzerland

Before we describe these great uprisings, a few words are in order about the negotiations SS General Wolff had begun with Dulles in Switzerland.[70] For several weeks in April there was no direct contact between them, although intermediaries kept up some liaison. Upon his return from Germany, where his family was now under surveillance, Wolff found it difficult to resume his plans. Then suddenly he reappeared in Lucerne on April 24, accompanied by his adjutant, Major Wenner, and by Lieutenant Colonel Viktor von Schweinitz of General von Vietinghoff's headquarters. Apparently Wolff hoped to sign the final armistice. Several days ensued before the Allied Combined Chiefs of Staff granted authorization for final signature.

By the 26th Wolff was worried lest his own headquarters in Fasano be taken by the partisans, who had already launched triumphant insurrections in most of the major cities. Deciding to head back to Italy, he gave full authority to his companions to sign the armistice. The Allies at last issued orders on the 27th for Schweinitz and Wenner to proceed to AFHQ in Caserta. They arrived there late the 28th and signed the unconditional surrender instrument on the 29th, to become effective May 2. By then, of course, the Germans had already been defeated in the field by the combined sinews of the Allies and the patriots. It may be noted in passing that soon after he crossed the frontier, Wolff was cut off and besieged in a villa near Como by the partisans. To rescue him from this hazardous situation and safeguard his usefulness, OSS ordered one of its liaison officers in the zone to return him to Switzerland. Later Wolff was permitted to cross the Austrian border to his headquarters, which by then had been transferred to Bolzano.[71]

Port of Genoa saved

The patriot insurrection in Genoa was probably the most valuable militarily and economically of all, for it helped save the vast

[70] See *supra*, Ch. xii, Enemy efforts to stave off insurrection.

[71] Feis, *Roosevelt, Churchill, Stalin*, pp. 583–596; Alexander, *The Italian Campaign*, pp. 62–66; Lanfranchi, *La resa degli ottocentomila*, p. 277 ff.

port facilities from complete destruction. In some respects the uprising was a "model," not only for Italy but all Europe, according to Communist historian Battaglia.[72] Some 3,100 poorly armed partisans, Gappisti, and Sappisti pitted themselves against a well-armed German garrison of about 6,000 men possessing heavy artillery. The foe, moreover, had in the port area 1,500 marines of the Italian X^{ma} MAS and 600 members of the Black Brigades, as well as some 3,400 of Graziani's Republican Army troops. The last group, however, showed no hostility to the patriots. The partisans' Ligurian Regional Military Command had drawn up careful battle plans for the city.

The enemy's first effort to destroy the port occurred on April 19, when he exploded several munitions dumps and sank some small vessels. Though he sabotaged an Italian aircraft carrier on the 21st and caused it to list badly, he was unable to sink it at the right point to block entry to the port. Whether he made any further efforts to sabotage the port is unclear from the conflicting testimony. On the 23rd General Guenther Meinhold, the German commander of land forces in the city, dispatched a delegate to the local archbishop to ask permission of the Ligurian CLN to evacuate his troops to Tortona, forty miles inland, in return for promising not to damage the city further. After an all-night session presided over by DC economist Paolo Emiliano Taviani, the CLN rejected the request.[73] Leftists were not ready to trust the enemy, and in any case they were committed to a policy of uncompromising insurrection.

On the morning of the 24th general insurrection began. The insurgents gained possession of public buildings, utilities, and many railway junctions in the province. In the city piazzas there was combat. The enemy kept control of the heights and began a pincers movement against the insurgents. That night fighting continued to be heavy; thousands of workers rose up, arming themselves as best they could. When the Germans threatened to bombard the city unless it surrendered, the CLN answered that if this bombardment occurred, the patriots would execute 1,000 prisoners. On the morning of the 25th, after the insurgents had

[72] Battaglia, *SRI*, p. 553.
[73] Paolo E. Taviani has written a *Breve storia dell'insurrezione di Genova* (4th ed.; Genoa, 1956).

captured several strong points, General Meinhold went to the archiepiscopate and at 7:30 p.m. (much to the surprise of the CLN) surrendered to Remo Scappini (PCI), President of the Ligurian CLN. It appears to have been the first recorded instance of a German senior officer surrendering to an Italian civilian. The Germans were ordered to consign their arms to the partisans and their prisoners to the Allies as soon as they arrived. The armistice went into effect at 9 a.m. on the 26th, but those Germans in Genoa who were under the command of Max Berninghaus paid no attention for a time to "traitor" Meinhold's agreement (ineffectually a drumhead tribunal sentenced him to death), so that fighting continued, especially around the harbor. It would appear that both the archbishop and those patriots who dismantled some of the mines can properly claim joint credit for saving the port from further sabotage.[74]

When Fifth Army units entered Genoa early the 27th they found that the partisans had 6,000 German prisoners in the city and some 12,000 more in the mountains. The patriots had suffered perhaps 400 dead and 850 wounded. On the 28th General Clark cited the exemplary work of the Ligurian CLN, which had installed a PLI man as prefect, a DC as vice-prefect, a PSIUP as mayor, a PRI as *questore*, and a PCI as vice-*questore*. Genoa's "stand-down" parade was scheduled for May 2.[75]

Milanese insurrection (April 24-26)

Milan was the second great industrial city to undergo the liberating insurrection. In this nerve center events rushed to a climax. On the evening of the 17th Mussolini transferred his headquarters from Salò to Milan's Prefectural Palace on Via Monforte.[76] Be-

[74] See Istituto storico della Resistenza in Liguria, *Atti della Commissione d'inchiesta sul salvamento del porto di Genova* (Genoa, 1951); Enrico Trinchieri, *Dal 23 al 26 aprile 1945 (contributo alla storia dell'insurrezione di Genova)* (Genoa, 1949); E. Trinchieri, *La resa di Villa Migone* (Genoa, 1950); Guenther Meinhold, "Come firmai la resa," Genoa *Secolo XIX*, April–May 1949.

Certain writers have asserted that SS General Wolff, to facilitate his own armistice negotiations, succeeded in countermanding further sabotage by the Germans. *Cf.* Lanfranchi, *La resa degli ottocentomila*, pp. 261–263; Silvestri, *Graziani, Mussolini, e l'antifascismo*, p. 553.

[75] Baccino, *Contributo alla storia della resistenza di Genova*, pp. 169–184; Longo, *Un popolo alla macchia*, pp. 437–439; Battaglia, *SRI*, pp. 552–557; Silvio Micheli, *Giorni di fuoco* (Rome, 1955), ch. "Il salvataggio del porto di Genova"; Harris, *Allied Military Administration of Italy*, pp. 300–303.

[76] Earlier Hitler had insisted that, if need be, Mussolini must transfer his govern-

fore quitting Lake Garda he apparently considered a last-ditch defense feasible. He had not yet lost confidence in the loyalty of his neo-Fascist forces, and he was uninformed of General Wolff's armistice bids.[77] In a cabinet meeting in Milan on the 20th the *Duce*'s chief party adviser, Pavolini, suggested again that they organize an ultimate defense system in Sondrio and the Valtellina redoubt northeast of Lake Como. There they could try to negotiate with the Allies, perhaps flee to Switzerland, and should worse come to worst, "die in beauty." Pavolini's bravado elicited scant support from the others, who sensed it was rather late to build up any Alpine Thermopylae, even though the "Tagliamento" Legion, a Black Brigade, and some other units were there. Death, no matter how transcendently beautiful its setting, held little attraction for them.[78]

For his part, Mussolini realized the gravity of the situation after he got to Milan. Already his son Vittorio had been seeking unsuccessfully an accord with the Allies through Cardinal Schuster. Hierarchs like Paolo Zerbino, Buffarini-Guidi, and Montagna also visited the archbishopric. So did Marshal Graziani.[79]

Many schemes seem to have raced through the *Duce*'s mind during this period. One of the strangest occurred on the 22nd: he would attempt to turn over power to the PSIUP and Pd'A in an effort to split the Resistance! For this maneuver he utilized Carlo Silvestri, a quondam Socialist journalist who in the 1920's had collaborated with the Anti-Fascist Concentration in France before he became soured and volunteered (in December 1943) to serve the *Duce* as an intermediary with his youthful Marxist associates.[80] Since the PSIUP and Pd'A were boycotting Bonomi's

---

ment to the Reich; but in the last days when the *Duce* made it clear that he preferred to take his chances in Italy, the *Fuehrer* changed his mind and advised Ambassador von Rahn to let Mussolini create his own myth. Dombrowski, *Mussolini: Twilight and Fall*, pp. 159–160.

[77] Regarding Mussolini's last weeks, see especially Tamaro, *Due anni di storia*, III, 507–576 ff.

[78] Cione, *Storia della RSI*, pp. 442–444; Salvatorelli and Mira, *Storia d'Italia nel periodo fascista* (Turin, 1957), p. 1118; Carli-Ballola, *Sdr*, pp. 286–287.

[79] Graziani, *Ho difeso la patria*, pp. 495–496.

[80] In impassioned tracts Silvestri has published many revelations, allegations, and counterallegations about the anti-Fascists: *I responsabili della catastrofe italiana* (Rome, 1946); *Turati l'ha detto* (Milan, 1946); *Contro la vendetta* (Milan, 1948); and *Mussolini, Graziani, e l'antifascismo* (1943–'45) (Milan, 1949).

second government, Mussolini and Silvestri hoped they might win their support. But the desperate bid was rejected flatly by Actionists Valiani and Lombardi and Socialists Pertini, Lelio Basso, and Corrado Bonfantini.[81]

On the 23rd General Cadorna, who had returned from Caserta four days earlier, convened the CG/CVL. Only representatives of the leftist triad attended. Aldo ("Guido") Lampredi, a prominent Venetian Communist, substituted for Longo, who had reason to believe that the enemy had identified him the day before. The Pd'A was represented by Avv. Corti instead of Parri; the PSIUP, by Avv. Stucchi, ex-commandant of the "Matteotti" units in Val d'Ossola. Cadorna reported on the discussions that he and Parri had had in liberated Italy. Lampredi expressed dismay at the news the Allies would approve local accords with the Germans whereby the latter would surrender only to the Allies in return for safeguarding industrial plants. He was also distressed that the Allies should demand that Fascist soldiers be treated as regular PW's. That same evening Arpesani (PLI) and Marazza (DC), who were negotiating with the Germans in Milan through Schuster's office, reported to Cadorna on their progress. But of greater import was the news that Mussolini himself was ready to talk to Cadorna.[82]

The *Duce* sent a Milanese industrialist, Gian Riccardo Cella, to request of Cadorna guaranties for the personal safety of the dictator, his hierarchs, and their families. Cella also asked assurances that the Fascist Militia be permitted to concentrate itself in Valtellina and surrender only to Anglo-Americans. Cadorna and Marazza answered that, if the *Duce* wished to surrender, he must come to the CLNAI in the sole place which the latter considered neutral—to Cardinal Schuster's archiepiscopate at Piazza Fontana. They warned the emissary that Mussolini must surrender unconditionally, for only in that way might he have the assurance of a regular trial. Cella promised to bring an early reply.[83]

On the morning of the 24th news of Genoa's insurrection was telephoned to the Milanese Insurrectional Committee, which since March was composed of Longo (PCI), Sereni (PCI), Per-

[81] L. Valiani, *L'avvento di DeGasperi: tre anni di politica italiana* (Turin, 1949), p. 9.
[82] Cadorna, *La Riscossa*, p. 249.
[83] *Ibid.*, pp. 249–250; Valiani, *Tutte le strade conducono a Roma*, p. 337.

tini (PSIUP), and Valiani (Pd'A). The committee also learned of the American crossing of the Po that day. It decided that the moment was at hand for insurrectionary strikes to break out in Milan. (The same day the General Command of the Garibaldi brigades issued insurrection orders to Veneto and Piedmont.) During the evening of the 24th some preliminary skirmishes occurred at the Pirelli rubber plants on the edge of the Lombard metropolis. But not till early on the 25th did the CLNAI, meeting in plenary session in the Collegio dei Salesiani convent in Via Copernico, issue the definitive order for insurrection. Cadorna published it that evening.[84] The decree terminated with a rhetorical flourish: "At this moment all the world is watching you! In the name of our martyrs, give proof of your valor! Don't forget those for whom you have fought and suffered so much. Long live Italy! Death to the Nazi-Fascist oppressors!" [85] Whatever the merits of the argument as to whether the Insurrectional Committee had the right to take action on its own, one thing was certain, Cadorna has vouchsafed: "It could not have been issued at a more opportune moment, and the results justified completely the risk taken." [86]

The plenary CLNAI meeting of the 25th (presided over by the new Socialist president Morandi) repeated the formula of "unconditional surrender," to be effected before 6 p.m. that day. This was the definitive answer to various bids the enemy had sent Resistance chieftains through Cardinal Schuster. The CLNAI next proceeded to issue three significant decrees. The first announced the insurrection and transfer of all civil and military power to the CLNAI and various regional and local CLN's. This was announced both in the name of the Italian "people" and as "delegate" of the Italian government; the next day the CLNAI added the CVL as a third fount of authority.[87]

A lengthy second decree established special popular courts of

[84] L. Valiani, "Personali ricordi," *Il Ponte*, xi (1955), p. 478; R. Cadorna, "Note e discussioni," *MLI*, No. 31 (1954), p. 44; Valiani, *Tutte le strade conducono a Roma*, p. 337; Longo, *Un popolo alla macchia*, p. 435; Battaglia, *SRI*, p. 558.
[85] Quoted in Maraldi, *Storia della seconda guerra mondiale*, p. 478.
[86] Cadorna, *La Riscossa*, pp. 254–255.
[87] Battaglia, *SRI*, p. 559; Catalano, *Storia del CLNAI*, p. 428. Signing the latter decree the 26th were Longo and Sereni (PCI); Parri and Valiani (Pd'A); Marazza and Augusto DeGasperi (DC); Arpesani and Filippo Jacini (PLI); and Morandi and Pertini (PSIUP).

assize, tribunals of war, and commissions of justice. By implication it ordered Mussolini's execution, for Article 5 stated, ". . . Members of the Fascist Government and the hierarchs of Fascism who are guilty of suppressing the constitutional guaranties, destroying popular liberties, creating the Fascist regime, compromising and betraying the fate of the country, and conducting it to the present catastrophe are to be punished with the penalty of death, and in less grave instances life-imprisonment." Those who organized Fascist squads that carried out deeds of violence and those who led the "insurrection" of October 28, 1922, were to be punished according to the Penal Code of 1889. Anyone guilty of crimes against the state since September 8, 1943, would be punished in accordance with the military laws of war in effect as of that time. The accused might defend himself if he could prove that he had prevented atrocities and destruction of national property. Or, if he had been forced to collaborate with the foe as a result of grave threats to his person or family, he could plead for leniency.[88] Unquestionably this was stern. "If the Liberation had occurred a year earlier," Valiani has averred, "the insurrectional movement would have shown much greater generosity. But the ferocious Nazi-Fascist repressions of the second half of 1944 had embittered the popular mind."[89]

A third decree of capital importance abrogated the neo-Fascist socialization edicts of October 12 and November 12, 1944, though it reaffirmed the provisions limiting profits. It abolished the neo-Fascists' factory councils and replaced them with national *consigli di gestione* ("management councils"), to be elected freely by the employees within three months after the Liberation. Thus the workers' representatives gained strategic posts from which to carry out purges in the factories. Technicians responsible for production would take over the specific work of the old factory head except in cases where *epurazione* decrees assigned authority to a "management commissioner." Any credits that had accrued to the workers during Fascist "socialization" were to be diverted to a special relief fund to be used in behalf of the laborers.[90] Meanwhile, the Economic Commission of the CLNAI issued addi-

[88] The decree is cited in Catalano, *Storia del CLNAI*, pp. 413-419; a supplementary one is quoted in *ibid.*, pp. 419-425.

[89] Valiani, *Tutte le strade conducono a Roma*, pp. 338-340.

[90] Battaglia, *SRI*, pp. 559-561; Catalano, *Storia del CLNAI*, pp. 404-406.

tional decrees designed to prevent black-marketing of scarce food supplies and to safeguard property.[91]

By mid-afternoon of the 25th, Milan's insurrectional strike was in full swing. Streetcar employees quit their posts en masse; businessmen and workingmen rallied to guard their plants from sabotage. Employees of the Pirelli rubber factory seized the German command post there. Defense of the Breda munitions plant proved more difficult. Municipal office buildings and radio stations were captured one by one. By early evening SAP brigades reached the edge of the city. Milan's uprising was relatively bloodless compared to Genoa's the day before or Turin's next day.[92] Allied liaison officer Salvadori reported that when he walked through the streets at 4 p.m. not a German or Fascist uniform could be seen, whereas only three hours earlier many had been visible: "All shops were closed and all trams had disappeared . . . , the city was silent. . . . At 4:30 p.m. I saw the first group of patriots, a patrol on bicycles. At 5:30 I saw the first truck with a red flag. At 6 I saw civilians attacking two German trucks. When I reached my lodgings I told my host: 'This is the end.' " [93]

Later that afternoon the CLNAI reconvened next door to a X^{ma} MAS detachment. Marazza, who had conferred with Cardinal Schuster, returned with news that Mussolini would arrive at the archbishopric at 5 p.m. The CLNAI designated Cadorna, Marazza (DC), and Riccardo Lombardi (Pd'A) to talk with him. According to Valiani, they were instructed "not to discuss, but to demand unconditional capitulation; to announce that in case of surrender, the Fascist troops would be treated according to international law, on the basis of agreements made with the Allied Command. The conference must not last more than an hour. If Mussolini agrees to surrender, he must be arrested and detained in the archbishop's office." [94] While the three went forth on their mission, Longo, Sereni, and Valiani stayed behind, nervously awaiting the outcome.

Mussolini arrived at the archiepiscopal palace somewhat before

[91] See "Documenti della Commissione Economica del CLNAI, Parte II," *MLI*, No. 51 (1958), pp. 38–46.
[92] Longo, *Un popolo alla macchia*, pp. 436–437.
[93] Massimo Salvadori-Paleotti, "The Last Hours in Milan with the Resistance," *The Commonweal* (April 5, 1946), p. 616.
[94] Valiani, *Tutte le strade conducono a Roma*, p. 341.

5 p.m. and first conversed alone with the cardinal, who received him "with pastoral charity" and indicated his hope that the *Duce* was willing to surrender as a prisoner of war and thus begin his expiation and save Italy from further bloodshed. Accompanying Mussolini to the rendezvous were Marshal Graziani, Interior Minister Zerbino, Undersecretary of the Presidency Barracù, Milanese Prefect Bassi, and Cella. In the antechamber with them sat some of the cardinal's close associates, including Don Giuseppe Bicchierai.

When the CLNAI representatives arrived about 6 p.m. Mussolini asked what dispositions they were ready to make. Marazza responded tersely, "Unconditional surrender." Then he continued, "After the Fascists have agreed to surrender, they may gather in a zone that roughly is bounded by the triangle Milan-Como-Lecco and enjoy immunity there when they give up their arms; with the exception that those who are guilty of specific crimes will be brought to court for trial." [95]

Stiffening, Mussolini observed that he had agreed to the meeting because various guaranties had been offered to him as well as to his high officials and their families. At this point General Cadorna commented that the Allies had decided that all the Militia, both conscripts and volunteers, should be guaranteed the usual treatment of prisoners of war. This appeared to relieve the hierarchs, one of whom observed quickly, "We are all in the Militia by virtue of our office." To this, Cadorna retorted, "Of course, this does not apply to specific war criminals." His interpretation cast a pall upon the Fascists.[96]

Graziani then declared flatly, "We shall not sign an accord behind the backs of the Germans." Taking exception, Marazza pointed out that the Germans already had discussed an armistice

---

[95] Graziani, *Ho difeso la patria*, p. 508.

[96] Eye-witness accounts are given in Cadorna, *La Riscossa*, pp. 250–253; Schuster, *Gli ultimi tempi di un regime*, pp. 162–170; Graziani, *Ho difeso la patria*, pp. 505–510; Riccardo Lombardi's interview with *Baltimore Sun* correspondent Howard M. Norton, May 1, 1945, and Lombardi's article, "Il libro bianco di Schuster," *Il Ponte*, II (1946), pp. 1053–1061. See also Valiani, *Tutte le strade conducono a Roma*, pp. 343–345; Amicucci, *I 600 giorni di Mussolini*, pp. 216–263; Cione, *Storia della RSI*, pp. 456–458; Lanfranchi, *La resa degli otto-centomila*, pp. 294–295; Vittorio Mussolini, "Mussolini mio padre," *Tempo* (Milan), XVIII, No. 5, Feb. 2, 1956; Tamaro, *Due anni di storia*, III, 591–599; Dombrowski, *Mussolini: Twilight and Fall*, pp. 161–172; Monelli, *Mussolini, Intimate Life of a Demagogue*, pp. 249–252.

with him personally. Confirming this, Cardinal Schuster also revealed that the Germans in Milan were delivering themselves into his hands with the understanding that they would become prisoners of the Anglo-Americans, who were fast approaching. Schuster vouchsafed further that at one point the Germans had offered to disarm the neo-Fascist Black Brigade. These revelations were too much for Mussolini. He jumped up and sputtered indignantly: "Once too often Germany has stabbed Italy in the back. The Germans have always treated us like slaves." He threatened to make a radio speech denouncing the alliance and resuming his freedom of action. The others pressed him to decide forthwith if he would surrender. Perhaps the *Duce* thought he had fallen into a trap; in any case, he replied that he would speak first with the German consul and would return his answer to the conferees by 8 p.m.

Mussolini and his hangers-on then left the archbishopric and repaired to the prefecture. The CLN delegation stayed. A few minutes later the German vice-consul arrived and was introduced. By that time two more CLNAI representatives, Arpesani (PLI) and Pertini (PSIUP), joined the group. The latter informed his colleagues of the course of the uprising. After hearing this, the Resistance spokesmen emphasized to the vice-consul the urgent need to surrender. He expressed his good intentions but declared that he was unable to communicate with his superior, SS General Wolff. A few minutes after the vice-consul departed Sereni (PCI) arrived. Lively discussion ensued among the underground titans. Apparently the leftists feared that the moderates might agree to a compromise with Mussolini.

By this time the erstwhile dictator's reply was overdue. Considerably worried by his procrastination, the CLNAI group decided to send him an ultimatum. Instead, to their dismay, they learned about 9 p.m. that he and Graziani, with several hierarchs, had fled. Quite possibly the Fascists believed the negotiations had passed into the hands of CLNAI extremists. According to Cadorna, the *Duce* might have gained such an impression from one of the Blackshirts who had an opportunity to leave the archiepiscopal palace in the early evening after Sereni joined the conferees.[97] It is known that Mussolini went to the prefecture, where

[97] Cadorna, *La Riscossa*, p. 253.

fewer than three dozen followers gathered about him in the court-yard. Already it was a matter of *sauve-qui-peut* for the Fascists. About 7:30 p.m. they sped away in an auto caravan, heading north to Como. Almost certainly Mussolini was thinking in terms of escape to Switzerland.[98]

Meanwhile, the Milanese insurrection proceeded on schedule through the night of the 25–26th. By dawn Finance Guards, led by Colonel Alfredo Malgeri who had secretly co-ordinated plans with the underground, occupied the prefecture and other govern-ment buildings.[99] Shortly thereafter the CG/CVL transferred its headquarters to the prefecture and the CLNAI also came out of hiding. In more or less continuous session now, it began to ex-ercise "all administrative and governmental powers" in Milan and Upper Italy. At noon it made its first regular broadcast over Radio Milano Libera,[100] and speedily it installed Riccardo Lombardi (Pd'A) as prefect and Antonio Greppi (PSIUP) as mayor.

During the afternoon of the 26th the "Pavia" division, com-posed of 1,000 well-armed men from the hilly Oltrepò, entered the metropolis, much to the relief of Resistance leaders.[101] By next morning other powerful forces, like Moscatelli's, arrived from Val d'Ossola and Val Sesia, where they had just taken many villages and the surrender of several thousand Nazi-Fascists.[102] German officers, meantime, assured Cadorna once more that their small but well-armed forces in the downtown Hotel Regina and elsewhere would not fight unless the patriots attacked them. Pru-dently, the latter did not. By afternoon of the 26th all opposition from the much more numerous Italian Fascist troops halted, the largest surrender being that of some 3,000 X^{ma} MAS marines who handed over their weapons to the patriots. "The insurrectional victory in Milan was relatively easy and it did not cost grave losses

[98] Graziani, *Ho difeso la patria*, p. 511; Amicucci, *I 600 giorni di Mussolini*, p. 263 ff.
[99] Col. Alfredo Malgeri, *L'occupazione di Milano e la liberazione* (Milan, 1947), p. 89 ff.; Cadorna, *La Riscossa*, pp. 255–256.
[100] Cadorna attended a CLNAI plenary session that evening, his first in several weeks. With sarcasm he noted that it discussed "interminably" a PCI proposal for broadening the CLN's to include the front organization "Difesa della Donna." *Ibid.*, p. 257.
[101] Regarding the Armed Resistance in the Pavia zone, see Franco Costa, "Ap-punti per una storia della resistenza nell'Oltrepò Pavese," *MLI*, No. 37 (1955), pp. 3–31.
[102] Cadorna, *La Riscossa*, pp. 255–257; Secchia and Moscatelli, *Il Monte Rosa è sceso a Milano*, pp. 607–647.

to the patriots," PCI political commissar Secchia has observed. The enemy "was taken by surprise, and above all he was demoralized by the flight of the top hierarchs, of Mussolini, of the ministers, of the Fascist Army leaders, of all the great dignitaries of the Militia and party, and by the flight of all those who had sworn to 'die in beauty.' . . ." [103]

On the evening of the 26th Salvadori spoke over Radio Milano Libera with Prefect Lombardi and eulogized the patriots' achievements.[104] Soon a few other Allied officials appeared, among them Colonel Poletti of AMG, who arrived Sunday morning the 29th by jeep well ahead of the troops.[105] He told CLNAI members that he was amazed at the admirable discipline he found. He tentatively approved their slate of nominations, and remarked jocularly that he would issue very few orders, as he knew how gifted Italians were in the arts of evading them.[106] On the 29th U.S. Major General Willis D. Crittenberger, Commander of IV Corps, entered Milan. He made a special point of welcoming the co-operation CLNAI was giving the Allies, and he concerted arrangements directly with Cadorna (sometimes without the knowledge of AMG Patriot Officers) for disarmament orders to be issued tactfully through the CG/CVL.[107]

Turin insurrection (April 26–28)

Turin's deliverance was much bloodier than Milan's. A general strike (including even the magistrates) was proclaimed as early as April 18, and during the ensuing week tension mounted rapidly. As soon as the CPLN learned that the U.S. 10th Mountain Division had crossed the Po on the 24th, it issued the order, "Aldo says 26 plus 1"—which signified that insurrection was to begin in Turin at 1 a.m., April 26.

Because of the presence of two German armored divisions under General Schlemmer west of Turin, Fifteenth Army Group Headquarters advised Colonel Stevens, British Liaison Officer in Turin, to delay the insurrection. Some patriots suspected, however, that the Allies really wished to enter Turin ahead of the mountain-

[103] Longo, *Un popolo alla macchia*, p. 437.
[104] Milan *L'Unità*, April 27, 1945; Salvadori, *Resistenza ed azione*, p. 296.
[105] NYT, March 31, 1947, 5:5.
[106] *Ibid.*, May 3, 1945, 3:2.
[107] Harris, *Allied Military Administration of Italy*, pp. 309–310, 315; *cf. infra*, Ch. XIII.

based guerrillas.[108] In any event, the CPLN labored amid much conflicting counsel on the 26th. They knew all too well that German units were heavily barricaded in the city center, and they were informed by the archbishop, Cardinal Fossati, that some of the Germans and *Repubblichini* were trying to devise a bargain whereby Turin would be proclaimed an "open city," provided the German troops could withdraw freely through it. In spite of all the pressures, the CPLN refused to negotiate. Instead, it transferred its seat of operations to a factory. (Workers already had taken over most of the city's large plants. They knew better than simply to barricade themselves inside; whenever German tanks approached they passed to the offensive, hurling "Molotov cocktails" at the vehicles.)

To the patriots' dismay, the Germans broke through the partisan barrier along the Dora River in the city the night of the 27–28th and escaped via the *autostrada* leading to Chivasso and Milan. Next morning, long-awaited partisan units from Monferrato entered Turin and found it free of the enemy. The CPLN moved from its factory locale to the more fitting Government Palace. Because General Schlemmer still had strong forces west of the city, Turin spent two more days in a state of continuous alarm. In vain, Colonel Stevens tried to persuade the patriots to dynamite the bridges. Fortunately, Schlemmer decided not to cross over them into the Piedmontese capital, and instead bypassed the city to the north via the Canavese. He was diverted at Vercelli northwestward toward Aosta.[109]

In the meantime the first motorized units of Japanese-Americans approached Alessandria on the 28th and found the patriots busily gaining armistice agreements from the foe.[110] Next day partisans freed Cuneo in accordance with their pre-arranged plan, despite some complications caused by a German division retreat-

---

[108] Ada Gobetti, *Diario partigiano*, pp. 396–414.

[109] Piero Pieri, "Torino e il Piemonte dall'8 settembre 1943 al 27 aprile 1945," *Nuova rivista storica*, xxxix (1955), pp. 290–300; O. Negarville, "L'insurrezione popolare e la presa di Torino," in *Venticinque aprile* (Turin, 1945), p. 103; Battaglia, *SRI*, pp. 564–569; Zandano, *La lotta di liberazione nella provincia di Vercelli, 1943–1945, passim*.

[110] Regarding the struggle in Alessandria province, see Giampaolo Pansa, "Appunti per una storia della Resistenza nella provincia di Alessandria," *MLI*, No. 55 (1959), pp. 3–40; and his "Lo sviluppo primaverile delle formazioni nella zona del Tobbio e il rastrellamento del 6–11 aprile 1944," *MLI*, No. 60 (1960), pp. 3–40.

ing from Liguria.[111] On the 30th Nisei troops entered Turin without having to fire a shot in the vicinity. They found the city under the efficient administration of the local CLN, just as it had intended that they should. Toward Val d'Aosta an American colonel took Schlemmer's surrender on May 3. (By that time Schlemmer had heard of Hitler's death and had decided that his oath to the *Fuehrer* was no longer valid.)

Some 2,500 patriots claimed credit for freeing Val d'Aosta well ahead of the arrival of French troops, who had to cross the Little St. Bernard Pass.[112] That the disputed valley managed to stay under Italian jurisdiction in the peace settlement was in no scant measure due to the timeliness and manner of its deliverance and to the intelligent reforms introduced by CLN administrators; [113] but it was also due to stanch support from the new American President Harry S. Truman, who was greatly annoyed when French forces under General Doyen pushed into Italy farther than the twenty kilometers they were supposed to and refused to obey orders issued by Anglo-American commanders. Within a few weeks Truman bluntly informed General De-Gaulle that all supplies except rations would be cut off from the French forces if they did not withdraw; at the same time he assured them that such withdrawal would not prejudice their claims to some border rectifications. In June they pulled back.[114]

Liberation of northeastern Italy

The last big sector of Italy to be emancipated was the northeast—Venezia Tridentina (Trentino), Venezia Euganea, and

[111] S. Micheli's chapter, "La liberazione di Cuneo," in his *Giorni di fuoco;* Monaco, *Pietà l'è morta*, pp. 176–184.
[112] Ricci (ed.), *Il contributo della Valle d'Aosta alla Guerra di Liberazione*, pp. 87–95; Roberto Dotti, "Guerra partigiana nella bassa valle d'Aosta," *MLI*, No. 31 (1954), pp. 3–27.
[113] On May 14 CLNAI President Morandi, prompted by Federico Chabod, issued, without reference to AMG or to the Rome government, a decree investing the new prefect of Aosta (Professor E. Passerin d'Entrèves) with authority to grant substantial autonomy to the valley by declaring both French and Italian as official languages. See A.P.E., "Autonomy in the Val d'Aosta," *The World Today* (June 1946), pp. 256–268; Harris, *Allied Military Administration of Italy*, p. 311. The Constitution of the new Italian Republic, drafted in 1947, granted formal autonomy to the valley as one of nineteen regional subdivisions of Italy.
[114] Truman, *Memoirs*, I, 239–242; Churchill, *Triumph and Tragedy*, pp. 493–494; Joseph C. Grew, *Turbulent Era: A Diplomatic Record of Forty Years, 1904–1945*, ed. by Walter Johnson (Boston, 1952), II, pp. 1513–1518; Harris, *Allied Military Administration of Italy*, pp. 318–328.

Venezia Giulia. The 10th Mountain Division had driven across the Po on the 24th and reached Verona on the 26th. Some of its units headed north toward Trent and Bolzano, the so-called "Central Redoubt" where *Wehrmacht* Commander-in-Chief von Vietinghoff had transferred his headquarters. Others veered westward into Lombardy and captured Brescia and Bergamo on the 28th, thus sealing off two strategic escape points for the Germans located between Lake Garda and Lake Como. Advance units of the IV Corps reached Como on the 28th and Milan on the 29th, as has been noted; other IV Corps units pushed on to Varese and Novara by May 2.[115]

In the northeast the Eighth Army crossed the lower Po on pontoon bridges April 25 and the Adige two days later. They were then ready to strike out northeastward in an attempt to get to Trieste before the Yugoslavs. The major transportation center of Padua was the first target; it was also the Venetian underground's chief *point d'appui*. Early on the 27th the Venetian Regional Command, acting on instructions from Milan, began its insurrection, though the Allies had called on the 26th merely "for more intensive disruptive action." [116] In Padua alone some 224 partisans were reported killed, while the enemy suffered approximately 500 deaths. About 12,000 Germans (including General von Arnim) and 5,000 *Repubblichini* were taken prisoners by the CLN. Fighting in the city had subsided when Indian and New Zealand contingents of the Eighth Army arrived on the 28–29th. Eighth Army commanders warmly complimented the Paduan resistants for their exemplary action, well-timed and co-ordinated with Allied operations.[117]

In Mestre, mainland suburb of Venice, fighting broke out as early as the 26th and patriots reported the loss of 110 men. But in Venice proper there were only a couple of hours of fighting on the 28th, thanks to a timely accord between the Venice CLN and the Germans, which safeguarded the port, explosive stores, and two liners, the *Vulcania* and *Gradisca*, from destruction. Thereafter the Germans obligingly provided charts of the port showing where mines had been sown. Thus when New Zealanders

[115] Starr, *From Salerno to the Alps*, pp. 433–434.
[116] Battaglia, SRI, pp. 570–572.
[117] *Ibid.*; Starr, *From Salerno to the Alps*, p. 437; Cox, *Road to Trieste*, pp. 171–173.

arrived on the 29th, the port was ready to function.[118] Through-out Venetia the chief electric company (Società Adriatica di Eletriccità) had prepared plans to flood the machine chambers of its power plants to keep the Germans from permanently demolishing them, but actually did not have to carry out these orders. On May 3 General Clark praised Venice's patriots for safeguarding the port, utilities, and works of art: "It may be said with truth that your city was captured from within by armed forces of the Corps of Freedom Volunteers with the support and encouragement of the entire population." [119]

Working in close harmony with II Corps units of the Fifth Army, and after much hard fighting, partisans helped free Vicenza on the 28th. On the 30th Bassano, Belluno, and Treviso gained their liberty. To the northeast in the Friuli, the rival "Osoppo" near the coast and "Garibaldi" groups in the uplands achieved unity in time for the final operations, which began on the 28th. Udine was captured by the partisans and Eighth Army after a violent struggle on May 1. In isolated sectors Italian patriot operations lasted in some cases until May 7—five days after the official armistice in Italy and three days after the first Allied forces reached the Carnic frontier of Austria. Some 32,000 prisoners were taken in the Friuli alone.[120]

Meanwhile, General Freyberg's 2nd New Zealand Division drove with all possible speed toward Trieste. But Tito's men, who had begun their offensive from the area of Bihac on March 20, beat them to Trieste, entering the city on April 30. That same morning the Italian CLN in Trieste (now in its fourth incarnation) sponsored its insurrection and rejected a Fascist suggestion that it join in a common front against the Yugoslavs. Italians managed to seize the radio and prison and to save the ports. But the Slovene OF also went into action and soon gained the upper hand. By May 2 Yugoslav authorities had arrested Italian CLN president Consulich and five other members, confiscated Italian property, and relabelled streets.[121] The New Zealanders made

[118] Ibid., pp. 177–183; Giovanni Ponti (ed.), L'insurrezione di Venezia, 26–29 aprile 1945: L'opera del Comando Piazza del Corpo Volontaria della Libertà. Relazioni e documenti (Venice, 1947), p. 50 ff.; Gavagnin, Vent'anni di resistenza, pp. 535–538; Harris, Allied Military Administration of Italy, p. 307.

[119] Gavagnin, Vent'anni di resistenza, p. 537; NYT, May 4, 1945, 1:6.

[120] Cox, Road to Trieste, pp. 187–188; Battaglia, SRI, pp. 570–574.

[121] Regarding underground publications in Trieste, see Carlo Ventura, "La

their first contact with Tito's warriors on May 1 at Monfalcone. Next day they entered Trieste, occupied the docks, and took the German surrender. Yugoslav Partisans controlled the city center.

Allied relations with Tito's forces rapidly worsened. Churchill and Truman kept in close consultation, as did the Combined Chiefs of Staff. Several advisors feared that Allied failure to check Tito would be a signal to the Italian Communists that the Allies were weak. Alexander and Clark quickly ordered Allied occupation of Gorizia and sent in additional troops to Trieste and along the Isonzo River, but they made no effort to occupy the eastern sectors of Venezia Giulia or the anchorage at Pola on the Istrian peninsula. For forty days the thorny northeastern frontier squabble remained the subject of high-level negotiations that tested the solidarity of the Allied coalition. Then on June 9 the United States, Britain, and Yugoslavia reached an accord whereby part of Venezia Giulia including Trieste was placed under "command and control" of the Supreme Allied Commander. Two thousand Yugoslav troops could remain in the area in a section assigned to them. AMG was to govern the area.[122]

Out of a total partisan force of 60,000 some 2,200 were killed and 1,800 wounded during the liberation of the entire Veneto (April 20–May 20). Enemy losses were claimed to be much higher (14,511). Some 140,292 prisoners were taken.[123] The Germans at von Vietinghoff's headquarters in Bolzano stood in great fear of the partisans, who attacked their Command on May 2, killing forty soldiers. A group of officers (headed by General von Senger rather than the frightened von Vietinghoff) who proceeded down the highway toward Verona to sign a formal armistice at General Clark's headquarters on May 4 were ambushed and probably would have been killed had it not been for the timely intervention of American officers.[124] Whereupon General

stampa clandestina a Trieste dal 1943 al 1945, Parte II: . . . dal maggio 1945 all'inizio dell'amministrazione alleata," *MLI*, No. 47 (1957), pp. 3–12.

[122] Churchill, *Triumph and Tragedy*, pp. 551–561; Truman, *Memoirs*, I, 244–253; Grew, *Turbulent Era*, II, 1476–1485; Ehrman, *Grand Strategy*, VI, 130–131; Feis, *Roosevelt, Churchill, Stalin*, pp. 628–632; Clark, *Calculated Risk*, pp. 443–448; Starr, *From Salerno to the Alps*, p. 400; Cox, *Road to Trieste*, pp. 1–23, 193–249; Valiani, *Tutte le strade conducono a Roma*, p. 351; Cadorna, *La Riscossa*, p. 273; P. A. Quarantotti Gambini, "L'ora di Trieste," *Mercurio* (*Anche l'Italia ha vinto*), II, No. 16 (Dec. 1945), pp. 373–387; Pietro Ferraro, "Giornate del Veneto," in *ibid.*; Battaglia, *SRI*, pp. 574–575.

[123] *Ibid.*, pp. 570–574.

[124] Clark, *Calculated Risk*, pp. 438–442.

Clark issued stern orders to the patriots to treat the surrendered Germans in accordance with international law.[125]

Mussolini's last hours

Historians and investigators who have sought to reconcile the often confusing and contradictory testimony of witnesses and alleged witnesses to Mussolini's flight, capture, and execution are confronted with an almost hopeless task. Of this, like so many other subjects, objective historical truth seems destined to remain a mirage; all that can be done is to give a bare outline of what seems to have transpired.[126]

Mussolini and his fleeing henchmen arrived in Como about 10 p.m., April 25. There they spent the rest of the night vainly trying to persuade Swiss frontier officials to let them across. Refused asylum, the harried fugitives mulled new schemes. Some of them argued that they should await the arrival of several thousand Black Brigadesmen, supposedly being led by Pavolini from Liguria and Piedmont. With their help a bastion might be erected either in the Valtellina or Spluga Pass northeast of the lake, and if the Nazis should continue resistance in Bavaria, Mussolini's band might conceivably join them. Apparently they decided upon this strategy. Leaving his wife and children in Como, the *Duce* and his small band wended their way up the narrow road along the western shore. At Cadenabbia they halted to inquire of Pavolini's whereabouts.[127]

Marshal Graziani left the group at that village, intending, he declared, to return to his headquarters near Como to make sure his troops would receive proper treatment as prisoners of war. En route he stopped at Cernobbia, where he happened to find SS General Wolff, who had been caught by the partisans after his return from armistice negotiations in Switzerland.[128] About noon on the 27th General Cadorna in Milan received

[125] NYT, May 5, 1945, 6:2; Harris, *Allied Military Administration of Italy*, pp. 305–307.

[126] The present account rests largely on the more-or-less judicious effort of the following writers to sift and assess the welter of testimony: Monelli, *Mussolini, the Intimate Life of a Demagogue*, pp. 253–271, 287–292; Salvatorelli and Mira, *Storia d'Italia nel periodo fascista*, pp. 1118–1121; Dombrowski, *Mussolini: Twilight and Fall*, pp. 175–241; Amicucci, *I 600 giorni di Mussolini*, pp. 267–287; Pini and Susmel, *Mussolini: l'uomo e l'opera*, IV, 517–539; and Ezio Saini, *La notte di Dongo* (Rome, 1950).

[127] Amicucci, *I 600 giorni di Mussolini*, p. 267 ff.

[128] Graziani, *Ho difeso la patria*, pp. 517–553.

word from Cardinal Schuster's office that Graziani had telephoned from Cernobbia that he was ready to surrender to Cadorna if the latter would send a protective escort to bring him to Milan. As it turned out, a lone American officer (Captain Emilio Q. Daddario ["Mim"], who had just come from the OSS outpost in Lugano) [129] subtracted Graziani from the CLNAI's control and escorted him to the Milano Hotel in Milan. According to Salvadori, this was in contradiction to instructions from Fifteenth Army Group Headquarters on the 24th. The latter had advised Allied forces not to release or transfer, except in most unusual circumstances, persons already imprisoned by the partisans as Axis collaborators. Rather, they should keep them for the Italian authorities, who would decide what action they might wish to take in accordance with their own purge program. These instructions had further counseled nonintervention in cases where partisans had independently taken punitive action prior to Allied arrival. Thereafter, however, no more independent actions should be permitted except as ordered by the proper authorities.[130]

On Sunday the 29th a group of Matteotti partisans surrounded the Milano Hotel with the intention of doing Graziani to death. Cadorna intervened hastily with the help of two Socialists, Stucchi and Mosna, and persuaded the crowd to permit them to transfer Graziani to a prison. While the CVL officials were inside the hotel, disgruntled onlookers blew up the automobile Cadorna had left at the hostelry door. At last Graziani was transferred temporarily to the same San Vittore prison that in previous months had slammed its doors on hundreds of captive anti-Fascists. On the night of the 29–30th Graziani signed a surrender instrument to General Crittenberger of the IV Army Corps, who had just arrived in Milan; by its terms all RSI troops were to be treated as regular PW's.[131] Years later Graziani stood trial in Italian courts on treason charges.[132]

[129] Icardi, *Aldo Icardi: American Master Spy*, pp. 181–184.
[130] Salvadori, *Resistenza ed azione*, pp. 297–298.
[131] Graziani, *Ho difeso la patria*, pp. 517–553; Cadorna, *La Riscossa*, pp. 258–263; Icardi, *Aldo Icardi: American Master Spy*, pp. 185–186.
[132] After numerous postponements the treason trial of Graziani by a special court of assize began in Rome in October 1948. Six months of heated proceedings elapsed before the court announced that it "lacked jurisdiction." Thereafter, Graziani was scheduled to be tried by a military tribunal. Alleged illness of the

Having lost their top military commander, Mussolini and his hierarchs moved on from Cadenabbia to near-by Menaggio the morning of the 26th. At last Pavolini caught up with them. But he did not have his vaunted column; that nebulous force was still far from Como. After appraising the situation, Pavolini returned to Como, intending to join his men when they arrived. Mussolini ordered his group to wait for Pavolini's force throughout the afternoon at Grandola, a village situated on a side road from Menaggio to Lugano. He also sent out Buffarini-Guidi and others to see if the side road into Switzerland was clear. Hardly had they embarked upon their reconnaissance mission when they were seized by Finance Guards who had gone over to the Resistance. Thoroughly alarmed by this intelligence, Mussolini ordered his harried band to move on. Toward evening they returned to Menaggio on the lakeshore, where to their dismay they found that local Fascist officials had vanished. That night Pavolini returned, still without his troops. Meanwhile, Mussolini's fugitives were joined by an automobile flying the Spanish flag; in it were Signorina Claretta Petacci, her brother Marcello, and his children, all equipped with presumably forged Spanish passports.[133]

On the morning of the 27th Mussolini and his minions decided once more to throw in their lot with the Germans. They joined a German convoy that consisted of an armored car, thirty trucks, and some 300 soldiers headed for the Alps. At Musso,

---

accused delayed the completion of the second trial. Finally, in May 1950, the military tribunal found him guilty of some of the charges and sentenced him to nineteen years' imprisonment (at the same time cancelling thirteen of them). Because of postwar amnesties and the nearly five years he had spent in detention, Graziani had only a few more weeks to serve. He was released on August 29, 1950. See NYT, Aug. 29, 1950, 6:6. The verbatim records of much of the first trial are available in Processo Graziani (3 vols.; Rome, 1948–1950). While awaiting trial Graziani wrote his apologia, Ho difeso la patria. Additional polemics by Graziani are to be found in Emilio Canevari, Graziani mi ha detto, pp. 42–89. An informative discussion of the trials has been written by Antonino Rèpaci, a judge of the Turin tribunal, "Il processo Graziani," MLI, No. 17/18 (1952), pp. 20–49, and "Le procès Graziani," Revue d'histoire de la deuxième guerre mondiale, III, No. 9 (Jan. 1953), pp. 30–37. Sympathetic essays about the general may be found in Graziani (Rome, 1956). Graziani died on January 11, 1955.

On the problem of trying the Fascists, see also Zara Algardi, Processi ai fascisti Anfuso, Caruso, Graziani, e Borghese di fronte alla giustizia. . . . Esame storico-giuridico. Pref. by Ferruccio Parri and Domenico R. Peretti-Griva (Florence, 1958).

[133] Amicucci, I 600 giorni di Mussolini, pp. 267–287.

fourteen kilometers north of Menaggio, a barricade thrown up by the 52nd Garibaldi Brigade at a turn in the narrow, walled road forced them to halt. The partisans had been alerted the night before of the German troop movement. After prolonged discussion, the German commander (Major Kritz) managed to work out a deal with "Pedro" (Count Pier Luigi Bellini delle Stelle), leader of the score of partisans, to let his soldiers proceed unmolested in return for handing over the Italian Fascists. This was the ultimate doublecross in the duplicity-steeped history of the Axis. In midafternoon the partisans began a detailed inspection of the convoy in the piazza of Dongo.

Fearing such a development, Mussolini had sneaked from the armored car into a truck loaded with a dozen German soldiers. In desperation he donned a German corporal's overcoat, a swastika-marked helmet, and even, according to one version, dark glasses. He pretended to snore as if in a drunken stupor. Between his knees was a Bren gun, though he did not try to use it. The partisan who searched the convoy quickly perceived that the "inebriate" was no youthful *Tedesco*. The well-known physiognomy of Mussolini could not possibly be camouflaged. A few yards away the terror-stricken Signorina Petacci was also quickly identified.

The partisans transferred the captive *Duce* temporarily to the town hall of Dongo while they awaited instructions from their superiors. Interrogated by local partisans who asked endless questions of why he had betrayed the Socialist movement, stabbed France in the back, and so on,[134] Mussolini, ever the polemicist, answered as best he could, trying to curry favor and usually blaming others for what had happened. Troubled to know how to keep his prisoner secure, "Pedro" later that afternoon shunted him to a Customs Guards barracks in the village of Germasino above Dongo. That night he picked up Signorina Petacci and

[134] Partisans in Dongo and its environs had experienced stern reprisals at the hands of the Fascists the previous year; they were in no forgiving mood in April. In this zone the Armed Resistance had its center in the Enrico Falck steel mills. A prominent DC who had served as his party's treasurer and held a major post in the CLNAI, Falck had conspired with his employees to slow production. In January 1945 he had been arrested by the Fascists along with many of his workers. See F. Parri's preface to Michele U. Bonafine, "Note sulla Resistenza a Dongo," *MLI*, No. 38/39 (1955), pp. 31–45.

about 3 a.m. removed the two prisoners during a heavy rainstorm to a farmhouse at Bonzanigo near Giulino di Mezzegra.[135]

In Milan, meantime, two prominent Communists who worked at the CG/CVL—Aldo Lampredi ("Guido") and Ing. Walter Audisio ("Colonello Valerio"), the latter a survivor of the international brigades in Spain and of prison on Ventotene—received word of the arrests. They went to General Cadorna on the evening of the 27th and informed him that they had a mandate from the CLNAI to proceed to the place of Mussolini's arrest and "render justice." Cadorna raised no objection. Next morning Valiani also sought out Cadorna, bearing the order of the CLNAI to execute Mussolini. Cadorna told him that this same order had been delivered the night before by Lampredi and Audisio. Valiani and Cadorna are in agreement that the final decision to execute the *Duce* was made by the Insurrectional Committee, composed of Longo, Sereni, Pertini, and Valiani.[136] In his memoirs Valiani has observed that the CLNAI decree of April 25 set forth the death penalty for all hierarchs and military personnel who did not surrender voluntarily. "Having refused to give himself up on insurrection day, Mussolini by his own action became an outlaw," Valiani has insisted.[137] Nevertheless, the CLNAI was still discussing the specific fate of Mussolini on the morning of the 27th. At that time Marazza (DC) suggested that it might be wise to consign him to the Allies (as indeed Article 29 of the Long Armistice demanded), but the majority preferred to hand him over to whatever partisan tribunal was nearest the place of capture. Salvadori assured the CLNAI that in an exceptional moment like this it was up to the CLNAI, which possessed interim governing authority, to decide upon the

---

[135] Salvatorelli and Mira, *Storia d'Italia nel periodo fascista*, p. 1119; Amicucci, *I 600 giorni di Mussolini*, pp. 277–287; Monelli, *Mussolini, the Intimate Life of a Demagogue*, pp. 253–265; Dombrowski, *Mussolini: Twilight and Fall*, pp. 185–208.

[136] Cadorna has written that he was well aware that the CLNAI for some time had been in general agreement that hierarchs as well as armed Militiamen guilty of specific crimes were to be executed as soon as their identity was ascertained. He consoled himself with the hope that American advance patrols near Como would demand that Mussolini be consigned to them as a war criminal, though he has emphasized that he himself would in no case have handed Mussolini over to the Allies for trial. *La Riscossa*, pp. 259–260.

[137] Valiani, *Tutte le strade conducono a Roma*, p. 350 ff.

laws to apply, but that as soon as the Allied troops arrived they would automatically have the right to take control of prisoners.[138]

Accompanied by a dozen partisans, Audisio and Lampredi arrived in Como early on the 28th. To their alarm they learned that American advanced units were nearing the city and that the local CLN planned to transfer the prisoners next day to Como and thence to Milan. If this should happen, they reasoned, Mussolini and his last-ditch supporters might end up before an Allied tribunal and might even escape the death penalty. After spending the morning in heated talks with the Como CLN and in a search for suitable trucks, Audisio and his escort drove on to Dongo, determined to take decisive action. As soon as they reached Dongo about 2 p.m., they informed the local partisan commander of their mandate. Audisio speedily separated from the fifty-one prisoners those seventeen hierarchs whose fate had been sealed by Article 5 of the CLNAI decree of the 25th. His next move was to convene the headquarters of the local brigade as a military tribunal on the basis of Article 14, which declared that during the state of emergency jurisdiction over Fascist criminals was entrusted to tribunals of war. Rapidly it went through the formality of ordering the death penalty for Mussolini and the seventeen *gerarchi*. Audisio then drove to the farmhouse in Bonzanigo where Mussolini and his mistress were held. He asked them to accompany him and drove them down the road toward the lake. At a certain point in the neighboring village of Giulino di Mezzegra he stopped and ordered them to stand against the garden wall of Villa Belmonte. Quickly he read out the execution order and then, after some difficulty in firing his automatic rifle, shot the spent dictator and his *amante*.[139] An act of revolutionary justice, the execution of Mussolini was, as Salvadori has commented, punishment for crimes hitherto unpunished.[140] On the other hand, whatever one may

[138] Salvadori, *Resistenza ed azione*, p. 297.

[139] Regarding Audisio's three versions of the execution, see Monelli, *Mussolini, the Intimate Life of a Demagogue*, pp. 265–269, and n. 40, pp. 289–292; Saina, *La notte di Dongo*; Dombrowski, *Mussolini: Twilight and Fall*, pp. 209–218. In an article, "Il y a 10 ans, la fin de Mussolini," *Historia*, No. 100 (1955), pp. 247–253, and No. 101 (1955), pp. 365–373, Monelli has argued that Mussolini was killed not by Audisio but by Pietro Gatti. Whatever the truth, Audisio exploited the deed and won a seat in the Senate of the Republic as his reward.

[140] Salvadori, *Resistenza ed azione*, p. 298.

have thought about Signorina Petacci, there seemed to be no cause for her summary execution.[141]

Leaving the bullet-ridden bodies in the rain in the custody of a pair of partisans for two hours, Audisio returned to Dongo in the late afternoon. This time it was the turn of the hierarchs who had been apprehended the previous day. He read out their death sentence and ordered them to line up before a firing squad on the piazza—much against the wishes of the mayor. The victims of the ensuing bloodbath were: Pavolini, Secretary of the PFR; Zerbino, Minister of Interior; Fernando Mezzasoma, Minister of Popular Culture; Ruggero Romano, Minister of Public Works; Augusto Liverani, Minister of Communications; Paolo Porta, Inspector of the PFR for Lombardy; Luigi Gatti, Prefect and Private Secretary of the *Duce*; Alfredo Coppola, President of the Fascist Cultural Institute; Ernesto Daquanno, Director of the "Stefani" News Agency; Mario Nudi, President of the Fascist Agricultural Confederation; Colonel Vito Casalinuovo of the GNR; Captain Pietro Salustri, personal pilot of the *Duce*; Signor Hintermayer, a journalist; Nicola Bombacci, the "excommunicated" PCI Deputy who had turned Fascist; and Marcello Petacci, brother of Claretta.[142] In Milan Achille Starace was felled the same day. Roberto Farinacci was shot at Vimercate after a summary trial.

The fate of the so-called "treasure of Dongo" that Mussolini and his entourage carried with them during their flight has remained a subject of controversy. It was alleged to have consisted of $90,000,000 worth of the Salò regime's gold bullion, foreign currency, Mussolini's personal funds, some three sacks of wedding rings contributed by Italian wives to help finance the Ethiopian War, and the jewelry of Signorina Petacci and the wives of some of the fleeing hierarchs. In addition, there were satchels containing some of Mussolini's correspondence with Hitler and a diary entitled "That the Italians May Know." Probably he hoped to use these as defense documents in case he came before an international tribunal.[143] In response to inquiries in 1945 the CG/CVL disclaimed any record of the treasure, and

[141] Dombrowski, *Mussolini: Twilight and Fall*, pp. 219–222.

[142] Salvatorelli and Mira, *Storia d'Italia nel periodo fascista*, p. 1120.

[143] Regarding these papers see Emilio Re, *Storia di un archivio: le carte di Mussolini* (Milan, 1946).

General Cadorna has commented that it was impossible to keep a minute check on the bookkeeping of the myriad patriot formations during the feverish liberation period.[144]

Meanwhile, word spread that Pietro Terzi, a leader of the 52nd Garibaldi Brigade, had turned the treasure over to Dante Gorreri, a Communist in Como, and that finally it had gone into PCI coffers. It was also to be alleged that several men who personally knew of the affair had been mysteriously killed. Efforts to indict Gorreri met with repeated frustrations because of the immunity he had gained after his election to Parliament.[145]

Late Saturday evening, April 28, 1945, Audisio brought the rain-soaked bodies of Mussolini, Petacci, and most of the hierarchs in a truck to Milan. Early next morning the corpses of the *Duce*, wearing the uniform of a squadrist Militiaman, and his mistress were laid out and then suspended headsdownward in a service station at Piazzale Loreto—the same square where on August 14, 1944, the German Command of Milan had publicly executed fifteen resistants as reprisal for a bomb explosion which had killed two Germans.[146] The bodies of Starace and Farinacci were also exhibited. Aroused by the emotions released upon the overthrow of a hated regime, an infuriated mob repeatedly kicked and spat upon the swinging cadavres.[147] After this lugubrious and disgusting display, the corpses of Mussolini and his mistress were buried secretly near Milan in Musocco cemetery in paupers' graves marked only with the numbers 167 and 166.[148] What was

[144] Cadorna, *La Riscossa*, pp. 270-271; *cf.* Saina, *La notte di Dongo, passim;* and Dombrowski, *Mussolini: Twilight and Fall*, pp. 223-227.

[145] Eventually this immunity was lifted in 1956. In April 1957 he and thirty-four other defendants were brought before the Padua Court of Assize. During the sensational trial Terzi testified that his brigade "decided to hand the treasure to the Communist Party because the Communists had fought harder than anyone else." A partisan driver told of loading five heavy suitcases aboard a Fiat and taking them to Gorreri in Como. The latter refused to concede the truth of any of these allegations. After nearly a million words of testimony from 381 witnesses, one of the jurors committed suicide and thus forced the judge to declare a mistrial in August 1957. Whether all the old witnesses and some thirty others who had not yet testified can be reassembled for a new trial and a verdict remains to be seen. *Time*, LXIX (1957), June 24, p. 34; Aug. 26, p. 28.

[146] After the insurrection this square was renamed Piazza dei Quindici Martiri ("Fifteen Martyrs Square").

[147] Eye-witness account of Bracker in *NYT*, April 30, 1945, 1:3.

[148] The government's efforts to hide the burial place proved futile. In the spring of 1946 some neo-Fascists led by Domenico Leccisi, who later was elected to Parliament, dug up the *Duce*'s corpse and spirited it away. In the casket they left a note: "Finally, oh *Duce*, you are with us. We shall surround you with roses." Several months passed before the police traced the body to the Franciscan

left of the dictator's brain was sent to the Army Institute of Pathology in Washington for study; experts there found it "normal."

The CLNAI deemed it expedient on the 30th to take note of the violent and repulsive scene at Piazzale Loreto and to issue a public statement that sought to put the affair into historical perspective:

". . . The shooting of Mussolini and his accomplices, ordered by the CLNAI, is the necessary conclusion of an historical era which leaves our country still covered by material and moral scars, and the conclusion of an insurrectional struggle which signified for the Fatherland the prerequisite for its rebirth and reconstruction. The Italian people could not begin a free and normal life—which Fascism for twenty years denied them—if the CLNAI had not timely demonstrated its iron decision to carry out a judgment which had already been pronounced by history.

"Only at the price of this neat break with a shameful and criminal past could the people have the assurance that the CLNAI is determined to pursue with firmness the democratic renovation of the country. Only at this price can there and must there occur in the forms of strictest legality, the necessary purging of the residues of Fascism at the end of the insurrectional phase.

"Fascism itself is the only responsible element for the explosion of popular hate, which on this single occasion has gone to excesses, and which is understandable only in the climate willed and created by Mussolini.

"The CLNAI, just as it has known how to conduct the insurrection—admirable for its democratic discipline, which infused

monastery of the Angelicum in Pavia, nineteen miles south of Milan, where it was found beneath an altar. To forestall any Fascist demonstrations, the authorities had the corpse furtively reinterred in a rural Capuchin monastery at Cerro Maggiore, fifteen miles northwest of Milan. Finally, in August 1957, the DC government of Premier Adone Zoli granted the *Duce's* 67-year-old widow, Rachele, permission to have the body laid to rest in the family vault at a cemetery near Predappio, sixty miles east of Bologna. Despite the government's insistence that there be no political demonstrations, a near riot occurred during the funeral ceremony when hundreds of neo-Fascist pilgrims chanted old slogans and stretched their arms in the outlawed salute. Signora Rachele at last felt impelled to cry out: "Finish it! Even in front of his bier you continue quarreling!" Only time will tell whether public burial of the ex-dictator beneath a tombstone engraved with a symbol of the fasces may contribute to the rise of an Italian version of the Napoleonic Legend. NYT, Aug. 31, Sept. 1, 2, 1957; *Newsweek*, L (Sept. 9, 1957), p. 52.

into all the insurgents a sense of responsibility in this great historic hour, and just as it has known how, without hesitation, to render justice to those responsible for the ruin of the Fatherland, intends that in the new epoch which is now opened to the free Italian people such excesses must not repeat themselves. . . ." [149]

Public discipline

That night Prefect Lombardi (Pd'A) announced over the Milan Radio, "In virtue of powers entrusted to me by the Allied Military Command for Lombardy, I order the immediate suspension of summary trials held by formations of volunteers or people styling themselves as such." He warned that both Italian authorities and AMG would take measures of "extreme severity against all those who infringe this order." [150]

Mob "justice" is reprehensible under any circumstances. No doubt northern Italy was lucky to experience as little of it as it did, when one considers the stratification and tensions of Italian society and the great emotional release of the insurrection, which spurred many to pay off their grudges freely. In Milan the crowds soon quieted down after venting their *sfogo* at Piazzale Loreto. The CLN's redoubled their efforts to discipline the Freedom Volunteers and the citizenry, and achieved remarkably good results, as most Allied officials on the scene have attested. Had there been no CLN's to exercise authority, the situation very likely would have been much worse.

In an address in Rome after the liberation, Parri praised the over-all accomplishments of the Resistenza Armata but conceded that "in the partisan movement there were the good and the bad, the heroes and the looters, the generous and the cruel; there was a people with its virtues and its vices. Then there were the partisans of the eleventh hour, in general a detestable race. And then the exploiters and profiteers of the partisan movement." [151] It was this irresponsible element which sullied some of the Resistance record. In some areas bands of ruffians, usually little more than adolescents, took advantage of the insurrectionary fervor to behave in highhanded fashion, "evening up scores" with those

[149] Quoted in Milan *La Libertà*, April 30, 1945.
[150] *NYT*, May 1, 1945, 3:1.
[151] Parri, "L'Italia partigiana," *Mercurio (Anche l'Italia ha vinto)*, II, No. 16 (Dec. 1945), pp. 9–20.

whose "faces they found unsympathetic." Some Allied officials reported that a dozen or more bodies were found nightly in the streets of Milan during the first few days after liberation.

While informal "military tribunals" were common during those very first days, soon "people's courts of assize" replaced them. By early June these, in turn, were superseded by AMG-approved "extraordinary courts of assize," which consisted of a judge and four lay members, selected from a panel of some 200 reliable anti-Fascists drawn up in each province by the CLN's.[152] Understandably, the preliminary courts committed some errors in their hasty adjudication of hundreds of accused; yet it should be kept in mind that the judges usually had before them fairly trustworthy information about the behavior of the accused during the preceding twenty months of extremely bitter civil war. Piedmont was the region where the greatest number of Fascists and enemy sympathizers were executed.[153] This was not surprising, for in Piedmont and in the Veneto the Resistenza Armata was more full-blown than anywhere else, and Piedmont had suffered a series of vicious *rastrellamenti*. Furthermore, industrialized Turin numbered far more Gappisti than did most other cities.

The number of people killed in northern Italy during the insurrectionary period cannot be agreed upon, either by observers at the time or by subsequent investigators. Certainly it was far less than the 300,000 that neo-Fascists in later years alleged had been slaughtered. Avv. Mario Scelba (DC), a postwar Minister of Interior, informed the Chamber of Deputies on June 24, 1952, that the correct figure was 2,344.[154] The writer Carlo Simiani

---

[152] Harris, *Allied Military Administration of Italy*, p. 285; cf. D. R. Peretti-Griva, "La magistratura italiana nella resistenza," *MLI*, No. 6 (1950), pp. 3–10; and A. Galante-Garrone, "Documenti sull'organizzazione clandestina della giustizia," *ibid.*, pp. 10–39.

[153] A confidential report to OSS, R. & A. Branch, May 11, 1945, indicated that according to "reliable reports," some 500 Fascists had been summarily executed in Milan and some 1,000 in Turin by May 6. Elsewhere the figures were much lower, it went on. See OSS, R. & A. Branch, Current Intelligence Study No. 18, "Political Results of the Liberation of North Italy," p. 2. General Trabucchi estimated 2,000 killed in Turin (*I vinti hanno sempre torto*, p. 214); cf. Harris, *Allied Military Administration of Italy*, pp. 303–305, and his Ch. XI, for AMG estimates.

[154] NYT, June 26, 1952. The Rome Istituto di Statistica calculated that deaths in Italy for all of 1945 by reason of judiciary execution and violent causes (acci-

estimated 40,000.[155] Probably the truth lay in between. Whatever the number, there was enough intemperance to enable neo-Fascist propagandists in postwar years to fan rather successfully the flames of a limited revulsion against the Resistenza Armata and, temporarily at least, to besmirch many of its worthier attributes.

---

dents, suicide, homicide), excluding war causes, were 5,896. If war causes were included, the figure would be 22,410. Cf. Battaglia, SRI, p. 575, n. 42.

[155] I giustiziati fascisti dell'aprile 1945 (Milan, 1949).

CHAPTER XIII · BALANCE SHEET

Contributions of the Resistenza Armata

THE CG/CVL scheduled its "stand-down" parades of the patriots in Milan and Turin for Sunday, May 6, 1945, in anticipation of their disarmament and demobilization. Two days before the ceremonies Prince Humbert appeared unexpectedly in Milan, voicing the desire to review the Freedom Volunteers as well as contingents of the Italian Army then en route to Milan. He pointed out that he had already attended similar ceremonies in Florence, Bologna, Parma, Verona, Bergamo, and Brescia without incident.[1] General Cadorna warned the Lieutenant-General of the Realm that he would blunder badly if he reviewed only the Italian units that had fought alongside the Fifth and Eighth Armies, and he explained that he would have to consult the staff of the CG/CVL with respect to reviewing the patriots. To the embarrassment of Humbert, Prefect Lombardi (Pd'A) avoided seeing him, and the CG/CVL refused to let him review the Freedom Volunteers. All Humbert could do was depart and hope for a more auspicious occasion to visit the antiroyalist capital of the Resistance.[2]

The parades took place on schedule. Decked in their distinctive colors, an impressive array of partisans marched past the reviewing stand in Milan where General Cadorna, CLNAI and CVL dignitaries, and several Allied officers stood. At the Turin ceremonies U.S. Colonel Marshall, who headed AMG in Piedmont, remarked in French to General Trabucchi of the Piedmontese CVL Regional Command, *"C'est beau et émouvant,"* but under his breath he was heard to add in English, "It is also fearsome." Allied fears of the Armed Resistance persisted long after the "beauty" of the occasion.[3]

A fitting climax to the Armed Resistance epic, these parades

---

[1] Bolla, *Colloqui con Umberto II*, p. 72; Milton Bracker in *NYT*, May 6, 1945, 12:5.

[2] Cadorna, *La Riscossa*, p. 272. On May 10 at a PSIUP conclave in Rome, Pertini boasted of having opened fire with a machine gun against the residence in Milan where Humbert was a guest. Tupini, *I Democratici cristiani*, p. 106.

[3] Trabucchi's own plans for slow demobilization of the patriots had been brusquely shelved. Trabucchi, *I vinti hanno sempre torto*, p. 229; Harris, *Allied Military Administration of Italy*, p. 356; Unclassified report for May 5–31, 1945, by British Lt. Col. L. E. Vining, Piedmont Regional Patriots Office, to AC Regional Commissioner, July 18, 1945.

memorialized the tenacious minority of northern patriots who had dared to stand firm against the cruel Nazi-Fascist overlords. A very large proportion of the resistants and their supporters had made the ultimate sacrifice since September 8, 1943—probably as many as one fifth of the total force of 200,000 who had participated at one or another time in the bloody underground struggle. It is impossible to harmonize fully the casualty lists compiled by the Italian Ministry of Foreign Affairs, CVL, ANPI, and other agencies; but whatever the precise number of casualties may have been, there can be no doubt that the "war of liberation" was also one of "expiation." [4]

Those who marched in the processions could be proud that the Resistenza Armata had been of considerable military value in the war against the Axis powers. By providing intelligence and a network for sabotage, the Italian resistants had often facilitated Allied operations, and in several instances had spared

[4] In 1946 the Ministry of Foreign Affairs reported 35,828 partisans dead; 21,168 injured; 9,980 civilians killed in reprisals; 412 civilians wounded. According to these statistics, the Veneto accounted for the greatest number of patriot casualties, and Tuscany the greatest number of civilians massacred. Ministry of Foreign Affairs, *The Italian Contribution to the War of Liberation against Germany* (Rome, 1946).

Later calculations suggest that the above figures erred on the low side. Salvadori has concluded that the casualties of the patriot movement in Upper Italy "exceeded those of the Allies for the entire Italian campaign." Salvadori, *SRI*, pp. 165, 30–31. In his official history of the Fifth Army, Starr has revealed that the 27 divisions and 7 corps which at one time or another fought under the Fifth Army in Italy suffered a total of 188,746 casualties (31,886 killed; 134,025 wounded in action; and 22,835 missing in action). By nationalities the total figures were: Americans, 108,642; British, 47,452; French, 27,671; Brazilians, 2,441; Italians, 1,570. Starr, *From Salerno to the Alps*, pp. 451–452. Precise casualty figures for the Eighth Army are not readily available.

Salvadori's calculations of patriot losses generally support those set forth in 1955 by Battaglia, the leading Communist chronicler of the Armed Resistance:

46,000 patriots and civilian hostages killed in combat or after being taken prisoner in national territory;

21,000 partisans wounded in national territory;

30,000 Italians killed abroad (in France, Balkans, et cetera) while fighting in various liberation movements;

33,000 Italian soldiers out of 615,000 interned in Germany between 1943 and 1945 who refused to serve in neo-Fascist units and never returned to their homeland;

8,000 Italian political deportees killed by Germans in extermination camps;

10,000 Italian soldiers in the Corps of Italian Liberation and other professional units fighting alongside the Allied Forces.

Roberto Battaglia and Giuseppe Garritano, *Breve storia della resistenza italiana* (Turin, 1955), pp. 336–337; Battaglia, *SRI*, p. 576, n. 48; and Longo, *Un popolo alla macchia*, p. 471.

civilians from needless bombardments. Furthermore, the wide-spread operations of the CVL had saved many Allied lives and had partially weakened the enemy by repeatedly forcing him to pull back many of his units from the front in order to comb out the partisans' mountain strongholds. The patriots had won their greatest glory by seizing control of northern cities hours and, in some cases, days ahead of the juncture of the Allies, who had scarcely bargained for such insurrections. They could also claim a good share of the credit for the preservation of electric power stations, industries, bridges, and port facilities from possible last-minute sabotage or destruction by the retreating foe (even though in some cases SS General Wolff may have issued orders not to commit such deeds lest they prejudice his armistice negotiations).

In a ten-point official report prepared on June 2, 1945, Lieutenant Colonel (G.S.) R. T. Hewitt, head of the Operations Section of the British Headquarters No. 1 Special Forces in Italy, noted that sabotage and "anti-scorch" had been uppermost in the minds of liaison officers during the final months, and that the patriots had executed these plans admirably.[5] Genoa's harbor, he explained, was "saved from complete demolition by the energetic action of the partisans, coupled by the perplexity of the German Command." "The partisan contribution to salvation of the economic structure of the country can be considered as the most relevant aspect of the role that they played in all the Italian campaign." Hewitt's judgment was generally confirmed in detailed reports submitted by AMG regional patriot officers. Commenting on the "excellent work performed by CLN prior to arrival of Allied Military Government," Hewitt noted that "what the CLN's did, they did well." "The prestige of the Italian Resistance Movement has never been higher than during recent weeks, as the result of the splendid work of the CLNAI and of its Regional and Provincial Committees." The Allies could have won the war in any case, Hewitt conceded, but victory could not have been "so rapid, so overwhelming, and at so low a price" without the aid of the Resistance.

[5] See his "Report on No. 1 Special Force Activities during April 1945," June 2, 1945. It is reprinted and discussed by Giorgio Vaccarino in "Il contributo della resistenza italiana in un documento alleato," *MLI*, No. 3 (Nov. 1949), pp. 3–23, and No. 4 (Jan. 1950), pp. 3–23.

Prime Minister Churchill, who had less of an axe to grind in the matter than Colonel Hewitt, voiced the same feeling in a message to Premier Bonomi on May 3, congratulating the Italian patriots for having "materially accelerated the liberation." Without the partisans the Allies "would have had twice as many casualties and would have needed twice as much time to reach their objectives." [6] The day before in Commons he paid tribute to all who had brought about the German surrender in the peninsula; he numbered among them "the free Italians who have played their part in clearing their country from the German-Fascist yoke." [7]

In a press conference at the end of April, Field Marshal Alexander generously conceded that Italy "had worked her passage," [8] and on May 3 he sent a message to CLNAI President Morandi and General Cadorna, congratulating them on their efficiency and the restoration of civilian administration.[9] Alexander was probably not making a virtue of necessity, for later in his official report on the last phase of the Italian campaign he wrote warmly that despite the enemy's "pitiless and unscrupulous" repressive measures, "the partisans willingly accepted the risks to which they exposed themselves and bravely did their best, and within the inevitable limitations imposed on them rendered valuable assistance to the Allied cause." [10]

An editorial in the Mediterranean edition of the U.S. Army newspaper, *Stars and Stripes*, summed up the G.I.'s assessment of the Italian Armed Resistance: "Our advance guards and armored troops entered cities full of Italian patriots. They were there in an extraordinary number. The Allied soldiers have finally felt that they were fighting to liberate people who really wanted to be free. After long months of the winter war, in the mud and the rain and the ruins, finally the Allied soldiers have seen another Italy." [11]

[6] Cited in Gavagnin, *Vent'anni di resistenza al fascismo*, p. 538.
[7] NYT, May 3, 1945, 3:1.
[8] Cited by Carter, *Italy Speaks*, p. 128.
[9] Harris, *Allied Military Administration of Italy*, p. 315.
[10] Alexander, *The Italian Campaign, 12th December 1944 to 2nd May 1945*, p. 19.
[11] OWI, "Italian News Bulletin," May 2, 1945. General Mark Clark has written, "The services which the Partisans performed were many, varied and important and included the capture of many towns and villages." *Calculated Risk*, p. 430.

It was largely because of this "other Italy" (which included, in addition to the patriot forces, the re-outfitted Italian combat groups that were integrated in the Allied armies) that a people which had been dazed and demoralized in 1943 could regain by 1945 much of their political and military self-respect. It was because of this "other Italy" that the nation could become a party to a peace treaty in 1947 that was far more generous than Italians could reasonably have expected on September 8, 1943.

Disarmament and demobilization

Allied fears that Italian Resistance forces would imitate Greek ones in refusing to turn in their arms proved only partly justified. Early in May the CG/CVL circulated orders for collecting the weapons. Usually the job was completed within a very few days. In the outlying Veneto, however, where there were thousands of PW's and where relations with Tito long remained tense, disarming of the "Osoppo" and "Garibaldi" brigades was delayed until mid-June. In Piedmont, where for a month the problems raised by French "liberators," German PW's, and remnants of Fascist military forces beclouded the situation, patriot leaders thought the disarming program too precipitate.[12] According to Field Marshal Alexander, the patriots' "loyalty to [the Allied] cause was shown again when, after the Allied Armies had completed the liberation of northern Italy, they laid down at ceremonial parades, in the presence of my representatives, the arms which they had proudly carried against the enemy." [13] Certainly the partisans relinquished most of the heavy equipment and many of the more antiquated rifles; however, extremist-minded guerrillas kept many side arms, in some cases as souvenirs, but more often for political considerations. At the end of June Allied officials estimated that 60 per cent of the arms had been turned in.[14] In later years Italian authorities unearthed dozens of caches of arms hidden by Communists and others for reasons best known

[12] Trabucchi, *I vinti hanno sempre torto*, pp. 232–237; Harris, *Allied Military Administration of Italy*, pp. 315–350, 355–358.
[13] Alexander, *The Italian Campaign, 12th December 1944 to 2nd May 1945*, p. 19.
[14] NYT, June 30, 1945, 7:1. According to Valiani, in Lombardy in May and June patriots turned in 102,652 rifles, 5,729 automatic weapons, 1,635 pistols, 354 cannons and mortars, and 31,261 hand grenades. *Tutte le strade conducono a Roma*, p. 353.

to themselves.[15] One can only guess what was the true percentage turned in.

Plans for demobilizing the underground fighters in the separation centers (which functioned until mid-July) were carried out as best they could in spite of the influx of "eleventh-hour patriots." If some Italian camp officials lacked imagination in handling the veterans, this was even truer of the Allied officers, very few of whom were temperamentally endowed to work easily with red-scarved, politically intoxicated veterans of the underground. Some Allied personnel concluded unfairly that these men were interested solely in tangible rewards.[16] Many of the patriots, for their part, resented the Allies' benevolent treatment of German PW's; understandably, they failed to appreciate the niceties of international law on the subject. The amount of mustering-out pay proved but a pittance in the face of spiraling inflation; even the supplement finally agreed to in June 1945 was quite inadequate. Reluctance of some industrialists to keep surplus workers on the pay roll, to assign job preference to former guerrillas, and to fulfill certain covert wage agreements made with clandestine labor leaders also bred resentment.[17]

Several Resistance spokesmen commented on the disparity between Rome's plans for treatment of Italian veterans and those adumbrated in Washington for American G.I.'s. Sogno suggested state-financed scholarships for younger veterans; but nothing came of it.[18] Longo proposed that the CLN's guarantee future employment and low-priced goods to the veterans through pro-

[15] In 1950 Interior Minister Scelba (DC) reported to the Chamber of Deputies that between January 1947 and June 1950 police had seized from partisan caches: 66 pieces of field artillery; 344 mortars; 1,543 heavy machine guns; 2,303 light machine guns; 6,444 Tommy guns; over 42,000 rifles and muskets; over 102,000 hand grenades; 244 tons of high explosives; 237 radio transmitters; and over 10,000,000 rounds of ammunition. NYT, Feb. 11, 1951.
As of August 31, 1951, the cumulative total of hidden arms confiscated included: 226,603 hand grenades; 33,888 pistols and revolvers; 159,975 rifles and muskets; 34,982 automatic rifles; 5,027 machine guns; 695 mortars and grenade launchers; 296 radio transmitters; 169 cannons; 29 tons of explosives; 19,756,401 rounds of ammunition. New York Herald Tribune, Jan. 6, 1952.
[16] Salvadori-Paleotti, "The Patriot Movement in Italy," Foreign Affairs, xxiv (1946), p. 549. General Trabucchi observed that Americans forgot that their own heroes in the Revolutionary War had been scorned by General Burgoyne as "rabble in arms, drunk with success and insolence." I vinti hanno sempre torto, p. 236.
[17] For details of these, see Harris, Allied Military Administration of Italy, p. 363.
[18] Milan La Libertà, May 5, 1945.

ducers' and consumers' co-operatives; but this too was ignored.[19] Communist leaders (who had quickly seen to it that only their most trusted men held command posts in the post-Liberation partisan formations) [20] were displeased that patriot units could not be recruited *en bloc* into the regular Army and police force. Not more than a quarter of the Volunteers of Liberty eligible to join these forces were permitted to be enrolled.[21]

When the CG/CVL officially dissolved itself on June 7, 1945, its leaders addressed a farewell message to the Freedom Volunteers, explaining that while "every effort has been made to obtain a just recognition of your sacrifices . . . , these attempts have not always been crowned with success. Circumstances independent of our will have often impeded them. The National Association of Italian Partisans [ANPI] will continue the work. But the great recompense lies in the consciousness on the part of all the fighters of the mountains and the cities that we have done together our duty as Italians. . . ." [22] And taking leave of his "boys" in Turin on May 20, General Trabucchi used the occasion to answer resolutely a query whether they really had made the world better: "I say to you it is, my lads, because the blood you shed is the seed from which social justice will germinate." [23]

Postwar frustrations spurred some to mutter darkly about returning "to the mountains." And here and there unseemly hooliganism spoiled the Resistance record. In a few lamentable instances, gangs of ex-partisans (or at least claimants to such status) went so far as to break into jails and machinegun Fascist prisoners. This they did in Ferrara and Modena on June 21, when they slaughtered thirty-five and wounded twenty-eight others.[24] On July 8 another band raided the Schio jail near Venice, slaying forty-seven political prisoners.[25] Fortunately, this kind of gangsterism ended soon after the new government of Ferruccio

[19] See his speech in Milan on June 6, published in CLNAI, *Verso il governo del popolo: primo convegno dei CLN regionali dell'Alta Italia, 6–7 giugno 1945* (Milan, 1945), p. 69.

[20] Cucchi and Magnani, *Crisi di una generazione*, pp. 36–37.

[21] When he became Chief of Staff in May 1945, General Cadorna insisted upon a rather restrictive system of admittance of Freedom Volunteers into the regular Armed Forces. *La Riscossa*, p. 292.

[22] Quoted in *ibid.*, p. 293.

[23] Trabucchi, *I vinti hanno sempre torto*, p. 244.

[24] *NYT*, June 22, 1945, 4:3; June 24, 7:1.

[25] *Ibid.*, July 9, 1945, 20:2; July 16, 3:2; July 31, 10:4; Dec. 21, 4:1.

Parri was installed in Rome. Nevertheless, misdeeds such as these inevitably cast a shadow on the entire patriot movement. Dozens of denigrators of the "criminal," "Communist" Resistance soon took advantage of the almost inevitable reaction and drummed out propaganda in the rotogravures and elsewhere against those who supposedly were interested only in massacring their fellow countrymen. At the other extreme, brazen Communist exploitation of the partisan veteran groups during the political and economic crises of 1946, 1947, and 1948 also tarnished the earlier multiparty reputation of the Resistenza.[26] It was hardly surprising, therefore, that more than a decade passed after the Liberation before the campaign to obtain full legal recognition of the CVL won success.[27]

"Vento del nord"

The chief disillusionment for the left-wing Resistance currents was political in nature. Much of the disenchantment was inevitable; seldom do the workaday realities of an imperfect world reflect the bright visions of a crusading era.

Italy was gripped by a strong revolutionary tide in May and June 1945. Just as in 1919, it seemed as if Italy were once more

[26] *Ibid.*, Aug. 28, 1946, 5:5; Oct. 25, 9:1; Sept. 3, 1947, 14:6; Sept. 17, 24:2, 5; Dec. 8, 1:7; Dec. 11, 1:2, 4; Feb. 2, 1948, 17:1; Feb. 6, 17:1.

[27] To be sure, Law No. 1317 of November 13, 1947, gave the CVL the same status as the regular Army. But a decision of the Tribunale Supremo Militare on March 26, 1954, upset this by declaring the partisans were not legally "belligerents," whereas soldiers in Mussolini's RSI were. This caused so much indignation that finally Parliament on March 25, 1958, approved a law which clarified beyond doubt that "the CVL is recognized, in every legal respect, as an organized military corps, included in the cadres of the Armed Forces of the State, for the activity carried out until the installation of the Allied Military Government in the specific localities." See Luca, "Un'incertezza eliminata," Rome *Il Mondo*, April 22, 1958, p. 4; *cf.* Achille Battaglia, "Il processo alla Resistenza," *ibid.*, Mar. 1, 1955, p. 3.

Meanwhile, another turn for the better had come on February 23, 1958, when the government of DC Premier Adone Zoli (himself a veteran of the Florence Resistance) granted permission to Parri's FIAP ("Italian Federation of Partisan Associations") to hold a public ceremony in Rome commemorating the CVL. (In postwar years many Freedom Volunteers had seceded from the Social-Communist-bossed ANPI and had organized their own veterans groups, like Parri's FIAP and GL, and General Cadorna's FIVL.) After the ceremony, neo-Fascists busied themselves "disinfecting" the scene. On March 14 the premier declared in the Chamber of Deputies that the flags of Resistance fighters were as deserving of honor as those of the regular Armed Forces—an observation that produced an outburst from a small band of neo-Fascist deputies, who brawled violently with the leftists. NYT, Feb. 24, 1958, 5:2; Mar. 15, 3:5.

on the brink of a real political and social revolution. The war experiences and the revolutionary upsurge throughout the world had stirred Italian laboring groups. Property owners were scared and uncertain of themselves. Those who had compromised with Fascism (and they were many) were anxious to save what they could from the debris; they were even ready to make quite a few concessions toward both democracy and socialism.

Yet the leftist tide failed to break down all of Italy's conservative dikes, and in less than three years it had largely spent itself. The three-year period of postwar readjustment did not end in a new Blackshirt dictatorship. Instead, it opened the way for a long era of Catholic government. The great majority of Christian Democrats were far from being Fascists; most were sincerely democratic. Yet in their accession to political power, as Professor Hughes has noted perceptively, the Christian Democrats were to make it fairly easy for many of the social groups who had once been *fiancheggiatori* of Fascism to reclaim influential positions in the economy and the government.[28]

How was it that the "quiet," moderate opposition gained the upper hand over the "militant," leftist opposition and frustrated many of the latter's revolutionary aspirations? At the moment of the northern insurrections in April 1945 the septentrional anti-Fascists of the left were confident that their CLN's could reshape the patterns of Italy's public life. Exuberantly they dreamed of the regeneration of the nation by their own new "democratic elite." They talked of a purifying *vento del nord* that would cleanse Italy of its decrepit Monarchy, its tainted politicians, its overcentralized prefectural bureaucracy, and its capitalistic monopolies. As early as April 26 the CLNAI expressed to the Rome Central CLN its unanimous hope that "in view of the reform of the government which certainly will follow the liberation of the North, . . . those ministries decisive for the conduct of the war and for democratic reconstruction of the country, and in particular the Ministry of the Interior, will be entrusted to men who have fought Fascism decisively." [29]

The Pd'A organ, *L'Italia libera*, circulating overtly in Milan

[28] Hughes, *The United States and Italy*, pp. 143–144.
[29] Archivio CLNAI, v/35, *Documenti del CLNAI*, p. 78, cited in Catalano, *Storia del CLNAI*, pp. 428–429.

on the 27th, went even further. Anxious to preserve the equal status it enjoyed with larger parties in the CLN circle, the Pd'A insisted that the CLNAI become the Provisional Government, with members of the local CLN's serving as a democratic advisory body until the Constituent Assembly could be elected. Make the CVL the shield of the new Republic, it further demanded.[30] The Pd'A editors seemed confident that the Rome politicians and Allied superintendents could be forced to accept such a semirevolutionary dispensation in order to avoid bloodshed.[31]

Echoes of the Milanese spirit were heard in Rome in those days. On Sunday, April 29, the Central CLN organized a celebration of the emancipation on Piazza Santi Apostoli, adjacent to the CCLN headquarters in Palazzo Guglielmi. The massed thousands greeted Negarville (PCI) enthusiastically when he denounced the Monarchy, and they cheered Cianca (Pd'A) and Nenni (PSIUP). The latter called on the Allies to erect no *cordon sanitaire* between North and South,[32] and to permit the patriots to keep their arms. Scelba (DC), who was suspected by the crowd of having royalist leanings, had great trouble making himself heard as the throng chanted, "Death to the King, royal family, and Badoglio!" Before a Labor Democrat could gain attention he had to reassure the audience that he thought a republic was necessary.[33]

On May Day in a solemn Milanese celebration of the patriot martyrs, Longo, the PCI firebrand in the North, went even farther. Milan must henceforth be the "moral capital and guide"

[30] *L'Italia libera* (Milan), April 27, 1945; Leo Valiani, *L'avvento di DeGasperi* (Turin, 1949), pp. 12–13; Calamandrei, "Rassegna della resistenza europea: funzioni rivoluzionari dei Comitati di Liberazione," *Il Ponte*, 1 (May 1945), pp. 138–140.

[31] Perhaps the Pd'A would have been less sanguine had it known that on April 18 U.S. Admiral Stone of the AC had ordered Premier Bonomi to withdraw from circulation the very first pamphlet to be published by Communist Scoccimarro's Ministry for Occupied Italy, "I CLN dell'Alta Italia—formazione e funzionamento," on the grounds that it implied erroneously that the Allies would approve the CLN political philosophy.

[32] The AC was seeking to impose a *cordon sanitaire économique* along the Gothic Line to prevent rapid depreciation of the currency in the North, but this proved a miserable failure. Harris, *Allied Military Administration of Italy*, pp. 289–291, 313.

[33] PWB, Central "D" Section, "Consolidated Report on Conditions in Liberated Italy," No. 66, May 1, 1945.

of Italy, he proclaimed. It must tell the politicians in Rome three things: (1) The northern patriots are not at all pleased with the wishy-washy way in which the purge was proceeding in the South. (2) A new, "popular" government must be placed in the hands of "energetic, determined" men who never have compromised with Fascism and who have known how "to accomplish the miracle of liberating their country." It "must be tied solidly to the masses and popular organizations arising out of the fire of the insurrection." (3) There must be wide participation by workers in factory administration. "We demand . . . that workers, clerks, and technicians participate in the manner set forth by the CLNAI in its decree regarding the administration of production on a level of absolute equality with the owners." [34]

"Consigli di gestione"

The important CLNAI decree to which Longo referred was that issued on April 17, establishing in larger industries *consigli di gestione* ("management councils")—a modernized version of the *consigli di fabbrica* ("factory councils") which Gramsci had pushed in imitation of Lenin's soviets after World War I. Perhaps the most far-reaching economic measure to be promulgated by the CLNAI, the decree had abrogated Mussolini's pseudosocialistic measures.

In the early postwar period three conceptions of "management councils" vied for acceptance: a radical Social-Communist proposal, a much more moderate Christian Democratic blueprint, and a middle-of-the-road Actionist plan.[35] A certain number of

---

[34] Quoted in Milan *L'Unità*, May 2, 1945.

[35] The Social-Communists hoped to establish *consigli di gestione* alongside the entrepreneurial and "administration council" ("*consiglio di amministrazione*")—whose prerogatives would remain unchanged—as an agency for handling technical matters and elaborating production plans. The *consigli di gestione* would be composed equally of representatives of capital and labor, and would be chaired by a person designated either by the *consiglio di amministrazione* or the entrepreneur. According to this plan, labor's representatives in effect would be technical co-managers of the factory.

The Christian Democrats preferred a less radical plan. They would have the new *consigli di gestione* replace those of *amministrazione*, to be sure, but the workers' representatives would hold a clearly minority status, based on the principle of employee stock-sharing.

The Actionists had still another plan for the *consigli di gestione* (or *consigli di controllo* or *d'azienda*, as they preferred to term them). They should be organs composed solely of representatives of the workers but should not share in the responsibility of factory management. Their function would be to check the con-

the Communist-dominated *consigli di gestione* were to be organized by "factory CLN's" in the North. But government officials in Rome, responsive to the protests of private enterprise, failed to extend legal recognition to them after the Liberation. Simultaneously the Allied Commission's Economic Section exerted subtle pressure against them on grounds they were "inefficient." As a result, most of them faded away in 1945 and 1946. The new Constitution of the Republic, drafted in 1947, reaffirmed their right to exist, however. In general, the revolutionary *consigli di gestione* were superseded by less pretentious *commissioni interne* ("internal commissions," or shop-stewards' committees), which had originated early in the century as liaison agencies between management and labor for the settlement of disputes over labor contracts. Suppressed by the Fascists, they had been rehabilitated during Badoglio's "45 days" and perverted by Mussolini's RSI during the ensuing two years. In their postwar incarnation these shop-stewards' committees operated chiefly as conciliatory and liaison bodies between management and labor, and were consulted in certain disciplinary and purge cases, in modifying hours of labor, and in administration of social-security funds.[36]

Advent of Parri

Within a week after the Liberation the hexpartite Rome Central CLN made it clear to Anglo-American overseers that they wished to go to Milan to consult the CLNAI on formation of a new government. At first the Allied Commission rejected this proposal, preferring to leave the management of political affairs in the hands of Bonomi's four-party government. After a few

---

sistency and integrity of business operations. Generally their role would be advisory, but decisions of major importance would be obligatory for management. See Giacomo Perticone and Bruno Caizzi's discussion in articles, "Consigli di gestione" and "Commissione di fabbrica" in Antonio Basso (ed.), *Dizionario di cultura politica* (Milan, 1946), pp. 153, 124.

[36] *Ibid.*; Catalano, *Storia del CLNAI*, pp. 404–406; Confindustria, *I consigli di gestione* (Rome, 1947), p. 20 ff.; Emilio Sereni, *CLN nella cospirazione, nella insurrezione, nella ricostruzione* (Milan, 1945), pp. 255–265, and *passim*; Dr. Cesare Merzagora, *I pavidi (dalla cospirazione alla Costituente)* (Milan, 1946), pp. 95–100, and *passim*; Riccardo Levi, "L'azione economica e sociale dei CLN dell'Alta Italia," *Il Ponte*, III (1947), 994–1000; and Maurice F. Neufeld, *Labor Unions and National Politics in Italian Industrial Plants* (Ithaca, 1954), pp. 20–30.

days, however, the AC did permit top-rung CLNAI men to fly to Rome on May 5 for such negotiations. The northern delegation consisted of Parri and Valiani (Pd'A), Pertini (PSIUP), Sereni (PCI), Arpesani (PLI), Marazza (DC), and Augusto DeGasperi (DC), brother of Alcide in Rome. In agreeing to this procedure, the CLNAI tacitly conceded its inferior status, though several ministers of the government in Rome two weeks later went to Milan for further talks. The crisis over reshaping the government persisted for more than a month.[37]

During the first weeks of post-Liberation euphoria many of the northern leaders (particularly those in the Pd'A) seemed to think that the victory of the Armed Resistance had suddenly expunged Italy's twenty-year record of tyranny. For the nonce they forgot that the Armed Resistance had been the work of a relatively small minority (albeit tenacious and respectable) of the total population. It was understandable that they were slow to appreciate fully the determination of Churchill (and the Americans, to a lesser degree) to prevent any ultraleftist political upheaval in Italy; after all, they had had little chance to witness at first hand the overwhelming military superiority of the Allies. Moreover, many of them had assumed Russia would throw her support behind a radically new political regime in Italy. Yet, as events quickly demonstrated, Stalin was quite willing to leave Italy to Anglo-American management so long as he could exercise similar undisputed sway over his sphere of eastern satellites.

The Communist position was rudely proclaimed by party chieftain Togliatti in a speech in Milan on May 21. The Mediterranean maestro of dialectical materialism rejected the northern Actionists' proposal for a new type of Central Consultative Assembly that would consist of delegates of the regional CLN's. Already the DC and PLI had vetoed this gambit, charging that it would subvert traditional patterns of parliamentary and prefectural government and give unwonted representation to the presumably minuscule Pd'A. Speaking the language of moderation, Togliatti now sided with these rightist currents and announced that the PCI would remain faithful to the earlier plan that Croce had outlined for an interim, appointive Consulta to

[37] Valiani, *L'avvento di DeGasperi*, pp. 1–14; Andreotti, *Concerto a sei voci*, pp. 47–49.

serve until the Constituent Assembly could be elected. To the dismay of the Actionists, Nenni's PSIUP supported Togliatti. It was clear that the two Marxist parties, linked by a "unity of action" pact, sensed that they and the Catholics would be postwar Italy's predominant *partiti di massa*. Henceforth they could afford to take their chances in the ballot boxes. They need no longer pay lip-service to "indissoluble unity" in the political round robin of the CLN's in which the minor parties (Pd'A, PLI, and DL) hitherto had exercised so unrealistic a share of power. The era of the CLN's was fast drawing to a close.

Incumbent Premier Bonomi [38] could not expect to continue in office, now that the two parties (PSIUP and Pd'A) which had boycotted his second government since November 1944 were anxious to get back into the seats of power. With six instead of four parties to be accommodated in the new cabinet (and with DL almost moribund), the center of gravity had to shift to the left. The candidacies of Nenni (PSIUP), Alcide DeGasperi (DC), Carandini (PLI), and Tarchiani (Pd'A) were long discussed, but Nenni and DeGasperi quickly became the major contenders. Catholic backers of DeGasperi pointed out correctly that since Nenni was linked to the Communists in a "unity of action" pact, he could hardly expect the Allies to endorse his candidacy. (Indeed, on May 20 an overzealous AMG official in Vercelli arrested Nenni for a few days for speaking in public without Allied permission.) [39]

While Italy's power-thirsty politicians wrangled over the composition of the new cabinet, AMG made ready to install itself in the North on June 1. This transfer of power signaled the denouement of the regional and local CLN's in the Po valley. On June 6 representatives of the CLNAI returned from Rome to attend a conclave in Milan of the regional CLN's. Many of them were dismayed to see AMG take over; a good many argued that it was both unnecessary and anachronistic, now that so many provinces in the Center and South had already been handed back

[38] In June Bonomi retreated into the political shadows and stayed there until 1948, when the old man was rewarded with the presidency of the newly elected Senate. He died three years later.

[39] Valiani, *L'avvento di DeGasperi*, pp. 14-15; Tupini, *I Democratici cristiani*, pp. 105-114; NYT, May 22, 1945, 10:1.

to direct Italian rule.[40] But the Allied Military Government plans could not easily be altered, and Churchill's policy makers were anything but elated about CLN "popular democracy" that implied both republicanism and considerable socialism. In Milan and certain other cities CLN-designated prefects continued in office until December 1945, and a good many CLN's demonstrated their skill in persuading AMG officers to approve some of their plans and nominees. The Allies were especially indebted to the CLNAI's Central Economic Commission for invaluable data it had amassed for them. Nevertheless, the CLN's direct legislative and executive role terminated on June 1. Except for some peripheral committees that lingered on for a few weeks in relative isolation, the multiparty organs of the Resistenza found themselves whittled down to advisory status as *giunte consultative*.[41]

Ruefully the reformist-minded wing of the CLNAI conceded by June 13 that its gusty *vento del nord* had all but blown itself out against the soporific sirocco and the prevailing westerlies from the Atlantic world. Cutting their demands, the CLNAI let it be known they would be content if only the new premier came from their ranks. The compromise was facilitated by Allied promises that this would hasten the practical suspension of some of the annoying armistice clauses. The CLN leaders then settled upon the candidacy of Ferruccio Parri, the Armed Resistance's most idealistic paladin. The selection of Parri on June 20 was, of course, no proof of the Action Party's strength but rather of the impasse among the ambitious *partiti di massa*; his weakness was to become apparent within a few weeks. Parri regarded his investiture as coming from the militant and semirevolutionary CLN hexarchy, not from the House of Savoy. Thus he looked upon his government as marking a clean break with the old Aventine tradition of the preceding anti-Fascist governments. He

[40] On May 10 the Allies handed over nine provinces in Tuscany, Umbria, and the Marches. On August 2 they turned over to the Rome government all areas except those north of Bologna.

[41] Harris, *Allied Military Administration of Italy*, pp. 353, 363–365; Sereni, *CLN nella cospirazione, nella insurrezione, nella ricostruzione*, p. 10 ff.; Mario delle Piane, *Funzione storica dei Comitati di Liberazione Nazionale* (Florence, 1946), p. 64; Calamandrei, "Funzione rivoluzionari dei Comitati di Liberazione," *Il Ponte*, 1 (May 1945), pp. 138–140; Valiani, "Intervento," *MLI*, No. 52/53 (1958), p. 208.

saw himself as the architect of far-reaching reforms of the Italian state and society.[42]

Though portfolios in his cabinet were assigned on the basis of fictional parity, the leftist triad dominated (DL was virtually nonexistent outside Rome). All told, there were twenty ministers and twenty-six undersecretaries of state—a new record! Fourteen of the ministers were natives of the North. Several had served in the previous Bonomi government. Four new ministries were created to handle postwar problems: Reconstruction; Food; Labor; and Postwar Assistance. Nenni (PSIUP) and Manlio Brosio (PLI) of Turin balanced each other as vice-premiers, the former being charged with preparing the Constituent Assembly, the latter the Consultative Assembly. While Togliatti (PCI) wormed his way into the Justice Ministry, Alcide DeGasperi (DC) tenaciously hung on to the Foreign Ministry (of special importance when the peace treay came up for negotiation) and he sought to retain the Interior Ministry. The latter post went to Premier Parri, however, with Spataro (DC) serving as undersecretary.[43]

Italy's new government head was a man of high aspirations—modest and appealing, yet a tragic figure. His friends in the underground had fondly nicknamed him "Zio Maurizio" ("Uncle Maurice"). As premier he preferred not to be called "Your Excellency" but simply "Professor Ferruccio Parri, President of the Council of Ministers." There was no doubt of his integrity and his patriotism. "Enough murders and reprisals; let us roll up our sleeves!" he besought his countrymen in his first broadcast on June 22, a day after partisan toughs had broken into Ferrara and Modena jails, as has been noted, and other demonstrators were active in Milan.[44] Premier Parri frankly told his people they

[42] Andreotti, *Concerto a sei voci*, pp. 62–86; Valiani, "The Italian Crisis," *The Nation*, Dec. 15, 1945, p. 656; Harris, *Allied Military Administration of Italy*, pp. 352–353; Hughes, *The United States and Italy*, pp. 145–151.

[43] Other members included: Ruini (DL), Reconstruction; Scoccimarro (PCI), Finance; Soleri (PLI), Treasury; Jacini (DC), War; Admiral DeCourten (Ind.), Navy; Cevolotto (DL), Aviation; Arangio-Ruiz (PLI), Public Instruction, with Achille Marazza (DC) undersecretary; Romita (PSIUP), Public Works; Gullo (PCI), Agriculture and Forests; LaMalfa (Pd'A), Transport; Scelba (DC), Posts and Telecommunications; Gronchi (DC), Industry and Commerce; G. Barbareschi (PSIUP), Labor and Social Welfare; Lussu (Pd'A), Postwar Assistance; and Enrico Molè (DL), Food. Andreotti, *Concerto a sei voci*, pp. 86–92; Tupini, *I Democratici cristiani*, pp. 113–114.

[44] On the 29th Justice Minister Togliatti also called for an end to impromptu justice. *NYT*, June 30, 1945, 5:1.

must have confidence in the Allies; it means "bread, coal, and credit." In order to shore up Italian claims for a generous peace, he soon asked the Allies for permission (they granted it unenthusiastically) to declare war on Japan.[45] Still, Italy could not hope to improve her status beyond that of a "co-belligerent." At the Potsdam Conference in July, Italy got nothing but an assurance that she would be eligible for membership in the United Nations after the peace treaty. President Truman did succeed in getting the conferees to agree that the Italian treaty should be first on the agenda of the Big Three Council of Foreign Ministers.

Though Parri wished to bring into Italian public life a sober, high-minded elite, he and many of his appointees lacked previous executive experience in Rome and failed to demonstrate conspicuous ability. They were handicapped, of course, by an entrenched bureaucracy which felt scant sympathy for their goals, by the intense rivalry among the parties within the government, by the splits within Parri's own Pd'A, and by the constant intervention of Anglo-American agencies.[46] Parri himself worked long hours and often slept in his office. Sometimes he became absorbed in details that might better have been assigned to others. This was unfortunate at a time when quick decisions were required on many fronts: fighting the inflation and black market which were reducing millions to destitution; compromising the Augean problem of *epurazione*; healing sectional wounds; handling noisy Sicilian separatists; defending the borders against Yugoslav and French pretensions; preparing for elections that would shape the political institutions of the new Italy; and satisfying some of the demands for land reform.

The three *partiti di massa* continued to elbow their way to the front, pushing Parri's Actionists and the others to the side. Togliatti proved himself one of the shrewdest politicians of the century. Convinced that any revolutionary adventures were futile in the presence of Anglo-American troops and in the absence of the Red Army, he eschewed inflammatory talk and sought to quiet the fears of the conservatives. For the present he bent his efforts toward welding a mighty party of proletarians and gain-

[45] Kogan, *Italy and the Allies*, pp. 116–117.
[46] Friedrich, *American Experiences in Military Government in World War II*, pp. 134–136.

563

ing supremacy in the Italian General Confederation of Labor (CGIL). At the same time he was careful to preserve his intimate working alliance with Nenni's PSIUP. Most important of all, perhaps, Togliatti was determined to hang on to the cabinet posts the PCI had won. To strengthen his power in the government, Togliatti invited DeGasperi to collaborate with him and Nenni in a tripartite regime.[47]

In all but the last effort, wily Togliatti met with success. To the dismay of the Actionists and the revisionist wing of Socialists (some of whom had dreamed of a union among themselves), Nenni played right along with the Communist "pied piper" by pushing through the PSIUP National Council on July 29–August 1, 1945, a motion calling for outright fusion with the PCI.[48] Thereupon, rightists Saragat and Silone in great alarm belatedly called an October meeting of the PSIUP Central Committee and persuaded it to renounce fusionism in return for renewing simply the "unity of action" pact which harked back to 1934 (except for the Molotov-Ribbentrop hiatus of 1939–1941). Nenni's party was destined to remain subordinate to Togliatti's, despite confusing propaganda to the effect that it would fortify its own independence and unity, champion individual freedom, and muffle its anticlericalism.[49]

The renewal of the pact deprived the Pd'A of its only conceivable strong ally and ended the tenuous partnership it had cultivated with the PSIUP on the side lines of Bonomi's second government (November 1944–June 1945). In the new *mise en scène* there was to be no enduring place for the Pd'A which, redoubtable though it was as an association of intellectuals, lacked grass-roots support outside Piedmont and some of the northern provinces. History was repeating itself: just as Carlo Rosselli's Giustizia e Libertà had been overtaken by the Social-Communist bloc in the era of the Popular Front and Spanish Civil War, so Parri's Action Party was being outmaneuvered by Togliatti's brilliant tactics, the realities of Anglo-American power,

[47] Hughes, *The United States and Italy*, pp. 148–149.
[48] PSI, *Almanacco Socialista* (Rome, 1946), pp. 315–338; and Emiliani, *Dieci anni perduti: cronache del PSI dal 1943 a oggi*, pp. 16–20.
[49] *Ibid.*, pp. 33–34; Elizabeth Wiskemann, "Socialism and Communism in Italy," *Foreign Affairs*, xxiv (1946), pp. 487–488.

and the mistakes of its own hotspurs.[50] Indeed, a good portion of the Actionists' trouble arose from the fact that they seldom could agree upon what they wished most to stress. Should it be revisionist socialism, or democratic liberalism, or Jacobinic conformity? And what should be their attitude toward totalitarian Communism? [51]

By September Parri's ill-starred government had taken two constructive steps: bestowal of autonomy on Val d'Aosta (advocated by the enlightened Resistance leaders from that sector), and convocation in Rome on the 25th of the long-bruited Consultative Assembly. Though its 429 members were all appointed, the Consulta helped bring a broader range of public opinion to bear upon the cabinet. The delegates came not only from the parties, including those outside the CLN magic circle, but also from the labor confederations, professional associations, and ex-parliamentarians untarnished by Fascism. As a gesture of defiance against the British, the Consulta enthusiastically chose Sforza to be its presiding officer.[52]

Parri was anxious to have national elections as soon as possible to settle the institutional issue. The royalists, on the other hand, felt that they had everything to gain by stalling; they much preferred a series of local administrative elections prior to the general ones. Nenni's Ministry of the Constituent Assembly made a modest beginning in drafting an electoral law and voting list. Yet, overburdened as he was with his High Commission for the Purge, Nenni could not carry out all his duties to the satisfaction of everyone. Inevitably such criticism was directed not only at him but also at Premier Parri.[53]

By autumn hostile forces had dragged up their heavy guns. A raucous, potentially neo-Fascist current which catered to the grievances of the "common man" and presented as a scapegoat everything related to the CLN's and the new government sprouted in

[50] Hughes, *The United States and Italy*, p. 149.

[51] As early as 1943 Croce had predicted that "only when the Action Party has provided itself with a coherent program will it be possible to determine [its fate]; perhaps then the Socialist and positively Communist elements in it will go to Socialism and to Communism, and the Liberal elements to Liberalism, for the whole question is one of method." *Quando l'Italia era tagliata in due*, p. 53.

[52] Grindrod, *The New Italy*, p. 30; Harris, *Allied Military Administration of Italy*, pp. 361–362; Friedrich, *American Experiences in Military Government in World War II*, p. 136.

[53] Wiskemann, *Foreign Affairs*, xxiv (1946), pp. 487–488.

the *Mezzogiorno* under the label, Fronte dell'Uomo Qualunque ("Common Man Front"). This equivocal, heavily subsidized conglomeration was directed by ex-playwright Guglielmo Giannini, who patterned much of his impudent propaganda upon the scatological spirit of D'Annunzio's *me ne fregismo*. Sounding the keynote for his petty bourgeois movement, Giannini liked to complain, "The Fascists deprived the Italians of their freedom, but no one yet has restored it to them." "We were better off when we were worse off!" He proposed a sit-down strike of "patriots" against the "politicians" and managed to entice all sorts of disgruntled folk in the South.

The immediate cause for the overthrow of Parri in November 1945 was the hostility that came from royalist Liberals and Christian Democrats within the cabinet. They had never subscribed unreservedly to either the political or the economic prospectus of the CLN's, and they received encouragement from the Allies.[54] For weeks they berated Parri and accused the CLN's of high-handedness. Their cumulative impatience at serving in the same cabinet with a majority of republican and socialistic ministers came to a head on the purge and the closely linked economic program calling for a capital levy and allocation of raw materials to favor small firms at the expense of the large trusts which had fattened under Fascism.[55] Resentful that Parri had appointed Togliatti Minister of Justice, the Liberals demanded as a safeguard against arbitrary arrests that Parri include in the cabinet some genro unaffiliated with the CLN's. Specifically they suggested ex-Premier Orlando. Well aware that this meridional octogenarian was not only opposed to the purge but to the idea of a republic, Parri refused, whereupon the conservative Liberals resigned. Though DeGasperi piously called for continuation of the CLN hexarchy, he knew well that the PLI would not change its mind. Soon he associated the DC with the PLI boycotters of Parri.

Advent of DeGasperi

Opposed thus by the centrists and rightists (and indirectly by the PCI and the Allies), Parri tendered his resignation on No-

[54] Hughes, *The United States and Italy*, p. 150.
[55] Kogan, *Italy and the Allies*, p. 124.

vember 24. Instead of presenting it privately to Prince Humbert as Bonomi had done in the spring, he preferred to present it to the antiroyalist CLN's who, in his view, had given him the mandate in the first place. Thus he called in CLN delegates from the North and a crowd of foreign journalists to hear a prepared speech delivered in a quiet, flat voice.[56] In this high drama he accused the entrenched social sets who previously had been fellow travelers of Fascism of deliberately undermining (he used the term *coup d'état*) his own cabinet. DeGasperi (who was the logical candidate for the succession) jumped up to contradict this assertion. While some of Parri's charges may have been unfair, few could deny that the collapse of his government marked the eclipse of the militant anti-Fascists. Whatever the merits of the charges and counterallegations, it was to be the "quiet" wing of anti-Fascism that henceforth shouldered major responsibility for finding a middle path against both the extreme rightist and leftist foes of liberal democracy.[57]

In the ensuing quest for a premier, three revenants (Orlando, Nitti, and Bonomi) were consulted so often by Prince Humbert that journalists nicknamed them "ONB" (the initials of the defunct Fascist youth organization).[58] But Nitti had been away from Italy so long that he could not easily comprehend its new tone; and Bonomi understood the problems too well to wish to tackle them again. Though favored by several rightists, Orlando was much too antiquated and monarchistic to inspire popular enthusiasm. In the absence of a unanimous bid, DeNicola did not wish the post. The leftists preferred Sforza, but he still faced the unconcealed hostility of the British.

Under the circumstances, 64-year-old Alcide DeGasperi seemed the proper choice to replace Parri (who later was named to the Senate). The wiry ex-mountain climber from the Trentino proved his stamina by hanging on to the political sacristy in the Viminale through seven consecutive ministries from December 10, 1945, to July 28, 1953—a record bested only by Mussolini.

[56] The tense atmosphere was captured verbally in Carlo Levi's collection of postwar political vignettes, *The Watch* (New York, 1951), p. 204.

[57] Hughes, *The United States and Italy*, pp. 150–151; Kogan, *Italy and the Allies*, pp. 123–125; Vittorio DeCaprariis, "Gli alleati in Italia," Rome *Il Mondo*, Mar. 26, 1957, p. 8; P. Calamandrei, "Desistenza," *Il Ponte*, 11 (Oct. 1946).

[58] Hilton-Young, *The Italian Left*, p. 184.

The austere and astute Christian Democrat could claim a post alongside Cavour as one of Italy's ablest statesmen. He was more than a match for Togliatti, whose party he expelled from the government in 1947. DeGasperi knew well that in Italy it was imperative to avoid any exclusively Catholic government, however. A man of stout democratic convictions, DeGasperi resisted firmly all attempts by the authoritarian and clerical wing of his party (*e.g.*, Luigi Gedda of Catholic Action) to set up a *monocolore* regime. DeGasperi's recognition of the need for collaboration between secularists and Catholics was remarkable and almost alien to Italian politics. Yet before his retirement in 1953, shifting political fortunes impelled DeGasperi to give up briefly his multiparty approach to government; and ever since Italy's Christian Democracy has been skating on the thinnest political ice, lacking a solid majority and having to make the choice between a political "opening to the left" (*i.e.*, to Nenni's Socialists) or one to the neo-Fascistic right.[59]

DeGasperi's first government in December 1945 represented a modest shift to the right, though Nenni remained vice-premier in charge of the Costituente and Togliatti stayed on as Minister of Justice. Romita, a moderate Socialist, took over the important Interior Ministry, while DeGasperi kept the Foreign Office.[60] All six CLN currents were included, but only the inner triad of mass parties held major posts. Right after DeGasperi's accession to office the Allies announced that AMG would turn over to him all the northern provinces except Venezia Giulia and Udine at year's end. The new premier announced that career prefects and bureaucrats would replace CLNAI appointees at the same time. The High Commission for Sanctions against Fascism would be dissolved by March 31, 1946.[61]

[59] Hughes, *The United States and Italy*, pp. 151–153; Valiani, *L'Avvento di DeGasperi*, pp. 23–24; Grindrod, *The Rebuilding of Italy*, pp. 65–66; Einaudi and Goguel, *Christian Democracy in Italy and France*, pp. 78–96.

[60] Other cabinet appointments included: Lussu (Pd'A), Vice-Premier for the Consulta; Scoccimarro (PCI), Finance; Corbino (PLI), Treasury; Brosio (PLI), War; Admiral DeCourten (Ind.), Navy; Cevolotto (DL), Aviation; Molè (DL), Public Instruction; Cattani, Public Works; Gullo (PCI), Agriculture and Forests; Lombardi (Pd'A), Transport; Scelba (DC), Posts and Telecommunications; Gronchi (DC), Industry and Commerce; Barbareschi (PSIUP), Labor and Social Welfare; LaMalfa (Pd'A), Reconstruction; and Gasparotto (DC), Postwar Assistance.

[61] AC *Weekly Bulletin*, Dec. 15, 1945, cited in Kogan, *Italy and the Allies*, p. 126. Expanded American aid helped buttress the new government.

In December 1945 Togliatti summoned the Fifth Congress of the PCI. With customary cunning he again offered Nenni's PSIUP the chance of fusion on the basis of equal representation in party offices, notwithstanding the PSIUP's inferior strength (as revealed in sundry local elections that winter). Proudly Togliatti claimed two million card-carrying Communists, a remarkable achievement in view of his party's brief span of legality and its weakness in the pre-Fascist era. The prestige it had won for itself in the Resistenza, the economic chaos in the country, and the previous conditioning of the Italian populace for a totalitarian-type party were some of the key factors in explaining the PCI's magnitude. Togliatti appealed unctuously for maintenance of the CLN's and the spirit of multiparty collaboration; [62] yet he also warned that it would not be possible to co-operate forever with DeGasperi's regime.[63]

In semicrisis throughout the winter, the PSIUP finally held its XXIV Congress in Florence between April 11 and 17, 1946. It decided to ignore the PCI fusion bid but continue the "unity of action" pact "for political, . . . not for ideological reasons." [64] Clearly the Socialists sensed the Communists' strength and hoped to capitalize on it without sacrificing their own individuality in the process.

Meanwhile, in February the Pd'A carved its epitaph at its Third Congress. With almost Calvinistic zeal, some delegates sought to uphold their "radical," "liberal-socialist" role, but others allowed themselves to sail along on a flood of words into authoritarian and collectivist ports.[65] The left-wing faction steered toward Nenni; the moderates (including Parri and La-Malfa) joined Pacciardi's stream of traditional and democratic republicanism; so did Sforza.[66]

[62] According to "heretics" Cucchi and Magnani, the old PCI directorate made sure it kept tight control of the party reins but admitted a few younger comrades to subsidiary posts. So long as Togliatti was in the cabinet, he saw to it that the provincial formations of partisan veterans kept inactive. *Crisi di una generazione,* p. 49.

[63] P. Togliatti, *Rinnovare l'Italia: Documenti del V° Congresso del PCI* (Rome, 1946), pp. 37–38 ff.

[64] Wiskemann, *Foreign Affairs,* xxiv (1946), pp. 484–493; Emiliani, *Dieci anni perduti,* pp. 35–47. Open schism within the PSIUP did not occur until January 1947, when Saragat's rightist group seceded.

[65] Massimo Salvadori-Paleotti, "Liberalism in Italy," *The Contemporary Review* (April 1949), p. 203.

[66] On the dissolution of the Pd'A, see also Roberto Battaglia, *Il Ponte,* ii

Referendum and the Republic

With the approval of the Consulta and of Prince Humbert, Premier DeGasperi announced on March 16 Decree-Law No. 98, calling for separate but simultaneous elections on June 2 for the Constituent Assembly and a referendum on the Monarchy. The referendum would be taken by single direct vote; the Costituente would be elected on the basis of proportional representation (in localities of more than 30,000). Royalist groups, together with the British, felt that it was safer to trust a popular referendum to uphold the Monarchy than to rely upon the Costituente to do so.[67] Moreover, the rightists succeeded in making sure that the Costituente would be confined to constitution-making and would possess no interim legislative powers, so that the parties could maintain their cabinet veto power over decrees. After the promulgation of Decree-Law No. 98, the Consulta withered away.

The national political contest got under way at once and aroused keenest interest. Despite their lack of familiarity with free election campaigns, the Italians behaved exemplarily, permitting bona fide parties to disseminate their propaganda unhindered. In preliminary local elections between March 10 and April 7, the Social-Communist Left (but not the Pd'A) showed surprising strength; clearly the future lay with the Marxians and the Catholics.[68]

By spring the attitudes of the parties toward the House of Savoy were well defined, except for the DC and PLI. DeGasperi hoped to straddle the issue; Gronchi and others to the left of center in his party were outspokenly republican; Jacini, most Catholic Actionists, and Vatican circles were stanch monarchists.

(March 1946), pp. 221-231; "La colpa è degli Azionisti: inchiesta del *Ponte*," *Il Ponte*, VII (1951), pp. 487-488; and commentaries of A. C. Jemolo, P. Togliatti, *et al*, "Inchiesta sul Partito d'Azione," *ibid.*, pp. 769-778, 901-915, 1466-1471.

[67] This was a reversal of the principle earlier embodied in Bonomi's Decree-Law No. 151. Harris, *Allied Military Administration of Italy*, pp. 205, 362, 383; Leo Valiani, "La battaglia per la sovranità della Costituente," *Il Ponte*, XIV (Supplement to Nov. 1958; special issue dedicated to Piero Calamandrei), pp. 80-94.

[68] Of 5,638 communes the DC (either alone or in coalition) won 2,326; the Social-Communists (either singly or in coalition) won 2,248; the Actionists, 11; Liberals, 97; Labor Democrats, 69; Republicans, 36; Qualunquists, 22. The remainder were won by independents on local lists. Tupini, *I Democratici cristiani*, p. 128.

When the DC held its First National Congress, April 24–27, however, the preference among card holders was three-to-one in favor of a republic.[69] Probably this ratio was smaller among apathetic peasants who held no *tessere*. The PLI endorsed the Monarchy on May 3.[70]

Such developments so disturbed the royalists that they embarked upon a desperate tack. Violating the truce pledge, they persuaded Victor Emmanuel III on May 9 to abdicate formally in favor of Humbert, in the hope that a "purified" House of Savoy would find greater response. The retiring monarch (whose political and diplomatic errors had cost him his own throne and the life of his daughter in a Nazi concentration camp) headed for Egypt. There death claimed him on December 28, 1947. Humbert II, Italy's "King of the May," held the throne for barely a month. Thoroughly incensed by the royal stratagem, republicans prevented the royalists from delaying the elections.

Two other attempts to influence the decision occurred. One was the announcement that the Allied Commission soon would be scrapped; that the Long Armistice thus would lose its validity and occupation costs would be negotiated directly between Italy and the occupant powers; and that all PW's would be repatriated at once.[71] Sponsors of this gambit almost certainly hoped that it would redound to DeGasperi's benefit. Actually the Allied Commission lingered on until January 31, 1947.

Pope Pius XII was responsible for the second electoral intervention. He deemed it expedient to offer moral counsel to Italians the day ahead of the election. Though he did not utter the words "monarchy" or "republic," he exhorted his listeners to choose between "Christianity" and "materialism," between the "champions" and the "wreckers of Christian civilization." [72]

Such maneuvers may have strengthened the Christian Democrats but they did not preserve the House of Savoy. When the votes were counted, of the almost 90 per cent of the eligible electorate who flocked to the polls on June 2 for the first unfettered national election in more than two decades, it was found that the Republic attracted 54.69 per cent (12,717,923) of the

[69] *Ibid.*, pp. 129–137.
[70] *NYT*, May 4, 1946, 6:4.
[71] Kogan, *Italy and the Allies*, pp. 117–118.
[72] *NYT*, June 2, 1946.

voters, and the Monarchy but 45.31 per cent (10,719,284).[73] Unhappily, however, the balloting reflected the growing sectional split in Italian political and economic life. Rome and all provinces to the north plumped solidly for the Republic. Emilia, Tuscany, and the Marches gave it the largest votes; Piedmont, the home of the reigning house, accorded the Republic 55 per cent of its ballots. Naples and the southern provinces, plus the islands, voted just as compactly and decisively to retain the Monarchy. In order to preclude disorders either by rebuffed royalists or jubilant republicans, Premier DeGasperi advised King Humbert II to leave Italy as quickly as possible. Reluctantly the sovereign complied; his airplane took off for Portugal on June 13 before the official canvass was announced. The last of the Savoyard dynasty was forbidden to return.

The June 2 elections also determined the composition of the Constituent Assembly.[74] The three *partiti di massa* accounted for 75 per cent of all the ballots, and the precarious balance between the Catholic Center and the Social-Communist Left at once became apparent. Except for three or four years after the April 18, 1948, parliamentary elections, this standoff was to remain a persistent problem of postwar Italian politics. The Christian Democrats easily won first place in 1946 for several reasons. The vast majority of Italians were nominally Catholic, and the rural groups as well as the women who now voted for the first time were susceptible to pressure from the clergy. Moreover, Catholic

[73] Istituto Centrale di Statistica, *Elezione per l'Assemblea Costituente e Referendum Istituzionale* (Rome, 1948), p. lxiv.

[74] The official tally showed:

Party	Votes	Percentage	Seats
Christian Democracy	8,083,208	35.2	207
Italian Socialist Party	4,744,749	20.7	115
Italian Communist Party	4,342,722	18.9	104
National Democratic Union (bloc of Liberals and Labor Democrats)	1,559,417	6.8	41
Common Man Front (Uomo Qualunque)	1,209,918	5.3	30
Italian Republican Party	997,690	4.3	23
National Liberal Bloc (royalist)	636,493	2.8	16
Action Party	333,758	1.5	7
Republican-Democratic Concentration	97,260	0.4	2
Unionist Movement	70,957	0.3	1
Social Christians	50,220	0.2	1
Other lists	826,488	3.6	9
Totals	22,952,880	100.0	556

Action, which was rapidly girding its organization in every diocese, campaigned vigorously for the DC. As direct heirs of Sturzo's PPI, DeGasperi's DC benefited from the prestige of its predecessor (which had been the country's second largest party prior to Fascism). It should be noted, too, that many Italians had grown bone-weary of long anticlerical political predominance since the Risorgimento. Finally, the DC attracted quite a number of ex-Fascists and *fiancheggiatori* who, though they were not enthusiastic about the party's political, religious, and economic program, regarded Christian Democracy at least as a "home-grown" institution that offered the safest bulwark against the greater evil of alien Marxism and the best hope for successful bargaining with the Western Powers at the peace table.

On the basis of preceding municipal elections, some observers had expected the PCI to come in second instead of third in June. None the less, the Communists' showing was impressive. In later elections the PCI was to advance into second place, expand its strength steadily southward, and become the largest Communist Party in western Europe. The Socialists, who had been a *partito di massa* before the Fascist night, demonstrated in 1946 that, despite their schismatic propensities, they still possessed much strength, especially in the factory cities. The so-called National Democratic Union, composed of quondam Liberals and Labor Democrats and parading such patriarchs as "ONB" and Croce, came in fourth and drew its chief support from the *Mezzogiorno*. The neo-Fascistic Uomo Qualunque ranked fifth. It was followed by the Republicans, the royalist National Liberal Bloc, and lastly the remnants of the Action Party. A cluster of splinter currents polled collectively a little more than a million votes.

On June 18, 1946, the Italian Republic was officially proclaimed in Montecitorio's Hall of the Wolf. With the hope of reconciling the royalist South, the Costituente elected Enrico DeNicola to be Provisional President of the Italian Republic on June 28. DeNicola, it will be recalled, was the Neapolitan jurist who in 1943–1944 had excogitated the formula of the Lieutenant-Generalcy of the Realm. The Constituent Assembly chose Saragat (PSIUP) to preside over its own labors. President DeNicola quickly entrusted Premier DeGasperi with the task of forming a

573

new cabinet, to be composed this time of only the four major anti-Fascist parties (DC, PCI, PSIUP, and PRI).[75] There was no question that the Catholic premier was determined to keep the pivotal posts out of Communist clutches; he retained for himself both the Foreign and Interior ministries. Before the month was out his government decreed general amnesties for Fascist political prisoners.[76]

The referendum of June 2, 1946, brought to an end the third chapter of the Italian people's breach with their unhappy past. First they had overturned Mussolini's dictatorship. Then they had repudiated his controversial superior, the timid King who had refused to sign Premier Facta's proclamation of a state of siege in October 1922, who had alienated many of his subjects by his aloofness during the Matteotti crisis, and who had disgusted still more of them by his precipitate flight from Rome on September 9, 1943. Finally they had rejected the idea of continuing the Monarchy under his son, Humbert II, who had grown to maturity in an atmosphere conditioned by the Fascist regime. Undeniably one of the prime causes of this ultimate action was the exhilarating experience of the Armed Resistance and the CLN's, which had given to many (particularly in the North) a vision of more dynamic mass participation in public affairs than Italians hitherto had been accustomed to. No doubt many people oversimplified Italy's modern history when they equated the Monarchy just with Mussolini's regime, but repudiation of the irresolute dynasty was certainly the logical first step toward clearing away the debris of dictatorship and building a renovated Italy.

European integration and the Constitution of the Republic

Though the militantly democratic wing of the Resistance was disheartened by the downfall of Premier Parri and the debacle of the purge, they could find some cheer in the noteworthy steps taken toward the integration of western Europe in the postwar years. Federalism was a principle of international organization

[75] The Liberals and Labor Democrats in the National Democratic Union and elsewhere were in a huff because of objections to the way of handling the referendum. The Actionists were no longer powerful enough to insist upon being included.
[76] NYT, June 22, 1946, 4:5.

that was dear to the hearts of the more enlightened leaders of the Actionist, revisionist Socialist, Christian Democratic, and Liberal parties. They and similar-minded veterans of the Resistance movements in other western European countries were chiefly responsible for the limited steps that thus far have been made to achieve the ultimate goal of a United States of Europe.[77]

The militant anti-Fascists could also take pride in at least many of the features of the 1948 Constitution of the Italian Republic, though many were disturbed by the inclusion of the Lateran Accords. Certainly it was the program of the Christian Democrats more than that of the laics that was most clearly incorporated in the Constitution.[78] And it is probably true that the balancing of forces between the totalitarian Communist-Socialists and the authoritarian "traditionalists" made it possible for Italy's minority of genuine democrats to nail down free republican institutions.[79]

Many of the Constitution's clauses, it should be admitted, long remained little better than pious expressions. With good cause, therefore, a handful of dauntless prophets of the Resistance, led by the late jurist and rector of the University of Florence, Piero Calamandrei,[80] set out to cleanse the civic temples of anachronistic remnants of Fascist laws and economic

[77] Regarding Italy and postwar federalism, see especially Altiero Spinelli, "The Growth of the European Movement since World War II," and other articles in C. Grove Haines (ed.), *European Integration* (Baltimore, 1957), a volume which grew out of a conference at the Bologna Center of the Johns Hopkins University in May–June 1956.

[78] Professor Mario Einaudi has observed that the Constitution reflected most of the Christian Democratic program in its six major areas: (1) preservation of the Lateran pacts; (2) expansion of a bill of rights to include freedom from want; (3) reinstatement of an elected Chamber of Deputies with a reorganized Senate, largely elected but also based partly on professional groupings, and inclusion of a referendum as a legislative device; (4) limitation of the power of the executive branch; (5) authorization of regional autonomy, especially for the border zones; and (6) provision for a Supreme Constitutional Court. *Christian Democracy in Italy and France*, pp. 39–50; cf. Guido Gonella, *Il programma della Democrazia Cristiana per la nuova Italia* (Rome, 1946).

[79] Massimo Salvadori, *NATO: A Twentieth Century Community of Nations* (Princeton, 1957), pp. 66–67.

[80] See P. Calamandrei, "La Costituzione e il programma politica della Resistenza," *Il Ponte*, XII (1956), pp. 161–163; Leopoldo Piccardi, "Calamandrei e la Costituzione," *ibid.*, pp. 95–113; Achille Battaglia, "Un giurista combattente," Rome *Il Mondo*, Oct. 9, 1956, pp. 1–2; and the special issue of *Il Ponte*, XIV (Nov. 1958), dedicated entirely to Piero Calamandrei. See also Grindrod, *The Rebuilding of Italy*, pp. 53–54; Webb, *Church and State in Italy, 1947–1957*, pp. 30–36.

practices.[81] They lamented the years of delay in implementing constitutional provisions for a Supreme Constitutional Court, a High Council of the Magistracy, a National Economic and Labor Council, use of the referendum, extension of regional autonomies, and guarantees of full freedom of religious expression. Their criticisms at last achieved some results a decade after the Liberation. Most praiseworthy was the establishment in 1956 of the Supreme Constitutional Court. Enrico DeNicola served as its first president.

Erection of this cornice upon the constitutional edifice of the new Italian Republic helped make it possible for many disconsolate survivors of the underground struggle to recognize more clearly that the constructive and reforming genius of the anti-Fascist Resistance was still at work. An increasing number of Italians were willing to agree that their nation had overcome at least some of the cynicism and apathetic acceptance of injustice and authoritarianism that had tarnished much of its history. If this was indeed true, then thousands who doggedly and idealistically had campaigned against Fascist tyranny for more than twenty years could claim part of the credit.

For at least in its finest moments the democratic and liberal wing of the anti-Fascist Resistance had sought to achieve national freedom in a free and interdependent world, a genuinely popular government under the rule of law, a secure defense of the dignity of man, and a deeper measure of social justice. In guiding Italy a few steps nearer to fulfillment of these aspirations, the democratic anti-Fascists' "Second Risorgimento" contributed substantially to the political and moral education of the Italian people—a contribution that surely will gain increasing recognition from the vantage point of the future.[82]

[81] Professor Salvemini discovered one law still in force in 1954 that called for fourteen years' imprisonment of any anti-Fascist exile who spread "false and tendentious rumors about the Fascist regime." "Coronamenti strutturali," *Il Ponte*, x (March 1954).

[82] The tenth anniversary of the Liberation called forth some tentative conclusions regarding the impact of the Resistance. See especially the essays of Achille Battaglia and Others, *Dieci anni dopo (1945–1955): Saggi sulla vita democratica italiana* (Bari, 1955); those in *Il Secondo Risorgimento: scritti di A. Garosci, L. Salvatorelli, C. Primieri, R. Cadorna, M. Bendiscioli, C. Mortali, P. Gentile, M. Ferrara, F. Montanari, nel decennale della Resistenza e del ritorno alla democrazia, 1945–1955* (Rome, 1955); and the special issue of *Il Ponte*, xi (April–May 1955).

Among many other perceptive analyses are H. Stuart Hughes, *The United States and Italy*; Muriel Grindrod, *The Rebuilding of Italy: Politics and Economics, 1945–1955*; Einaudi and Goguel, *Christian Democracy in Italy and France*; Antonino Rèpaci, *Fascismo vecchio e nuovo*; and Roberto Ducci, *Questa Italia: saggio sul fascismo e dopo* (Verona, 1948).

Somewhat more specialized appraisals include Alessandro Galante-Garrone, "Aspetti politici della guerra partigiana in Italia," *Acropoli*, II (1946), pp. 150–164; A. Garosci, "I risultati politici della guerra partigiana," *Nuovi Quaderni di Giustizia e Libertà*, No. 5/6 (Jan.–Aug. 1945), pp. 5–12; L. Valiani, "La politique de la Résistance italienne," *Revue d'histoire politique et constitutionelle*, No. 1 (Paris, 1951), pp. 118–132; Franco Antonicelli, "La resistenza è in piedi," *Il Ponte*, VI (1950), pp. 68–77; Salvadori, *SRI*, pp. 31–33; Valiani, *Tutte le strade conducono a Roma*, pp. 357–359; and Cadorna, *La Riscossa*, pp. 276–279.

BIBLIOGRAPHICAL NOTE

IN VIEW OF the many references in the preface and in the footnotes to source materials, it is superfluous to add here any detailed bibliographical discussion. To make a comprehensive listing would be an enormous task. Mention need be made of only a few of the major works that themselves contain specialized bibliographies on the subject of the anti-Fascist Opposition and Armed Resistance which will help provide the researcher with a point of departure for further investigation.

The relevant sections in the *Bibliografia storica nazionale*, published annually since 1939 by the Giunta Centrale per gli Studi Storici (Bari: Laterza), list all articles, books, and reviews published in Italy. An equally indispensable compilation is *Libri e riviste d'Italia: notiziario bibliografico mensile*, ed. Centro di Documentazione della Presidenza del Consiglio della Repubblica Italiana, Rome.

For an over-all interpretation of Italy during the Fascist era the fundamental work is Luigi Salvatorelli and Giovanni Mira, *Storia d'Italia nel periodo fascista* (Turin, 1957), and its earlier version, profusely illustrated, *Storia del fascismo: l'Italia dal 1919 al 1945* (Rome, 1952), both of which contain a limited number of source references. In the multivolume *Questioni di storia contemporanea*, ed. Ettore Rota (Milan, 1953), there are excellent bibliographical essays by Nino Valeri, "Sulle origini del fascismo," III, pp. 733–758, and Paolo Alatri, "Benito Mussolini: nota biografica e bibliografica," III, 759–796. The bibliographical discussions of Piero Pieri, "Fascismo e resistenza," and Aldo Garosci, "Partiti e leaders politici," in the special issue of the review, *Itinerari* (Genoa), IV, No. 22/23/24 (Dec. 1956), dedicated to the late Professor Gaetano Salvemini ("Prospettive storiografiche in Italia"), are very useful. Also to be noted are Aldo Garosci, *Pensiero politico e storiografia moderna* (Pisa, 1954), and my own article, "Italian Historical Scholarship: A Decade of Recovery and Development, 1945–1955," *Journal of Modern History*, XXVIII (Dec. 1956), pp. 374–388.

On the subject of the *émigrés* one should consult the most up-to-date list of writings by and about them: G. Silvano Spinetti, *Bibliografia degli esuli politici sotto il fascismo* (Rome, 1959), which supplements Michele Cantarella, "A Bibliography of Italian Writers in Exile," in *Neither Liberty Nor Bread: The Meaning and Tragedy of Fascism*, ed. Frances Keene (New York and London, 1940). Other specialized references for this period will be found in Aldo Garosci, *Storia dei fuorusciti* (Bari, 1953); his *La vita di Carlo Rosselli* (2 vols.; Milan-Florence, 1945); Alessandro Schiavi, *Esilio e morte di Filippo Turati, 1926–1932* (Rome, 1956); and my article, "The Italian Anti-Fascist Emigration, 1922–1943," *Journal of Central European Affairs*, XII (April 1952), pp. 20–55.

Regarding the Catholic opposition there are helpful references to sources in Daniel A. Binchy, *Church and State in Fascist Italy* (London, 1941); Edith Pratt Howard, *Il Partito Popolare Italiano* (Florence, 1957); Richard A. Webster's recently published *The Cross and the Fasces: Christian Democracy and Fascism in Italy* (Stanford, 1960); and a few in Arturo Carlo Jemolo, *Chiesa e stato in Italia negli ultimi cento anni* (4th ed.; Turin, 1955).

For the crisis of World War II the best bibliographical starting point for works published prior to 1949 is Franco Ravà and Giorgio Spini, "Fonti documentarie e memorialistiche per la storia della crisi dello stato italiano (1940–1945)," *Rivista storica italiana*, LXI (1949), pp. 404–431, 574–602. The Ufficio Storico of the Corpo Stato Maggiore of the Italian Army has published a helpful *Saggio bibliografico sulla seconda guerra mondiale* (Rome, 1955). A long alphabetical listing of books (but not articles, and without commentary) dealing chiefly with the Armed Resistance (and in some cases its antecedents) may be found in *Resistenza: panorama bibliografico*, ed. Alfonso Bartolini, Giulio Mazzon, and Lamberto Mercuri, with preface by Ferruccio Parri (Trapani, 1957). Stefano Merli, on behalf of the Istituto Rodolfo Morandi, is preparing an elaborate classified bibliography of the anti-Fascist struggle. Paolo Monelli, *Roma, 1943* (5th ed.; Milan, 1948) and *Mussolini: piccolo borghese* (Milan, 1950), include a number of citations, as does Agostino degli Espinosa, *Il regno del Sud (8 settembre 1943–4 giugno 1944)* (Rome, 1946; Florence, 1955). Though written from a decidedly neo-Fascist slant, Attilio Tamaro, *Due anni di storia, 1943–1945* (3 vols.; Rome, 1948–1950), is a chronicle with useful references and many photographs. On the broader topic of postwar evaluations of the Fascist era, consult Emiliana P. Noether, "Italy Reviews its Fascist Past: A Bibliographical Essay," *The American Historical Review*, LXI (July 1956), pp. 877–899.

Probably the most notable group of scholars collecting information about the Resistance is the Istituto Nazionale per la Storia del Movimento di Liberazione in Italia, established in 1949 at Piazza Duomo 14, Milan, by former Premier Ferruccio Parri, and including on its executive committee Franco Antonicelli, Mario Bendiscioli, Mario Dal Pra, Giorgio Vaccarino, Bianca Ceva, and several others. This institute houses the archives of the CLNAI and the CVL and publishes the trimonthly review *Il Movimento di Liberazione in Italia: Rassegna di Studi e Documenti*, which contains much historical and bibliographical information. On the basis of these archives Franco Catalano has written a valuable, documented book, *Storia del CLNAI* (Bari, 1956). The institute has sponsored several important conclaves for the study of the Resistance. Their fruitful results have been summarized in *MLI*, No. 22 (1953), No. 34/35 (1955), No. 52/53 (1958), No. 56 (1959), and No. 57 (1959).[1] The institute was host to the Second International Congress on the History of the European Resistance Movements in March 1961,[2] the theme of this conference being "The Allies and the European Resistance Movements." Franco Venturi and Ferruccio Parri presented the major paper on Italy. All the proceedings will be published. Meanwhile, the Italian Radical Party sponsored eight seminars between April 30 and June 20, 1959, on the subject of the Italian anti-Fascist struggle between 1919 and 1947.[3] The American Historical Association at its December 1960 meeting in New York devoted one session to the World War II underground movements, including the one in Italy.

In Milan the Istituto Giangiacomo Feltrinelli has gathered praiseworthy collections on the Italian Resistance, an idea of

---

[1] See also Giampaolo Pansa, "Vecchio e nuovo nella storiografia della resistenza," *Rivista storica del socialismo*, II, No. 7/8 (1959), pp. 710–722.

[2] The first international congress met in Liége, September 14–17, 1958. It was organized by the Belgian Federation of History Teachers under the patronage of the King of the Belgians. See its *General Report*, prepared by Henri Michel of France, and the paper on Italy by Giorgio Vaccarino.

[3] See papers of N. Valeri, L. Salvatorelli, F. Schiavetti, A. Garosci, A. Spinelli, N. Chiaromonte, F. Parri, and U. LaMalfa in *Lezioni sull'antifascismo* (Bari, 1960).

which can be gained from its newly published *Bibliografia*, edited by Laura Conti (Milan, 1961). It is also encouraging research in this field. There are also important regional collections on the Armed Resistance, especially in Turin. In the great libraries of Paris, Washington, New York, Harvard, and Stanford, to name but a few, there are significant collections. Current periodicals like *Il Ponte*, *Il Mondo*, *Rinascita*, and *Rivista storica del socialismo*, as well as such older ones as *Stato Operaio*, *Nuovi Quaderni di Giustizia e Libertà*, and *Mercurio*, have published much information that is pertinent.

Though marred by a distinctly Communist bias, Roberto Battaglia's detailed *Storia della resistenza italiana (8 settembre 1943–25 aprile 1945)* (2nd ed.; Turin, 1953) is a very helpful contribution and provides a detailed bibliography broken down by regions. Luigi Longo, *Un popolo alla macchia* (Milan, 1947), is equally Communist-inspired; it includes a number of bibliographical references. Renato Carli-Ballola, *Storia della resistenza* (Milan, 1957), written from the Socialist Party standpoint, includes some new references. Leo Valiani's autobiographical *Tutte le strade conducono a Roma* (Florence, 1947) and his archive-based *Dall'antifascismo alla resistenza* (Milan, 1959) offer important interpretations of the struggle by an Action Party leader. General Raffaele Cadorna, *La Riscossa: dal 25 luglio alla liberazione* (Milan, 1948), is also autobiographical in tone and is written from a more conservative standpoint. Needless to say, practically every major figure in the Resistance has written one or more articles.

Approaching the subject from foreign vantage points are the numerous important works of Massimo Salvadori, including his autobiographical *Resistenza ed azione* (Bari, 1951) and his brief *Storia della resistenza italiana* (Venice, 1955); Norman Kogan, *Italy and the Allies* (Cambridge, Mass., 1956), which summarizes cogently the diplomacy of the wartime period; H. Stuart Hughes' sympathetic and interpretive *The United States and Italy* (Cambridge, Mass., 1953); Howard McGaw Smyth's authoritative article, "The Armistice of Cassibile," in *Military Affairs* (Spring 1948); the recent official study by Charles R. S. Harris, *Allied Military Administration of Italy, 1943–1945* (London, 1957), in *History of the Second World War: United King-*

dom Military Series, ed. J. R. M. Butler; and the relevant chapters by Elizabeth Wiskemann and others in the *Survey of International Affairs, 1936–1946*, volume, *Hitler's Europe*, ed. Arnold and Veronica M. Toynbee (London, 1954). Not to be ignored are parts of the memoirs of Winston S. Churchill, Cordell Hull, Harry Hopkins, Field Marshals Alexander and Montgomery, General Clark, Field Marshal Kesselring, and others. Only a portion of Allied documentation in Alexandria, Virginia, pertaining to the wartime Resistance has been declassified. A partial history of OSS is being written.

From the perspective of a decade after the Liberation, one should note the often perceptive essays by Achille Battaglia and Others, *Dieci anni dopo* (1945–1955): *saggi sulla vita democratica italiana* (Bari, 1955); [4] and Aldo Garosci and Others, *Il Secondo Risorgimento* (Rome, 1955).

---

[4] For a Marxist criticism of this, see Gastone Manacorda, "Dicci anni dopo o del modo di scrivere la storia recente," *Società*, xi (June 1955), pp. 543–558.

INDEX

601

Parri, Ferruccio, 29–30, 52–54, 60, 71–73, 90, 211–13, 253, 278–79, 291–92, 312–13, 327, 342, 357, 362–63, 368–70, 380, 424–25, 433n, 435, 451, 464, 467–68, 498, 500n, 502, 522–23n, 544, 553–54, 561–63, 569, 573–74; arrested (Dec. 1944), 470–71f; clarification of Cadorna's status, 440–44; mission to South (Nov.–Dec. 1944), 456–58, 463–69; premiership (June–November 1945), 558–67; radicalism, 171–73; reports to CLNAI on Allied plans (1945), 506–11

Partigiano Alpino, 352

partisan warfare, *see* Resistenza Armata

Partito Comunista Italiano, *see* PCI

Partito d'Azione, *see* Pd'A

Partito Liberale Italiano, *see* PLI

Partito Nazionale Fascista, *see* PNF

Partito Popolare Italiano, *see* PPI; Catholics

Partito Repubblicano Italiano, *see* PRI

Partito Socialista Italiano di Unità Proletaria, *see* PSIUP; Socialists

Passerin d'Entrèves, Ettore, 295, 531n

Passoni, Rag. Piero, 279n

Pastor, Ludwig, 97n

Pastore, Giulio, 216

Pastore, Ottavio, 113n, 188n

Patch, General Alexander M., 423n

Paternò, Emanuele, 86, 93n, 101

Paternò, Prefect (Florence), 409

Paterson, New Jersey, 200

Patriot Office, 410–13. *See also* ACC; Bonomi government

Patriots Branch (ACC), 410–13, 509. *See also* ACC; Resistenza Armata

Pavelič, Ante, 184

Pavese, Cesare, 95n, 353

Pavia, 93n, 168; "Pavia" division, 528, 543n. *See also* Oltrepò Pavese

Pavolini, Alessandro, 235n, 262–63, 267, 373, 378, 402, 407, 421, 521, 535, 541

Pavone, General Giuseppe, 310–11, 314, 319

PCI (Partito Comunista Italiano), 59–60, 63, 65–66, 68–69, 71, 75, 79n, 82–84, 93, 95, 106, 109f, 131, 146f, 173, 187, 207, 211, 216, 220, 222, 238n–39, 245, 249–53, 269, 271–72, 274, 277–82n, 285–90, 301, 304, 310, 314, 324n, 327, 333–34, 338, 342–44, 347–55, 368–70, 385, 388–89n, 391, 393, 397n, 415, 419, 423, 427–28, 430–31, 435–36, 440–44, 452–53, 461–63, 468–69, 483–85, 488, 490, 497, 514, 522–23n, 527, 529, 534, 539, 541–42, 553–54, 556, 560, 562; activities abroad (1939–1943), 187–206; attitude toward King after Aventine, 42–43; Aventine era, 16–17, 19–24; catastrophes of 1927–1928, 117–19; clandestine apparatus, 114–17f; CLNAI representation, 356–57; conspiracies, 110–30; Constitution (1948), 575–77; DeGasperi first government, 566–69f; DeGasperi second government, 574; Directive No. 16 re insurrection (April 10, 1945), 512–13; directorate, 488; Fifth Congress (1945), 569; Fourth Congress (1931), 126–27; Gappisti, 373–75f; general strikes of March 1944, 370–72; Gramsci in prison, 119–21; infiltration of Fascist mass organizations, 166–69; intervention in Spanish Civil War, 149–54f; isolation (1928–1934), 121–30; Lyon (Third) Congress, 111–13; Military Command, 370; northern strikes (March 1943), 207–10; "open letter" debate (Nov. 1944–Feb. 1945), 474–76; organized labor, 304–06; origins of PCI, 9n–11n; Parri government, 558–67; partisan forces (1943–1945), 290–91f; Popular Front era, 178–80; *svolta* (1930), 124–25; *svolta* (Aug. 23, 1939), 179; *svolta* (1944), 336–39; Togliatti's leadership abroad, 113–14; "unity of action" pact with Socialists (1934f), 130f, 294, 394; Venezia Giulia problem, 381–84f; victory of Republic, 570–74; Youth Federation, 115–16, 124

Pd'A (Partito d'Azione), 29, 161, 164n, 171, 179n, 207, 218, 238n–

Stevenson, Adlai E., 335
Stiatti, 194n
Štoka, Franz ("Rado"), 444–45
Stone, Commodore Ellery, 329n, 392, 556n
Storoni, Enzo, 221n
Strone, Val, 436
Strong, Brigadier Kenneth W. D., 247, 249, 254
Stucchi, Avv. G. B. ("Colonel Federici"), 282n, 435, 442, 488, 522, 536
Studi politici (Rome), 95
Studium, 97
Stura, 377, 416, 421
Sturzo, Don Luigi, 6–7, 48–49, 55, 142, 162, 197, 201, 205, 215–16, 478, 573
Suardo, Giacomo, 232n
Šubašič, Dr. Ivan, 445
Sudetenland, 164
Suez Canal, 141
Suhling, Major William, 434
Superti, Ettore, 430–31
Supreme Constitutional Court, *see* Constitutional Court
Sweden, 309, 459
Switzerland, 26n, 46–47, 52, 55–56, 59, 66–67, 76, 82, 95n, 114, 124n, 138, 150, 165, 185, 191, 193, 195–96, 198, 205, 271, 302, 308, 312, 358, 362, 369, 380, 394, 402, 424, 430–31, 435–36, 456, 470, 485–86, 491–92, 495–96, 498, 500–01, 507, 521, 528, 535, 537; emigration to (Sept. 1943f), 281–83f; Resistance center in World War II, 195–96f
Syndicalists, *see* Anarcho-Syndicalists
Syracuse, 254

Tabet, Duccio, 200
Tacchi-Venturi, Fr. Pietro, S.J., 105
Tagliacozzo, Enzo, 171n, 178, 200, 203n
"Tagliamento" legion, 521
Tagliamento River, 302
Tampa, 200
Tangier, 244–45
Taranto, 118n, 316, 321, 331n
Tarchiani, Alberto, 50, 60–61, 64–67, 78, 108, 134, 136, 166, 189, 195,

201–02, 206, 309–10, 324n, 342–43, 359, 560
Targetti, F., 282n
Tarvisio, 241–42, 245
Tasca, Angelo ("A. Rossi"), 10n, 79n, 114, 120, 122–23, 131, 178–80, 188, 194–95
Tassinari, Renato, 262n–63
"Taurinense" division, 277
Taviani, Paolo Emiliano, 519
Taylor, Brigadier General Maxwell D., 255–56, 320
Tedeschi, Dr. Alessandro, 35
Teheran Conference, 317n
Temple, Major, 469
Tenda Pass, 420
Tenth Torpedo-boat Flotilla, *see* X^{ma} MAS
Teramo, 299, 360, 405
Terra, Stefano, 196
Terracina, 384
Terracini, Benvenuto, 177n
Terracini, Umberto, 10n, 117–18, 190, 431
Teruzzi, Attilio, 234n
Terza Brigata Liguria, 376
Terzi, Pietro, 542
Testa, Alfredo, 159n
Thaon di Revel, Grand Admiral, 224
Third International, *see* Comintern
Third Panzer Grenadiers, 257
Thomas, Ivor, MP, 197n
Tibaldi, Professor Ettore, 295
Tiber River, 13, 385
Ticino, 55–56
Tino, Adolfo, 95, 172n, 213, 238n, 282n
Tirano, 196
Tito, Marshal Josip, 110, 277, 280, 302–03, 320n, 358, 363, 367, 395, 424, 452, 489–91, 501, 534, 551; and Resistenza Armata (Sept. 1943–June 1944), 381–84f; (June–November 1944), 444–47
Todt labor service, 277, 279
Togliatti, Palmiro, 10n, 20, 63, 83–84, 106, 111, 113–14, 121–29n, 132–33, 152, 158n, 163, 167, 179, 187f, 206–07, 281, 286, 291, 324, 341–43n, 370, 389, 391, 394–95, 410, 412n, 461–62, 559–60, 562–64, 566, 568–

617

Zamboni, Anteo, 38
Zanatta, Carlo, 142
Zanetti, Armando, 45, 95
Zanetti, Avv. Piero, 74
Zaniboni, Tito, 33–36, 51, 331
Zanoni, Arturo, 161
Zanotti, A., 282n
Zanotti-Bianco, Umberto, 69
Zanussi, General Giacomo, 249n, 254n–55n
Zara, 218, 264n, 445

Zari, Pietro, 73n
Zelka, Mata ("General Paul Lukacs"), 151
Zerbino, Paolo, 521, 526, 541
Zevi, Bruno, 171n, 178, 200, 203n
Zimmermann, SS General, 372
Zimmerwald, 193n
Zinoviev, Gregory, 10n, 111
Zoli, Avv. Adone, 272, 279n; as premier, 543n, 554n
Zurich, 47, 56, 76, 82, 189, 196, 495